FOUNDATIONS OF
LAW

CASES, COMMENTARY, AND ETHICS

FIFTH EDITION

DELMAR CENGAGE Learning

Options.
Over 300 products in every area of the law: textbooks, online courses, CD-ROMs, reference books, companion websites, and more – helping you succeed in the classroom and on the job.

Support.
We offer unparalleled, practical support: robust instructor and student supplements to ensure the best learning experience, custom publishing to meet your unique needs, and other benefits such as Delmar Cengage Learning's Student Achievement Award. And our sales representatives are always ready to provide you with dependable service.

Feedback.
As always, we want to hear from you! Your feedback is our best resource for improving the quality of our products. Contact your sales representative or write us at the address below if you have any comments about our materials or if you have a product proposal.

Accounting and Financials for the Law Office • Administrative Law • Alternative Dispute Resolution • Bankruptcy Business Organizations/Corporations • Careers and Employment • Civil Litigation and Procedure • CLA Exam Preparation • Computer Applications in the Law Office • Constitutional Law • Contract Law • Court Reporting Criminal Law and Procedure • Document Preparation • Elder Law • Employment Law • Environmental Law • Ethics Evidence Law • Family Law • Health Care Law • Immigration Law • Intellectual Property • Internships Interviewing and Investigation • Introduction to Law • Introduction to Paralegalism • Juvenile Law • Law Office Management • Law Office Procedures • Legal Nurse Consulting • Legal Research, Writing, and Analysis • Legal Terminology • Legal Transcription • Media and Entertainment Law • Medical Malpractice Law Product Liability • Real Estate Law • Reference Materials • Social Security • Sports Law • Torts and Personal Injury Law • Wills, Trusts, and Estate Administration • Workers' Compensation Law

DELMAR CENGAGE Learning
5 Maxwell Drive
Clifton Park, New York 12065-2919

For additional information, find us online at:
www.delmar.cengage.com

FOUNDATIONS OF
LAW

CASES, COMMENTARY, AND ETHICS

FIFTH EDITION

Ransford C. Pyle
University of Central Florida

Carol M. Bast
University of Central Florida

DELMAR
CENGAGE Learning™

Australia • Brazil • Japan • Korea • Mexico • Singapore • Spain • United Kingdom • United States

DELMAR
CENGAGE Learning™

Foundations of Law: Cases, Commentary, and Ethics, Fifth Edition

Author: Ransford C. Pyle and Carol M. Bast

Vice President, Career and Professional Editorial: Dave Garza

Director of Learning Solutions: Sandy Clark

Senior Acquisitions Editor: Shelley Esposito

Managing Editor: Larry Main

Senior Product Manager: Melissa Riveglia

Editorial Assistant: Danielle Klahr

Vice President, Career and Professional Marketing: Jennifer Baker

Marketing Director: Deborah Yarnell

Marketing Manager: Erin Brennan

Marketing Coordinator: Erin DeAngelo

Production Director: Wendy Troeger

Production Manager: Mark Bernard

Content Project Manager: Chris Chien

Senior Art Director: Joy Kocsis

Senior Technology Product Manager: Joe Pliss

For product information and technology assistance, contact us at
Cengage Learning Customer & Sales Support, 1-800-354-9706

For permission to use material from this text or product, submit all requests online at **www. cengage.com/permissions.**
Further permissions questions can be e-mailed to
permissionrequest@cengage.com

Library of Congress Control Number: 2010924100

ISBN-13: 978-1-4354-4084-5
ISBN-10: 1-4354-4084-6

Delmar
5 Maxwell Drive
Clifton Park, NY 12065-2919
USA

Cengage Learning is a leading provider of customized learning solutions with office locations around the globe, including Singapore, the United Kingdom, Australia, Mexico, Brazil, and Japan. Locate your local office at: **international. cengage.com/region**

Cengage Learning products are represented in Canada by Nelson Education, Ltd.

To learn more about Delmar, visit **www.cengage.com/delmar**
Purchase any of our products at your local college store or at our preferred online store **www.ichapters.com**

NOTICE TO THE READER

Publisher does not warrant or guarantee any of the products described herein or perform any independent analysis in connection with any of the product information contained herein. Publisher does not assume, and expressly disclaims, any obligation to obtain and include information other than that provided to it by the manufacturer. The reader is expressly warned to consider and adopt all safety precautions that might be indicated by the activities described herein and to avoid all potential hazards. By following the instructions contained herein, the reader willingly assumes all risks in connection with such instructions. The reader is notified that this text is an educational tool, not a practice book. Sine the law is in constant change, no rule or statement of law I this book should be relied upon for any service to any client. The reader should always refer to standard legal sources for the current rule or law. If legal advice or other expert assistance is required, the services of the appropriate professional should be sought. The publisher makes no representations or warranties of any kind, including but not limited to, the warranties of fitness for particular purpose or merchantability, nor are any such representations implied with respect to the material set forth herein, and the publisher takes no responsibility with respect to such material. The publisher shall not be liable for any special, consequential, or exemplary damages resulting, in whole or part, from the readers' use of, or reliance upon, this material.

Printed in the United States of America
1 2 3 4 5 6 7 15 14 13 12 11 10

CONTENTS

CHAPTER 2 Ethics   39

CHAPTER 3 Sources of the Law: Cases   73

CHAPTER 4   Sources of the Law: Legislation   96

CHAPTER 7 Procedure in Civil Cases 179

CHAPTER 8   The Law of Criminal Procedure   209

CHAPTER 9   Criminal Law   244

CHAPTER 10 Torts, Personal Injury, and Compensation   270

CHAPTER 14 Administrative Law and Procedure   391

Appendices   412

PREFACE

The goals of this edition have not changed from prior editions. Many new cases have been added and others have been removed. New features have been added, as noted later, but the body of the text remains as expository comments and condensed judicial decisions. Thus, this preface reissues many of Ransford Pyle's comments from prior editions. Dr. Pyle was the sole author of the first through third editions, and he brought me in as second author on the fourth edition. Dr. Pyle turned the book over to me to prepare this fifth edition, an endeavor that I gladly accepted; he will remain as first author because he was the one who inspired the book's creation.

Foundations of Law is intended for introductory law courses at the postsecondary, undergraduate level of instruction, particularly paralegal programs, pre-law and legal studies programs, and business law courses that aim at a broader base than the "legal environment of business" text. I taught for nearly three decades in a program that began as a strictly paralegal program but gradually changed in student orientation to primarily pre-law students. My goal has always been to impart the basic knowledge of American law and the American legal system that I considered any undergraduate ought to have, regardless of whether he or she wanted to be paralegals or lawyers or simply wanted to acquire an understanding of the law. I have found that the needs of students have not changed even if their aspirations have shifted.

Foundations approaches the law from a lawyer's viewpoint, as opposed to that of a social scientist, covering basic fields of the law such as property, contracts, torts, and criminal law, as well as procedure in both civil and criminal cases. I have included historical and societal commentary where I think it helpful in understanding the law; I would have liked to include much more, but I have found that covering most of the basic fields and legal concepts is quite enough for a one-semester course.

NEW FEATURES

New to this edition are "You Be the Judge" features that provide students with some facts that might be the basis of a lawsuit and ask them to determine how they would decide the case. Students may or may not agree with the way in which actual controversies involving the facts were decided. These features can be used to generate class discussion or as student assignments.

A number of cases excerpted in the book contain concurring and dissenting opinions. Questions at the end of the chapters require students to access these opinions and delve into their reasoning.

The Student CD-ROM contains legal research and legal analysis tips to accompany Chapters 1 through 6. These tips supplement and enrich the content of those chapters without interfering with the flow of the print text. Students can be introduced to legal research of cases and statutes through coverage of this material.

ORGANIZATION

The basic topics of the course reflect our legal tradition, as well as the basic fields found in the law and in legal education. The organization of chapters is simple and, I think, logical. I ease students into the study of law with a narrative chapter on the legal profession (formerly two chapters, one on lawyers and one on paralegals). The second chapter covers legal ethics. I have experimented with saving this chapter for the last in my course with the thought that legal ethics are better understood after a full acquaintance with the law, but, because the first chapter on the legal profession necessarily addresses what lawyers do and what others may not do, legal ethics, and especially unauthorized practice of law, follows some of the issues raised in the first chapter. Chapters 3 and 4 introduce the sources of the law in terms of cases and legislation. (Some have suggested the inclusion of a chapter on the Constitution as a source of law, but I have always felt that the Constitution, though essential to understanding some of our law, is primarily an allocation of power rather than a source of law. The Constitution is referenced where necessary [e.g., criminal procedure].) Chapters 5 and 6 introduce the American court system. Chapters 7 and 8 deal with procedure—civil and criminal, respectively. Chapters 9 through 13 discuss major fields of substantive law. Chapter 14 deals with administrative law and procedure, focusing on the latter. Appendix A, "How to Read a Case," is ordinarily read by students early in the course to prepare them for the many judicial opinions in the text. Appendix B contains the complete text of the United States Constitution, a document I frequently consult during class, having failed to memorize it as I should have.

CHAPTER FORMAT AND FEATURES

The body of the text in each chapter consists of narrative and commentary on the law and legal system, interspersed with edited cases—that is, judicial opinions—to illustrate or expand on the comments. Within each edited case, references to other cases have been shorted to retain only the case names. Legal terms mentioned in the commentary and cases are boldfaced in the text and defined in the margins. This is helpful to both student and teacher, with the caveat that my experience is that many students rely on learning these definitions for exams to the neglect of reading text or cases, apparently not believing my assertions that they will suffer when they encounter my exams.

A major undertaking in each new edition has been the inclusion of many new cases. To some extent this process updates the cases, but more importantly I have tried to weed out cases that proved inferior as learning tools and replace them with cases that are more effective in this regard. Review questions are found at the end of each chapter. I have reintroduced reading review questions (a feature from the second edition) in each chapter; these are ten or so questions that test students' absorption of important words and concepts in each chapter. They are not deep questions but instead are designed to test whether the reader has a basic knowledge of the chapter. I have often resorted to these questions when I have covered a chapter and have a few minutes left in class before time runs out. They may also be useful for instructors who hold review sessions before tests, but their primary purpose is to provide a self-test for students when they finish a chapter.

At the request of some instructors, we have included some open-ended discussion questions at the end of each chapter. These were intended for those who wish to deal in general terms with legal issues. One of the reasons I enjoy teaching an introductory law class is that rarely does a week go by without an interesting legal event emerging from the shadows. These events demonstrate that law is vital and dynamic, a welcome contrast for students to black-letter law learning and the more routine features of practice. These critical thinking questions are optional for the instructor: I would use these questions as part of my quasi-Socratic approach, whereas my coauthor will probably not use them because she uses significant class time for student presentation of cases. It goes without saying that instructors should employ their own teaching talents and follow their own goals, in keeping with the composition of their audience.

I have retained the "Scenarios" ("Review Problems" in a few instances) at the end of each chapter. These are designed to make readers apply chapter concepts to hypothetical cases, cases either loosely based on actual cases or situations that are looming on the legal horizon.

Supplemental Teaching Materials at a Glance

SUPPLEMENT	WHAT IT IS	WHAT'S IN IT
Student CD-ROM	CD-ROM that provides additional material to help students understand the important concepts in the course.	• Legal Research Tips and Legal Analysis Tips for Chapters 1 to 6
Online Instructor's Manual	Resources for the Instructor, posted online at: http://www.paralegal.delmar.cengage.com/ in the Online Resources section	• Instructor Manual with sample course syllabi; answers to text questions; useful web sites; test bank and answer key • PowerPoint® Presentations
Instructor Resources CD-ROM	Resources for the Instructor, available on CD-ROM	• Instructor Manual with sample course syllabi; answers to text questions; useful web sites; test bank and answer key • Computerized Testbank in ExamView with many questions and styles to choose from to create customized assessments for your students • PowerPoint® Presentations
Online Companion™	Additional resources for the Student, posted online at: http://www.paralegal.delmar.cengage.com/ in the Online Companions section	• Helpful web links

Web Page

Come visit our website at http://www.paralegal.delmar.cengage.com/, where you will find valuable information such as hot links and and sample materials to download, as well as other Delmar Cengage Learning products.

Please note that the Internet resources are of a time-sensitive nature and URL addresses may often change or be deleted.

ACKNOWLEDGMENTS

The authors and Delmar Cengage Learning would like to thank the following reviewers for their many suggestions:

Chelsea Campbell
Lehman College
Bronx, New York

Mark Ciccarelli
Kent State University
Liverpool, Ohio

Regina Dowling
Brandford Hall Career Institute
Windsor, Connecticut

Jane Jacobs
Community College of Philadelphia
Philadelphia, Pennsylvania

Diane D'Amico Juettner
Mercy College
Ferry, New York

Clark Silliman
Edmonds Community College
Lynnwood, Washington

Deborah Vinecour
SUNY Rockland Community
 College
Suffern, New York

TABLE OF CASES BY CHAPTER

TABLE OF CASES
ALPHABETICAL

CHAPTER 1

LAW AND THE PROFESSION OF LAW

INTRODUCTION

We all know what the law is; we use the term every day with considerable confidence that our listeners know perfectly well what meaning we attach to this word, even though it may have quite a few shades of meaning. Nevertheless, almost no one can come up with a definition of the term that would satisfy the critical scrutiny of a diverse segment of speakers of American English. Rather than foray into the semantic, philosophical, and scholarly features of definition, let us limit our inquiry to the practical side of the law since this book is designed as an introduction for those who are considering the practice of law as a career field. We hope the text will also serve those who simply want to know more about the field, but the focus will be practical or, better said, an introduction to the practical. This simplifies our definitional quandary: *Law* is what lawyers do, what judges decide, what legislators make. Law is more than that, broader than that, but let us leave any such expansions for another book.

In a sense, this chapter covers what the law says the law is. In particular, we will look at what it is that lawyers do when they are described as "practicing law." Be forewarned, however: even the practice of law is hard to define. Lawyers are licensed to practice law and unlicensed individuals are prohibited from practicing law, but the courts and the professional associations that make the prohibitions have had a difficult time delineating what exactly constitutes those activities that are strictly the practice of law. Some things—for example, representing someone before a court of law—are nearly universally considered the territory of lawyers, while others, such as giving someone advice as to the conduct of affairs, are not always easy to label or recognize as legal advice.

The people we call *lawyers* or, alternatively, *attorneys* may be identified by the custom of licensing. One definition of a lawyer, then, is one who is licensed to practice law. What exactly a lawyer is licensed to do is problematic. Bar associations and state supreme courts have often despaired of finding a definition; in the latter part of this chapter, we examine an area called "the unauthorized practice of law" in an attempt to discern what the practice of law is by looking at what those without licenses may not do. Some of this inquiry accompanies our discussion of legal assistants, or *paralegals*, who are essential adjuncts to lawyers and law firms.

An important theme of this chapter concerns the broad range of advice and services that lawyers provide to the public. "Lawyering" is not simply a matter of giving legal advice, drafting legal documents, and appearing in court. Contemporary American life is complex in large part because of the regulation of all spheres of human endeavor. In many ways, law defines and regulates life, love, and death, not to mention property, business, crime, and injury. The first author, having taught in higher education for nearly three decades, would today give advice that did not occur to him 30 years ago to anyone embarking on a teaching career: "Don't sign that teaching contract until you have shown it to an attorney; and make sure you consult an attorney who specializes in academic contracts." It would be wise, in fact, to consult an attorney before making any important decision: buying a house, getting married, making a will, starting or investing in a business. Lawyers have a wealth of knowledge by virtue first of their legal training and second because they spend their days anticipating and solving myriad problems. As a result, they can provide a great deal of advice about the law and about many of life's problems.

Let us, then, inquire into who lawyers are and how they become lawyers. Thereafter we discuss what lawyers do, what they should not do, and what others may not do. All of this is important information about the legal profession, but it is also an important first step toward understanding law and the legal system. Lawyers in general maintain and direct the law and its system. Those special lawyers we call *judges* enforce and define the law. Formal lawmaking is the province of legislators, who need not be lawyers but often are and who almost never draft legislation without legal consultation.

THE LAW AND THE LAWYER

Lawyers are named after the subject matter of the profession, the law. Unfortunately, the field of law is not as easily described as, say, electrical engineering. The problem of precisely defining law may be left to legal philosophers and scholars of **jurisprudence**. The primary concern of this study is with law in operation or "in practice." Lawyers are called professionals, but are also referred to as *practitioners,* referring to the professional application of learned skills. The practice of law includes a great variety of services furnished by lawyers to their clients.

For practical purposes, *law* may be defined as a process, a system, or a set of rules governing society. As a process, law can be viewed as the means by which rights and duties are created and exercised. As a system, law interconnects rules governing society with a hierarchy of courts served by the legal profession and the police. As a set of rules,

jurisprudence
Commonly defined as the science or philosophy of law; it is generally concerned with the nature of law and legal systems.

law is a complex code of conduct and values formally established and published, backed by the threat of enforcement. This last view of law as rules is what law students regularly study and what the public generally views as the law.

Failure to understand law as system and process, however, leads to a distorted view of law and lawyers. For example, nonlawyers often regard **plea bargaining** as an unethical device used by criminal defense lawyers to circumvent justice. Plea bargaining makes sense only in the context of the pressures and problems inherent in the administration of criminal justice. It has become an indispensable aid (some might say a necessary evil) in resolving criminal cases in the context of overcrowded jails, overburdened court **dockets**, and overworked **prosecutors**.

One must never forget that law continually undergoes change. Not only do the rules change, but the legal system also changes. As society changes, so must law. Law has a particularly important place in American society, which is extremely diverse and complex in comparison with other societies. The various parts of American society express differing and often conflicting values, so a major task of law is to convert values into functioning rules. In recent times, America has encountered major value confrontations over issues such as racial discrimination, same-sex marriage, the death penalty, and abortion. Although these are social, political, and even spiritual issues, Americans have looked to law and the legal system for their resolution.

The law we discuss in the following chapters is American law, the law of the American legal system as practiced by the legal profession. It might more properly be labeled "Anglo-American law," as we have more than nine hundred years of unbroken legal tradition from England. The severing of political bonds with England in 1776 did not bring a corresponding break with the English legal tradition. In fact, it has been argued convincingly that the American colonials were fighting for the rights normally accorded Englishmen in England but denied to Americans by colonial governments.

Law is concerned with rights, duties, obligations, and privileges and their enforcement. Under the U.S. constitutional model, political authority is divided among the executive, legislative, and judicial branches of government. The study of law generally focuses on the judiciary because the courts in our system are entrusted with interpreting the law, and it is in the courts that disputes between opposing sides are resolved.

Disputes form the heart of our legal system, which has evolved as an **adversarial system** in which legal battle is waged by conflicting parties employing legal counsel to take their sides before an impartial judge and, if necessary, an impartial jury. The practice of law commonly involves advancing and protecting the interests of a client in a dispute, but equally important is the prevention of disputes. No ethical lawyer would write a **will** or **contract** or close a real estate transaction hoping that **litigation** will result. The test of a well-written will is whether its provisions are carried out uncontested; the test of a good contract is whether it has resolved all reasonably foreseeable conflicts in advance and allows the contracting parties to perform their obligations to their mutual satisfaction. Perhaps it is in this area of preventive law, in which lawyers foresee and avoid future problems, that they do their best work and provide their most valuable services. The public rarely recognizes that lawyers routinely perform this function. The uncontested will, the contract that is not **breached**, and the transaction that runs smoothly do not make headlines. For most lawyers, however, an appreciative and satisfied client is one of the frequent personal rewards of the practice of law.

plea bargaining
One accused of a crime can "bargain" through her attorney with the prosecutor; the bargain usually involves an agreement by the accused to plead guilty in return for favorable treatment, such as a lenient sentence, reduction to a lesser charge, or probation in lieu of incarceration.

docket
The court calendar of proceedings.

prosecutor
The attorney charged with prosecuting criminal cases on behalf of a state or the United States; a public employee commonly titled state attorney, district attorney, or United States. attorney.

adversarial system
The U.S. legal system in which litigants, typically represented by attorneys, argue their respective sides in a dispute before an impartial judge and jury.

will
A document through which a person directs how his or her property will be distributed after the person's death.

contract
An agreement that creates a legal relationship and obligations between two or more parties.

BECOMING A LAWYER

litigation
A dispute brought to court; derived from the Latin *lis*, which means lawsuit.

breach of contract
When a party fails to render the performance required by a contract.

bar
The term used to refer collectively to licensed members of the legal profession.

bench
Drawn from the term referring to the seat occupied by judges in court; refers to all judges collectively.

disbarment
The most severe professional disciplinary sanction, canceling an attorney's license to practice law.

bar examination
A written test required of an applicant for a license to practice law.

J.D.
The basic law degree; stands for "juris doctor" and is equivalent to the more traditional LL.B.

LL.B.
The basic law degree, a "bachelor of laws," replaced in most law schools today by J.D. (juris doctor).

To represent a client before a court, a person must become a member of the bar. In a general sense of the term, the **bar** refers to licensed members of the legal profession, the community of American lawyers, just as the term **bench** refers to all judges collectively. Requirements for membership, however, differ from state to state, and membership in one state bar does not confer membership in another state. In most states, licensing is regulated by the state supreme court with the assistance of the state bar association to which members pay annual dues. The state bar associations are responsible for maintaining standards of conduct within the profession and for determining misconduct or assisting the court in disciplining members for misconduct with a variety of sanctions, the most severe of which is **disbarment**. Bar disciplinary boards are particularly concerned about misconduct in relations with clients, such as misuse of client funds or the failure to provide promised services. Bar associations also engage in review and reform of laws and provide a sounding board and even lobbying activities for the legal profession. If a state attempts to place new restrictions or taxes on lawyers, for example, they will be quick to respond through their respective bar associations. The authority and activities of the different associations vary considerably from state to state.

Admission to the bar requires one to pass a **bar examination** and submit to scrutiny by the bar association. As shown in Exhibit 1-1, bar examination passage rates vary from state to state; and some law school graduates take the examination two or more times before they pass. Traditionally, bar membership has required that each candidate be approved on the basis of moral character, as determined by the licensing association. In earlier times, the character and competence of an applicant for admission to the bar was vouched for by members of the bar; today, some states conduct extensive inquiry into each applicant's background.

Approval of an application to take the bar examination generally requires completion of law school and the receipt of a law degree, usually called a **J.D.** (Juris Doctor) or **LL.B.** (Bachelor of Laws), although some states allow senior law students to take the examination prior to graduation. Admission to law school normally requires completion of a four-year undergraduate degree.

Law School

To understand how lawyers think, some appreciation of the law school experience is helpful. Law school provides a type of rigorous training that formally and informally molds a certain sort of thinking. Strict emphasis on critical and analytical reasoning sets a high standard for legal debate and discussion, but some have argued that the focus is too narrow.

Admission to law school is highly competitive. Prestige and reputation are important in the legal profession and equally so to the law student because placement and salary upon graduation from law school depend upon the prestige of the law school and performance in law school. Entry to law school is based principally on undergraduate grade point average and scores obtained on the **Law School Admissions Test (LSAT)**. The more prestigious the law school, the higher one's grades and scores must be to obtain admission. Intense competition is characteristic of law students and happily encouraged by their professors, most of whom were once law school achievers.

EXHIBIT 1-1 2008 BAR EXAMINATION PASSAGE RATE*

SELECTED STATES	FIRST TIME TAKING EXAM	SUCCESSIVE TIME(S) TAKING EXAM
California	71%	30%
Florida	81%	30%
Illinois	91%	50%
Indiana	84%	49%
Louisiana	66%	54%
Massachusetts	89%	42%
Michigan	82%	29%
New Jersey	85%	43%
New York	81%	35%
Ohio	88%	43%
Oklahoma	93%	58%
Pennsylvania	87%	43%
South Dakota	95%	43%
Texas	84%	49%

*Source: National Conference of Bar Examiners

Among law schools, the most elite are considered "national law schools" because their orientations as well as their reputations are national. Yale Law School in New Haven, Connecticut, for example, is not a training ground for Connecticut lawyers but an entree to large New York law firms, the so-called Wall Street firms, which represent national business interests. The archetype of the perfect new **associate** just hired by a law firm is the person who went to Harvard Law School, became editor of the *Harvard Law Review*, and served a year or two as a **law clerk** for a United States Supreme Court **Justice**. Such credentials would guarantee a handsome salary at a top law firm.

Law school training continues to follow a model established in the 1890s by Dean Christopher Columbus Langdell of the Harvard Law School. He invented the **case method** in which students read judicial opinions, or cases, rather than treatises about law, formerly the dominant method of studying law. Langdell reasoned that the practice of law in the United States was based on discovering the law through judicial decisions because it was in the courts that law was interpreted and explained. A natural corollary to the case method is the *Socratic dialogue* between professor and student. Instead of lecturing, the law professor asks questions of the students about cases they have been assigned to read, so as to determine the issues and reasoning in the opinions. For the first-year law student, this is a grueling and often humiliating experience, which has been called a "game that only one (the professor) can play." It is a rite of passage in which

Law School Admissions Test (LSAT)

A written, largely multiple-choice, test required for admission at most law schools.

associate

The title usually given to a full-time member of a law firm who has not yet been elevated to partner.

law review

Publication issued by most accredited law schools, on a quarterly basis, with scholarly articles and comments on legal issues.

law clerk
A law school student who works summers or part time for private attorneys; also, top law students who obtain clerkships with judges after graduating from law school.

Justice
The title given to the judges of the Supreme Court of the United States and to the judges of the appellate courts of many of the states.

case method
A means of studying law that consists of reading judicial opinions (cases) and analyzing them under the law professor's questioning; since its introduction by Dean Langdell at Harvard Law School, this method has been the standard approach to law school instruction in the United States.

bailiff
An officer of the court charged with keeping order in the courtroom, having custody over prisoners and the jury.

court reporter
A person who makes verbatim recordings of court proceedings and other sworn statements, such as depositions, which can be reduced to printed transcripts.

students are forced to shed their former ways of thinking and reacting to issues and problems and begin to "think like lawyers." This method of teaching has been seriously criticized as promoting tunnel vision, but it succeeds in its goal of fostering analytical thinking and objective argument. Because of this criticism, however, many law schools have in recent years shown greater sensitivity to the needs of students, offering counseling and tutoring by staff and peers.

The human product of an American law school has read hundreds of judicial opinions and spent countless hours finding his or her way through an extensive law library but may never have been in a courtroom and may not know the difference between a **bailiff** and a **court reporter**. In recent years law schools have initiated or expanded the number of **clinical programs**, in which students practice law under the supervision of an instructor. In addition, many law students gain experience by serving as law clerks for law firms during the summers between academic years. Despite this occasional practical education, law schools focus on developing an attitude of mind that seeks the relevant legal issue in each human transaction and applies a technical, analytical approach to solving problems.

Obtaining a License to Practice Law

To represent a client in legal matters, an attorney must be licensed in the jurisdiction in which she or he practices. Each state has its own requirements for admission to practice, and the federal courts have their own requirements. Many states relax their requirements for long-term members of the bar of other states, but the process by which the newly graduated law student becomes an attorney follows a similar pattern in most states.

Application for licensing generally requires graduation from a law school approved by the American Bar Association (ABA) (in some states, nonapproved law schools are allowed). The applicant must also show good moral character, but the extent to which this is scrutinized depends on the state. *Moral fitness* is difficult to define and must be determined on a case-by-case basis; in the real world, bar examiners are especially concerned about defects in character that suggest a potential for betraying a client's trust or deceiving a court. For example, an individual previously convicted of **perjury** would be a poor candidate for the practice of law, having already demonstrated a disregard for the integrity of the justice system. Finally, admission is usually predicated on a passing score on the bar examination. What constitutes a passing score is determined by the examiners and often varies from state to state, giving some states the reputation as "hard" states for passing the bar.

Bar Examination

Upon completion of law school or just before graduation, aspiring candidates face the dreaded ordeal of the bar examination. This generally consists of two or three days of a written examination, which in most states consists of two parts. One part is the **Multistate Bar Examination**, a standardized national test that contains 200 multiple-choice questions on general legal topics such as property, contracts, and constitutional law. Each question is based on a hypothetical fact situation, and the examination requires a thorough knowledge of **black-letter law**. This mentally exhausting part of the examination lasts six hours.

The "Multistate" tests candidates' knowledge of general principles of law, but most states also require a second part that addresses law specific to the state administering the examination. This part of the examination often requires written essay questions based on hypothetical legal disputes and resembles the sorts of examinations typically given as final examinations in law school. Applicants must then wait several weeks, or even months, to receive the final results. Each state licensing board or supreme court is free to establish its own standards, so a passing grade on the Multistate in one state may be a failing grade in another. In most states, between 65 and 90 percent of examinees pass. A failing candidate can usually retake the examination, though some states limit the number of times the examination can be taken.

The bar examination not only establishes a minimum standard of competence for lawyers but also represents a psychological ordeal shared by attorneys; most recall the experience quite vividly. The Multistate in particular calls for an approach for which law students have not been prepared, namely, to marshal a broad knowledge of the law and apply it all at once to a series of multiple-choice questions. For this reason, most applicants take a bar review course lasting several weeks prior to the examination itself. Whereas law students have been accustomed to limiting their study to a particular subject over the course of an academic term, the bar examination requires the applicant to recall the sum of three years of legal study.

In most states, a license to practice law is predicated on membership in the state bar association. This signifies an **integrated bar**. Because the bar also acts as a lobbying organization, some members may object when their dues are spent on political efforts with which they disagree.

Attorney Employment

The vast majority of new bar members join private law firms, but significant numbers obtain employment as government attorneys or as **house counsel** for private corporations. A few brave souls decide to "hang out their shingles" and begin practicing law as sole practitioners or jointly with one or more law school colleagues. Despite three years of intensive training, few law school graduates are prepared for the demands of practice. They are unfamiliar with law office routine and management, including collecting for services rendered, the peculiarities of court systems, and standard practice areas such as interviewing clients and negotiating settlements. Successful practice requires interpersonal skills that are sorely neglected in law school. In addition, law school focuses on major legal issues presented in casebooks with national distribution. A law school graduate, before preparing for the bar exam, is likely to be totally ignorant of many areas of state law. A new lawyer is unlikely to know how to process a **bankruptcy**, do a tenant eviction, get a **zoning variance** from a city, or even conduct a **real estate closing**. Because of their unfamiliarity with so many features of day-to-day practice, new lawyers are most comfortable in the company of more experienced practitioners and their legal staff.

The competitive spirit of law school also directs many new lawyers to large firms. Already oriented toward achievement and success, graduating law students often

clinical programs
Programs found in most law schools, and sanctioned by the courts and the bar, in which students provide legal services to the public under the supervision of law professors; some schools require enrollment, but in most law schools "clinic" is a voluntary course for credit.

perjury
Knowingly making a false statement under oath in a judicial proceeding; the false statement must concern a material issue or fact in the proceeding.

Multistate Bar Examination
A standardized national test of general legal subjects, such as property, contracts, and constitutional law.

black-letter law
Lawyers' slang for the basic, well-established rules of law.

integrated bar
A state bar association in which membership is required in order to practice law.

house counsel
Full-time attorneys employed by many corporations and other businesses as part of the administrative staff; distinguished from "outside counsel."

bankruptcy
Generally, the situation in which a person, business, or government cannot or will not pay its debts, so its property is entrusted to a "trustee in bankruptcy" who distributes the property to creditors.

zoning variance
Exception to or specific modification of a zoning code or ordinance. It is customary in the United States for local governments to create *zones* within city and county boundaries with restrictions primarily on the form of use, for example, agricultural, residential, commercial, etc.

real estate closing
Culmination or completion of a real estate transaction(s), at which numerous documents are signed and exchanged, payment is made, and property deeds are transferred.

pro se **(Latin)**
"For oneself," "in one's own behalf." American law recognizes not only the right to be represented by an attorney but also the right to represent oneself in court.

measure themselves by starting salaries and the prestige of the law firms they join. Big-city law firms compete with each other for top law school graduates, and the largest Wall Street firms offer starting salaries more than twice the average.

Fortunately for our society, not all law graduates are driven to enrich themselves. It is very common for a graduate to return to his or her hometown to assume a respected position among friends and associates. Lawyers who choose this path inevitably find that the rewards of service to the community outweigh monetary compensation. The practice of law, like most other professions, offers an opportunity for personal satisfaction difficult to find in other kinds of employment.

Some law school graduates have specific goals for their training, such as preserving the environment, providing legal services to the poor, prosecuting criminals, or serving as elected legislators. The legal profession provides a unique foundation for contributing to change or improvement of one's society.

Obtaining prestigious employment, however, does not guarantee a successful career. New attorneys in a firm are called *associates*, a position from which they may never advance. The traditional course of a legal career in a private firm entails working for a few years as an associate and then being invited to become a partner in the firm, which means moving from collecting a salary to sharing in the profits of the firm. In the largest firms, only a small number of associates are ever asked to become partners. Associates who do not make partner commonly move to other firms or set up their own practices. This brutally competitive system has been improved somewhat in many firms by the establishment of intermediate positions like senior associate or junior partner. This allows firms to reward attorneys without forcing a partnership decision.

The pressures on attorneys to perform do not consist simply of providing good services to clients. A law firm is also a business, and attorneys who do not add significant profits to the business by way of new clients and many hours of work that are billable to clients are unlikely to become partners in a firm. For some, the advantage of employment with government or a private corporation is that an attorney is more often measured by the quality of work rather than the quantity of business generated. See Exhibit 1-2 for types of employment for law school graduates.

Paralegals must understand the stresses involved in the work of attorneys in order to work better with their employers. One of the advantages of paralegal work over that of an attorney is that paralegals do not bear ultimate responsibility for the outcome of clients' problems. The difference in stress can be great. Paralegals occupy a position similar to corporate lawyers in that performance is measured by the quality of their work.

An attorney licensed by the state bar may decide not to practice law and elect inactive status, as the physician/attorney did in *Applebaum v. Rush University Medical Center*. An attorney on inactive status maintains some contact with the legal community and can resume active status later without having to retake the state bar examination; however, an attorney on inactive status is precluded from practicing law. Although a person is entitled to represent himself or herself in court (appear *pro se*), Applebaum ran afoul of the state ethics rules when he filed a lawsuit representing himself in his capacity as administrator of his father's estate.

EXHIBIT 1-2 TYPE OF EMPLOYMENT FOR 2008 LAW SCHOOL GRADUATES*

Private practice	56.2%
Business	13.4%
Judicial clerk	9.6%
Other	6.2%
Public interest (including public defenders)	5.4%
Government	4.4%
Academic	2.3%
Unknown	1.2%

*Source: The Association for Legal Career Professionals

Michael APPLEBAUM, Special Adm'r of the Estate of Joseph APPLEBAUM, Deceased, Appellant

v.

RUSH UNIVERSITY MEDICAL CENTER

Supreme Court of Illinois

No. 105905

899 N.E.2d 262 (Ill. 2008)

The circuit court of Cook County certified the following question of law . . .:

"Whether the nullity rule should be applied in a wrongful death action where the plaintiff is an attorney who has passed the bar and was on inactive status at the time of the filing of the complaint, was the special administrator, sole beneficiary and son of the decedent and prior to the hearing on the motion whose license was reinstated." . . .

This **interlocutory appeal** has its genesis in a medical malpractice complaint filed on December 1, 2005, in the circuit court of Cook County. Plaintiff, Michael Applebaum, filed suit as special administrator of the estate of Joseph Applebaum, against Rush University Medical Center and other defendants, seeking damages for the estate pursuant to the Wrongful Death Act . . . and the Survival Act . . . stemming from defendants' alleged misconduct in treating decedent. Plaintiff is decedent's only child and the sole beneficiary of his estate, which had no creditors and was not opened to probate. . . .

Plaintiff signed the complaint as "Attorney for Plaintiff." The record reveals that plaintiff is a physician who received an Illinois license to practice law in 1988. The Attorney Registration and Disciplinary Commission (ARDC) has no record of plaintiff ever having been disciplined or being the subject of a public disciplinary proceeding. Plaintiff remained on "active" status with the ARDC until January 6, 2005, when, pursuant to our Rule 756(a)(5) . . ., he voluntarily changed his registration to that of an "inactive status attorney." This change in status occurred nearly one year prior to the filing of the medical malpractice complaint. . . .

The trial court . . . disagreed with defendants that this case required application of the nullity rule. Noting that the purpose of the nullity rule is to protect the public against unskilled and unscrupulous persons representing them in legal proceedings, the trial court found that the instant medical malpractice action filed by plaintiff—who has a law degree, who has been duly licensed in Illinois and never disciplined, who had resumed active status with the ARDC prior to the dismissal hearing, and who sought redress through this suit for alleged harm suffered by his father—did not present any of the concerns intended to be remedied by application of that rule. In addition, the court was troubled by the fact that applying the nullity rule and dismissing the action would foreclose any possibility of recourse for decedent's alleged injuries. . . .

[W]here a person who is not licensed to practice law in Illinois attempts to represent another party in legal proceedings, this rule permits dismissal of the cause, thereby treating the particular actions taken by that person as a nullity. *Sperry.*

It has long been settled that the inherent power to define and regulate the practice of law in this state resides in this court. *Sperry.* . . . The fundamental difference between an individual who has satisfied the licensing requirement—but runs afoul of a technical or administrative rule—and a person who has no license to practice law was highlighted in *Brigham.* In light of the framework of our rules, the plain language of Rule 756(a)(5), and our precedent as set forth in *Brigham* and *Sperry*, we reject the argument advanced by defendants, based upon the holding of the appellate court below, that plaintiff's inactive status is the equivalent of plaintiff being unlicensed, and that his filing of the complaint in this action constitutes the unlicensed practice of law calling for application of the harsh sanction of the nullity rule to void his actions. . . . We emphasize that an individual who has (i) graduated from law school; (ii) satisfied this court's character and fitness requirements; (iii) passed the bar examination; and (iv) obtained a license to practice law in this state does not become "unlicensed" by simply choosing to change his or her ARDC registration status from active to inactive. . . .

As discussed, in light of the specific facts in this case, we hold that the purposes served by applying the nullity rule—the protection of the public and the integrity of the court system from the harm presented by representation by unlicensed individuals—are not present here. Accordingly, the appellate court erred in concluding that the nullity rule should be imposed in this case.

We do note, however, that although plaintiff at all times remained licensed, Rule 756(a)(5) provides that he was no longer "eligible" to practice law on the date he filed the medical malpractice complaint by virtue of the fact that he was on inactive status. It is well settled that our rules are not mere suggestions; rather, "[t]hey have the force of law, and the presumption must be that they will be obeyed and enforced as written." . . . Attorneys are not free to ignore our rules, and, if they are found to have violated these precepts, they will be subject to appropriate discipline. . . .

For the foregoing reasons, we answer the certified question in the negative.

Case Questions

1. Why would a licensed attorney choose not to practice law?
2. Why would an attorney choose to go on inactive status rather than let his or her license lapse?
3. What is the nullity rule and what is its purpose?
4. Why do you think that Applebaum filed the case in violation of state ethics rules?
5. Should the practice of law be regulated by the highest court in the state or by the state agency responsible for regulating most occupations in the state?

Case Glossary

certify a question
    A procedure by which a lower court asks a higher court to answer a specific question posed by the lower court.

interlocutory appeal
    An appeal of a matter crucial to the lower court decision prior to the lower court reaching a final decision of the case.

WHAT LAWYERS DO

The United States has more than a half a million lawyers. They are assisted by more than two hundred thousand paralegals. Obviously, a great deal of legal work exists to support this workforce. What exactly do lawyers do?

Acquisition of knowledge in law school is merely the first step in becoming a competent attorney; this knowledge must be put into practice. Just as the LSAT is an imprecise predictor of performance in law school, law school grades are an imperfect predictor of success in the practice of law. Even the bar examination fails to measure many qualities essential to future success. An attorney is not simply a repository of legal knowledge and technical skills. An attorney is a problem solver who must rely on imagination, creativity, common sense, and psychology as well as the analytical skills learned in school. The rules that make up the body of the law are abstractions that take on meaning only in the course of human events. Attorneys are frequently addressed as "counselor," and this perhaps comes closer than any other word to the true nature of their work. Attorneys act as providers of legal services, advisors, counselors, negotiators, and agents for their clients.

Many states have attempted to define what lawyers do in order to clarify what is meant by *unauthorized practice of law (UPL)* because each state prohibits the unauthorized practice of law and punishes violations with fines and injunctions and (on rare occasions) with jail. In our legal system, we insist that crimes be clearly expressed by **statute.** Nevertheless, expressing what is prohibited as UPL has been difficult because it is difficult to articulate precisely what *only* lawyers may do.

statute
A law enacted by the legislative branch of government declaring, commanding, or prohibiting something.

An example of the dilemma posed by defining the practice of law can be found in an opinion of the Supreme Court of South Carolina, which has, as in most jurisdictions, the final say on rules of the bar. The South Carolina Bar Association, through a subcommittee, proposed rules for the unauthorized practice of law and submitted them to the Supreme Court of South Carolina with the following response:

> We commend the subcommittee for its Herculean efforts to define the practice of law. We are convinced, however, that it is neither practicable nor wise to attempt a comprehensive definition by way of a set of rules. Instead, we are convinced that the better course is to decide what is and what is not the unauthorized practice of law in the context of an actual case or controversy. . . .
>
> We urge any interested individual who becomes aware of such conduct [which might constitute unauthorized practice of law] to bring a **declaratory judgment** action in this Court's original jurisdiction to determine the validity of the conduct. *In re South Carolina Bar,* 309 S.C. 304, 422 S.E.2d 123 (1992)

declaratory judgment
A binding judgment that specifies the rights of the parties but orders no relief. It is the appropriate remedy for the determination of an actionable dispute when the plaintiff's legal rights are in doubt.

Although the court enumerated specific exceptions to unauthorized practice of law (e.g., CPAs working within their area of expertise and persons certified to represent parties before state agencies), it clearly preferred the case-by-case approach to defining the practice of law, or the unauthorized practice of law, to an arbitrary set of rules. If we recognize the different roles of bar and court, the decision makes more sense. Of course it would be fine to have a clear set of rules, but the practice of law is ever changing. Law firms are growing into huge businesses in which individual lawyers are highly specialized and assisted by staffs which perform tasks that only lawyers performed in the past. Bar associations, when dealing with unauthorized practice of law, are concerned with protecting their members from nonlawyers' encroachment into their activities. The courts are also concerned with the rights of members of the public to give and receive assistance in the conduct of their affairs. As we will see in Chapters 3 and 4, deciding cases and making rules are different processes; not all problems can be resolved in advance by a set of rules.

In many states, the highest court in the state has the authority to punish someone for unauthorized practice of law. Usually the court delegates the task of investigating the facts supporting unauthorized practice of law claims; in Delaware, for instance, the Supreme Court of Delaware gives this responsibility to the Office of Disciplinary Counsel, as shown in *In re Estep*. The office makes findings of fact and may recommend to the court a particular sanction. The court reviews the findings of fact and imposes sanctions. Estep was an accountant with his own area of expertise but had crossed into the practice of law by engaging in estate planning.

What is the court to do when someone continues to engage in unauthorized practice of law in contravention of the court's prior order? A court has the inherent authority to discipline someone who disobeys its order, as in *In re Estep*.

In the Matter of Ralph

v.

ESTEP, Respondent

No. 647, 2006

Supreme Court of Delaware

933 A.2d 763 (Del. 2007)

The Respondent, Ralph V. Estep, is a public accountant with an office in Wilmington, Delaware. The Respondent is not authorized to practice law in Delaware or any other jurisdiction. On October 30, 2006, this Court issued an order directing that the Respondent cease and desist the unauthorized practice of law ("**Cease and Desist Order**").

On December 11, 2006, the Office of Disciplinary Counsel ("ODC") filed a Petition for a **Rule to Show Cause** in this Court, alleging that the Respondent was in violation of the Cease and Desist Order. . . .

In the [June 6, 2006] Admissions, the Respondent agreed that the "drafting of wills and trusts by a non-lawyer who is not authorized to practice law by the Delaware Supreme Court constitutes the unauthorized practice of law. . . ." The Respondent further agreed that "acting in a representative capacity in the Register of Wills, giving legal advice on matters relating to Delaware estate law, and drafting legal documents for use in the Register of Wills by a non-lawyer each constitutes the unauthorized practice of law. . . ." The Respondent agreed that he would "not draft wills

and trusts, act in a representative capacity in the Register of Wills, give legal advice on matters relating to Delaware estate law, or draft legal documents for use in the Register of Wills and he would not advertise legal services related to 'wills,' 'trusts,' 'estate,' 'probate,' 'estate administration,' and 'estate and probate services' as services provided by his firm in any manner including print ads, yellow pages, billboards, on his letterhead, or elsewhere." . . .

This Court has exclusive authority and jurisdiction over matters involving the legal profession and the practice of law in the State of Delaware. Pursuant to that authority, this Court established the Board on the Unauthorized Practice of Law. This Court designated the ODC to evaluate, investigate and prosecute all matters relating to the unauthorized practice of law. . . .

The unauthorized practice of law is prohibited so that members of the public will receive legal representation only from a person who has demonstrated his or her competence to practice law by passing the bar examination, as well as the character and fitness examination, and who is subject to the Delaware Lawyers' Rules of Professional Responsibility. As this Court explained fifty years ago:

> The profession thus established arose out of a public necessity for the exclusion from the practice of law of unqualified persons. The attorney thus became an officer of the court and an important adjunct to the administration of justice. The profession from the very start was affected with a public interest and was created for the protection of the public.

Originally, anyone could practice law, but for the protection of the public it was found necessary to circumscribe that right. The advance of civilization and its material things has done nothing to change that fundamental fact. The existence of the legal profession is continued for the assistance of the public under limitations imposed by the court. Violations of those limitations are punished by the court through its process of citation for **contempt**. The admission of attorneys to practice, and the exclusion of unauthorized persons from practice lie within the province of this court. A violation of this court's exclusive right to license attorneys at law by presuming to practice law without such license is a contempt of its authority and punishable as such. . . .

[T]he issue is whether the Respondent engaged in the unauthorized practice of law as defined and agreed to by him in his Admissions and voluntary assurances to this Court that constituted the basis for the Cease and Desist Order. . . .

Respondent met with Burch and her granddaughter, Susan Cooper ("Cooper"), on November 3, 2006, to discuss estate planning. This consultation was typical of Respondent's meetings with other estate planning clients. For example, Cooper took Burch to Respondent to draft a will. Cooper, her grandmother, Respondent and a "tall young lady" from Respondent's office were the only people present during the initial meeting. No Delaware lawyer was present. After interviewing Burch and taking detailed notes during this meeting, Respondent provided his notes to Leonard Kingsley ("Kingsley"), an attorney admitted in Pennsylvania and New Jersey. Kingsley, who is not admitted to practice law in Delaware, then drafted a power of attorney, will and irrevocable trust for Burch as directed by Respondent. Respondent employed largely the same procedure regarding his estate planning work for Welsh, Abbott and Titus. . . .

Kingsley always received instructions from Respondent as to what documents to draft. After Kingsley prepared the legal documents, he returned them electronically to Respondent's office. With only two exceptions, Kingsley never met with Respondent's clients. The documents were then forwarded to Thomas McCracken, Esquire ("McCracken"), a member of the Delaware Bar. Kingsley never met with McCracken to discuss the documents.

Respondent and McCracken had a business agreement that was memorialized in a Memorandum of Understanding. Respondent testified that McCracken would draft documents, meet with clients and answer questions about the documents. But, Respondent's testimony on this point was directly contradicted by Kingsley and McCracken, both of whom testified that Kingsley, not McCracken, drafted the legal documents based on Respondent's instructions. The Board specifically found that Kingsley did the drafting, not McCracken.

McCracken received the draft legal documents electronically from Respondent but, unlike Kingsley, he did not receive Respondent's personal notes. McCracken played no role in determining what estate planning documents were prepared for Respondent's clients. Indeed, it is uncontroverted that none of Respondent's clients ever met McCracken before executing their legal documents. Their first introduction to their own lawyer was only moments before these documents were signed.

The Board found that Respondent's clients were intentionally misled about McCracken's role. When Respondent and McCracken met with clients to execute legal documents, the clients were presented a letter prepared by Respondent, but printed on McCracken's letterhead and signed by McCracken. This letter falsely informed the clients that McCracken "prepared the legal documents" to carry out the client's wishes. It also falsely stated that Respondent "and [McCracken] have decided that these documents will effectively carry out your intent from the estate and tax planning consultation you had with [Respondent]." Contrary to these representations, McCracken did not prepare the legal documents, nor did he form or express any opinions about whether the legal documents effectively carried out the client's intent. . . .

Respondent's business arrangements with Kingsley and McCracken constitute a transparent, nefarious attempt to circumvent the Cease and Desist Order and continue with "business as usual". . . . The Board found that the Respondent violated the Cease and Desist Order by engaging in the conduct set forth in Counts II, III, IV, V, VI, VII, [VIII], IX and X of the Amended Petition but that the conduct alleged in Counts I and XI was not contemptuous. The Board's findings of fact are supported by clear and convincing evidence and the product of a logical deductive reasoning process. Accordingly, those factual findings by the Board are accepted by this Court and will constitute the basis for imposing sanctions upon the Respondent. . . .

The Court holds the Respondent in contempt for violating the Cease and Desist Order, by engaging in the conduct set forth in Counts II-X of the Amended Petition. . . .

In addition to disgorging the foregoing fees in the amount of $17,868.75, the Respondent is fined $2000 for each of the nine counts of contemptuous conduct. Therefore, the Respondent is ordered to pay the Clerk of this Court $35,868.75 within thirty days of the date of this Opinion.

This Court's Cease and Desist Order shall remain in full force and effect. Any further violations by the Respondent will be sanctioned in an escalated manner that is commensurate with such repeat offenses.

Case Questions

1. What is the problem with a Delaware accountant meeting with clients and giving them estate planning advice?
2. What was the problem with Kingsley drafting the documents?
3. What was the problem with McCracken's role?
4. Why is the court concerned with an attorney licensed in another state drafting documents for Delaware clients?

Case Glossary

In the matter of
Indicates that this case does not involve two parties; that is, this is not plaintiff versus defendant. "In the matter of" is converted to "In re" in references, so that this case would be referred to as *In re Estep*.

cease and desist order
A court directive prohibiting someone from continuing to take a specific action.

rule to show cause
A court directive that someone appear in court to explain why the court should not take the contemplated action (in this case, why Estep should not be held in contempt).

contempt
An action taken in violation of a prior court directive.

§

The Lawyer as Provider of Legal Services

The public most commonly pictures the lawyer as a furnisher of services in legal problem solving. Although this may be the primary function of an attorney, the following sections reveal that attorneys also play many other roles.

The dramatic popular image of the lawyer focuses on the trial lawyer, when in actuality very few attorneys spend a significant portion of their time in court. Many lawyers never try cases, and most trial lawyers spend most of their time preparing for trial. Lawyers are basically problem solvers. Sometimes the problems are actual disputes that may lead to lawsuits and eventually to trial. Most disputes never reach the trial stage but are settled with the lawyer acting principally as negotiator or conciliator.

Much of the work that lawyers do has nothing to do with disputes. Many client problems do not involve an adversary but range from matters as simple as changing one's legal name to something as complicated as obtaining approval for a major airport. Potential adversaries may be lurking on the sidelines, but most problems require legal help largely because they have legal consequences. Incorporating a business must be accomplished in accordance with state law; writing a will must be done with formalities dictated by state law. Although these things may be done without an attorney, it is wiser and safer to employ professional services.

Most lawyers are specialists, whether they realize it or not. Some, for instance, handle only tax matters; others, who may call themselves general practitioners, may refuse to handle criminal or divorce cases. The body of the law is immense and constantly growing. No lawyer can adequately keep up with the changes in all areas of the law. If a lawyer accepts a case in an area in which she is not expert, it is her duty to educate herself before proceeding.

Because of specialization, the distribution of legal work for any particular lawyer varies considerably, but we may make some generalizations about how lawyers spend their time. They talk with clients, first to understand the problem, then to explain its legal ramifications to the client. They write many letters—to clients, to other attorneys, to a large variety of other sources—to request information. They are constantly reading. They read contracts furnished by their clients; they read wills and deeds and many other legal documents to assess their clients' duties, rights, and risks. They read a lot of "law," which may be research focused on a particular problem or dispute or may be designed to keep them current in areas of law of particular concern. Lawyers must be well informed about matters affecting their clients. It has been said that some lawyers specializing in **medical malpractice** cases know more about many fields of medicine than the average physician. In short, the attorney must know enough to provide competent legal representation to a client, an ethical duty imposed by every state bar association. (See Chapter 2 on current ethical codes.)

In short, lawyers must rely on their communication skills; they talk, they write, and they read. Those who view lawyers merely as clever manipulators of words fail to recognize that a primary function of law in our society is to reduce rules of conduct to precise language that can be applied to real situations. Lawyers exercise their verbal skills with knowledge of the law and supported by analytical training. In a legal context, words often are not used in the manner of casual speech. The attorney must use not only legal terms in a precise way but ordinary words as well. When dealing with the written word, attorneys read with a verbal microscope, analyzing each word and phrase for its legal implications. They are adept at what we might call "legal semantics." Anyone can memorize rules or fill out forms, but training, experience, and intelligence are required to use the special language of the law.

Lawyers are also organizers. Many transactions require detail and coordination. The merger of two corporations, for example, is a complex transaction that should be performed without leaving loose ends. Lawyers serve in such transactions to ensure that no legal problems will arise that could have been foreseen and avoided during the negotiations. They establish an orderly process to facilitate a smooth transition. Similarly, preparation for trial requires a step-by-step process in which all necessary information is collected and organized in a way that builds a logical and convincing presentation of the client's side of the lawsuit. As the case is built, it must be constantly reevaluated; lack of proper organization will produce poor results.

medical malpractice
A form of professional misconduct restricted to negligence in the medical field; an important field of legal specialization.

YOU be the JUDGE   *Unauthorized Practice of Law*

Which of the following acts, if performed by a layperson, constitute unauthorized practice of law?

- Publishing a packet of materials providing information on how to obtain a divorce.
- Selling a packet of materials providing information on how to obtain a divorce.
- Meeting with individuals contemplating divorce and advising them on a course of action.
- Helping individuals prepare documents for their divorce.

See State v. Winder, 348 N.Y.S.2d 270 (N.Y. App. Div. 1973).

The Lawyer as Advisor

Clients consult lawyers when they feel they need legal advice. Many transactions and events take place in our society that have legal significance, and common sense dictates that they be entrusted at least in part to someone knowledgeable regarding their legal ramifications. Most of these probably involve property transactions in some way, but those who are accused of a crime or are seeking compensation for injury can best protect their interests by employing an attorney.

A person making a will or buying a residence is involved in important property planning. For most, purchasing a home constitutes the largest investment of a lifetime, and the consequences of such a transaction should not be left to chance and ignorance. This transaction involves two principal areas of law: the law of real property and the law of contracts. Property law has evolved over many centuries and contains many relics of the past that present hidden traps for the unwary or the uninformed. The buyer may be presented with a standard contract for sale that provides reasonable protections for buyer and seller or may be confronted with a contract that was designed primarily for the benefit of the seller. In either case, the buyer is unlikely to understand the full import of the many clauses contained in the document. An attorney who is well versed in property law can explain the contract and advise the client about its possible dangers and how to deal with them.

As an advisor in these circumstances, the attorney does not give only legal advice. The attorney is likely to have a wealth of practical knowledge that has nothing to do with law, strictly speaking, such as the current state of local real estate prices, the most favorable mortgage rates, and planned or proposed development in the area. The attorney may know that the airport is about to change its flight paths in such a way that flights will pass directly over the home in question. Such information may be more valuable to a client than the explanation of rights and duties or the legal consequences of the contract itself.

Attorneys may be successful for many reasons, including politics and even luck, but most attorneys succeed because they provide valuable services. They are in a position to acquire a great deal of practical knowledge because they deal on a daily basis with countless problems that arise in the course of practice. An attorney who specializes in wills and **trusts,** for example, has seen countless examples of what can happen when

trust
A device whereby title to property is transferred to one person, the trustee, for the benefit of another, the beneficiary.

someone dies if relatives and in-laws fight over the deceased's **estate**. Writing a will for a client may appear to be a technical legal matter, yet an attorney's knowledge of human nature will influence the legal advice given.

This role of the lawyer as personal, practical advisor is also important with business clients. Many businesses frequently require legal help. Not only are they concerned with making contracts and buying and selling, but they must also be concerned with employee relations, government regulation, and taxation, not to mention the type of business organization that is appropriate to the enterprise. It is common for a close relationship to develop between an attorney and a business client. The attorney comes to understand the business and its needs, and the client often turns to the attorney for advice of a business and personal nature. The client also enjoys the **attorney-client privilege**, which allows the client to treat the attorney as a confidante who may be told matters that could not be disclosed to anyone else.

The Sixth Amendment to the United States Constitution guarantees a criminal defendant a certain level of advice and assistance from an attorney, often referred to as *effective assistance of counsel*. Although a court usually discusses **ineffective assistance of counsel** in the context of a criminal case, the term can be used in a civil case to indicate that a client suffered because the attorney's advice was not accurate. Does a client have any recourse when an attorney (or a paralegal in the attorney's law firm) wrongly advises the client and the court rules against the client because of the advice? In *Aris v. Mukasey*, the paralegal in the firm told Aris that no court hearing was scheduled; that information, the attorney's failure to file a document in court, and the attorney's continuing failure to provide advice were so far below the expected standard that Aris was nearly deported. At the time the case was decided, Mukasey was the Attorney General.

estate
Has several legal meanings; when used in reference to a decedent, it means the property rights to be distributed following death.

attorney-client privilege
Legal protection whereby confidential statements made by a client to an attorney may not be disclosed to others by the attorney without the client's permission.

ineffective assistance of counsel
Advice and assistance of an attorney that falls below the standard expected by the legal community.

Garfield Livern St. Valentine ARIS

v.

Michael B. MUKASEY

United States Court of Appeals, Second Circuit

Docket No. 07-1211-ag

517 F.3d 595 (2d Cir. 2008)

With disturbing frequency, this Court encounters evidence of ineffective representation by attorneys retained by immigrants seeking legal status in this country. We have previously indicated that ineffective assistance of counsel can constitute an "exceptional circumstance" warranting the reopening of a **deportation** order entered *in absentia*. . . . We write today to establish what we would have thought self-evident: A lawyer who misadvises his client concerning the date of an immigration hearing and then fails to inform the client of the deportation order entered *in absentia*

(or the ramifications thereof) has provided ineffective assistance. We further clarify that such misadvice may constitute ineffective assistance of counsel even where it is supplied by a paralegal providing scheduling information on behalf of a lawyer.

Petitioner Garfield Livern St. Valentine Aris, a native and citizen of Jamaica, seeks review of a decision of the Board of Immigration Appeals ("BIA") denying his motion to rescind an order of deportation entered *in absentia* and reopen his deportation proceedings. . . . The Immigration Judge ("IJ"), Sandy Hom, ordered Aris deported on May 3, 1995, following his failure to appear at the hearing scheduled for the previous day. . . .

In 1983, at the age of twelve, Aris entered the United States as a lawful immigrant. Aris's wife, daughter, stepdaughter, and mother all reside in the United States and are citizens of this country. Aris financially supports his wife and stepdaughter. He has no close family members in Jamaica.

The Immigration and Naturalization Service ("INS") issued an order to show cause charging that Aris was subject to deportation based on [a] 1991 cocaine conviction.... After he received the order to show cause, Aris hired David Scheinfeld of David Scheinfeld & Associates, PLLC to represent him in the immigration proceedings.

On April 15, 1994, accompanied by an associate from the firm, Aris attended a hearing before the IJ. Aris conceded deportability, and the IJ scheduled a hearing for May 2, 1995. In addition, the IJ granted Aris permission to apply for discretionary relief . . . , but required that Aris do so by the end of business that day. Counsel failed to file the application for § 212(c) relief, which in and of itself likely constitutes ineffective assistance of counsel in light of the equities of Aris's case. . . .

On May 2, 1995, having heard nothing from his lawyer, Aris phoned the law firm to check the status of the hearing. Aris spoke to a paralegal at the office who told him something to the effect that the firm calendar did not indicate any hearing scheduled for that day and that no attorneys were available to speak with him. Aris states that he relied on this information and did not appear at the May 2, 1995 hearing.

Evidently, the paralegal subsequently telephoned the immigration court, learned there was in fact a hearing scheduled, and tried to obtain an adjournment. But by the time she reached the court, the determination had been made to deport Aris. No one from the law firm ever contacted Aris to inform him that the paralegal had been mistaken concerning the hearing date or that he had been ordered deported *in absentia.*

Aris did receive a letter, dated September 25, 1995, informing him that the INS had made arrangements for his deportation. Aris took the letter to a lawyer at the firm, who assured Aris that he would take care of everything.

[A lawyer at the firm took steps, which were ineffective in resolving the situation, but the lawyer failed to keep Aris informed and for nearly ten years Aris assumed that the matter had been resolved. After applying for United States citizenship, Aris was arrested on the outstanding deportation order. Aris contacted another lawyer, who was also ineffective. Aris's family found an prominent law firm that agreed to represent Aris pro bono.] New counsel promptly investigated the various errors committed by Aris's prior counsel and filed disciplinary complaints against them with the New

York and New Jersey bars. New counsel also collected the necessary documents and moved before the BIA to reopen Aris's deportation proceedings, rescind the order entered *in absentia,* and remand the case to the immigration court. Aris's motion alleged ineffective assistance of prior counsel. It finally explained for the first time that Aris failed to appear at the May 2, 1995 hearing because a paralegal at his first lawyer's office wrongly informed him that there was no hearing scheduled for that day. . . .

We now join our sister circuits in concluding that, under BIA precedent . . . a lawyer's inaccurate advice to his client concerning an immigration hearing date can constitute "exceptional circumstances" excusing the alien's failure to appear at a deportation hearing, *see In re Grijalva-Barrera* and meriting the reopening of an *in absentia* deportation order. . . . The importance of quality representation is especially acute to immigrants, a vulnerable population who come to this country searching for a better life, and who often arrive unfamiliar with our language and culture, in economic deprivation and in fear. In immigration matters, so much is at stake—the right to remain in this country, to reunite a family, or to work. . . . Members of the bar enjoy a monopoly on legal practice, "a professionalized system designed in large part around [their] needs." David Luban, *Lawyers and Justice* 286 (1988). And for that reason, among others, lawyers have a duty to render competent services to their clients. *See* Robert W. Gordon, *The Independence of Lawyers,* 68 B.U.L. Rev. 1, 6 (1988) ("These freedoms are usually analyzed as part of a social bargain: they are public privileges awarded in exchange for public benefits."). When lawyers representing immigrants fail to live up to their professional obligations, it is all too often the immigrants they represent who suffer the consequences.

We appreciate that, unfortunately, calendar mishaps will from time to time occur. But the failure to communicate such mistakes, once discovered, to the client, and to take all necessary steps to correct them is more than regrettable—it is unacceptable. It is nondisclosure that turns the ineffective assistance of a mere scheduling error into more serious malpractice.

In sum, to the extent there was any uncertainty, we hold today that the logic of *In re Grijalva-Barrera* applies with equal force where the communication at issue involves the incorrect—and uncorrected—advice of a paralegal speaking on behalf of an attorney as to the scheduling of an immigration hearing. In addition, *In re Grijalva-Barrera* applies to comments, such as the one at issue in the instant case, concerning whether or not a hearing appears on the law firm's official schedule.

Mr. Aris's prior attorneys failed spectacularly to honor their professional obligation to him and to the legal system they were duty-bound to serve. Governmental authorities, whatever their roles, must be attentive to such lapses that so grievously undermine the administration of justice. Accordingly, we remand so Aris may have his § 212(c) application considered on the merits. . . .

For the reasons set forth above, we GRANT the petition for review, VACATE the decision of the BIA and REMAND this case for further proceedings consistent with this opinion.

Case Questions

1. Why does the court state that the action of a nonattorney (the paralegal) was a basis for the finding of ineffective assistance of counsel?

2. Why did the court call the person who accompanied Aris to the April 15, 1994, hearing "an associate"?

3. Whose responsibility was it to make sure that the hearing was properly scheduled on the law firm calendar?

4. According to the court, why are attorneys the only individuals allowed to practice law?

5. What is the distinction between ineffective assistance of counsel and legal malpractice?

Case Glossary

deportation

Removal of someone not a United States citizen from the United States and transfer to the country of origin.

in absentia

Without physical presence; here, without the client or attorney being present.

§

The Lawyer as Counselor

The role of counselor includes the role of advisor and more. The term is commonly used to refer to legal counsel, but in fact attorneys are often called upon to do much more. Certain areas of the practice of law entail personal counseling skills beyond legal skills, most notably divorce law. Lawyers must be prepared for the fact that clients deliver to them problems that the clients are not competent to handle themselves. When dealing with a client seeking divorce or one accused of a crime, the lawyer must be aware that the client is dealing with intensely emotional personal problems as well as immediate legal problems. Law school training rarely prepares the new attorney for this kind of conflict.

Although the function of the lawyer is to resolve a client's legal difficulties, the close personal and confidential relationship that often develops between lawyer and client can put the attorney in a role similar to that of a mental health counselor. Some lawyers avoid this role by taking a distant, strictly professional attitude toward their clients, but others feel that this can seem callous and insensitive to a client who may be very much in need of caring and understanding. To clients who may be full of guilt and pain and have low self-esteem, personal rejection by the person they are looking to for solutions can make them feel very alone.

On the surface, the lawyer's responsibility would seem to end with the furnishing of legal services, but the nature of the relationship between attorney and client affects the quality of the services rendered. A divorcing spouse or an incarcerated person may well be in an emotional state that weakens his or her ability to achieve a reasonable legal solution. Persons suing for compensation for personal injury often face loss of work, medical expenses, and other financial difficulties that render them vulnerable to unfair negotiations with an insurance company or corporation that views the dispute as merely a business transaction. An attorney insensitive to these personal problems may do a client a disservice.

Attorneys must also learn that a fine line must be drawn between caring and understanding and emotional involvement with a client's problems. It is one thing to have a personal relationship with a client and quite another to have a social or even romantic relationship. Taking a cue from mental health counselors, the lawyer should maintain a professional attitude without losing sight of the fact that clients are human beings deserving respect and understanding.

 ***Disbarred or Suspended Attorney Performing Law-Related Services***

- May a law firm hire a disbarred or suspended attorney to perform paralegal services?
- What type of supervision must the attorney provide under the circumstances?

See chart III of the 2009 Survey of Unauthorized Practice of Law Committees, accessible at http://www.abanet.org; *In re* Juhnke, 41 P.3d 855 (Kan. 2002).

The Lawyer as Negotiator

The attorney must give each client the best representation possible. In the adversarial legal system, a lawyer often appears to be the "hired gun," using all the tricks of the trade to destroy the opposing party. This picture misrepresents the role of the lawyer, who is more often a negotiator, mediator, and conciliator. In a personal injury case, for example, the attorney must weigh a number of factors besides winning. If a person injured in an auto accident is suing an insurance company, both sides will have made an estimate of reasonable compensation. Their estimates are based on past experience, both in negotiations and with awards made by juries and judges. If the initial estimates, which are kept secret, are close, it is likely that the two sides can come to an agreement early in the process. If this happens, a number of advantages accrue to the client. First, the client will not experience the considerable unpleasantness of a trial. Second, the client will not endure prolonged negotiations. Third, the expenses, including attorneys' fees, will be minimized.

The client in this case is best served by an attorney who is a persuasive negotiator and can convince the other parties that it is in their best interests to present reasonable offers of compensation. The attorney not only negotiates with the insurance company's attorney but also must apprise the client of the risks and strategies on both sides, so that the client has reasonable expectations. Although the client must make the final decision to accept or reject an offer of settlement, the attorney commonly acts as a mediator between the two sides, ultimately persuading the client that an offer should be accepted. It should be noted, however, that some insurance companies adopt a strategy of nonnegotiation, in which case the plaintiff's attorney must assume an aggressive and threatening posture.

The adversarial role is especially problematic in divorce cases. The legal process of divorce tends to aggravate an already painful and frequently hostile relationship between husband and wife. The best interests of clients go beyond maximizing economic benefits and parental rights. If minor children are involved, the divorcing parents need to establish at least a minimal basis of cooperation for the children's sake. A court battle is likely to leave everyone severely scarred emotionally. Nowhere are ethical and professional duties more perplexing than in divorce law. Divorce does not make unhappy people happy. Perhaps no other area of the practice of law produces so many dissatisfied clients. Interpersonal skills in negotiation, mediation, and conciliation are just as essential as legal skills in this field.

Negotiating skills are essential in commercial law as well. In business and real estate transactions, in contracts, and in structuring business organizations, the objective is usually to establish agreement among all concerned within the requirements of the law. Though different parties have different self-interests, business transactions are normally entered into because everyone benefits. The attorney acts as a facilitator and negotiator, at the same time protecting the client's interests. In some long-standing business relationships based on personal trust, legal counsel may actually be intrusive. If agreements have customarily been cemented with a handshake, the sudden appearance of a contract written by an attorney may be insulting and could damage the relationship. Again, the lawyer's legal skills must be tempered with sensitivity.

PARALEGALS/LEGAL ASSISTANTS

Origins

Today the terms **paralegal** and **legal assistant** are used interchangeably, though there has been some debate over which term is more descriptive. In some cities and even in individual law firms, the terms may be used to differentiate two jobs that also different in prestige, though there is no clear indication of which is higher. Thus, some lawyers and some legal staffers insist on two different meanings; it is simply a matter of custom. As with other areas of employment, the more skill and judgment required in a job, the more prestige that job is likely to carry.

Tasks assigned to paralegals today were, in times past, assigned to staff of the law firm or done by the lawyers themselves, that is, until *paralegal* came to be recognized as an essential job in law firms. Paralegals assist lawyers in providing legal services to clients, but there are a number of things paralegals cannot do because they are not licensed to practice law, a matter discussed later in this chapter. Because paralegals are employees of lawyers and law firms, the nature of their work depends largely on how their work is defined by their employers. Nevertheless, the types of tasks they perform have become increasingly standardized, in part because of the uniformity of the formal training they are receiving in educational institutions.

Although the paralegal profession is relatively recent in origin, lawyers have been using legal assistants in some form since the founding of our republic. Before bar associations, bar examinations, and law schools, it was the custom in the legal profession to learn law by apprenticeship in a law office, often called "reading the law." Except for those affluent enough to study law at the **Inns of Court** in London, early nineteenth-century lawyers learned law by assisting lawyers for a period of time, taking what opportunities

paralegal (legal assistant)
Generally, an employee in a law office who performs legal tasks under attorney supervision but who is not licensed to practice law. Some states allow paralegals to provide limited legal services without supervision. "Paralegal" as a title and a job is usually interchangeable with "legal assistant."

Inns of Court
Place in London where English lawyers were trained; for centuries, students learned the law there by association with legal scholars, lawyers, and judges.

they could to read cases and treatises about the law. This often took on an aspect of exploitation at low wages, but eventually the novice was sponsored by his employer to be accepted into practice by the courts of his jurisdiction. This form of legal education qualified bar applicants in most states well into the twentieth century, and contemporary law school students continue to serve much the same function when they work as law clerks in law offices during summer vacations from law school. It would be appropriate to refer to these students as paralegals, though the customary label is *clerk*. In communities with large law schools, law students and paralegals often compete for employment.

Before the rise of paralegalism, many lawyers trained their legal secretaries to perform legal tasks beyond the usual scope of secretarial work, and some attorneys still prefer this approach to hiring formally trained assistants. Many present-day paralegals were trained in this way. As the attorney's practice increased, the secretary was gradually converted into a full-time paralegal, and a new secretary was hired to do the secretarial/administrative work. The advantage of such an arrangement was that the lawyer was able to take an employee with whom a good working relationship had been established and train that person to do the specific auxiliary tasks the lawyer needed. The disadvantage was that both the lawyer and the secretary took time away from their work for the training.

The paralegal position would never have been invented had it not proven economically advantageous to law firms. The prime movers in paralegalism have been the largest law firms in the largest American cities. In large law firms, attorneys tend to be highly specialized, which tends to produce attorneys who are very knowledgeable and competent within their field of practice. They charge premium fees because they can provide quick delivery of high-quality legal services to large corporate and affluent private clients. However, this can be accomplished effectively only if the firm is a well-managed business. The lawyers are freed to concentrate on important tasks by the assistance of a competent staff, consisting primarily of law office managers, paralegals, and secretaries. The more support staff a lawyer has, the more time the lawyer can devote to delivering legal services and the more money can be brought into the firm. In many instances this benefits the clients, who can be billed for paralegal research, for example, at a significantly lower rate than the attorney's hourly rate. In short, paralegals came to occupy defined positions in large law firms simply because they were part of a rational allocation of work that improved the quality of legal services at the same time that it increased profit for the firm.

 *Business Cards and Law Firm Letterhead*

- Under what circumstances is it appropriate for a paralegal to give the paralegal's business cards to law firm clients?
- May a law firm list a paralegal on the law firm letterhead?

See comment to Guideline 5 of the ABA Model Guidelines for the Utilization of Paralegal Services, accessible at http://www.abanet.org/.

Paralegal Training

Because paralegals are as yet unlicensed, no formal training is required (but see California Business and Professions Code, § 6450 et seq.). As mentioned, many paralegals have been trained at work by their supervising attorney; some have even trained themselves. While we may call some persons paralegals by virtue of the completion of formal training, others are best defined by the nature of the work they do. In addition, many individuals working in law firms perform secretarial work as well as legal work that goes beyond what would normally be expected of a legal secretary. Whether we call such individuals legal secretaries or paralegals is presently a matter of choice.

Paralegal training is not currently monopolized by any one type of institution. This is unusual because training in most fields is clearly either vocational or academic. Paralegals should be viewed as professionals who must possess not only technical skills but also a firm grounding in the subject matter of their field, which is law. A *professional* is a person who applies a body of knowledge to aid people in solving their problems.

Perhaps an analogy with the English legal profession will be helpful. In England, the legal profession is divided into barristers and solicitors. **Solicitors** perform the day-to-day tasks of handling commercial transactions and advising clients with legal problems. **Barristers** are similar to what we in America call *trial lawyers;* they take from solicitors cases that cannot be resolved by negotiation and must be decided by trial in court. Although English solicitors have broader authority than American paralegals, the two are similar in the sense that their authority stops short of representation in court. Nevertheless, paralegals, like solicitors, are often present during trials to advise and assist the trial attorney. Solicitors are not merely technicians; rather, they must have an intimate knowledge of the law so as to adequately represent the interests of their clients.

Parallels with the English system are obvious, and recognition of paralegalism as a profession in its own right is imminent. To take their place beside the time-honored professions, paralegals must possess more than technical skills. They must also acquire a broad body of knowledge to help them exercise wise and effective judgments. With this in view, paralegal training takes on a serious mission.

Academic institutions conform to the traditions of academic training and the requirements of regional accrediting agencies, which monitor the activities of the institutions that seek continuing approval. The American Bar Association (ABA) has added its own approval process, which entails a detailed initial approval application and periodic review to maintain approval. Any program that has obtained ABA approval has received careful attention to ensure that it meets stringent requirements. Because the approval process is voluntary as well as costly and time consuming, many fine programs have declined to seek ABA approval. The American Association for Paralegal Education (AAfPE) plays a significant role in discussing and setting standards for paralegal programs.

Regional accreditation subjects an educational institution as a whole to intense scrutiny but does not necessarily subject its paralegal program to the same scrutiny; this is largely up to the institution itself. An institution like a community college or university that has both regional accreditation and ABA approval has undergone scrutiny through two processes. Though neither of these guarantees high quality, they demonstrate that a program has met important minimal standards. A less formal but nonetheless important measure of any program is its reputation among local attorneys. Like law schools

solicitor
A lawyer in England who handles all legal matters except trial work.

barrister
An English lawyer who specializes in trial work.

and the legal profession in general, reputation and prestige are very important. Good programs that graduate good paralegals will ultimately be recognized through the legal grapevine because attorneys have a serious interest in hiring competent paralegals.

Paralegal training programs can also be divided into degree programs and certificate programs. Degree programs are more typical of traditional academic programs, like those found in community college, college, and university settings, where a degree such as Associate of Science, Associate of Arts, or Bachelor of Arts is awarded. In these programs, the institution usually requires that the academic training meet a general standard that may require courses in addition to paralegal courses. In certificate programs, a certificate of satisfactory completion is conferred, and the programs usually limit themselves to the particular field of study. *Certificate programs* should not be confused with *certification* by the National Association of Legal Assistants (NALA), which conducts an optional examination of qualified paralegals leading to the designation *Certified Legal Assistant* and *Certified Paralegal.* Although this designation has no official legal status, NALA was an early entry into the paralegal field, assigning itself the mission of establishing standards for practicing paralegals; certification, like passing a bar exam, is evidence of professional knowledge and competence.

 *Legal Fees*

- May an attorney charge a client for paralegal services even though the amount charged is above the amount the attorney is paying the paralegal for performing the services?
- May an attorney compensate a paralegal for bringing a client to the law firm?

See Richlin Sec. Serv. Co. v. Chertoff, 128 S. Ct. 2007 (2008). Also see comment to Guidelines 8 and 9 of the ABA Model Guidelines for the Utilization of Paralegal Services, accessible at http://www.abanet.org/.

Curriculum

Paralegal courses echo those taught in law school. Both train legal practitioners, and the subjects are necessarily similar. Because of the variety of paralegal programs, the curriculum and pedagogy vary far more than they do in law school. Nevertheless, the basic subjects have changed little in name over the years. Both the law and legal curricula divide law into two major areas: **substantive law** and **procedural law**. (The distinction is extremely important in the law and perhaps should not be introduced here in what is largely descriptive content; but, like so many important legal themes and concepts, no obvious learning sequence presents itself.) Procedural law is aptly named because it deals with procedure: such things as **pleading, evidence, motions,** and **jurisdiction.** Substantive law in one sense covers all that is not procedural or, more specifically, the basic law of legal rights and duties. *Procedural law* is the means by which rights and

substantive law
The part of law that creates, defines, and regulates rights; compare to *procedural law,* which deals with the method of enforcing rights.

procedural law
The part of the law that deals with procedures and the proper or authorized method of doing things.

pleadings
Written formal documents framing the issues of a lawsuit, consisting primarily of what is alleged on the one side (for example, the plaintiff's complaint) or denied on the other (for example, the defendant's answer).

evidence
The information presented at trial; the rules of evidence are part of the procedural law.

motions
Requests that a judge make a ruling or take some other action.

jurisdiction
The authority, capacity, power, or right of a court to render a binding decision in a case.

duties may be enforced. *Substantive* is derived from *substance,* which is often contrasted with *form.* We are inclined to elevate substance over form in our personal values; but, in law, form—that is, procedure—is the structure that creates system rather than chaos and anarchy.

The word *right* conjures up fundamental rights, such as freedom of speech and equality before the law, but legal process is far more often involved in more mundane rights and duties. For example, the law recognizes that each of us has a right to be free of physical attack by others, to enjoy a reputation unsullied by malicious lies about our character, to enjoy our privacy, and to use our property in most ways that do not intrude on the rights of others. Furthermore, each of us has a duty to not deprive others of those same rights. The substantive law delineates those rights. Later chapters of this book, which discuss contracts, torts, and property law, among other issues, contain basic treatment of substantive rights and duties. The chapters on civil procedure and criminal procedure deal with basic procedural law. These subjects and others form a basic curriculum for both law schools and paralegal programs.

The difference between curricula of law schools and paralegal programs lies not so much in subject matter as in method. The case method discussed earlier in this chapter is a staple of law schools but is used sparingly in undergraduate education. This book, by the way, uses a modified case method: case excerpts are found in each chapter, but the bulk of the book consists of descriptive comments about the law. Paralegal programs typically include more courses based on practice, whereas law schools relegate this field to on-the-job training or the so-called clinical courses, which are usually voluntary programs. Law schools are often the battlegrounds for theoretical disputes about law, such as feminist legal theory and the radical critique that in the late twentieth century challenged the traditional business—some might call "patriarchal"—focus of law school training. Paralegal training tends to avoid theoretical issues, except to the extent that such issues are encountered in a four-year curriculum that emphasizes a liberal arts focus over vocational training. The emphasis, of course, depends not merely on the formal curriculum but also on the orientation of the faculty.

Paralegals regularly receive training in law office skills that is absent from law school training. These may include computer program use, law office management, and specific legal clerical tasks. Paralegal training tends to be far more task oriented than law school training, which emphasizes analytical and verbal training. Paralegals frequently serve as interns, doing many of the tasks law students perform as summer law clerks. Many paralegals ultimately decide to go on to law school to be transformed into attorneys. See Exhibit 1-3 for types of employment for paralegals.

What Paralegals May Not Do

Before we discuss what paralegals actually do, it may be helpful to clarify what they may *not* do. This summary does not include all the areas in which paralegals may run into difficulties, such as splitting fees with attorneys, soliciting business for attorneys, and other ethical problems covered in Chapter 2; for now we confine the discussion to work tasks.

Problem areas are subsumed into what is called *unauthorized practice of law.* Some things may be done legally only by licensed attorneys, and most states have

EXHIBIT 1-3   TYPE OF EMPLOYMENT FOR PARALEGALS ANSWERING 2008 SURVEY*

Private law firm	64%
Insurance company	2%
Public sector/Government	8%
Self-employed	1%
Health/Medical	1%
Bank	1%
Corporation	18%
Court System	1%
Nonprofit corporation, foundation, or association	2%

Source: The Association of Legal Assistants

a statute that restricts the practice of law to attorneys. Limited exceptions may be made for realtors and accountants, for example, within their respective fields, and paralegals may enjoy limited privileges if the state has specifically authorized them. Those few states that have addressed this issue by statute have largely been concerned with what paralegals cannot do rather than with what they can do. It is incumbent upon paralegals to become familiar with the restrictions and privileges in effect in their state. Because many states are currently investigating the need for and desirability of regulating and licensing paralegals, we can anticipate that the range of permissible activities for paralegals will vary widely among the states and gradually settle into basic principles recognized nationally. Several national paralegal associations and the American Bar Association encourage uniformity among the states. In the meantime, individual paralegals must stay informed of the requirements of their states.

Despite variations among the states, it is possible to arrive at general principles because there is a consensus on what an attorney's license permits. Lawyers are privileged to provide legal advice and legal representation to clients. *Legal advice* means advising a client about legal rights and duties and especially about the proper course of action as it relates to the law. For instance, a paralegal may properly advise someone, "I think you ought to see a lawyer," but it would not be proper to say, "I think you ought to file a motion to dismiss." This extends even to matters of law clearly within the paralegal's knowledge and competence. *The temptation to advise must be resisted.* This proscription extends beyond actual clients—whenever a paralegal gives legal advice, she may be engaged in the unauthorized practice of law. The line is not always easy to draw. Consider the example of a friend laboring under the misconception that the **statute of limitations** is four years when the paralegal knows it to be only two. Should she quietly sit by and let her friend lose a suit? Without advising the friend on a course of legal action, the paralegal can certainly

statute of limitations

A federal or state law that specifies time limits within which suits must be filed for civil and criminal actions; they vary from state to state and from action to action.

question the friend's knowledge and suggest a visit to an attorney or provide a copy of pertinent state statutes, without interpretation that might constitute legal advice.

Legal representation includes a number of important activities, including representation before a court, which is the privileged domain of attorneys. This monopoly of the bar is necessary to exercise control over attorneys who act improperly and to enable clients who are improperly represented to sue their attorneys for malpractice. Nonlawyers may not represent others in court, may not sign documents submitted to the court in any proceeding, and may not sign any documents that call for an attorney's signature. The paralegal is not an agent of a client and must avoid any appearance of being one. There may be limited exceptions to this rule, but paralegals act at their peril in such matters and must be very clear on state law when interviewing clients or engaging in negotiations.

Observing two cardinal rules can avoid the dangers of legal representation by the paralegal. First, the client must always be aware that the paralegal is not an attorney. In any consultations with a client in which the paralegal may participate, especially in initial contacts, the status of paralegal should be made clear to the client. Letters written on law firm stationery (some states do not allow paralegals' names on the letterhead) should make clear that the letter is not from an attorney, for example, "As Mr. Clinton's paralegal, I have been asked to write concerning . . . [signed] Erin Summer, Paralegal." Even this might not be sufficient if legal advice is offered. Many clients do not know that paralegals are not lawyers.

The second rule concerns attorney supervision. As long as the paralegal is under the control and supervision of an attorney and the attorney exercises supervision properly, nearly all potential problems are avoided. Many legal documents, including pleadings, are prepared by paralegals and signed by lawyers. The attorney is responsible for ascertaining the paralegal's competence to prepare the documents and must review and amend the documents before signing them. Responsibility rests with the supervising attorney, who may be disciplined by the court or the bar association for problems created by a failure to supervise properly, but the paralegal must be aware of the dangers of such situations. Other activities that could constitute unauthorized practice of law include:

1. Negotiating fees or legal representation on behalf of the attorney
2. Discussing the merits of a case with attorneys for the other side
3. Assisting others in the unauthorized practice of law

 ***Becoming a Certified or Registered Paralegal***

Several states have voluntary programs that allow paralegals to hold themselves out as being certified or registered paralegals. Consider the following questions:

- What is the benefit of qualifying as a certified paralegal?
- What education or experience or both should be required?
- Should there be ethics requirements?
- Does certification or registration allow a paralegal to perform legal services independent of an attorney?

- What continuing education should be required for the paralegal to renew certification or registration?
- Does your state have such a program? If so, what are the requirements to participate?

To see how North Carolina, Ohio, and Texas have answered these questions, see http://www.nccertifiedparalegal.gov/; http://www.ohiobar.org (accessible under "certification"); http://txpd.org. California restricts the use of "paralegal" and "legal assistant" to someone with knowledge of the law (as gauged by education or work experience or both) and who fulfills continuing education requirements. Cal. Bus. & Prof. Code §§ 6450–6456.

Licensing/Certification/Registration

legal technician

Person who provides legal services for compensation without attorney supervision.

The terms *paralegal* and *legal assistant* both imply attorney supervision. There are also a number of persons now calling themselves **legal technicians**, who provide legal services without attorney supervision. A movement toward licensing appears to have started in California, where a significant number of independent paralegals risked legal sanctions for providing services to the public. Although the California Bar Association disapproved the proposed licensing of paralegals in November 1990, the issue survives. Several states have formalized licensing bills in the state legislatures, including Illinois, Minnesota, Washington, and Oregon. In 1994, Arizona followed other states in postponing comprehensive regulation and licensing. Until a consensus is built in the bar of at least one state or until someone frames a case for the courts, the problem of regulation is likely to be tabled for the time being, but it will not go away as long as the number of nonlawyers offering legal services continues to increase. The current issue is likely to shift from *whether* to license paralegals to who will be responsible for regulating them.

At least four states have given semiofficial status to paralegals through voluntary certification and registration programs. Certification and registration may not fully resolve the problem of what paralegals and others may or may not do, but it does assure minimal qualifications in a field in which anyone can use the label "paralegal." Bar associations would seem to be the appropriate organizations for regulating paralegals because of their long experience in establishing standards of legal competence to practice law.

The North Carolina Bar Association began certifying paralegals in July 2005. Individuals not certified by the North Carolina Bar Association may perform paralegal tasks under the supervision of an attorney. This implies, of course, that certified paralegals could provide services without attorney supervision, but that is clearly not the case. "The Plan," as it is called, continues to require attorney supervision except when a nonlawyer is by law allowed to represent someone (e.g., Social Security Disability cases).

In 2005, Florida faced the problem of a legislature demanding paralegal standards, so that The Florida Bar Association began once again to address the problem, preferring to assume responsibility for registration rather than allow the legislature to adopt standards or delegate authority to another agency.

Supreme Court of Florida

In re AMENDMENTS TO THE RULES REGULATING THE FLORIDA BAR-FLORIDA REGISTERED PARALEGAL PROGRAM

No. SC06-1622

Nov. 15, 2007

PER CURIAM.

This matter is before the Court on the petition of The Florida Bar proposing that the Court amend the Rules Regulating the Florida Bar by adopting chapter 20, the Florida Registered Paralegal Program. . . .

Background

The Bar undertook its study of the issue of paralegal certification or registration in 2005 when legislation to institute a regulatory scheme for paralegals was introduced before the Florida Legislature. The Bar opposed the proposed legislation, in part because it believed that any regulation of paralegals should be in the judicial, rather than the legislative, branch. The President of The Florida Bar at the time, Alan Bookman, appointed the Special Committee to Study Paralegal Regulation (Committee) to study the status of paralegals in Florida. The Committee had twenty-four members, including four paralegals, three paralegal educators, Representative Juan Zapata (the proponent of one of the bills), and attorneys from various geographic areas and areas of practice in Florida.

After much study and debate and a complete public airing of the issue, including a public hearing in October 2005, The Florida Bar, on August 15, 2006, filed its "Petition to Amend the Rules Regulating the Florida Bar to Add Chapter 20-Florida Registered Paralegal Program" (hereinafter "petition"). The Board of Governors approved the filing of the petition and unanimously approved the petition's proposed amendments and actions. The Bar published the instant proposals in *The Florida Bar News* and posted the proposals on its website. The notice directed readers who wished to comment on the proposals to file their comments directly with the Court after the Bar filed its report. . . .

The Court commends the many members of the paralegal profession and the paralegal organizations who filed comments on both sides of this issue. It is clear from the well-reasoned arguments received that all of the commenters are desirous of establishing high professional standards for the paralegal profession. While we are cognizant that the adoption of chapter 20 does not go as far as some would like, we nevertheless believe this is a first, prudent step toward the desired end. It behooves us to tread with caution in implementing a registration program for professionals who have hitherto been largely self-regulated, so that the efficacy of the program being adopted and its impact on both the legal and paralegal professions can be assessed before any mandatory plan is instituted. . . .

The Court need not address whether it has jurisdiction to "regulate" the paralegal profession because the rules proposed by the Bar that the Court adopts in this opinion do not establish "regulation" of the paralegal profession. Rather, they create a registration program, participation in which is purely voluntary. The Bar urges the Court to approve this voluntary registration plan for members of a profession who perform work that is clearly related to the practice of law. We do so because we believe the program will inure to the benefit of the public. . . .

Discussion

The new chapter 20 creates the Florida Registered Paralegal Program. It provides for voluntary registration of paralegals who meet certain minimum educational, certification, or work experience criteria and who agree to abide by an established code of ethics in exchange for the ability to refer to themselves as Florida Registered Paralegals.

[The preamble to chapter 20] states the purpose of the chapter. It also makes it clear that the chapter is not intended to set forth the duties a paralegal may perform or be deemed relevant in charging or awarding fees for the services rendered by nonlawyer employees. . . .

Rule 20-2.1 . . . defines a "paralegal" to be someone with education, training, or work experience who works under the direction and supervision of a member of the Bar and who performs specifically delegated substantive legal work for which the Bar member is responsible. A "Florida Registered Paralegal" [FRP] is someone who meets the definition of a paralegal who also meets the requirements for registration set forth in rules 20-3.1 and 20-4.1. The rule also defines "paralegal work experience" and approved paralegal programs. . . .

Rule 20-5.1 provides that some individuals will be ineligible either to register as an FRP or to renew an already-existing registration. One such category is anyone who is currently suspended or disbarred or who resigned in lieu of discipline from the practice of law in any state or jurisdiction. Persons in the identified categories will still be able to work as unregistered paralegals in the employ of an attorney. . . .

[R]ule 20-6.1 . . . establishes the continuing education requirements for FRPs and specifies which courses or seminars will satisfy this requirement. . . .

Rule 20-7.1 . . . establishes the Code of Ethics and Responsibility governing FRPs. The code does not alter an attorney's obligation to supervise nonlawyer employees or to follow Florida's Code of Professional Responsibility.

We strongly emphasize, for the benefit of members of The Florida Bar, that the primary responsibility of monitoring the conduct and activities of all paralegals, whether they are FRPs or not, still rests with the lawyer by whom the individual paralegal is employed and under whose direction the paralegal performs substantive legal work. This responsibility cannot be delegated, and this voluntary registration program does not relieve the lawyer of that critical responsibility. . . .

[Eight rules in s]ubchapter 20-8 . . . establish the complaint and disciplinary process for violations of the Code of Ethics and Responsibility for FRPs established by subchapter 20-7. . . .

Rule 20-8.1 provides for district paralegal committees, at least one committee for each appellate district. Each committee will have at least three members, including at least one FRP and one Bar member. The rule provides for the appointment, terms of office,

and disqualification of committee members, a chair, vice-chair, and secretary. . . .

Rule 20-8.2 sets out the duties and authority of the district paralegal committees. The committees receive and evaluate complaints against FRPs and have the authority to remove or revoke a FRP's registration. The registration of a FRP may be suspended or revoked for any of an enumerated list of occurrences. . . .

Review of the district committee's actions is limited and does not involve the Court. A revocation or nonrenewal decision goes to the designated reviewer for the committee, who may affirm the decision, ask the committee to reconsider its decision, or refer the matter to the Disciplinary Review Committee (DRC) of The Florida Bar. The DRC may confirm, reject, or amend the designated reviewer's recommendation, in whole or in part. The DRC reports its findings to the Board of Governors of The Florida Bar, which may confirm, reject, or amend the DRC's recommendation, in whole or in part. The board is the last level of review. . . .

Conclusion

Accordingly, we amend the Rules Regulating the Florida Bar by adoption of chapter 20 establishing the Florida Registered Paralegal Program as reflected in the appendix to this opinion. These new rules shall become effective on March 1, 2008, at 12:01 a.m.

Case Questions

1. Which branch of state government should regulate paralegals: the legislative branch or the judicial branch? Why?
2. What is the distinction between regulating paralegals and creating a paralegal registration program?
3. Is a Florida Registered Paralegal permitted to provide legal services without being supervised by an attorney?
4. Why is a suspended or disbarred attorney prohibited from becoming a Florida Registered Paralegal?
5. What benefits are there to a paralegal becoming a Florida Registered Paralegal?

What Paralegals Do

Once impermissible tasks are eliminated, paralegals may do anything from typing and filing to preparing **appellate briefs**. An efficiently run law office will clarify the boundaries between paralegal work and the work of the rest of the office staff. Routine typing and filing should be assigned to the secretarial staff simply because such tasks do not effectively utilize the knowledge and skills of the paralegal.

Rather than catalog the myriad tasks that a paralegal can do, it is more instructive to consider what a paralegal *might* do in a case. In a complex case that may result in litigation, a paralegal may be assigned extensive duties of management and coordination. A supervising attorney can delegate tasks to a trusted and experienced paralegal to free the attorney from time-consuming, routine activities. In our hypothetical case, the attorney is working on a **contingency fee** basis, so the final fee will be the same regardless of who performs the work. In such a situation, the use of paralegals, who presumably earn considerably less than the supervising attorney, is very cost efficient. Keep in mind that consultations with the attorney should be frequent, and the attorney should directly supervise the paralegal's work. Depending on the complexity of the case, a paralegal may actually supervise other paralegals.

Hypothetical case: The parents of a five-year-old boy who has a rare form of cancer consult a personal injury firm concerning a possible lawsuit against a business adjacent to their residence that has been investigated for and charged with dumping toxic waste in back of the business premises. It has been determined by a public investigating agency that some of the effluent has caused contamination of the well water serving the surrounding neighborhood. The parents have received information that the particular chemicals disposed of have been linked elsewhere with their son's form of cancer. After a preliminary investigation, the law firm decides that the business wrongfully dumped toxic waste that caused contamination of the water supply, that a strong case can be made for a causal connection between the contamination and the child's cancer, and that the injuries sustained were sufficient to pursue the case on a contingency fee basis. What are some of the tasks that might be assigned to the paralegal working on the case? (This hypothetical may remind the reader of the movie, *Erin Brockovich*, which was similar with multiple plaintiffs. Brockovich may be this country's most famous paralegal.)

Numerous tasks could be performed by a paralegal assigned as case manager. A paralegal may be put in charge of many tasks and report directly to a supervising attorney. Some tasks may be delegated to a secretary or another assisting paralegal. Without a paralegal, some tasks, such as telephone calls to collect information and arrange meetings, would be performed by a legal secretary, while others would be performed by an attorney.

An attorney may prefer to have the paralegal present from the outset in any consultations with a client. In fact, the client may see the paralegal first in an interview to determine the nature of the case. All this depends on the practices of the firm and the relationship between attorney and paralegal. An advantage of having a paralegal present is that the client can be introduced in a setting in which the client perceives the paralegal as a trusted assistant to the attorney. In addition, the paralegal can take notes, thus freeing the attorney from having to talk and take notes at the same time. If the paralegal is not present, the attorney must later take time to explain the case to the paralegal.

appellate brief
A formal statement submitted to the appellate court. When a case is appealed, the appellant submits a written statement to the appellate court raising legal issues to be decided. The appellee then has a period within which to file an appellee's brief, challenging the appellant's arguments on the issues.

contingency fee
Arrangement between an attorney and a client under which the attorney receives compensation in the form of a percentage of the money recovered in a lawsuit; used predominantly in personal injury cases.

The paralegal will engage in some investigative activities. The facts as represented by a client are necessarily incomplete. Facts must thus be collected from other sources to get a complete picture and also to minimize any distortions the client may have conveyed. A report of the agency investigating the dumping of wastes will be sought. Any action taken against the business will be researched and its status followed through any final decision. The paralegal may make a visit to the site to take pictures of the client's property and its relation to the property on which the chemicals were dumped. The paralegal may question neighbors named by the client who have suffered illness(es) they believe to have been caused by the dumping of waste. In short, a full picture of the background and context in which these events took place should be established, both through informal investigation and questioning and through public and private records.

discovery

A pretrial procedure in which parties to a lawsuit ask for and receive information such as testimony, records, or other evidence from each other.

Pretrial preparation also involves formal devices for collecting information from the opposing party, called **discovery**. The paralegal can be instrumental in the pretrial process. He can arrange for depositions to be taken of the employees of the business and any other witnesses for the opposition. During the case, the attorney will develop what is often loosely called the "theory" of the case, that is, the most probable legal basis for winning the case, tying it into the facts of the case. It is called *theory* for two reasons. First, no one can be certain that the judge or jury will agree until the final decision. Second, the approach and even the basis for the lawsuit may change as the factual basis becomes clearer. Like a scientific theory, the theory of the case is a tentative explanation or working hypothesis that remains to be proved and may be adjusted if it is not working.

interrogatories

Pretrial written questions sent from one party to the other party in a lawsuit; one of several *discovery* devices.

In a good working relationship, attorney and paralegal share the story of a case and develop a strategy to deal with it. If a paralegal enjoys the confidence of the attorney, the paralegal can formulate questions for depositions, draft **interrogatories** to opposing counsel to obtain basic information, and participate in and sometimes direct other discovery processes such as requesting documents from the other side. The fact that the attorney is responsible for reviewing and approving or signing appropriate documents does not prevent the paralegal from doing most of the work. Oral depositions must be arranged at times convenient to attorneys for both sides as well as the person to be deposed. It is more economical for a paralegal or secretary to make such arrangements than an attorney. The case manager can track the process on the attorney's calendar to see that these tasks are completed. Obviously secretaries can perform such tasks, but it is more efficient to have someone in charge of the details of a particular case to ensure that everything has been done.

transcript

A written verbatim version of an oral statement. In law, transcripts are used most frequently in reference to depositions and trials.

Whether or not the paralegal is directly involved in the deposition itself, in a complicated case it is essential that the deposition be summarized and indexed. The court reporter typically reduces the deposition to a verbatim written **transcript**, which can often run to several hundred pages. Long transcripts are unmanageable without summaries and references to the pages of important topics discussed. Summarizing and indexing should be done by someone familiar with the case and its theory. This is a time-consuming job that can be accomplished by a paralegal, allowing better time management by the attorney.

Extensive legal research will be necessary in the case. As much as possible, the client's legal position must be bolstered by persuasive legal authority. This is not only important to persuade the trial judge, but is also instrumental in negotiations with opposing counsel. If a defendant's attorney is convinced that, under the law, the client has a losing case, focus will change from fighting the case to saving the client money by a favorable negotiation. A strong case built on solid research is an essential part of the negotiation process. Although some attorneys insist on doing most or all of the legal research, many paralegals are accomplished researchers. The most important ingredients in good research are thoroughness and perseverance.

Management of a complex case requires an orderly filing system. The many documents that accumulate in the course of the case must be readily available for review and preparation for trial. In our computer age, file management has been made much easier. Many software packages are available for litigation files, and a program can be tailored for specific styles of organization. Material can be stored by computers in ways that make retrieval fast and efficient. Nevertheless, a human being is still necessary to record and file the material on the computer, and paralegal case managers often perform or delegate and oversee these responsibilities.

Writing can also be an important activity for the paralegal. In complex litigation, a paralegal case manager may at many points in the case have a greater mastery of the legal and factual details of the case than the attorney, who as the decision maker has an overview of the case. The attorney may ask the paralegal to write memoranda about the case, and especially the legal issues of the case, so that the major issues are summarized in an analytical form that makes a quick review of the case and its status possible. Although analysis and writing require more skill than does research, experience is a great teacher. The fortunate paralegal works for an attorney who will take time to help build these skills.

Paralegals can also be instrumental in maintaining good client relations. One of the most frequent client complaints is difficulty in reaching attorneys by phone and in receiving return calls. Paralegals often have direct contact with clients and may have a better feel for clients' concerns. Clients may be reluctant to discuss all their concerns with the attorney, especially if they think of that five-dollar-a-minute clock ticking. The paralegal is often a more sympathetic and patient listener and can reassure the client that the case is proceeding in a timely fashion as well as relay the client's concerns to the attorney. Clients often feel that nothing is happening in their case if their attorney has not corresponded with them for some time. It is helpful for a client to know that more than one person is concerned about the case. The paralegal can call, receive calls, make sure that copies of letters and legal documents are sent to the client, and in other ways make the client appreciate that the case is receiving attention. The paralegal can also alert the attorney to angry clients and help head off unpleasant confrontations.

The tasks performed by paralegals are too numerous to catalog completely, but the following lists give some indication of paralegal duties in two specialized areas of the law. They borrow heavily from lists prepared by the Subcommittee on Legal Assistance of the New York State Bar Association:

Real Estate Transactions

1. Review the contract for sale of real property.
2. Request and obtain title searches.

3. Request and obtain survey of the property.

4. Prepare deeds.

5. Review title opinion and/or title insurance documents.

6. Prepare and review closing statements.

7. Forward, receive, and track documents for closing.

8. Monitor closing file for completeness and accuracy.

9. Track deadlines.

Wills and Trusts

1. Maintain files and indexes.

2. Conduct initial interview with fiduciary.

3. Prepare and file probate documents.

4. Arrange for publication and service of citation.

5. Prepare application for tax identification number.

6. Value assets.

7. Transfer property to trust.

8. Prepare decedent's final income tax return.

9. Prepare estate tax return.

10. Prepare applications for life insurance benefits.

11. Inventory investments, bank accounts, etc.

12. Pay decedent's debts and costs of administration.

13. Cancel credit cards.

14. Prepare final accounting.

15. Prepare final probate petition.

Similar lists could be compiled for corporate paralegals, tax paralegals, bankruptcy paralegals, or paralegals in virtually any other specialty field of law. The lists indicate the variety of formal document preparation and management required for activities involving property transfers. A great deal of work is required to ensure that these events are handled accurately, completely, and in a timely fashion.

 *Acts Constituting the Practice of Law*

Which of the following acts are delegable by an attorney to a paralegal, and which constitute unauthorized practice of law?

- A paralegal investigating and researching facts.
- A paralegal obtaining information from clients.
- A paralegal conducting a real estate closing without an attorney present.

- A paralegal conducting a deposition.
- A paralegal appearing in court.

See comment to Guideline 2 of the ABA Model Guidelines for the Utilization of Paralegal Services, accessible at http://www.abanet.org, and chart II in the 2009 Survey of Unauthorized Practice of Law Committees, accessible at http://www.abanet.org.

SUMMARY

Law school training and admission to the bar are the first steps in becoming a competent attorney. Although law school imparts a basic knowledge of important fields of the law, it emphasizes the development of analytical skills and does not provide either training for the daily tasks of the practice of law or the communication skills necessary for rendering valuable legal services. Law students often clerk in law offices during summer terms to gain experience in the practical side of the profession.

Lawyers are problem solvers; they help remove the legal hurdles from a client's path. Sometimes this means fighting a legal battle in the courtroom, but more often it involves resolving a dispute without going to trial. Perhaps attorneys spend an even greater portion of their time preventing disputes and aiding in personal and business transactions by anticipating and avoiding potential conflicts.

The practice of law entails many skills that are not taught in law school and are often absent from the popular image of the lawyer. These are primarily interpersonal communication skills that cast the attorney in the role of advisor, counselor, and negotiator.

The last years of the twentieth century witnessed a boom in large law firms and a trend toward specialization even in small ones. This accompanied an increase in personnel and technology. This same period saw the establishment of paralegal employment as an essential adjunct to the law office, part of a more businesslike emphasis in the legal profession. Paralegals, or legal assistants, perform a variety of tasks in law offices that depend largely on the needs of the firm. Paralegals today do many things that only lawyers did in the past, but there are certain things only lawyers may do, and anyone else who attempts to engage in these activities risks being charged with unauthorized practice of law. Representing clients in court and giving final legal advice top the list of activities that require membership in the bar. Independent paralegals, often called "legal technicians," must therefore walk a fine line. Licensure for paralegals has been considered for several years but has yet to come to pass.

KEY TERMS

adversarial system	bench	disbarment
appellate brief	black-letter law	discovery
associate	breach of contract	docket
attorney-client privilege	case method	estate
bailiff	clinical programs	evidence
bankruptcy	contingency fee	house counsel
bar	contract	ineffective assistance of
bar examination	court reporter	counsel
barrister	declaratory judgment	Inns of Court

integrated bar	LL.B.	*pro se*
interrogatories	marital settlement	prosecutor
J.D.	agreement	real estate closing
jurisdiction	medical malpractice	solicitor
jurisprudence	motions	statute
Justice	Multistate Bar	statute of limitations
law clerk	Examination	substantive law
law review	paralegal (legal assistant)	transcript
Law School Admissions	perjury	trust
Test (LSAT)	plea bargaining	will
legal technician	pleadings	zoning variance
litigation	procedural law	

CHAPTER REVIEW QUESTIONS

1. What is law as . . . a. Process? b. System? c. A set of rules?
2. Why has plea bargaining become necessary?
3. What is the adversarial system?
4. What is meant by the "bar"?
5. What are the basic qualifications for becoming a licensed attorney?
6. What is the traditional approach to teaching law in American law schools?
7. What are the principal roles of attorneys?
8. What may lawyers do that paralegals may not do?
9. What is the unauthorized practice of law?
10. What justifies granting lawyers a monopoly over representation before a court?

CRITICAL THINKING QUESTIONS

1. What criteria would you use to measure the success of an attorney?
2. Do the system and process under which a person becomes an attorney encourage a profession of privileged elitists?

CYBER EXERCISES

1. The United States Department of Labor, Bureau of Labor Statistics, publishes information on a wide range of careers in its *Occupational Outlook Handbook*, which is available online at http://www.bls.gov/ under "publications." Research the information available in the *Occupational Outlook Handbook* for someone seeking to become a paralegal and answer the following questions:
   a. How many jobs were held by paralegals and legal assistants?
   b. Where were paralegals and legal assistants employed?
   c. What is the job outlook for paralegals and legal assistants?
   d. What are the projected earnings for paralegals and legal assistants?

2. The United States Department of Labor, Bureau of Labor Statistics, publishes information on a wide range of careers in its *Occupational Outlook Handbook*, which is available online at http://www.bls.gov/ under "publications." Research the information available in the *Occupational Outlook Handbook* for someone seeking to become an attorney and answer the following questions:
    a. How many jobs were held by attorneys?
    b. What percentage of attorneys were self-employed, and where did the balance of attorneys work?
    c. What is the job outlook for attorneys?
    d. What are the projected earnings for attorneys?

3. Information concerning the Law School Admission test is accessible at http://www.lsac.org/.
    a. Is there a recommended major for someone planning to attend law school, and what are the traditional majors for those planning to attend law school?
    b. What courses might a first-year law school student expect to take?
    c. What are the fields in which an attorney might specialize, and which of these appeals most to you?

4. The *Official Guide to ABA-Approved Law Schools* is accessible at http://official-guide. lsac.org/. Provide answers to the following questions using the guide:
    a. What are the law schools in your state?
    b. What is the median grade point average and median LSAT score for at least three of the law schools in your state (or region)?
    c. Using your grade point average and your projected (or actual) LSAT score, what are the schools at which you have a 50% likelihood of being accepted?

5. The ABA Model Guidelines for the Utilization of Paralegal Services, accessible at http://www.abanet.org, provide guidance to an attorney working with a paralegal. Provide answers to the following questions using the guidelines:
    a. Which three tasks may not be delegated by the attorney to the paralegal?
    b. How should the attorney introduce the paralegal to clients, other attorneys, and court personnel?
    c. When working with a paralegal, what steps should an attorney take to safeguard client confidential information?

6. The NALA Code of Ethics and Professional Responsibility is accessible at http://www.nala.org/. Provide answers to the following questions using the code:
    a. What restrictions does the code place on services performed by a paralegal even if the services have been properly delegated by and supervised by an attorney?
    b. What activities are prohibited to the paralegal?
    c. What duty does the paralegal have when initially meeting with a client, attorney, court personnel, or member of the public?
    d. What is the relationship between the NALA Code and attorney ethics rules?

7. The *2009 Survey of Unauthorized Practice of Law Committees* is accessible at http://www.abanet.org. The survey includes charts with state-specific information. Review the charts and provide the following information concerning your state:
    a. Does your state define the practice of law, and, if so, where can one locate the information?
    b. Does your state define unauthorized practice of law, and, if so, where can one locate the information?

SCENARIO

marital settlement agreement

A contract between spouses concerning division and ownership of property acquired during the marriage and entered into in contemplation of separation or divorce.

You have been working as a paralegal for five years for an attorney specializing in divorce and family law. A close friend comes to you for help. He says that his wife has filed for divorce and has presented him with a **marital settlement agreement** drawn up by her attorney, and he wants you to read it and tell him what you think of it. You have prepared many of these agreements yourself and know that in your jurisdiction the judges routinely approve such agreements when signed by both parties unless they appear grossly unfair to one party. Your friend says that the agreement appears to him to reflect his oral agreements with his wife before she consulted an attorney. He has consulted several attorneys, and all want at least $1,500 to represent him. He says he cannot afford this additional expense and will not hire an attorney unless absolutely necessary. If you do not read the agreement, he says, he will simply take his chances by signing it. He knows you are a paralegal and not licensed to practice law.

What are the ethical considerations?

1. Does it matter whether your friend pays you for this service?
2. Must you advise your friend to consult an attorney?
3. Must you refuse to read the agreement?
4. If you read the agreement and are convinced that it is fair and legally sound, can you so inform your friend?
5. If you read the agreement and have doubts about some of its clauses, what can you tell your friend?
6. Can you advise your friend with a disclaimer to the effect that you are not an attorney, that your advice may be incorrect, and that he should consult an attorney?

Student CD-Rom

For additional materials, please go to the CD in this book.

Online Companion™

For additional resources, please go to http://www.paralegal.delmar.cengage.com

CHAPTER 2

ETHICS

INTRODUCTION

The study of ethics is a branch of philosophy. The **ethics** discussed in this chapter is more appropriately labeled **legal ethics**, which has developed over the past century from an intuitive sense of duty and responsibility to an explicit set of rules governing the professional conduct of attorneys. Violation of the rules subjects attorneys to disciplinary action.

It must be cautioned at the outset that a strong sense of right and wrong will not guarantee avoidance of violations of professional ethics, though it certainly minimizes the danger. The practice of law involves duties to clients, to the public, to the courts, and to colleagues. Lawyers have access to sensitive, confidential information about their clients, and that information must often necessarily be shared with law office staff. In the representation of clients, attorneys are frequently faced with ethical dilemmas that are not easily solved. Ethical codes are designed to provide answers to most of these dilemmas, but they cannot precisely address every possible situation. Clients can be unpredictable and even unscrupulous, consciously or unconsciously putting attorneys in positions that lead to unfavorable outcomes. Only by strictly following the ethical codes and acting in utmost good faith can attorneys avoid the many traps that the practice of law entails.

In the past two decades, the legal profession has expended great effort to define and refine the principles governing the ethical conduct of attorneys. More than any other profession, the legal profession has embarked on a campaign to identify and police unethical conduct and fulfill its primary duty of serving the public and the legal system.

ethics
Concerns right or proper conduct and often refers to the fairness and honesty of a person's character. In philosophy, it covers the area of inquiry into right conduct.

legal ethics
Synonymous with "professional responsibility"; the legal profession promulgates specific rules to cover important areas of professional misconduct and disciplines transgressors.

HISTORY OF ETHICAL RULES

Formulating ethical principles has been an ongoing task of the American Bar Association (ABA), which established Canons of Ethics as early as 1908. The ABA has no disciplinary authority, but it is the appropriate forum for discussing ethical principles because it represents the bar nationwide. The Canons are general statements of principle urging proper conduct. They have been elaborated over the years through the addition and amendment of *Disciplinary Rules* and *Ethical Considerations,* which describe more specifically conduct that is subject to discipline (*Disciplinary Rules*) and conduct that, though improper, is not subject to discipline (*Ethical Considerations*).

In 1970, these principles were crystallized in the ABA's *Model Code of Professional Responsibility* and were quickly adopted by nearly all states. Once these principles were adopted, the Multistate Bar Examination devised a separate ethics test, which most states then made a part of their state bar examination. The ABA additionally provided advisory opinions on specific applications of the *Model Code,* and many state bar associations have similarly answered ethical questions posed by their members via the issuance of formal opinions.

In 1983, after several years of intense study and dialogue, the ABA reformulated legal ethics in the *Model Rules of Professional Conduct.* The *Model Rules* (as distinguished from the earlier *Model Code*) attempted to reflect changes in the legal profession; for instance, the former prohibition against advertising legal services was found by the U.S. Supreme Court to be an unconstitutional invasion of freedom of speech. The *Model Rules* also addressed conduct more specifically, narrowing the principles to increase clarity and enforceability. The *Model Rules* did away with *Disciplinary Rules* and *Ethical Considerations,* substituting "shall" and "shall not" ("a lawyer shall not seek to influence a judge, juror . . . except as permitted by law or the rules of court") as language warranting disciplinary action and "may" ("a lawyer may refuse to offer evidence that the lawyer reasonably believes is false") as language expressing conduct that is discretionary and not subject to disciplinary action.

The *Model Code* must be discussed along with the more recent *Model Rules* for three reasons:

1. The basic principles are quite similar.
2. Because the *Model Code* was the initial set of rules adopted by the states, a host of opinions and judicial decisions serve as precedents for interpretations of the *Rules.*
3. The *Model Rules* have not received the same degree of acceptance from state bar associations as the *Model Code* previously enjoyed.

 *Attorney Conflict of Interest*

An attorney representing an elderly couple prepared a durable power of attorney, which they signed. The durable power of attorney gave an "attorney-in-fact" power to act on the couple's behalf and named the attorney as their attorney-in-fact. Was it an unethical conflict of interest for the attorney both to draft the durable power of attorney and to be named in the document as attorney-in-fact?

After answering the question, consider whether the following information would alter your answer:

- The attorney borrowed a large sum of money from the couple without informing the couple of the loan.
- The attorney did not prepare anything in writing documenting the loan transaction.

See *In re* Williams, 659 S.E.2d 100 (S.C. 2008).

 *Attorney Conflict of Interest in Divorce Case*

Is it a conflict of interest for an attorney to represent both the husband and the wife in a divorce, when the attorney had represented the husband in the past and the wife trusts the husband and the attorney?

After answering the question, consider whether the following information would alter your answer:

- The attorney drafted the documents for the wife to file for divorce.
- The husband contacted the attorney and had the attorney draft the documents.
- The wife did not discuss the property settlement agreement with the attorney prior to signing it.
- The attorney assumed that the wife was receiving one half of the marital property but did not investigate the value of the property.
- The property was worth $82,500, but the settlement agreement gave the wife $8,807.

See Ishmael v. Millington, 50 Cal. Rptr. 592 (Cal. Dist. Ct. App. 1966).

THE *MODEL CODE* AND THE *MODEL RULES*

The Canons of Professional Responsibility of the *Model Code* are listed here with corresponding sections of the *Model Rules*. Although the same issues are addressed, a comparison reveals a distinct difference. The Canons somewhat resemble the Ten Commandments, a moral code to live by, whereas the *Model Rules* reflect a more sophisticated legislative approach, organized into related subject areas with specific proscriptions that provide better guidance to disciplinary boards and tribunals. The *Model Rules* are eminently more practical, both in terms of enforcement and in terms of the clarity provided to attorneys.

Keep in mind that the Canons were extensively supplemented by *Disciplinary Rules* and *Ethical Considerations* that spelled out specific problems. Nor does displaying the

Model Rules in this way show their higher degree of organization. The *Model Rules* were published with supplementary comments that address problems routinely confronted by attorneys and are a practical improvement over the *Model Code* as guidelines for attorneys. Nevertheless, because the *Model Rules* are more specific and more clearly enforceable, not all sectors of the bar have been satisfied with them, and the states have not received the *Model Rules* with the same wholehearted approval that the *Model Code* received.

 ***Attorney Use of Email Scanned by Computer***

An email service provider attaches advertisements relevant to the text of the email message. The advertisements are generated by a computer scanning the email text and attaching pertinent advertisements after the email has been sent and prior to the email being received by the intended recipient. Is it ethical for an attorney to send emails using this service provider?

After answering the question, consider whether the following information would alter your answer:
- The email contains no confidential information.
- The email contains confidential information.

See N.Y. St. B. Ass'n. Comm. Prof. Eth. Op. 820 (Feb. 8, 2008).

CODES FOR LEGAL ASSISTANTS

Legal assistant organizations have also formulated ethical codes designed specifically for paralegals. Because paralegals are not licensed, infractions of the rules do not incur any legal sanctions. This fact should not obscure the need for paralegals—and other office staff, for that matter—to be aware of legal ethics. When a paralegal in a law firm breaches ethical standards, he very likely subjects his attorney supervisor to disciplinary action. For example, if a paralegal discloses a client's confidential statements to someone outside the firm, an ethical breach has occurred and the supervising attorney may be held responsible. The ABA has promulgated *Model Guidelines for the Utilization of Legal Assistant Services,* which hold the attorney responsible for paralegal conduct under the attorney's direction or delegation and effectively assign attorneys the duty of ensuring that paralegals are aware of professional ethics. Legal ethics prohibit attorneys from assisting in the unauthorized practice of law, a violation of legal ethics more likely to be committed by a paralegal than a lawyer because the paralegal is unlicensed. There is, of course, a sanction that can be imposed on a paralegal: employment termination.

One of the most common ethical dilemmas for a paralegal occurs when an attorney delegates tasks that should be performed only by an attorney. Experienced paralegals are knowledgeable and competent and could, for example, often provide clients with sound legal advice, but are ethically prohibited from doing so. Paralegals commonly draft legal documents for attorneys. When an attorney submits or files such documents without reading them, an ethical breach has occurred even if the document is without a blemish, although the breach is not likely to come to anyone's attention. A paralegal is put in a delicate position when she becomes aware that this is happening; it is difficult to chastise the boss.

The National Association of Legal Assistants drafted a *Code of Ethics and Professional Responsibility* in 1975, the most recent revision of which was published in 1995. It is composed of nine canons, in the ABA tradition, but, in contrast to the old ABA *Model Code,* concentrates on the unauthorized practice of law. When and if paralegals are licensed, we can anticipate more specific prohibitions like the ABA's *Model Rules.*

Ethical standards have always required attorneys to provide "zealous representation" to their clients. Canon 7: "A lawyer should represent a client zealously within the bounds of the law." Attorneys are, however, officers of the court and thereby charged with a duty to uphold the judicial system, as well as to maintain the dignity of the courts and the legal profession. A problem often arises when an attorney's zeal for a client's case or cause exceeds the boundaries of proper practice. In the *Tweedy* case, attorney Craig Tweedy seems to have become so zealous in his involvement in some cases that he acted improperly. Among the allegations not included in the case excerpts were "communication with a person who is represented by counsel" and "false and reckless statements about a judge." The primary issue, however, dealt with "his continued filing of frivolous and vexatious motions and pleadings after being directed by two levels of federal courts not to do so." He was suspended from practice before the federal courts in Oklahoma, and this resulted in the Oklahoma Bar Association bringing complaints.

Tweedy demonstrates the limits of ethical considerations. When attorneys act improperly, judges are usually quick to admonish them and the improprieties usually end. When the conduct occurs in the courtroom, a judge may threaten contempt of court, which ordinarily frightens the attorney into an apology and the exercise of restraint. Tweedy's conduct was interesting in that he went too far in certain cases but was otherwise cooperative and appropriate in his conduct. An important feature of the case is the issue of disbarment. The Oklahoma Supreme Court indicates its reluctance to invoke this most serious of professional disciplinary actions.

State of Oklahoma ex rel. Oklahoma Bar Association

v.

Craig R. Tweedy

Supreme Court of Oklahoma

2000 OK 37, 52 P.3d 1003

May 9, 2000

As Corrected May 18, 2000.

The Complainant Oklahoma Bar Association (OBA) brought disciplinary proceedings against Respondent Attorney, Craig R. Tweedy (Respondent)[.] . . .

The allegations against Respondent in Complaint I had their genesis in his handling of three separate matters in the United States District Court for the Northern District of Oklahoma (Northern District) and the United States Court of Appeals for the Tenth Circuit (Tenth Circuit), between 1986 and 1993. Both courts sanctioned Respondent for pursuing baseless legal claims and remedies in the three cases. The

Tenth Circuit eventually disbarred Respondent and the Northern District suspended him from practice for three years. The Northern District refused to subsequently reinstate Respondent upon the expiration of his three-year suspension. . . .

After a hearing, the PRT [Professional Responsibility Tribunal] found there was clear and convincing evidence that Respondent violated the ORPC [Oklahoma Rules of Professional Conduct], Rule 3.2 by making frivolous claims and contentions, Rule 8.2 by making false or reckless statements concerning the qualifications or integrity of a judge, Rule 8.4(d) by conduct prejudicial to the administration of justice, and Rule 1.1 by incompetent representation of clients. The PRT also found that Respondent violated the RGDP Rule 1.3 by conduct that discredits the legal profession. . . .

Upon these findings, the PRT recommended Respondent be disbarred for "his continued filing of frivolous and vexatious motions and pleadings after being directed by two levels of federal courts not to do so," for his refusal to acknowledge the unprofessional nature of his conduct, and for being suspended and denied reinstatement by the Northern District and disbarred by the Tenth Circuit. . . .

In considering the PRT's recommendations, we review the entire record de novo[.] . . .

III. COMPLAINT I, COUNT I, GRAHAM LITIGATION

In 1987, Respondent entered his appearance for the plaintiff, Graham, in her suit alleging wrongful termination, discrimination and harassment against American Airlines (Graham 1). The case was tried in the Northern District over a period of days. After the trial, in August of 1989, the court entered judgment for the defendant, American Airlines. After judgment in Graham 1, Respondent filed two cases in the state district court in Tulsa County regarding the same claim (Graham 2 and Graham 3). . . . American Airlines removed both cases to the [federal courts.] . . .

During the course of the Graham litigation, Respondent filed a myriad of post-trial motions. . . . In addition, he commenced two appeals to the Tenth Circuit both of which he later sought to dismiss. He also sought two **writs of mandamus** in the Tenth

Circuit. Ultimately the Tenth Circuit sanctioned Respondent, indicating that "[t]he record in this case is replete with multiple and vexatious filings by Plaintiff . . . so numerous and multiplicative we . . . have determined that sanctions are appropriate in this case."

. . . Regardless of his convictions to Graham's cause, Respondent was required to heed the law regarding the method of attacking judgments and the mandates of the Oklahoma Rules of Professional Conduct. Respondent failed in this regard. We find that the evidence establishes, by a clear and convincing standard, that Respondent's actions, as alleged in Count I, Complaint I, were prejudicial to the administration of justice. . . .

[The court goes on to the *Mullen* and *Burggraf* cases, which involved conduct strikingly similar to the *Graham* case. Other misconduct is discussed and the court notes throughout that Tweedy denied all wrongdoing and "either blamed the federal judicial system, his opposing parties, or a favored relationship between the two."]

An attorney must be zealous in his advocacy on behalf of his clients, but the rule is not without limits and the attorney must remain within the bounds of the law and ethical considerations. Respondent's conduct in the Graham, Mullen, and Burggraf litigation exceeded these bounds.

In imposing discipline, our purpose is not to punish the involved attorney, but to inquire into his continued fitness to practice law with a view to safeguarding the public, the courts and the legal profession. . . .

. . . Respondent has consistently cooperated with the OBA throughout this proceeding. Also, Respondent has apparently practiced law throughout the pendency of this matter without any further grievances. Both these factors tend to mitigate the severity of the punishment.

The PRT has recommended that Respondent be disbarred. We reject that recommendation for two primary reasons. . . . [First . . .] A review of cases in which this Court imposed disbarment as a discipline reveals the existence of conduct of a more serious degree of culpability.

Second, we are persuaded that the discipline imposed by the Northern District and Tenth

Circuit (the jurisdictions in which the misconduct occurred) has effectively served to deter Respondent from subsequent acts of professional misconduct. Respondent has apparently practiced law in the intervening seven years without any reported grievances. In view of this recent record, we are convinced that we can fulfill our purpose to protect the public and the courts generally by crafting a discipline short of disbarment.

For the reasons stated herein, Respondent is suspended from the practice of law for a period of six (6) months from the effective date of the filing of this pronouncement opinion. Respondent is ordered to pay costs in the amount of $1,340.25 relating to the investigation and disciplinary proceedings against

him not later than ninety (90) days after this opinion becomes final.

Case Questions

1. What seems to be the line between zealous representation of a client and overzealous representation?
2. Why did the court mete out a less severe penalty than had been recommended?

Case Glossary

writ of mandamus
An order requiring a public official to perform a duty.

DISCLOSURE

Many ethical problems can be resolved or mitigated by full disclosure to clients. Some conflict-of-interest situations may be eliminated by disclosure of the conflict to the client and opposing party and consent by both to continued representation. Even if an attorney represents a client in the mistaken belief that the ethical problem has been resolved, evidence of full disclosure indicates a good faith attempt by the attorney to resolve the ethical problem and may mitigate any resulting disciplinary action. Written documentation of disclosure is best.

In addition to disclosure to the parties, ethical questions over which some uncertainty exists may be addressed to an appropriate state bar ethics committee for an opinion on the ethical issues, if such a procedure is available.

 *Outsourcing Paralegal Services to India*

Is it ethical for an attorney licensed in the United States to hire paralegals in India to perform paralegal work? Consider the following additional information:
- A licensed attorney would review the paralegal's work and contact the client.
- The paralegal will have access to confidential client information.
- The attorney may or may not inform the client that the paralegal work is being outsourced to India.

To see how the Florida Bar answered these questions, see Fla. Bar Op. 07-2 (2008), accessible through http://www.floridabar.org.

DEFINING THE PRACTICE OF LAW

The practice of law may be defined in two ways as it relates to professional ethics. The first definition addresses the question of whether an attorney is rendering legal services. For example, a lawyer may engage in **mediation** activities, which does not entail providing legal services and therefore is not covered by legal ethics per se, but any linkage of mediation services and the practice of law raises ethical problems. For example, an attorney might mediate a divorce between husband and wife and then represent one of them in the divorce or refer them to the attorney's firm for representation. Such action would give rise to ethical problems of conflict of interest and confidentiality constituting a serious breach of ethics. Thus, an attorney may engage in activities other than the practice of law, but such activities must be consistent with the attorney's professional responsibilities.

The practice of law is defined differently when addressing the question of the unauthorized practice of law (UPL). In this instance, it is not so much what lawyers do as what may be done *only* by lawyers that defines the practice of law. For ethical purposes, the practice of law is best defined in the context of unauthorized practice of law, which is subject to criminal and civil sanctions by the courts. In applying these sanctions, the courts have been forced to address the definition of the practice of law.

mediation

A form of conflict resolution often used in conjunction with litigation or as an alternative to it. Mediation deals with adversarial parties, as in divorce mediation, but is not an adversarial process. The mediator's task is to facilitate agreement and resolution, bringing the parties together without taking sides.

UNAUTHORIZED PRACTICE OF LAW

The following discussion should be supplemented with a review of the comments already made on this subject in Chapter 1.

Each state restricts the practice of law to licensed attorneys and provides for a penalty, commonly criminal, to enforce these prohibitions. The problem lies in defining what constitutes the practice of law, which varies widely among the states. From an ethical standpoint, the restrictions on providing legal services can be justified only by an interest in protecting the public and not in preserving a professional monopoly. There are two issues regarding protection of the public: (1) the public should be protected against incompetence, and (2) some agency, usually a court, must have the power to protect the public. Licensing protects the public by requiring a level of competence necessary to obtain the license and by establishing authority to revoke the license for misconduct. Those without licenses can be punished for practicing law.

Lawyers are agents of their clients; they can represent clients before the court, sign certain documents on behalf of their clients, and act as direct contacts in matters in which they represent their clients. Because of this agency relationship, the lawyer is held to ethical standards in representing clients and can be disciplined for misconduct and even sued by the client for breach of the limits of the relationship. Abuse of the representation can have serious consequences to the client and so justifies this control over attorney misconduct. Unlicensed persons providing legal services are much less subject to the scrutiny of the court and the profession.

The practice of law is much less narrow than the practice of other professions, such as medicine and dentistry. For example, lawyers give advice on the conduct of personal and business affairs, but so do many others, such as accountants, real estate brokers, stock brokers, insurance agents, bankers, and so on. These persons commonly give advice concerning the legal consequences of their clients' personal and business decisions. In fact, advice that could be considered legal is furnished by just about everyone. Anyone arrested for speeding, anyone buying land, or anyone getting a divorce can find many people offering advice on the legal aspects of each of these. When are such people practicing law?

This question is by no means easy to answer, as a review of court cases on unauthorized practice of law attests. It is not sufficient to define the practice of law, as some early cases did, as what lawyers traditionally do. Lawyers do a great many things that do not require legal expertise. For the purposes of unauthorized practice of law, the issue has come down to identifying what it is that only lawyers may do. Although the states vary considerably on the specific activities restricted to lawyers, three activities are universally identified:

1. Legal representation before a court
2. Preparation of legal documents (or having documents prepared under attorney direction and supervision)
3. Giving legal advice

Note that the first two categories relate to the attorney-client agency relationship under control of the court, whereas the third category is concerned with legal competence.

For instance, Louisiana regulates the practice of law with the following statutes:

> It is a crime for a non-lawyer to practice law, hold himself out as an attorney, or advertise that he alone or jointly has an office for the practice of law.

La. Rev. Stat. Ann. § 37:213.

> The practice of law is defined as appearing as an advocate, drawing papers, pleadings or documents, performing any act in connection with pending or prospective court proceedings or, if done for consideration, the advising on the "secular" law and doing any act on behalf of another tending to obtain or secure the prevention or redress of a wrong or the enforcement or establishment of a right.

La. Rev. Stat. Ann. § 37:212.

Legal Representation before a Court

Because of the technical requirement of procedural law, as well as the intricacies of specific kinds of lawsuits, a litigant without a lawyer is severely disadvantaged, especially if the opposing party has legal representation. In our legal system, it is not required that a person have an attorney to bring or defend a suit (i.e., she may represent herself), but a person may not be represented by someone other than a licensed attorney. The court relies on the competence and accountability of attorneys.

A successful outcome to a trial generally requires legal skills, experience, and knowledge of a high order; the adversarial system does not work fairly when one of the parties lacks legal representation. However, many court appearances involve routine matters that do not involve legal argument or expertise and could easily be managed by legal staff acting on behalf of an attorney, at a great savings to clients without risk.

The appearance of the attorney in court is certainly necessary when a legal argument may ensue or rights and duties of clients are decided; otherwise, the court need only be reassured that an attorney is ultimately responsible for the action taken. The legal system and the practice of law would be more efficient and less costly if paralegals were authorized to perform a number of routine tasks. Nevertheless, no nonlawyer should ever appear in court to represent a client unless absolutely certain that this is permissible.

Many administrative agencies, like the Social Security Administration, permit representation by any person of the claimant's choosing. Before undertaking such representation, a nonlawyer should ascertain the extent and scope of such representation under the agency's rules and regulations and make certain that the person represented consents (in writing) to such representation with full knowledge that the representative is not a member of the bar.

Although the *Alexander* case is more than forty years old, the court struggles with a continuing problem: What is, and what is not, the practice of law? The law student clerk charged with unauthorized practice of law might today be described as a paralegal. The trial court took a broad view of the practice of law, a protectionist attitude toward the bar, and was perhaps affronted by the appearance of a nonlawyer in the courtroom. The appellate court, however, showed a progressive attitude toward the allocation of legal services benefiting the bench, the bar, and the public.

Note that the individual in question was not prosecuted for unauthorized practice of law but was disciplined by the court for contempt of court, a sanction available to a judge for punishing misconduct in court.

PEOPLE of the State of Illinois, Plaintiff-Appellee

v.

Walton ALEXANDER, Defendant-Appellant

Appellate Court of Illinois, First District, Fourth Division

53 Ill. App. 2d 299, 202 N.E.2d 841 (1964)

This is an appeal from a judgment order adjudging defendant guilty of contempt of court for the unauthorized practice of law. The Supreme Court transferred this case to our court and it is to be considered here as a direct contempt.

Defendant is a clerk employed by a firm of attorneys and is not licensed as a lawyer, although he is studying to be an attorney. On October 19, 1962, defendant

was present in court when the case of *Ryan v. Monson* was called. Thereafter, he prepared an order spreading of record the fact that after a trial of the case of *Ryan v. Monson* the jury had disagreed and continuing the case until October 22. The trial judge added to that order "a mistrial declared."

Before entering the contempt order, the court issued a rule to **show cause** and a hearing was held at which only defendant testified. He was examined by his attorney, cross-examined and also interrogated by the judge. . . .

In his testimony defendant stated that after the case was called on October 19, he and plaintiff's attorney in the *Ryan v. Monson* case stepped up; that the judge inquired whether they knew of the disagreement by the jury; that the court requested that an order be prepared spreading the mistrial of record; that both defendant and plaintiff's lawyer sat down at a counsel's table and defendant wrote the order which they then presented to the judge in **chambers**.

An order of court reciting the verdict of a jury or setting out its failure to agree on a verdict is the responsibility of the court and the court clerk is usually ordered by the court to enter an order showing the result of a jury's deliberations. This is reflected in *Freeport Motor Casualty Co. v. Tharp*, 406 Ill. 295, at 299, 94 N.E.2d 139, at 141. . . .

The preparation of an order, in the instant case, with the collaboration of opposing counsel was a ministerial act for the benefit of the court and a mere recordation of what had transpired. We cannot hold that this conduct of defendant constituted the unauthorized practice of law.

The opinion of the trial court also states as a basis for contempt that on October 22 the judge inquired of defendant whether the case of *Ryan v. Monson* was settled and that defendant answered in the negative. It appears that on that date the court held the case for trial. Defendant testified that he advised the court that the trial attorney was actually engaged in a trial in the Federal Court. The court held that the appearance of defendant constituted the unauthorized practice of law.

Plaintiff contends that any appearance by a non-lawyer before a court for the purpose of apprising the court of an engagement of counsel or transmitting to the court information supplied by the attorney in the case regarding the availability of counsel or the status of the case is the unauthorized practice of law.

In the case of *People ex rel. Illinois State Bar Ass'n v. People's Stock Yards State Bank*, 344 Ill. 462, at page 476, 176 N.E. 901, at page 907, wherein a bank was prosecuted for the unauthorized practice of law, the following quotation is relied upon:

"According to the generally understood definition of the practice of law in this country, it embraces the preparation of pleadings, and other papers incident to actions and special proceedings, and the management of such actions and proceedings on behalf of clients before judges and courts * * *."

Since this statement relates to the appearance and management of proceedings in court on behalf of a client, we do not believe it can be applied to a situation where a clerk hired by a law firm presents information to the court on behalf of his employer.

We agree with the trial judge that clerks should not be permitted to make **motions** or participate in other proceedings which can be considered as "managing" the litigation. However, if apprising the court of an employer's engagement or inability to be present constitutes the making of a motion, we must hold that clerks may make such motions for continuances without being guilty of the unauthorized practice of law. Certainly with the large volume of cases appearing on the trial calls these days, it is imperative that this practice be followed.

Case Questions

1. The court distinguishes between appearance in court "in behalf of a client" and appearance "in behalf of the attorney-employer." Is this a relevant distinction?
2. Is there an implied distinction between "management of proceedings" and routine clerical activities? What is meant by "ministerial act"?

Case Glossary

show cause

A court may issue a rule to show cause when it wants a hearing on the question of why it should not take certain action. A party shows cause by providing a compelling reason to prevent the action.

chambers

The private office of a judge where matters not required to be heard in open court can be discussed and appropriate orders issued.

motion

Generally, a formal request by a party for a ruling by the court in favor of that party. There are many types of motions; dismissal motions are discussed in Chapter 7.

Preparation of Legal Documents

This category refers to "preparation of legal instruments and contracts by which legal rights are secured." A major function of paralegals is the preparation of such documents; real estate agents ordinarily prepare contracts for sale that allocate legal rights and duties in great detail; and accountants prepare tax forms. Thus, the word *preparation* may be a poor choice, as it is not the preparation per se that is at issue but the final product at the time the document or instrument takes legal effect. The person with ultimate responsibility for the document must be licensed to practice law.

In many instances, paralegals prepare documents that are signed by attorneys. There is no ethical problem with this as long as the supervising attorney reads and approves the document prior to signing. Many documents require little skill in draftsmanship, sometimes only requiring that names, dates, and the like be inserted into a standard form. Nevertheless, the attorney is responsible for the legal sufficiency of documents prepared for clients. There is a danger that an attorney with a large workload assisted by a seasoned, competent paralegal may place too much reliance on the paralegal and begin signing documents without reading them, even when the documents are not standard forms. The concern here is not the competence of the paralegal but a proper allocation of responsibility.

In reality, a paralegal may be more knowledgeable about a particular legal matter than an attorney, but in theory the paralegal is a trained technician and the attorney is a legal analyst. This is an excellent combination of skills to serve clients; paralegal and attorney working as a team provide legal services of high quality. If the attorney, however, relies on the paralegal entirely, the equation fails; the client has not received the services contracted.

Giving Legal Advice

Paralegals must be careful not only to refrain from giving legal advice but also to avoid even giving that impression. It is important that each client clearly understand that the paralegal is not a lawyer and is not licensed to practice law. Clients will often seek advice from paralegals, especially when the attorney is temporarily unavailable. Paralegals possess a competence and knowledge of the law that tends to encourage clients and friends to ask for legal advice.

Defining *legal advice* is not an easy task either because there is a fine line between providing information and giving advice. For example, it is neither unethical nor an unauthorized practice of law to sell standard legal forms (office supply stores regularly sell legal forms). Nor is furnishing typing services improper. A logical conclusion might be that assisting a person by typing information into the blanks on a standard legal form is not improper or illegal. In the course of filling out a form, however, a client may ask a question concerning the legal consequences of an item in the form.

As a practical matter, the paralegal should be alert and wary about making statements to a client. Statements that may induce the client to do or refrain from doing something that may have legal consequences may be construed as legal advice. There is a big difference between saying "Don't do that" and "You ought to talk to an attorney before doing that." When pressed for advice, the paralegal must always refer the questions to the attorney. Although often a conduit or messenger between attorney and client, the paralegal must exercise care in conveying information or advice. Even when instructions are unambiguous, such as "Tell the client to go ahead and sign the contract," a paralegal should ascertain the exact instructions to be conveyed and indicate to the client that the instructions are those of the attorney. Of course, it is far better for the attorney to communicate directly with the client.

Ironically, a paralegal is more constrained in giving legal advice than is the man-in-the-street. The justification for this is that the paralegal is knowledgeable in the law, so paralegal advice is likely to be construed as correct and thus be acted upon. Presumably, individuals understand that legal advice from the man-in-the-street has no authority behind it. Paralegals must be aware of their special vulnerability in this regard. In coming years, the boundaries of paralegal responsibilities will undoubtedly undergo significant clarification. It should be noted that at present the states differ significantly in where they draw these boundaries.

CONFIDENTIALITY

Perhaps the most important topic in legal ethics is confidentiality. In the course of legal consultation, a client typically reveals information that is personal, private, and often secret. Legal services are predicated on the assurance that none of these private facts will be disclosed to third parties beyond the attorney and the attorney's staff. To deal effectively with client affairs, the attorney must be fully informed about all matters relating to the client's need for legal service and advice. For this reason, statements made in confidence to an attorney by a client are privileged and may be disclosed only with the consent of the client or when special circumstances provide clear exceptions to the rule.

The privilege extends to law firm employees who necessarily have access to confidential material in order to provide legal services, including especially legal secretaries, clerks, and paralegals. Although paralegals are not subject to disciplinary actions for improper disclosures, a supervising attorney can be held responsible both under attorney disciplinary rules and by a possible suit by the client.

The paralegal must be scrupulous in protecting clients' confidences. It is a great temptation for attorneys and paralegals alike to relate the facts of an interesting case to friends and associates outside the law firm, but any disclosure incurs the risk that the listener may identify a client and thereby learn facts that are privileged. If third parties not covered by the privilege learn confidential communications, the disclosures may lose their confidential status. Extreme caution must be exercised in discussing specific matters involving specific clients. Attorneys and law firms routinely warn staff about confidentiality, but paralegals must also constantly remind themselves of their responsibilities toward the firm's clients.

Confidentiality can lead to bizarre predicaments, as illustrated by the following real-life situation. A woman was working as an intake paralegal for a Legal Aid office that provided legal services in civil cases for indigents. As such, she interviewed prospective clients for the office. A woman seeking divorce came to the office and was accepted as a client. The attorney in charge of the case was encountering difficulties finding the woman's husband to serve notice of the pending divorce action. It so happened that the husband later came to the office for legal representation. In the course of collecting intake information, the paralegal recognized that the man was the husband of a client of the office. Although the office could not represent both husband and wife, it was now in possession of the husband's address and telephone number—but that information was now considered privileged information because the husband had furnished it in confidence while attempting to establish a lawyer-client relationship.

Although the attorney for the wife was informed that the husband had furnished this information, she and the paralegal concluded that it might be improper to give it to the wife's attorney, so the husband's file was locked away where the attorney did not have access to it. (Fortunately, the husband's whereabouts were discovered through another source.) The lesson, however, is that the paralegal and the attorney were appropriately sensitive to the confidentiality question.

A client's actions may render disclosures nonconfidential. Statements made before third parties who are not covered by confidentiality are disclosable (*see People v. Mitchell*). If, for instance, the client brings a friend along to a meeting with the attorney and the friend has no relation to the case, statements made at the meeting are not confidential. Attorneys and paralegals are careful to exclude third parties from discussions, especially when confidential statements are expected. The problem with nonconfidential statements is that their content is subject to discovery by the opposing side, and in criminal cases the third parties may be required to disclose the statements on the witness stand.

Whether or not the confidential attorney-client relationship applies depends on the circumstances. Even though an attorney may have represented a client in the past, statements made with regard to an unrelated current problem may not be confidential if the client has not expressed an intention to retain the attorney in the current matter.

In contrast, the attorney-client relationship may be understood to be ongoing. A client who employs an attorney on all business matters may implicitly intend all business statements to be confidential. A client may also pay an attorney a **general retainer** with the understanding that the attorney and client have a continuing relationship. Once confidentiality is established, the confidentiality does not end with the termination of client representation, though it may not extend to subsequent nonconfidential information.

general retainer
The first payment made in hiring an attorney. A general retainer occurs when a client furnishes a sum of money to an attorney to ensure that the attorney will represent the client in whatever legal matters may arise.

The duty to preserve the confidentiality of a client differs somewhat from the lawyer-client privilege. This is an evidentiary rule designed to protect a client by preventing the disclosure of confidential communications. The Restatement of Law (Third), Law Governing Lawyers, sets out four elements necessary for invoking the lawyer-client privilege: (1) a communication (2) made between privileged persons (3) in confidence (4) for the purpose of obtaining or providing legal assistance for the client.

The rationale for the privilege is based on the need for the client to make disclosures to the attorney so that the attorney may effectively represent the client's interests. Presumably, the attorney is far better at assessing the relevance of facts and developing a legal theory to aid the client than the client could without an attorney. A frank discussion between attorney and client is protected by the privilege. Many clients would probably be unwilling to disclose pertinent facts if the information were not protected by the privilege.

The effect of the privilege is to foreclose the attorney from disclosing the confidential communications in legal proceedings. The attorney may not be required to disclose these communications; and the privilege is absolute in that the relevance of the communications to a legal proceeding or to the truth has no bearing. Only the specific exceptions made by the law can intrude on this privilege that belongs to the client.

The PEOPLE of the State of New York,
Respondent

v.

John C. MITCHELL, Appellant

Court of Appeals of New York

58 N.Y.2d 368, 448 N.E.2d 121 (1983)

Defendant was a resident of Waterloo, New York, and, at the time these events occurred, he was under **indictment** for causing the stabbing death of his girlfriend, Audrey Miller, in February, 1976. He was represented on that charge by Rochester attorney Felix Lapine. In January, 1977, defendant went to Rochester to take care of some personal matters and registered at the Cadillac Hotel. On the evening of January 5 while sitting at the hotel bar, he met O'Hare McMillon. They had two or three highballs and then were seen to leave the bar about 11:00 p.m. and take the elevator to the floor on which Mitchell's room was located. No one saw either of them leave defendant's room that night or the next morning, but in the afternoon of January 6, on a tip from attorney Lapine, the police went to defendant's hotel room and found the partially clad dead body of O'Hare McMillon on the bed. She had been stabbed 11–12 times in the face, chest and back. At least four of the wounds were sufficient to cause her death by exsanguination.

After leaving the hotel room that morning, defendant went to attorney Lapine's office. Lapine was not in but defendant met and spoke to a legal secretary, Molly Altman, in the reception area. She testified that he seemed nervous and as if he was looking for someone. Apparently he could not find whomever it was he was looking for so he left only to return a minute later and start telling her about what happened the night before. She testified that he said: "he wanted to go out and have a last fling * * * he had been out drinking and met a girl and then he woke up in the morning and she was dead. He had stayed there all night and then he walked out again."

While he was talking to Ms. Altman, Judith Peacock, another legal secretary, entered the reception area. She testified that defendant was kind of rambling on but he said that: "he had laid next to someone all night and they didn't move, and he [was] in a bar and * * *

in a hotel * * * this person who he had laid next to was black and he was worried because when the black people find out about it, they protect their own and he would be in danger." She also testified that he muttered something about a knife.

Ms. Pope-Johnson entered the room. She asked defendant what was wrong and he told her: "that there was a dead body and he felt that he had done it and that the person was dead, that she was dead because of being stabbed."

Shortly thereafter, Lapine entered the office and talked privately with defendant. After defendant left Lapine called the police and had them check defendant's hotel room. The body was discovered, defendant's identification learned from the hotel registration and defendant found and arrested at a bar near the courthouse.

* * *

On this state of the record, we conclude that defendant has not met his burden of establishing that when he spoke to these unknown women in a common reception area, his statements were intended to be confidential and made to an employee of his attorney for the purpose of obtaining legal advice. The only evidence identifying the women came from Lapine who responded to a question whether he had "any female employees" by saying "Yes, Robin Pope-Johnson." She, it turns out, was the last woman in the office to hear defendant's inculpatory statements and even if statements made to her at the time could have been privileged, the privilege was lost because of the prior **publication** to nonemployees and the utterance of the statements to Pope-Johnson in front of the non-employees. . . . Taking this view we need not consider whether the statements could be privileged because of an ongoing retainer between defendant and Lapine or if they could be privileged if made to the attorney's employee before a formal retainer was agreed upon.

Case Questions

1. What circumstances argued most strongly for defeating the attorney-client privilege?
2. What argument can be made in Mitchell's behalf?

Case Glossary

indictment
  A written accusation by a grand jury charging the accused with a crime. Also called a "true bill."

When the grand jury does not indict, it is called a "no bill."

publication
  Making a statement publicly, orally, or in writing, i.e., to a third person.

Exceptions to Confidentiality

A client may create an exception to the attorney-client confidentiality privilege either by (1) the client voluntarily disclosing otherwise confidential information (as in *People v. Mitchell*) or (2) the client consenting to the attorney's disclosure of otherwise confidential information.

Although confidential statements about past crimes and misconduct are privileged, a client's intention to commit a crime in the future is not. An attorney has an ethical duty to attempt to dissuade a client from committing a crime and a duty to inform appropriate authorities if unable to dissuade the client. The ABA *Model Rules of Professional Conduct* require the attorney to disclose information in two instances: (1) "[t]o prevent a client from committing a crime" and (2) "[t]o prevent a death or substantial bodily harm to another." The most difficult case arises when a client plans to commit perjury at trial and, despite the attorney's admonitions, proceeds to lie on the witness stand. Attempted withdrawal by the attorney at that stage of the process will ordinarily be refused by the court, but the attorney also is not free to disclose the confidences that would reveal the perjury.

The ABA *Model Rules of Professional Conduct* allow the attorney to disclose otherwise confidential client information when necessary to protect the attorney in a conflict with the client. This exception, for example, would allow the attorney to comply with ethics rules and to disclose client information as part of the attorney's claim or defense in a civil or criminal matter.

If the purpose of attorney-client confidentiality is ultimately protection of the public—so that individuals can protect their interests by revealing their secrets to their lawyers—is the violation of confidentiality mitigated by the fact that disclosure of a client's privileged statements leads to a public benefit?

 *Attorney Use of Metadata in Digital Document Sent by Opposing Counsel*

When an attorney receives a digital document from opposing counsel, is it ethical for the attorney to search for metadata, review metadata, or use metadata to benefit the client?

After answering the question, consider whether the following information would alter your answer:
  • The metadata contains no confidential information.
  • The attorney knows that opposing counsel is not aware that a digital document contains metadata.

- The metadata contains confidential information.
- Rule 4.4(b) of the ABA *Model Rules of Professional Conduct* provides, "A lawyer who receives a document relating to the representation of the lawyer's client and knows or reasonably should know that the document was inadvertently sent shall promptly notify the sender."

See ABA Formal Op. 06-442 (2006); Ala. Bar Ethics Op. 2007-02 (2007); Colo. Bar Ethics Op. 119 (2008); D.C. Bar Ethics Op. 341 (2007); Fla. Ethics Op. 06-2 (2006); Me. Bar Ethics Op. 196 (2008); Md. Bar Ethics Op. 2007-09 (2007); N.Y. Bar Ethics Op. 749 (2001); Pa. Bar Ethics Op. 2009-100 (2009) for various ways in which bar associations have dealt with this issue. Search the American Bar Association website (http://www.abanet.org) for "metadata."

CONFLICTS OF INTEREST

A common conflict-of-interest problem arises when an attorney leaves one firm for another and the second firm represents a party suing or being sued by a client of the former firm. The risk of disclosure of attorney-client confidences by the attorney to the new employers raises serious ethical concerns. Extreme cases are not difficult to decide. If the attorney worked on the client's case at his first employment, it would be clearly unethical to work for the opposing party. However, if an attorney moves from one large law firm to another and had no exposure to the case at either firm, the risk of disclosure is minimal. The risk can be further minimized by erecting a "Chinese wall" between the attorney and those dealing with the case; that is preventing access to the case file and warning all concerned not to discuss the case with the firm-switching attorney. If no exception is made, an attorney working for a large firm becomes a "typhoid Mary," virtually unemployable at other large firms for fear the firm may have or may take on a client who may be involved in a dispute against a client of the other firm.

Because paralegals regularly deal with confidential material, an identical problem arises: The entire firm may be disqualified from representing a client if the court concludes that the risk of improper disclosure cannot be purged. In fact, some paralegals will have contact with a greater number of files than any single attorney.

This particular form of conflict of interest poses a practical as well as an ethical problem because the firm representing a client can request that the court disqualify an opposing firm's representation. This action has resulted in numerous reported court decisions that not only clarify the ethical principles but also give them the force of law. In *Silver Chrysler Plymouth, Inc. v. Chrysler Motors Corp.*, 518 F.2d 751 (2d Cir. 1975), the court articulated the "substantially related" test subsequently adopted by the courts of many jurisdictions. *Silver Chrysler* distinguished between the activities of a lawyer or law clerk at a former law firm that were substantially related to representation in a current case at a second law firm employing the attorney. The court thereby attempted to distinguish situations in which a distinct risk of confidential disclosures exists from those in which the risk is insignificant.

Common sense tells us that an attorney cannot represent both sides in an adversarial proceeding. Law firms are often put in the difficult position of representing clients who inadvertently become legal adversaries. Disclosure of the conflict and even waiver of objection by the parties may not be sufficient. Attorneys owe undivided loyalty to their clients. A fairly common exception to the rule is the uncontested divorce. In general, parties to an uncontested dispute may be represented by a single lawyer or a single law firm, provided that disclosure of the representation and consent by the parties are evident. It may be that businesses that are in an amicable ongoing relationship may dispute the terms of a contract but not wish to undermine their relationship. Still, there are dangers and these occur with some frequency in divorce. What begins as an amicable divorce often ends as battle royale.

A criminal defendant charged with a felony is in an especially precarious position, being subject to serving time in prison. In a criminal case with multiple defendants, there may be an attorney for each defendant, to avoid having a single attorney represent two defendants in the case whose version of the facts may differ. The prosecuting attorney's office typically has a certain amount of discretion in handling a case and the defendant may receive more favorable treatment if the defendant's attorney can stay on good terms with the prosecution. In *State v. Cottle*, the attorney was doing something worse than representing two defendants in a single criminal case: Cottle's attorney had been indicted by the same prosecuting attorney's office that had returned an indictment against Cottle.

STATE of New Jersey, Plaintiff-Respondent

v.

Mylee COTTLE, Defendant-Appellant

Supreme Court of New Jersey

194 N.J. 449, 946 A.2d 550

Argued Oct. 22, 2007.

Decided May 6, 2008.

In this case, an attorney representing a juvenile charged with murder in Essex County kept secret from his client that he—the attorney—had been indicted for criminal stalking in the same county. Indeed, the attorney did not disclose to his client that both simultaneously were criminal defendants being prosecuted by the Essex County Prosecutor's Office. With the consent of the Prosecutor's Office, but unknown to his client, the attorney later gained admission into the Essex County Pretrial Intervention (PTI) Program. Despite his pending indictment and his obligation to report to the Prosecutor's Office as a condition of his enrollment in the PTI program, the attorney continued to

represent the juvenile, even through a jury trial. Tried as an adult, the juvenile was convicted of murder.

In this appeal, we must determine whether the attorney's representation of the juvenile constituted an intolerable conflict of interest, rendering that representation constitutionally ineffective and requiring the grant of a new trial. Presented here is the unseemly appearance of an attorney entangled in a conflict that pitted his personal welfare against his professional obligations to his client. We now hold that an attorney has a per se conflict of interest when both he and his client are simultaneously under indictment in the same county and being prosecuted by the same prosecutor's office. Without an informed waiver made in court and on the record, prejudice will be presumed, rendering the representation ineffective. The undisclosed conflict in this case denied the juvenile the effective representation of counsel guaranteed to him under . . . the New Jersey Constitution and therefore he is entitled to a new trial.

In May 1995, defendant Mylee Cottle, then seventeen years old, was charged in an Essex County juvenile complaint with murder and related weapons offenses. In June 1995, for a fee of $10,000, defendant's family retained Steven Olitsky, Esq., to defend [Cottle] against those charges. Olitsky did not advise defendant or his family that just three months earlier an Essex County grand jury had returned a six-count indictment against him for third-degree stalking. . . .

In February 1996, after a waiver hearing in the Chancery Division, Family Part, at which Olitsky represented defendant, the court determined that defendant would be tried as an adult in the Law Division, Criminal Part. . . .

In April 1996, with the consent of the Essex County Prosecutor's Office, a Superior Court judge admitted Olitsky into PTI for a period of three years. . . . PTI is a statewide program that allows eligible defendants charged with first-time, non-violent offenses to avoid prosecution by receiving supervisory or rehabilitative treatment for a period not to exceed three years. . . . If a defendant successfully completes the program, the criminal charges are dismissed. . . . Olitsky was obliged to "have each client sign an acknowledgment of his participation in the PTI program" and then to "submit a copy of [the acknowledgment] to the PTI program and to the Prosecutor's Office." . . . At no time did Olitsky inform defendant or the Cottle family about his indictment in Essex County and his participation in PTI.

On December 9, 1996, the Disciplinary Review Board (DRB), which reviews charges of professional misconduct filed against attorneys, issued a decision recommending that this Court suspend Olitsky from the practice of law for three months for commingling personal and client funds in 1994 in violation of *Rules of Professional Conduct* (RPC) 1.15(a) and 8.4(c). . . . That same day—the first day of defendant's murder trial—Olitsky kept from his client the looming ethical problems that would result in this Court suspending Olitsky for three months, effective May 16, 1997. . . .

The jury found defendant guilty of all three counts in the indictment. The trial court sentenced defendant to a term of life imprisonment with thirty years of parole ineligibility on the murder conviction and to a concurrent five-year term with a two-year parole disqualifier on the unlawful possession of a weapon conviction. . . .

In December 2001, defendant filed a petition for post-conviction relief (PCR) based on claims of ineffective assistance of counsel, and a motion for a new trial based on newly-discovered evidence. With regard to the ineffective-assistance-of-counsel claim, defendant alleged that Olitsky (1) failed to disclose to him that he was under criminal indictment and facing professional discipline at the time of the murder trial; (2) was "distracted and intimidated from [providing] an effective defense" because the Essex County Prosecutor's Office was investigating his own misconduct; (3) did not "effectively consult" with defendant before trial; (4) failed to contact alibi witnesses who would have provided information that defendant was not at the crime scene at the time of the murder; (5) neglected to obtain the employment records of defendant's brother Hassan, which would have impeached Walker's claim to having seen Hassan with defendant on the evening of the murder; (6) permitted defendant to appear in prison garb in full view of two jurors; and (7) erroneously advised defendant not to testify under the mistaken belief that defendant's juvenile record could be used for impeachment purposes. . . .

Defendant, moreover, presented Olitsky's extensive ethics history, detailing the attorney's personal and financial travails and psychiatric treatment during the time period he represented defendant. After defendant's trial, Olitsky was not only disbarred for professional misconduct (unrelated to defendant's trial), but also failed to successfully complete the PTI program. . . .

The paramount obligation of every attorney is the duty of loyalty to his client. . . . A client charged with a crime places his fate in the hands of his attorney, who stands between him and the considerable power of the State—a power mostly exercised through the office of the county prosecutor. The stakes are high in a criminal case with the client's freedom often hanging in the balance. With so much on the line, an attorney's self-interest should never interfere with the duty of unstinting devotion to the client's cause. An attorney should never place himself in the position of serving a master other than his client or an interest in conflict with his client's interest. . . . Surely, the attorney must never be perceived as having a reason to curry some personal favor with the prosecutor's office at the expense of his client.

Those simple yet fundamental assumptions underlie our Rules of Professional Conduct. RPC 1.7(a)(2) specifically prohibits a lawyer from representing a client if "there is a significant risk that the representation of one or more clients will be materially limited . . . by a personal interest of the lawyer." The sole exception to that rule is when the "client gives informed consent, confirmed in writing, after full disclosure and consultation," and even then the lawyer may represent a client only if he "reasonably believes that [he] will be able to provide competent and diligent representation to [the] client" and "the representation is not prohibited by law." . . .

While under indictment, Olitsky represented defendant at a juvenile waiver hearing, a critical proceeding for any juvenile . . . and his adversary in that matter was the same adversary in his own case—the Essex County Prosecutor's Office. In such circumstances, it is not difficult to imagine that Olitsky might not have had the zeal to engage in a bruising battle with the very prosecutor's office that would be weighing his fate. Given his own criminal jeopardy and its threat to his professional career, Olitsky surely had no personal incentive—even if it were in his client's best interest—to take on the office that he would need to help him. Like many first-time charged criminal defendants, Olitsky pursued enrollment in PTI, but the way would

be smooth only with the cooperation and consent of the Prosecutor's Office. . . .

Olitsky was under indictment and subject to prosecution during the entire period of his representation of defendant. It was Olitsky's dependence on the Prosecutor's Office, which was pursuing a murder conviction against his client, that undermined his own professional independence. . . . This was a scenario fraught with the real potential of impairing an attorney's zealous advocacy on behalf of a client.

Case Questions

1. What legal ethics problems had the attorney had in the past, aside from the conflict of interest in representing Cottle?
2. How is the attorney's duty of loyalty related to the duty to avoid a conflict of interest?
3. Did Cottle's family have any duty to investigate the quality of legal representation the attorney would provide?
4. If you or a family member needed legal representation, how would you choose an attorney to hire?

§

SOLICITATION

solicitation

In legal ethics, using improper means to drum up business. For example, the practice of "ambulance chasing," such as approaching hospital patients to solicit business, is unethical.

For many years, the legal profession banned the advertising of legal services as a form of improper solicitation; many disciplinary cases considered such issues as listings in the Yellow Pages, the sending of Christmas cards, the size of law office signs, and so on. In 1977, the U.S. Supreme Court, in *Bates v. State Bar of Arizona,* 433 U.S. 350, held that the ban on advertising violated First Amendment freedom of speech. Since that time, ethical concerns have aimed at distinguishing advertising from **solicitation**. The bar continues to attempt to thwart "ambulance chasing," the practice of hunting down injured parties and twisting their arms to hire the attorney. Although *Bates* made it clear that attorneys were free to announce their services to the public in general, the aggressive solicitation of individual clients is still condemned. Typically, ethics rules prohibit the attorney from directly contacting an individual unless the attorney previously had some type of past relationship with the prospective client.

An attorney is also prohibited from soliciting through another person, including a paralegal. Paralegals must be careful in generating business for the attorneys for whom they work. It is very tempting, when hearing a story of a personal injury or some other promising legal case, to encourage a visit to the law office, but paralegals must be cautious in their treatment of such situations. Certainly it is unethical to loiter at the hospital handing out business cards to accident victims, but it is not necessary to keep one's employment a secret or, when asked, to recommend an attorney. Suggesting that a person seek legal help is ethical if the paralegal has not sought out clients. The paralegal should not disparage other attorneys, encourage a person to switch from one attorney to another, or criticize an attorney's handling of a client. When learning of possible misconduct by an attorney, the paralegal should discuss the matter with an associate who is an attorney, who has an ethical duty to address attorney misconduct.

FEES

The *Model Rules* treat fee arrangements with much more specificity than did the *Model Code.* Fees are based on contracts between the attorney and the client and should be specifically discussed by the attorney with the client. Whenever fees have not been adequately explained to a client, a potential conflict emerges. If at all possible, a contract signed by the client should clearly explain the basis on which the fees are established. When the *Model Rules* were debated, the framers wanted to require that all fee arrangements be in writing, but sole practitioners and rural lawyers argued that this would hurt their relationships with many of their clients, so the writing was not made mandatory.

A recurring issue regarding fees concerns *contingency fees,* whereby the attorney is paid a percentage of the award or recovery received by the client. There is a strong national movement favoring limitations on contingency fees. Personal injury cases are typically based on contingency fees, which are unethical in criminal cases and divorce proceedings. It is essential that the client understand that the percentage does not include costs other than the attorney's services. In cases using expert witnesses, the costs can be quite large; the client must made be aware of this, as well as of the fact that the client must pay the costs regardless of who wins the case.

Work performed by a paralegal is commonly billed to a client. Ordinarily the paralegal's work is charged at a rate significantly less than that for an attorney though not necessarily proportional to the compensation paid the paralegal. Clients should not be charged for attorney's work if paralegals actually did the work, nor should they be billed for more time than was actually spent. The latter is not only unethical but illegal as well. Even though paralegals may not be responsible for the billing, they should not participate, actively or passively, in a fraud on the client.

REPORTING MISCONDUCT

Ethics rules typically require an attorney to report the ethics violation of a fellow attorney. Although lawyers are understandably reluctant to inform on each other, this rule is clear, and failure to report misconduct is an ethical violation. The object is not simply to punish the wrongdoer but to protect the public and the legal system. Choice of the authority to which the misconduct should be reported depends on whether the misconduct is a professional matter or a matter before the court.

The duty of paralegals to report misconduct is more problematic. If the misconduct is also criminal, a legal duty to report a crime falls upon the paralegal. If the misconduct is of a professional, noncriminal nature, the duty is less clear. There is an ethical duty in an abstract sense, but not one that subjects the paralegal to discipline, as the paralegal is not a member of the bar. If misconduct results in an injury to a client, the paralegal who overlooks the misconduct may be viewed as contributing to the injury. In any event, such matters must be treated with great delicacy. Accusations of misconduct can have serious ramifications for an attorney. The paralegal is quite vulnerable as well, having a subordinate position in the legal hierarchy. In such a situation, it is to be hoped that the paralegal knows a lawyer who can give counsel. If the misconduct can be corrected, approaching the wrongdoer rather than informing may be the best policy. In any event, diplomacy and caution should be exercised.

Judges likewise have a duty to report an attorney who is unable to competently represent a client. In *Johnson*, the court commented on the string of mistakes made by the attorney for the defendant; the attorney's failure to follow court rules and proofread documents prior to filing them were so egregious that the appellate court reported the attorney to the Wisconsin Office of Lawyer Regulation.

Shawn JOHNSON, Plaintiff-Respondent

v.

ROMA II-WATERFORD, LLC and Roma's E.T., Inc., Defendants-Appellants

Court of Appeals of Wisconsin

No. 2008AP1396

2009 WI App 77

April 8, 2009

Roma II-Waterford, LLC, is appealing the circuit court's order granting **default judgment** to Shawn Johnson. . . .

On September 13, 2007, Johnson filed a summons and complaint [and] Roma II filed an answer on November 13, 2007. The answer was incomplete. While it responded to Johnson's general allegations and the allegations comprising her first cause of action, it did not respond to the other three causes of action. It was also oddly paragraphed. It started with paragraphs one through eleven and then skipped to paragraphs twenty-three and twenty-four, which denied the first cause of action.

Johnson responded with a motion for default judgment and supporting affidavit that she filed on December 17, 2007. In that motion, she sought a default judgment on the second, third and fourth causes of action. Roma II reacted by filing an amended answer and counterclaim on December 19, 2007.

A hearing on Johnson's motion was held on January 28, 2008. Johnson asked the court to ignore Roma II's amended answer because it was filed after Johnson had moved for default judgment and to grant her a default judgment on her second, third and fourth causes of action. Roma II's attorney, Patrick J. Hudec, explained to the court . . . that the first answer was a draft that a new secretary had printed from a computer file and he had signed and filed it by mistake. He complained that counsel for Johnson did not make a courtesy call to point out the incomplete answer rather than file a motion for a default judgment. . . . Johnson's counsel replied that when counsel signs a pleading, he is certifying that he has read the pleading, and Hudec cannot be heard to claim excusable neglect.

The trial court granted Johnson a default judgment after first acknowledging that the original answer was "clearly a mistake," but going on to hold that "there has to be some good justification or reason for the mistake." The court commented that the signer of the pleading is certifying that the contents are correct and that implies "that the signer of the document had reviewed the document for its correctness." . . . The court concluded that the mistake did not rise to the level of "excusable mistake or excusable neglect or whatever the terms are used in the cases." The court failed to discuss the amended answer that had been filed in response to the motion for a default judgment. . . .

Before addressing the merits, we are obliged to explain that Hudec's "mistake" in signing and filing an incomplete answer appears not to be an isolated incident but a pattern of gross and inexcusable inattention to details. We have already explained that at the hearing on Johnson's motion for a default judgment on January 28, 2007, Hudec made a representation to the court that he had filed an affidavit in opposition to the motion. He had to retract that representation when both Johnson's attorney and the court remarked that they had not received his affidavit.

But Hudec's egregious conduct did not end in the circuit court. It continues here with his failure to insure a proper final order or judgment was in the record when he filed his notice of appeal.... We also struck his reply brief, filed on behalf of Roma II, because it was not timely filed . . . and he failed to serve a copy of it on Johnson. . . .

Hudec's problems in this court do not stop with his ignoring the rules of appellate practice. In the table of contents of his principal brief, he states the first issue is:

Did the trial court err in granting a default Judgment where a timely answer was filed but mistakenly in an early draft form that did Respond to all causes of action?

Skipping to the statement on oral argument and publication, Hudec writes:

In this case, the attorney dictated final changes over the shoulder of a secretary who then printed off an earlier draft and that mistake was not caught prior to signing the document.

We will not detail other errors. We are left shaking our heads! Frankly, we are at a loss to understand what is clearly Hudec's intentional disregard of the rules and the details, including his failure to proofread. . . .

The court granted default judgment solely because Roma II did not join all of the issues. . . . This would be a simple case but for Roma II filing an amended answer, joining all of the issues only two days after Johnson moved for a default judgment. The filing of an amended answer joined all of Johnson's causes of action because Roma II was at liberty . . . to file an amended answer within six months of the filing of Johnson's summons and complaint. Johnson filed her summons and complaint on September 13, 2007; she filed her motion for default judgment on December 17, 2007; and Roma II filed its amended answer on December 19, 2007. . . .

Given that Johnson had been served with the answer and amended answer and both documents had been timely filed, she was also required to establish that she would be prejudiced by the court's not striking Roma II's answers and granting her a default judgment. . . . She did not establish prejudice and the court did not discuss prejudice and make a finding that Johnson or the court would be prejudiced by permitting Roma II's answers to stand.

We reject Roma II's request that we review "what type of mistakes, in this 'new electronic age,' should call into play equitable and remedial relief." Whether counsel prepares pleadings with a quill pen and foolscap, a typewriter and bond paper, or a computer and pdf file there is an obligation to pay attention to details. We see no reason to construct different rules for computer-based errors; the novelty of an error inherent in a method of preparation does not justify different rules and relief. . . .

In conclusion, Roma II's answer and amended answer were timely and joined all of the issues of law and fact. The court erred in granting default judgment because Johnson failed to (1) move to strike the amended answer before moving for a default judgment and (2) establish that either she or the court would be prejudiced if default judgment was not granted. . . .

[The court stated in a footnote:]

We will forward a copy of this opinion to the Office of Lawyer Regulation pursuant to the requirement of SCR 60.04(3)(b) (2008)[:]

A judge who receives information indicating a substantial likelihood that a lawyer has committed a violation of the rules of professional conduct for attorneys should take appropriate action. A judge having personal knowledge that a lawyer has committed a violation of the rules of professional conduct for attorneys that raises a substantial question as to the lawyer's honesty, trustworthiness or fitness as a lawyer in other respects shall inform the appropriate authority.

Case Questions

1. Whose responsibility is it to make sure that the correct version of a document is filed?
2. Does an attorney have any ethical obligation to inform opposing counsel of an error that might easily be corrected?

3. Do you think that the tone of the court's opinion would have been different had Hudec been more careful in the past?
4. Should Johnson's attorney be disciplined for failing to filed a motion to strike the amended complaint before moving for a default judgment?

Case Glossary

default judgment
A judgment entered by the court for the plaintiff when the plaintiff filed a complaint that the defendant failed to answer.

TRUST ACCOUNTS

One of the most common reasons for attorney discipline involves the misuse of client funds. This is considered by disciplinary committees to be one of the most serious transgressions. Clients deposit funds with attorneys for a number of reasons besides paying fees. Money held for a client must never be commingled (mixed) with an attorney's personal accounts, nor should separate **trust accounts** be commingled in any way. Accurate record keeping is essential to properly account for monies received and disbursed.

trust account

In the practice of law, a special bank account in which fees paid by clients are kept until an attorney may properly claim the funds for fees or expenses.

The easiest way to get into ethical trouble as an attorney is to mishandle client funds. Attorneys frequently have large sums of money passing through their hands. They must never put these funds in the wrong account, but mostly they must not make client funds available for their own personal use or accounts until funds are clearly owing to them (e.g., when they have earned money for work completed). In *Au*, Au's troubles with mishandling trust account funds and sharing legal fees with a nonlawyer were compounded by him lying to the disciplinary hearing committee that was investigating the ethics charges against him. The court viewed Au's mishandling of client trust account funds as so serious that it disciplined him even though no client had suffered any actual injury.

OFFICE OF DISCIPLINARY COUNSEL,
Petitioner

v.

Ronald G.S. AU, Respondent

Supreme Court of Hawai'i

No. 26517

107 Haw. 327, 113 P.3d 203

June 7, 2005

The Disciplinary Board (the Board) filed a report and recommendation to suspend Respondent Ronald G.S. Au (Au) from the practice of law for a period of two years. The Board bases its report and recommendation on a hearing committee's findings of fact and conclusions of law. . . .

On November 26, 2003, the hearing committee also filed its forty-seven-page findings of fact, conclusions of law, and recommendation for discipline. The hearing committee found, among other things, that Au falsely testified

- that Au first paid his clients and then deposited the clients' settlement checks into Au's office account,
- that Au had no client referral agreement with [nonlawyer "runner"] Yoshimoto, and
- that the fees Au paid Yoshimoto for Labrador's two personal injury matters were for Yoshimoto's investigative services.

The hearing committee further found that, instead of testifying truthfully, Au attempted to mislead and deceive the [Office of Disciplinary Counsel (ODC)] and the hearing committee regarding his dealings with Yoshimoto. When the hearing committee gave Au opportunities to recant his false testimony, Au refused. . . .

With respect to ODC [case number] 95-242-4701, the hearing committee concluded that Au misrepresented the holding of a published court opinion . . . to Judge Heely. . . .

With respect to ODC 97-213-5407, the hearing committee concluded that, in several instances, Au improperly[:]

deposited his clients' settlement proceeds into his office account . . .[;]

paid for certain litigation costs by using funds from his client trust account . . .[;]

deposited unearned fees into his office account, rather than his client trust account. . . [;]

reimbursed his client trust account . . .[;]

failed to withdraw funds from his client trust account . . .[;]

falsely certified that he had complied with client trust account requirements . . .[; and]

paid fees to a non-lawyer "runner" in exchange for client referrals, and, in so doing, Au also inflated his contingency. . . .

With respect to ODC 98-064-5555, the hearing committee concluded that Au deposited a client's payment for legal fees into Au's personal business account before Au earned the fees. . . .

When Au (1) misrepresented the holding of a published opinion to a judge and (2) falsely certified that he had maintained his clients' funds in accordance with HRPC Rule 1.15, Au violated his duty to refrain from dishonesty under HRPC Rule 3.3(a)(1) and HRPC Rule 8.4(c). . . .

When Au misrepresented the holding of a published opinion to a judge, Au violated his duty to provide competent representation under HRPC Rule 1.1.

When Au (1) misrepresented the holding of a published opinion to a judge and (2) improperly used a non-lawyer "runner" to obtain client referrals, Au violated his duty to maintain personal integrity under HRPC Rules 3.3(a)(1), 7.2(c), 8.4(a), and 8.4(c). . . . Au engaged in intentional conduct involving dishonesty, fraud, deceit, or misrepresentation that seriously adversely reflected on Au's fitness to practice law. . . .

When Au mishandled his clients' funds, Au knew or should have known that he was dealing improperly with client property, and Au caused potential injury to his clients. . . . The record shows that Au committed a significant portion of his misconduct with an intentional and/or knowing state of mind. . . . Au's misconduct does not appear to have caused actual harm to his clients. However, Au's misconduct caused potentially serious injury to his clients. Furthermore, Au's misconduct seriously harmed the integrity of the legal system. . . .

Of the ten possible aggravating factors that ABA Standard 9.22 . . . recognizes, the hearing committee found the following six aggravating factors with respect to Au:

[1.] Dishonest or selfish motive (ABA Standard 9.22(b)). Respondent [Au] was motivated by monetary gain by the use of a runner and in depositing unearned fees into his Office Account. . . .

[2.] A pattern of misconduct (ABA Standard 9.22(c)). Respondent [Au] has engaged in a pattern of misconduct in his accounting practices. In addition, Respondent [Au] has also a pattern of misrepresentation in his citation of the Sherry 2 decision, his denial of the accuracy and completeness of the tapes and transcripts of the August 16 and 29, 1994 conversations, his filing false annual registration statements, and his false testimony regarding payment to his clients prior to negotiating the settlement checks.

[3.] Multiple offenses (ABA Standard 9.22(d)). Respondent [Au] There are multiple, unrelated instances of unethical conduct in this matter.

[4.] Submission of false evidence, false statements, or other deceptive practices during the disciplinary process (ABA Standard 9.22(f)). As stated above, Respondent [Au] falsely testified at the Formal Hearing (1) that he first paid his clients, then deposited the settlement checks into his Office account; (2) that he had no illicit referral agreement with Mr. Yoshimoto; and (3) that he paid Mr. Yoshimoto investigation fees for services rendered to Ms. Labrador.

[5.] Refusal to acknowledge wrongful nature of conduct (ABA Standard 9.22(g)). Although Respondent [Au] has acknowledged that he committed certain acts, he has denied that those acts were unethical. Respondent [Au] falsely denied hiring Wayne Yoshimoto as a runner and paying him illicit referral fees. When given opportunities to recant this false testimony, he refused. Instead of addressing the issues in good faith, he repeatedly made baseless arguments and attempted to divert attention from his misconduct to irrelevant issues, such as the qualifications of the person who transcribed the tapes and his dealings with other lawyers.

[6.] Substantial experience in the practice of law (ABA Standard 9.22(i)). Respondent [Au] was admitted to practice in 1963 and has practiced for most of the past 40 years. . . .

Of the thirteen possible mitigating factors that ABA Standard 9.32 . . . recognizes, the hearing committee found only two with respect to Au: . . .

[1.] Absence of prior disciplinary record (ABA Standard 9.32(a)). Respondent [Au] has no prior discipline.

[2.] Correction of Accounting Practices; Lack of Material Economic Harm to Clients Due to Accounting Practices. When Respondent [Au] learned that his accounting/bookkeeping practice were improper, he corrected them. His improper practices do not appear to have caused any material economic harm to any client or third party. . . .

Based on the forgoing analysis, we hereby accept the hearing committee's findings of fact and conclusions of law. However, we reject (a) the hearing committee's recommendation to publicly censure and disbar Au and (b) the Board's recommendation to suspend Au from the practice of law for two years. Under the circumstances of this case, disbarment would be too severe a sanction, and yet a suspension of less than five years would be insufficient to reflect our concern for the protection of the public, the legal profession, and the courts from Au's unprofessional conduct. Therefore, an order suspending Au from the practice of law for a period of five years will be entered contemporaneously with the filing of this opinion.

Case Questions

1. Why is it unethical to share legal fees with someone who is not an attorney?
2. What is the rationale behind disciplining at attorney for trust account violations when no client was harmed by the attorney's actions?

MALPRACTICE

malpractice

Professional negligence; those who are licensed professionals are held to a higher standard of care for their services than is required in ordinary negligence.

Disciplinary action is not the only risk facing an attorney. When a client has been injured by the negligence or intentional misconduct of an attorney, the client may bring a civil action for **malpractice**, seeking compensation from the attorney for the injury. *Malpractice* usually refers to professional negligence, and *negligence* in turn refers to a cause of action falling in the class of private suits called *torts*, explained in greater detail in Chapter 10. Ordinary negligence occurs when a person fails to exercise reasonable care and because of carelessness causes injury to another person or to property. Persons (usually licensed) holding themselves out as professionals are held to a professional rather than an ordinary standard of care. After all, lawyers are hired because of their presumed competence and skill in legal representation. The lawyer who fails to meet the standards of the profession should compensate those injured by this failure. Much of a lawyer's work involves judgments that may prove mistaken but are nevertheless defensible even in retrospect. It may not be difficult in such situations for an attorney to get other attorneys to testify that the judgment was within the standards of the profession. The most provable instance of attorney malpractice occurs when an attorney negligently allows a statute of limitations to run, barring further action on a client's lawsuit. There may be other consequences from such conduct as well.

 *Legal Malpractice*

The basis of a legal malpractice action is that the attorney's conduct falls below the standard of care expected of the attorney. Each party to the lawsuit might call experts to testify as to the standard of care and whether the defendant's actions met the standard of care. A question might arise as to whether there is a statewide standard of care or, instead, whether there are different standards of care for different areas of the state. Would the standard of care differ depending on the area of law in which the attorney is practicing? What are the justifications for a statewide standard of care, a local standard of care, and a standard of care peculiar to the area of law?
See Chapman v. Bearfield, 207 S.W.3d 736 (Tenn. 2006).

MISCONDUCT OUTSIDE THE PRACTICE OF LAW

Attorneys are subject to disciplinary action for conduct unrelated to the practice of law. Violations of the law by attorneys, such as driving while intoxicated, may be scrutinized by the bar in addition to criminal charges. Criminal or improper conduct that reflects on an attorney's fitness to practice law may result in sanctions. An attorney may act to undermine the integrity of the legal system even when not acting in the role of an attorney, as President Clinton discovered to his dismay. He had testified falsely, albeit with a semantic deftness that seemed at first to be technically truthful. He was understandably reluctant to reveal his sexual improprieties with Monica Lewinsky, but the false testimony that he gave presented the court and the bar with a transgression that begged for inquiry. As Judge Wright concluded in *Jones v. Clinton,* in such matters the president must be treated like other citizens, like other attorneys.

These days, a substantial part of the practice of law can be conducted via email, with many of the emails containing confidential client information. Unauthorized accessing of law firm emails is illegal and, if done by an attorney, is unethical. In *Markins*, Markins was an attorney but his illegal activity was apart from his practice. Unfortunately, the activity resulted in him and his attorney wife being fired and him being disciplined.

LAWYER DISCIPLINARY BOARD, Petitioner

v.

Michael P. MARKINS, a Member of the West Virginia State Bar, Respondent

Supreme Court of Appeals of West Virginia

No. 33256

222 W. Va. 160, 663 S.E.2d 614

Decided May 23, 2008.

In this lawyer disciplinary proceeding, Respondent Michael P. Markins ("Respondent") objects to the sanctions recommended by a Hearing Panel Subcommittee of the Lawyer Disciplinary Board ("Board") for violations of the West Virginia Rules of Professional Conduct ("Rules"). . . .

At all times relevant, Respondent was employed as an associate attorney at the law firm of Huddleston Bolen, LLP ("Huddleston"). . . . His wife, also an attorney, was similarly employed at the law firm of Offutt, Fisher & Nord ("OFN"). In late October or early November of 2003, Respondent began accessing his wife's OFN e-mail account without her permission or knowledge. . . . Respondent testified that the purpose of reading his wife's e-mails was to secretly monitor her activities because he believed she had become involved in an extramarital affair with an OFN client. Respondent further testified that, initially, he improperly accessed only his wife's account and later, that of another attorney, an OFN partner. . . . Eventually, however, Respondent's curiosity got the better of him, and he began accessing the e-mail accounts of seven other OFN attorneys. Obviously, Respondent did so without either the knowledge or permission of the account holders. . . .

It is undisputed that Respondent improperly accessed the e-mail accounts of OFN attorneys on more than 150 occasions. In so doing, Respondent learned personal information about certain attorneys which had been relayed confidentially via e-mail. With regard to confidential client information that had been accessed by Respondent, Mr. Offutt was particularly concerned with the fact that OFN and Huddleston,

Respondent's employer, represented co-defendants in a large mass tort case that was in litigation during the time period at issue. In March, 2006, Respondent, along with other lawyers whose firms were involved in the mass litigation, was monitoring the trial from the Hampton Inn in Beckley, West Virginia. While monitoring the proceedings, Respondent gained unauthorized access into various OFN e-mail accounts from the Hampton Inn's IP account. According to Mr. Offutt, Huddleston's mass tort client had a contractual relationship with and a claim for indemnity against OFN's client. Though the claim was not then being litigated, Mr. Offutt testified that information included in the firm's e-mail system would have been "helpful" to Huddleston's client. However, neither Huddleston nor OFN found evidence that any information between OFN attorneys and its client in that case had been compromised. . . .

In March 2006, Respondent's wife, who had been completely unaware of Respondent's misconduct, told Respondent that someone had been breaking into OFN e-mail accounts and that the firm was getting close to finding out who it was. Shortly thereafter, Respondent revealed to his wife that it was he who had been improperly accessing the OFN e-mail accounts. The following day, Mr. Offutt, who had learned from the computer expert's investigation that Respondent was responsible for the unauthorized access of the e-mail accounts, inquired of Respondent's wife if she was aware of Respondent's actions. Though she had just learned of Respondent's misconduct, she denied any knowledge of it to Mr. Offutt. Immediately thereafter, Respondent's counsel contacted Mr. Offutt and others at the firm to disclose his actions. Both Respondent and his wife were eventually terminated from employment by their respective law firms as a result. . . .

On December 18, 2006, the Board filed a Statement of Charges against Respondent, alleging violations of . . . the West Virginia Rules of Professional Conduct. The Board alleged violations of Rule 8.4(c) "[b]ecause Respondent engaged in the repetitive unauthorized access of [OFN] e-mail accounts by improperly using various e-mail account passwords assigned to various [OFN] attorneys." Under Rule 8.4(c), "[i]t is professional misconduct for a lawyer to: . . . (c) engage in conduct involving dishonesty, fraud, deceit or misrepresentation."

The Board also alleged violations of Rule 8.4(b), "[b]ecause Respondent's repetitive unauthorized access of [OFN] e-mail accounts was criminal in nature . . . and adversely reflected on his honesty, trustworthiness or fitness as a lawyer[.]" . . . Under Rule 8.4(b), "[i]t is professional misconduct for a lawyer to: . . . (b) commit a criminal act that reflects adversely on the lawyer's honesty, trustworthiness or fitness as a lawyer in other respects[.]" The Board further alleged there to be "aggravating factors," stating that "Respondent's conduct involved multiple offenses and a pattern of misconduct, was for a selfish motive, and constituted illegal acts." . . .

In the instant matter, we are mindful of the mitigating factors presented by Respondent, including the unique circumstances which motivated his misconduct in the first place. However, there are also several aggravating factors which this Court cannot ignore or minimize. . . . Though Respondent initially accessed his wife's OFN e-mail account with motives very personal to his marriage, his misconduct eventually became more rampant. Out of simple curiosity, he broke into the e-mail accounts of eight of his wife's unsuspecting co-workers on almost a daily basis for over a two-year period. He did not cease or disclose his actions until he learned OFN's computer experts were on the verge of discovering who was behind the unauthorized intrusions. Moreover, in addition to confidential personal information, Respondent viewed confidential financial information intended to be read exclusively by OFN partners. With regard to confidential client information, in one instance, his firm and OFN represented separate co-defendants which had interests adverse to each other because Respondent's client had an indemnity claim against OFN's client.

Presently, there is no evidence that Respondent has used or misused the information he improperly accessed from OFN. Nevertheless, we must recognize that OFN has suffered negative consequences from Respondent's actions. Not only was OFN forced to expend valuable time and resources to investigate the matter, but it was also required to disclose the unfortunate events to its clients, opening itself up to potential law-suits and professional embarrassment. Moreover, one is unable to predict or tangibly quantify the future impact of Respondent's misconduct on OFN or on Respondent's former law firm in terms of attracting new clients.

Finally, we recognize that with the widespread use of computer e-mail as an important method of communication between and among attorneys and their clients comes the potentiality that the communication might be improperly infiltrated. This Court does not take lightly the fact that, in this case, it was an attorney who repeatedly accessed the confidential e-mails of other attorneys without their knowledge or permission. Thus, the imposition of a suitable sanction in a case such as this is not exclusively dictated by what sanction would appropriately punish the offending attorney, . . . but, just as importantly, this Court must ensure that the discipline imposed adequately serve as an effective deterrent to other attorneys, . . . "to protect the public, to reassure it as to the reliability and integrity of attorneys and to safeguard its interest in the administration of justice." . . .

For the reasons stated above, we adopt the Board's recommendations and hereby impose the following sanctions upon Respondent: (1) Respondent is suspended from the practice of law in West Virginia for a period of two years; (2) upon reinstatement, Respondent's private practice shall be supervised for a period of one year; (3) Respondent is ordered to complete twelve hours of CLE in ethics in addition to such ethics hours he is otherwise required to complete to maintain his active license to practice, said additional twelve hours to be completed before he is reinstated; and (4) Respondent is ordered to pay the costs of these proceedings.

Case Questions

1. Why was Markins's wife fired?
2. Do you think that the result would have been different had Markins refrained from accessing the emails of attorneys other than his wife?

CASE NOTE: The case contained a majority opinion, excerpted above, and a concurring opinion. The concurring opinion is dealt with in questions at the end of this chapter.

SUMMARY

The legal profession is governed by a code of professional ethics that is enforced by the courts and the profession. Each state has an ethical code for lawyers. The ABA has been the leader in developing ethical codes, adopting the *Model Code of Professional Responsibility* in 1970 and the *Model Rules of Professional Conduct* in 1983. Most states have adopted these codes nearly verbatim, so there is considerable uniformity in principle, at least.

The interpretation of the codes by the courts shows some disparities, especially in defining the unauthorized practice of law, which is of special concern to paralegals because they risk unauthorized practice of law if they engage in activities permitted only to licensed attorneys, namely:

1. Legal representation before a court

2. Preparation of legal documents (without attorney supervision)

3. Giving legal advice

The unauthorized practice of law may be prosecuted under criminal statutes or by the court as contempt of court.

Confidentiality of client statements is protected by the attorney-client privilege, which extends to law office personnel. Paralegals must take great pains not to disclose confidential information from or regarding clients to persons not covered by the privilege. The attorney-client privilege belongs to the client and not the attorney. Major exceptions to the privilege apply when a client proposes to commit a crime or when the client sues the attorney.

Confidentiality gives rise to problems of conflict of interest when an attorney or a paralegal changes employment from one firm to another. If the new firm represents a party adverse to a party represented by the firm from which the new employee came, the risk that confidential information may be disclosed to the disadvantage of a former client is great. The entire new firm may be disqualified. However, in this age of large law firms, lawyers and paralegals frequently have no contact with a client of the firm in which they work. As a result, the courts and the *Model Rules* have adopted the "substantially related" test: The adverse representation must be substantially related to matters with which the attorney dealt in prior employment. Law firms must additionally take pains to isolate the attorney from the case, the so-called Chinese wall approach.

KEY TERMS

ethics	malpractice	trust account
general retainer	mediation	
legal ethics	solicitation	

CHAPTER REVIEW QUESTIONS

1. What is the difference between the *Model Code* and the *Model Rules*?

2. What is the severest form of professional punishment for an attorney?

3. How may a paralegal be punished for professional misconduct?

4. What does *UPL* stand for?
5. What constitutes attorney malpractice?
6. How can potential conflicts of interest be avoided?
7. What is a *retainer*?
8. What may lawyers do that paralegals may not?
9. What is the consequence of speaking to your attorney in front of a third party?
10. What constitutes solicitation?

CRITICAL THINKING QUESTIONS

1. Is there something about the practice of law that causes the public to hold lawyers in low esteem?
2. What are the problems inherent in writing a set of rules to govern the professional conduct of professionals who are adept at manipulating the language of rules to mean different things to different people?

CYBER EXERCISES

1. The *Model Rules of Professional Conduct* are found at the ABA website, http://www.abanet.org. Using the *Model Rules,* answer the following questions:
   a. Does an attorney who meets with a prospective client but declines to represent the prospective client owe any duty to safeguard information revealed by the prospective client in the meeting?
   b. In litigation, does an attorney have any duty to inform a judge of a case adverse to the position of the client?
   c. Is it ethical for an attorney to communicate with an individual represented by another attorney?
   d. What duty, if any, does an attorney have to report another attorney for violating an attorney ethics rule?
   e. What duty, if any, does an attorney have to report a judge for violating a judicial ethics rule?
2. Nearly every state has attorney ethics rules (sometimes referred to as *rules of professional responsibility* or *rules of professional conduct*). Many states model their ethics rules on the ABA *Model Rules of Professional Conduct.* Links to attorney ethics rules of various states and the ABA *Model Rules* are found at the ABA website, http://www.abanet.org. You may also be able to access your state's attorney ethics rules from the website of your state's bar association.
   a. Does your state have attorney ethics rules?
   b. Where did you find these ethics rules?
   c. Are your state's attorney ethics rules modeled on the ABA *Model Rules of Professional Conduct*?
   d. What are the projected earnings for paralegals and legal assistants?
3. In the past, an experienced attorney usually mentored a new attorney and explained the expectations of other attorneys in the community. Some have

complained of a lack of civility in the legal profession, and a growing number of state or local bar associations have established professionalism codes designed to educate new attorneys on community expectations. The professionalism codes differ from the ethics rules in that an attorney cannot be disciplined for violation of the professionalism code. Links to attorney professionalism codes are found at the ABA website, http://www.abanet.org.

    a. Does your state have a professionalism code?

    b. Where did you find the professionalism code?

    c. What types of provisions appear in the professionalism code, and what types of conduct are addressed?

    d. Even though there is no sanction attached to an attorney's violation of a professionalism code, do you think that the professionalism code will have an effect on attorney behavior?

4. The *Model Rules of Judicial Conduct* are found at the ABA website, http://www.abanet.org. Using the *Model Rules,* answer the following questions:

    a. Is it ethical for a judge to inform a police officer of the judge's position in order to escape a traffic ticket?

    b. Is it ethical for a judge to joke about the nationality of someone appearing before the judge?

    c. What is the judge's role in discussing settlement with parties to a lawsuit?

    d. When is a judge required to disqualify himself or herself from hearing a case?

    e. Is a judge allowed to practice law?

5. Nearly every state has judicial ethics rules, with many states modeling their judicial ethics rules on the ABA *Model Rules of Judicial Conduct.* Links to judicial ethics rules of various states and the ABA *Model Rules* are found at the ABA website, http://www.abanet.org. You may also be able to access your state's judicial ethics rules from the website of your state's court of last resort.

    a. Does your state have judicial ethics rules?

    b. Where did you find these ethics rules?

    c. Are your state's judicial ethics rules modeled on the ABA *Model Rules of Judicial Conduct?*

6. Opinions of the Supreme Court of Appeals of West Virginia are accessible at a number of websites, including the website for West Virginia state courts, http://www.state.wv.us/wvsca. The court decided *Lawyer Disciplinary Bd. v. Markins,* 663 S.E.2d 614 (W. Va. 2008), on April 1, 2008. The case contained a majority and a concurring opinion (the majority opinion is excerpted in this chapter). Locate the case at the West Virginia state courts website and answer the following questions concerning the concurring opinion:

    a. Why would a justice write a concurring opinion rather than join in a majority opinion?

    b. How does Justice Starcher's opinion fit within the definition of a concurring opinion?

    c. What sanction would Justice Starcher have imposed and why?

SCENARIO

Part I

You are defending a man accused of murder; we will call him Sammy. He has a history of crime and violence. The incident giving rise to the murder charge involved an altercation he had with another man on the street. Both Sammy and his victim, Joey, have been involved in the drug trade. Sammy shot Joey in front of witnesses, whose testimony made it virtually impossible to defeat the accusation that Sammy shot Joey. Because the two men had a long history of hostility, you feel the only possible defense for Sammy is self-defense. Sammy has told you that he believed Joey had a knife and was reaching for it when Sammy fired his pistol. It becomes clear that the self-defense argument is weak since Sammy and Joey were sufficiently far apart that Sammy was not in immediate danger from Joey's knife, especially considering that Sammy was armed with a pistol. Sammy asks if his case would be a lot better if he had thought that Joey had a gun. Of course, you acknowledge that would be a better scenario for self-defense, but you and Sammy both know that Joey did not have a gun and Sammy did not believe he had a gun. Nevertheless, Sammy offers to testify that he saw the glint of something in Joey's hand that he thought was a gun.

You tell Sammy that such testimony would be perjury and attempt to dissuade him from making such statements. When he insists, you tell him that you will withdraw from the case and tell the judge of the proposed perjury (it is one thing to keep a client's statements of past crimes confidential and quite another to refuse to disclose proposed criminal acts). Sammy reluctantly agrees. When put on the witness stand, however, Sammy tells the gun, rather than the knife, story. As he begins to tell this story, what should you do?

Before answering the question, consider the following proposed standard:

ABA Project on Standards for Criminal Justice; Proposed Defense Function Standard 4-7.7 (2d ed. 1980)

(a) If the defendant has admitted to defense counsel facts which establish guilt and counsel's independent investigation established that the admissions are true but the defendant insists on the right to trial, counsel must strongly discourage the defendant against taking the witness stand to testify perjuriously.

(b) If, in advance of trial, the defendant insists that he or she will take the stand to testify perjuriously, the lawyer may withdraw from the case, if that is feasible, seeking leave of the court if necessary, but the court should not be advised of the lawyer's reason for seeking to do so.

(c) If withdrawal from the case is not feasible or is not permitted by the court, or if the situation arises immediately preceding trial or during the trial and the defendant insists upon testifying perjuriously in his or her own behalf, it is unprofessional conduct for the lawyer to lend aid to the perjury or use the perjured testimony. Before the defendant takes the stand in these circumstances, the lawyer should make a record of the fact that the defendant is taking the stand against the advice of counsel in some appropriate manner without revealing to the court the client's intent to perjure himself. The lawyer may identify the witness as the defendant and may ask appropriate questions of the defendant when it is believed that the defendant's answers will not be perjurious. As to matters for which it is believed the defendant will offer perjurious testimony, the lawyer should seek to avoid direct examination of the defendant in the conventional manner; instead, the lawyer should ask the defendant if he or she wishes to make any additional statement concerning the case to the trier or triers of the facts. A lawyer may not later argue the defendant's known false version of facts to the jury as worthy of belief, and may not recite or rely upon the false testimony in his or her closing argument.

The difficulty of adhering to these standards might best be examined by a mock examination in which someone plays the witness and someone the witness's attorney in an unscripted and spontaneous exchange.

Does it matter that the judge will very likely know exactly what is going on and the jury will be very curious?

Part II

Sammy is convicted of murder, and he files a habeas corpus petition on the grounds that he was denied "effective assistance of counsel" as guaranteed by the United States Constitution's right to counsel. He argues that you turned against him and were no longer zealously defending him. He claims this on the basis of your attitude following his proposal to use the gun defense and later at the trial when you suddenly stopped fighting in his behalf.

Have you violated ethical principles?

Is there substance to his argument that he was not properly represented?

Note that these two questions are independent.

Student CD-Rom

For additional materials, please go to the CD in this book.

Online Companion™

For additional resources, please go to http://www.paralegal.delmar.cengage.com

CHAPTER 3

SOURCES OF THE LAW: CASES

INTRODUCTION

The law in practice revolves around disputes and problems. The primary forum for dispute resolution is the court. Even though most disputes brought to lawyers do not result in trials, the courts, through their spokespersons, the judges, are the final arbiters of what the law is. Because courts are the last legitimate resort of disputants, judges must decide. No matter how difficult or complex a case, the judge may not plead ignorance, frustration, or indecision. In deciding a case, the judge must provide reasons and rules, the final product of the process of adjudication. Without reasons and rules, decision making is purely political. This is particularly true in the U.S. constitutional system, in which the lines between the judicial function and the administrative and legislative functions are relatively distinct.

Where does a judge find the rules? The judicial imagination is not sufficient authority, even though some judicial decisions seem to suggest otherwise. There are several sources of the law, the primary ones being the Constitution, legislation, and prior judicial decisions. This last is the subject matter of this chapter.

JUDICIAL RESTRAINT

judicial restraint
An accepted, customary policy of courts to restrict themselves to consideration of the questions presented to them and to restrain from legislating or interfering unduly with the executive or legislative branches. The principle also refers to the customary restraint federal courts exercise to leave questions of state law to state courts.

supremacy clause
Article VI of the U.S. Constitution, which provides: "This Constitution and the laws of the United States which shall be made in pursuance thereof; and all treaties made, or which shall be made, under the authority of the United States, shall be supreme law of the land, and the Judges in every State shall be bound thereby, any thing in the Constitution or laws of any State to the contrary notwithstanding."

judicial review
Review by an appellate court of a determination by a lower court; also, the power of the federal courts to declare acts contrary to the Constitution null and void.

In the American judiciary, a principle has evolved called **judicial restraint**. The United States Constitution set the stage by separating executive, legislative, and judicial functions into the three basic branches of government. Taking their cues from European Enlightenment thinkers of the eighteenth century, the framers of the Constitution established a political charter designed to break completely from the archaic remnants of feudalism, in which power and status were based on the accident of birth and society was ruled by an aristocracy with ultimate power residing in the monarch. The Constitution, by contrast, attempted to create a "government of laws and not of men" and allocated authority to the three branches of government in such a way that each could serve as a check on the other.

From the beginning, the president and the members of Congress were elected officials and ipso facto involved in politics and the political process. The political nature of the courts was not clearly defined in the Constitution, and it can fairly be said that Chief Justice John Marshall, who dominated the United States Supreme Court during the early nineteenth century, single-handedly defined the role of the federal judiciary. Among the important doctrines Marshall established, two stand out as fundamental principles that have guided American law ever since:

1. Marshall argued that the U.S. Constitution was the "law of the land," meaning that no law or official act that violated the Constitution was lawful; the Constitution stood as the guiding light superior to every other law. Because the U.S. Supreme Court is the final interpreter of the meaning of the Constitution, this doctrine of constitutional supremacy provided the Supreme Court with great political power. This phrase in the Constitution is referred to as the **supremacy clause**. The power of the court to examine legislative and executive acts is called **judicial review**.

2. This power was severely limited by another principle established by Marshall, which was dubbed *judicial restraint.* Because ultimate authority resides in the Court, which is made up of judges who are appointed for life subject only to removal by impeachment, it is necessary that judges restrain themselves from actively entering the political arena. This can be effectively accomplished by judges devoting themselves to deciding cases according to existing law. In simple terms, this means that judges interpret the law rather than make it, the latter function being reserved to the legislature. Ideally, judicial decisions are based on the authority of legal principles already in existence and not on the moral, political, or social preferences of the judges.

Although such situations rarely arise, a court on occasion must determine whether it has the power to decide a case. One would think that if Congress passed a statute authorizing a court to take a particular action, then the court would have the authority to take the action. The judge in *Beck* decided otherwise.

In re Petition of Captain William BECK and Sea Tow Services of the Palm Beaches, Inc. d/b/a Sea Tow Palm Beach and Certain Vessels, for a License to Engage in Maritime Salvage on the Coast of Florida, pursuant to 46 U.S.C. § 80102, Petitioners

and

United States of America, Intervenor

United States District Court, S.D. Florida

Case No. 07-80534-CIV

526 F. Supp. 2d 1291

Dec. 6, 2007.

THIS MATTER is before the Court upon Petitioners' Petition For A License To Engage In Maritime Salvage On The Coast Of Florida. . . .

This action was brought by Petitioners for the issuance of a license to engage in the business of salvaging on the coast of Florida, pursuant to 46 U.S.C. § 80102. Section 80102 [lists] the criteria a petitioner must meet before a judge of a United States district court in Florida may issue such a license to the vessel and its master. These criteria include whether the "vessel is sea worthy and properly equipped for the business of saving property shipwrecked and in distress," and whether "the master is trustworthy and innocent of any fraud related to property shipwrecked or saved on the coast." . . .

It is highly unusual, if not unheard of, for a United States district court judge to engage in the survey and inspection of a ship and her captain. . . . The Court has carefully reviewed the filings herein and has otherwise considered all possible constitutional constructions of § 80102. However, for the reasons expressed below, the Court finds that it is without **jurisdiction** over this action and therefore must deny the instant Petition and dismiss this action. . . .

The practice of "salvaging" is rooted in the maritime cultures of ancient Greece and Rome, where mariners would rescue vessels, persons, and cargo from distress, and as payment for their efforts they would receive a portion of the cargo, or some other pecuniary award if no cargo was rescued. The particular statute at issue

here was passed in its original form when Florida was still a territory. Act of May 23, 1828, 4 Stat. 291. . . . If a person engaged in salvaging without the requisite license, he forfeited whatever recovery to which he was otherwise entitled.

In 2006, Title 46 of the United States Code was re-codified by Congress [and] the statute . . . was amended into its present form. . . .

Before the Court may act in any matter, it must first determine whether it has jurisdiction over the cause and parties before it. This Court's exercise of jurisdiction is limited by Article III, Section 2 of the United States Constitution to "cases" and "controversies" that arise between certain entities and persons. U.S. Const. art. III, § 2. The term "case" has been loosely defined as a suit "instituted according to the regular course of judicial procedure." *Mushkrat.* The term "controversy" is less comprehensive than the term "cases" and "it includes only suits of a civil nature." *Mushkrat.* The preposition "between" found in Article III, Section 2 naturally denotes a relationship among at least two, possibly more, individuals or entities, that, in a legal sense, is adversarial. . . .

Thus, for the Court to exercise jurisdiction over a case it must necessarily involve two parties, in pursuit of an honest and actual antagonistic assertion of one party's rights against the other. . . . Where there is such a concrete case that contemplates an immediate and definite determination of the legal rights of the parties in an adversary proceeding, the judicial power may be appropriately exercised. . . . However, the Court may not act upon a party's petition or complaint that does not present the Court with a "case" or "controversy" upon which its judicial power may extend. . . . This limitation moors the federal courts to their constitutional mandates and keeps them from drifting into the executive or legislative functions of government. . . .

Turning to the instant Petition, the paradigm constructed for proceedings under § 80102 falls outside the norms that traditionally govern proceedings before this and every other federal court. A petition for a license under § 80102 is filed *ex parte.* There is no adversarial party to contest the qualifications of a petitioner and his salvaging ship under § 80102. Rather, the Court itself is charged with acting as both the adversary and the judge. . . .

In the alternative, if a reviewing court were to find that the proceedings outlined in § 80102 present a case or controversy such that a district court of Florida could properly exercise its jurisdiction in adjudication of the instant Petition, or if a reviewing court found that the current procedural posture of this action with the United States as an intervening Party constituted a case or controversy, the Court would still deny the instant Petition, because the Court lacks the power to issue licenses. . . .

It is well established that laws passed by Congress and duly signed by the President are presumed constitutional. It is only in the rare instance when the dictates of a statute force a court to act in a manner that is otherwise not authorized by the Constitution that it will decline to act in the manner prescribed by Congress. . . .

It is the governing principle of our republic that our federal government is divided into three distinct and independent branches that abstain from and oppose encroachment on each other. . . . Article III of the United States Constitution states that "[t]he judicial power of the United States shall be vested in one supreme Court and in such inferior Courts as Congress may from time to time ordain and establish." U.S. Const. art. III, § 1. The term "judicial power," as it is used in the Constitution, is defined as the power to hear and determine those matters which affect life, liberty, or property, by declaring for the parties what the law is, and their rights in conformity thereto. . . . With the investiture of the judicial power in the nation's federal courts there is also a natural limitation put upon them: federal courts may only act in a manner that is consistent with judicial action. . . . This inherent limitation to the Court's power also applies to the other branches of government, as legislative power is vested only in the Congress through Article I, Section 1, and the executive power is vested in the President alone through Article II, Section 1 of the Constitution. Thus, the President may not pass legislation, and Congress may not act in an executive capacity. . . .

Applying the principle of a natural limitation to federal courts' judicial power means that "neither the legislative nor the executive branches, can constitutionally assign to the judicial any duties, but such as are properly judicial, and to be performed in a judicial manner." . . . Since Congress cannot delegate to the courts power that is beyond what has been vested in them by the Constitution, the actions of the judiciary must remain consistent with the manner and function of actions contemplated in a judicial act. . . .

In the instant action, the crux of the Court's inquiry is whether the power to issue licenses, as directed under 46 U.S.C. § 80102, is a judicial act as contemplated in the Vesting Clause's use of the term "judicial power." . . . The issuance of licenses for salvaging off the coast of Florida is not an action taken in furtherance of carrying out a judicial act or part of the Court's governance of the proceedings before it. . . . Thus, the Court finds that Congress's purported delegation of authority upon the district courts of Florida to issue licenses under § 80102 would extend this Court's exercise of power beyond the "judicial power" granted to it in the Vesting Clause of Article III. Therefore, if it were later determined that the instant action constitutes a case or controversy, the Court is nevertheless powerless to act pursuant to § 80102 and issue a license to Petitioner for salvaging on the coast of Florida.

The Court notes that Petitioner is engaged in the business of salvaging and that he seeks to comply with the governing law by having the Court issue a license, as prescribed by § 80102, for him to lawfully engage in the same. . . . Petitioner urges this Court to strike this statute down as unconstitutional. . . . However, because the Court does not have subject matter jurisdiction over this action, it may not exercise its judicial power to do so. Therefore, the Court looks to Congress's speedy repeal of this constitutionally infirm statute.

Case Questions

1. Why does the court state that a lawsuit must be based on an adversarial proceeding?
2. What differentiates the judicial, legislative, and executive branches of government?
3. Why is issuing licenses not a judicial act?
4. Why can't the court declare the statute unconstitutional?
5. How is this case an example of a court exercising judicial restraint rather than making law?

Case Glossary

jurisdiction
   The power of a court to decide a case.

THE COMMON LAW

The American legal system is said to follow the **common law tradition** inherited from England. We are perhaps unique, along with England, Canada, Australia, and New Zealand, in enjoying more than nine hundred years of virtually uninterrupted legal evolution since the Norman Conquest of England in 1066. Since that time, England has not been invaded by foreign powers imposing their own legal institutions, nor have political or legal revolutions seriously disrupted the steady development of English law. When the British came to America, they brought their law with them. The American Revolution made a political break with the mother country and established a more democratic political organization, but it did not change the fundamental process of the law. When our judges sought legal authority for their decisions, they logically turned to the basic principles of English law, which they knew and trusted even if they did not trust George III.

When the Normans organized England into a unified kingdom, they eliminated the pockets of local authority and jurisdiction characteristic of continental European countries at the height of the Middle Ages. Although local legal process continued for a time for purely local matters, England gradually became a nation in the true sense of the word and gave birth to the "common law of England," under which developed a body of law common to all citizens of the nation. This undoubtedly led eventually to the reverence for the rule of law in the minds of the British people.

The **common law** has come to mean something more than simply English law. In American jurisprudence, the common law refers to judge-made law, distinguishing it from continental European legal systems, which are civil law systems. From the seventeenth century onward, with the rise of European nationhood, centralized governments were formed that required corresponding national legal institutions. Rather than building on existing custom and institutions, these governments compiled sets of laws into codes, borrowing heavily from the *Corpus Juris* of the Roman Emperor Justinian, the first European to attempt to collect and organize legal principles into comprehensive written form. This movement had significantly less impact on England, which had long enjoyed a central government and a national court system.

Although the sources of English law included edicts of the monarch and acts of Parliament, the daily life of the law was conducted in the courts, where pronouncements of the law were made on matters great and small. Today we are accustomed to view the legislature as the source of new law and expect judges to exercise judicial restraint by merely interpreting and enforcing the laws, but this was not always so. Until well into the nineteenth century, the English Parliament, the U.S. Congress, and the various state legislatures were by modern standards virtually inactive. The law was declared by judges, relying on traditional principles, in the process of resolving disputes. In modern times, society and polity have grown more complex at an accelerating rate, and it is no longer possible to deal with modern problems by relying on slowly evolving legal principles. As a result, modern legislatures have assumed the major burden of lawmaking, and the courts have assumed a sharply reduced role.

common law tradition

In the first century after the Norman Conquest, the Normans established a legal regime for the entire kingdom of England, with laws common to all inhabitants of the realm. Under that system, three common law courts were established (King's bench, common pleas, exchequer). The decisions of these courts and especially the decisions of the appeals of these courts became binding precedents on lower courts under a doctrine called *stare decisis.*

common law

Judge-made law.

JUDGES MAKE LAW

It is currently part of the American democratic folklore that judges merely interpret but do not "make" law. The fallacy of this notion lies in the fact that the power to interpret the law inevitably leads to making the law. Every time a judge is called upon to interpret the law, lawmaking occurs. Because judges ordinarily rely on the authority of existing law, judicial interpretation of the law invokes changes that are nearly imperceptible, but when faced with novel or difficult cases, judges occasionally formulate statements of the law that form important new principles.

It may be helpful to give an example of judicial lawmaking. In the landmark case of *MacPherson v. Buick Motor Co.*, 217 N.Y. 382, 111 N.E. 1050 (1916), Justice Cardozo of the New York Court of Appeals wrote an opinion that ushered in a new era in liability of manufacturers for injuries caused by their products, leading many years later to the field of **product liability**. Mr. MacPherson sued for injuries caused by the collapse of a defective wooden spoke wheel on the Buick he had purchased. The company defended against the suit on the grounds that it had sold the car to a dealer, which had in turn sold the car to MacPherson. Because Buick did not have a contractual relation with MacPherson, it was not liable, stated attorneys for the company. In a carefully reasoned opinion, Cardozo explained why the company could not be protected by the traditional principle of **privity of contract**, and held the company liable. The appearance of the automobile on the American scene put in the hands of the American public a potentially dangerous machine. Cardozo held that the manufacturer was responsible for inspection of the vehicles it sold and refused to allow the manufacturer to pass liability on to the dealer under the guise of privity of contract. In handing down his decision, Cardozo charted a course for compensation law in the United States.

What is a court to do when asked to decide whether a statutory term applies but the court is unsure of what the term means because the statute fails to provide a definition? There is no mechanism allowing the court to ask the legislature what the term means. What should the legislature do when the court interprets the previously undefined term, but not to the legislature's liking? If the legislature then amends the statute to define the term, can the legislature define the term differently than it was defined by the court?

product liability
A branch of tort law that assigns liability to a manufacturer when injury occurs due to a "dangerously defective product." It dispenses with traditional requirements of proving fault, as in intentional torts and negligence.

privity of contract
The relationship between two parties to a contract. Originally, this was a bar to a suit brought by a consumer against a manufacturer when the consumer bought through a dealer rather than directly from the manufacturer. Modern product liability law does away with this impediment.

John L. HALE and Robbin Hale, husband and wife, Petitioners

v.

WELLPINIT SCHOOL DISTRICT NO. 49, a municipal corporation, Respondent

Supreme Court of Washington, En Banc

No. 80771-0

165 Wash. 2d 494, 198 P.3d 1021

Decided Jan. 15, 2009.

Until 2007, the Washington Law Against Discrimination (WLAD), chapter 49.60 RCW, contained no definition of the term "disability." In 2006, this court found that the meaning of "disability" as used in the WLAD

was consistent with the definition found in the federal Americans with Disabilities Act of 1990 . . . *McClarty.* In reaction, the legislature rejected the *McClarty* definition and amended the WLAD to provide a new statutory definition of "disability." Being careful not to reverse *McClarty*, the legislature explicitly declared [that] the new statutory definition applied retroactively to causes of action occurring the day before the *McClarty* opinion was filed and to causes of action occurring on or after the effective date of the amendment. We are asked to determine whether this retroactive amendment to a statute previously construed by this court violates separation of powers. We hold that under the facts of this case, it does not. . . .

John Hale was hired by the Wellpinit School District (Wellpinit) in February 2002 to provide student support services at Wellpinit High School. . . . Hale suffered from an anxiety disorder and depression. Feeling that the work environment was exacerbating his condition and that he was receiving no help in trying to improve the situation, Hale left his position with Wellpinit on March 20, 2003.

In 2006, Hale filed suit in Stevens County Superior Court against his former employer, Wellpinit, alleging negligent infliction of emotional distress, breach of contract, and disability discrimination under the WLAD. The WLAD claim alleged that Hale was disabled and that Wellpinit had failed to accommodate his disability by failing to intervene and stop the abusive conduct Hale felt was exacerbating his anxiety disorder. Wellpinit filed a motion for partial summary judgment alleging that Hale had failed to establish that he was disabled under the WLAD. On March 30, 2007, the trial judge granted Wellpinit's motion for partial summary judgment on the WLAD claim, finding that there was no issue of material fact regarding whether Hale was disabled as that term is defined under *McClarty.*

In April 2007, following the dismissal of Hale's accommodation claim, the legislature passed Substitute Senate Bill 5340, 60th Leg., Reg. Sess. (Wash. 2007) (S.S.B.), which statutorily defined "disability" under the WLAD. The new legislative act explicitly declared that the definition applied retroactively. Hale filed a motion for reconsideration arguing that in light of the legislature's amendment of the WLAD and its retroactive effect, partial summary judgment should have been denied because his condition qualified as a disability under the new definition. . . .

That the United States Constitution has endured since drafted in 1787 is a testament to the fact that its creators understood both the need for a stronger national government and mistrusted power. . . . In response to this desire for a stronger yet limited national government, the delegates [to the Constitutional Convention] adopted a plan based largely on the concept of separation of powers. They hoped to ensure liberty by defusing and limiting power. Separation of powers created a clear division of functions among each branch of government, and the power to interfere with the exercise of another's functions was very limited. . . . The doctrine recognizes that each branch of government has its own appropriate sphere of activity. . . .

Within this framework, the fundamental function of the judicial branch is judicial review. This includes the authority to interpret the law. *Marbury* judicial review was also familiar to the delegates who convened in 1787. . . .

The doctrine of separation of powers is reciprocal. "Unlike many other constitutional violations, which directly damage rights retained by the people, the damage caused by a separation of powers violation accrues directly to the branch invaded." *Carrick.* The judicial branch violates the doctrine when it assumes " ' "tasks that are more properly accomplished by [other] branches." ' " *Carrick.* The legislature's role is to set policy and to draft and enact laws. " ' "[T]he drafting of a statute is a legislative, not a judicial, function." ' " *Sedlacek.* Both the legislature and the judiciary intrude upon the other's authority cautiously so as not to violate the doctrine of separation of powers.

The separate branches must remain partially intertwined to maintain an effective system of checks and balances. *Carrick.* The art of good government requires cooperation and flexibility among the branches. Each must act with a spirit of interdependence. Washington State has enjoyed a rich history of cooperation and harmony among its three branches of government. Each branch has given deference to the others and all three have acted interdependently in exercising authority. . . .

As respondents correctly note, statutory amendments are generally presumed to be prospective only. The retroactive application of laws may violate the ex post facto doctrine, affect vested rights and violate due process, or affect other judicial functions. There are also many policy reasons that disfavor changing the law retroactively. Retroactive changes in the law alter the status quo and may disturb a party's reasonable reliance on what the law formerly said and may cause manifest injustices. However, where no constitutional prohibition applies, an amendment may act retroactively if the legislature so intended or if it is curative. . . .

In the absence of a clear declaration by the legislature regarding retroactivity of an amendment, it may be helpful to characterize changes to a statute as "clarifying" or "restorative" or "curative" or "remedial" to assist in determining legislative intent. However, here the legislature was quite clear that S.S.B. 5340 amending RCW 49.60.040 was remedial and retroactive. The amendment was in direct response to our decision in *McClarty*, which the legislature believed "failed to recognize" that WLAD is independent from the federal ADA of 1990. The legislature has expressed its intent unequivocally, and we find the nature of the amendment unhelpful in analyzing the separation of powers issue.

"[I]t is this court's obligation to determine and carry out the intent of the legislature." *City of Redmond*. Determining the collective intent of the legislature is not always an easy task. This is particularly true when we are called upon to interpret a law that was passed decades ago. Sometimes the legislative body was not as artful as it could have been in choosing the words for the text of the bill it has passed. Occasionally, try as the court may, the legislature is disappointed with the court's interpretation. As recently expressed by a distinguished member of the legislature, sometimes the court must consider legislation passed by the legislature, shake its head and think, "what were they thinking?" And then of course there are times when the legislature reads an opinion of the court and says the same thing.

In passing S.S.B. 5340, the legislature acted wholly within its sphere of authority to make policy, to pass laws, and to amend laws already in effect. As originally passed, the WLAD did not define "disability." In *McClarty*, this court, in a five to four opinion, interpreted the act and concluded [that] the definition of "disability" in the ADA was more consistent with the intent of the legislature. The legislature thereafter exercised its authority to amend the act and change the definition of "disability" retroactively. The legislature was careful not to reverse our decision in *McClarty* nor did the legislature interfere with any judicial function. The legislature has not threatened the independence or integrity or invaded the prerogatives of the judicial branch. We hold that the adoption of S.S.B. 5340 did not violate the separation of powers doctrine. Indeed, the court's efforts to express the intent of the legislature in . . . *McClarty* and the legislative response in S.S.B. 5340 should serve as a model of how two separate and independent branches of government can work together in harmony and in the spirit of reciprocal deference to the other's important role and function in the art of governing.

Case Questions

1. Why was the state legislature careful to carve out a short window of time to which the amendment was inapplicable?
2. What is the benefit of interpreting a state statute consistent with a similar federal statute?
3. What is the disadvantage of interpreting a state statute consistent with a similar federal statute?
4. Why did the court mention that *McClarty* was a five-to-four decision?

STARE DECISIS

Today the importance of the common law tradition lies largely in the principle of **precedent**, or stare decisis, by which judicial lawmaking is rendered orderly, predictable, and legitimate. The principle of **stare decisis** dictates that in making decisions judges should follow prior precedents. In practice, this means that disputes involving similar fact situations should be decided by similar rules. Former decisions are thus called *precedents* and are examined for guidance in making present decisions. When the court is faced with a novel fact situation (**case of first impression**) and formulates a rule to decide the case, the court "sets a precedent" that should be followed should a similar case arise.

As an example, let us suppose that a state court is faced with the following situation: A man and woman who have been living together for several years without benefit of marriage separate; the woman sues the man for breach of contract, claiming that when they entered into a cohabitation arrangement, the man promised to share his earnings equally with her if she refrained from employment and provided him with homemaking services and companionship, to which she agreed. The man defends on the basis of an established principle of contract law that a contract to perform illegal acts is unenforceable. Because sexual cohabitation is illegal in the state and that was the purpose of any promises that might have been exchanged, claims the man, the contract cannot be enforced.

Assuming the court has never been faced with this precise situation before, it must apply the rules of contract law and set a precedent for cohabitation agreements. Judging from similar cases already decided in several states, the court will probably rule that a cohabitation agreement is enforceable like any other contract unless its purpose is compensation for sexual services. Once this precedent has been set, the next dispute over a cohabitation agreement should be decided by application of the same rule. In this way, the first case is precedent for the second. If the rule is applied in many similar cases over a period of time, the court is likely to refer to it as a "well-established principle of law."

The force of a precedent depends upon the court that hands it down. A precedent is considered binding on the court that sets it and all lower courts within its jurisdiction. In a typical state court system, decisions can be rendered at three levels: trial court (lowest), court of appeals (intermediate appellate), and state supreme court (highest). Decisions of the highest state court are binding on all state courts. Decisions of courts of appeals are binding on that court and on lower courts within its jurisdiction. There is frequently more than one court of appeals, each with specific regional jurisdiction within the state. The hierarchy of federal courts also follows this pattern.

It sometimes happens that different courts of appeals within the same system (i.e., a state or the federal system) will formulate different rules for the same fact situation, creating considerable confusion. Trial courts in the First Circuit may feel bound by a different rule than those in the Fifth Circuit, and courts in the Third Circuit, whose court of appeals may not have decided an equivalent case, may be in a quandary about whether to follow the First Circuit rule or the Fifth Circuit rule. The logical solution is to obtain a ruling from the highest court, which is at liberty to adopt either rule or even a different rule, which would then be binding on all the courts within its jurisdiction.

The quagmire of American jurisdiction can be clarified by certain important principles. First, not only are federal and state court systems separate, but state and federal laws are separate as well. Where federal law is concerned, federal courts set the precedents, and the U.S. Supreme Court has final authority in declaring what the law is. In matters of state law, state courts have authority, and the highest court of a state has final authority to declare what the state's law is. Many Americans labor under the misconception that the U.S. Supreme Court is the final authority for interpreting state law. On the contrary, the highest court of each state is the ultimate authority for the law of that state. One of the reasons for the confusion arises from the supremacy clause of the U.S. Constitution, under which the U.S. Supreme Court may declare state law, whether judicial precedent or state statute, invalid if it is deemed to be in violation of the U.S. Constitution. This power of the U.S. Supreme Court is not derived from any authority to define state law but from authority to interpret the meaning of the U.S. Constitution, which is the "supreme law of the land."

The *Li* case is an example of a court overruling a well-established precedent and thus substituting a new rule. The issue facing the Supreme Court of California was whether to abolish the doctrine of contributory negligence and replace it with the doctrine of comparative negligence. Negligence is discussed in some detail in Chapter 10 (on torts),

precedent

Prior decisions of the same court, or a higher court, which a judge must follow in deciding a subsequent case presenting similar facts and the same legal problem. Precedent consists of the rule applied in a case and encompasses the reasoning that requires it. In a given decision, the precedent may be distinguished from *dictum,* which includes extraneous or conjectural statements not necessary to the decision and that are not binding on future decisions.

stare decisis

The doctrine that judicial decisions stand as precedents for cases arising in the future. It is a fundamental policy of our law that, except in unusual circumstances, a court's determination on a point of law will be followed by courts of the same or lower rank in later cases presenting the same legal issue. It means to "stand by a decision." The conventional translation (probably not very helpful) is "Let the decision stand."

case of first impression

A case presenting a fact situation that has never been decided before by that court.

but in lay terms, negligence occurs when one person injures another by failing to exercise care (for example, if someone carelessly causes an auto accident). Because negligence is grounded in fault, the courts in the nineteenth century developed the doctrine of *contributory negligence,* which held that a negligent defendant would not be liable if it could be shown that the plaintiff's negligence also contributed to the injury. It soon became apparent that the doctrine was inequitable in cases in which the defendant's negligence was great and the plaintiff's negligence was minimal. For example, railroad workers commonly worked under dangerously unsafe conditions and sometimes contributed to their own injuries through momentary inattention. Gradually the states began to replace contributory negligence with the doctrine of *comparative negligence,* which apportioned fault between plaintiff and defendant so that the plaintiff, even if also negligent, could recover a diminished amount if the jury found the plaintiff less responsible for the cause of the injury (e.g., plaintiff 20 percent at fault and defendant 80 percent at fault).

In *Li,* the plaintiff made an improper turn through an intersection and was struck by the defendant, who was racing to pass through the intersection while the stoplight was yellow. The case was heard without a jury. The judge found both plaintiff and defendant negligent and entered a judgment in favor of the defendant based on California law. The plaintiff then appealed in the hope that she could persuade the Supreme Court of California to overrule prior precedent, in which effort she was successful.

A careful reading of the case reveals that four of the six justices ruling on the case wanted to change the law. Their decision was complicated by the fact that although contributory negligence originally arose through judicial decision, the California legislature had enacted a statute in 1872 establishing the doctrine of contributory negligence. In a lengthy discussion of the statute and its history (omitted here), the court concluded that the statute had not been intended to permanently establish contributory negligence as the law of the state.

LI

v.

YELLOW CAB COMPANY OF CALIFORNIA
et al., Defendants and Respondents

**13 Cal. 3d 804, 532 P.2d 1226,
119 Cal. Rptr. 858 (1975)**

In this case we address the grave and recurrent question [of] whether we should judicially declare no longer applicable in California courts the doctrine of **contributory negligence**, which bars all recovery when the plaintiff's negligent conduct has contributed as a legal cause in any degree to the harm suffered by him, and hold that it must give way to a system of **comparative negligence**, which assesses liability in direct proportion to fault. . . .

It is unnecessary for us to catalogue the enormous amount of critical comment that has been directed over the years against the "all-or-nothing" approach of the doctrine of contributory negligence. The essence of that criticism has been constant and clear: the doctrine is inequitable in its operation because it fails to distribute responsibility in proportion to fault.

* * *

It is in view of these theoretical and practical considerations that to this date 25 states have abrogated the "all or nothing" rule of contributory negligence and have enacted in its place general apportionment statutes calculated in one manner or another to assess liability in proportion to fault. In 1973 these states were joined by Florida, which effected the same result by judicial decision. (*Hoffman v. Jones* (Fla. 1973) 280 So. 2d 431.) We are likewise persuaded that logic, practical experience, and fundamental justice counsel against the retention of the doctrine rendering contributory negligence a complete bar to recovery—and that it should be replaced in this state by a system under which liability for damage will be borne by those whose negligence caused it in direct proportion to their respective fault. . . .

It is urged that any change in the law of contributory negligence must be made by the Legislature, not by this court. Although the doctrine of contributory negligence is of judicial origin . . . subsequent cases of this court, it is pointed out, have unanimously affirmed that . . . the "all-or-nothing" rule is the law of this state and shall remain so until the Legislature directs otherwise. . . .

[There follows a discussion of why the court may nevertheless abolish the doctrine of contributory negligence, followed by a discussion of the different forms of comparative negligence adopted in the other states.]

For all of the foregoing reasons, we conclude that the "all-or-nothing" rule of contributory negligence as it presently exists in this state should be and is herewith superseded by a system of "pure" comparative negligence, the fundamental purpose of which shall be to assign responsibility and liability for damage in direct proportion to the amount of negligence of each of the parties.

* * *

The judgment is reversed.

* * *

CLARK, J., dissenting. . . . [T]he Legislature is the branch best able to effect transition from contributory to comparative or some other doctrine of **negligence**. Numerous and differing negligence systems have been urged over the years, yet there remains widespread disagreement among both the commentators and the states as to which one is best. . . . This court is not an investigatory body, and we lack the means of fairly appraising the merits of these competing systems. Constrained by settled rules of judicial review, we must consider only matters within the record or susceptible to judicial notice. That this court is inadequate to the task of carefully selecting the best replacement system is reflected in the majority's summary manner of eliminating from consideration all but two of the many competing proposals—including models adopted by some of our sister states.

By abolishing this century-old doctrine today, the majority seriously erodes our constitutional function. We are again guilty of judicial chauvinism.

Case Questions

1. Is abolishing contributory negligence a question more properly addressed by the legislature than the court? (Consider this question when reading the section comparing adjudication and legislation.)
2. If the court sets a "bad" precedent, must it wait for the legislature to rectify the mistake?
3. What if the California legislature, after the decision in *Li,* passed a law unequivocally declaring that contributory negligence and not comparative negligence was the law of California? Does a legislature have authority to do this? Must the court follow the statute?

Case Glossary

contributory negligence
A principle by which recovery will be denied to a plaintiff for defendant's negligence if plaintiff is also found to have been at fault. It is an affirmative defense that has been replaced by *comparative negligence* in most states.

comparative negligence
A principle whereby damages are apportioned between plaintiff and defendant according to their relative fault in a negligence case where both are found to have been at fault.

negligence
A cause of action based on a failure to meet a reasonable standard of conduct, which failure results in an injury.

§

DISTINGUISHING CASES

Stare decisis requires that the same rule be applied in future cases with identical fact situations. However, virtually every case differs in some respect, large or small, from preceding cases. Legal arguments commonly revolve around the comparison of the facts of the instant case with the precedents. Arguing against the application of precedent in a given case entails *distinguishing* the facts of the instant case from those of the precedents. The differences, of course, must arguably call for a different rule. Let us take a fairly simple (perhaps simpleminded) example. At common law, "every dog has one bite." The owner of a dog was not liable when his dog bit the first time but was liable thenceforth. In contrast, a person keeping a wolf would be liable upon the first bite. The owner of a wolf could not rely on dog precedents, but the owner of a collie could rely on cocker spaniel precedents. The difference between a dog bite and a wolf bite is legally meaningful (i.e., we can reasonably justify the difference). On the one hand, a dog is a tame, domesticated animal, and its propensity to bite is not known by its owner before it actually bites. A wolf, on the other hand, is a wild animal. Keeping a wild animal puts a duty on its owner to maintain sufficient control to keep the animal from causing harm. The difference between dogs and wild animals makes legal sense. Caveat: We won't go into the difference between pit bulls and golden retrievers. Suffice to say that dog ownership is today governed by statutes and local ordinances; the common law rule usually does not apply.

In *L.M.*, the juvenile was arguing for a change in state law that would have given him the right to a jury trial. He was fighting an uphill battle because *McKeiver*, a U.S. Supreme Court opinion from 1971; *McClarty*, a 1984 state court decision; and *L.A.*, a state court decision from 2001, had all held that a juvenile has no right to a jury trial. Apparently, this was not an easy decision for the court. The majority opinion is excerpted here; one justice concurred and one justice dissented. Questions at the end of the chapter concern the concurring and dissenting opinions.

In the Matter of L.M.

Supreme Court of Kansas

No. 96,197

286 Kan. 460, 186 P.3d 164

June 20, 2008.

L.M. seeks review of the Court of Appeals decision affirming his juvenile adjudication for aggravated sexual battery and being a minor in possession of alcohol. L.M. claims that he should have received a jury trial and argues that sweeping changes to juvenile justice procedures in Kansas since 1984 merit renewed scrutiny under applicable constitutional protections. . . .

L.M. is challenging the constitutionality of K.S.A. 2006 Supp. 38-2344(d), which provides that a juvenile who pleads not guilty is entitled to a "trial to the court," and K.S.A. 2006 Supp. 38-2357, . . . which gives the district court complete discretion in determining whether a juvenile should be granted a jury trial. . . .

L.M.'s first argument relies on the Sixth Amendment to the United States Constitution, which provides in pertinent part:

"In all criminal prosecutions, the accused shall enjoy the right to a speedy and public trial, by an impartial jury of the State and district wherein the crime shall have been committed. . . ."

L.M. further relies on the United States Constitution's Fourteenth Amendment Due Process Clause, which provides in relevant part:

"No State shall make or enforce any law which shall abridge the privileges or immunities of citizens of the United States; nor shall any State deprive any person of life, liberty, or property without due process of law. . . ."

Kansas has previously resolved this issue against L.M.'s position. Twenty-four years ago, under the statutes then controlling the disposition of juvenile offender cases, this court held that juveniles do not have a constitutional right to a jury trial under either the federal or state constitutions. *Findlay*. . . .

The *Findlay* court also adopted the United States Supreme Court's reasoning in *McKeiver*, where a plurality of the Court held that juveniles are not entitled to a jury trial under the Sixth and Fourteenth Amendments to the Constitution.

In *McKeiver*, the United States Supreme Court addressed the constitutionality of the Pennsylvania and North Carolina juvenile justice systems, neither of which afforded juveniles the right to a jury trial. Although the resulting plurality opinion held that juveniles are not entitled to a jury trial under the federal constitution, the justices could not agree on the reasoning to support that holding. Four of the justices supported their decision with . . . 13 policy considerations and assumptions or speculations about the impact of jury trials on juvenile proceedings. . . . Justice Harlan concurred with the result. . . . Justice Brennan also concurred with the result but relied on the concept of fundamental fairness. . . . Justices Douglas, Black, and Marshall dissented, stating that "neither the Fourteenth Amendment nor the Bill of Rights is for adults alone." *McKeiver*. . . .

L.M. recognizes the import of *Findlay* and *McKeiver* but asks us to overturn *Findlay*. We begin our analysis by noting that the Kansas Legislature has significantly changed the language of the Kansas Juvenile Offender Code (KJOC) since the *Findlay* court decided this issue 24 years ago. The juvenile code is now called the Revised Kansas Juvenile Justice Code [KJJC]. . . .

In 1982, the KJOC was focused on rehabilitation and the State's parental role in providing guidance, control, and discipline. However, under the KJJC, the focus has shifted to protecting the public, holding juveniles accountable for their behavior and choices, and making juveniles more productive and responsible members of society. These purposes are more aligned with the legislative intent for the adult sentencing statutes, which include protecting the public by incarcerating dangerous offenders for a long period of time, holding offenders accountable by prescribing appropriate consequences for their actions, and encouraging offenders to be more productive members of society by considering their individual characteristics, circumstances, needs, and potentialities in determining their sentences. . . .

Besides amending the 1982 version of the KJOC to reflect the purpose and provisions included in the adult criminal code, the legislature has removed some of the protective provisions that made the juvenile system more child-cognizant and confidential, a key consideration in the *McKeiver* plurality decision. . . .

These changes to the juvenile justice system have eroded the benevolent parens patriae character that distinguished it from the adult criminal system. The United States Supreme Court relied on the juvenile justice system's characteristics of fairness, concern, sympathy, and paternal attention in concluding that juveniles were not entitled to a jury trial. *McKeiver*. Likewise, this court relied on that parens patriae character in reaching its decision in *Findlay*. However, because the juvenile justice system is now patterned after the adult criminal system, we conclude that the changes have superseded the *McKeiver* and *Findlay* Courts' reasoning and those decisions are no longer binding precedent for us to follow. Based on our conclusion that the Kansas juvenile justice system has become more akin to an adult criminal prosecution, we hold that juveniles have a constitutional right to a jury trial under the Sixth and Fourteenth Amendments. As a result, K.S.A. 2006 Supp. 38-2344(d), which provides that a juvenile who pleads not guilty is entitled to a "trial to the court," and K.S.A. 2006 Supp. 38-2357, which gives the district court discretion in determining whether a juvenile should be granted a jury trial, are unconstitutional.

In reaching this conclusion, we are mindful of decisions in other jurisdictions rejecting the argument that changes to the juvenile justice system have altered its parens patriae character. . . . We are also mindful that many of the state courts that have addressed this issue in one form or another have declined to extend the constitutional right to a jury trial to juveniles. . . .

While there is wide variability in the juvenile offender laws throughout the country, it nevertheless seems apparent to us that the KJJC, in its tilt towards applying adult standards of criminal procedure and sentencing, removed the paternalistic protections previously accorded juveniles while continuing to deny those juveniles the constitutional right to a jury trial. Although we do not find total support from the courts in some of our sister states, we are undaunted in our belief that juveniles are entitled to the right to a jury trial guaranteed to all citizens under the Sixth and Fourteenth Amendments to the United States Constitution.

The State relies on our more recent decision in *L.A.* to support its argument that juveniles are not entitled to a jury trial. However, we do not find *L.A.* persuasive. The *L.A.* court relied on *Findlay* without analyzing the distinctions between the KJOC and the KJJC. As a result, it did not address the issue presented in this case. . . .

The district court and the Court of Appeals acted in accordance with our prior precedent in *Findlay*. However, we agree with L.M. that *Findlay* is no longer applicable because of the legislative overhaul to the juvenile justice code. The right to a jury trial in juvenile offender proceedings is a new rule of procedure; it does not operate retroactively. It does not create a new class of convicted persons, but merely raises " 'the possibility that someone convicted with use of the invalidated procedure might have been acquitted otherwise.' " *Drach.* This right will apply only to cases pending on direct review or not yet final on the date of filing of this opinion. Because L.M. was tried without a jury, his adjudication is reversed and this matter is remanded to the district court for a new trial before a jury.

Case Questions

1. What was the vote on the plurality decision in *McKeiver*?
2. Why is a plurality opinion difficult to deal with under the doctrine of stare decisis?
3. Did it make sense for the court to distinguish *L.A.* (a 2001 case in which the court stated that there was no right to a jury trial) from *L.M.*?
4. Why does the court make the point that the right to a jury trial is procedural?

ADJUDICATION VERSUS LEGISLATION

legislation
The act of giving, making, or enacting laws; preparation and enactment of laws; lawmaking, ordinarily the prerogative of legislatures or legislative bodies.

adjudication
The formal act of deciding disputes by a court or tribunal.

Although judges may be said to "make law," they do so in a way quite unlike that of legislators. **Legislation** is a very different process with a different orientation. Whereas adjudication can be said to be *particularized,* in the sense that cases focus on particular events and particular parties, legislation is *generalized* in that it is designed to make rules that apply to everyone.

Adjudication: Narrow Focus on Past Events

Judges resolve disputes between parties; **adjudication** refers to the process of making these decisions. In the American system, a person (which can also be a business, a corporation, or a city) files a lawsuit against another to redress an injury or to establish rights and duties. When a case reaches trial, the judge is faced with past events that have been framed by attorneys for both sides for submission to the judge for resolution. Ordinarily, only the facts of the events relating to the dispute are relevant to the resolution of that dispute. Evidence presented at trial will reveal those facts in great detail in order to determine which rule of law is applicable. The judge will decide which laws are relevant to the facts as determined by the evidence presented in court. Thus, the process of adjudication focuses on past events specific to one dispute, and only the law the judge deems appropriate to that case will be applied.

In short, the judge looks through a magnifying glass at one case and declares what law is applicable. If law is made in the process, it is a by-product of the case. The function of the judge is to settle the dispute, not to determine how the law will apply to other cases in the future. The judge will look to the authority of the past to make the decision.

Legislation: Universal Application and Future Effect

The characteristics of legislation are universal application and future effect. Legislators do not resolve individual cases, though they are often motivated by dissatisfaction with the outcomes of cases decided in the courts. For example, the *Baby M* case in New Jersey (*In re Baby M,* 109 N.J. 396, 537 A.2d 1227 [1988]), in which a surrogate mother fought unsuccessfully to gain custody from the couple who had arranged to adopt the baby, resulted in many legislatures, including New Jersey, enacting laws regulating surrogate mother contracts. But the New Jersey legislature did not decide the *Baby M* case or change the ruling of the court; its enactment governed contracts between surrogate mothers and adoptive parents in future cases.

The legislative process typically operates by first recognizing a problem and then, through investigation and deliberation, attempting to solve the problem by enacting a law. When the legislative process is complete, the law is a matter of public record, and everyone must comply or risk legal consequences. Only rarely can legislation apply retroactively. The surrogate mother case brought to public attention the moral issues in the commercialization of pregnancy and adoption. Some people felt that such contracts should be illegal or unenforceable, some felt that the natural mother should have the option to revoke the contract, and others felt that ordinary contract law provided sufficient protection. State legislatures deliberated these questions and arrived at laws designed to deal with the question. These laws, however, did not change adoptions that had already taken place but instead served as the legal standards that would govern surrogate mother contracts subsequent to enactment of law.

The *Colby* and *Higgins* cases illustrate the difference between legislation and adjudication and illuminate the judicial attitude exemplified in the doctrine of stare decisis. American courts in the nineteenth century created or expanded immunity to suit for several categories of parties, including charitable institutions, the subject of *Colby* and *Higgins.* Immunity from suit leaves an injured party without a remedy, and in the twentieth century the courts and legislatures of our country began to question the wisdom and legality of immunity to suit. The rise of the insurance industry made such immunities obsolete. Individuals and institutions can protect themselves from catastrophic losses by purchasing insurance. The Supreme Judicial Court of Massachusetts was presented with an archaic principle of charitable immunity that it had created a century before. By the time these cases were decided, nearly every other state had abolished charitable immunity by statute or by the highest state court overruling its own prior decisions.

Even though the court was inclined to abolish charitable immunity, it found itself in a dilemma. Because the precedents were clear (i.e., charitable institutions were immune from suit according to a well-established line of precedents), the Supreme Judicial Court was reluctant to change the rule suddenly—but at the same time the doctrine of charitable immunity had just as clearly been discredited as a principle of American law. Charitable institutions should be able to rely on the law as stated by the courts. Why should a nonprofit hospital buy insurance if it cannot be sued?

Edwin A. COLBY, Administrator

v.

CARNEY HOSPITAL

356 Mass. 527, 254 N.E.2d 407 (1969)

The plaintiff **administrator** brings this action of tort and contract for the death and conscious suffering of his **intestate**. The defendant hospital set up, among other things, the defence of charitable immunity. The plaintiff demurred to this part of the answer, stating that it "does not set forth a valid or legal defense, in that said defense as alleged violates and abrogates certain rights, privileges and immunities granted to, and preserved for the citizens of the Commonwealth" under arts. 1, 10, 11, 12, 20, and 30 of our Declaration of Rights and also under the Fifth and Fourteenth Amendments to the Constitution of the United States. A judge in the Superior Court overruled the **demurrer**, and the plaintiff appealed.

The demurrer was rightly overruled. Nothing has been brought to our attention suggesting that the doctrine of charitable immunity is repugnant to any provision of the Constitutions of the United States and the Commonwealth.

In the past on many occasions we have declined to renounce the defence of charitable immunity set forth in *McDonald v. Massachusetts Gen. Hosp.,* 120 Mass. 432, and *Roosen v. Peter Bent Brigham Hosp.,* 235 Mass. 66, 126 N.E. 392, 14 A.L.R. 563. We took this position because we were of [the] opinion that any renunciation preferably should be accomplished prospectively and that this should be best done by legislative action. Now it appears that only three or four States still adhere to the doctrine. . . . It seems likely that no legislative action in this Commonwealth is probable in the near future. Accordingly, we take this occasion to give adequate warning that the next time we are squarely confronted by a legal question respecting the charitable immunity doctrine it is our intention to abolish it.

Order overruling demurrer affirmed.

John HIGGINS

v.

EMERSON HOSPITAL

328 N.E.2d 488 (Mass. 1975)

This appeal brings before us the issue whether, by reason of the language in *Colby v. Carney Hosp.,* 356 Mass. 527, 528, 254 N.E.2d 407 (1969), we should hold that the defense of charitable immunity is not available to the defendant hospital. . . .

The plaintiff brought an action in tort and contract for injuries allegedly sustained by him on June 17, 1970, while he was an inpatient at the defendant hospital. The case was tried on June 20, 1974, before a Superior Court judge and a jury. The plaintiff's attorney made an opening statement that asserted the facts of the plaintiff's accident and injury, including a stipulation that the defendant hospital . . . was operated exclusively for charitable purposes. The judge thereupon **directed verdicts** for the defendant as to both counts of the plaintiff's declaration.

. . . The parties and the judge have clearly considered that the single issue is whether, by reason of the *Colby* case, or any other consideration, we should hold that charitable immunity is not applicable in this case. We hold that the doctrine is applicable and the judge properly directed verdicts for the defendant as to both counts.

The injury here occurred after the date of the decision of the *Colby* case (December 23, 1969), but before the effective date, September 16, 1971, of [the statute] which abolished the doctrine of charitable immunity. We have since held that the statute is not retrospective in effect . . . , and it is thus clear that the plaintiff here takes no benefit from the statute.

The plaintiff contends that, because of the intimation in the *Colby* case as to the possible future abolishment of charitable immunity, that doctrine is not applicable in this case. He argues that from the date of the decision the various charitable institutions, as well as the insurance industry and members of the public, were clearly given notice of and could conform their conduct in reliance on the fact that claims of charitable immunity raised with respect to incidents occurring after the date of the decision, December 23, 1969, would be rejected.

He further contends that had the Legislature not acted on the subject matter in 1971 there would be no question that this court would rule the charitable immunity doctrine abolished as to the instant case.

We reject the arguments. In *Colby v. Carney Hosp.*, 356 Mass. 527, 528, 254 N.E.2d 407, 408 (1969), we said that any renunciation of the doctrine of charitable immunity "should be accomplished *prospectively* and that this should be best done by legislative action" (emphasis supplied). At no time has this court abolished the doctrine. In *Ricker v. Northeastern Univ., supra,* _____ at _____, 279 N.E.2d at 672, we said, speaking of the *Colby* case, "This language does not by itself abolish the doctrine of charitable immunity as of December 23, 1969 . . . [the language] makes it clear that no change of the doctrine was then being made." The Legislature chose to act subsequent to the *Colby* decision. We recognize the factual distinction between the instant case and the *Ricker* case, to wit, that the injury to Ricker occurred prior to December 23, 1969, the date of our decision in the *Colby* case, while the injury underlying this action occurred subsequent to that decision. Nevertheless, we see no persuasive reason now to rule, as in practical effect the plaintiff urges here, that the doctrine of charitable immunity does not apply to an injury which occurred after December 23, 1969, but before the effective date of [the statute].

* * *

Judgment affirmed.

Case Questions

1. If the court was so clearly opposed to charitable immunity, why did it not simply abolish it in *Colby*?
2. Because the doctrine of charitable immunity was a judicial creation in the first place, why did the court look to the legislature to abolish it?
3. How do these cases express the judicial attitude toward precedent in Massachusetts?
4. If you had been Higgins's attorney in *Higgins v. Emerson Hospital,* would you have predicted a win or a loss in the Supreme Judicial Court?

Case Glossary

administrator
A person appointed by a court to manage the distribution of the estate of a deceased person.

intestate
A person who dies without a will. Also used as an adjective to refer to the state of dying without a will.

demurrer
A motion to dismiss a case, alleging that the complaint is insufficient to state a legal cause of action.

directed verdict
The judge may order a verdict against the plaintiffs when they have failed to meet their burden of proof. Formerly the judge ordered the jury to enter a verdict against the plaintiff. Today the judge grants a motion for a directed verdict and enters a judgment.

OBITER DICTUM

Not everything that is expressed in an opinion is precedent. The author of an opinion is free to make comments that go beyond the immediate issues to be decided. The remarks, opinions, and comments in a decision that exceed the scope of the issues and the rules that decide them are called **dictum** (plural **dicta**), from the older Latin phrase **obiter dictum**, and are not binding on future cases. As we have already seen, the process of adjudication commonly results in the making of new rules or the interpretation of existing rules. This is an unavoidable result of the necessity of resolving disputes. However, when a judge attempts to expand an argument to issues or facts not before the court in the dispute, adjudication ends and legislation begins. Although these statements are worthy of consideration in subsequent cases, they are not considered binding precedent and need not be followed; they are *dicta* rather than rule.

dictum (dicta, obiter dictum)

Dictum is a Latin word meaning "said" or "stated." *Obiter* means "by the way" or "incidentally." *Obiter dictum,* then, means something stated incidentally and not necessary to the discussion, usually shortened to *dictum* or its plural *dicta*. In law, it refers to a part of a judicial decision that goes beyond the scope of the issues and is considered mere opinion and not binding precedent.

Analytically, the way to distinguish *dictum* from the rule of law is to determine the legal and factual issues presented by a dispute and analyze the reasoning that leads to their resolution. Anything outside this reasoning and the rule behind it is *dictum.*

This can be applied to the *Colby* and *Higgins* cases. In *Colby,* the court faced the issue of whether charitable immunity was still the rule in Massachusetts. Although the court expressed its disapproval of the rule, it nevertheless followed prior precedent and held that charitable immunity was still in effect, even while suggesting that it would be better for the legislature to abolish the doctrine. The court added that it intended to abolish the doctrine the next time it was faced with the same issue. This assertion of the court's future intentions was *dictum.* When the trial court in *Higgins* was faced with the same issue five years later, it upheld charitable immunity and directed verdicts in favor of the defendant. The trial court was legally correct because the Supreme Judicial Court in *Colby* had not abolished the doctrine but merely expressed its intention to do so. The Supreme Judicial Court agreed with the lower court that the doctrine had not been abolished by the court and indicated that its expression of future intentions had no legally binding force on Massachusetts courts. As a practical matter, the fact that the legislature had subsequently abolished charitable immunity meant that the Supreme Judicial Court need not take it upon itself to abolish the doctrine, which only affected those unfortunate few who were injured prior to the legislative act.

NONBINDING AUTHORITY

In practical terms, the law consists of state and federal constitutions, statutes, and judicial opinions. If a trial court in Rhode Island is faced with a difficult legal issue, it will attempt to determine the applicable law by resorting to Rhode Island statutes and case law that conforms to mandates of the Rhode Island and federal constitutions. It is bound by these authorities alone. Nevertheless, the court may confront an issue that clearly demands judicial resolution and for which the usual binding sources of the law provide little or no guidance. Typically this arises in a case of first impression, in which the factual situation giving rise to the dispute has never been decided by a court of the state nor been addressed by the state legislature.

Reasoning from Authority

To arrive at a reasonable solution, the court will use the best authority it can find. It may reason from existing state law using logic and analogy to infer a rule. For instance, until recently state courts universally rejected the notion that a professional license was property that could be used to establish property settlements upon divorce. This was particularly problematic in cases in which spouses, usually wives, had worked to support their husbands through professional school, only to be divorced soon afterward, when their professional husbands had not yet practiced long enough to acquire much property to be divided between husband and wife. In attempting to classify professional licenses, the courts, though admitting that a license clearly had value for its holder, noted that the licenses did not have the usual attributes of property (namely, they could not be transferred, sold, leased, or given away) and noted that they could be revoked by the licensing authority. Although many courts obviously felt that this traditional definition of property resulted in an injustice to many wives, they felt compelled to follow the law. Finally, in *O'Brien v. O'Brien*, 489 N.E.2d 712 (N.Y. 1985), the New York court defined professional licenses as "marital property," justifying its departure from prior law on the basis of recent divorce legislation that provided a broad definition of marital property in divorce. Of course, the *O'Brien* decision was only binding on New York courts. The definition of "marital property" is a matter of state law, and New York had used a definition broader than that of other states.

Law from Sister States

When binding authority is absent, the court often looks to nonbinding authority from other states. An issue unique in one state may very well have been decided in another. It seems reasonable to examine such decisions to see whether the rules handed down and the reasoning behind them are applicable to the law of the state faced with a case of first impression. Often the pioneering state will give its name to the principle; for example, one of the comparative negligence rules mentioned in *Li* as the "50 percent" rule might also be referred to as the "Wisconsin rule," as opposed to the "Florida rule," which is normally referred to as "pure" comparative negligence.

Decisions of other state courts are commonly referred to as **persuasive authority**; they command respect because they represent the law of another American jurisdiction even though they are not binding outside that jurisdiction. The persuasiveness of such authority is greatest in areas of common law, especially torts, and weakest in decisions based on statutory interpretation. For example, in the area of family law, there is considerable variation among the states concerning divorce law, so the reasoning of the court of one state may be considered inappropriate in another by virtue of differences between their respective statutes. For example, California is a **community property** state, whereas New York is an **equitable distribution** state, making California decisions regarding the distribution of property upon divorce largely inapplicable to New York cases. In contrast, because the **Uniform Commercial Code (UCC)** has been adopted in every state except Louisiana, decisions interpreting the UCC are often used as persuasive authority.

Secondary Sources

In addition to cases from other states, there exists a vast array of legal materials used in arguments by lawyers and opinions by judges that are not officially the law anywhere; these materials are called **secondary authority**. Principal among these are law review articles, **treatises**, and the **Restatements of the Law**. Law review articles written by legal scholars commonly address contemporary problems in the law and suggest carefully reasoned solutions. For example, the surrogate motherhood question that arose in New Jersey in the *Baby M* case gave rise to numerous articles critiquing the court's decision and discussing appropriate solutions to the issues raised. Treatises by eminent scholars are often cited in cases, and the Restatements are especially respected because they attempt to provide a general statement of American law rather than focus on any particular state.

In addition to cases of first impression, courts, usually the highest state courts, are sometimes presented with cases that reveal serious weakness in prior precedents and urge that those earlier cases be overruled. In rationalizing the departure from what otherwise appears to be binding precedent, the court will muster all the available persuasive authority and secondary authority it can.

---

persuasive authority
Authority that carries great weight even though not qualifying as precedent; for example, decisions of other state courts.

community property
A regime in which the earnings of husband and wife during marriage are owned equally by both; eight states borrowing from French (Louisiana) or Spanish (Texas west to California) law incorporated the concept of community property into marital law.

equitable distribution
Legal scheme of property ownership designed to equalize the marital shares of husband and wife for purposes of divorce.

Uniform Commercial Code (UCC)
Commonly referred to simply as the UCC, a set of comprehensive statutes governing most commercial transactions; has been adopted in every state except Louisiana.

secondary authority
Authoritative statements of law other than statutes and cases, such as law review articles, treatises, and the Restatements.

treatises

In the legal context, scholarly books about the law, usually covering one of the basic fields of law, such as torts or contracts, or a significant subfield of the law, such as workers' compensation.

Restatements of the Law

Compilations of general interpretations of major fields of common law, sponsored and published by the American Law Institute (founded in 1923).

Because cases raise serious legal issues and judges are entrusted with the administration of justice, decisions are not mechanical products of legal scholarship. Much attention is given in written opinions to fairness to the parties and the consequences to society of the rules that are constructed or enforced. The search for authority on which to base a rule helps to ensure that judges do not act merely on their own personal value systems but instead reflect a consensus of the wisdom of their peers. This is the legacy of the common law, a system of judicial decision making that has endured many centuries of political and social change and has perhaps greatly assisted in making those changes.

Precedent and Unpublished Cases

In the 1960s and 1970s, appellate courts found their caseloads increasing significantly. This tendency has continued since that time without a corresponding increase in the number of appellate judges or the amounts of their budgets. Faced with numerous cases that could be decided on well-established precedents and offered little of interest to anyone other than the parties, judges in the past few decades have increasingly decided that some decisions were not worthy of inclusion in the reporters. These cases are deemed "unpublished" because they do not appear in the official printed reports. This practice allowed judges to skimp on writing, focusing their attention simply on the facts and issues necessary to explain the decision to the parties without the extensive discussion needed for opinions serving as stare decisis. Of course, the decisions were "official" in the sense that they decided the winners and losers, adjudicating the rights of the parties; but they were not published in the usual sources that attorneys would research. Recently, though, these unpublished opinions have been made available on Westlaw and Lexis, the two primary legal databases, as well as by other sources, so that they are readily searchable on the Internet.

These unpublished decisions were deemed by many jurisdictions not to have precedential force. An apparently logical conclusion followed that attorneys should not cite them. Federal Rule of Appellate Procedure 32.1, adopted in 2006, provides that a court may not limit an attorney from citing to an unpublished federal case decided on or after January 1, 2007; however, this rule is arguably effective only for the United States Courts of Appeals.

SUMMARY

The Anglo-American legal tradition has a rich history of judge-made law known as the common law. It is governed by the principle of stare decisis, which urges that the courts abide by past precedents unless there is a compelling reason to depart from them. The process of adjudication focuses on disputes, in contrast to the legislative process, which enacts general laws for future application.

In determining and interpreting the law, courts base decisions on authority, principally statutes and prior case law. When these do not provide a clear answer to the case at hand, secondary authority may be used as the source of reasoning and rules.

The statements of the law made in higher courts must be followed by the lower courts, but the force of precedent applies only to that part of the decision pertinent to the facts of the dispute before the court and not to incidental statements of the author of a judicial opinion.

KEY TERMS

adjudication	judicial restraint	Restatements of the Law
case of first impression	judicial review	secondary authority
common law	legislation	stare decisis
common law tradition	persuasive authority	supremacy clause
community property	precedent	treatises
dictum (dicta, obiter dictum)	privity of contract	Uniform Commercial
equitable distribution	product liability	Code (UCC)

CHAPTER REVIEW QUESTIONS

1. What is meant by *judicial review?* On what constitutional provision is it based?
2. What political purpose encouraged the establishment of judicial restraint? Why is it called a *doctrine?*
3. How did the phrase *common law* originate?
4. Why is the statement "judges do not make law" inaccurate?
5. What is the Latin phrase expressing the principle of precedent?
6. By what authority can the U.S. Supreme Court invalidate state laws?
7. What are the two characteristics of legislation?
8. What is the practical significance of *obiter dictum?* (see *Colby* and *Higgins*)
9. What is a *case of first impression?*
10. What are examples of secondary sources?

CRITICAL THINKING QUESTIONS

1. What alternatives are there to stare decisis?
2. Should judicial opinions be written in "plain English" so the average person can understand them?

CYBER EXERCISES

1. Opinions of the Pennsylvania Supreme Court are accessible at a number of websites, including the website for Pennsylvania state courts, http://www.aopc .org/. The Pennsylvania Supreme Court decided *Freed v. Geisinger Medical Center*, 971 A.2d 1202 (Pa. 2009) on June 15, 2009. The case contained a majority and a dissenting opinion. Locate the case at the Pennsylvania state courts website and answer the following questions concerning the case:
   a. Why did Freed file the lawsuit?
   b. What did the Pennsylvania Supreme Court hold in *Flanagan*?

    c. How did the Pennsylvania Supreme Court distinguish *Miller* and *McClain*, on the one hand, and *Flanagan*, on the other hand?

    d. What effect did the Pennsylvania Supreme Court's decision in *Freed* have on *Flanagan*?

    e. What three conclusions did the court reach regarding its prior decision in *Flanagan*?

    f. Does the new rule announced by the court apply prospectively or retroactively, and why?

    g. What conclusion would Justice Eakin have reached?

    h. What was Justice Eakin's reasoning?

    i. Do you find the majority or the dissenting opinion more persuasive?

2. Opinions of the Kansas Supreme Court are accessible at a number of websites, including the website for Kansas state courts, http://www.kscourts.org/. Go to that website and locate *In re L.M.*, a case excerpted in this chapter. The case contained a majority opinion, a concurring opinion, and a dissenting opinion. Using *In re L.M.*, answer the following questions:

    a. What conclusion would Justice Luckert reach?

    b. What was the basis for this conclusion?

    c. What conclusion would Justice McFarland reach?

    d. How does Justice McFarland compare the juvenile system and the adult system?

    e. What does Justice McFarland mean by stating that "the majority's decision is contrary to the weight of authority"?

    f. Did Justice McFarland find any persuasive authority from other jurisdictions to support the majority's conclusion?

3. The state courts of your state probably have a website. Find the website and answer the following questions concerning the website:

    a. What is the URL for the website? (If there are multiple websites, provide the URL for each such website.)

    b. Is the full text available for state court cases, and for which courts are opinions available?

    c. What information do you need (such as party names, docket number, date of decision, etc.) to access opinions?

    d. For which years are full-text opinions available?

SCENARIO

A case from Chapter 2, *Johnson v. Roma Waterford, LLC*, is designated as an "unpublished disposition." A note preceding the case states:

> See Rules of Appellate Procedure, Rule 809.23(3), regarding citation of unpublished opinions. Unpublished opinions issued before July 1, 2009, are of no precedential value and may not be cited except in limited instances. Unpublished opinions issued on or after July 1, 2009, may be cited for persuasive value.

Given the history and importance of precedence, how does Rule 809.23(3) conflict with this system?

Here is the scenario. The appellant filed an appeal electronically five minutes after midnight on August 2, 2009. The appellee argued that the appeal should be dismissed because the deadline for filing was August 1, 2009. Thus, the appeal had not been filed within the requisite time limits. The appellant contended that the court should make an exception because the appellant submitted the appeal a few minutes before midnight, but the court did not show it as having been filed until after midnight.

In making its case, the appellant wanted to cite to an unpublished opinion of the Wisconsin Court of Appeals, dated June 1, 2009, that contained similar facts; however, Rule 809.23(3) precluded citation to the unpublished opinion. In the June 1, 2009, opinion, the court had made an exception because the appeal was late due to factors outside appellant's control.

The three-judge panel that will decide whether the appeal should be dismissed does not contain any of the three judges who participated in the June 1, 2009, unpublished decision; thus, the panel may be unaware of the June 1, 2009, unpublished decision. The appellant's attorney fears incurring the wrath of the court by citing to an unpublished opinion in contravention of Rule 809.23(3); however, the attorney has an ethical obligation to zealously represent the client by bringing authority favorable to the client to the court's attention. What should the attorney do?

The issue of whether unpublished opinions are precedent, persuasive authority, without value, or even disallowed is very controversial. These questions go to the essence of stare decisis and the proper role of bench and bar. Try to state the reasons for both sides in this case in the context of the significance of decision and precedent in our legal system.

Student CD-Rom

For additional materials, please go to the CD in this book.

Online Companion™

For additional resources, please go to http://www.paralegal.delmar.cengage.com

CHAPTER 4

SOURCES OF THE LAW: LEGISLATION

INTRODUCTION

Historically, judicial decisions have played the major role in the evolution of Anglo-American law, but the courts as the source of law have been eclipsed in modern times by the ascendancy of legislatures as primary lawmaking bodies.

EVOLUTION OF LEGISLATION

During most of the development of Anglo-American law, the pronouncement of law was accomplished by courts deciding cases in which customs, practices, and informal principles of conduct were formalized in written decisions. Although Anglo-American law largely escaped the **codification** movements that revolutionized continental European law, the nineteenth century brought a new attitude in America with regard to legislation. The English Parliament enacted numerous statutes over the centuries that clarified or changed the common law, but its legislative output was minor in comparison to the courts as a source of law.

    The American situation was different. The United States had approved a written federal constitution that allocated political authority among the three branches of government, providing specific important spheres of authority for Congress. (See Appendix B; U.S. Const. Art. I, §§ 1 and 8.) The legal profession and the courts were viewed by some with suspicion because of the elitist tradition of these institutions in England and colonial America. Congress, in contrast, was elected by the people and thus viewed as representative of the people. It was natural that antiaristocratic sentiment in the new

codification

May refer to the simple process of turning a custom or common law rule into legislation but usually refers to the making of a *code,* that is, a set of written rules.

republic would turn to Congress and the state legislatures for lawmaking, which is their constitutional and customary function.

The last half of the nineteenth century saw a major movement toward codification in the United States. In addition to the reasons previously given for favoring legislation, two others provided impetus. First, Americans had learned through revolution and the establishment of the Constitution that the people could guide their own destiny by making law through their representatives, in a democratic and rational process. Second, the country was undergoing rapid change and development, and Americans were disinclined to preserve ancient customs simply because they were ancient. Americans were ambitious and ready for change. Awaiting the evolution of legal principles through the cumbersome and conservative judicial process was probably never truly part of the American character.

The most renowned spokesman for codification was David Dudley Field, a New York lawyer who was appointed to a law revision commission that authored the *Code of Civil Procedure* enacted in 1848, often called simply the "Field Code." Although Field advocated and authored several other codes as well, their reception in New York and other eastern states was poor. Western states, on the contrary, wholeheartedly jumped at the chance for ready-made law, perhaps because their brief history and lack of tradition made them impatient for a system of laws from which they could set new horizons.

The complex problems of the twentieth century encouraged timely responses from legislative bodies, which have become politically very powerful, often seeming to eclipse the common law tradition. Although the states differ in the extent to which they have codified state law, every state has enacted a complex body of statutes that serves as a principal source of law. The rise of the power of legislatures is reflected in the courts, which now defer to the statutes. Nevertheless, because disputes over the law must ultimately be resolved in the courts, the meaning of legislation is decided by the courts and applied to specific cases.

THE NATURE OF LEGISLATION

In Chapter 3, legislation was distinguished from judge-made law by its characteristics of "universal application and future effect." The line drawn between the characteristics of legislation and adjudication has not always been clear. In the past, legislatures often passed special bills to define narrow rights of individuals or local entities, but this practice has always been viewed with suspicion (see the 1851 case of *Ponder v. Graham*). When a legislative body narrows its focus to resolve a particularized dispute, its actions may be challenged in court as violating the principle of separation of judicial and legislative powers embodied in federal and state constitutions.

Legislation strives to reduce principles of law to a coherent written form in which the intent of the law can be determined from the words alone: statutes are pure rules, often without policy statements or statements of intent. In this respect they differ in nature from the common law, which, while relying on past precedent when available, may be characterized as customary law because it is based on unwritten principles of justice and proper conduct rooted in the values of society and is elaborated in often lengthy critical comments in the decisions. The rules in judicial decisions are formulated to apply to the case before the court and are tailored to that dispute. They express an underlying principle rather than an exact rule, as is the case with legislation. The reasoning is as much a part of the rule as the precise statement of the rule in the decision.

The common law treats law as an evolving process. Ultimately, it is what a case comes to stand for rather than what it actually states. For example, the landmark school case *Goss v. Lopez*, 419 U.S. 565 (1975), which defined the rights of public school students regarding certain disciplinary actions, is frequently cited as establishing a constitutional right to a public education. In fact, *Goss v. Lopez* did not hold that the U.S. Constitution established such a right but rather that once a state (Ohio) established such a right, it could not take that right away without due process of law. Nonetheless, if the U.S. Supreme Court or state courts dealing with state law declare that *Goss v. Lopez* holds that there is a constitutional right to a public education, then that principle becomes the law, regardless of the actual language of the prior case. Because all states provide public education, the distinction is largely academic, but the point here is that judicial statements of law are not always taken literally in the way that statutes are. Because judicial decisions are narrowly framed by reference to particularized disputes, the rules they express frequently require further refinement and explanation when used as precedent for subsequent cases.

This distinction may be shown more simply by the difference in attitude of a court in dealing with legislation as opposed to judicial precedent. The court "interprets" statutes, that is, attempts to determine the meaning of the words and phrases in the statute, whereas the specific rules laid down in cases are examined to determine the underlying principles on which they are based. For example, in *Goss v. Lopez*, the majority concluded with the statement:

> We should also make it clear that we have addressed ourselves solely to the short suspension, not exceeding 10 days. Longer suspensions or expulsions for the remainder of the school term, or permanently, may require more formal procedures.

In so stating, the court made its ruling quite limited, leaving clarification for future cases. Such an imprecise approach would be unacceptable for legislation.

The end result of legislation is the enactment of written laws with an **effective date** and publication in the statute books. From the lawyer's point of view, the quality of legislation is measured by its clarity and lack of ambiguity. Because lawyers must be able to predict the outcomes of their clients' disputes, carefully framed statutes are an important aid. Still, legislators are not clairvoyant; they cannot predict every future scenario and provide for every possibility. Numerous cases arise in which the applicability of a statute to a particular case is unclear. A court may ultimately be asked to define the statute's application to a real-life dispute. Keep in mind, however, that when statutes are later found to be faulty or unclear, the legislature is free to amend or change the statute to reflect legislative intent.

What happens when a lawsuit is filed pursuant to a state statute and the state legislature amends the state statute during the pendency of the lawsuit? The first step may be to examine the effective date of the statute, which often is effective **prospective** rather than **retroactive (retrospective)**. This usually means that if the lawsuit is grounded in facts occurring prior to the statutory effective date, the lawsuit is unaffected by the

effective date [of a statute]
The date on which the statute can first be applied.

prospective
Occurring in the future; with respect to a statute, enforcement or application of the statute as to circumstances occurring on or after the statute's *effective date*.

retroactive (retrospective)
Applying to past circumstances or occurrences; with respect to a statute, enforcement or application of the statute as to events and actions that occurred before the statute became law.

statutory amendment. Under the **ex post facto clause** of the U.S. Constitution, it is unconstitutional for a state to pass a statute putting someone at a disadvantage for a past action. Most state constitutions have a similar provision. In *Ackison*, the Ohio legislature amended state statutes so that they applied retroactively to pending lawsuits.

ACKISON, Appellee, et al.,

v.

ANCHOR PACKING COMPANY et al.,
Appellants

Supreme Court of Ohio

Nos. 2007-219, 2007-415

120 Ohio St. 3d 228, 897 N.E.2d 1118

Decided Oct. 15, 2008.

In May 2004, Linda Ackison, widow and administrator of the estate of Danny Ackison, filed suit against her husband's former employer and multiple other defendants alleging that her husband's illness and death were caused by long-term exposure to asbestos in his workplace. . . .

On September 2, 2004, . . . legislation extensively revised state laws governing asbestos litigation and was in response to the legislative finding that "[t]he current asbestos personal injury litigation system is unfair and inefficient, imposing a severe burden on litigants and taxpayers alike." H.B. 292, Section 3(A) (2), 150 Ohio Laws, Part III, 3988. . . .

Among other sections, this bill enacted [Ohio Revised Code] 2307.91, 2307.92 (requirements for prima facie showing of physical impairment in certain asbestos claims), and 2307.93 (filing of reports and test results showing physical impairment; dismissals). These provisions establish certain threshold requirements. Among these requirements are that no person shall bring or maintain certain kinds of asbestos claims (including claims alleging a nonmalignant condition) without filing with the court certain qualifying medical evidence of physical impairment, and that such evidence must be supported by the written opinion of a competent medical authority stating that the claimant's exposure to asbestos was a substantial

contributing factor to his medical condition. . . . The claim of any plaintiff who does not file the required preliminary medical evidence and physician's statement is to be administratively dismissed "without prejudice" with the court retaining jurisdiction, meaning that a plaintiff would not be barred from reinstating the claim in the future when and if the plaintiff could meet the threshold evidentiary requirements. . . . The legislation also provides that the threshold evidentiary requirements and administrative-dismissal provision be applied to all asbestos cases pending in Ohio courts, regardless of whether they were filed before or after the effective date of [the new statutes].

The trial court determined that the revised asbestos legislation applied to Ackison and that the legislation did not impair any substantive rights so as to violate Section 28, Article II of the Ohio Constitution. The trial court also administratively dismissed Ackison's claims because Ackison had failed to file the statutorily required documentation. . . .

The court of appeals reversed and reinstated the case. In its opinion, the court of appeals held that the retroactive application to Ackison's claim of the . . . evidentiary requirements was unconstitutional. The court stated that because Ackison's suit had been filed prior to the effective date of the statutory changes, she had a vested substantive right to pursue recovery for her husband's illness and death under the statutes that were in effect at the time her complaint was filed.

The court of appeals certified that its decision conflicted with three cases from the Twelfth District Court of Appeals, each of which held that retroactive application of the . . . standards was not unconstitutional. . . .

We accepted jurisdiction and recognized the conflict on the following question: "Can R.C. 2307.91, 2307.92, and 2307.93 be applied to cases already pending on September 2, 2004?" . . .

"Though the language of Section 28, Article II of the Ohio Constitution provides that the General Assembly 'shall have no power to pass retroactive laws,' Ohio courts have long recognized that there is a crucial distinction between statutes that merely apply retroactively (or 'retrospectively') and those that do so in a manner that offends our Constitution." *Bielat v. Bielat.* . . .

[A] statute is presumed to apply prospectively unless expressly declared to be retroactive. . . . If a statute is clearly retroactive, though, the reviewing court must then determine whether it is substantive or remedial in nature. . . .

In determining whether a statute is substantive or remedial, we have established the following parameters:

"A statute is 'substantive' if it impairs or takes away vested rights, affects an accrued substantive right, imposes new or additional burdens, duties, obligation[s], or liabilities as to a past transaction, or creates a new right. * * * Conversely, remedial laws are those affecting only the remedy provided, and include laws that merely substitute a new or more appropriate remedy for the enforcement of an existing right." *Cook.* . . .

We have previously concluded that R.C. 2307.92 and 2307.93 "do not relate to the rights and duties that give rise to this cause of action or otherwise make it more difficult for a claimant to succeed on the merits of a claim. Rather, they pertain to the machinery for carrying on a suit. They are therefore procedural in nature, not substantive." *Norfolk S. Ry. Co. v. Bogle.* . . .

Ackison's chief argument in this regard is that before the enactment of [the statute], asbestos-related conditions were compensable under Ohio law when there was merely an alteration of the lungs (such as pleural thickening), irrespective of whether any impairment or disease had developed. Assuming for purposes of argument that the common law can be sufficiently settled

to give rise to a vested right to its application, we must find, in order to accept her argument, that common-law liability existed in Ohio for asymptomatic pleural thickening at the time Ackison's claim was filed. . . .

When R.C. 2307.91(FF)(1) and (2) are read in pari materia, it appears that the two subsections were intended to require that asbestos exposure be a significant, direct cause of the injury to the degree that without the exposure to asbestos, the injury would not have occurred. Thus, the statute reflects the common-law requirement that asbestos exposure be both a cause in fact and the direct cause of the plaintiff's illness. This is an embodiment of the common law, not an alteration of it. Because we hold that R.C. 2307.91(FF) does not alter the common law that existed at the time Ackison filed her claim, the statute is not unconstitutionally retroactive and may be applied to her pending claim. . . .

For the reasons expressed herein, we hold that the requirements in 2307.91, 2307.92, and 2307.93 pertaining to asbestos-exposure claims are remedial and procedural and may be applied without offending the Retroactivity Clause of the Ohio Constitution to cases pending on September 2, 2004.

Case Questions

1. After the trial court "administratively dismissed" the lawsuit, could Ackison have refiled the lawsuit?
2. How does the court distinguish between substantive and remedial (procedural) statutes?
3. What is the court's explanation for concluding that the statutory amendment did not alter any right that Ackison had prior to the amendment?

CASE NOTE: Two justices dissented from the majority opinion and one of the two wrote a dissenting opinion. The dissenting opinion is dealt with in questions at the end of this chapter.

THE LEGISLATIVE PROCESS

Although individual states are free to regulate and order the process of lawmaking, we find a common pattern by which principles are enacted into law. The following discussion describes a formal political process. It does not take into account the influence on legislation of informal political activities, the conflicts inherent in the two-party system, lobbying, interest groups, constituencies, and the like because their interaction varies from issue to issue and locality to locality.

Among the many problems that arise in our society, some come to the attention of lawmakers as problems that may be helped by the enactment of laws. Typically, legislators serve on legislative committees that deal with a defined area of interest. These committees are assigned to conduct an examination of proposed legislation and frame the law. In studying the problem, the committee collects a wide range of data and information and often conducts hearings on the subject. The purpose is to frame the legislation in the best way to solve the underlying problem, and this is best accomplished if legislators are fully informed about the problem so they can estimate the effectiveness of the solution. Each legislature has rules by which the proposed legislation reaches the floor of the legislature for open debate and vote. All states except Nebraska have a **bicameral** legislature modeled on the U.S. Senate and House of Representatives; the different views of these two bodies often require compromise before a law is passed.

The process is quite different from adjudication in that the legislators must weigh and forecast the general effect of the law in the future, taking into consideration the effects on all who may be subject to the law. Enactment into law creates a public record and serves as notice to the public of the requirements of the law.

The hallmark of the legislative process is discussion and debate. (Note that their absence was criticized implicitly in the legislative divorce that the Supreme Court of Florida invalidated in *Ponder v. Graham.*) Passage of a bill into law ultimately requires open debate within the legislative body, which may be quite extensive regarding complex or controversial legislation, or quite brief concerning laws on which there is a general consensus or lack of interest.

Ponder reflects a fundamental difference between legislative and adjudicative functions in our political system, but it also reveals an interesting facet of the history of family law. In England, prior to American independence, family law matters were handled by ecclesiastical courts. There was no divorce in the modern sense, although a cumbersome procedure involving common law courts and an act of Parliament could result in a legal divorce. It was rare and, practically speaking, available only to men of influence and power. Because the United States did not incorporate ecclesiastical courts into its legal system, family law eventually fell within the purview of the courts of equity (see Chapter 6 for a discussion of courts of law and equity) rather than the common law courts. In the meantime, several state legislatures borrowed from the English practice of legislative divorce and passed special acts divorcing married couples.

Under the principle of **separation of powers**, each of the three branches of government is charged with carrying out a distinct governmental function, and no branch may usurp the power given to another branch of government. A court may hold a statute unconstitutional if it strays into adjudicating rather than legislating; the court in *Ponder* did just that. A court may hold that it is without jurisdiction over the case, as the court did in *In re Beck* (excerpted in Chapter 3), if the legislature purports to assign a court duties that are outside the court's responsibilities of adjudicating. In the past century, state legislatures have regulated marriage and divorce through statute, and the courts have assumed the task of granting divorces and determining the rights of divorcing parties. When *Ponder v. Graham* was decided, this separation of function was still evolving.

ex post facto clause

A provision of the U.S. Constitution, Article I, § 10, prohibiting a state from passing a statute with retrospective application.

bicameral

Refers to a legislature with two bodies, such as a House of Representatives and a Senate; only Nebraska has a single, or *unicameral,* legislature.

separation of powers

Effect of the constitutional prohibition on any branch of government carrying out a government function of another branch. The federal government is divided into three branches, with the legislative branch responsible for passing legislation, the judicial branch responsible for interpreting law and deciding cases, and the executive branch responsible for carrying out law. The powers of each branch are separate and unique to that branch.

William G. PONDER, Executor of Archibald Graham, Appellant

v.

Mary GRAHAM, Appellee

4 Fla. 23 (1851)

[Mary Graham was not satisfied with the provisions made for her by her husband, Archibald Graham, in his will, and petitioned to take her **dower** right to one-third interest in his estate in lieu of the will. Ponder was appointed under the will to distribute Archibald's estate and challenged Mary's right on the ground that she was not lawfully married to Archibald. The jury found for Mary and the court awarded her a one-third interest in Archibald's real estate.]

The facts of the case are succinctly these: The respondent, then Mary Buccles, about the year 1820, in South Carolina, intermarried with one Solomon Canady. Some time afterwards, they removed to, and resided in Georgia, but soon, in consequence of domestic dissensions, separated. Mary went to reside with Graham, a bachelor, and continued to live with him, under circumstances from which an adulterous **cohabitation** might be inferred.

In 1832, and while the said cohabitation continued, a bill was passed by the Legislative Council of the then Territory of Florida, entitled "An act for the relief of Mary Canady."

By this act, the Legislative Council, for the cause expressed in the preamble, assumed to judge and declare that the said Mary Graham was thereby divorced from her said husband, Solomon, and that the bonds of matrimony subsisting between them, were thereby to be entirely and absolutely dissolved, as if the same had never been solemnized. . . . There does not appear to have been any petition, **affidavit**, or proofs—a reference to a committee to ascertain the facts, or any notice to the absent husband. In 1834, the cohabitation between Mary and the testator still subsisting, the ceremony of marriage is celebrated between them, and from the time up to the period of the testator's death, which occurred in 1848, he lived with her, and acknowledged her as his wife, and in his will he provides for her by that name, and in that relation.

* * *

The main question raised in this case, as to the power of a Legislative body, *as such,* to grant divorces, is not altogether a new one. It has been investigated by some of the American Courts, and grave constitutional questions have been necessarily involved in the discussion; and yet the question still remains an open one—opinions clashing—nothing settled. . . .

No one doubts the right of the people by their constitution, to invest the power in the Legislature, or any where else; but the question is, when the constitution is silent on the subject, in what department of government does this authority rest? [M]uch, if not the whole difficulty, has arisen from overlooking some of the great principles which enter into the constitutional government of the States, and from not preserving the obvious distinction between legislative and judicial functions—by confounding the *right* which a legislative body has to pass *general laws* on the subject of divorce, with the *power* of dissolving the marriage *contract.*

* * *

[The court goes on to dispute the notion that the English Parliament granted divorces, noting that both ecclesiastical courts and common law courts were required to rule on a divorce before it went for approval by the House of Lords, which served as the English supreme court as well as a legislative body.]

In every respect in which I have been able to see this case, I can find no reason to sustain the act of the legislature. It appears by the record, that the parties were domiciled in the State of Georgia, where, it is alleged, the desertion and ill treatment occurred. The wife, living with the testator, Graham, removed to Florida—while the husband returned to Carolina, his former residence. The bill was introduced into the legislature one day, and passed the next. It is very clear that this divorce would not be recognized by the courts of Georgia or Carolina, were any rights asserted under it in those States. . . . I am, therefore, of [the] opinion that the act of the Legislative Council of February 11th, 1832, was in conflict with the organic law of Florida and the Constitution of the United States, and is, therefore, void.

Per Curiam—Let the judgment of the court below be reversed.

Case Questions

1. What does Mary Graham get as a result of this decision?
2. What are the relative powers of legislature and court with regard to divorce?

Case Glossary

dower
Property interests acquired in a husband's estate upon marriage. At old common law, a wife was entitled to one-third of her husband's real property upon his death. Today, husband and wife have the same rights as surviving spouses, but these vary from state to state.

cohabitation
Living together in a marital-like relationship; sometimes simply refers to a sexual relationship.

affidavit
A statement in writing sworn to before a person who is authorized to administer an oath.

JUDICIAL INVALIDATION OF LEGISLATION

Although the courts are bound to uphold legislation, there are two grounds on which courts have struck down legislation:

1. *Defective procedure.* The passage of the law may have been procedurally defective as measured by state law. Because our legislatures have been operating for many decades, the legal requisites of statutory enactment are well known and generally orderly, so procedural challenges rarely succeed.

2. *Unconstitutionality.* The law itself may violate principles of state or federal constitutions. Statutes may also be declared unconstitutional in substance rather than procedure. A statute may be unconstitutional "on its face," meaning that a careful reading of the statute reveals that it violates some constitutional prohibition; or a statute may be unconstitutional in its effects or applications, which is more difficult to establish.

JUDICIAL DEFERENCE TO LEGISLATION

Our constitutional system allocates legislative powers to Congress and authority to decide cases and "controversies" to the federal judiciary. This constitutional mandate has been followed by state constitutions, and so the principle of separation of legislative and judicial functions has become a fundamental part of our legal system. Inherent in this scheme is the notion that legislatures make law and courts interpret and enforce them.

This does not abolish the common law system, which is still held in high esteem. Nevertheless, legislatures have surpassed the courts as the major source of new law. The evolution of a complex society and legal system in America brought these two legal institutions into direct and frequent confrontation. The separation of powers and the self-imposed custom of judicial restraint ultimately resulted in judicial subservience to statutes. If a statute is procedurally correct and constitutional in substance, American courts are bound to enforce it. Individual judges and courts have expressed dislike for particular statutes at the same time that they have upheld them. If the legislature passes a "bad" law, it is the job of the legislature, not the courts, to revise the law. Courts often send strong messages to the legislature by way of their written decisions (e.g., the Supreme Judicial Court of Massachusetts in the *Colby* case), but the legislature may or may not heed these messages.

In the evolutionary process of defining legislative and judicial functions, legislative bodies have also been subject to certain constraints. Although legislatures enact laws and even provide for the means of enforcement by establishing and funding regulatory, judicial, and law enforcement agencies, the task of enforcement is not a legislative function. The courts are the final arbiters of disputes that arise under the laws, whether common law or legislation. The power of the legislature to make the rules is counterbalanced by the power of the judiciary to interpret and apply them. It is not uncommon for a court to give lip service to the language of a statute at the same time that its interpretation of the statute makes serious inroads into the statute's intended purpose. Lawmaking and interpretation take place in a political, social, and economic environment that is often more influential than legal technicalities or even the Constitution.

The *Papachristou* case held a Jacksonville, Florida, vagrancy ordinance unconstitutional both on its face and in its potential for abuse by the police—an abuse made apparent from the facts of the various parties to the case. Note that local legislative bodies, such as a county commission or a city council, enact pieces of legislation, commonly called **ordinances**, which have the force of law and are subject to the same constitutional requirements as state and federal statutes. The principal challenge to the ordinance in *Papachristou* was based on the principle of **void for vagueness**, which applies to a statute that "fails to give a person of ordinary intelligence fair notice that his contemplated conduct is forbidden by the statute." This principle is based on the notion that statutes serve as public notice of the conduct required by law. If a law cannot be understood as written, it does not furnish notice. The void-for-vagueness doctrine is derived from the constitutional requirement in the Fourteenth Amendment that no state shall "deprive any person of life, liberty, or property, without due process of law."

The Jacksonville ordinance included peculiar language that came from much earlier English "poor laws" used to control the working class:

> Rogues and vagabonds, or dissolute persons who go about begging, common gamblers, persons who use juggling or unlawful games or plays, common drunkards, common night thieves, pilferers or pickpockets, traders in stolen property, lewd, wanton and lascivious persons, keepers of gambling places, common railers and brawlers, persons wandering or strolling around from place to place without any lawful purpose or object, habitual loafers, disorderly persons, persons neglecting all lawful business and habitually spending their time by frequenting houses of ill fame, gaming houses, or places where alcoholic beverages are sold or served, persons able to work but habitually living upon the earnings of their wives or minor children shall be deemed vagrants and, upon conviction in the Municipal court shall be punished as provided for Class D offenses. [Jacksonville Ordinance Code § 26–57.]

ordinance

Legislation at the local level, typically created or passed by city councils or county commissions.

void for vagueness

A constitutional principle of substantive due process used to invalidate legislation that fails to give a person of ordinary intelligence fair notice that his or her contemplated conduct is forbidden by the legislation.

Margaret PAPACHRISTOU et al., Petitioners

v.

CITY OF JACKSONVILLE

405 U.S. 156 (1972)

The facts are stipulated. Papachristou and Calloway are white females. Melton and Johnson are black males. Papachristou was enrolled in a job-training program sponsored by the State Employment Service at Florida Junior College in Jacksonville. Calloway was a typing and shorthand teacher at a state mental institution located near Jacksonville. She was the owner of the automobile in which the four defendants were arrested. Melton was a Vietnam war veteran who had been released from the Navy after nine months in a veterans' hospital. On the date of his arrest he was a part-time computer helper while attending college as a full-time student in Jacksonville. Johnson was a tow-motor operator in a grocery chain warehouse and was a lifelong resident of Jacksonville.

At the time of their arrest the four of them were riding in Calloway's car on the main thoroughfare in Jacksonville. They had left a restaurant owned by Johnson's uncle where they had eaten and were on their way to a night club. The arresting officers denied that the racial mixture in the car played any part in the decision to make the arrest. The arrest, they said, was made because the defendants had stopped near a used-car lot which had been broken into several times. There was, however, no evidence of any breaking and entering on the night in question.

Of these four charged with "prowling by auto[,]" none had been previously arrested except Papachristou[,] who had once been convicted of a municipal offense.

* * *

[The court goes on to describe each of the arrests of the several petitioners—including those in companion cases, which were consolidated upon appeal—none of whom were engaged in conduct that would be criminal except for the ordinance.] . . . [Heath and his companion] and the automobile were searched. Although no contraband or incriminating evidence was found,

they were both arrested, Heath being charged with being a "common thief" because he was reputed to be a thief. The codefendant was charged with "loitering" because he was standing in the driveway, an act which the officers admitted was done only at their command.

* * *

This ordinance is void-for-vagueness, both in the sense that it "fails to give a person of ordinary intelligence fair notice that his contemplated conduct is forbidden by the statute," *United States v. Harriss*, 347 U.S. 612, 617, and because it encourages arbitrary and erratic arrests and convictions.

Living under a rule of law entails various suppositions, one of which is that "[all persons] are entitled to be informed as to what the State commands or forbids."

* * *

The Jacksonville ordinance makes criminal activities which by modern standards are normally innocent. "Nightwalking" is one. . . .

"[P]ersons able to work but habitually living upon the earnings of their wives and minor children"—like habitually living "without visible means of support"—might implicate unemployed pillars of the community who have married rich wives.

"[P]ersons able to work but habitually living upon the earnings of their wives or minor children" may also embrace unemployed people out of the labor market, by reason of a recession or disemployed by reason of technological or so-called structural displacements.

* * *

Another aspect of the ordinance's vagueness appears when we focus, not on the lack of notice given a potential offender, but on the effect of the unfettered discretion it places in the hands of the Jacksonville police. . . .

A direction by a legislature to the police to arrest all "suspicious" persons would not pass constitutional muster. A vagrancy prosecution may be merely the cloak for a conviction which could not be obtained on the real but undisclosed grounds for the arrest. . . .

The Jacksonville ordinance cannot be squared with our constitutional standards and is plainly unconstitutional.

Reversed.

Case Questions

1. What was the purpose of the Jacksonville ordinance?
2. Why did this decision invalidate vagrancy statutes throughout the United States?
3. What constitutional provision supports the void-for-vagueness doctrine?

STATUTORY INTERPRETATION

For the legal practitioner, the most important problem with legislation is interpretation. Over the course of many years, a number of principles have been developed to guide the courts in resolving disputes over the meaning of statutes. The principles governing statutory interpretation are commonly called **rules of construction**, referring to the manner in which courts are to **construe** the meaning of statutes. The overriding principle governing statutory interpretation is to determine the intent of the legislature and give force to that intent. The rest of this section discusses some of the rules and priorities employed to further this goal.

Legislative Intent

The underlying purpose behind statutory construction is the search to determine **legislative intent.**

The Plain Meaning Rule

The **plain meaning rule** states simply that if the language of a statute is unambiguous and its meaning clear, the terms of the statute should be construed and applied according to their ordinary meaning. Behind this rule is the assumption that the legislature understood the meaning of the words it used and expressed its intent thereby. This rule operates to restrain the court from substituting its notion of what the legislature *really* meant if the meaning is already clear.

Application of the plain meaning rule may in fact undermine legislative intent and can actually be used to evade legislative intent. Although legislation is usually carefully drafted, language is by its nature susceptible to ambiguity, distortion, or simple lack of clarity. Because legislation is designed to control disputes that have not yet arisen, the "perfect" statute requires a degree of clairvoyance absent in the ordinary human being, including legislators, so that a statute may apply to a situation not foreseen by the legislators, who might have stated otherwise had they imagined such a situation.

The plain meaning rule obviates the need to pursue any lengthy inquiry into intent. Consider the nature of the legislative process. First, legislative intent is difficult to determine. The final product of the legislative process, the statute, would thus seem to be the best evidence of legislative intent. Legislatures are composed of numerous members who intend different things. In many instances, legislators do not even read the laws for which they vote. To believe that there is a single legislative intent is to ignore reality. Many

---

rules of construction

A tradition of customs for statutory interpretation.

construe

The verb from which the noun *construction* is derived; very close in meaning to *interpret*.

legislative intent

That which the legislature wanted or intended to achieve when it enacted a statute; the determination of which is the goal of the court when the language of a statute is in question, ambiguous, or called into doubt.

plain meaning rule

A rule of statutory construction stating that if the language of a statute is unambiguous, the terms of the statute should be construed according to their ordinary meaning.

statutes are the result of compromise, the politics of which are not a matter of public record and cannot be accurately determined by a court. The precise language of the statute, then, is the best guide to intent. If, in the eyes of the legislature, the court errs in its application of the statute, the legislature may revise the statute for future application.

Limitations on the Plain Meaning Rule

Adherence to the plain meaning rule is neither blind nor simpleminded. A statute that is unambiguous in its language may be found to conflict with other statutes. Statutes are typically enacted in "packages," as part of a legislative effort to regulate a broad area of concern. Thus, for example, alimony is ordinarily defined in several statutes embraced within a package of statutes covering divorce, which in turn may be part of a statutory chapter on domestic relations. The more comprehensive the package, the more likely some of its provisions may prove to be inconsistent. A sentence that seems unambiguous standing alone may be ambiguous in relation to a paragraph, a section, or a chapter.

Language must thus be interpreted in its context. In fact, this principle often operates to dispel ambiguity. Comprehensive statutes commonly begin with a preamble or introductory section stating the general purpose of the statutes collected under its heading. This statement of purpose is intended to avoid an overly technical interpretation of the statutes that could achieve results contrary to the general purpose.

The preamble is frequently followed by a section defining terms used in the statutes. This, too, limits the application of the plain meaning rule, but in a different way: The definitions pinpoint terms that have technical or legal significance to avoid what might otherwise be nontechnical, ordinary interpretations.

On occasion, a provision in a statute may turn out to defeat the purpose of the statute in a particular set of circumstances; the court is then faced with the problem of giving meaning to the purpose of the statute or the language of the clause within the statute. In *Texas & Pacific Railway v. Abilene Cotton Oil Co.*, 204 U.S. 426 (1907), the U.S. Supreme Court was called upon to interpret the Interstate Commerce Act, which set up the Interstate Commerce Commission (ICC) and made it responsible for setting rates and routes for the railroads. A disgruntled shipper sued the railroad under an old common law action for "unreasonable rates." The Act had a provision, commonly included in legislation, stating that the Act did not abolish other existing remedies. However, the court reasoned that if persons were able to bring such actions any time they were unhappy with the rates, the rate structures established by the ICC would have little meaning, depending instead upon what a particular jury or judge considered reasonable. The court limited the effect of the clause and argued that Congress could not have intended for the clause to be used to completely undermine the purpose of the Act; "in other words, the act cannot be held to destroy itself."

The court will not ordinarily disregard the plain meaning of a statute, especially in a criminal case.

Aids to Statutory Interpretation

Single statutes do not exist in a legal vacuum. They are part of a section, chapter, and the state or federal code as a whole. Historically, statutes developed as an adjunct to the traditional common law system that established law from custom.

Like case law, statutory construction relies heavily on authority. *Interpretation* is a formal reasoning process in the law, which in our legal tradition depends less on the creative imagination than on sources of the law. In the reasoning process, an overriding judicial policy insists that the body of laws be as consistent and harmonious as possible. It was for this reason that the court held, in *Abilene Oil*, that the statute "cannot be held to destroy itself."

If a clause seems to conflict with its immediate statutory context, it will be interpreted so as to further the general legislative intent, if such can be ascertained. In a sense, this is simply intelligent reading; words and phrases take their meaning from their contexts. The principle can be extended further, however. Statutes taken from different parts of a state or federal code may be found to conflict. The court will interpret the language to harmonize the inconsistency whenever possible. Legislative intent may become quite obscure in such situations because the presumption that the legislature meant what it said is confronted by the problem that it said something different elsewhere. In reconciling the conflict, the court may use its sense of overall legislative policy and even the general history of the law, including the common law. The obvious solution to these conflicts is action by the legislature to rewrite the statutes to resolve the inconsistencies and provide future courts with a clear statement of intent.

Strict Construction

Words by their nature have different meanings and nuances. Shades of meaning change in the context of other words and phrases. Tradition has determined that certain situations call for broad or liberal construction, whereas others call for narrow or **strict construction**, meaning that the statute in question will not be expanded beyond a very literal reading of its meaning.

strict construction
Narrow interpretation by a very literal reading; criminal statutes in particular are *strictly construed.*

"Criminal statutes are strictly construed." This rule of construction has its source in the evolution of our criminal law, in particular, in the many rights we afford those accused of crime. Out of fear of abuse of the criminal justice system, we have provided protection for the accused against kangaroo courts, overzealous prosecutors, and corrupt police. It is an accepted value of our legal system that the innocent must be protected even if it means that the guilty will sometimes go free.

Although many basic crimes, such as murder, burglary, and assault, were formulated by the common law in the distant past, today most states do not recognize common law crimes but instead insist that crimes be specified by statute. We consider it unjust for someone to be charged with a crime if the conduct constituting the crime has not been clearly prohibited by statute. Conversely, if a statute defines certain conduct as criminal, "ignorance of the law excuses no one" (*ignorantia legis neminem excusat*). If public notice of prohibited conduct is an essential ingredient of criminal law, strict construction is its logical conclusion. If conduct is not clearly within the prohibitions of a statute, the court will decline to expand the coverage of that statute.

aggravated
Circumstance that increases the severity of a crime.

A second category of statutes that are strictly construed is expressed by the principle that "statutes in derogation of the common law are strictly construed." State legislatures frequently pass laws that alter, modify, or abolish traditional common law rules. The principle that such changes are narrowly construed not only shows respect for the common law but also reflects the difference between legislative and judicial decision making.

Whereas judicial decisions explain the reasons for the application of a particular rule, allowing for later interpretations and modifications, statutes are presumed to mean what they say. The intent of the legislature is embodied in the language of the statute itself, which if well drafted can be seen to apply to the situations for which it was intended.

A statute should stand alone, its meaning clear. Unfortunately, this is not always possible. If there is some question of meaning, a statute that appears to conflict with prior principles of the common law can be measured against that body of law. In other words, the court has recourse to a wealth of time-tested principles and need not strain to guess legislative intent. This is particularly helpful when the statute neglects to cover a situation that was decided in the past. If the statute is incomplete or ambiguous, the court will resolve the dispute by following the common law.

In *Flores-Figueroa*, Flores-Figueroa had pled guilty to two counts of misuse of immigration documents and one count of entry without inspection but pled not guilty to two counts of **aggravated** identity theft. At a **bench trial**, the judge found him guilty and sentenced him to six and a quarter years on all of the counts. Without his conviction under the aggravated identity theft statute, his sentence would have been reduced by two years. The United States Supreme Court granted his **petition** for **writ of certiorari**, and the case became one of the hundred or so cases in which the Court issued a full opinion during its 2008–2009 term.

bench trial
A case decided by a judge, without a jury.

petition
A written request.

writ of certiorari
An order of an appellate court to a lower court requiring the lower court to provide a certified record of a case so that the appellate court can review the case; the method used by the United States Supreme Court to invoke its discretionary jurisdiction over a case.

Ignacio Carlos FLORES-FIGUEROA, Petitioner

v.

UNITED STATES

Supreme Court of the United States

No. 08-108

129 S. Ct. 1886

Decided May 4, 2009.

A federal criminal statute forbidding "[a]ggravated identity theft" imposes a mandatory consecutive 2-year prison term upon individuals convicted of certain other crimes *if,* during (or in relation to) the commission of those other crimes, the offender "*knowingly* transfers, possesses, or uses, without lawful authority, *a means of identification of another person*." 18 U.S.C. § 1028A(a)(1) (emphasis added). The question is whether the statute requires the Government to show that the defendant *knew* that the "means of identification" he or she unlawfully transferred, possessed, or used, in fact, belonged to "another person." We conclude that it does. . . .

Petitioner Ignacio Flores-Figueroa argues that the statute requires that the Government prove that he *knew* that the "means of identification" belonged to someone else, *i.e.,* was "a means of identification *of another person*." The Government argues that the statute does not impose this particular knowledge requirement. The Government concedes that the statute uses the word "knowingly," but that word, the Government claims, does not modify the statute's last phrase ("a means of identification of another person") or, at the least, it does not modify the last three words of that phrase ("of another person"). . . .

Ignacio Flores-Figueroa is a citizen of Mexico. In 2000, to secure employment, Flores gave his employer a false name, birth date, and Social Security number, along with a counterfeit alien registration card. The Social Security number and the number on the alien registration card were not those of a real person. In 2006, Flores presented his employer with new counterfeit Social Security and alien registration cards; these cards (unlike Flores' old alien registration card) used his real name. But this time the numbers on both cards were in fact numbers assigned to other people.

Flores' employer reported his request to U.S. Immigration and Customs Enforcement. Customs discovered that the numbers on Flores' new documents belonged to other people. The United States then charged Flores with two predicate crimes, namely, entering the United States without inspection . . . and misusing immigration documents. . . . And it charged him with aggravated identity theft, . . . the crime at issue here. . . .

There are strong textual reasons for rejecting the Government's position. As a matter of ordinary English grammar, it seems natural to read the statute's word "knowingly" as applying to all the subsequently listed elements of the crime. The Government cannot easily claim that the word "knowingly" applies only to the statutes first four words, or even its first seven. It makes little sense to read the provision's language as heavily penalizing a person who "transfers, possesses, or uses, without lawful authority" a *something*, but does not know, at the very least, that the "something" (perhaps inside a box) is a "means of identification." Would we apply a statute that makes it unlawful "*knowingly* to possess drugs" to a person who steals a passenger's bag without knowing that the bag has drugs inside? . . .

The manner in which the courts ordinarily interpret criminal statutes is fully consistent with this ordinary English usage. That is to say[,] courts ordinarily read a phrase in a criminal statute that introduces the elements of a crime with the word "knowingly" as applying that word to each element. . . . For example, in *Liparota v. United States*. . . , this Court interpreted a federal food stamp statute that said, " 'whoever knowingly uses, transfers, acquires, alters, or possesses coupons or authorization cards *in any manner not authorized by [law]*' " is subject to imprisonment. . . . The question was whether the word "knowingly" applied to the phrase "in any manner not authorized by [law]." . . . The Court held that it did, . . . despite the legal cliche "ignorance of the law is no excuse."

More recently, we had to interpret a statute that penalizes "[a]ny person who—(1) knowingly transports or ships using any means or facility of interstate or foreign commerce by any means including by computer or mails, any visual depiction, if—(A) the producing of such visual depiction involves the use of a minor engaging in sexually explicit conduct."

18 U.S.C. § 2252(a)(a)(A). . . . In issue was whether the term "knowingly" in paragraph (1) modified the phrase "the use of a minor" in subparagraph (A). . . . The language in issue in *X-Citement Video*. . . was more ambiguous than the language here not only because the phrase "the use of a minor" was not the direct object of the verbs modified by "knowingly," but also because it appeared in a different subsection. . . . Moreover, the fact that many sex crimes involving minors do not ordinarily require that a perpetrator know that his victim is a minor supported the Government's position. Nonetheless, we again found that the intent element applied to "the use of a minor." [*X-Citement Video.*]

The question, however, is whether Congress intended to achieve this enhanced protection by permitting conviction of those who do not *know* the ID they unlawfully use refers to a real person, *i.e.,* those who do not *intend* to cause this further harm. And, in respect to this latter point, the statute's history (outside of the statute's language) is inconclusive. . . .

Finally, and perhaps of greatest practical importance, there is the difficulty in many circumstances of proving beyond a reasonable doubt that a defendant has the necessary knowledge. Take an instance in which an alien who unlawfully entered the United States gives an employer identification documents that *in fact* belong to others. How is the Government to prove that the defendant *knew* that this was so? The Government may be able to show that such a defendant knew the papers were not his. But perhaps the defendant did not care whether the papers (1) were real papers belonging to another person or (2) were simply counterfeit papers. The difficulties of proof, along with the defendant's necessary guilt of a predicate crime and the defendant's necessary knowledge that he has acted "without lawful authority," make it reasonable, in the Government's view, to read the statute's language as dispensing with the knowledge requirement.

We do not find this argument sufficient, however, to turn the tide in the Government's favor. For one thing, in the classic case of identity theft, intent is generally not difficult to prove. For example, where a defendant has used another person's identification information to get access to that person's bank account, the Government can prove knowledge with little difficulty. The same is true when the defendant has gone through someone else's trash to find discarded credit card and bank statements, or pretends to be from the victim's bank and requests personal identifying information. Indeed, the examples of identity theft in the legislative history (dumpster diving, computer hacking, and the like) are all examples of the types of classic identity theft where intent should be relatively easy to prove, and there will be no practical enforcement problem. For another thing, to the extent that Congress may have been concerned about criminalizing the conduct of a broader class of individuals, the concerns about practical enforceability are insufficient to outweigh the clarity of the text. Similar interpretations that we have given other similarly phrased statutes also created practical enforcement problems. . . . But had Congress placed conclusive weight upon practical enforcement, the statute would likely not read the way it now reads. Instead, Congress used the word "knowingly" followed by a list of offense elements. And we cannot find indications in statements of its purpose or in the practical problems of enforcement sufficient to overcome the ordinary meaning, in English or through ordinary interpretive practice, of the words that it wrote.

We conclude that § 1028A(a)(1) requires the Government to show that the defendant knew that the means of identification at issue belonged to another person.

Case Questions

1. Did the Court use the plain meaning rule in deciding the case?
2. Was legislative intent or legislative history helpful in deciding the case?
3. Did the Court strictly or loosely construe the statutory language?
4. Do you think that the Court captured Congress's intent?
5. Were the facts in this case something that Congress anticipated in passing the statute?
6. Was there anything else the Court could have done to make interpretation of the statute easier as applied to Flores-Figueroa?

CASE NOTE: Three Justices were not in total agreement with the majority opinion. Justices Scalia and Alito concurred in part and each wrote a separate opinion. Justice Thomas joined in Justice Scalia's opinion. These concurring opinions are dealt with in questions at the end of this chapter.

Legislative History

If the application of a statute remains unclear in its language and in its written context, the intent of the legislature may be ascertained by researching the statute's **legislative history**. This includes the records and documents concerning the process whereby the statute became law. The purpose and application of the statute may sometimes become clear with these additional materials. Several committees may have held hearings or discussions on the law during its enactment that have become part of the public record and demonstrate the concerns of legislators and the reasons for enactment. Inferences may be made based on different drafts of the statute and the reasons expressed for the changes. If two houses of the legislature began with different language, the final compromise language may also suggest conclusions. Legislative debates may similarly clarify legislative intent.

Research into legislative history can be a lengthy process involving extensive analytical skills; nonetheless, an examination of the entire process for a particular enactment will tend to dispel plausible but incorrect interpretations of legislative intent. The informal politics of negotiation and compromise, however, are not always reflected in the record, so the reasons for the final decisions on the language of the statute may remain obscure.

legislative history
Recorded events that provide a basis for determining the legislative intent underlying a statute enacted by a legislature; the sources for legislative history include legislative committee hearings and debates on the floor of the legislature.

In this day and time, one would suppose that a statute prohibiting one from driving while intoxicated would cover a teenaged driver who was high when he caused the death of another teenager and serious injury to others. Perhaps fearing a negative reaction by the press, the New York Court of Appeals (the highest New York state court) applied each of the canons of construction discussed in this chapter before concluding that "intoxication" did not include being high on a drug.

The PEOPLE of the State of New York, Appellant

v.

Vincent LITTO, Respondent

Court of Appeals of New York

8 N.Y.3d 692, 872 N.E.2d 848, 840 N.Y.S.2d 736

June 27, 2007.

Over the last 97 years, the Legislature has crafted and repeatedly refined statutes with the goal of removing from the road those who drive while intoxicated. This appeal centers on the phrase "driving while intoxicated" in Vehicle and Traffic Law § 1192(3). Based on the language, history and scheme of the statute, we conclude that the Legislature here intended to use "intoxication" to refer to a disordered state of mind caused by alcohol, not by drugs.

On the evening of January 13, 2004, defendant Vincent Litto, 19 years old, was driving south in Brooklyn on a four-lane road, with three passengers in his car. Traveling at 50 miles an hour on a road on which cars moved at an average speed of 30 miles an hour, defendant picked up a can of "Dust-Off" from the dashboard and sprayed it into his mouth. About 45 seconds later, he veered into oncoming traffic and crashed into a vehicle driven by Andrea Sett. One of the passengers in Sett's car, 17-year-old Kristian Roggio, was killed. Sett, another passenger, defendant and two of his passengers were injured, some seriously.

Dust-Off contains a hydrocarbon, difluoroethane, which assists as a propellant and gives a person who "huffs" it a "high." . . . The People submitted 14 counts to the grand jury-[including] one count [of] operating a motor vehicle while in an intoxicated condition (Vehicle and Traffic Law § 1192(3)).

The question posed in this case is whether a driver can be prosecuted under Vehicle and Traffic Law § 1192(3) for "driving while intoxicated" while under the influence of a drug or other unlisted substance. . . . The legislative history of the statute and its scheme reveal that the Legislature's intent has been to treat a driver's use of alcohol differently from a driver's use of drugs, and that the prohibition of driving while intoxicated under subdivision 3 of section 1192 is part of the strategy to prevent the "drinking driver" from using the roadways.

Section 1192 of the Vehicle and Traffic Law is entitled: "Operating a motor vehicle while under the influence of alcohol or drugs." The law provides:

"1. Driving while ability impaired. No person shall operate a motor vehicle while the person's ability to operate such motor vehicle is impaired by the consumption of alcohol.

"2. Driving while intoxicated; per se. No person shall operate a motor vehicle while such person has .08 of one per centum or more by weight of alcohol in the person's blood as shown by chemical analysis of such person's blood, breath, urine or saliva, made pursuant to the provisions of section eleven hundred ninety-four of this article.

"2-a. Aggravated driving while intoxicated; per se. No person shall operate a motor vehicle while such person has .18 of one per centum or more by weight of alcohol in such person's blood as shown by chemical analysis of such person's blood, breath, urine or saliva made pursuant to the provisions of section eleven hundred ninety-four of this article.

"3. Driving while intoxicated. No person shall operate a motor vehicle while in an intoxicated condition.

"4. Driving while ability impaired by drugs. No person shall operate a motor vehicle while the person's ability to operate such a motor vehicle is impaired by the use of a drug as defined in this chapter.

"4-a. Driving while ability impaired by the combined influence of drugs or of alcohol and any drug or drugs. No person shall operate a motor vehicle while the person's ability to operate such motor vehicle is impaired by the combined influence of drugs or of alcohol and any drug or drugs. . . .

"9. Conviction of a different charge. A driver may be convicted of a violation of subdivision one, two or three of this section, notwithstanding that the charge laid before the court alleged a violation of subdivision two or three of this section. . . ."

Vehicle and Traffic Law § 114-a, in the same chapter—chapter 71 of the Consolidated Laws—as section 1192, provides: "The term 'drug' when used in this chapter, means and includes any substance listed in section thirty-three hundred six of the public health law." Public Health Law § 3306 is an extensive schedule of controlled substances. Neither difluoroethane nor the more general hydrocarbon is on the list and, therefore, defendant in this case could not have been charged under Vehicle and Traffic Law § 1192(4). . . .

The Court's primary goal is to interpret a statute by determining, and implementing, the Legislature's intent. Analysis begins with the language of the statute itself. Next, in construing a statute, the courts frequently "follow the course of legislation on the subject, the lineage of the act being thought to illuminate the intent of the legislature" [citation to state statute]. The Court additionally looks to the purposes underlying the legislative scheme. . . . That method is particularly apt in this case in which the Legislature itself, over the course of the century, has repeatedly refined the statute as society has evolved, science has progressed and new problems have emerged. . . .

The plain meaning of the language of a statute must be interpreted "in the light of conditions existing at the time of its passage and construed as the courts would have construed it soon after its passage" (*People v. Koch*). . . . [The opinion included at least four pages of a description of the legislative history of section 1192 and related statutes. The court reviewed the 1910 statute, which was the precursor to section 1192, the definition of "intoxication" in the 1910 and 1914 editions of a law dictionary, the original version of section 1192 passed in 1929, and amendments in 1941, 1959, 1960, 1966, 1970, and 2006 to the statute and related statutes.]

The legislative history not only manifests legislative intent to employ the term "intoxicated" to refer to persons inebriated by alcohol and to prevent them from driving, but also reveals a scheme by which the statute would reach that goal. This Court must determine "the consistency" of the Legislature's reaching its goal "with the purposes underlying the legislative *scheme*" (*Sheehy* . . .). . . .

In two respects, the People's construction of Vehicle and Traffic Law § 1192(3) is out of step with the statutory scheme. First, the scheme of section 1192 provides for different levels or kinds of proof to establish violations of the statute. Thus, a prosecutor must show impairment by alcohol to prove a violation of subdivision 1—resulting in a traffic infraction. Subdivision 1 is a lesser-included offense of subdivisions 2 and 3. Subdivisions 2 and 2-a require a showing of a specific amount of blood alcohol content to result in a per se criminal violation, whereas subdivision 3—"in an intoxicated condition"—allows for a circumstantial showing of inability to operate a motor vehicle while under the influence of alcohol. Confirming this scheme, subdivision 9 explicitly permits a conviction under subdivision 1, 2 or 3 even when the charge alleges a violation of either subdivision 2 or 3. If subdivision 3 were now read, as the People urge, to allow for any drug to be included as part of the definition of "intoxication," then one who has committed a misdemeanor under subdivision 3 could not, in contravention of the legislative plan, be found to have committed the lesser-included offense of driving while impaired by alcohol under subdivision 1.

Second, while the legislative history from 1910 is unavailable, the history thereafter shows that the Legislature has consistently presumed that the initial statute was created to prevent drunk driving. Although, as the People argue, the goal of the Legislature may be advanced by including use of drugs in the definition of "intoxication," the Legislature has repeatedly and definitively concentrated on precise mechanisms to prevent deathly accidents related to alcohol. . . . Including driving while under the influence of limitless "drugs" as a violation of driving while intoxicated has not been part of that mechanism.

In 1960, the Legislature added section 1192(1) to assure that not all drivers who were under the influence of alcohol would be criminally liable. This Court determined that this subdivision and subdivision 3 were not unconstitutionally vague (*see Cruz* . . .). The Court concluded that, as to subdivision 1, evident from the statutory language and scheme, the issue was "whether, by voluntarily consuming alcohol, this particular defendant has actually impaired, to any extent, the physical and mental abilities which he is expected to possess in order to operate a vehicle as a reasonable and prudent driver." . . . "Intoxication," the Court stated, "is not an unfamiliar concept" and is "intelligible to the average person." The standard to determine intoxication is "whether the individual's consumption of alcohol has rendered him *incapable* of employing the physical or mental abilities needed to, for instance, form a specific intent". . . . These terms, the Court continued, have an accepted meaning "long recognized in law and life" [(*Cruz*)]. The Court thus upheld the Legislature's scheme.

The addition in 1966 of subdivision 4 demonstrates the Legislature's desire to add the use of drugs to that of alcohol for further prevention of deaths on the highway. Were drugs included in the definition for "intoxication" under subdivision 3, the Legislature would have had no reason to add another misdemeanor. Rather, the Legislature, after careful study and debate, concluded that a driver could be convicted for impairment by drugs—and then only by explicitly enumerated drugs. . . .

Only last year, focusing its attention on strengthening the statute, the Legislature added one provision to prohibit driving while using alcohol—aggravated driving while intoxicated, subdivision 2-a—and another provision to prohibit driving while using a combination of "drugs or of alcohol and any drug or drugs"—subdivision 4-a. The Legislature unambiguously employed the term "intoxicated" for the level of alcohol, and the terms "alcohol" and "drugs" for the combination.

If defendant did what the prosecution charges, then his conduct was reprehensible—his voluntary inhalation of hydrocarbon while driving resulted in the death of a young woman and serious injuries to others. Perhaps gaps exist in the law and the prosecution should not have to rely on the 12 other counts charged. However, a determination by this Court that intoxication in Vehicle and Traffic Law § 1192(3) includes the use of any substance would improperly override the legislative policy judgment.

Case Questions

1. What did the court find to be the legislature's intent?
2. How did the court use the plain meaning rule?
3. What did the court say about the context of the statute under which Litto was charged?
4. What was the impact of the definition of "drug"?
5. Did the court strictly construe the statute?
6. What did the legislative history show?

A Caveat on Statutory Interpretation

We have touched here on only a few of a multitude of rules of interpretation employed by the courts in resolving issues of statutory meaning. In fact, there are so many rules and exceptions to them that the courts enjoy considerable freedom to select the rules that support the interpretation that a given court or judge favors. For example, any specific rule may be avoided by declaring that it conflicts with the primary intent of the legislature. There is a subjective element to this analysis that affords a court great discretion.

Courts ordinarily attempt to give force to legislative intent. They are assisted by a great variety of technical rules of construction that have been developed in the precedents of prior judges faced with the problem of statutory meaning. But the thinking of judges differs from that of legislators. Judges not only deal with abstract rules but on a daily basis must also resolve difficult problems with justice and fairness. Very few judges will blindly follow a technical rule if the result would be manifestly unfair. They can justly reason that the legislature never intended an unjust result. When arguing the interpretation of a statute, a lawyer or paralegal must keep in mind the importance of persuading the court that the proposed interpretation is not only correct but also fair and just.

As you know from Chapter 1, a lawsuit must be filed within a certain time period, the statute of limitations. A **tolling statute** suspends the running of the time period under the statute of limitations as long as a given circumstance exists. In *Prosperi*, the government claimed that the statute of limitations on criminal charges had not run because the United States had been at war.

tolling statute

A statute that stops the clock on the running of a statute of limitation while a given circumstance exists.

UNITED STATES of America

v.

Robert PROSPERI, Gregory Stevenson, Gerard McNally, Marc J. Blais, John J. Farrar, and Keith Thomas

United States District Court, D. Massachusetts

Criminal No. 06-10116-RGS

573 F. Supp. 2d 436

Aug. 29, 2008.

In this case, the court is asked to determine whether the United States is presently at war, and if so, with whom. Defendants are charged with conspiracy, mail fraud, and the making of false statements in connection with the federally-financed Central Artery Tunnel Project (CA/T). . . .

The CA/T project, colloquially known as the "Big Dig," is a multi-billion dollar interstate highway construction project. The CA/T involves the building or reconstruction of nearly eight miles of highway bisecting the City of Boston, almost half of it underground. . . . Defendants are former employees of Aggregate Industries, N.E. (Aggregate), a major concrete supplier to the CA/T. Defendants are accused of recycling stale and adulterated concrete, and submitting false batch reports to conceal their fraud. Approximately 5,000 of the 500,000 concrete loads that Aggregate delivered to the CA/T are alleged to have failed to conform to contract specifications. . . .

Defendants contend that the acts of highway project fraud and mail fraud alleged to have been committed prior to May 3, 2001 (eighty-five counts in total), are **barred** by the five-year federal statute of limitations. The government, for its part, maintains that these counts are saved by the Wartime Suspension of Limitations Act (Suspension Act), 18 U.S.C § 3287. The government argues that the Suspension Act **tolled** the running of the statute of limitations as of September 18, 2001, the date on which Congress authorized the use of military force against the Taliban government of Afghanistan; or alternatively, as of October 10, 2002, the date of the authorization of the use of military force in Iraq. The Suspension Act provides (with appropriate emphasis) as follows.

When the United States is at war the running of any statute of limitations applicable to any offense (1) involving fraud or attempted fraud against the United States or any agency thereof in any manner, whether by conspiracy or not, or (2) committed in connection with the acquisition, care, handling, custody, control or disposition of any real or personal property of the United States, or (3) committed in connection with the negotiation, procurement, award, performance, payment for, interim financing, cancellation, or other termination or settlement, of any contract, subcontract, or purchase order which is connected with or related to the prosecution of the war, or with any disposition of termination inventory by any war contractor or Government agency, shall be suspended until three years after the termination of hostilities as proclaimed by the President or by a concurrent resolution of Congress. . . .

Congress has not exercised its power under Article I, Section 8, clause 11 of the United States Constitution to "declare war." Aside from a formal declaration of war, the Suspension Act gives no explicit indication of the type of military action that Congress intended to trigger a tolling of a limitations period under the Act. As a result, this case requires the court to make the determination of what it means for the United States to be "at war" within the meaning of the Act.

The judicial branch has a constitutionally-based policy of abstaining when "a question [is] too fraught with gravity even to be adequately formulated when not compelled." *Ludecke v. Watkins.* . . . The reluctance to assay into "political thickets," *see Baker v. Carr. . . ,* is rooted in the case or controversy requirement of Article III and the Court's original understanding that the Constitution does not authorize it to render advisory opinions, even when requested to do so by the political branches. . . .

One might think of this case—which involves a political issue of great sensitivity—as one counseling abstinence. There are cases, however, that leave no choice to a court but to interpret statutory or contractual language that depends on the determination of the existence of a declared or undeclared state of war. . . . The question posed here is the meaning of the phrase "at war" as it appears in the Suspension Act. So framed, the question would appear to be one of straight-forward statutory construction. There are numerous statutes in the United States Code that take effect only in times of war. . . . The parties, however, have not identified—nor has the court uncovered—a statute comparable to the Suspension Act with its unusual mix of a pecuniary element with an "at war" requirement. The **canons of construction** dictate that "courts must presume that a legislature says in a statute what it means and means in a statute what it says." *Barnhardt v. Sigmon* . . .

Here, although the words "at war" may, in a general sense, mean exactly what they say, their meaning in the specific context of the Suspension Act—a tolling statute—is not as certain as might appear at first blush. . . . The "at war" clause of the Suspension Act has not been the subject of extensive judicial review—in fact only one district court has been called upon recently to decide its meaning. That court determined that the Act's tolling provisions apply only when Congress

exercises its Article I power to formally declare war. *See United States v. Shelton.* . . . This court . . . believes that *Shelton* reads the Suspension Act to incorporate a condition precedent that is not found in its text or legislative history. Under the *Shelton* reading, only a war on a "massive and pervasive" scale (like World War II), that is sufficient to provoke Congress into a formal declaration of war (and does so) triggers the Act. The *Shelton* formulation thus does not capture the Korean War or the Vietnam War, two of the largest, bloodiest, and most expensive military campaigns in our nation's history (nor does it capture the conflicts in Iraq and in Afghanistan). Moreover, it does not answer very persuasively the question of why the Act is to take effect when Congress declares a war that is neither massive nor pervasive, say against Mexico or Spain, and yet not when Congress stops short of a formal declaration in more formidable circumstances like Korea and Vietnam.

The *Shelton* reading of the Suspension Act would be defensible if there was some indication in the Act (or its legislative history) that Congress meant the tolling provision to apply only during declared wars of an all-consuming nature like the Second World War. But there is not. Had Congress intended the phrase "at war" to serve as a limitation, it would have written the modifier "declared" into the Act as it has in other statutes. . . .

While resort to legislative history is discouraged when the plain words of a statute speak without ambiguity, to the extent that the *Shelton* decision may raise questions about the meaning of its text, it is appropriate to look to the origins of the Suspension Act. . . . [The court examines the passage of the Act in 1921 and amendments to it.]

Congress twice in two years confirmed (or at least, acknowledged) the President's power as Commander-in-Chief to send U.S. forces into combat abroad [in passing the Authorization for the Use of Military Force (AUMF) in 2001 and] . . . the Authorization for the Use of Military Force Against Iraq (AUMFAI) [in] 2002. While not formal declarations of war, the AUMFs signified the commitment of Congress "to pursue vigorously the war on terrorism through the provision of authorities and funding requested by the President." AUMFAI, at 1501. [The court reviewed various definitions of "war," the scope of the conflicts, and the government's actions to deal with terrorist threats.] . . .

The tolling provisions of the Suspension Act apply "until three years after the termination of hostilities as proclaimed by the President or by a concurrent resolution of Congress." As the government posits, a strong case can be made, given the continuing expenditures and loss of life in Iraq and Afghanistan, that the United States remains at war. It is nonetheless incumbent on the court, under the test it proposes, to identify a clear demarcation point at which the tolling provisions of the Suspension Act cease to run. . . . On December 22, 2001, the United States formally recognized and extended full diplomatic relations to the new government of Hamid Karzai. . . . Accordingly, the statute of limitations with respect to the Afghan conflict, expired on December 22, 2004. Similarly, on May 1, 2003, President Bush, while aboard the USS *Abraham Lincoln,* proclaimed that "[m]ajor combat operations in Iraq have ended. In the Battle of Iraq, the United States and our allies have prevailed. And now our coalition is engaged in securing and reconstructing that country." Consequently, with regards to the Iraq conflict, the statute of limitations expired on May 1, 2006. . . .

For the foregoing reasons, the motion to dismiss is *DENIED.* The AUMF, which authorized the Afghanistan War, tolls the limitations period from September 18, 2001, to December 22, 2004. The Iraq War Authorization tolls the limitations period from October 10, 2002, to May 1, 2006. The court therefore will deem the Suspension Act to toll the limitations period for defendants' alleged offenses from September 18, 2001, to May 1, 2006.

Case Questions

1. Why should a court shy away from answering political questions and rendering advisory opinions?
2. What do you suppose was the motivation for Congress to toll the statute of limitations if the nation was at war?
3. Does it make sense to apply the tolling statute during the conflicts in Afghanistan and Iraq?
4. Does the court's application of the tolling statute conflict with the principle that criminal statutes are strictly construed?

Case Glossary

bar
   To defeat or estop.
tolled
   Held in abeyance; kept from running.
canons of construction
   Rules of statutory interpretation.

STATUTE AND PRECEDENT

It would be a mistake to think that the existence of a statute suspends the common law principle of precedent. Although a statute may supersede a common law rule, the court's interpretation of the statute is law. When researching a case covered by statute, it is not enough to look merely to the statute. One must also look at the cases that have interpreted the statute. In many instances, the application of a statute to a client's case is clear; if any doubt exists, judicial decisions must be examined.

SUMMARY

In modern times, legislation has replaced the common law as the major source of changes in the law. Legislative bodies enact laws to be applied generally to future situations rather than to decide existing disputes, which is the task of the courts. Unless they are procedurally defective or unconstitutional, statutes must be enforced by the court without changing or distorting their language. For cases in which the application of a statute is unclear, the courts have developed a multitude of rules of construction with the purpose of ascertaining the intent of the legislature. Once a higher court has interpreted the meaning of a statute, that decision becomes precedent for it and lower courts. The legislature always has the option of rewriting the statute for clarification or revision or if it objects to the interpretation the court has given it.

KEY TERMS

aggravated	legislative history	rules of construction
bench trial	legislative intent	separation of powers
bicameral	ordinance	strict construction
codification	petition	tolling statute
construe	plain meaning rule	void for vagueness
effective date	prospective	writ of certiorari
ex post facto clause	retroactive (retrospective)	

CHAPTER REVIEW QUESTIONS

1. Why was the United States fertile ground for codification?
2. When does legislation cross the line into adjudication? (*See Ponder v. Graham.*)
3. What is the hallmark of judicial process?
4. On what basis may courts invalidate legislation?
5. Define the *void-for-vagueness* doctrine.
6. Describe the *plain meaning rule.*
7. What is the underlying purpose guiding statutory construction?
8. Why is strict construction applied to criminal statutes?
9. What is legislative history?
10. What is the relation of legislation and precedent?

CRITICAL THINKING QUESTIONS

1. Why must the courts search for statutory intent? Why are legislatures unable to clearly express their intentions?
2. Is the legislature inherently more democratic than the judiciary? If so, does that mean it makes better law?

CYBER EXERCISES

1. The United States Supreme Court interpreted 18 U.S.C. § 1028A in *Flores-Figueroa v. United States,* a case excerpted in this chapter. The Cornell University Law School website, http://www.law.cornell.edu/, is an extremely reputable website that you can use to access the statute. Using that website, locate the statute and answer the following questions:
    a. In *Flores-Figueroa*, the Court states that the defendant is subject to a mandatory consecutive two-year prison term under 18 U.S.C. § 1028A(a)(1), yet that portion of the statute does not make the prison term consecutive. Why does the Court state that the two-year term is consecutive?

    b. Section 1028A(a)(1) references "any felony violation enumerated under subsection (c)." Which felony violation is relevant to Flores-Figueroa?

    c. What is the prison term for someone convicted of a "terrorist offense"?

    d. Is the prison term concurrent or consecutive?

    e. How would a court determine if someone has committed a terrorist offense?

2. Opinions of the United States Supreme Court are accessible at a number of websites, including the United States Supreme Court website, http://www .supremecourtus.gov/. Go to that website and locate *Flores-Figueroa v. United States*, a case excerpted in this chapter. The case contained a majority opinion and two concurring opinions, one written by Justice Scalia and the other written by Justice Alito. Using *Flores-Figueroa*, answer the following questions:

    a. Both Justice Scalia's opinion and Justice Alito's opinion state "concurring in part and concurring in the judgment." What does this mean? Do their opinions differ from a "concurring opinion"?

    b. With which portion of the majority opinion does Justice Scalia agree?

    c. With which portion of the majority opinion does Justice Scalia disagree, and why?

    d. With which portion of the majority opinion does Justice Alito agree?

    e. With which portion of the majority opinion does Justice Alito disagree, and why?

3. Opinions of the Ohio Supreme Court are accessible at a number of websites, including the Ohio Supreme Court website, http://www.sconet.state.oh.us/. Go to that website and locate *Ackison v. Anchor Packing Co.*, a case excerpted in this chapter. The case contained a majority opinion and a dissenting opinion. Using *Ackison*, answer the following questions:

    a. According to Justice Pfeiffer, what was the legislative intent behind the new legislation?

    b. According to Justice Pfeiffer, was the new legislation substantive or procedural, and why?

    c. How does the tone of the dissenting opinion differ from the tone of the majority opinion?

    d. How does the last paragraph of the dissent (preceding the appendix) relate to principles introduced in this chapter?

    e. Do you think that the majority opinion made law or interpreted the new legislation?

4. Same-sex marriage is currently a hot topic, and states are dealing with this topic by provisions in the state constitutions, by statute, and by case law. Much information on same-sex marriage is available at http://www.freedomtomarry.org/. Using that website, answer the following questions:

    a. Which states have dealt with same-sex marriage by provisions in the state constitutions, and to what effect?

    b. Which states have statutes sanctioning same-sex marriage?

    c. Which states have dealt with same-sex marriage by case law, and to what effect?

d. Would a state that has not spoken on the legality of same-sex marriage recognize the validity of a same-sex marriage sanctioned by another state?

e. What if a same-sex couple marry in a state allowing same-sex marriage, move to a state prohibiting same-sex marriage, and then decide to divorce?

5. The statutes of your state are probably accessible online from a website maintained by your state. Find the website and answer the following questions:

a. What is the URL for the website?

b. What information did you find helpful in navigating the website?

c. What information does *Zimmerman's Research Guide* (available online) provide concerning the statutes of your state?

REVIEW PROBLEM

Lawmaking does not always follow the ideal plan.

In addition to the state and federal constitutions, the major sources of our law, as outlined in Chapters 2 and 3, are the courts and the legislatures. A basic premise of modern American law is that the enactments of the legislature are law, albeit sometimes invalidated by the courts or later revised by the legislature. More problematic is the conclusion that courts make laws. The history of the common law acknowledges this fact even though much of the common law has been codified or abrogated by legislation. The court-as-lawmaker conclusion rests on somewhat weaker ground when we argue that the interpretation of statutes results in making law. Many, especially judges, would have us see this as merely interpretation and not lawmaking. After all, the courts are merely expressing "legislative intent." However, one might argue that a law is not a law until the court tells us what it means. After all, the legislature cannot enforce the law. To paraphrase Oliver Wendell Holmes, Jr., "The law is what the court says it is."

What Is the Law?

Yes, at some level Holmes, the judge, was right. If you go to court wondering whether your or your opponent's interpretation of the law is right, rest assured, the judge will let you know which of you is correct. As a practical matter, of course, we cannot wait for judgment. We need to know the law before we act, before we advise our clients on how to act. We cannot afford to wait for the judge to tell us. We need to know when to challenge others' interpretation of the law and when to yield. In life we must assess the cost of following the rules as well as the cost of bending them. A fundamental premise of a modern democratic society is that the law is knowable.

Some rules are not exactly laws. Chapter 4 ended with a discussion of statutory construction and a case concerning the so-called plain meaning rule (of statutory construction). The rules of statutory construction are often referred to as "guidelines," "canons," and even "rules of thumb." In the *Courchesne* case (following), the majority in at least one statement refers to a rule of construction as a law, but that is not the general view. The canons of statutory construction are a bit like *stare decisis,* binding but not law—a judicial policy. One might even call these "customs." The crux of the problem in *Courchesne* was what a fairly recent enactment of the Connecticut legislature (the

General Assembly) meant. The legislature passed a law providing for the death penalty in cases of "murder of two or more persons at the same time or in the course of a single transaction," where "the defendant committed the offense in an especially heinous, cruel, or depraved manner." Robert Courchesne stabbed and killed a woman who happened to be pregnant. A caesarean section was performed and the child lived for 40 days before dying. The facts were sufficient for a prosecution and conviction under the multiple-murder statute. In an effort to avoid the death penalty, the defendant argued, *inter alia,* that the plain meaning (or ultimate meaning; he would have been happy with either) of the statute was that the state must establish a heinous, cruel, or depraved manner for *both* victims.

The majority agreed that the defendant's reading of the statute was "linguistically" more "logical" than the state's reading that the statute required aggravating circumstances for only one of the murders, suggesting that the plain meaning favored the defendant. Nevertheless, an agonizingly lengthy discussion of legislative history by the majority concluded that the intent of the legislature was to allow the death penalty when the murder of only one of the victims was heinous. It is common for opinions examining legislative history to be protracted, but *Courchesne* was undoubtedly stretched because of the equally lengthy dissent. The length of the majority and dissenting opinions indicates the importance of one issue; namely the majority's assertion that the plain meaning rule should be abandoned.

Without necessarily condoning the murder of pregnant women, we can sympathize with the defendant, who is hearing that his argument is "logical" but he must die anyway. Note, too, how peculiar it is that rules of statutory construction are changed in a death penalty case, when we know that criminal statutes are strictly construed and death penalty cases viewed with special scrutiny. Apparently the plain meaning rule, in the view of a majority of Connecticut's justices, is not a law. If it were a law, established by precedent, it is difficult to imagine that a court would overrule that precedent to invoke the death penalty. (The first sentence of Justice Zarella's dissent describes the majority's opinion as "breathtaking.")

The Holistic Approach: The Majority Opinion

Justice Borden, the author of the majority opinion, disavows the plain meaning rule, arguing that the search for legislative intent should be based on all the pertinent evidence that may help to explain the meaning of a statute. This we will call the "holistic approach."

After conceding that the defendant's reading of the multiple-murder statute is linguistically logical, despite the state's different interpretation, Justice Borden then proceeds to discuss the statute in context and, more particularly, in comparison with the capital crime of kidnap-murder, where the same "heinous" language is used to allow the death penalty and has been found not to require that both the kidnap and the murder be heinous. The majority suggests that to require both (or all) the murders to have been carried out in a "heinous, cruel, or depraved manner" would achieve a bizarre result. This is perhaps a reasonable position: Why should a defendant escape the death penalty simply because one of the victims was not murdered as viciously as another?

After this lengthy analysis (with a great deal more analysis yet to come), the opinion then tackles the plain meaning rule. [From the majority opinion in *State v. Courchesne*, 816 A.2d 562, 576 (Conn. 2003):]

> We take this opportunity to clarify the approach of this court to the process of statutory interpretation. For at least a century, this court has relied on sources beyond the specific text of the statute at issue to determine the meaning of the language as intended by the legislature. [Citations] For that same period of time, however, this court often has eschewed resort to those sources when the meaning of the text appeared to be plain and unambiguous. [Citations]
>
> In 1994, however, we noted a dichotomy in our case law regarding whether resort to extratextual sources was appropriate even in those instances where the text's meaning appeared to be plain and unambiguous. In *Frillici v. Westport*, supra, 231 Conn. 430–31 n.15, we stated: "It is true that, in construing statutes, we have often relied upon the canon of statutory construction that we need not, and indeed ought not, look beyond the statutory language to other interpretive aids unless the statute's language is not absolutely clear and unambiguous. [Citations] That maxim requires some slight but plausible degree of linguistic ambiguity as a kind of analytical threshold that must be surmounted before a court may resort to aids to the determination of the meaning of the language as applied to the facts of the case. . . . It is also true, however, that we have often eschewed such an analytical threshold, and have stated that, in interpreting statutes, we look at all the available evidence, such as the statutory language, the legislative history, the circumstances surrounding its enactment, the purpose and policy of the statute, and its relationship to existing legislation and common law principles. [Citations] This analytical model posits that the legislative process is purposive, and that the meaning of legislative language (indeed, of any particular use of our language) is best understood by viewing not only the language at issue, but by its context and by the purpose or purposes behind its use."
>
> Since then, we have not been consistent in our formulation of the appropriate method of interpreting statutory language. At times, we have adhered to the formulation that requires identification of some degree of ambiguity in that language before consulting any sources of its meaning beyond the statutory text. See, e.g., *MacDermid, Inc. v. Dept. of Environmental Protection*, 257 Conn. 128, 154, 778 A.2d 7 (2001) ("if the language of a statute is plain and unambiguous, we need look no further than the words themselves because we assume that the language expresses the legislature's intent" [internal quotation marks omitted]). We refer herein to that formulation as the "plain meaning rule," which we discuss in further detail later in this opinion. At other times, we have . . . adhered to a more encompassing formulation that does not require passing any threshold of ambiguity as a precondition of consulting extratextual sources of the meaning of legislative language. See, e.g., *Bender v. Bender*, supra, 258 Conn. 741.
>
> We now make explicit that our approach to the process of statutory interpretation is governed by the Bender formulation, as further explicated herein. The first two sentences of that formulation set forth the fundamental task of the court in engaging [in] the process of statutory interpretation, namely, engaging in a "reasoned search for the intention of the legislature," which we further defined as a

reasoned search for "the meaning of the statutory language as applied to the facts of [the] case, including the question of whether the language actually does apply." . . . That formulation admonishes the court to consider all relevant sources of meaning of the language at issue—namely, the words of the statute, its legislative history and the circumstances surrounding its enactment, the legislative policy it was designed to implement, and its relationship to existing legislation and to common-law principles governing the same general subject matter. Id. We also now make explicit that we ordinarily will consider all of those sources beyond the language itself, without first having to cross any threshold of ambiguity of the language [emphasis added].

[Later the majority makes the change even clearer:]

Thus, this process requires us to consider all relevant sources of the meaning of the language at issue, without having to cross any threshold or thresholds of ambiguity. Thus, we do not follow the plain meaning rule [emphasis added].

[The majority goes on to challenge the Zarella dissent, which characterizes the legislative history approach as fraught with unreliability:]

In sum, we have confidence in the ability of this court to ascertain, explain and apply the purpose or purposes of a statute in an intellectually honest manner. . . .

Thus, the dissent regards the use of legislative history as unreliable evidence of legislative intent, and as insidious in the sense that it permits the court to interpret a statute to reach a meaning that the court wants it to have, based on the court's own policy preference, rather than that of the legislature.

The Structured Approach: The Dissenting Opinion

Justice Zarella, in a vigorous and lengthy dissent, asserts that "statutory text should be the polestar of a court's search for the meaning of a statute," with the plain meaning rule as the starting point.

ZARELLA, J., with whom SULLIVAN, C. J., joins, dissenting. The majority's opinion is nothing short of breathtaking. The majority expressly abandons the plain meaning rule and fails to apply the rule of lenity in a death penalty case in which the majority states that the text of the statutory provision at issue favors the defendant's interpretation. Moreover, application of the tools of interpretation that the majority employs in reaching its conclusion leads to a flawed assessment of the rationality of the legislature's choices in drafting this state's death penalty statute. I believe, for reasons distinct from those offered by the majority, that the text of the statute at issue suggests that the defendant's interpretation of the statute should be rejected. I am not convinced, however, that the statute is clear and unambiguous, which, under well established law, is constitutionally required if this court is to reject the defendant's interpretation. Finally, in my view, the majority's abandonment of the plain meaning rule in favor of an alternative and novel method of statutory interpretation represents an incorrect deviation from our traditional mode of statutory interpretation and an impermissible usurpation of the legislative function. Accordingly, I dissent.

I also strongly disagree with the majority's proposition that adherence to the plain meaning rule leaves this court vulnerable to criticism of being "result-oriented." On the contrary, it is the majority's case-by-case approach to statutory interpretation that is subject to such criticism inasmuch as it encourages as a virtue unfettered discretion in utilizing the various tools of statutory construction. Such an approach expands the judiciary's power to the detriment of the legislature by allowing courts to depart from the plain meaning of the law under the guise of interpretation. Indeed, the majority's nebulous relativistic approach, under which all factors are considered, and under which no factor aside from the text is taken as a priori more informative than any other, virtually guarantees that there will be some evidence for nearly any interpretation that a court may wish to advance. . . .

[Justice Zarella outlines a four-step approach to statutory interpretation as follows:]

The process of statutory interpretation involves a reasoned and ordered search for the meaning of the legislation at issue. In other words, we seek to determine the meaning of statutory language as would be understood by a reasonable person reading the text of the statute.

In determining this objective meaning, we look first and foremost to the words of the statute itself. If the language of a statute is plain and unambiguous, we need look no further than the words themselves, unless such an interpretation produces an absurd result. In seeking the plain meaning of a statute, we generally construe words and phrases "according to the commonly approved usage of the language"; General Statutes § 1-1(a); in the context of the entire statute and employ ordinary rules of grammar. In addition, we may apply the ordinary canons of judicial construction in seeking the plain meaning, recognizing that such canons are not infallible in aiding the search for plain meaning.

When, and only when, the meaning of a statute cannot be ascertained in this fashion, we next eliminate all possible interpretations that render the statutory scheme incoherent or inconsistent. If more than one reasonable interpretation of the statute remains, we next consider the statute's relationship to other existing legislation and to common-law principles governing the same general subject matter and eliminate any interpretations incompatible with this legal landscape.

If ambiguity still remains, we seek to uncover the meaning of the statute by way of review of the statute's legislative history and the circumstances surrounding its enactment. Finally, if we are still left with an ambiguous statute after resort to all the foregoing tools of statutory interpretation, we apply any applicable presumptions in reaching a final interpretation.

The Aftermath

That *Courchesne* was viewed as abandoning the plain meaning rule can be seen by the reaction of the Connecticut General Assembly, which enacted a law making the plain meaning rule a law:

The meaning of a statute shall, in the first instance, be ascertained from the text of the statute itself and its relationship to other statutes. If, after examining such text and considering such relationship, the meaning of such text is plain and unambiguous and does not yield absurd or unworkable results, extratextual evidence of the meaning of the statute shall not be considered.

Public Acts 2003, No. 03–154, § 1. This section was signed into law by the governor on June 26, 2003, to become effective October 1, 2003; *Courchesne* was decided on March 11, 2003.

Now, here is a problem for you: Can the Supreme Court of Connecticut throw out the new statute enforcing the plain meaning rule as a violation of separation of powers, claiming that the legislature cannot tell the judiciary how to interpret statutes? Of course, the court can say whatever it wants—what will it say? In contrast, is not the abandonment of the plain meaning rule overstepping the separation of powers? Is the court saying, "We are not bound to give your statutes their ordinary meaning"?

To tax your brains a little further, consider this: Custom may be more sacred than law. More to the point, once custom must be articulated as law, it may lose its power. The plain meaning rule as a custom flows from a premise of judicial restraint and deference to legislation. When the court in *Courchesne* diminished the plain meaning rule, it may have disturbed a natural balance between the judiciary and the legislature. It would appear from the haste with which the legislature responded that this was so. The new law might be called a "rule of sore thumb," thumbing the nose of the legislature at the judiciary. This in turn is no doubt related to the polarization of politics over judicial activism and the appointment of judges. Speaking of politics, the irony of *Courchesne* is that the majority took a liberal activist approach in order to approve the death penalty, even though it felt the defendant's reading of the statute was linguistically correct, whereas the conservative approach of the dissent would have benefited the murderer. Why could the majority not simply have said that the statute is ambiguous with regard to whether both murders must have been heinous and then resorted to legislative history? Why did the majority go out of its way to jettison the plain meaning rule? We arrive at the anomalous result of the court finding that the legislature intended something different from what it said. The court is saying, "We see that the most logical reading of the statute would prevent Courchesne from being executed, but our analysis of the legislative history leads us to believe that the legislature would have wanted Courchesne executed." If that were true, why did the Connecticut General Assembly immediately reintroduce the plain meaning rule?

At the time of this ruling, Connecticut had not executed anyone since 1960. In 1995, the legislature changed the law regarding means of execution from electrocution to lethal injection. Finally, on May 13, 2005, Michael Ross was executed, but only because he dropped all appeals and asked to be executed. Were it not for Michael Ross, it would seem that all the time and energy spent on this was academic.

The courts of Alaska and Texas have also expressed disfavor of the plain meaning rule, Alaska as long ago as 1978 ("We reject the so-called 'plain meaning' rule as a strict exclusionary rule." *North Slope Borough v. Sohio Petroleum Corp.*, 585 P.2d 534 [Alaska 1978]). Will this minority trend be followed in other states? In a more recent case (*FDIC v. Caldrello*, 830 A.2d 767, at 774–75 [Conn. App. Ct. 2003]), a Connecticut court acknowledged the *Courchesne* majority opinion's abandonment of the plain meaning rule, noting by footnote without comment its reinstatement by the Connecticut General Assembly. Nevertheless, the court of appeals followed the plain meaning of the statute "because the defendants have not presented us with any extratextual support for any other interpretation of the words and we have found none." Does this mean that *Courchesne* is the law? More importantly, does this signal the demise of judicial restraint and deference to legislation, at least in Connecticut?

Query Why did the state insist on using the multiple-murder statute in the first place? Sometimes prosecutors reach for the death penalty because they can get death-qualified jurors (prospective jurors who are against the death penalty can be excluded) in order to have a more conservative, prosecution-oriented jury. Consider the following: *Courchesne* was not a "spree" or Columbine High school type of shooting. Connecticut had not executed anyone for more than thirty years.

Query On the Connecticut Supreme Court website (http://www.jud.state.ct.us/), Justice Borden's biographical sketch indicates that he teaches a course in statutory interpretation at the University of Connecticut School of Law. Does this influence your evaluation of the opinion?

CHAPTER 5
TRIAL AND APPELLATE COURTS

INTRODUCTION

Like any human institution, the legal system has its faults, but it has within it the means to diminish or eliminate its own weaknesses. A major means of correcting mistakes in the system lies in the appellate process, which provides the opportunity to litigants to challenge the propriety of the results of trial. Ambrose Bierce, in his *Devil's Dictionary*, defined *appeal* as "in law, to put the dice into the box for another throw." This is not quite true; the appellate process aims at rectifying serious mistakes made in the course of trial. The appellate courts are there to ensure that the rules of the game are enforced.

THE ADVERSARY PROCESS

The American legal system is based on certain assumptions that are responsible for its organization and structure, its strengths and its weaknesses. The system is a competitive one that reflects the political process and the competitive market economy. In the legal arena, this competitive form is referred to as the **adversarial system**. Every legal system must assert justice as its primary goal in order to claim legitimacy. Our system maintains that justice can best be achieved on the basis of rules that provide a fair procedure for those engaged in a dispute. The procedure embodies a search for truth by allowing disputing parties to present their cases through partisan, legally competent agents before an impartial tribunal. The agents are duly licensed attorneys, and the impartial tribunal is composed of a disinterested judge and a disinterested jury.

The adversarial process has been likened to a game and a fight, but as a game it has serious consequences and as a fight it is controlled by numerous rules that attempt to

adversarial system

The U.S. legal system in which litigants, typically represented by attorneys, argue their respective sides in a dispute before an impartial judge and jury; often contrasted with an inquisitorial system in which an accused is questioned by officials without rights of defense in a relentless search for the truth.

make the fight fair and civilized. Whichever metaphor is used, the judge may be viewed as an "umpire," ensuring that the rules are followed and each party is treated with fairness.

Although there may be several parties to a lawsuit, there are only two sides. Each side is provided with equal opportunity to present its evidence and arguments and to challenge the evidence and arguments from the other side. It is to be expected that each side will present a very different picture of the dispute, but the underlying assumption is that objective observers will be able to come close to the truth of the events behind the dispute and that the judge, trained and experienced in the law, will be able to weigh the legal arguments of both sides and come to a correct application of the law in each case.

Critics of the adversarial system point to certain inherent weaknesses: the partisanship of the attorneys often operates to cloud the truth rather than reveal it; judges and juries are neither objective nor totally disinterested; the competitive market model reflects a patriarchal, elitist, capitalist bias that prevents litigants from obtaining equality before the law; the system is old-fashioned, awkward, and inefficient. There is some truth to all of these criticisms, yet the Anglo-American legal system has made remarkable achievements that have been out of reach for legal systems based on different models.

FACT AND LAW

To understand the difference between trial and appellate courts, an appreciation of the fact/law distinction is necessary. As the modern court system has developed, the functions of judge and jury have become distinct. The word **trial** refers to *trial of fact;* the factfinder at trial is also called the **trier of fact**. In jury cases, the jury is the trier of fact; if there is no jury (for example, if the parties have waived a jury trial), the judge, sometimes simply referred to as the *court,* is the trier of fact. The trier of fact determines, from the evidence presented, the facts of the case in dispute. Once the facts are determined, appropriate law is applied. Decision, declaration, and determination of the law are the sole province of the judge. The jury's factfinding is called the **verdict**, and upon the verdict the judge makes a **judgment**, which determines the respective rights and obligations of the parties.

Facts in a legal case must be distinguished from what is considered fact in the layperson's sense of the word and from what might be considered scientific fact. Although the purpose of trial is to get at facts and truth, neither of these is clear at the outset, or there would be no need for a trial; if both parties agree to all the facts relevant to a case, there is nothing left to do but apply the law—no jury is necessary. In a trial, each side presents a different version of the facts. The jury, or the judge in a nonjury trial, must decide what actually happened based on inferences and conclusions drawn from the evidence. The jury (or judge) may believe one side and disbelieve the other, or it may conclude that the truth lies somewhere in between. In many cases, the truth is not readily apparent.

Sometimes fact determinations are supported by very persuasive evidence, but sometimes they are not. Suppose, for example, two litigants were involved in a head-on collision, and each asserts that the other crossed the median line and caused the collision. Assuming that one is telling the truth, how is the jury to determine the facts months after the accident? The jury would be very much aided by disinterested eyewitnesses who confirmed one version rather than the other. Expert witnesses may be called upon to reconstruct the accident by skid marks, the position of the cars after the accident, and

---

trial

A judicial examination, in accordance with the law, of a criminal or civil action. It is an "on-the-record hearing," which means the determination is to be made on the basis of what is presented in court. It is a trial of fact with judgment entered on the law.

trier of fact

Also called *factfinder;* the entity that determines fact in a trial. In a jury trial, the jury is entrusted with factfinding; in a bench trial, the judge necessarily must find the facts as well as make conclusions of law.

verdict

The factfinding by a jury. For example, in a civil case, the jury might find the defendant liable in a dollar amount; in a criminal case, the verdict is usually *guilty* or *not guilty* of each criminal charge.

judgment

The official decision of a court about the rights and claims of each side in a lawsuit; usually a final decision after trial based on findings of fact and making conclusions of law.

the nature of the injuries. Nevertheless, eyewitnesses and expert witnesses can be as equivocal as the participants. Jurors may rely on other inferences: the experience of the drivers, the evidence that one driver had been drinking, and the demeanor of the parties as witnesses (one may seem honest and sincere, the other furtive and evasive). The absolute truth may never be known, but the jury is obliged to draw conclusions about the facts. If standards of scientific proof of fact were required, cases could not be resolved.

Under the adversarial system, then, the facts are assumed to be as concluded by the trier of fact. Even though inferences drawn by the trier of fact may differ from the absolute truth, the assumption of the legal system is that when impartial, reasonable persons deliberate about the facts, their conclusions are as close to the truth as possible and that the process of arriving at the facts is fair to both parties.

Distinguishing fact from law is not a simple matter. Generally, facts are concerned with what happened—answers to the questions of who, when, what, and how. These are **questions or issues of fact**. A **question of law** involves the application or meaning of the law. As a rule of thumb, questions of law and fact are distinguished by whether a particular question requires legal training or knowledge. For example, whether or not the defendant in an auto accident/negligence case was drinking prior to the accident is a question requiring no special legal training. A judge is no better qualified to answer that question from the evidence presented than a layperson, thus identifying this as a question of fact. In contrast, the issue of whether particular evidence of the defendant's drinking is admissible in court is a question of law; the judge is trained and experienced in the rules of evidence and must decide which evidence may properly be presented and which is inadmissible.

The fact/law distinction is not important only for the assignment of labor between judge and jury; it can be critical on appeal. Once a trial has reached final judgment, a disappointed party may seek reversal on appeal. The appellate courts treat questions of law and questions of fact quite differently. Questions of law decided by the trial court judge are not treated deferentially by an appellate court that disagrees. For example, if the trial judge gave the jury an instruction that the appellate court concludes was an incorrect statement of the law, the appellate court would **substitute its judgment** for that of the trial court and order a new trial if the improper instructions constituted **prejudicial error (reversible error)**. Factfinding by judge or jury, however, is treated by the appellate court with great deference and will be overturned only if it is **clearly erroneous** or without **substantial evidence** to support it. This standard makes it extremely difficult to challenge factfinding on appeal (see Exhibit 5-1).

Questions of law and questions of fact are not always distinct. For example, the meaning of words may be either a law or a fact question. The common meaning of a word is a question of fact; the interpretation of a legal term is a question of law. Although judges may not be more competent than laypersons to define *tree, employee* may be used in either a legal sense or an everyday sense. So, if *employee* is used in a statute, its meaning would seem to be a question of law. However, it may not have been used with any particular legal reference and may have been used simply as an ordinary term. Whether a person is an employee for the purposes of inclusion in a collective bargaining unit under the National Labor Relations Act could be treated as either a question of law or a question of fact. Who decides which it is? The judge, of course, or, as put by Isaacs: "Whether a

question (issue) of fact

A question for the jury in a jury trial or for the judge in a bench trial. Fact questions are evidentiary questions concerning who, when, where, and what.

question of law

A question for the judge; that is, a question as to the appropriate law to be applied, or the correct interpretation of the law.

substitution of judgment

The standard of review of conclusions of law made by a lower court.

prejudicial error (reversible error)

Mistakes made at trial that are sufficiently serious to prejudice the result.

clearly erroneous

The test or standard used at the appellate level to determine if *judicial* factfinding at trial constitutes prejudicial error. Highly deferential toward the trial court.

substantial evidence

The test or standard used at the appellate level to determine if *jury* factfinding at trial constitutes prejudicial error. Often used interchangeably with *clearly erroneous.*

EXHIBIT 5-1 FACT/LAW DISTINCTION

LABEL OF THE STANDARD	ISSUE	DEFERENCE PAID TRIAL COURT OR JURY
Substitution of judgment	Law	None—appellate court "substitutes its judgment" for that of trial court.
Clearly erroneous	Fact	Great deference—This is commonly applied to the trial judge's factfinding.
Substantial evidence	Fact	Great deference—When referring to jury factfinding, appellate courts rarely overturn findings of fact.

particular question is to be treated as a question of law or a question of fact is not in itself a question of fact, but a highly artificial question of law" (22 COL. L. REV. 1, 11–12 [1922]).

A criminal defendant may file a motion to suppress, which, if granted, may easily mean that the prosecution must dismiss the case for lack of evidence. As in *Deines*, denial of a motion to suppress often leads the defendant to plead guilty or nolo contendere, with the defendant allowed in some jurisdictions to contest the trial court's denial of the suppression motion. Because the court considers the motion to suppress prior to trial, the court must make findings of fact and then apply the law to determine whether crucial evidence should be suppressed.

STATE of Montana, Plaintiff and Appellee

v.

Todd DEINES, Defendant and Appellant

Supreme Court of Montana

No. DA 08-0371

2009 MT 179, 351 Mont. 1, 208 P.3d 857

Decided May 19, 2009.

The procedural issue on appeal is whether the District Court correctly denied Deines' motion to suppress evidence of driving under the influence of alcohol obtained after Montana Highway Patrol Trooper Michael Briggs (Briggs) stopped Deines for running two red lights. Deines argues that the District Court "misapprehended the effect of the evidence before it" and that this Court should extend a line of cases that

"view with distrust" the failure of law enforcement officers to preserve a record of particular evidentiary matters. Thus, the relevant legal issue presented in this appeal is whether the failure of a police officer to record events creating particularized suspicion for a traffic stop should be viewed with distrust in the judicial assessment of particularized suspicion, when the means to record events are readily available to the officer. . . .

At about 10:38 p.m. on November 24, 2007, Trooper Briggs was waiting in his patrol car at the intersection of Towne Street and Meade Avenue in Glendive for the traffic light to turn green so he could turn left and travel northwest on Towne Street. The light turned green, Briggs turned left, and after traveling a short distance, he noticed Deines' truck traveling in the opposite direction on Towne Street. Briggs testified that he watched Deines' truck drive through a red light at Towne and Meade in his driver's side rearview mirror. Briggs made a U-turn to follow Deines' truck and observed Deines run another red light on Towne and Kendrick. Briggs turned on his overhead lights to initiate a traffic stop after Deines stopped for a red light at Towne and Merrill. Briggs' patrol car was equipped with a video camera that was activated automatically when the overhead lights were engaged.

When Briggs commented that Deines had run two red lights, Deines insisted that the lights were in fact green. Briggs asked Deines' girlfriend, who was also in the truck, whether she noticed that the lights were red. She responded that she did not because she was looking down at her purse. As a result of the traffic stop, Briggs arrested Deines for DUI. Prior to conducting field sobriety tests, Deines told Briggs, "I'm sorry what I did at those stoplights." Deines' preliminary breath test revealed a .132 blood alcohol content (BAC). . . .

The District Court held a hearing on the motion [to suppress] on June 10, 2008, and denied the motion on June 12. Deines pled nolo contendere and reserved his right to appeal the denial of his motion to suppress all evidence for lack of particularized suspicion. Deines now appeals the denial of his motion to suppress. . . .

We review a district court's decision to grant or deny a motion to suppress to determine whether the court's underlying findings of fact are clearly erroneous and whether the court correctly interpreted and applied the law to those findings. "A trial court's findings are clearly erroneous if they are not supported by substantial credible evidence, if the court has misapprehended the effect of the evidence, or if our review of the record leaves us with a definite and firm conviction that a mistake has been made." *State v. Lewis*. . . .

The District Court found that "patrolman Briggs' observation of the Defendant's vehicle from his outside mirror going through a red light and his observation of the Defendant immediately in front of him driving through a second red light is particularized suspicion that justified the officer's stop of the Defendant's vehicle."

Deines argues that the District Court's finding that Briggs had particularized suspicion is clearly erroneous because the court misapprehended the effect of Briggs' testimony by failing to consider that Briggs did not record Deines running the second red light when the means to do so was readily available. Deines argues that this Court should extend a line of cases that advise Montana courts to "view with distrust" the failure of law enforcement to preserve a record of particular evidentiary matters. . . .

[The court reviewed its prior decisions in four cases.]

We decline to extend this "viewed with distrust" precedent to the facts in this case. *Grey, Cassell, Lawrence,* and *Gittens* all concern the unique circumstances requiring Miranda warnings. The U.S. Supreme Court required Miranda warnings in order to protect a detainee's constitutional privilege against self-incrimination from the "inherent coercion" of custodial interrogation. . . . This line of "viewed with distrust" cases mostly relate to police officers gathering evidence in the controlled environment of a police station. This Court has explicitly recognized that circumstances, such as Mirandizing a suspect in the field at the time of arrest, may preclude the creation of a tangible record. . . . Although Briggs' patrol car was equipped with a video camera, Briggs was not interviewing a suspect at the police station, and there is no allegation that Deines' privilege against self-incrimination was infringed due to a failure to receive Miranda warnings in the face of the inherent coercion of custodial interrogation.

Siegal presents the closest factual circumstances to the case at bar. *Siegal* is the rare "viewed with distrust" case involving an investigation outside of the police station. However, this "viewed with distrust" discussion is not binding. The *Siegal* opinion specifically prefaced the analysis quoted above as "future guidance to the courts," which went well beyond the holding of the case. Consequently, the Court's discussion in dicta, that the officer's failure to videotape the gathering of thermal imaging evidence would be viewed with distrust in the judicial assessment of the interpretation of those results, proves of questionable validity. . . .

To view a sworn police officer's statements that he observed actions contributing to particularized suspicion with distrust merely because he failed to videotape his observations in the field would stretch our long-established jurisprudence well beyond constitutional necessity and reason. Deines presents no justification for questioning the District Court's factual determination. This Court has long adhered to the well-established rule that factual determinations are within the purview of the trial courts.

It is not this Court's function, on appeal, to reweigh conflicting evidence or substitute our evaluation of the evidence for that of the district court. We defer to the district court in cases involving conflicting testimony because we recognize that the court had the benefit of observing the demeanor of witnesses and rendering a determination of the credibility of those witnesses.

Gittens. To single out a particular class of witness and suggest that their testimony should be viewed with distrust is a considerable departure from well-established precedent and a significant erosion of the role of the trier of fact. The District Court weighed the conflicting testimony of Officer Briggs and Deines and determined that Officer Briggs' account was more credible. Deines has not convinced us that the District Court's findings of fact were clearly erroneous.

In addition, Deines provides no reason to believe that videotaping the events preceding the traffic stop would have done anything but further corroborate Officer Briggs' testimony. Briggs was not required to take initiative to procure video evidence that Deines alleges would assist his defense. Deines' suggestion that Briggs' failure to videotape him running a second red light amounts to destruction of exculpatory evidence is not supported by our caselaw or the facts. Briggs could have particularized suspicion for the stop based solely on his personal observations. . . .

We conclude that there is no reason to view with distrust the failure of a police officer to record events creating particularized suspicion for a traffic stop. The District Court's finding that Officer Briggs had particularized suspicion to stop Deines was not clearly erroneous and the denial of Deines' motion to suppress was correct.

Case Questions

1. Why did the appellate court defer to the finding that the police officer had particularized suspicion to stop Deines?
2. What was the basis for the court distinguishing the four "viewed with distrust" cases from *Deines*?
3. Why did the court not view the "viewed with distrust" language from *Siegal* as binding?

TRIALS AND TRIAL COURTS

A trial is an "on-the-record" evidentiary hearing. *On the record* refers to the requirement that the facts be determined exclusively on the basis of evidence presented at trial. Evidence of disputed facts is presented by both sides. The plaintiff attempts to establish facts substantiating claims against the defendant, and the defendant attempts to counter the plaintiff's case by questioning and objecting to the plaintiff's evidence, as well as by presenting additional evidence. Evidence takes several forms, including witness testimony, **physical evidence**, and documents. The evidence forms the **record**. Naturally, the jury will make factual inferences based on common sense and experience gained outside the trial, but it is improper for jurors to use knowledge of events that gave rise to the dispute acquired outside of the record. It would be improper, for instance, for a juror to visit the scene of the crime or ask questions of witnesses or bystanders.

physical evidence
Physical objects introduced as evidence, such as a gun, a lock, drugs, and so on.

record
All the evidence presented at trial, whether or not recorded.

jury instructions
Detailed directions (instructions) given by the judge to the jury about its functions in the lawsuit.

Jury Instructions

The jury is given detailed **jury instructions** by the judge about its functions in the lawsuit. Judges' explanations of the proceedings before and during the trial vary, but the most important instructions are given to the jury at the close of the evidence as the jury prepares to deliberate its verdict. These instructions provide only as much explanation of the law as is needed for the jury to dispose of factual questions. For example, in a lawsuit for slander, the judge would instruct the jury about the facts it would need to find to hold the defendant liable for slander namely, (1) the utterance alleged to be slanderous was communicated to a third party and (2) injured the reputation of the plaintiff. In addition, the judge would instruct the jury that if it found the statement to be true, the defendant would not be liable. The jury would also be instructed on what would constitute compensation for injuries sustained. The specifics of these instructions could vary considerably from case to case.

In short, the court delineates the facts that the jury must decide in making its verdict according to the nature of the case, confining the jury to its factfinding function. When the jury reaches a consensus on the facts and presents the judge with its results, the judge makes conclusions of law and enters a judgment.

Before and during trial, the judge makes a series of decisions on the law. The most important of these concern motions to dismiss the lawsuit in favor of one of the parties, admission of evidence and the propriety of its presentation, and instructions to the jury. In each decision, the judge applies legal principles, which the judge could interpret or apply incorrectly. The correctness of the judge's rulings forms the basis for appeal.

Clark County School District v. Virtual Education Software illustrates the interplay between jury findings of fact and the appellate court feeling free to substitute its judgment on the law for that of the trial court. In *Clark County*, the issue of first impression was the type of claim the plaintiff could make for statements the school district employee had made about the plaintiff's product. The trial court assumed that that plaintiff was claiming that the defendant had defamed the plaintiff and thus gave the jury instructions about the facts the jury would need to find to hold the school district liable for defamation. Although the jury's findings of fact would have been sufficient to support a defamation claim, the highest court in Nevada decided that the plaintiff's claim more properly should have been for business disparagement.

CLARK COUNTY SCHOOL DISTRICT,
A Nevada Political Subdivision, Appellant

v.

VIRTUAL EDUCATION SOFTWARE, INC.,
A Nevada Corporation, Respondent

Supreme Court of Nevada

No. 50313

213 P.3d 496

Aug. 6, 2009.

In this appeal, we consider . . . whether allegedly defamatory statements made about a business's product provide a basis for defamation per se or for business disparagement.

We . . . conclude that when allegedly defamatory statements concern a business's product and the plaintiff seeks to redress injury to economic interest, the claim is one for business disparagement, not defamation per se. . . .

Appellant Clark County School District (CCSD) and Clark County Education Association (CCEA), the local teachers' union, are parties to a collective bargaining agreement, which sets the terms and conditions of employment for CCSD teachers. The agreement includes a provision for teachers to enhance their salaries by obtaining additional degrees, taking either upper-division, graduate-level courses or completing professional development courses offered by CCSD. However, educational courses that are not credit bearing toward a degree may be excluded from the courses eligible for salary enhancement. In addition, CCSD may deny credit for courses that it deems are of a "frivolous nature."

Respondent Virtual Education Software, Inc. (VESI), is a Nevada corporation that markets and sells computer-based instruction for educators and business professionals. . . .

Dr. George Ann Rice, the associate superintendent of CCSD's human resources department in 2002, had the responsibility for making the final determination as to whether a course complied with the collective bargaining agreement. Because of concerns regarding the academic rigor of VESI courses and their compliance with the collective bargaining agreement, Dr. Rice asked her administrative assistant to research and evaluate the VESI courses. . . .

After reviewing VESI's courses, Dr. Rice's assistant noted several concerns with the academic quality of the courses. . . . As a result, Dr. Rice determined that the courses did not comply with the requirements of the collective bargaining agreement between CCSD and CCEA for salary enhancement. . . . On November 6, 2002, Dr. Rice sent a letter to VESI's president, with copies to other school administrators and CCSD counsel, explaining CCSD's decision to deny salary advancement credit for VESI courses. . . .

VESI filed a complaint with the district court, alleging five causes of action against CCSD, including defamation. The district court dismissed all but VESI's defamation claims. . . . VESI based its claims for defamation on Dr. Rice's November 6, 2002, letter to VESI's president, and at least 12 communications to CCSD teachers, including e-mails sent by CCSD administrative staff. . . .

At trial, VESI presented its case-in-chief, offering evidence that it had suffered an economic downturn, but only tenuously indicated that any economic damages were proximately caused by CCSD's statements. . . . The jury returned a special verdict form, finding that four of the six communications constituted defamation by CCSD. Specifically, the jury found that, in addition to Dr. Rice's November 6, 2002, letter, three e-mail communications to individual CCSD teachers were defamatory. All three e-mails were written by Dr. Rice's assistant to individual teachers. The first e-mail provided, in part:

> This is not a new policy. The contract states that courses must be credit bearing towards a degree and courses such as those offered by VESI have only

recently come to our attention as violating contract. Be wary of these 3rd party entities. If the university offering credit will not include them even as an elective in their program, there is something remiss with the course.

The second e-mail provided, in part:

> Credit bearing toward a degree does NOT mean a particular individual must be in that degree program, only that the university offering it values the course enough to allow at least elective credit w/i their own university. VESI is a consulting agency and many of the courses have been deemed "[frivolous.]" None of the colleges sponsoring the courses offer degree credit for them so, yes, they should not be taken for salary growth.

The third e-mail communication provided:

> Thank you for your recent letter to Dr. Rice regarding VESI courses. The 3 classes you have already taken . . . will be allowed for salary growth. . . but as they do not comply with the CCEA Negotiated agreement, please be sure any future courses are upper division or graduate credits and are listed in a degree program of the university offering the credit.

The jury awarded damages of $161,024 to VESI. The district court also found that VESI met its offer of judgment and was therefore entitled to an award of attorney fees. Thereafter, the district court awarded VESI prejudgment interest and attorney fees and entered judgment in VESI's favor in the total amount of $340,622.40. CCSD appeals. . . .

A claim for defamation per se primarily serves to protect the personal reputation of an individual. But where communications concern the goods or services provided by a business entity, a plaintiff generally seeks to redress injury to economic interests. . . . The elements required to prove a cause of action for business disparagement differ from the elements required to prove classic defamation and, necessarily, defamation per se. To succeed in a claim for business disparagement, the plaintiff must prove: (1) a false and disparaging statement, (2) the unprivileged publication by the defendant, (3) malice, and (4) special damages. Notably, the principal differences between defamation per se and business disparagement concern the elements of intent and damages. As opposed to defamation, which merely requires some evidence of fault amounting to at least negligence, business disparagement requires something more, namely, malice. Malice is proven when the plaintiff can show either that the defendant published the disparaging statement with the intent to cause harm to the plaintiff's pecuniary interests, or the defendant published a disparaging remark knowing its falsity or with reckless disregard for its truth. . . .

[A] cause of action for business disparagement requires that the plaintiff set forth evidence proving economic loss that is attributable to the defendant's disparaging remarks. Lastly, if the plaintiff cannot show the loss of specific sales attributable to the disparaging statement, the plaintiff may show evidence of a general decline of business. Nonetheless, the general decline of business must be the result of the disparaging statements and the plaintiff must eliminate other potential causes.

We thus conclude that VESI failed as a matter of law to establish the elements of intent and damages for a claim of business disparagement. First, although there was substantial evidence for the jury to conclude that the information contained in the e-mail communications was false and disparaging, VESI failed to prove that CCSD maliciously intended to cause VESI pecuniary loss, or that CCSD acted with malice because it knew the statements were false or acted in reckless disregard of their falsity. CCSD drafted the e-mail communications in response to individual teachers' inquiries regarding whether CCSD would accept VESI courses for salary enhancement. Although there was some indication that the statements in the e-mails may be false, VESI did not present evidence for the jury to conclude that CCSD acted with reckless disregard when it responded to teachers' questions or concerns regarding VESI's courses. . . .

[W]e reverse the jury's verdict as to the . . . three e-mail communications since the verdict was improperly based on a claim for defamation per se. Because VESI sought compensation for economic loss for defamatory statements about its products, VESI's claim was one for business disparagement and not defamation per se. Further, VESI could not have proven the elements of business disparagement because it did not produce sufficient evidence of malice or of special damages that were proximately caused by CCSD's disparaging statements.

Case Questions

1. Why should the claim have been for business disparagement rather than defamation?
2. How do the elements of defamation differ from the elements of business disparagement?
3. How did the plaintiff fail to establish intent?
4. How did the plaintiff fail to establish damages?

APPELLATE COURTS

The courts above the trial court level to which appeals may be taken are called **appellate courts**. The most common arrangement in the state hierarchy echoes that of the federal court system (see Exhibit 5-2), with an intermediate appellate court and a court of last resort (e.g., Colorado Court of Appeals, Colorado Supreme Court). Some states, like Florida (see Exhibit 5-3), have a two-tiered trial court system in which one court handles cases of lesser import, often limited by a dollar amount, and misdemeanor cases, whereas the other court has jurisdiction over felonies and civil cases above the specified dollar amount. In this arrangement, the "higher" court may serve as an appellate court for cases decided in the lower court. Illinois is a state with a single trial court, an intermediate appellate court, and a court of last resort (see Exhibit 5-4).

Although the drama of the courtroom receives the greatest amount of attention from the media and the public, legal professionals are primarily concerned with appellate court decisions because of stare decisis. Trial courts interpret and apply the law, but appellate courts state the law with greater authority. Because they establish

appellate courts
As distinguished from *trial courts,* courts that function primarily to correct errors of the lower, trial courts and do not ordinarily serve as factfinders. The two common forms of appellate courts are intermediate appellate courts, usually called courts of appeal(s), and the highest courts, usually called supreme courts.

EXHIBIT 5-2   FEDERAL COURTS

TYPE OF COURT	NAME OF FEDERAL COURT
Court of last resort	United States Supreme Court
Intermediate appellate court	United States court of appeals
Trial court	United States district court

EXHIBIT 5-3   FLORIDA STATE COURTS

TYPE OF COURT	NAME OF COURT
Court of last resort	Florida Supreme Court
Intermediate appellate court	district court of appeal
Upper-level trial court	circuit court
Lower-level trial court	county court

EXHIBIT 5-4   ILLINOIS STATE COURTS

TYPE OF COURT	NAME OF COURT
Court of last resort	Supreme Court of Illinois
Intermediate appellate court	appellate court
Trial court	circuit court

appellant

The party bringing an appeal against the other party, the *appellee.*

appellee

The party against whom an appeal is brought.

precedent for future cases, appellate courts not only settle disputes but also have an impact beyond the case at hand.

The appellate process is quite different from trial. The appellate court does not retry facts, nor does it call witnesses. It receives a record from the trial court, which includes a written transcript of the testimony at trial, exhibits introduced during trial, copies of the pleadings and motions filed with the court before and during trial, and written briefs submitted by the attorneys for **appellant** and **appellee** arguing the issues raised on appeal.

Attorneys for the parties are given a limited time to make oral arguments before the appellate court, during which the appellate judges may ask questions concerning the case. Deliberation of the case following oral argument is governed by the customs of the particular court, but at some point a vote is taken, and usually a single judge will be assigned to write the opinion for the court in consultation with the other judges. Judges disagreeing with the result may write dissenting opinions; judges agreeing with the result may wish to add comments in a concurring opinion. There can be a considerable lapse of time between the oral argument and the issuance of a written opinion, depending largely on the complexities of the legal issues raised and the extent of disagreement among the judges.

Although the appellate court is limited to the record before it with regard to the dispute, its research of the law and its legal arguments may go beyond the cases and arguments made by attorneys for appellant and appellee in their briefs and oral arguments. Because decisions of the appellate courts may establish precedent for future cases, appellate judges are not concerned simply with resolving the dispute at hand; they must also consider the impact of their interpretation of the law on future cases. At trial, the judge is constrained to proceed in a timely fashion, making rulings that will not delay the process and issuing a decision as soon as possible to define the rights of the parties. By contrast, the appellate process may be described as deliberative. The attorneys representing the parties have the opportunity to reflect on their arguments and craft carefully reasoned briefs, and the appellate court will take the time necessary to examine the law to write a reasoned decision. Steadily rising caseloads in appellate courts have put pressure on the courts, but it is fair to say that cases of great import receive corresponding attention by appellate courts.

Appellate courts have two primary functions in deciding appeals: (1) resolve the dispute and (2) state the law. Many cases raise minor issues, dispute well-established rules, or have no particular merit (e.g., many criminal appeals are at government expense, so the convicted party has nothing to lose by appealing). When no significant issue of law is decided or if prior law is followed, many jurisdictions do not require that the opinion be published. In some instances the court will write a cursory **memorandum decision** or **per curiam opinion** that disposes of the case without elaborate reasoning. Lengthy reasoning is reserved for cases that raise new or controversial legal issues.

As at the trial level, court rules govern the procedure to be followed in pursuing an appeal, in part to ensure that the process is fair. An appellate court has the authority to sanction a party who fails to follow appellate court rules. In *Alva*, the attorney filed the appeal six minutes late, and this untimely filing resulted in the appeal being dismissed. Although dismissal of the appeal is quite harsh, the court indicates that the late filing was only one of the mistakes made by the attorney.

memorandum decision (per curiam opinion) A court's decision that gives the ruling (what it decides and orders done) but no opinion (reasons for the decision). A *memorandum opinion* is the same as a *per curiam opinion*, which is an opinion without a named author, usually a brief and unanimous decision.

Sergio ALVA; Luz Alva; Silvio Alva, Plaintiffs-Appellants

v.

TEEN HELP, a partnership; Worldwide Association of Specialty Programs, a corporation; Resource Realizations, a corporation; R & B Billing, a corporation; Dixie Contract Services, a corporation; Teen Escort Services, a corporation; Ken Kay; Robert B. Lichfield; Karr Farnsworth; Brent M. Facer, Defendants-Appellees

United States Court of Appeals, Tenth Circuit

No. 04-4012

469 F.3d 946

Nov. 22, 2006.

Plaintiffs Sergio Alva and his parents, Luz and Silvio Alva, appeal from the district court's grant of summary judgment to Defendants Teen Help, World Wide Association of Specialty Programs, R & B Billing, Dixie Contract Services, Robert Lichfield, Karr

Farnsworth and Brent Facer (Defendants). Because Plaintiffs' notice of appeal is untimely, we dismiss this appeal for lack of jurisdiction. . . .

Defendants did not contest the timeliness of Plaintiffs' notice of appeal. Nevertheless, because it appeared to be untimely, we required Plaintiffs to show cause why this appeal should not be dismissed for lack of jurisdiction and also permitted Defendants to file a brief. We specifically directed the parties to discuss *Eberhardt* and *Kontrick*, two recent [United States] Supreme Court cases suggesting [that] time prescription rules are sometimes mistakenly regarded as jurisdictional. After reviewing Plaintiffs' response to the order to show cause and Defendants' brief, we conclude [that] the requirement for a timely notice of appeal in a civil case is not a "claim-processing rule" subject to forfeiture under either *Eberhardt* or *Kontrick* but a jurisdictional prerequisite to our review. . . .

Both 28 U.S.C. §2107(a) and Rule 4(a) of the Federal Rules of Appellate Procedure require a notice of appeal in a civil case to be filed with the district clerk within thirty days after the judgment or order appealed from is entered. A judgment is deemed entered when the judgment is set forth on a separate document . . . and entered in the civil docket.

Here, the judgment, which was set forth on a separate document, was entered in the civil docket on Wednesday, December 17, 2003. Pursuant to Rule 26(a) of the Federal Rules of Civil Appellate Procedure, Plaintiffs had until Friday, January 16, 2004, to file their notice of appeal. Although the notice of appeal was dated January 16, 2004, it was not filed until 12:06 A.M. on January 17, 2004. Thus, it is untimely. . . .

The late filing is consistent with Plaintiffs' cavalier approach to litigation. On November 25, 2002, the district court issued a scheduling order setting July 15, 2003, as the factual discovery deadline. Plaintiffs did not conduct any discovery. When Defendants filed their motion for summary judgment on August 5, 2003, Plaintiffs sought a motion to stay the hearing on Defendants' motion until after they deposed the individual defendants and to compel the individual defendants to appear for their noticed depositions. (Although Plaintiffs had noticed the individual defendants' depositions for August 20 and 21, 2003, Defendants informed Plaintiffs they would not appear without a court order because the depositions were scheduled after the discovery deadline.) The district court denied the motion to stay and to compel, finding Plaintiffs had been dilatory:

> [Plaintiffs'] eleventh hour effort to depose the individual Defendants was the *sole* discovery effort made by Plaintiffs since they brought this action in February 2000. Indeed, Plaintiffs have not propounded a single interrogatory, request for admission or request for production. They have not issued a single subpoena or taken a single deposition. . . .

Nothing in Plaintiffs' response to the order to show cause convinces us to the contrary. In it, their attorney states he was aware January 16 was the last day to file a notice of appeal and that he personally filed the appeal on January 16 just before midnight but that when he withdrew the document from the time-stamp slot, it indicated it was filed at 12:06 A.M. He does "not understand why it was stamped 12:06 or know whether the stamp clock was precisely calibrated on that day. . . . At the time, [he] regarded the stamped date as inaccurate and de minimis, and so proceeded with the appeal." . . . He noted on the docketing statement that "[he] had filed the Notice of Appeal on time, but that the stamp date was January 17." (*Id.*) No further explanation was offered. In any event, he claims he made every effort to meet the deadline and emphasizes no one, except this Court, has ever objected to the late filing. Had someone objected, he states he would have moved for an extension of time under Rule 4(a)(5) on the grounds of excusable neglect. In summary, he claims "[i]t would be inequitable, after more than two years of waiting for a decision, and after all of [Plaintiffs'] briefing and additional submissions . . . , to dismiss this case for lack of jurisdiction over a barely tardy appeal, an issue that, if not apparent on the face of the Notice itself, was plainly and forthrightly raised by the Docketing Statement and Case Summary within 60 days of the appeal[ ] being filed." . . .

By his own admission, counsel knew the appeal was six minutes late according to the court's file stamp. That file stamp, not counsel's watch or memory, controls. Knowing the notice of appeal was late according to court records, counsel could have and should have filed a motion for extension of time with the district court. . . . Most probably such a request would have been granted if timely made. . . .

To the extent Plaintiffs are asking this Court to find excusable neglect and extend the time for filing their notice of appeal, we have no authority to do so. Only the district court may do so and only under limited circumstances and for a limited time. Because that time has passed without a request from Plaintiffs or action by the court, the bar fell, fatally.

As we explain, a timely notice of appeal in a civil case is jurisdictional, not merely compliance with a "claim processing rule" subject to forfeiture for failure to object. Therefore counsel's failure to timely act cannot be excused for want of an objection from opposing counsel. Nor can counsel's failure be excused based upon a good faith reliance on *Eberhardt* or *Kontrick*. *Eberhardt* was decided in 2005 and *Kontrick* was decided only days before counsel filed the notice of appeal. . . .

The subject-matter jurisdiction of lower federal courts is within the plenary control of Congress. U.S. CONST., art. III, § 1. In 28 U.S.C. § 1291, Congress provided:

> The courts of appeals (other than the United States Court of Appeals for the Federal Circuit) shall have jurisdiction of appeals from all final decisions of the district courts of the United States, the United States District Court for the District of the Canal Zone, the District Court of Guam, and the District Court of the Virgin Islands, except where a direct review may be had in the Supreme Court. . . .

For nearly sixty years we have treated the timely filing of a notice of appeal in both criminal and civil actions as mandatory and jurisdictional. . . . However, two recent Supreme Court cases appear (at least at first blush) to call into doubt this long line of precedent. . . .

Neither *Eberhardt* nor *Kontrick* affects the jurisdictional nature of the timely filing of an civil appeal. *Kontrick* involved bankruptcy rules 4004 and 9006; *Eberhardt* involved criminal procedural rules 33

and 45. None of these rules derive expressly from a statute. Rule 4(a), on the other hand, implements 28 U.S.C. § 2107. And that statute is specifically mentioned in *Kontrick* as an example of a jurisdictional provision containing a "built-in time constraint[ ]." . . .

Even assuming, *arguendo,* that *Eberhardt* can be read as calling into question the jurisdictional nature of 28 U.S.C. § 2107, as well as Rule 4(a), we decline to upset past precedent without an express ruling to that effect. . . . When a statute unambiguously constrains our jurisdiction, rules implementing that constraint have passed muster with Congress and sixty years of jurisprudence have cemented the jurisdictional nature of a timely notice of appeal in civil cases, it is not the place of a court of appeals to engage in a contrary flight of fancy. Excursions into that rarified air are the exclusive province of the United States Supreme Court.

Notwithstanding the jurisdictional nature of the timely filing of an appeal, nothing in *Kontrick* or *Eberhardt* upsets our ability to enforce our own rules. In both cases, *a party* sought to enforce a rule after the court had reached the merits. In both cases, the Supreme Court held *the party* had forfeited its right to invoke the rule. Neither case involved a court enforcing a rule. Indeed, a holding that a court may not enforce its own rules unless a party timely invokes them would be nonsensical. Such a holding would place a court at the mercy of the parties.

Case Questions

1. Why did the court, on its own, raise the question of whether the late filing had an impact on the court's jurisdiction?
2. Why did the court characterize the plaintiffs' attorney's approach to litigation as "cavalier"?
3. What would have been an easy method for dealing with the late filing?

Prejudicial Error

The appellate court examines the record and arguments to determine whether prejudicial (also called *reversible*) error occurred at the lower court level. The court does not impose an impossibly perfect standard on the trial court but must determine whether mistaken actions constitute grounds for reversal. For example, the court may conclude that although one of the instructions to the jury was not an exact statement of the law, given the facts and circumstances of the case, a precise statement of the law would not have changed the jury's verdict. This would be considered *harmless error* that did not prejudice the case and would not be grounds for reversal. In some instances the appellate court may agree with the trial court's result but disagree with its reasoning, in which situation the court may substitute its reasoning in an affirming opinion or **remand** the case for the lower court to rewrite the decision in accord with the appellate court's instructions. A remand for a new decision would also be appropriate when no error was committed in factfinding but there was prejudicial error in the application of law. For instance, the appellate court might hold that the trial court had no authority to award **punitive damages**, so that portion of the decision would be deleted, leaving the award of **compensatory damages** intact.

Reversible error may or may not call for a new trial. The appellate court might find, for example, that the trial court was incorrect in ruling that the statute of limitations had not run, thereby barring further suit. The appellate court may conclude that the trial court was wrong in granting a plaintiff's motion for judgment notwithstanding the verdict, the effect of which was to reject the verdict in favor of the defendant and enter a judgment in favor of the plaintiff; the result of the appellate reversal would be to reinstate the jury's verdict and enter a judgment in favor of the defendant. In contrast, the appellate court might find that instructions to the jury or a ruling on the admissibility of evidence so prejudiced the factfinding process that the error can be corrected only by a new trial.

In short, reversible error refers to reversal of the *judgment* of the lower court. Because the judgment is based on findings of fact and conclusions of law, either or both could constitute harmful error, and the order of the appellate court is designed to correct the error in the most expeditious manner.

In the murder trial at issue in *Carruthers v. State,* the evidence was conclusive that Carruthers slit Jannette Williams's throat and stabbed her 11 times in the chest. On appeal, there was no credible argument against the guilty verdict. In murder cases in Georgia, however, once guilt has been determined, the jury must then choose between life imprisonment and death in the sentencing phase of the trial. Prosecutor and defense attorney are likely to make impassioned arguments before the jury to persuade the jurors of either of these sentences. On occasion, the prosecutor may go too far and make improper remarks that an appellate court may find to be prejudicial. The appeal in this situation presents a special feature: because murder trials have two phases, error in the sentencing phase may be separable from the trial-of-fact phase. The jury has been dismissed, however; what is the court to do?

remand

Sending a case back to a lower court; done by a higher court.

punitive damages

Sometimes awarded beyond mere compensation (see *compensatory damages*) to punish a defendant for outrageous conduct in tort.

compensatory damages

Amount awarded to an injured party to make her whole; that is, in tort, to compensate for all injuries, and in contract, to put the nonbreaching party in the position he would have been in if the contract had been performed.

Anthony **CARRUTHERS**

v.

STATE

Supreme Court of Georgia

528 S.E.2d 217 (2000)

Anthony Carruthers was convicted of the malice murder of Jannette Williams and sentenced to death. Carruthers contends that the assistant district attorney made several improper arguments that warrant reversal of the death sentence. Finding no reversible error in the guilt/innocence phase of Carruthers' trial, we affirm the jury's verdict of guilt on all charges. However, because we conclude that the trial court erred in allowing the state to urge the jury to follow the religious mandates of the Bible rather than Georgia law, we reverse the sentence of death and remand the case for another jury to consider the proper sentence for the murder. . . .

The United States Constitution and the Georgia Constitution guarantee criminal defendants the right to due process at trial. In addition, OCGA § 17-10-35 requires this Court to review the death sentence to determine whether it "was imposed under the influence of passion, prejudice, or any other arbitrary factor."

Carruthers filed a motion in limine to exclude during closing argument any Bible passages that appealed to the passion of the jury and would encourage it to impose a death sentence based on religion. During a pre-argument hearing, the prosecutor said that he intended to cite passages from the Books of Romans, Genesis, and Matthew. The defendant objected to the biblical references, but the trial court overruled the objection and allowed the three passages.

During closing argument, the state urged the jury to impose a death sentence because the Bible states that society must deter criminals by taking the life of persons who kill other people. The state argued as follows:

> Now, ladies and gentlemen, let me talk to you a moment about some biblical references that help us in this case. Deterrence is very important and the Bible suggests to us why deterrence is appropriate. Romans tells us that every person is subject to the governing authority, every person is subject. And in Matthew it tells us, who sheddeth man's blood by man shall his blood be shed for in the image of God made [he] man. For all they who take the sword shall die by the sword, and this is a message that is very clear, that society must deter criminals.

This Court has noted its concern about the use of biblical authority during closing arguments in death penalty trials. . . . By quoting these texts during closing arguments, prosecutors may "diminish the jury's sense of responsibility and imply that another, higher law should be applied in capital cases, displacing the law in the court's instructions."

Although we have long declined to disapprove of passing, oratorical references to religious texts in arguments by counsel, we have distinguished those fleeting references from more direct references that urge that the teachings of a particular religion command the imposition of a death penalty. In contrast to biblical law, Georgia law gives the jury the discretion to recommend life imprisonment or death, provides stringent procedures and safeguards that must be followed during the trial, and permits the jury to impose the death penalty only in limited circumstances.

In addition, we have specifically disapproved of a prosecutor quoting verses from the Bible to support the death penalty. In *Hammond v. State*, we concluded that it was improper for the assistant district attorney to argue that the defendant had violated the law of God that "whoever sheds the blood of man by man shall his blood be shed." Despite this disapproval and repeated admonitions, prosecutors have continued to quote the Bible and urge its teachings, and trial courts have continued to permit the arguments.

Unlike previous cases, however, where the defendant failed to object to the state's religious arguments at trial, the defense in this case anticipated the argument and tried to prevent it by filing a motion in limine, but the trial court denied the motion. Because the defendant received an adverse ruling on his objection, the standard of review in this case is not whether the improper argument in reasonable probability changed the result of the trial, but simply whether the argument was objectionable and prejudicial.

It is difficult to draw a precise line between religious arguments that are acceptable and those that are objectionable, but we conclude that the assistant district attorney in this case overstepped the line in directly quoting religious authority as mandating a death sentence. In citing specific passages, he invoked a higher moral authority and diverted the jury from the discretion provided to them under state law. . . .

Therefore, we find that Carruthers' right to due process as secured by OCGA § 17-10-35, the Georgia Constitution, and the Constitution of the United States was abridged when the trial court allowed the inappropriate arguments from the Bible over objection. Because we cannot conclude beyond a reasonable doubt that the violation of Carruthers' state and federal constitutional rights was harmless, we reverse the jury's death sentence and remand the case for resentencing. . . .

Judgment affirmed in part and reversed in part. All the Justices concur, except Carley, J., who concurs in part and dissents in part.

CARLEY, Justice, concurring in part and dissenting in part.

. . . A reversal of the death sentence on this basis runs counter to the long-standing principle that "the range of discussion (during closing argument) is wide—very wide. . . . [The prosecutor's] illustrations may be as various as are the resources of his genius; his argumentation as full and profound as his learning can make it; and he may, if he will, give play to his wit, or wing to his imagination." "Counsel may bring to his use in the discussion of the case well-established historical facts and may allude to such principles of divine law relating to transactions of men as may be appropriate to the case." Counsel for the State may forcibly or even extravagantly attempt to impress upon the jury "the enormity of the offense and the solemnity of their duty in relation thereto." *Conner v. State.* . . . Here, the prosecutor used Biblical references only to illustrate the historical and moral underpinnings of deterrence as a justifying factor for imposing the death penalty. He did not improperly argue that Carruthers deserved to die for any reason other than that authorized under the secular law of this state. Instead, he made only an emotional exhortation that our contemporary reliance upon the deterrent effect of capital punishment has its roots in religious teachings. In the State's argument, the Bible did not supplant applicable statutes, but rather explicated those enactments. . . .

In *Conner v. State*, supra at 122 (5), this Court noted that it had never "invalidated a death penalty simply because the prosecutor made an impassioned argument to the jury during the sentencing phase of the trial." With today's opinion, that is no longer true. Henceforth, death sentences are subject to reversal if an emotional argument by the State does not satisfy the sensibilities of a majority of the Justices on this Court. . . .

Case Questions

1. What was improper about the prosecutor's remarks with regard to sentencing?
2. What was the basis of the dissent's disagreement concerning the propriety of the prosecutor's remarks?

IMPACT OF THE APPELLATE SYSTEM

Appellate courts serve as a brake on the arbitrariness of trial judges as well as a forum for establishing uniformity in the interpretation of the law. The right to appeal is a fundamental custom of our legal system. Trial court judges naturally dislike being reversed, so the threat of appeal that lurks behind every case encourages them to conform to the law as stated by higher authority. In states having both intermediate courts and courts of last resort, a disappointed litigant has two opportunities for appellate review of the case. Courts of last resort have great discretion in choosing cases for review and decline to hear most cases. Intermediate appellate courts also have significant discretion in the cases they hear and the time they wish to devote to a case.

These factors limit the numbers of appeals, as does the prohibitive cost. Not only are substantial attorney's fees involved in preparing for appeal, but the cost of reproducing the trial transcript in a lengthy trial is an economic burden as well. Appeals therefore tend to involve cases in which the cost of appeal is borne by the government, as in criminal cases, or that involve significant amounts of money. Some appeals are subsidized by outside groups that have an interest in setting a precedent or in representing appellants, such as in a civil rights action. Because of these factors, appeals are not a representative sample of the cases that go to trial.

Appellate decisions also affect lawyers, who must evaluate their client's chances by predicting the outcome of trial and appeal. Most cases are settled without going to trial or appeal; settlement is encouraged by well-established principles of law that allow attorneys to assess whether a case is a winner or a loser. Indirectly, the costs of trial and appeal encourage litigants to make realistic decisions about whether to proceed.

In *Irby*, the compensation board made the initial decision to award death benefits. After a court reversed the board's decision, the Alaska court of last resort decided that the board had been correct. Because the lower court's error was prejudicial, the Alaska Supreme Court remanded to give the lower court the opportunity to reinstate the board's decision.

Edward P. IRBY, Deceased, and Cartrie Irby, Edward P. Irby II, and Hannah C. Irby, Beneficiaries, Appellants

v.

FAIRBANKS GOLD MINING, INC., and Old Republic Insurance Co., Appellees

Supreme Court of Alaska

No. S-12680

203 P.3d 1138

March 20, 2009.

This appeal concerns the timeliness of a March 2004 workers' compensation claim. Edward Irby disappeared in an apparent industrial accident on April 13, 1997. Irby's wife promptly petitioned the Fairbanks district court for a presumptive death certificate, but in October 1997 the district court jury determined there was insufficient evidence to presume Irby dead. In 2003 Irby's son filed a second presumptive death petition; the jury in this second proceeding decided in October 2003 that Irby was presumed dead in the industrial accident. Irby's widow filed a workers' compensation claim for herself and her children in March 2004. The Alaska Workers' Compensation Board rejected Irby's employer's contention that the claim was untimely and awarded death benefits. The employer appealed to the superior court, which reversed. It held that the one-year statute of limitations, AS 23.30.105(a), began running on April 13, 2002, when Irby was presumed dead per AS 13.06.035(5),

and that the March 2004 claim was therefore untimely. Applying **tolling** principles and because Irby's family acted reasonably in pursuing a presumptive death certificate before filing a claim for workers' compensation benefits, we hold that the claim was timely and remand for reinstatement of the board's decision and order. . . .

Edward Irby worked as a truck driver at the Fort Knox Mine, operated by Fairbanks Gold Mining, Inc. The event resulting in this workers' compensation claim happened about two days after Irby began training to operate a bulldozer. On April 13, 1997, the bulldozer Irby was operating traveled backward down a steep slope into a tailing pond and broke through the ice. The bulldozer was completely submerged. No one saw the accident, but Irby's shift supervisor, observing that Irby was not at his assigned location, discovered the accident site shortly after Irby was last seen. . . .

In a workers' compensation appeal from the superior court we directly review the board decision. Application of the relevant statute of limitations is a legal question involving no agency expertise; accordingly, we substitute our judgment, adopting the rule of law that is most persuasive in light of precedent, reason, and policy. The board's factual findings are reviewed to see if they are supported by substantial evidence. "Substantial evidence is 'such relevant evidence as a reasonable mind might accept as adequate to support a conclusion.'" . . .

We have previously stated that even though the defense of statute of limitations is a legitimate defense, we look on it with disfavor and "will strain neither the law nor the facts in its aid." We have identified several policies served by limitations periods: providing defendants with notice of the nature of adverse claims and barring plaintiffs who have slept on their rights, as well as protecting against prejudice from stale claims. Here, Fairbanks Gold had notice of the claim: it indicated in a 1997 letter to its workers' compensation carrier that the first jury verdict stayed Cartrie's claim for benefits and that the claim would "go into excess" at some point. In 1998 its workers' compensation carrier instructed Fairbanks Gold to leave a reserve on that claim. The evidence also suggests that the Irbys did not sleep on their rights. Cartrie promptly filed the first presumptive death petition only seven weeks after the accident. In 1998 Cartrie contacted Fairbanks Gold, the workers' compensation adjuster, and board staff seeking advice about pursuing a claim for benefits and information about reports or other evidence related to the accident. In 2000 she again contacted Fairbanks Gold to see if it had any new information about the accident. The record also shows that the Irbys contacted the Fairbanks court in 1999 and again in 2002 about filing another presumptive death petition. Finally, nothing indicates that any evidence became more stale between the running of the five-year presumptive death period and the time Edward II filed the second presumptive death proceeding.

Under the doctrine of equitable tolling, when a party has more than one legal remedy available, the statute of limitations is tolled while the party pursues one of the possible remedies. In *Gudenau v. Sweeney Insurance, Inc.*, we adopted a three-part test for equitable tolling: (1) the alternative remedy must give notice to the defendant; (2) the defendant must not be prejudiced; and (3) the plaintiff must have acted reasonably and in good faith. The initial remedy must be pursued in a judicial or quasi-judicial forum. A party is generally entitled to the full statutory period after the circumstances which justify equitable tolling abate.

Because the statute of limitations on workers' compensation death benefits runs from the time of death and because Fairbanks Gold insisted that Irby was still alive, the Irby beneficiaries needed to establish a date of death or presumed death.... Here, Cartrie had more than one way to pursue a finding of Irby's death. To obtain a presumptive death certificate from the

state, she could either file a presumptive death petition in district court or, after five years had elapsed, begin a superior court proceeding, presumably in probate....

Cartrie initially chose to file a presumptive death petition in district court shortly after Irby's disappearance. Her actions were reasonable: a district court presumptive death hearing is the only way to obtain a certificate of presumptive death without waiting five years, and, given the circumstances of Irby's disappearance, it was not unreasonable for her to think that a jury would find that he had died at the mine.

After the first jury decided that the evidence was insufficient to presume that Irby was dead, Fairbanks Gold filed its second **controversion** with the board, specifically relying on the jury verdict. Because the 1997 verdict did not establish the presumptive death, and because Fairbanks Gold took the position that as a result of that verdict no workers' compensation benefits were payable, Cartrie cannot be faulted for failing to file a claim for benefits after the jury returned its 1997 verdict. In effect, given the jury's verdict in 1997, the time in which to file a claim was not yet running.

In addition, when Cartrie contacted the board in 1998, she received conflicting advice. One staff member suggested that the statute of limitations had already run, while a second indicated that filing for death benefits could be "premature." The insurance adjuster offered her no information about pursuing a claim, even though she had no attorney at the time. Based on Fairbanks Gold's controversion and the conflicting advice she received from the board, it was reasonable for Cartrie not to file a workers' compensation claim immediately.

It was also reasonable for the Irbys to wait for the five-year presumptive death period to pass before taking further action. The parties agree that there was no time limit by which the Irbys needed to refile a presumptive death petition. Here, Edward II filed the second presumptive death petition about six years after Irby's disappearance. The one-year delay in filing beyond the five-year presumptive death period was not per se unreasonable. As we noted earlier, the Irbys inquired of Fairbanks Gold and the court during the time between the first jury verdict and the filing of the second presumptive death petition....

Fairbanks Gold had ample notice of the circumstances of the accident, the two presumptive death petitions, and the workers' compensation claim. . . . The board's finding that Fairbanks Gold had ample opportunity to investigate and defend the claim indicates that Fairbanks Gold was not prejudiced by any delay in pursuing a presumptive death certificate before filing a claim for death benefits.

We conclude that there are no genuine factual disputes as to any of the elements of equitable tolling and that the parties had a fair opportunity to dispute parallel issues before the board. The Irbys satisfy the elements of equitable tolling: the Irbys' pursuit of a presumptive death certificate and related inquiries gave adequate notice of the claim to Fairbanks Gold; Fairbanks Gold was not prejudiced; and the Irbys acted reasonably and in good faith in pursuing a presumptive death certificate before filing their claim for death benefits, particularly in light of Fairbanks Gold's December 1997 controversion. Their claim was filed within a reasonable period of time for equitable tolling purposes because it was filed within one year of the jury verdict which found that Irby was presumed to have died in the April 1997 accident.

Case Questions

1. What are legitimate reasons for invoking the statute of limitations?
2. Why do you think that the court disfavors a defendant relying on the statute of limitations as a defense?
3. How did the widow act reasonably in pursuing death benefits?
4. How did the widow satisfy the elements of the doctrine of equitable tolling?

Case Glossary

toll
Suspension of the running of a time period.
controversion
In a dispute, one party's statement of the facts.

MISCELLANEOUS JUDICIAL DUTIES

In attempting to learn the law, one tends to concentrate study on appellate decisions, which provide authoritative statements of the law. Most of these are appeals from final judgments from trials, but judges engage in many other duties that consume much time and energy.

Trial Courts

Lower court judges must act on a number of problems that are not truly adversarial in nature but that require orders from a court. The advent of **no-fault divorce**, for example, has converted a formerly adversarial proceeding into one that frequently involves a judge simply approving a marital settlement agreement negotiated by the divorcing parties through their attorneys. A five- or ten-minute hearing disposes of the matter. The major purpose of no-fault divorce laws has been to diminish the adversarial aspect of divorce and give the parties rather than the court control over their own destinies. Of course, if the parties cannot agree on the distribution of marital assets, alimony, and child support, the proceedings take on the former adversarial character, forcing the judge to decide these issues.

Some actions, like a legal name change, in which no defendant is involved, are rather perfunctory actions requiring a court order. Others, like **garnishment** of wages, can be adversarial but usually are not. In addition, the court must take action on issues prior to trial and enforce judgments after trial. Also, depending on the jurisdiction, judges may spend a good deal of time on purely administrative duties.

no-fault divorce
Contemporary method divorce that does away with the need to prove fault (i.e., state grounds) against the other spouse.

garnishment
An action by which one who is owed a debt may collect payments through a third party, often an employer.

Appellate Courts

In general, appellate courts are responsible for overseeing the orderly process of the court system. This includes not only hearing appeals but also ruling on requests for delays in the appellate process, staying decisions of lower courts, applications for bail, and so on. Appellate courts may also be involved in matters relating to admission to the bar and disciplinary actions.

Appellate courts also have responsibility for administrative duties, managing their own activities, as well as some supervisory functions over the lower courts. Onerous administrative duties are often bestowed on the chief judge of a district or circuit court or the chief justice of a supreme court. The time spent in administrative duties may be directly related to the staff available to a judge.

Unlike trials, which are conducted by a single judge, appellate proceedings involve three or more judges, usually an odd number to prevent evenly divided decisions. Assignment of duties also becomes an administrative matter, as someone must make the assignments. Many appellate courts have panels of judges, from which a subset is selected, to hear certain cases. The U.S. Court of Appeals is the most familiar example.

The *Lee* case is an example of the regulatory feature of appellate courts. The newspaper in the case was charged with contempt of court for violating a "gag" order of the court in a juvenile case by publishing letters from the parents. The newspaper petitioned for a **writ of prohibition**, which is a common law remedy asking an appellate court to restrain a lower court from doing something it has no authority to do.

writ of prohibition
An order by a higher court directing a lower court not to do something.

MINNEAPOLIS STAR AND TRIBUNE COMPANY, La Crosse Tribune Company, and Northwest Publications, Inc., Petitioners

v.

Honorable Robert E. LEE, Judge of County Court for Houston County, Respondent

Court of Appeals of Minnesota

353 N.W.2d 213 (1984)

Facts

The petitioners request a writ of prohibition. In June 1984, the trial court issued an order that all parties in what was presumably a juvenile dependency case cease and desist from publishing letters or statements having to do with the proceeding. Subsequently, the minor's parents wrote two letters to the editor of a newspaper in the area. On July 27, 1984, the trial court, believing the letters to be a violation of its order, ordered a contempt hearing. . . .

Issue

May a court issue an order forbidding publication of information about a juvenile case obtained from involved parties and at the contempt hearing which was open to the public?

Analysis

* * *

Prior restraints of speech have long been deemed unconstitutional except in the most drastic of situations.

* * *

Such a restraint must be "necessitated by a compelling governmental interest, and * * * narrowly tailored to serve that interest."

* * *

In this case, the governmental interest is not constitutional but statutory: privacy in a juvenile proceeding. It is an important and substantial government interest, but also with limits.

* * *

In this case, there has been no showing of any illegality; the trial court simply wanted to stop people from reading about the case. [The trial court judge] said he wanted to protect the child and have a better relationship between Houston County Social Services and the parties. Such an interest does not rise to the level required to justify a prior restraint. The order violated a fundamental constitutional right. Although the court's motives were honorable, nonetheless it was a violation of a fundamental right. There is no adequate remedy at

law to redress such a violation and, therefore, the writ must issue.

Decision

The trial court's order was an unconstitutional prior restraint of speech. It is hereby vacated.

The writ of prohibition is granted.

Case Questions

1. Why does the court note that there is no adequate remedy at law?
2. Could a court ever use a gag order prior to trial?
3. Under what provision of the Constitution was this case decided?

Case Glossary

prior restraint

An action by the government to impose limits on the exercise of free speech, especially publication, prior to its exercise, as distinguished from punishing a person after publication.

SUMMARY

In the United States, the judicial system has a hierarchy that is divided into trial and appellate courts. The function of the trial court is to resolve disputes between parties in an adversarial process in which an impartial and disinterested judge presides over the presentation of evidence of fact by attorneys for the two sides. When a jury is present at trial, it determines issues of fact, whereas the judge applies the law in the conduct of the trial and renders a judgment on the verdict. In a nonjury trial, the judge serves as the trier of fact and then applies the law.

The distinction between law and fact is important on appeal. The appellate court does not try facts, although it is sometimes called upon to determine whether the trial record indicates that factfinding at the trial was clearly erroneous, warranting reversal. This is a much higher standard than the appellate court exercises in reversing an application of law by the trial judge. On questions of law, the appellate court is free to substitute its judgment for that of the lower court and need not show any deference to the lower court. As a result, most reversals are based on legal rather than factual arguments.

For an appellant to win a reversal on appeal, the appellate court must be convinced that there was reversible error at the trial level. Reversible error is a mistake in the law or the facts that was so prejudicial to the appellant that a different result might have resulted if the mistake had not occurred. Minor mistakes may be deemed to be nonprejudicial or harmless error. In some cases reversible error requires a new trial; in others the error can be corrected by the appellate court or remanded to the lower court to write a new decision and order.

The appellate process provides a means to make the actions of trial courts consistent with the law, decide new issues of law, and protect litigants from misapplication of the law.

KEY TERMS

adversarial system
appellant
appellate courts
appellee
clearly erroneous
compensatory damages
garnishment
judgment
jury instructions

memorandum decision
   (per curiam opinion)
no-fault divorce
physical evidence
prejudicial error (reversible
   error)
punitive damages
question (issue) of fact
question of law

record
remand
substantial evidence
substitution of judgment
trial
trier of fact
verdict
writ of prohibition

CHAPTER REVIEW QUESTIONS

1. What are some of the criticisms of the adversary process?
2. What is the jury's factfinding called?
3. What is the rule of thumb that distinguishes questions of fact from questions of law?
4. What is meant by "on the record" in reference to a hearing?
5. What does an appellate court use for its consideration of a case?
6. What is meant by *prejudicial error?*
7. Why are appellate cases an unrepresentative sample of trial cases?
8. What are common grounds for appeal?
9. Who is the trier of fact in a case?
10. Does an appellate court accord more deference to trial court factfinding or conclusions of law?

CRITICAL THINKING QUESTIONS

1. Are there any classes of disputes that are not well suited to resolution through an adversarial process?
2. Should trial or appellate judges be elected?

CYBER EXERCISES

1. Opinions of the Montana Supreme Court are accessible at a number of websites, including the website for Montana state courts, http://www.montanacourts.org/. Appellate briefs are accessible at the website. The Montana Supreme Court

decided *State v. Deines*, 208 P.3d 857 (Mont. 2009) on May 19, 2009. The case contained a concurring opinion. Locate the case at the Montana state courts website and answer the following questions concerning the case:

    a. According to Justice Nelson, what was the "view with distrust" line of cases intended to do?

    b. According to Justice Nelson, why was the "view with distrust" sanction adopted?

    c. How might the appellate briefs in *Deines* be helpful in performing legal research?

SCENARIO

Return to Chapter 3 and the *Colby* and *Higgins* cases. *Higgins* declared that the single issue on appeal is "whether, by reason of the *Colby* case, or any other consideration, we should hold that charitable immunity is not applicable in this case."

Treat the *Higgins* decision as if it were the trial court decision—*Higgins* affirms the trial court, so this should not be difficult—and write a new appellate decision to explain why the trial court decision is weakly reasoned and unfair to the plaintiff/appellant. In other words, you are writing a new appellate decision that reverses the trial court instead of affirming it. Give the reasons why the court now abolishes charitable immunity and explain what its effects and limits will be in light of legislation on the matter. Although an appellate decision commonly cites a wealth of authorities, you may treat this simply as a well-reasoned policy statement. You can cite *Colby* and, if appropriate, the *Ricker* case cited in *Higgins*.

This exercise should not only make you think about trial and appeal but also make you look at both sides of the argument. (The author often has his students write an appellate brief and then make them write the brief for the appellee without having told them in advance that this was the next writing assignment.)

CHAPTER 6

STATE AND FEDERAL COURTS

INTRODUCTION

The United States has a unique court system. Whereas most developed countries have a hierarchical court system in which all courts are subordinate to a central supreme court, the United States has two separate court systems, federal and state; also, each state is independent from every other and is free within constitutional limits to make its own laws and administer its own system of justice. This chapter discusses the interrelationships of this court system and the ramifications of those interrelationships.

THE UNITED STATES CONSTITUTION

The U.S. Constitution allocates power between the federal and state governments. The aspects of the Constitution discussed here are far more important and complex than this summary treatment suggests, but acquaintance with certain constitutional provisions is essential for an understanding of state and federal court systems.

    When the American colonies united into a federal republic, their representatives framed a charter, the United States Constitution, which allocated governmental authority between state and federal governments. The Constitution reflects a certain distrust of government based on the experience of abuses of traditional legal principles by the British colonial governors under a monarchy. Not only was there a distrust of government in general but also a degree of mutual distrust among the states due to differences in local economies (e.g., plantation economies of Virginia and the Carolinas versus commercial economies of New York, Massachusetts, and Pennsylvania) and differences in size and population (e.g., Rhode Island versus New York). As a result, the Constitution was framed to limit the power of the federal government while preserving governmental autonomy among the states.

The Constitution was viewed as a granting of power by the states to the federal government such that the federal government's powers were limited to those enumerated in the Constitution. All other governmental authority remained with the states, without need to specify that authority in the Constitution itself. This principle is embodied in the Ninth and Tenth Amendments:

> AMENDMENT IX. The enumeration in the Constitution of certain rights shall not be construed to deny or disparage others retained by the people.

> AMENDMENT X. The powers not delegated to the United States by the Constitution, nor prohibited by it to the States, are reserved to the States respectively, or to the people.

This language reflects that the federal government exercises its authority "by grant," whereas the states exercise authority "by reservation." Note that this language is the language of property law, such as when a property owner transfers or "grants" property rights to another, "reserving" those rights not granted. Like a property transaction, the grant of power is a contract between the people and the government. This is not merely a philosophical point; constitutional cases may best be conceptualized as enforcing property rights in a contractual relationship in which the federal government is bound by the original bargain.

The scope of federal control over the states can be expanded or restricted by constitutional interpretation. In the twentieth century, it was greatly expanded by a broad interpretation of the *commerce clause,* Article I, § 8, cl. 3, which gives Congress power to regulate interstate commerce. Because most business is in some way involved in interstate commerce, Congress is allowed pervasive regulation of American business. In contrast, in recent decades the U.S. Supreme Court has recognized inherent privacy rights into which neither the states nor the federal government may intrude (e.g., abortion rights).

Supreme Law of the Land

Article VI, § 2, of the Constitution provides that the Constitution "shall be the supreme law of the land." It was early established by the U.S. Supreme Court that this clause meant that neither state nor federal legislatures could enact laws in conflict with the Constitution, nor could any official or agency of government act in violation of the Constitution (refer to *judicial review* in Chapter 3). Because the U.S. Supreme Court is the ultimate authority with regard to the interpretation of the Constitution, it can exercise significant authority over state action.

The doctrine of **preemption** governs the conflict between federal and state statutes. Although the Constitution allocates authority between the federal government and the

preemption
The principle or doctrine that federal statutes that overlap or are in conflict with state statutes will take precedence and prevail (be preferred), even to the point of invalidating state statutes entirely.

states, that authority is often overlapping. In particular, the authority over regulation of interstate commerce is given to the federal government and, in the twentieth century, the U.S. Supreme Court interpreted the interstate commerce clause of the Constitution to give the federal government broad powers. Because states have the authority to regulate state businesses, it happens from time to time that state and federal law conflict. The question then arises as to whether the federal law *preempts* state law, which it usually does.

In *Wyeth*, a professional musician suffering from a migraine headache visited a local medical clinic. The method by which drugs were administered to treat her headache (intravenous push injection) resulted in her losing her arm. As one might expect, she sued everyone involved, including the drug manufacturer. The drug manufacturer relied on a preemption defense; it claimed that it could provide no stronger warning label than that allowed by the United States Food and Drug Administration (FDA), the federal administrative agency that regulates warning labels on prescription drugs. The drug company argument was that the comprehensiveness of FDA regulation of drug warnings precluded an additional warning of the danger posed by intravenous administration of the drug.

WYETH, Petitioner

v.

Diana LEVINE

Supreme Court of the United States

No. 06-1249

129 S. Ct. 1187, 173 L. Ed. 2d 51

Decided March 4, 2009.

Directly injecting the drug Phernergan into a patient's vein creates a significant risk of catastrophic consequences. A Vermont jury found that petitioner Wyeth, the manufacturer of the drug, had failed to provide an adequate warning of that risk and awarded damages to respondent Diana Levine to compensate her for the amputation of her arm. The warnings on Phernergan's label had been deemed sufficient by the federal Food and Drug Administration (FDA) when it approved Wyeth's new drug application in 1955 and when it later approved changes in the drug's labeling. . . .

Levine's injury resulted from an IV-push injection of Phernergan. On April 7, 2000, as on previous visits to her local clinic for treatment of a migraine headache, she received an intramuscular injection of Demerol for her headache and Phernergan for her nausea. Because the combination did not provide relief, she returned

later that day and received a second injection of both drugs. This time, the physician assistant administered the drugs by the IV-push method, and Phernergan entered Levine's artery, either because the needle penetrated an artery directly or because the drug escaped from the vein into surrounding tissue (a phenomenon called "perivascular extravasation") where it came in contact with arterial blood. As a result, Levine developed gangrene, and doctors amputated first her right hand and then her entire forearm. In addition to her pain and suffering, Levine incurred substantial medical expenses and the loss of her livelihood as a professional musician.

After settling claims against the health center and clinician, Levine brought an action for damages against Wyeth, relying on common-law negligence and strict-liability theories. Although Phernergan's labeling warned of the danger of gangrene and amputation following inadvertent intra-arterial injection, Levine alleged that the labeling was defective because it failed to instruct clinicians to use the IV-drip method of intravenous administration instead of the higher risk IV-push method. More broadly, she alleged that Phernergan is not reasonably safe for intravenous administration because the foreseeable risks of gangrene and loss of limb are great in relation to the drug's therapeutic benefits. . . .

The evidence presented during the 5-day jury trial showed that the risk of intra-arterial injection or perivascular extravasation can be almost entirely eliminated through the use of IV-drip, rather than IV-push, administration. . . . While Phernergan's labeling warned against intra-arterial injection and perivascular extravasation and advised that "[w]hen administering any irritant drug intravenously it is usually preferable to inject it through the tubing of an intravenous infusion set that is known to be functioning satisfactorily," the labeling did not contain a specific warning about the risks of IV-push administration. . . .

[T]he jury found that Wyeth was negligent, that Phernergan was a defective product as a result of inadequate warnings and instructions, and that no intervening cause had broken the causal connection between the product defects and the plaintiff's injury. It awarded total damages of $7,400,000, which the court reduced to account for Levine's earlier settlement with the health center and clinician.

On August 3, 2004, the trial court filed a comprehensive opinion denying Wyeth's motion for judgment as a matter of law. After making findings of fact based on the trial record (supplemented by one letter that Wyeth found after the trial), the court rejected Wyeth's pre-emption arguments. It determined that there was no direct conflict between FDA regulations and Levine's state-law claims because those regulations permit strengthened warnings without FDA approval on an interim basis and the record contained evidence of at least 20 reports of amputations similar to Levine's since the 1960's. The court also found that state tort liability in this case would not obstruct the FDA's work because the agency had paid no more than passing attention to the question whether to warn against IV-push administration of Phernergan. In addition, the court noted that state law serves a compensatory function distinct from federal regulation. . . . The Vermont Supreme Court affirmed. . . .

The question presented by the petition is whether the FDA's drug labeling judgments "preempt state law product liability claims premised on the theory that different labeling judgments were necessary to make drugs reasonably safe for use." . . .

Our answer to that question must be guided by two cornerstones of our pre-emption jurisprudence. First, "the purpose of Congress is the ultimate touchstone in every pre-emption case." *Medtronic*. Second, "[i]n

all pre-emption cases, and particularly in those in which Congress has 'legislated . . . in a field which the States have traditionally occupied,'. . . we 'start with the assumption that the historic police powers of the States were not to be superseded by the Federal Act unless that was the clear and manifest purpose of Congress.'" *Lohr*.

In order to identify the "purpose of Congress," it is appropriate to briefly review the history of federal regulation of drugs and drug labeling. [The Court's review of this history is omitted.] . . .

The FDA's premarket approval of a new drug application includes the approval of the exact text in the proposed label. Generally speaking, a manufacturer may only change a drug label after the FDA approves a supplemental application. There is, however, an FDA regulation that permits a manufacturer to make certain changes to its label before receiving the agency's approval. Among other things, this "changes being effected" (CBE) regulation provides that if a manufacturer is changing a label to "add or strengthen a contraindication, warning, precaution, or adverse reaction" or to "add or strengthen an instruction about dosage and administration that is intended to increase the safe use of the drug product," it may make the labeling change upon filing its supplemental application with the FDA; it need not wait for FDA approval. . . .

Of course, the FDA retains authority to reject labeling changes made pursuant to the CBE regulation in its review of the manufacturer's supplemental application, just as it retains such authority in reviewing all supplemental applications. But absent clear evidence that the FDA would not have approved a change to Phernergan's label, we will not conclude that it was impossible for Wyeth to comply with both federal and state requirements. . . .

Impossibility pre-emption is a demanding defense. On the record before us, Wyeth has failed to demonstrate that it was impossible for it to comply with both federal and state requirements. The CBE regulation permitted Wyeth to unilaterally strengthen its warning, and the mere fact that the FDA approved Phernergan's label does not establish that it would have prohibited such a change. . . .

Wyeth also argues that requiring it to comply with a state-law duty to provide a stronger warning about IV-push administration would obstruct the purposes and objectives of federal drug labeling regulation.

Levine's tort claims, it maintains, are pre-empted because they interfere with "Congress's purpose to entrust an expert agency to make drug labeling decisions that strike a balance between competing objectives." Brief for Petitioner 46. We find no merit in this argument, which relies on an untenable interpretation of congressional intent and an overbroad view of an agency's power to pre-empt state law....

If Congress thought state-law suits posed an obstacle to its objectives, it surely would have enacted an express pre-emption provision at some point during the FDCA's 70-year history.... Its silence on the issue, coupled with its certain awareness of the prevalence of state tort litigation, is powerful evidence that Congress did not intend FDA oversight to be the exclusive means of ensuring drug safety and effectiveness....

In advancing this argument, Wyeth relies not on any statement by Congress, but instead on the preamble to a 2006 FDA regulation governing the content and format of prescription drug labels. In that preamble, the FDA declared that the FDCA establishes "both a 'floor' and a 'ceiling,'" so that "FDA approval of labeling ... preempts conflicting or contrary State law." It further stated that certain state-law actions, such as those involving failure-to-warn claims, "threaten FDA's statutorily prescribed role as the expert Federal agency responsible for evaluating and regulating drugs."...

This Court has recognized that an agency regulation with the force of law can pre-empt conflicting state requirements. In such cases, the Court has performed its own conflict determination, relying on the substance of state and federal law and not on agency proclamations of pre-emption. We are faced with no such regulation in this case, but rather with an agency's mere assertion that state law is an obstacle to achieving its statutory objectives....

[T]he FDA's newfound opinion, expressed in its 2006 preamble, that state law "frustrate[s] the agency's implementation of its statutory mandate," does not merit deference.... Indeed, the "complex and extensive" regulatory history and background relevant to this case undercut the FDA's recent pronouncements of pre-emption, as they reveal the longstanding coexistence of state and federal law and the FDA's traditional recognition of state-law remedies—a recognition in place each time the agency reviewed Wyeth's Phernergan label.

In short, Wyeth has not persuaded us that failure-to-warn claims like Levine's obstruct the federal regulation of drug labeling. Congress has repeatedly declined to pre-empt state law, and the FDA's recently adopted position that state tort suits interfere with its statutory mandate is entitled to no weight. Although we recognize that some state-law claims might well frustrate the achievement of congressional objectives, this is not such a case.

Case Questions

1. Why do you think that, after the clinic and the clinician settled, the drug manufacturer did not?
2. What two basic concepts does the Court rely on in analyzing the preemption defense?
3. What were the Court's reasons for failing to accord the 2006 FDA opinion more weight?

Due Process

The most important phrase in the Constitution for operation of the legal system is the **due process clause** of the Fifth and Fourteenth Amendments. The Fifth Amendment provides that no person "shall be deprived of life, liberty or property, without due process of law." Because this applied only to the federal government, the Fourteenth Amendment was ratified in 1868, including the language "nor shall any State deprive any person of life, liberty, or property, without due process of law." In this way actions by state officials, legislatures, and courts become federal constitutional issues if denial of due process is alleged.

Due process is an elusive concept at best. It has been defined as requiring "fundamental fairness" in judicial process and prohibiting legislation that is "unreasonable, arbitrary, or capricious." These are subjective concepts—fairness and reasonableness are in the eyes of the beholder. As long as the court has the last word, what the court says is fair is fair, and what the court says is reasonable is reasonable. Unbridled power of the judiciary is mitigated, however, because the principles of *stare decisis* and judicial restraint constrain judges from arbitrarily imposing their views on society, and the appellate process encourages trial court judges to stay within the bounds of established law.

Due process has been divided into procedural and substantive due process. **Procedural due process** treats the issues of notice and hearing. **Notice** requires that a person threatened with legal action or whose legal rights are being affected be notified in such a way as to be able to prepare to protect those rights. **Hearing** requires that the form and nature of legal proceedings be fundamentally fair (e.g., an impartial tribunal, right to counsel, right of cross-examination, etc.). **Substantive due process** requires that legislation be reasonable, that it have a legitimate purpose, that it use reasonable means to effect a reasonable end, and so on. The void-for-vagueness doctrine is an example of a reasonableness test.

Because the fairness and reasonableness standards of due process have been developed on a case-by-case basis, to understand due process one must become acquainted with the principal cases that have interpreted it. But judges tend to perceive as unfair what most citizens perceive as unfair, so the anger and frustration that a person may feel toward treatment at the hands of the law or the courts will often strike a resonant chord in the minds of judges. Whenever the government acts to the detriment of an individual, a due process argument lurks in the background.

It is not possible to catalog all the possibilities for denial of due process, but consider the following in terms of potential lawsuits against government:

1. A state university has a policy not to release course transcripts if a student has a debt outstanding to the university. George Shylock fails to be admitted to law school because his transcripts were not sent due to an outstanding $2.00 library fine he failed to pay. George had not been notified of the fine and now must wait an additional year to enter law school.

2. The Town of Uppercrust, Connecticut, passes a new zoning plan that requires residential building lots to be at least half an acre in area. Mohammed Hussein owns a lot that is four-tenths of an acre, sufficient under the old ordinance for a building site, but his application for a variance (an exception to the ordinance) is denied, so he cannot build on his lot.

3. Under state law, a person can be convicted of manslaughter if involved in a fatal auto accident while driving intoxicated, even if the intoxication did not contribute to the accident.

4. In a rulemaking hearing held by the Interstate Commerce Commission, representatives of the railroad and trucking industries are permitted to offer oral testimony of expert witnesses concerning the impact of proposed transportation regulations but are not permitted to cross-examine witnesses.

due process clause

The Fifth Amendment and the Fourteenth Amendment to the U.S. Constitution, which guarantee that law administered through courts of justice is equally applied to all under established rules that do not violate fundamental principles of fairness. The process that is due before government may deprive a person of life, liberty, or property.

procedural due process

Due process that is concerned with the fairness of *notice* and *hearing* provided by government in the adjudication of rights and duties.

notice

In law, represents the requirement of timely notification of the opposing party. Under *procedural due process,* the fairness of legal procedure requires that a party have sufficient notice to prepare a response to legal action.

hearing

The presentation of evidence and argument before a tribunal. Under *procedural due process,* the hearing (usually the trial) must be fair and evenhanded. Most of the elements of a fair hearing have been established by custom and precedent.

substantive due process

A theory of due process that emphasizes judging the content of a law by a subjective standard of fundamental fairness; the government may not act arbitrarily or capriciously in making, interpreting, or enforcing the law.

equal protection of the laws

A constitutional guaranty specifying that every state must give equal treatment to every person who is similarly situated or to persons who are members of the same class; this protection is a requirement of the Fourteenth Amendment, originally enacted to protect former slaves.

standing

A person's right to bring a lawsuit because he or she is directly affected by the issues presented, having a stake in the outcome of the suit.

These hypothetical situations raise additional constitutional issues. The zoning case would be challenged as taking private property without just compensation under the Fifth Amendment; the manslaughter case would undoubtedly raise the Eighth Amendment issue of cruel and unusual punishment. Due process questions are commonly raised along with other issues.

Equal Protection

The Fourteenth Amendment also prohibits states from denying "any person within its jurisdiction the **equal protection of the laws**." This language was designed originally to protect former slaves from discriminatory treatment after the Civil War. Its coverage, however, has been expanded to invalidate all laws and procedures that unreasonably discriminate. It has been invoked when classes of persons have been treated unequally by the law; for instance, alimony statutes in many states provided alimony only for women, thus discriminating against men, or public schools budgeted more for male athletics than female athletic programs, discriminating against women. The discriminatory aspect of the law may be more subtle, such as when cable TV companies objected to regulation of their broadcasting that was not also applied to noncable broadcasting. All laws by their nature discriminate—drunken-driving statutes discriminate against drinkers—but such forms of discrimination are benign, protecting society and its members. Equal protection of the laws is designed to protect a stigmatized group from discrimination.

Cases and Controversies

Article III of the Constitution vests judicial power in the "Supreme Court, and in such inferior courts as the Congress may from time to time ordain and establish" (see Exhibit 6-1). Article III, § 2, refers to judicial power over "cases" and "controversies." These words have been interpreted by the U.S. Supreme Court to restrict access to the federal courts in several ways, the most important of which concerns the question of **standing**. In our legal system, not every person may seek redress for every deprivation of a legal right. Standing is a limitation on who may bring an action. In general, only a person who has a "personal stake in the outcome" of a case may bring suit. This gloss on the Constitution encourages litigants to frame their suits in terms of property rights, but even in the violation of abstract rights, such as freedom of speech, suits are limited to those persons directly affected. A person may not sue the government for the abuse of power if that abuse is unrelated to the person desiring to sue.

Case and controversy have also been interpreted as referring to actual disputes between real parties. Not every slight, rebuke, or annoyance is a legal matter. The courts also refuse to hear cases concerning remote or hypothetical questions. This does not mean that some injury or wrong must necessarily have already occurred, but there must at least be an immediate threat of invasion of a right. In the *Waddell* case, a high school referee's call was taken all the way to the Georgia Supreme Court.

EXHIBIT 6-1 U.S. FEDERAL COURTS

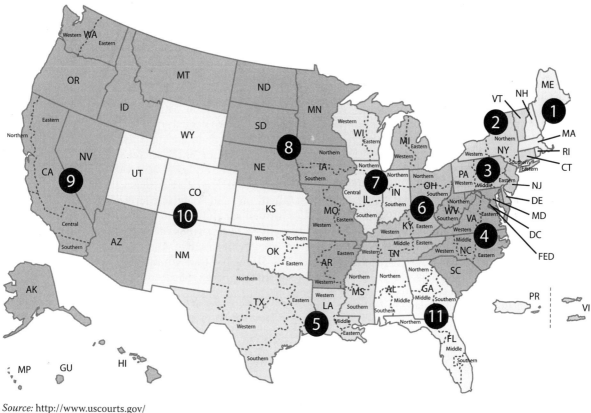

Source: http://www.uscourts.gov/

GEORGIA HIGH SCHOOL ASSOCIATION

v.

WADDELL et al.

Supreme Court of Georgia

248 Ga. 542, 285 S.E.2d 7 (1981)

On October 23, 1981, a football game was played between R.L. Osborne and Lithia Springs High Schools, members of region 5 AAAA established by the Georgia High School Association. The winner of this game would be in the play-offs, beginning with Campbell High School.

The score was 7 to 6 in favor of Osborne. With 7 minutes, 1 second, remaining in the game, Osborne had the ball on its 47 yard line, 4th down and 21 yards to go for a first down. Osborne punted but "roughing the kicker" was called on Lithia Springs. The referee officiating the game with the approval and sanction of the Georgia High School Association assessed the 15 yard penalty, placed the ball on the Lithia Springs 38 yard line, and declared it was 4th down and 6 yards to go.

The rules of the National Federation of State High School Associations provide that the penalty for roughing the kicker shall be 15 yards *and* 1st down. There is a dispute as to whether the Osborne coaches properly protested to the referee, before the ball was put in play, the error in the referee's failing to declare a 1st down.

From Lithia Springs' 38, Osborne punted again. Lithia Springs received the punt and drove down the field to score a field goal. Now 2 points behind, Osborne passed. Lithia Springs intercepted and scored again. The final score was Lithia Springs over Osborne, 16 to 7.

* * *

On November 12, suit was filed in the Superior Court of Cobb County by parents of Osborne players against the GHSA. Hearing was held on November 13. The court found that it had jurisdiction, found that the referee erred in failing to declare an automatic first down, and found that a protest was lodged with the proper officials of GHSA. The court found that the plaintiffs have a property right in the game of football being played according to the rules and that the referee denied plaintiffs and their sons this property right and equal protection of the laws by failing to correctly apply the rules.

The court then entered its order on November 13 canceling the play-off game between Lithia Springs and Campbell High School scheduled for 8 p.m. that evening and ordered ". . . that Lithia Springs High School and R.L. Osborne High School meet on the football field on November 14, 1981 at an agreed upon time between the parties and resume play at the Lithia Springs thirty eight yard line with the ball being in the possession of R.L. Osborne High School and it be first down and ten yards to go for a first down and that the clock be set at seven minutes one second to play and that the quarter be designated as the fourth quarter."

Asserting that the trial court's order was erroneous under *Smith v. Crim*, 240 Ga. 390, 240 S.E.2d 884 (1977), and would disrupt the play-off games not only between Lithia Springs and Campbell but succeeding play-offs, the GHSA filed a motion for **supersedeas** in this court on November 13, 1981, and the court entered its order suspending the trial court's order, pending further order of this court.

In *Smith v. Crim, supra*, we held that a high school football player has no right to participate in interscholastic sports and has no protectable property interest which would give rise to a due process claim. Pretermitting the question of "state action" which is the threshold of the 14th Amendment, we held that Smith was not denied equal protection by the rule of GHSA there involved. Similarly we find no denial of equal protection by the referee's error here. Were our decision to be otherwise, every error in the trial courts would constitute a denial of equal protection. We now go further and hold that courts of equity in this state are without authority to review decisions of football referees because those decisions do not present judicial controversies. The stay granted by this court on November 13, 1981, is hereby reaffirmed.

All the Justices concur.

Case Questions

1. Why is "state action" the threshold question for an inquiry into a denial of equal protection of the law under the Fourteenth Amendment?
2. Why did the football players have no right and no property interest to qualify for due process protection?
3. Did the players receive fair procedure?

Case Glossary

supersedeas

An order staying the execution of judgment by a trial court; suspension of the trial court's power, as when an appeal halts the court's power to execute judgment.

Full Faith and Credit

Article IV of the Constitution begins "**Full faith and credit** shall be given in each State to the public acts, records, and judicial proceedings of every other State." As a practical matter, this means that the courts of each state must recognize the validity of the laws and judicial orders of other states. Divorce provides a useful example. Frequently, after divorce, an ex-husband ordered to pay child support or alimony moves to another state and stops making payments. The ex-wife may bring an action in the state to which the former husband has moved to collect arrears in payments. In the action, the court must recognize the validity of the divorce and the order to make payments.

Full faith and credit has some limitations. A court may find that the law or court order of another state is repugnant to public policy, a rare occurrence. This statement will undoubtedly be tested in the light of legalization of same-sex marriage (e.g., Massachusetts). What happens when a same-sex married couple moves to a state that does not allow such marriages? Another basis for denying recognition is jurisdiction. One state may conclude that the court of another state did not have jurisdiction over the matter in the first place. Jurisdiction is the first issue in any case. A court without jurisdiction has no authority and its orders no validity. For example, husband and wife separate and live in different states. One brings a divorce action in one state and the other in another state. Only one state should have jurisdiction—two conflicting divorce decrees make no legal or practical sense. A court may conclude that the court of another state did not have jurisdiction and refuse to enforce its orders.

This may have unanticipated results; consider the following case. Many years ago, a man from North Carolina obtained a "quickie" divorce in Nevada, immediately remarried in Nevada, and returned to North Carolina with his new wife. North Carolina charged and convicted him of bigamy, and the case went to the U.S. Supreme Court twice. This created the anomalous situation in which a man was a "bigamist for living in one state with the only one with whom the other state would permit him lawfully to live" (Justice Douglas, *Williams v. North Carolina*, 317 U.S. 287 [1942]). The Court required North Carolina to respect the Nevada decree (with vigorous dissenting opinions). The advent of no-fault divorce since this case was decided has mitigated the need for divorce havens like Nevada, but jurisdictional problems can still create a tangled web in divorce cases.

SUBJECT MATTER JURISDICTION

Although jurisdiction may properly be treated as part of civil and criminal procedure, the distinction between federal and state court systems is grounded on jurisdiction as well. The power and authority of a court in a particular dispute are based on jurisdiction. We repeat: Without jurisdiction, a court has no authority; its orders are not valid. **Subject matter jurisdiction** refers to the kinds of disputes a court has the authority to decide. For example, the Constitution provides that the federal government has exclusive control over **bankruptcy**, **patent**, **trademark**, **copyright**, and **admiralty**. A state court has no power to decide a bankruptcy case; if it should do so, its orders would have no validity.

General and Limited Jurisdiction

Courts are classified as having **general** or **limited subject matter jurisdiction**. Courts of general jurisdiction have authority to decide a wide variety of cases

case and controversy

Terms used in Article III, § 2, of the U.S. Constitution regarding the judicial power; the terms have been interpreted to mean that the courts have authority over real disputes between real parties, as opposed to hypothetical disputes or nonadversarial parties. The courts do not answer questions about the law, but decide actual disputes.

full faith and credit

The Constitution requires that each state respect the legal pronouncements of sister states, "Full faith and credit shall be given in each State to the public acts, records, and judicial proceedings of every other State" (Article IV).

subject matter jurisdiction

The jurisdiction of a court to hear and determine the type of case before it. For example, in Florida, election contests are heard in the circuit court but not in county court. The reference to Leon County in "the Circuit Court for Leon County" refers only to the location of the court—it is a circuit court, not a county court.

bankruptcy

Generally, the situation in which a person, business, or government cannot or will not pay its debts; its property is entrusted to a "trustee in bankruptcy" who distributes the property to creditors.

patent

An exclusive right, granted by the government, to use one's invention.

trademark

A distinctive mark, in symbols or words, used to distinguish products of manufacturers or merchants.

copyright

A right in literary property, giving an author exclusive rights over her or his works for a limited period of time.

admiralty

Branch of law pertaining to maritime commerce and navigation.

and apply the full range of judicial remedy and relief. Major trial courts in each jurisdiction fit into this category. However, most states have also established courts of limited jurisdiction to handle only a restricted class of cases. A probate court, for example, handles matters concerning decedents' estates (many probate courts also have jurisdiction over some areas of law relating to juveniles). Thus, a probate court does not hear cases of tenant evictions. Some states divide their courts into criminal and civil courts; Texas even divides appeals into civil and criminal appeals at the supreme court level.

There is a wide variety of lower courts handling minor matters with limited subject matter jurisdiction; one example is small claims court (limited to cases involving a low maximum monetary amount and having limited remedial powers—it cannot grant divorces, issue injunctions, etc.). Municipal courts are common in the United States, typically handling violations of city ordinances and other minor civil and criminal matters. Many of these lesser courts are conducted with less formality than higher trial courts. Small claims courts are designed to provide litigants with an inexpensive means of resolving disputes. Lawyers do not usually participate, court reporters are usually not present (and therefore no transcript is made), and court costs are minimal; the judge tends to take a more active role in the process because the litigants are unfamiliar with the technicalities of the law.

FEDERAL SUBJECT MATTER JURISDICTION

Federal jurisdiction applies to two categories of cases: (1) federal question cases and (2) diversity of citizenship cases (see Exhibit 6-2).

Federal Question Cases

The Constitution provides that the federal courts have jurisdiction over cases arising under the Constitution, laws, and treaties of the United States. These are called **federal question** cases. A case may directly raise a constitutional issue, or the issue may

EXHIBIT 6-2   BASES FOR FEDERAL COURT JURISDICTION

Federal question	A case arising under the United States Constitution, laws, and treaties of the United States
Diversity of citizenship	Each plaintiff is from a state or country different from each defendant and the amount being disputed is more than $75,000

arise under a federal statute enacted by Congress (e.g., federal civil rights violations, environmental protection issues).

Each state (and the District of Columbia) has at least one U.S. District Court, the federal trial court to which federal question cases are brought. Many cases involve both state law and federal questions and may be brought in state courts, which must then decide issues of both state and federal law. For instance, the drunken-driving manslaughter case in our hypothetical situations considered earlier would begin as a state prosecution in which the defendant would raise defense arguments based on the due process and cruel and unusual punishment clauses of the U.S. Constitution as well as their counterparts in the state constitution (and factual defenses, of course). If convicted, the defendant could appeal to the state court of appeals and the state supreme court and then petition the U.S. Supreme Court for a **writ of certiorari** on the federal constitutional issues.

A case originating in the federal district court will stay in the federal system even if an issue of state law must be decided. A case originating in the state courts will remain in the state court system until decided or denied consideration by the state's highest court, from which appeal is made (by way of **certiorari**) to the U.S. Supreme Court. A defendant may challenge federal question jurisdiction in a case in a U.S. District Court, which would force the case into state court if the challenge is successful. Similarly, a defendant may petition the U.S. District Court for removal from state court to the federal court and will succeed if the federal court concludes that the case could have been brought originally in the federal court.

Keep in mind that state courts have the final authority to declare state law, and federal courts have final authority to declare federal law. State courts will thus use federal cases to determine federal law, while federal courts will rely on decisions of state courts where state law is concerned. The exceptions to this are: (1) if state and federal laws overlap and conflict (e.g., certain state and federal labor laws may give rise to an inconsistency between them), state law must yield to federal law and (2) any state statute or court decision that is held to be in conflict with the U.S. Constitution is invalid and without authority as to the part that is unconstitutional.

Federal question cases commonly arise in those areas in which the federal government has a special stake by virtue of the authority it has through the Constitution regarding interstate commerce, copyright, patent, bankruptcy, the military, customs, and so on. In each of these areas, a body of federal law has been developed by Congress and defined by the federal courts.

The Federal Trade Commission Act, a federal act regulating sale of commercial products to consumers, allows the Federal Trade Commission (FTC) to sue a company for fraud where false advertising statements induced the consumer to purchase the company's product. In *QT*, the company claimed that its bracelet provided quick relief from chronic pain. The magistrate judge who tried the case enjoined the advertising and ordered the company to transfer some $16 million to the FTC for distribution to defrauded consumers.

general subject matter jurisdiction
A court's authority to hear and decide a broad range of cases.

limited subject matter jurisdiction
A court's restricted authority to decide only certain kinds of cases; for example, a probate court hears only cases concerning decedents' estates.

federal question
Issues in cases arising under the Constitution, laws, and treaties of the United States, over which federal courts have subject matter jurisdiction.

writ of certiorari
A writ issued by a higher court to a lower court requiring the certification of the record in a particular case so that the higher court can review the record and correct any actions taken in the case that were not in accordance with the law.

certiorari
To be informed of; to be made certain in regard to.

FEDERAL TRADE COMMISSION, Plaintiff-Appellee

v.

QT, INC., Q-Ray Company, Bio-Metal, Inc., and Que Te Park, Defendants-Appellants

United States Court of Appeals, Seventh Circuit

No. 07-1662

Decided Jan. 3, 2008.

WIRED Magazine recently put the Q-Ray Ionized Bracelet on its list of the top ten Snake-Oil Gadgets. See http://blog.wired.com/gadgets/2007/11/10-awesome-gadg.html.

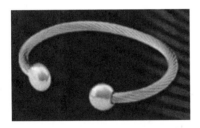

The Federal Trade Commission has an even less honorable title for the bracelet's promotional campaign: fraud. In this action under 15 U.S.C. §§ 45(a), 52, 53, a magistrate judge, presiding by the parties' consent, concluded after a bench trial that the bracelet's promotion has been thoroughly dishonest. The court enjoined the promotional claims and required defendants to disgorge some $16 million (plus interest) for the FTC to distribute to consumers who have been taken in.

According to the district court's findings, almost everything that defendants have said about the bracelet is false. Here are some highlights:

- Defendants promoted the bracelet as a miraculous cure for chronic pain, but it has no therapeutic effect.
- Defendants told consumers that claims of "immediate, significant or complete pain relief" had been "test-proven"; they hadn't.
- The bracelet does not emit "Q-Rays" (there are no such things) and is not ionized (the bracelet is an electric conductor, and any net charge dissipates

swiftly). The bracelet's chief promoter chose these labels because they are simple and easily remembered-and because Polaroid Corp. blocked him from calling the bangle "polarized".

- The bracelet is touted as "enhancing the flow of bio-energy" or "balancing the flow of positive and negative energies"; these empty phrases have no connection to any medical or scientific effect. Every other claim made about the mechanism of the bracelet's therapeutic effect likewise is techno-babble.
- Defendants represented that the therapeutic effect wears off in a year or two, despite knowing that the bracelet's properties do not change. This assertion is designed to lead customers to buy new bracelets. Likewise the false statement that the bracelet has a "memory cycle specific to each individual wearer" so that only the bracelet's original wearer can experience pain relief is designed to increase sales by eliminating the second-hand market and "explaining" the otherwise-embarrassing fact that the buyer's friends and neighbors can't perceive any effect.
- Even statements about the bracelet's physical composition are false. It is sold in "gold" and "silver" varieties but is made of brass.

The magistrate judge did not commit a clear error, or abuse his discretion, in concluding that the defendants set out to bilk unsophisticated persons who found themselves in pain from arthritis and other chronic conditions.

Defendants maintain that the magistrate judge subjected their statements to an excessively rigorous standard of proof. Some passages in the opinion could be read to imply that any statement about a product's therapeutic effects must be deemed false unless the claim has been verified in a placebo-controlled, double-blind study. . . .

Nothing in the Federal Trade Commission Act, the foundation of this litigation, requires placebo-controlled, double-blind studies. The Act forbids false and misleading statements, and a statement that is plausible but has not been tested in the most reliable way cannot be condemned out of hand. The burden is on the Commission to prove that the statements are false. . . .

Now for the remedy. Defendants do not contest the terms of the injunction. They do, however, say that the financial award was excessive. The magistrate judge set as his goal the disgorgement of the profits that defendants made while the Q-Ray Ionized Bracelet was heavily promoted with infomercials on late-night television. Disgorging profits is an appropriate remedy. But defendants say that the record does not contain evidence about their profits. True, the FTC compiled balance sheets showing profits running in the millions every year. These should not be considered, defendants insist, because when Que Te Park (defendants' principal investor and CEO) testified about the subject, he was asked only whether he could "see" the enterprise's net income (he conceded that he could), not whether the figures are correct, and the FTC's lawyer then forgot to offer the balance sheets themselves as evidence.

This is too clever by half. The FTC made estimates of profits from the Q-Ray Ionized Bracelet business and gave defendants an opportunity to respond. They chose not to do so. Park's noncommittal answers avoided any risk of prosecution for perjury but did not meet the FTC's prima facie showing. The magistrate judge was entitled to treat the evasion as an admission that the FTC's computation is in the ballpark. A monetary award often depends on estimation, for defendants may not keep (or may conceal) the data required to make an exact calculation. Defendants' business was a profitable one; that much, at least, they concede. (It is so profitable that they continue to carry it on despite the injunction that requires them to stop making most of their old claims for its efficacy. Today it is sold with testimonials and vaporous statements.) A court is entitled to proceed with the best available information; if defendants thought that their profits for these years were below $16 million, they should have produced their own figures—for once the FTC produces a reasonable estimate, the defendants bear the burden of showing that the estimate is inaccurate.

Although defendants complain that the magistrate judge failed to separate ill-got gains from legitimate profits, they offer no reason to think that any of their profits are "legitimate." Defendants' sole business is the sale of Q-Ray products.

On top of paying $16 million (plus interest) into a fund for distribution to all of their customers, defendants must refund the full purchase price of some bracelets purchased over the Internet. Defendants' infomercials promised buyers that the purchase price would be refunded any time during 30 days after the sale if the buyers were not satisfied with their bracelets. Defendants honored that promise for bracelets purchased by telephone but not for bracelets purchased from their web sites. Internet purchasers were allowed only 10 days to return their bracelets. The district court held that defendants must refund the purchase price of anyone who bought from the web sites and returned the merchandise between days 11 and 30. Defendants protest that their web sites disclosed the 10-day refund period, but this does not meet the FTC's point. The infomercials promised a 30-day return period, then suggested that customers purchase online. Anyone who followed that advice received only a 10-day return period. The disclosure of this shorter period was buried several clicks away in the web site. The district court was entitled to conclude the switch deceived reasonable persons who relied on what the infomercials told them.

Case Questions

1. What is a snake-oil gadget?
2. What is the rationale for requiring truth in consumer advertising?
3. Is federal regulation of consumer advertising necessary?

Diversity of Citizenship Cases

Article III of the Constitution placed suits between citizens of different states under federal jurisdiction. This jurisdiction is not exclusive, so a plaintiff of Maryland suing a defendant from Virginia may elect to sue in a state court (most likely Virginia) or in a U.S. District

diversity of citizenship

The subject matter jurisdiction of federal courts to hear cases between citizens of different states.

Court. The differences in state citizenship are referred to as **diversity of citizenship**, and jurisdiction is based on the status of the parties without regard to the subject matter of the case; that is, no federal law other than the diversity clause of the Constitution is required. Diversity cases additionally require that the amount in controversy exceed $75,000.

Diversity jurisdiction requires total diversity—if there are multiple plaintiffs or defendants and any plaintiff is a citizen of the same state as any defendant, diversity jurisdiction will be denied. Like federal question cases, a petition for removal (to the federal court) is available to the defendant if the plaintiff elects to bring the suit in the state court. The petition, however, is not available if suit is brought in the defendant's state. The rationale for this exception is based on the original purpose of the diversity clause. When the Constitution was framed, it was feared that parties might face prejudice when suing or being sued in a state other than their own. Federal jurisdiction was made available on the belief that federal courts would be less inclined to partiality. Thus, when a defendant is sued at home, the rationale for federal jurisdiction no longer holds.

William M. FINE, et al., Plaintiffs

v.

DELALANDE, INC., Defendant

United States District Court, S.D. New York

545 F. Supp. 275 (1982)

This lawsuit began on April 1, 1982, in the New York Supreme Court, New York County, the same day on which the defendant Delalande, Inc. filed an action in this Court against the plaintiffs herein based upon claimed diversity of citizenship. Delalande removed this action from the state court on April 20, 1982, pursuant to 28 U.S.C. § 1441(c).

By motion docketed May 5, 1982, the *Fine* plaintiffs seek the remand of this action to the state court as improvidently removed, because Delalande, Inc. is a citizen of New York by reason of its principal place of business of this state.

For purposes of 18 U.S.C. § 1441, a corporation is deemed to be a citizen of the state wherein it has its principal place of business, and of the state of its incorporation. 28 U.S.C. § 1332(c).

For reasons discussed more fully in this Court's Memorandum and Order of this date in the companion *Delalande* action, 545 F. Supp. 268, familiarity with which is assumed, this Court finds that Delalande has its principal place of business in New York. Accordingly, there is not complete diversity because at least eleven of the plaintiffs are also citizens of New York.

Plaintiff's motion to remand this action to the state court is granted.

Case Questions

1. If Delalande's principal place of business is New York, on what basis was it claiming diversity of citizenship?
2. Why would the plaintiff prefer state court or the defendant federal court?

In the *Fine* case, both sides filed suit on the same day, one in state court and one in federal court. As the case indicates, a corporation may be a "citizen" of more than one state for the purposes of diversity jurisdiction. Although a defendant sued in state court may petition for removal to federal court, claiming diversity jurisdiction, a defendant sued in federal court in a diversity case may move to remand to the state court, claiming a lack of diversity jurisdiction. Note that a removal should be distinguished from a *remand,* which in a diversity case would seek a transfer from a federal court back to the state court. Both removal and remand may be distinguished from a motion to dismiss for lack of jurisdiction.

Many have argued that the diversity clause no longer makes sense and unnecessarily clogs federal courts, which ought to be deciding cases of federal rather than state law.

The *Erie* Doctrine

In 1938, the U.S. Supreme Court decided the case of *Erie Railroad v. Tompkins,* 304 U.S. 64, which altered the nature of diversity cases forever. Tompkins was injured by a train while walking along a path beside the railroad tracks, when an open door on a refrigerator car hit him. Tompkins was a citizen of Pennsylvania, and the incident occurred in Pennsylvania; but Erie was a New York corporation. Tompkins brought a diversity case in federal court in New York and was awarded $30,000 in damages. The Second Circuit Court of Appeals affirmed the award, but the railroad petitioned and received certiorari from the U.S. Supreme Court.

At issue was the substantive law to be followed in a diversity case. The trial judge instructed the jury that the railroad was liable under general law if the jury found simple negligence. The railroad argued from the beginning that the common law of Pennsylvania, the site of the injury, should apply. Under Pennsylvania law, Tompkins would be considered a trespasser, as he was walking on the railroad's right of way, so the railroad would not be liable to a trespasser on the basis of ordinary negligence; it would be liable only if the jury found gross negligence (i.e., wanton and reckless misconduct). In Pennsylvania, a landowner such as the railroad owes a lower duty of care to a trespasser than to nontrespassers. For this reason, Tompkins's attorneys chose to bring the case in federal court rather than the Pennsylvania state court.

Section 34 of the Federal Judiciary Act of 1789 had provided for the recognition and application of state common law in appropriate cases, but in *Swift v. Tyson,* 41 U.S. 1 (1842), the Court had held that the federal courts were free to disregard specific decisions of state common law in favor of general principles of common law.

The effect of *Swift v. Tyson* was to encourage the creation of a general federal common law that could differ significantly from the law of a particular state. This would encourage litigants for whom diversity jurisdiction was available to select the court, state or federal, in which they would have the greatest likelihood of success—precisely what Tompkins's lawyers did. In *Erie,* the Supreme Court overruled *Swift v. Tyson* and declared that, henceforth, the federal courts in diversity cases would follow the common law of the state.

Mr. Tompkins lost his case.

Erie has been applied to substantive law but not procedure—when suing in federal court, federal procedure is followed.

In the *Brown* case, like the *Fine* case, the principal issue is diversity jurisdiction. Once the court determines it has jurisdiction, the case is summarily dismissed by interpreting state law as *Erie* requires. The *Brown* plaintiff is suing for wrongful discharge, but she is an "at-will" employee, which means that she does not have an employment contract that guarantees a period of employment, so she can be discharged at any time.

Some states allow suits for wrongful discharge by at-will employees; Missouri does not. Why is the plaintiff trying desperately to get into a Missouri state court? The answer may lie in the *Erie* doctrine itself. Although the federal court in a diversity case will be extremely reluctant to upset established Missouri precedent, the plaintiff might be able to persuade a Missouri court to overrule precedent in light of a trend in other states to recognize an action for wrongful discharge of an at-will employee.

Deborah BROWN, Plaintiff

v.

SOUTHLAND CORPORATION, et al., Defendants

United States District Court, E.D. Missouri, E.D.

620 F. Supp. 1495 (1985)

Plaintiff, a resident of Missouri, brought this action for damages in the Circuit Court of the City of St. Louis against Southland Corporation, a Texas corporation, and Clyde Tinsley, a resident of Missouri.

The action arises out of the circumstances surrounding plaintiff's discharge from defendant Southland Corporation's (Southland) employment. Plaintiff was employed as the store manager of a "7-Eleven" store owned by defendant Southland at the time of her discharge in May 1980. Plaintiff alleges that she was wrongfully discharged pursuant to a corporate policy implemented to cover-up top-level employees' negligence. . . .

28 U.S.C. § 1441(b) gives a defendant who meets certain requirements the right to remove a civil action from a state court to a federal district court on the basis of diversity of citizenship. The requirement of complete diversity between plaintiffs and defendants is fully applicable to § 1441(b). A federal court, however, will not allow removal to be defeated by the collusive or fraudulent joinder of a resident defendant. . . .

In the present action, plaintiff's complaint alleges that Tinsley was the zone manager with ultimate supervisory responsibility over the store where plaintiff worked. In support of his removal petition, defendant Tinsley submitted affidavits and plaintiff's own deposition statements to the effect that at the time of the occurrences alleged in plaintiff's complaint, he was not the zone manager of the district in which plaintiff's store was located and that he had no involvement in the said occurrences. Plaintiff states in her deposition that she never spoke with defendant Tinsley. Plaintiff has not disputed this evidence. The Court concludes that defendants have met their burden of proving that defendant Tinsley was improperly joined and dismisses him pursuant to Rule 21, Fed.R.Civ.P. Accordingly, plaintiff's motion to remand is denied.

The next matter for consideration is defendants' motion to dismiss for failure to state a claim. Plaintiff does not allege any contractual or statutory provision that would bar her termination. In Missouri, it is firmly established that an at-will employee cannot maintain an action for wrongful discharge. . . .

The above rulings dispose of all claims in plaintiff's complaint against each defendant. Judgment for defendants.

Case Questions

1. Why does the plaintiff want the case remanded to state court?
2. What reasons are given for denial of the petition to remand?
3. What result does *Erie* achieve in this case?

CONFLICT OF LAWS

Separate state jurisdictions within one nation have also presented a special problem called **conflict of laws** or *choice of law*. Suppose two Connecticut residents are involved in an auto accident in Massachusetts. With a Connecticut plaintiff and a Connecticut defendant, suit is logically brought in Connecticut, although it could be brought in Massachusetts where the accident occurred. Should Connecticut or Massachusetts law apply? This is a conflict-of-laws problem. Whatever state is chosen for the suit (the *forum* state), its procedural laws will be followed; but a question may arise as to which forum's substantive law should apply. In some respects this parallels the issue in *Erie:* the result of the lawsuit should not depend on the choice of the forum. Because of differences in state law, a defendant may be liable under the law of one state but not under the law of another, making the defendant's state of residence the determining factor in the result.

Conflict-of-laws rules resolve this problem to some extent. Each state has its own rules to decide the choice of law. If the Connecticut plaintiff sues in Connecticut, Connecticut choice of law must apply. Assuming that Connecticut is in no way involved with the accident (i.e., the accident and its causes occurred wholly within Massachusetts), the substantive law of Massachusetts would apply, just as it would if the case were brought in Massachusetts. Connecticut law would require that the substantive law of Massachusetts govern the outcome of the case.

There is logic to this result. Whether conduct is wrongful should be determined by the law of the place where the conduct occurs. The Connecticut driver in Massachusetts must obey Massachusetts law. To illustrate, many states allow a driver to turn right at a red light after stopping and determining that it is safe to turn. Suppose a resident of such a state follows this custom in a state that does not allow turning on red. It would certainly be no defense, either civil or criminal, that the driver's home state has a different rule. Suppose that the turn on red caused an accident and that an injured party sued the nonresident in his home state. Should the defendant's conduct be judged differently because it is legal in his home state, the state where the suit was brought? No, wrongful conduct should not be magically transformed into proper conduct by the choice of the forum.

Unfortunately, conflict of laws is not always this simple. Suppose, for example, that the two drivers were crossing the Connecticut-Massachusetts border as the accident occurred. The wrongful act of one driver may have occurred in Connecticut, but the injuries were inflicted in Massachusetts. Choice of law will depend on the conflict-of-laws principles of the forum state. In tort cases like an auto accident, two rules are generally applied. The ancient rule, *lex loci delicti*, or "the law of the place of the wrong," holds that choice of law will fall on the site of the last act necessary to make the actor liable, that is, where the tortious act is complete. In recent times another test, called the **significant relationship test**, has been adopted in many states. Under this test, all the circumstances of the tort are considered in deciding which state has the greatest connection with the wrong.

Contract cases present far more problems for conflict of laws. As a somewhat absurd, but not impossible, example, consider the following:

> Two corporations with nationwide activities negotiate a complex contract. One corporation is incorporated in California, the other in New York. The contract is

---

conflict of laws

Also called *choice of law;* concerns the problem that arises when there is a question about which state's law should apply in a particular case.

***lex loci delicti* (Latin)**

"The law of the place of the wrong." In a *conflict-of-laws* question in a tort action, this ancient rule held that the court would apply the law of that place (state) where the last act necessary to complete the tort occurred or the last act necessary to make the actor liable occurred.

significant relationship test

The modern rule followed in a *conflict-of-laws* setting; it is used in both tort and contract contexts and makes the court apply the law of the state that had the most "significant relationship" to the cause of action.

negotiated and signed in Illinois. The contract is to be performed primarily in Texas but is breached in Louisiana. The contract specifically provides, "in case of breach, this contract will be construed under the law of Michigan." The California corporation sues the New York corporation in New Jersey, its principal place of business.

Theoretically, the law of one of several states might be chosen. If suit is brought in New Jersey and the New Jersey court agrees that it has jurisdiction, the choice of law would depend on New Jersey rules concerning conflict of laws. New Jersey conflict-of-laws rules may be very different from those of Texas or Illinois. Most states give great weight to the agreement of the parties to specify the law that governs, here that of Michigan. Many contracts are silent in this regard, though, and there may be policy reasons for not enforcing that part of the contract.

There are several conflict-of-laws principles with regard to contracts, and frequently different rules apply to different circumstances. Like torts, there has been a strong trend toward the significant relationship test, which aims at choosing the state having the greatest connection with the contract. Except for those rare experts on conflict of laws, anyone with a problem in this area can anticipate doing considerable research. To achieve the best results, one should consider which state's law might apply, which would be most favorable, and which of the possible forum states has conflict rules that would invoke the favorable state's law.

In the *Newman* case, a conflict-of-laws problem becomes a pivotal issue because the plaintiff might well lose in New York and win in Illinois. Note that the case was filed in a federal court in New York, which under *Erie* followed New York law, specifically New York conflict-of-laws rules, to determine whether New York or Illinois law should apply. *Newman*, a suit for damages for the cost of re-creating a lost manuscript, was decided in the days before photocopying and word processing. Today the court might hold the plaintiff contributorily negligent for not making a copy of the valuable lost manuscript.

Although the court does not discuss them in detail, it uses two of the traditional bases for choice of law in contract cases: (1) the place where the contract was made and (2) the place where the contract was performed.

NEWMAN

v.

CLAYTON F. SUMMY CO.

Circuit Court of Appeals, Second Circuit

133 F.2d 465 (1943)

Appellee, a composer, sent a manuscript, insured for $500, by Railway Express from Florida to appellant, a music publisher, in Chicago. Appellant later procured appellee's permission to send the manuscript to appellant's New York office. But, unknown to appellee, appellant, in shipping the script to New York, also by Railway Express, described the package as containing merely "sheet music." The script was lost in transit. Appellee, having retained no copy, spent considerable time in reproducing the script and later contracted with another publisher who published it under a royalty agreement.

* * *

The manuscript had no market value and was unique, so that it was proper to measure its value by the reasonable worth of the time and effort spent by appellee in reproducing it. On the basis of evidence, the verdict was not excessive. And appellee's failure to keep a copy of her script did not bar recovery. . . .

Appellant asserts that the trial judge erred in instructing the jury as follows: "What is the duty which the bailee, the Summy Company, owed to the bailor, Miss Newman? Being a **bailment**, the Summy Company owed the plaintiff the duty of exercising reasonable care in handling her manuscripts and in dealing with her manuscripts. * * * Negligence is usually defined in these words: Negligence is the failure to exercise a care commensurate to the hazard. That is, the amount and kind of care that would be exercised by an ordinarily prudent person in the same or similar circumstances, or that degree of diligence which the manner and the nature of the employment make it reasonable to expect. The question, therefore, that you must decide is whether the defendant failed in its duty to observe that degree of care in looking after the manuscript which had been entrusted to it." Appellant maintains that the judge should have instructed the jury that it was not liable unless it was grossly negligent because, appellant claims under *Erie R.R. v. Tompkins*, 304 U.S. 64 . . . New York law governs. By the law of New York where the trial was held, appellant was a gratuitous bailee, and a gratuitous bailee is not liable except for **gross negligence**. There is, however, no need for us to consider what would be the law of New York applicable to such a transaction occurring in New York, for here we must apply the New York doctrine of conflict of laws and that doctrine is to the effect that the applicable legal rules are those of Illinois. There can be no doubt that the arrangements for the bailment were made in Illinois, and that "performance," i.e., the shipment of the manuscripts, occurred in that state. In such circumstances, the New York courts hold that the Illinois law as to bailments should be applied.

Turning then to the Illinois decisions, it appears that the rule is that, regardless of whether or not there was a **gratuitous bailment** or one for "mutual benefit," the bailee must use the same care as he would with respect to his own property; there is no discussion of "gross negligence." . . .

The instruction given by the trial court in the instant case was not literally in accord with the language used in those cases. Perhaps the differences are not substantial. But even if they are, that is of no import, since, in the trial court, appellant did not except to the instruction on the ground of any such differences but only because of the failure to give instructions as to gross negligence. Accordingly there was no reversible error.

The judgment of the trial court is affirmed.

Case Questions

1. Why is a different standard of care applied to gratuitous bailment and bailment for hire in New York?
2. To what law (and why) does the federal court look to determine what substantive law to apply?
3. What would be an example of a bailment for hire? A gratuitous bailment?

Case Glossary

bailment
When the owner of personal property delivers possession without intent to pass title, such as when one leaves an automobile with an auto mechanic.

gross negligence
Negligence reflecting a reckless disregard for the rights of others; in contrast to *ordinary negligence*, which is commonly characterized by simple carelessness or inattention.

gratuitous bailment
A bailment for which no compensation is made.

LAW AND EQUITY

History has left the American legal system with an arbitrary division of remedies into *legal* and *equitable*. **Legal remedies** refer to relief granted by common law courts, and **equitable remedies** to those afforded by courts of **equity**, also called **chancery**. Although this subject is usually treated under the heading of remedies, it is related to jurisdiction because many states restrict equitable jurisdiction to their highest trial courts.

legal remedy
A remedy under the common law, as distinguished from an *equitable remedy*.

equitable remedy

A special remedy, such as an injunction or specific performance, not available at common law.

equity

A system for ensuring justice in circumstances where the remedies customarily available under conventional law are not adequate to ensure a fair result. Also see *chancery*.

chancery

Equity, equitable jurisdiction, a court of equity; a court that administers justice and decides controversies in accordance with the rules, principles, and precedents of equity and that follows the forms and procedure of chancery; as distinguished from a court having the jurisdiction, rules, principles, and practice of the common law.

writ

A written order directing that a specific act be performed.

complaint

The initial pleading in a civil action in which the plaintiff alleges a cause of action and asks that the wrong done to the plaintiff be remedied by the court.

The existence of legal and equitable remedies can be adequately understood only in historical context. Anglo-American law began with the administrative organization of England in the aftermath of the Norman Conquest (A.D. 1066). Although the Normans left local tribunals in operation, often applying principles of former English law, the organization of a centralized kingdom included the establishment of laws common to the entire kingdom; hence the name *common law.* Courts were established that had jurisdiction over the common law. In these courts, actions were initiated by **writs**, a word that does not have an exact counterpart in modern law. A writ stated a cause of action, so it is similar to the modern pleading we now call a **complaint**. But writs had specific names, such as the writ of **trespass** *quare clausum fregit,* which corresponds to our modern cause of action for trespass to land, or the writ *de ejectione firmoe,* corresponding to modern ejectment or eviction. The writs were essentially formulas applied to recognized legal wrongs, almost like a catalog of actions in which a party would fill in the blanks. Each action was required to fit precisely into a specific writ. In the first years of the common law courts, new writs were constantly created as different disputes arose that varied from already established actions. Gradually, however, the system crystallized, and the common law courts became formal and rigid, resisting the establishment of new writs so that novel cases that did not fall within established writs were rejected by the courts.

This development did not leave litigants without a remedy, however, because from the beginning subjects of the kingdom enjoyed the right of petitioning the king for justice. As more and more cases arose that were not recognized by the common law courts, parties sought relief from the king, who then presented these cases to the chancellor, originally an ecclesiastical office staffed by priests—not to be confused with ecclesiastical courts under the authority of the church that applied the principles of canon law. Because of a gradually mounting caseload, chancery developed its own courts independent of the common law courts and referred to as *courts of equity.* Courts of law and equity existed side by side until recent times, when the states merged law and equity into a single court having authority to order both legal and equitable remedies. Despite the merger, features of the historical differences between the two courts are still important in modern legal practice.

Courts of equity treated the cases before them somewhat differently than the common law courts. Because petitions in equity sought special justice and presented novel situations, equity courts required greater flexibility and discretion than common law courts. The aim of equity was to provide relief appropriate to merits of the case; thus, courts of equity were described as *courts of conscience,* governed by the moral issues of the case rather than *stare decisis.* Theoretically this is still true today: a judge sitting in equity is not bound by precedent. As a practical matter, modern judges rule in equity on the basis of authority (that is, prior equity cases), and expect attorneys to provide precedential authority in their arguments. Nonetheless, because judges sitting in equity sometimes exercise discretion and ignore precedent, appeal from a case in equity is frequently premised on the basis of "abuse of discretion" by the lower court judge. If a judge departs from well-established principles of equity as revealed by prior cases, an appellant may use this effectively to persuade an appellate court that the lower court judge abused discretion. Thus, justices sitting in equity are urged to follow consistent principles in a manner similar to *stare decisis* in the common law.

Jury Trials

Because courts of equity exercised moral authority and originally were cloaked with the spiritual authority of the clergy and the secular authority of the king, juries were deemed unnecessary and inappropriate. This custom remains today; there is no right to a jury trial in a case seeking equitable relief alone. The merger of law and equity compounds the jury question, as both legal and equitable remedies may be sought in the same suit, and legal as well as equitable issues may be raised in a suit for equitable relief.

Adequacy of Remedy at Law

Equitable jurisdiction was always discretionary. Because equity courts were originally established to provide remedies when the common law was unavailing, the equity courts refused to hear cases if there was an adequate remedy at law. This became the threshold question in every equity action. The usual common law remedy is *damages,* specifically, monetary compensation for an injury or wrong. There are a number of specific common law actions, such as **replevin** and **ejectment**; various extraordinary remedies titled *writs* (e.g., **writ of mandamus**, writ of prohibition) are common law remedies.

To invoke the equitable jurisdiction of the court, the claim must be based on some special feature that monetary compensation will not redress. A common request for equitable relief is for an injunction, usually a prohibitory injunction, which asks the court to order someone *not* to do something. Injunctions are based on an alleged threat of imminent and irreparable injury, asking equity to prevent the injury rather than waiting for the injury to occur and then suing for damages. Affirmative injunctions requiring a party to act (e.g., requiring a school to desegregate) are viewed less favorably by the courts because of enforcement problems.

Inadequacy of legal remedy is often asserted when the subject matter of a contract is unique or irreplaceable. For example, if someone has made a contract to purchase and the seller refuses to deliver the goods, the remedy of **specific performance** may be sought on the grounds that the goods have some unique quality, such as a family heirloom or a one-of-a-kind work of art. Real property (i.e., land and its improvements) has long been regarded as unique, making available the remedy of specific performance for contracts for the sale of real property. If the goods may be readily purchased elsewhere on the market, however, the remedy is to purchase them and sue the original seller for the difference between the cost of replacement and the cost under the contract. Money damages would then be an adequate remedy because the final cost would correspond to the price promised under the contract.

Campbell Soup Company had a practice of making **output contracts** with farmers, providing seed and agreeing to purchase the entire crop at prices fixed in advance. The Wentz brothers were Pennsylvania farmers who grew Chantenay carrots for Campbell. During the 1947 season, because of the scarcity of these carrots, the price per ton rose to $90. Because the contract price was $30, the Wentz brothers were not eager to honor the contract; they sold 62 of their 100 tons of carrots to Lojeski, who sold half of them to Campbell. Ordinarily, Campbell could pursue a legal remedy by purchasing the carrots elsewhere at the market price and suing for the difference between the market and contract prices and so receive the benefit of its bargain. Unfortunately, the carrots were unavailable on the market. Campbell was also undoubtedly concerned about

trespass

Originally covered a wide variety of wrongs, one species of which, trespass *quare clausum fregit,* constituted "trespass to land," which is a wrongful intrusion on the land of another.

replevin

A common law cause of action to recover personal property wrongfully possessed by another person.

ejectment

A common law cause of action designed to return rightful possession of real property; commonly called *eviction* in modern landlord/tenant law.

writ of mandamus

An order requiring a public officer to perform a duty.

specific performance

An equitable remedy that asks the court to order a party to a contract to perform the terms of the contract.

output contract

A contract that binds the buyer to buy and the seller to sell the entire product produced by the seller.

the possibility of other farmers under contract acting similarly in the future and so brought suit for specific performance, an equitable remedy asking the court to order performance of the contract.

CAMPBELL SOUP CO.

v.

WENTZ et al.

CAMPBELL SOUP CO.

v.

LOJESKI

United States Court of Appeals, Third Circuit

172 F.2d 80 (1948)

On January 9, 1948, Campbell, suspecting that defendant was selling its "contract carrots," refused to purchase any more, and instituted these suits against the Wentz brothers to enjoin further sale of the contract carrots to others, and to compel specific performance of the contract. . . .

We think that on the question of adequacy of the legal remedy, the case is one appropriate for specific performance. It was expressly found that at the time of the trial it was "virtually impossible to obtain Chantenay carrots in the open market." This Chantenay carrot is one which the plaintiff uses in large quantities, furnishing the seed to the growers with whom it makes contracts. It was not claimed that in nutritive value it is any better than other types of carrots. Its blunt shape makes it easier to handle in processing, and its color and texture differ from other varieties. The color is brighter than other carrots. It appears that the plaintiff uses carrots in 15 of its 21 soups. It also appeared that it uses these Chantenay carrots diced in some of them and that the appearance is uniform. . . .

The trial court concluded that the plaintiff had failed to establish that the carrots, "judged by objective standards," are unique goods. . . . [T]hat the test for specific performance is not necessarily "objective" is shown by the many cases in which equity has given it to enforce contracts for articles—family heirlooms and the like—the value of which was personal to the plaintiff.

. . . Here the goods of the special type contracted for were unavailable on the open market, the plaintiff had contracted for them long ahead in anticipation of his needs, and had built up general reputation for its products as part of which reputation uniform appearance was important. We think if this were all that was involved in the case, specific performance should have been granted.

The reason that we shall affirm instead of reversing with an order for specific performance is found in the contract itself. We think it is too hard a bargain and too one-sided an agreement to entitle the plaintiff to relief in a court of conscience. . . . This form has quite obviously been drawn by skillful draftsmen with the buyer's interests in mind.

[The Court then discusses the contract paragraph by paragraph, demonstrating that it gives Campbell numerous powers and protections while affording no protection to the farmers, and concludes that the contract is "unconscionable."]

. . . That equity does not enforce unconscionable bargains is too well established to require elaborate citation.

. . . As already said, we do not suggest that this contract is illegal. All we say is that the sum total of its provisions drives too hard a bargain for a court of conscience to assist.

The judgments will be affirmed.

Case Questions

1. How is it that the appellate court totally disagreed with the trial court yet affirmed the trial court's decision?
2. What is Campbell Soup's remedy in future cases like this?
3. What is meant by "unconscionable"?

Clean Hands Principle

Although equity is not bound by *stare decisis*, a number of principles of equity have developed over the years, and are expressed in the form of **equitable maxims**. A maxim is often stated in a form resembling a moral commandment. One has already been discussed: Equity will not intervene if there is an adequate remedy at law. Other maxims reflect the moral basis for equitable relief, an important one of these maxims being the **clean hands doctrine**. Because equity is a court of conscience based on moral principles that dispenses special justice, an equity court may refuse to give relief if the petitioner has not acted in good faith or is otherwise undeserving of special consideration.

Statutes of Limitations and Laches

Another difference between legal and equitable remedies arises in the context of delay in bringing suit. Common law actions may be barred by statutes of limitations. Each state has legislated that suits must be brought within a certain period of time, usually measured in years. Some statutes creating causes of action fix the period within which suit may be brought. Unless the state legislature has otherwise specified a time period, equity follows the maxim expressed by the word **laches**. Rather than fixing precise periods of time, laches may be used as a defense to an action in equity if the action is unreasonably delayed to the prejudice of a party who has changed position during the delay. Circumstances might dictate that a party bring an action very promptly or, conversely, that because no one was harmed by a long delay, no injustice would occur by allowing the action.

Domestic Relations

Prior to the establishment of the American republic, family law matters fell within the jurisdiction of ecclesiastical courts and were governed by canon law. With the American separation of church and state, the law of domestic relations, having no common law precedent, fell within equity jurisdiction. This has had a profound effect on the law, as equity entails great discretion. This is generally appropriate because, with divorce and custody questions, problems tend to be particularized and each case must be examined on its own merits. No-fault divorce, however, has discouraged divorce contests and encouraged parties to negotiate the conditions of custody and the division of property. State legislatures have been active in recent years in setting the standards for child support and providing the means to collect it.

Language

It is important to note that the historical separation of law and equity has given rise to different terms. Because equity actions are brought by petition, the parties to an action in equity are called *petitioner* and *respondent* rather than their common law equivalents, *plaintiff* and *defendant*. Judges sitting in equity are in some jurisdictions referred to as **chancellor** or **master in equity**.

---

equitable maxim

A general rule or principle guiding decisionmaking in courts of equity, often serving the function that *precedent* would serve in a common law court.

clean hands doctrine

An *equitable maxim* according to which a court of equity will refuse to provide a remedy to a petitioner who has acted in bad faith (with "unclean hands").

laches

An equitable principle roughly equivalent to a statute of limitations at common law; it prevents a party from bringing a petition (suit) when there has been unreasonable delay in doing so.

chancellor (master in equity)

A judge of a court of chancery or court of equity.

SUMMARY

The American legal system is complicated by the existence of separate state and federal jurisdictions. Not only do these have different spheres of authority, but the states themselves are also independent jurisdictions. The division of judicial power is expressed in the U.S. Constitution, which grants specific power to the federal government and reserves the remaining authority to the states. The Constitution is the supreme law of the land, and no official act, law, or judicial order may violate it. The federal judiciary exercises significant authority over state law under the due process and equal protection clauses of the Fourteenth Amendment. The Constitution also requires that the states honor the acts, laws, and judicial orders of other states under the full faith and credit clause.

The Constitution also dictates subject matter jurisdiction of the federal courts, which have jurisdiction over federal question cases (those arising under the Constitution, laws, and treaties of the federal government) and diversity of citizenship cases (those given federal jurisdiction because of the grant of authority over citizens of different states). In diversity cases, by virtue of the decision in *Erie Railroad v. Tompkins*, the federal courts apply state law rather than developing a general federal common law.

In cases in which there is some question as to which state's substantive law should apply, each state has its own rules, called conflict of laws, to determine whether it should apply its own law or that of a state more closely involved with the facts giving rise to the lawsuit.

A further complication in the American legal system is the historical existence of common law courts and courts of equity. Equity court first arose several centuries ago in England to provide remedies for disputes that the common law courts would not hear. Equity developed special remedies differing from the usual common law remedy of monetary compensation (damages) and developed its own principles based on moral principles. As a result, equitable remedies are more flexible and less bound by precedent than legal remedies. One important feature that distinguishes law from equity is the traditional absence of the right to a jury in equity.

Today law and equity have merged, so that American judges provide both equitable and legal relief, and legal and equitable remedies may be requested in the same suit. Nevertheless, many of the traditional differences have been maintained.

KEY TERMS

admiralty	diversity of citizenship	hearing
bankruptcy	due process clause	laches
case and controversy	ejectment	legal remedy
certiorari	equal protection of the laws	*lex loci delicti*
chancellor (master in	equitable maxim	limited subject matter
equity)	equitable remedy	jurisdiction
chancery	equity	notice
clean hands doctrine	federal question	output contract
complaint	full faith and credit	patent
conflict of laws	general subject matter	preemption
copyright	jurisdiction	procedural due process

replevin   subject matter jurisdiction   writ
significant relationship test   substantive due process   writ of certiorari
specific performance   trademark   writ of mandamus
standing   trespass

CHAPTER REVIEW QUESTIONS

1. How does the division between state and federal governments in the United States differ from other countries?
2. How was the authority of the federal government established?
3. How was the authority of the states established?
4. What form of due process is particularly aimed at legislation?
5. What is *standing?*
6. To whom does *full faith and credit* apply?
7. To what does *subject matter jurisdiction* refer?
8. What kinds of cases are referred to as *federal question cases?*
9. How did courts of equity arise?
10. What is the biggest difference between law and equity?

CRITICAL THINKING QUESTIONS

1. Should we do away with some or all jury trials?
2. Does diversity of citizenship jurisdiction make sense today?

CYBER EXERCISE

Opinions of the United States Supreme Court are accessible at a number of websites, in particular http://www.supremecourtus.gov. The United States Supreme Court decided *Wyeth v. Levine,* 129 S. Ct. 1187 (2009) on March 4, 2009. The case contained both concurring and dissenting opinions in addition to the majority opinion excerpted in this chapter. Locate the case at the United States Supreme Court website and answer the following questions concerning the case:

a. Why did Justice Breyer, who joined in the majority opinion, write a concurring opinion?
b. Did Justice Thomas also join in the majority opinion?
c. Why did Justice Thomas write a concurring opinion?
d. What is Justice Alito's main argument in his dissenting opinion?
e. Do you agree more with the majority opinion, Justice Thomas's concurring opinion, or the dissenting opinion, and why?

REVIEW PROBLEM

Whereas Chapters 3 and 4 covered sources of the law, Chapters 5 and 6 dealt with the structure of authority, particularly within the courts. *Li v. State of Oregon* deals with the interplay of law, constitution, different branches of government, and different levels of government, along with the sovereignty of the people, in amending the state constitution. When these interrelationships come into conflict, courts inevitably become involved to determine where authority lies and how it must be exercised under the law. This case is offered as a test of what has been learned in the last few chapters.

When the county commissioners of Multnomah County (Portland), Oregon, decided that the Oregon Constitution required them to grant marriage licenses to same-sex couples, they must have known a legal battle would ensue. It culminated in *Li v. State*, which outlines the legal authority of all aspects of state government with regard to marriage, and much more. This case should not be read merely to consider the issue of same-sex marriage and equal protection; the court rather neatly sidesteps that one. As a matter of fact, focusing on that issue will prevent the reader from understanding the case. Divisive issues such as the legality of same-sex marriage, abortion, and the death penalty present moral issues that society cannot reconcile, so they end up in court. A careful reading of *Li* shows how the court concentrates on legal process to resolve the problem in an orderly fashion. In so doing, the court deals with the relation of local versus state authority; legislative versus administrative authority; and the authority to make the laws, to interpret them, and to carry them out. In addition, we have an example of the authority and power of the people to amend the state constitution within the context of majority rule versus rights claimed by a minority.

The opinion seems to say that the proponents of same-sex marriage in Oregon ought to pursue rights to *benefits* as domestic partners rather than the right to marry. The opinion also hints that this court might well refuse to recognize an out-of-state marriage as against the public policy of the state of Oregon. The case also shows the relation of the courts. The court of appeals certified the question for the Oregon Supreme Court, probably recognizing that the issue would ultimately be decided by that court anyway. The Oregon Supreme Court did not hesitate to find the trial court in error.

As you read *Li v. State*, you must resist the temptation to agree or disagree with the reasoning because you like or dislike the result. Suspend any biases until you have read the case objectively. Imagine that you were to argue against this decision before the U.S. Supreme Court: would your cause be served if your argument were based on the homophobic bias of the Oregon Supreme Court? Note, by the way, the absence of a dissenting opinion.

Li

v.

State

Supreme Court of Oregon

338 Or. 376, 110 P.3d 91 (2005)

The dispute underlying this declaratory judgment case began when the Chair of the Multnomah County Board of Commissioners ordered the Records Management Division of Multnomah County (the county) . . . to issue marriage licenses to same-sex couples who applied for such licenses from the county. Pursuant to those licenses, approximately 3,000 same-sex couples participated in individual marriage ceremonies conducted by various officials empowered under Oregon law to perform marriages. Those officials forwarded the documentation generated by each ceremony to the State Registrar, who maintains a central record of marriages performed in Oregon. The State Registrar, however, refused to register the documents on the ground that same-sex marriages do not comport with the provisions of ORS [Oregon Revised Statutes] chapter 106, which regulates marriages performed in Oregon. As a result, the plaintiffs in this case—nine same-sex couples, . . . the advocacy group Basic Rights Oregon, the American Civil Liberties Union, and the county (collectively, plaintiffs)—brought this action against the State of Oregon, the Governor, the Attorney General, the Director of the Department of Human Services, and the State Registrar (collectively, the state) seeking a declaration that the statutes prohibiting same-sex couples from marrying on the same terms as opposite-sex couples violated Article I, section 20, of the Oregon Constitution. Article I, section 20 . . . provides: "No law shall be passed granting to any citizen or class of citizens privileges, or immunities, which, upon the same terms, shall not equally belong to all citizens." . . .

Our review begins with ORS 106.010, which defines marriage in Oregon . . . : "Marriage is a civil contract entered into in person by males at least 17 years of age and females at least 17 years of age, who are otherwise capable, and solemnized in accordance with ORS 106.150."

Although the phrase "entered into in person by males * * * and females" suggests that marriage in Oregon is a contract between a male and female, it is not necessarily dispositive. However, when that phrase is read in context with other statutes relating to marriage, no doubt remains. ORS 106.150(1) . . . requires the parties to a marriage to declare that "they take each other to be *husband and wife*." . . . ORS 106.041(1) . . . requires the official conducting the marriage ceremony "to join together as *husband and wife* the persons named in the license."

Although the legislature has not defined the terms "husband" or "wife" for the purposes of ORS chapter 106, . . . we give those words their "plain, natural and ordinary meaning." . . . Here, by their respective dictionary definitions, "husband" means "a married man," and "wife" means a "married woman." *Webster's Third New Int'l Dictionary* 1104, 2614 (unabridged ed 2002). As a result, although nothing in ORS chapter 106 expressly states that marriage is limited to opposite-sex couples, the context that ORS 106.150(1) and

ORS 106.041(1) provide leaves no doubt that, as a statutory matter, marriage in Oregon is so limited.

In November 2004, while the appeals were pending, Oregon voters adopted Ballot Measure 36 (2004), a voter-initiated amendment to the Oregon Constitution aimed at defining marriage as a relationship between one man and one woman. That amendment, which became effective on December 2, 2004, provides:

> "It is the policy of oregon, and its political subdivisions, that only a marriage between one man and one woman shall be valid or legally recognized as a marriage." . . .

Based on the foregoing, we conclude that the use of the word "policy" in Measure 36 is intended to signal a presently enforceable tenet of Oregon constitutional law. And, with respect to the remaining text, there is no ambiguity regarding the measure's substantive effect. Today, marriage in Oregon—an institution once limited to opposite-sex couples only by statute—now is so limited by the state constitution as well. As the later-enacted (and more specific) constitutional provision, Measure 36 resolves any prospective claims that plaintiffs may have had under Article I, section 20, to obtain marriage licenses. The claims of the five same-sex couples that they are entitled as a matter of state law, now or hereafter, to obtain marriage licenses and to marry thus fail. . . .

Plaintiffs also raise issues concerning the effect of Measure 36 on the remaining same-sex couples, who received licenses and participated in marriage ceremonies before that measure became effective. . . . As we explain below, the county did not have authority to issue the licenses for the marriages in question. . . .

[Oregon case law establishes] that the state and, more specifically, the legislature, is the locus of power over marriage-related matters in Oregon. If that power is broad enough to preempt other states' contrary marriage policies, it inescapably is broad enough to preempt similar policies generated by a political subdivision of this state, such as the county. . . . We conclude that Oregon law currently places the regulation of marriage exclusively within the province of the state's legislative power. . . .

[Citing the *Cooper* case, the county argued that county officers are sworn to uphold the state constitution and may not act in violation of the law. The county commissioners, after consultation with the county attorney, had concluded that the Oregon Constitution required same-sex couples to be issued marriage licenses.]

But when *Cooper* [*v. Eugene School Dist. No. 4J*] is read properly, it contains no hint that the duty to be mindful of the state and federal constitutions somehow grants to a governmental official powers not otherwise devolved by law on that official to take actions and fashion remedies that, under any other circumstances, would constitute *ultra vires* acts. In reaching a contrary conclusion in the appeals before us here, the county erroneously transmogrified a governmental official's ongoing obligation to support the constitution into an implied grant of authority, respecting any laws that the official must administer, to prescribe remedies for any perceived constitutional shortcomings in such laws *without regard to the scope of the official's statutory authority to act.* . . .

In summary, we conclude as follows. First, since the effective date of Measure 36, marriage in Oregon has been limited under the Oregon Constitution to opposite-sex couples. Second, Oregon statutory law in existence before the effective date of Measure 36 also limited, and continues to limit, the right to obtain marriage licenses to opposite-sex couples. Third, marriage licenses issued to same-sex couples in Multnomah County before that date were issued without authority and were void at the time that they were issued, and we therefore need not consider the independent effect, if any, of Measure 36 on those marriage licenses. In short, none of plaintiffs' claims properly before the court is well taken. . . .

The judgment of the circuit court is reversed, and the case is remanded to the circuit court with instructions to dismiss the action.

Queries:

1. Can an amendment to a constitution be unconstitutional?
2. In *Goodridge v. Department of Public Health,* 14 Mass. L. Rptr. 591, the Supreme Judicial Court of Massachusetts held the ban on same-sex marriages to be unconstitutional. What happens when an Oregon same-sex couple goes to Massachusetts, marries, and returns to Oregon?

Student CD-Rom

For additional materials, please go to the CD in this book.

Online Companion™

For additional resources, please go to http://www.paralegal.delmar.cengage.com

CHAPTER 7
PROCEDURE IN CIVIL CASES

INTRODUCTION

Procedural law is the oil that greases the legal machine. No area of law has more theoretical or practical importance. From a theoretical perspective, procedural law informs us about the basic premises of the legal system itself. The adversarial premise of the American legal system maintains that our system is based on competition and that individuals act in their own self-interest and cannot be trusted unless their power positions are equalized by a disinterested and perhaps indifferent tribunal. The fact that we preserve the jury system suggests that we do not even trust the impartiality of our judges. The rules that exclude evidence suggest that we do not trust the capacity of juries to sift good evidence from bad.

The theoretical premise at the heart of our procedure is; if the means by which conflict in society is resolved are fair and equal, justice will, on the whole, be achieved. Acceptance of this premise is a virtual catechism of lawyers. When criminal defense attorneys are asked, "Would you defend a guilty man? Would you help a guilty man be acquitted and go free?," the answer is usually the same: "Every person is entitled to competent legal representation; it is not for the attorney to judge; it is the job of the prosecution to prove guilt beyond a reasonable doubt." This response can be understood only in the context of a system that places procedure on a pedestal.

The practical importance of procedure is equal to its philosophical importance. Rights have no meaning without a means to enforce them. Without a procedure for enforcement, the statement of a right is merely symbolic.

Each state and the federal system have compiled their own set of rules of civil procedure, which henceforth are referred to as "the rules." These treat some procedural questions with great specificity, allowing little room for interpretation, but other questions may be adequately understood only by researching rules of court, judicial interpretations, or even local procedural customs. The competent practitioner must have a thorough understanding of the rules of the jurisdictions in which practice is to be conducted, but that is beyond the scope of the treatment of civil procedure here. What follows is merely a model and an overview.

Procedure is arbitrary and technical, yet it is always subject to attack for its fairness under the due process clause of the Fourteenth Amendment. Cases concerning procedural due process tend to be exceedingly complex and difficult. One of the reasons for this may be that the social values underlying the rules are obscure at best. In comparison, substantive areas of law, such as tort and contract, may rely on values supported by a general consensus. For example, in contract law, it is a premise of our society that a person should fulfill lawful promises; in tort law, it is a premise that a person who wrongfully injures another should compensate the injured party. In contrast, is there any fundamental reason that a jury may not be exposed to hearsay evidence, that a hearing be adversarial rather than mediatory in nature, or that a complaint must state a cause of action?

PROCEDURAL FRAMEWORK OF LEGAL DISPUTES

As shown in Exhibit 7-1, a basic model of the legal processing of a dispute underlies American procedural law. In its minute details, it differs from jurisdiction to jurisdiction, but the basic idea is the same. Keep this model in mind as you proceed through the chapter.

DETERMINING THE PROPER COURT FOR THE SUIT

In addition to the problems of subject matter jurisdiction discussed in Chapter 6, a number of obstacles may arise concerning the exercise of the court's authority in a particular case.

EXHIBIT 7-1   PROCEDURAL FRAMEWORK OF LEGAL DISPUTES

1. One who proposes to seek relief through the legal system must formally state to a court the basis for a grievance, and the grounds asserted must amount to a grievance that the law recognizes as enforceable.
2. The opponent in a legal action must be notified of the suit and given the opportunity to prepare a defense.
3. Prior to a trial, the parties to a lawsuit will have every reasonable opportunity and means to become fully informed of the factual and legal arguments of the other side.
4. If a dispute proceeds to trial, the trial will be conducted as an adversarial proceeding in which each side has every opportunity to challenge the evidence and arguments of the other side.
5. In an adversarial trial, decisions of the court must be based on the evidence and arguments presented in court before an impartial tribunal.
6. Any departure from procedural rules will provide a basis for challenging the fairness of the process.
7. Procedural error takes precedence over substantive goals. The corollary to this is that if the procedure was fair, the results cannot be questioned except in extraordinary circumstances.

Service of Process

Notification of the defendant in a lawsuit is accomplished by **service of process**. This refers to the presentation to the defendant of a copy of the complaint, along with a summons informing the defendant that an answer to the complaint must be served on the plaintiff's attorney within a specified number of days, commonly 20. It is an essential component of procedural due process, the other being a (fair) hearing. *Service* refers to presentation of the documents; service of the complaint and summons is **original service**. (After original service, documents may be served on the attorneys for the parties by mail.) **Process** refers to the document commanding a party to do or not do something. At common law, original process was formerly called an *original writ* or *writ of process*. In equity, it was called a *subpoena*. Today, original process is usually simply called a *summons*.

Service of process is effected by filing the complaint and summons with the court, followed by presentation to the defendant of the complaint and summons by one authorized to do so, typically a sheriff or deputy or a U.S. Marshal for federal cases. Private process servers may also be authorized by the law and are typically used if the defendant may be purposely avoiding service or is difficult to locate. Deputies and marshals have many duties and cannot be expected to go to great efforts in serving process in civil cases. Attorneys commonly offer assistance in locating defendants, such as informing the sheriff of the defendant's place of work or the hours the defendant is likely to be at home. The place, time, and manner of service of process must be in accord with the rules or other statutes of the jurisdiction in which process is served. The different methods of accomplishing service of process are described later in this subsections and are summarized in Exhibit 7-2.

service of process
Delivery of a summons, writ, complaint, or other process to the opposite party or other person entitled to receive it, in such manner as the law prescribes.

original service
The first presentation of legal documents to the defendant, after which service is usually made to the defendant's attorney.

process
In criminal law, the document commanding a party to do or not to do something; see *service of process*.

EXHIBIT 7-2 SERVICE OF PROCESS

METHOD OF SERVICE	DESCRIPTION
Personal service	Presenting the summons and the complaint personally to the defendant
Substituted service	Presenting the summons and the complaint to someone other than the defendant, such as someone living in the defendant's home
Publication	Publication of a legal notice in an authorized periodical

personal service

The presentation of the summons and complaint upon the defendant personally.

substituted service

Service of process to someone other than the defendant, such as a relative living at the defendant's abode; requirements are usually defined by statute.

publication

In reference to *service of process,* a means of service by publishing notice in the legal section of a newspaper periodically as prescribed by statute.

Presenting the summons and complaint personally to the defendant is called **personal service** and is the ideal form of service, especially in jurisdictions in which the defendant signs a paper, thus assuring the court that the defendant was properly notified of the suit and making it difficult for the defendant to challenge the service later. The rules or statutes also provide for **substituted service**, whereby process can be served on someone other than the defendant, such as a relative living at the defendant's abode. Substituted service that does not strictly comply with the law is invalid. If a diligent search for the defendant fails to reveal the defendant's whereabouts, service may also be made by publication in a newspaper of general circulation. **Publication** refers to the publication of a legal notice in an authorized periodical, such as a newspaper of general circulation. Again, the manner of service by publication must strictly follow the law.

The rules provide for service in special situations. Business entities, for example, call for different service: a corporation may be served by service upon an authorized agent of the corporation; partnerships may be served by service upon a partner. Minors, prisoners, military personnel on active duty, legal incompetents, and the like may call for special treatment.

Service of nonresidents is accomplished under the authority of **long-arm statutes,** with the cooperation of the officers of the defendant's state of residence. If the nonresident is present in the state in which the suit is filed, personal service within that state is effective. A lawsuit may be brought in a state court against a nonresident and the nonresident may even be served in his home state, but that does not necessarily confer personal jurisdiction. In *Cockrell v. Hillerich & Bradsby Co.,* a South Carolina plaintiff attempted to include a Massachusetts defendant in the case by using the South Carolina long-arm statute.

COCKRELL

v.

HILLERICH & BRADSBY CO., James A. Sherwood, University of Massachusetts at Lowell Baseball Research Center, the National Federation of State High School Associations, and the South Carolina High School League

Supreme Court of South Carolina

363 S.C. 485, 611 S.E.2d 505 (2005)

Facts

On March 16, 2002, Ryan Cockrell, a thirteen-year-old seventh grader, was pitching in a Greenwood High School junior varsity baseball game. A line drive ball off the bat of an opposing player hit Ryan in the head[,] causing severe injuries. The bat was an aluminum bat manufactured by defendant Hillerich & Bradsby Company d/b/a Louisville Slugger (Hillerich). The respondents, the University of Massachusetts at Lowell Baseball Research Center (Research Center) and James Sherwood (Sherwood), a mechanical engineering professor and the Director of the Research Center, certified the bat as meeting certain National Collegiate Athletic Association (NCAA) regulations. . . .

Issue

Did the circuit court err in granting the respondents' motion to dismiss for lack of personal jurisdiction?

Discussion

I. Background

Typically, aluminum bats substantially outper-form traditional wooden bats and other metal bats. However, aluminum bats also increase the risk to pitchers and other infield players because the high speed of the balls batted off these bats decreases these players' reaction time [the time within which players have to react]. The NCAA developed a maximum-batted exit speed and certain weight and length requirements for aluminum bats and announced that the respondents would test and certify that all aluminum bat models meet these requirements.

After the respondents have certified a bat model, a permanent certification mark must be clearly displayed on the barrel end of each bat. . . . We note the certi-fication of a bat means simply [that] it has passed the standards which the NCAA has set forth. It does not mean the bat has been otherwise tested for safety.

II. Personal Jurisdiction

Sherwood is a resident of Massachusetts and the Research Center is a corporation with its principal place of business in Massachusetts. . . .

Specific jurisdiction over a cause of action arising from a defendant's contacts with the state is granted pursuant to the long-arm statute. S.C. Code Ann. § 36-2-803 (2003). . . . Because South Carolina treats its long-arm statute as coextensive with the due process clause, the sole question becomes whether the exercise of personal jurisdiction would violate due process. . . .

Due Process/Sufficient Minimum Contacts

Due process requires that there exist minimum contacts between the defendant and the forum state such that maintenance of the suit does not offend tra-ditional notions of fair play and substantial justice. . . . Further, due process mandates that the defendant pos-sess sufficient minimum contacts with the forum state, so that he could reasonably anticipate being haled into court there. . . . Without minimum contacts, the court does not have the "power" to adjudicate the action. . . . The court must also find that the exercise of jurisdiction is "reasonable" or "fair." . . .

Under the fairness prong, the court must consider: (1) the duration of the activity of the nonresident within the state; (2) the character and circumstances of the commission of the nonresident's acts; (3) the inconvenience resulting to the parties by conferring or refusing to confer jurisdiction over the nonresident; and (4) the State's interest in exercising jurisdiction. . . .

The appellant alleges the following facts support finding the respondents purposefully availed themselves of the laws of South Carolina. The Research Center was the exclusive testing and certification facility for all bats used in schools under the auspice[s] of the NCAA and the National Federation of State High School Associations . . .

[The court draws an analogy with *Moosally v. W. W. Norton & Co.*, a libel case in which the plaintiffs sued the author of a book about a battleship explosion that placed the blame for the explosion on the plaintiffs. *Moosally* held sale of the book nationally, as well as in bookstores in South Carolina, did not meet the test of minimal contacts.]

The Court of Appeals concluded that South Carolina does not have specific personal jurisdiction over a defendant who is the producer of a nationwide television program and the author of a book distributed nationwide who would directly profit from the sale of his books. Likewise, we conclude that South Carolina also does not have personal jurisdiction over the respondents in this case. The bats did not arrive in South Carolina through the respondents' efforts. As the NCAA regulations state, "[u]se of the certification mark to advertise or promote the sale or distribution of bats is expressly prohibited." Hillerich unilaterally dis-tributed and sold them in South Carolina. The respon-dents had no control over the distribution of the bats and did not profit from their sale. The respondents merely certified the bats as having met the NCAA rules, which is clearly less activity than producing a nationwide television program or authoring a book. . . .

In conclusion, we hold the respondents do not have the minimum contacts with South Carolina necessary to comply with the due process requirements. Accordingly, the trial court correctly granted the respondents' motion to dismiss due to lack of personal jurisdiction.

Case Questions

1. Why would the long-arm statute apply to Hillerich, the bat maker, even if it was not a South Carolina company?
2. Why is there a need for long-arm statutes in the first place?

long-arm statutes

Statutes that provide a state with jurisdiction over persons or entities ordinarily beyond its territory and usual jurisdiction.

seduction

Inducing (usually by deception or promise to marry) a person (usually a chaste, unmarried woman) to have sex.

Service other than personal service will be scrutinized carefully by the judge if the defendant does not answer and does not appear for a judicial proceeding. Judges are understandably reluctant to determine the rights of an absent defendant.

The *Wyman* case presents several interesting procedural features, some of which are difficult to reconstruct because of the age of the case. In 1937, personal service of process was preferred even more than today. At that time, the causes of action for seduction and breach of promise to marry were recognized in most states as in Florida, which later abolished them, but they were in disrepute, particularly in New York, which may explain why the complaint was filed in Florida rather than New York. (**Seduction** is one of the so-called **heart-balm suits**, along with **breach of promise to marry**, **criminal conversation**, and **alienation of affections**, which were designed to compensate for loss of or interference with intimate relationships. Most states have abolished such causes of action through what have come to be known as *anti–heart-balm statutes.*) Because the defendant did not answer the Florida complaint, the Florida court entered a **default judgment**, which the plaintiff then attempted to enforce in New York.

WYMAN

v.

NEWHOUSE

Circuit Court of Appeals, Second Circuit

93 F.2d 313 (2d Cir. 1937)

This appeal is from a judgment entered dismissing the complaint on motion before trial. The action is on a judgment entered by default in a Florida state court, a jury having assessed the damages. The recovery there was for money loaned, money advanced for appellee, and for seduction under promise of marriage.

* * *

Appellant and appellee were both married, but before this suit appellant's husband died. They had known each other for some years and had engaged in meretricious relations.

The affidavits submitted by the appellee deemed to be true for the purpose of testing the alleged error of dismissing the complaint established that he was a resident of New York and never lived in Florida. On October 25, 1935, while appellee was in Salt Lake City, Utah, he received a telegram from the appellant, which read: "Account illness home planning leaving. Please come on way back. Must see you." Upon appellee's return to New York he received a letter from appellant stating that her mother was dying in Ireland; that she was leaving the United States for good to go to her mother; that she could not go without seeing the appellee once more; and that she wanted to discuss her affairs with him before she left. Shortly after the receipt of this letter, they spoke to each other on the telephone, whereupon the appellant repeated, in a hysterical and distressed voice, the substance of her letter. Appellee promised to go to Florida in a week or ten days and agreed to notify her when he would arrive. This he did, but before leaving New York by plane he received a letter couched in endearing terms and expressing love and affection for him, as well as her delight at his coming. Before leaving New York, appellee telegraphed appellant, suggesting arrangements for their accommodations together while in Miami. She telegraphed him at a hotel in Washington, D.C., where he was to stop en route, advising him that the arrangements requested had been made. Appellee arrived at 6 o'clock in the morning at the Miami Airport and saw the appellant standing with her sister some 75 feet distant. He was met by a deputy sheriff who, upon identifying appellee, served him with process in a suit for $500,000. A photographer was present who attempted to take his picture. Thereupon a stranger introduced himself and offered to take appellee to his home, stating that he knew a lawyer who was acquainted with the appellant's attorney. The attorney whom appellee was advised to consult came to the stranger's home and seemed to know about the case. The attorney invited appellee to his office, and upon his arrival he found one of the lawyers for the appellant there. Appellee did not retain the Florida attorney to represent him. He returned to New York by plane that evening and consulted his New York counsel, who advised him to ignore the summons served in Florida. He did so, and judgment was entered by default. Within a few days after the service of process, the appellant came to New York and sought an interview with the appellee. It resulted in their meeting at the home of the appellee's attorney. She was accompanied by her Florida counsel.

These facts and reasonable deductions therefrom convincingly establish that fraud [was] perpetrated upon him by the appellant in falsely representing her mother's illness, her intention to leave the United States, and her love and affection for him, when her sole purpose and apparent thought was to induce him to come within the Florida jurisdiction so as to serve him in an action for damages. Appellant does not deny making these representations. All her statements of great and undying love were disproved entirely by her appearance at the airport and participation in the happening there. She never went to Ireland to see her mother, if indeed the latter was sick at all.

In asking for judgment based on these Florida proceedings, appellant relies upon article 4, section 1, of the United States Constitution, providing that "Full Faith and Credit shall be given in each State to the public Acts, Records, and Judicial Proceedings of every other State." . . .

This judgment is attacked for fraud perpetrated upon the appellee which goes to the jurisdiction of the Florida court over his person. A judgment procured fraudulently, as here, lacks jurisdiction and is null and void. A fraud affecting the jurisdiction is equivalent to a lack of jurisdiction. The appellee was not required to proceed against the judgment in Florida. . . .

Judgment affirmed.

Case Questions

1. Did the Florida trial court have any reason to believe that the service of process was accomplished by fraud?
2. Does the court's opinion suggest a union of a conniving plaintiff and an unscrupulous attorney?

In Personam Jurisdiction

In personam or **personal jurisdiction** refers to the authority of the court to determine the rights of the defendant in a lawsuit. (Personal jurisdiction over the plaintiff results from the plaintiff's filing the suit.) When service of process is deficient or not in accordance with law, the court does not have personal jurisdiction over the defendant. The defendant may simply be beyond the reach of the court. If a resident of Oregon is involved in an accident in Oregon with a resident of California, the Oregon resident can object to personal jurisdiction in California; California would have personal jurisdiction under its long-arm statute only if the accident occurred in California.

Appearance by the defendant in court confers personal jurisdiction despite deficient service of process. In many jurisdictions, the defendant may enter a **special**

heart-balm suits
Now largely discredited lawsuits for emotional injuries, such as *seduction, breach of promise to marry, criminal conversation,* and *alienation of affections.*

breach of promise to marry
A cause of action based on breaking off an engagement to marry.

criminal conversation
Causing a married man or woman to commit adultery. Despite its name, this is a tort, not a crime, and it has generally been abolished in most states as a cause of action.

alienation of affections
Taking away the love, companionship, or help of another person's husband or wife; still recognized in a few states.

default judgment
May be entered against a party that fails to file a required document in a lawsuit, particularly for failing to file an answer.

in personam (personal) jurisdiction
The power a court has over the person of a defendant to subject that person to decisions and rulings made in a case.

special appearance
An appearance in court by a defendant, for the purpose of challenging personal jurisdiction, that does not confer personal jurisdiction, as an appearance would otherwise do.

appearance solely for the purpose of contesting personal jurisdiction, and the appearance will not be construed as conferring personal jurisdiction. Challenges to personal jurisdiction must follow the rules if the defendant is to avoid a waiver of defenses to personal jurisdiction. Of course, a nonresident may remain silent and later challenge jurisdiction of the original court if the plaintiff attempts to enforce a judgment under full faith and credit in the defendant's home state, but a significant risk is involved because the defendant's state might reject the defenses and enforce the judgment, leaving the defendant without an opportunity to defend the case on its merits.

In Rem Jurisdiction

Under certain circumstances, the purpose of a suit may be to determine the status of property rather than to determine personal rights; in such a situation, an **in rem action** may be brought. *Rem* is from the Latin word *res*, roughly translated as "thing." Courts generally have jurisdiction over real and personal property located within their jurisdictions. In rem proceedings are often brought to prevent the removal of property from the jurisdiction, typically in **attachment** proceedings to secure court control over property subject to a debt. Some actions involve property but operate only between parties to the suit and hence are called **quasi in rem**. Conceptually, it is difficult to distinguish quasi in rem from in personam actions. In rem actions are fairly rare because the primary purpose of most lawsuits is to determine the respective rights of persons.

Certain real property actions in equity are in rem or quasi in rem actions, such as suits to quiet title or to remove a cloud on title. These suits are usually brought in connection with a real estate transaction when an attorney (or title company) discovers some potential defect in the title that should be cleared up before the transaction is completed. For example, a person can acquire title by adverse possession; that is, someone without rightful possession of real property who nevertheless enters on the land and occupies it for a certain number of years (20 at common law, less under most state statutes) may acquire title. The presence at some past time of adverse possession may raise doubts about title that can be settled by an in rem suit. Essentially, then, the suit is against the property rather than against specific persons. Whenever the parties are known, caution suggests that they should be included as defendants.

Another example of an in rem action is a suit for divorce. In theory, the **res** in a divorce action is the marriage—divorce has the effect of changing the status from married to unmarried. In practice, courts are extremely reluctant to treat divorce actions as in rem proceedings because ordinarily divorce actions involve the adjudication of personal rights. Alimony and child support, for example, are considered in personam questions.

These examples demonstrate that in rem proceedings must be restricted to special circumstances; frequently, as in attachment, they are ancillary to a larger in personam suit. Whenever a known person's rights are involved, personal jurisdiction should be established to prevent a later attack on the judicial order.

In Personam, in Rem, and Quasi in Rem Compared

In personam, in rem, and quasi in rem (see Exhibit 7-3) are difficult to distinguish in the abstract. The cases, the history, and the difference between jurisdictional definitions

EXHIBIT 7-3   BASES OF JURISDICTION

TYPE OF JURISDICTION	DESCRIPTION
In personam (personal) jurisdiction	The authority of the court to determine the rights of the defendant in a lawsuit
In rem jurisdiction	The authority of the court to determine the status of property
Quasi in rem jurisdiction	The authority of a court to determine the status of property to satisfy a personal claim and used when the defendant cannot be served personally

have left the distinctions quite confused. With this confusion in mind, the following is designed as a rule-of-thumb guide:

- In personam jurisdiction has a party—a person—as a defendant.

Example: Johnson sues Jackson for breach of contract.

- In rem jurisdiction has property as a defendant.

Example: State seizure of property for taxes.

- Quasi in rem jurisdiction brings suit against property to satisfy a personal claim.

Example: A plaintiff sues for attachment and sale of property to satisfy a debt owed by another party who has property located within the forum state but is beyond the reach of the personal jurisdiction of the court.

Quasi in rem is used when personal jurisdiction would have been obtained if the defendant could have been served personally. In this situation, the court has in rem jurisdiction over property within the state but does not have in personam jurisdiction over out-of-state residents who have no contact with the state other than their ownership of property located within the state.

The distinctions are often obscure, and an inherent due process issue always lurks when rights may be affected without opportunity to be heard. This problem of definition underscores the difficult problems of civil procedure: namely, measuring very technical rules and concepts against the broad, flexible concept of due process.

Venue

Venue refers to the place where jurisdiction is exercised. Venue is easily confused with jurisdiction, but the two must be clearly distinguished. For example, the issue of whether a case should be heard in a state or federal court is a matter of subject matter jurisdiction, as discussed in Chapter 6. Venue concerns the question of which court within a system should be the *place* where jurisdiction is exercised. An example from divorce law in Florida may clarify this problem.

Florida circuit courts have jurisdiction over divorce cases (now called "dissolution of marriage"). The jurisdictional requirement for bringing a divorce action is that the petitioner must have resided in the state for six months prior to bringing the action. The action may be brought in any circuit in the state; in fact, some actions are brought

in rem action
A lawsuit brought to enforce rights in a thing against the whole world, as opposed to one brought to enforce rights against another person; see *in personam jurisdiction*.

attachment
Formal seizure of property to bring it under the control of the court; usually done by getting a court order to have a law enforcement officer take control of the property.

quasi in rem
Describes an action that is really directed against a person but is formally directed only against property.

res

Thing. (In Latin, nouns have different forms for subjective and objective positions in the sentence. Thus, *res* is the same noun as the *rem* in "in rem," except that the latter takes a different ending because it follows the preposition. Note that "in personam" also adds an "m" to "persona" because it follows the preposition.)

venue

Place; specifically, the place where jurisdiction is exercised. Many courts may have jurisdiction over a case, but it is filed in only one place (venue).

forum non conveniens

Doctrine stating that if two or more courts both have proper *venue* for a case, a judge of one such court may rule that the lawsuit must be brought in the other court for either the convenience of or fairness to the parties.

complaint

The initial pleading in a civil action, in which the plaintiff alleges a cause of action and asks that the wrong done to the plaintiff be remedied by the court.

answer

A pleading that responds to the complaint, admitting and denying specific allegations and presenting defenses.

in a venue far from the residences of either party to the action in order to avoid local public scrutiny. However, if the respondent objects to the place where the suit is filed, venue may be challenged, and the court will transfer the case to the circuit in which the respondent resides. It is not that the original court does not have jurisdiction but, rather, that another court with similar jurisdiction is determined to be the more appropriate site of the lawsuit.

The divorce example is based on the allegation of *inconvenient venue,* commonly referred to by the Latin phrase **forum non conveniens**. Another venue challenge is based on the allegation that a party cannot obtain a fair trial where the action has been brought (e.g., the plaintiff may have unusual influence over the local population so that the defendant fears that a fair trial is difficult or impossible).

PLEADINGS

Many technical problems may arise concerning proper and necessary parties to a lawsuit, that is, who may or must be included in the lawsuit. Problems of multiple plaintiffs or defendants, class action suits, and other special problems must be left to a more detailed study of litigation and procedure. Discussion here is limited to the basic documents that frame the issues for trial.

Modern pleading borrows heavily from both law and equity. The basic documents of pleading, the **complaint** and the **answer**, echo the procedure of equity, which required the suitor to file a **petition** or bill in equity. The petition initiated the suit much like a complaint does today, except that the petition was a lengthy recitation of the facts of the case, much restricted today in a complaint. After the bill was filed, a **subpoena** was issued requiring the respondent to appear, and the respondent provided an answer, which presented the respondent's defenses, thereby closing the pleadings and requiring the plaintiff to go forward to prove the allegations.

Equity also provided for **joinder,** which consolidated related claims and related parties, thus avoiding the necessity of hearing numerous cases. If a respondent had a claim against the petitioner, this could be brought through a *cross-bill,* analogous to the modern **counterclaim**.

Equity also provided for petitioner's (and later respondent's) discovery of information possessed by the adverse party in order to prepare for hearing.

All these features of equity procedure were incorporated, albeit with changes, into modern pleading. Common law procedure, which was complex and formal, had two principal objects. First, it was necessary for the plaintiff to fit the case into a *form of action* that would support the court's issuance of a corresponding writ or order to the sheriff to compel the defendant to satisfy the plaintiff's claim or appear in court to show cause why he or she need not do so. The form of action corresponds to the **cause of action**, still required in modern pleading; the specific facts required by the formula for each form of action correspond to the **elements** presently required to state a cause of action.

Second, common law pleading was designed to focus the lawsuit on a single issue, and it did this by a series of responsive pleadings back and forth between plaintiff and defendant until the issue was clearly framed. This was a highly technical process with numerous pitfalls. The parties were not allowed to present multiple actions or defenses, and any attempt to do so would result in a holding for the other side.

The advantage of common law pleading was its precision; the disadvantages were its inflexibility and technicality. The advantages of equity procedure were its flexibility and attention to substance over technicality; its disadvantage was the time-consuming process of setting the case for hearing, as the relative simplicity and flexibility of equity procedure often failed to focus the case and restrain the parties.

Modern code pleading attempts to borrow the advantages of both processes while minimizing their disadvantages. Equity pleadings are restricted to the allegation of **ultimate facts** rather than the more detailed **evidentiary facts**. Rather than focusing on a single issue, the pleadings are designed to establish a cause of action and present defenses. Issues are narrowed largely by the pretrial process, including discovery, a concept borrowed from equity. Liberalized pleading allows complaints to be amended, shifting emphasis toward substantive rather than purely technical issues. It must be noted, however, that civil procedure is by its nature technical, and inattention to the rules can be costly.

The Complaint

The complaint is designed to inform the court and the defendant that a lawsuit has been filed, invoking the attendant legal process. The complaint itself—that is, the document filed with the court and served on the defendant—may be divided into several parts:

1. The **caption** is the heading of the complaint and identifies the court in which the complaint is filed, the names of the parties to the suit, and the case number of the suit (assigned by the clerk). The caption begins each document filed with the court. Below the case number (on the right underneath the name of the court) or below the caption itself is the label of the document, e.g., "COMPLAINT," "ANSWER," "MOTION FOR SUMMARY JUDGMENT."

2. The first paragraph of the complaint contains the jurisdictional allegation, which states the grounds for subject matter jurisdiction of the court wherein the complaint has been filed.

3. The remaining numbered paragraphs of the complaint present a brief allegation of general facts designed to state a cause of action and provide notice to the defendant of the basis for the suit.

4. The complaint ends with a **prayer for relief**, sometimes called the **wherefore clause** because it traditionally begins with something like "WHEREFORE, the Plaintiff prays for judgment. . . ."

A complaint must allege enough facts to inform the defendant of the factual basis for the suit and be sufficient to include all the elements of a cause of action. The complaint can be found insufficient no matter how long or how short.

 *Sufficiency of the Complaint*

A complaint is more than 100 pages in length, but problems with organization and grammar make it difficult for the defendant to determine the claims against it. Should the court dismiss the complaint **with prejudice**, which means that the plaintiff could not file an amended complaint?

petition

A formal, written request, addressed to a person or body in a position of authority, that alleges a cause of action; sometimes also known as a *complaint* or *pleading*.

subpoena

A court's order to a person that he or she appear in court to testify in a case.

joinder

The bringing in of a new person who joins together with the plaintiff as a plaintiff or the defendant as a defendant.

counterclaim

A cause of action brought by a defendant against the plaintiff in a single case; e.g., in an auto collision, both drivers often sue each other, with one filing a complaint and the other counterclaims.

cause of action

Subject of a statement required to bring a lawsuit, identifying the theory or law under which the plaintiff is suing. The court must recognize the action (suit) as one of the many kinds that the court can decide. In a sense, a cause of action is a label for a type of lawsuit. For example, slander, breach of contract, invasion of privacy, and trespass are causes of action.

elements

The specific parts of a *cause of action* that must be alleged and proved to make out that cause of action.

ultimate facts

The general statements of fact that support a cause of action; for example, the allegations of fact in the complaint. Compare to *evidentiary facts.*

evidentiary facts

The specific facts presented at trial, as distinguished from the more general *ultimate facts.*

caption

The heading of a court paper, which usually includes the names of the parties, the court, and the case number.

prayer for relief

Also known as *demand for relief;* the portion of a complaint or claim for relief that specifies the type of relief to which the plaintiffs feel they are entitled and that they are requesting. See *wherefore clause.*

wherefore clause

The *prayer for relief;* the final clause in a complaint that asks the court for some sort of remedy: "Wherefore, the plaintiff prays that. . . ." *Wherefore* means "for this reason."

After answering the question, consider whether the following information would alter your answer:

- The plaintiff has amended the complaint three times.
- The trial court previously put the plaintiff on notice of the deficiencies of the complaint.

See *Arena Land & Inv. Co. v. Petty,* 69 F.3d 547 (10th Cir. 1995).

The Answer

To defend the suit, the defendant must file an answer, although other procedural devices to attack the complaint are also available at this time. The answer is responsive to the complaint and admits allegations in the complaint that the defendant does not wish to contest. It contains denials of allegations in the complaint that the defendant disputes, which allegations then become questions for proof and argument. The answer may also contain **affirmative defenses**, which contain matter not included in the complaint that the defendant alleges will prevent the plaintiff from obtaining relief. For example, the defendant may contend that the statute of limitations has run, thus barring the plaintiff's suit. If the plaintiff cannot overcome this defense, the suit must be dismissed. The answer may also present a *counterclaim*, which is a claim by the defendant against the plaintiff that must contain sufficient allegations to state a cause of action on its own.

The Reply

Although filing an answer usually ends the pleadings, the plaintiff must file a **reply** if the defendant has made a counterclaim, in order to present denials and defenses to the counterclaim. Affirmative defenses do not necessarily require the filing of a reply, but the cautious attorney may do so to avoid certain technical problems later on.

DISCOVERY

Discovery refers to pretrial devices for obtaining information relevant to the suit. It is a modern adaptation of procedures in equity and has come to play a major role in civil cases. Long delays in bringing suit to trial are most often related to the discovery process, which has been severely criticized for its contribution to delays and the resulting costs that give a significant advantage to wealthy parties. Although it is unethical to delay as a strategy for wearing down an opponent or as leverage to induce settlement and is subject to sanctions in some states, it is difficult to prove that attorneys have used procedural devices solely for the purpose of delay. Defense attorneys in personal injury suits have little incentive to effect prompt resolution of a case—their clients are not eager to pay sooner than necessary, and the attorneys continue to receive compensation as the process is prolonged. This is not purely self-serving on the attorneys' part. In the end, the client may save a great deal of money in the settlement, despite increased attorneys' fees. Also, any eagerness to settle tends to be regarded as weakness by the other side. This is one of the prices we pay for having an adversarial system that encourages both sides to employ strategies, tricks, and traps to win.

The discovery process involves a great deal of work that currently is often accomplished by paralegals. It requires knowledge of the law and the legal system but does not require the pivotal decision making that is the responsibility of the attorney.

 *Discovery Sanction*

During discovery, the defendant initially produced for the plaintiff all but one page of a five-page contract. The plaintiff realized that the page was missing and requested the defendant to produce the missing page. The defendant refused to produce the missing page until the one-year discovery period was almost over. What sanction should the court impose for the defendant's delay?

See Camp Takajo, Inc. v. SimplexGrinnell, Ltd. P'ship., 957 A.2d 68 (Me. 2008).

Depositions

A primary tool of discovery is the **deposition**. It consists of an oral questioning of a witness or the parties themselves; attorneys for both sides are present, and a court reporter records verbatim the questions and answers for later transcription. The ostensible purpose of the deposition is to gather information, but it serves also to gauge the credibility of the witness and to make a record of statements under oath to preserve testimony for trial, usually effectively preventing witnesses from later changing their testimony. The merits of a case are usually reevaluated following the deposition of an important witness, based on the information gathered and the impact the witness is likely to make on judge and jury. Settlement offers are often raised or lowered following a deposition.

Attorneys often arrange for a deposition through their paralegals; scheduling can be difficult because the attorneys and the witness (*deponent*) must all be available at the same time. Although several depositions may be taken in succession on the same day, attorneys frequently arrange one deposition at a time, prolonging the pretrial period for several months or even years.

Paralegals frequently draft questions for depositions and may even sit beside an attorney and pass notes concerning objections and follow-up questions to responses made by the deponent.

Interrogatories and Requests for Admissions

Attorneys submit written questions, called **interrogatories**, to the opposing party asking for specific information, usually information not easily denied, such as vital statistics, employment, and historical facts of the case. Time of reply is often protracted, although undue delay may be countered by motions to the court to compel compliance. **Requests for admissions** ask the opposing party to admit specific facts, which once admitted may no longer be put in dispute, thereby narrowing the issues for trial.

with prejudice
A dismissal with prejudice precludes the plaintiff from filing an amended complaint in the lawsuit.

affirmative defense
A claim made by the defendant that, if it prevails, will negate the plaintiff's case.

reply
A pleading made by a plaintiff when a defendant makes a counterclaim or affirmative defenses that require a response.

deposition
Oral examination of a witness transcribed by a court reporter. Ordinarily, attorneys for both sides are present, one having requested the deposition. A deposition is part of the pretrial procedure called *discovery* and is usually conducted without any participation by the judge.

interrogatories
Pretrial written questions sent from one party to the other party; a discovery device.

Requests for Documents and Mental and Physical Examinations

A party may demand the **production of documents** and records relevant to the case (e.g., business records, receipts) as well as mental and physical examinations of a party if it can be shown that an examination is relevant to the case (this is especially common in personal injury actions).

Scope of Discovery

Discovery inquiry is measured by very broad standards and is not limited by the more restrictive standards of admissibility applied to evidence at trial. Discovery is normally conducted through the attorneys without the intervention of the judge, who may have little knowledge of what is happening. The court becomes involved only when the process breaks down and a party seeks an order from the court requiring the other party to comply with the discovery process.

In theory, discovery is based on the rationale that justice is served by both sides being fully informed and prepared for trial. It is a counterpoise to the "gunslinger" approach to trial in which trial becomes a battle of wits between great performers—a view favored by popular dramatists. In practice, the trial is a performance that has been carefully rehearsed: both sides are aware of the facts and arguments of the other, the only uncertainty being the unpredictability of the jury.

On the surface, discovery appears to be a reasonable feature of the search for truth and equalization of the positions of the parties. In fact, it is as much subject to subterfuge as any other part of a lawsuit. Deponents are prepared for depositions as are witnesses for trial and are warned by attorneys not to expand on their answers, to answer merely "Yes" or "No" to questions that can be answered simply by yes or no responses. Answers to interrogatories are drafted by attorneys, rather than the parties, to provide as little information as possible. In short, discovery has become a negotiating tool used as much for strategic purposes as for investigation. It is a part of a lengthy pretrial process devoid of judicial scrutiny, encouraging continual reevaluation of a case for negotiating settlement. More than any other feature of civil procedure, discovery is responsible for pretrial settlements. The question remains whether this mechanism is fairer, more efficient, or more just than procedure without it.

The discovery process typically proceeds without the involvement of the court. When one party is uncooperative, the other may ask for the court's intervention. If this fails to bring the uncooperative party into line, the court may impose sanctions, including dismissal of the case.

PRETRIAL HEARING

In a great many cases, a **pretrial conference** or **hearing** is held at an advanced stage of the pretrial process. It is frequently held in the judge's chambers rather than in open court and is attended by the judge and attorneys for the parties. A general discussion is held on the issues of the case and the merits of the claim. Matters such as discovery, logistics, and the like are discussed as well. Ostensibly the pretrial hearing helps the judge assess the progress of the pretrial process and plan for trial time. Depending on the judge and the jurisdiction, the "pretrial" is often used to encourage settlement. The judge may urge the attorneys to focus on real issues and suggest areas for compromise. Attorneys may show a willingness to settle in the pretrial hearing that they were reluctant to show previously. The judge may express some impatience with frivolous claims and issues and ask the attorneys to submit written arguments on questions of law.

Depending on the judge, the attorneys may come away from the conference with a clear idea of where the judge stands on the law and even the judge's attitude toward the merits, weaknesses, and defenses with regard to the claim. It is not that the judge prejudges the lawsuit, but a frank discussion of the case takes place in which the judge can act as a mediator to resolve the dispute and obviate the need to go to trial. It is often in the interests of all present to forgo the time and expense of trial. At the pretrial conference, the adversaries finally come face-to-face with the one person whose job it is to resolve the dispute.

PROCEDURE AT TRIAL

Trial is conducted as an orderly sequence of steps. The model presented here is followed quite generally in federal and state courts.

Jury Selection

The means and manner of selecting a jury vary considerably among jurisdictions, and even different judges differ in the extent to which they wish to control the process. The jury pool is typically selected from the list of registered voters within the jurisdiction, a number of whom are called for jury duty when the court is in session. From a number larger than the number of jurors required in a case, the jury will be selected by an examination called *voir dire*, during which the attorneys and/or the judge will ask the prospective jurors questions with regard to their qualifications to serve in the case. In addition to statutory disqualifications, jurors who are prejudiced with regard to the parties or subject matter of the case or who cannot reasonably be expected to judge the facts impartially may be excluded from the jury. An attorney who wishes to exclude such a juror makes a **challenge for cause**. These are unlimited in number, on the theory that no party should be tried by a biased jury. Cases that receive widespread publicity prior to trial may involve lengthy voir dire in the attempt to find impartial jurors, though the problem is usually encountered in sensational criminal trials.

In addition to challenges for cause, each party is allowed a specific number of **peremptory challenges**, which allow the parties to exclude jurors they suspect are unsympathetic to their side of the case but who are not otherwise disqualified. Attorneys do not give reasons for exercising peremptory challenges.

Jury selection is extremely important. Cases commonly go to trial because there are two believable versions of the facts or simply because the facts could be viewed to favor either side. A case may be won or lost on the basis of jury selection. After all, a decision on the value of "emotional distress" or an award of punitive damages is arbitrary and subjective.

In *Grundy*, Sumner went to the emergency room for treatment for nausea and was seen by Dr. Dhillon, who performed some tests and admitted her. Later that day

voir dire

The examination of potential jurors to qualify them for the trial.

challenge for cause

In qualifying jurors during *voir dire*, either party may challenge the seating of a juror for bias or other disqualification. Challenges for cause are unlimited.

peremptory challenge

Exclusion of a juror that does not require justification. Each side is allowed a limited number of peremptory challenges, as dictated by statute.

Sumner was feeling better and voluntarily left the hospital. She refused to return to the hospital until the early hours of the next day. The emergency room physician gave her antibiotics. Sumner died later that same month.

Grundy, the administrator of Susanne Sumner's estate, filed a wrongful death action against the emergency room treating physician and the physician's employer. After the wrongful death action was unsuccessful, Grundy requested a new trial because one of the jurors failed to disclose information on voir dire, with the undisclosed information possibly being the basis of a challenge for cause.

GRUNDY, Admr., Appellee

v.

DHILLON et al., Appellants

Supreme Court of Ohio

No. 2007-1292

900 N.E.2d 153

Decided Dec. 11, 2008.

A jury rejected appellee John Grundy's claims that appellants, Dr. Jagprit Singh Dhillon and Emergency Professional Services, Inc., negligently caused the death of Susanne Sumner in treating her at the Trumbull Memorial Hospital emergency room. Grundy moved for a new trial, arguing that a juror had failed to disclose during voir dire that one of his family members had been treated at Trumbull Memorial Hospital emergency room and that the juror had a low opinion of the hospital's standard of care.

This case presents the question[ ] of . . . the showing required to establish that a juror's nondisclosure of material information on voir dire is sufficient to warrant a new trial. We hold . . . that to obtain a new trial on that ground, the moving party must show that a juror failed to answer honestly a material question on voir dire and that the moving party was prejudiced by the presence on the trial jury of a juror who failed to disclose material information. To demonstrate prejudice, the moving party must show that an accurate response from the juror would have provided a valid basis for a for-cause challenge. Because we conclude that the court of appeals failed to accord sufficient deference to the trial court's findings in ruling on the motion and incorrectly applied the legal standard, we

reverse the court of appeals' judgment and reinstate the jury verdict. . . .

In *Pearson*, counsel for the plaintiff in a personal-injury action moved for a new trial based on the failure of no fewer than four jurors to disclose, in response to a question to the array during voir dire, prior accidents involving themselves or their family members. The trial court denied the motion, concluding that the plaintiff had not been prejudiced by the jurors' sitting on the case. The trial court also found that the jurors did not deliberately fail to answer the questions, but had difficulty remembering the particulars of the accidents. This court held that the record revealed no abuse of discretion by the trial court in making those findings or in rejecting the motion for a new trial. . . .

[T]he [Grundy] trial court found that "it is not evident that Juror Krusely gave false information to questions put to him, but rather that he did not volunteer all information that he may have [had] if other specific questions were asked." The record supports this determination.

Grundy's trial counsel asked the entire panel the following question: "How about members of your family? Have you ever taken a member of your family to the Trumbull Memorial Emergency Room?" One juror (not Krusely) answered, "yes." Grundy's lawyer asked that juror, "About that, any experiences that you think will influence your decision making on this case?" Before that juror replied, Grundy's lawyer immediately commented on how emergency rooms have changed over the years and explained the two different divisions within the emergency department and the hospital's practice of subletting its emergency department to an outside group. Another juror made a comment in response to the lawyer's comment about emergency room doctors not being employees of the hospital.

Grundy's trial counsel then asked several new questions simultaneously and directed those questions to Krusely. The lawyer asked: "Do you believe it is reasonable to expect that Emergency Professional Services, Inc., if they are going to sublet the emergency room in our community hospital, would hire qualified doctors to handle the emergency room? You think that is a reasonable expectation? What do you expect from an emergency room doctor?" Krusely then answered the questions put directly to him, as follows:

"I don't like the idea of it being a primary care. * * * I think the emergency room has an obligation to save your life, to not make it any worse, to not necessarily cure you, but at least to get you on the road to where maybe I need to send you to a professional tomorrow. I'll make an appointment with a bone specialist or whatever you happen to need."

Q: "Sort of, what is going on?"

A: "Yes."

Q: "And not necessarily cure you, but at least identify what the problem is?"

A: "Certainly. I don't think everything can be cured in the emergency room setting."

Q: "I agree, is that a reasonable expectation?"

A: "Yes."

Q: "Anybody else? Yes, Sir?"

After this colloquy, Grundy's trial counsel moved on to question another juror. During this discussion with Juror Krusely, Grundy's trial counsel did not follow up with him specifically on the question about whether he or his family had been treated at Trumbull Memorial Hospital emergency room.

The trial court's finding that Krusely did not give false information, but only failed to volunteer information, is supported by the record of the voir dire. Under the circumstances of the questioning here, we cannot say that Juror Krusely's failure to raise the topic again when the questioning returned to him amounted to a deliberate failure to disclose material information in response to a question put to him or the panel.

The trial court also found that "there is no evidence in the record that Juror Krusely actually had a

remembrance of the subject events at the time he was questioned during voir dire." The record also supports that determination. At the hearing on the motion for a new trial, Krusely testified that the incident in which he took his child to Trumbull Memorial Hospital emergency room occurred four years before the trial in this case. When asked if he had "at any time [during voir dire] knowingly or deliberately attempt[ed] to conceal information" from the lawyers, Krusely answered: "Absolutely not." Krusely also testified (in response to the judge's question at the hearing):

"Do I remember everything I have ever done? No, Sir. But I certainly, certainly did not try to hide anything, and I certainly answered everything honestly.

"Quite frankly, I believe in two and a half weeks of hearing about this case and this 22 year old girl, made me remember about my son who happens to be 22 years old. Had I been reminded of it earlier, I would have certainly relayed that incident."

The trial court's assessment of this evidence was not an abuse of discretion.

Additionally, Grundy's trial counsel later during voir dire asked Krusely—twice—whether he could be fair in deciding the case. Both times, Krusely responded that he could. Such responses would cut against any basis for a for-cause challenge to juror Krusely. . . .

The trial court's opinion also suggested that if any party had had reason to excuse Krusely had he disclosed his son's experience at Trumbull Memorial emergency room, it would have been the defendants, not the plaintiff. Thus, the trial court implicitly rejected any argument that Grundy had had a valid challenge of juror Krusely for cause. Such a determination, under the circumstances of this case, was not an abuse of discretion.

Case Questions

1. Why does the court discuss *Pearson*?
2. Are you persuaded by Krusely's version of the facts?
3. What facts did the trial court rely on in denying the motion for a new trial?
4. Why would the defendants have been the ones more likely to excuse Krusely?

Conduct of the Trial

With the jury selected, the trial begins with **opening statements** by each side, plaintiff first and then defendant, who may reserve opening remarks until later. Opening statements are designed to inform the jury of the nature of the case and the facts each side proposes to show or dispute. In a **bench trial** (a nonjury trial), opening statements are usually waived because the judge ordinarily does not need to be prepared in this way.

The plaintiff then presents the evidence that forms the **case-in-chief**. The plaintiff has the **burden of proof**, meaning that there must be sufficient proof of the allegations of the complaint to sustain a verdict in favor of the plaintiff if the evidence is believed. This is called making a **prima facie case**.

Questioning of witnesses proceeds with the party calling the witness conducting a **direct examination**, followed by **cross-examination** by the other side. Cross-examination aims at showing flaws in the witness's testimony or discrediting the witness. The initial party then has the opportunity to **redirect** questions concerning issues raised "on cross." This is followed by **recross**.

When the plaintiff finishes the case-in-chief, the defendant produces witnesses favorable to the defense, who are questioned in similar fashion, with the defense conducting the direct examination. The plaintiff then has the opportunity to present evidence rebutting the defendant's presentation, followed by rebuttal by the defendant.

Finally, each side makes a **summation**, or **closing argument**, before the jury, with the defendant usually first (in opposite order of the opening statements). The function of the closing argument is to summarize the evidence and present an interpretation of the facts consistent with the evidence that favors the party making the argument. Considerable latitude is given the attorneys in their closing arguments, provided they stay within the scope of the evidence presented and conduct themselves properly.

Verdict and Judgment

Before the jury retires to deliberate the facts, the judge **charges** them, that is, gives instructions to the jurors. The jury returns when it reaches consensus and reads the verdict before the court. The judge then asks each juror if he or she concurs in the verdict. After dismissing the jury, the judge may enter judgment on the verdict immediately or wait for a period, during which the parties may make posttrial motions.

In a nonjury trial, the judge is the trier of fact, so no verdict is entered, though the judgment should include findings of fact beyond what would be appropriate in a jury trial. Final judgment is in written form, dated and signed by the judge and filed with the court records.

THE RULES OF EVIDENCE

Evidentiary rules form an independent subject for study that cannot be treated in satisfactory fashion here. In general, the rules of evidence are designed to exclude evidence that is irrelevant, repetitious, or unreliable. They help to prevent filibustering (delaying tactic) by attorneys representing losing causes. Nevertheless, the rules also reveal a distrust of the jury. Much that is excluded could be helpful in learning the truth but is not admissible because of questions of reliability, thus questioning the jury's ability to weigh the import of unreliable evidence. Because the jury may find facts based only on the evidence that it hears and sees, it often receives a limited picture of the circumstances of the case.

The ancient forerunner of the modern jury was composed of members of the community who knew the defendant and could judge the veracity of the plaintiff's claim. Today the jurors are strangers to the parties as well as the facts and are limited by the rules of evidence in what they can know of the case.

Two examples of evidentiary rules may illustrate this problem. First, one rule of evidence holds that a nonexpert witness, or layperson, may not give opinion testimony. A person qualifying as an **expert witness**, let us say a psychiatrist, may express an opinion on the facts of the case as long as the opinion is within the expert's field of expertise. As a result, an eyewitness friend of the defendant may not declare that the defendant was "insane," whereas a psychiatrist who entered the case long after the events took place may talk at length about how Oedipal conflicts caused the defendant to act as he did.

Second, the **hearsay rule** excludes from testimony out-of-court statements made by a person not present in court ("My friend told me that Joe had been drinking"). There are more than a dozen major exceptions to the hearsay rule, but it excludes what might otherwise be extremely relevant evidence on the grounds of unreliability and lack of opportunity to cross-examine the person who made the statement.

MOTIONS

Parties to a case have at their disposal numerous motions that ask the court to take particular action by granting or denying the motion. Because the ruling on each motion requires the exercise of legal judgment and therefore raises a question of law, denial of a motion may be the basis for appeal by the **movant** (person making the motion), and granting the motion may provide a basis for appeal by the **nonmoving party** on the ground of prejudicial error. The discussion here is confined to a handful of motions that are designed to terminate the case favorably to the moving party if granted. They have several names but much in common; their differences depend largely on their timing, and so they are often classified as pretrial, trial, and posttrial motions.

Fact/Law Distinction

To understand the function of these motions, one must keep in mind the purpose of trial. Trial refers to trying facts. Assuming a typical jury trial of a damage suit, the plaintiff must prove the elements of a cause of action and the amount of the damages. The jury must find facts supporting each element and fix the dollar amount of damages in order for the plaintiff to recover. The only issues before the jury are those of disputed fact. If no facts are in dispute, the jury has no function. The parties may stipulate the truth of certain facts, thus taking those fact questions out of dispute. For example, in a suit for damages, the defendant might acknowledge liability for compensation to the plaintiff, not disputing the amount claimed as compensation by the plaintiff but arguing that punitive damages are not allowed under the circumstances of the case. Whether

direct examination
The first questioning of a witness in a trial by the side that called the witness.

cross-examination
The questioning of an opposing witness during a trial or hearing.

redirect
The questioning of a witness by the party that called the witness following *cross-examination*.

recross
The questioning of a witness by the party that did not call the witness following *redirect*.

summation (closing argument)
Each lawyer's presentation of a review of the evidence at the close of trial.

charges [to the jury]
Jury instructions, given to the jurors before their deliberations.

expert witness
A witness who is qualified (by education, licensing, experience, etc.) to offer opinion testimony, which would be objectionable in a "lay" witness.

hearsay rule

Excludes from testimony out-of-court statements made by a person not present in court; a complex rule with many exceptions.

movant

The party making a motion.

nonmoving party

The party against whom a motion is made.

mistrial

A trial that the judge ends and declares will have no legal effect because of a major defect in procedure or because of the death of a juror, a deadlocked jury, or other major problem.

judicial notice

The judge recognizing a certain fact as true without a party furnishing evidence; ordinarily judicial notice is taken on the basis of common knowledge of a fact.

punitive damages are allowable is a legal question. If the judge agrees with the defendant's argument, there would be no task for the jury; if the judge disagrees, the jury must determine whether the facts of the case warrant punitive damages according to the instructions given the jury by the judge. If the jury finds punitive damages appropriate, the amount must be fixed by the jury.

The simple model of dispute resolution describes a two-step process in which (1) facts are determined from the evidence presented and (2) law is applied to the facts to establish the prevailing party and the form of relief, if any, to be awarded. This assumes, first, that facts will be found—this is almost always the case, but on rare occasions the jury finds it impossible to reach a consensus, resulting in a **mistrial**. The model also assumes that the law is there to be found and applied. This is somewhat problematic because the judge will always make conclusions of law, but the peculiarities of a given case may present novel legal issues not easily answered on the basis of existing law.

If no material facts are in dispute, the only task before the court is to apply the law. Whether there are facts in dispute is a question of law for the judge. The judge may take the case out of the hands of the jury or take a fact question away from jury determination by converting it into a question of law. This sleight of hand is justified with language such as "reasonable persons could not disagree. . . ." The rationale here is that the jury is needed only if some doubt exists with regard to the facts. If the judge concludes that no doubt exists, even though the parties dispute the facts, the question can be decided "as a matter of law" ("reasonable persons could not disagree"). Disputed facts should normally go to the jury; a judge who oversteps the authority to decide facts will be reversed on appeal.

In its simplest form, the conversion of a fact question into a question of law is seen in the taking of **judicial notice**. The court may relieve a party of the burden of proving a fact by taking judicial notice of that fact. Ordinarily, notice is taken on the basis of common knowledge of a fact (it is dark in Omaha at midnight; Mario Cuomo was governor of New York in 1989). Of course, self-evident facts are rarely disputed, so the court need not bother with such questions, but sometimes facts that seem clear are nevertheless disputed, as when a party attempted to argue that wine is not intoxicating and the judge took judicial notice of the fact that wine is an intoxicating beverage.

In the 1940s, the great silent film actor Charlie Chaplin was sued by Joan Berry over paternity of her daughter, Carol Ann Berry. Chaplin agreed to pay support for the child if blood tests indicated that he could be the father. To the contrary, the blood tests showed that he could *not* have been the father. Carol Ann had blood type B, while Joan had A and Charlie had O. Because Carol Ann must have inherited B from a parent who had a B or AB type blood, Charlie could not have been the father. Joan won a suit that was characterized by histrionics, including putting Charlie and Carol Ann side by side to show a family resemblance. The court refused to take judicial notice of the blood tests as conclusive and sent the case to the jury, which concluded that Charlie was the father. Although judicial notice is usually reserved for matters of common knowledge, the question arises as to whether the court should take factfinding away from the jury when scientific certainty compels a factual conclusion. Compare *State v. Gray*.

Note that bastardy, usually called *paternity*, proceedings are "quasi-criminal" proceedings used to establish paternity for related civil suits. The court uses **preponderance of the evidence** rather than **guilt beyond a reasonable doubt** as the standard of proof.

STATE OF OHIO ex rel. HOPE A. STEIGER, COMPLAINANT

v.

BRUCE GRAY, DEFENDANT

Juvenile Court of Ohio, Cuyahoga County

145 N.E.2d 162 (1957)

Complainant, an unmarried woman, filed a complaint in bastardy alleging that the defendant is the father of her child born to her December 1, 1956.

Defendant himself did not testify on his own behalf. He called but one defense witness—Dr. Roger W. Marsters, a clinical pathologist, who had been appointed by the court to conduct the blood grouping tests of the child, the complainant and the defendant, as requested by the defendant. . . .

Dr. Marsters' qualifications as an expert serologist were not questioned by the complainant. He testified that he carefully tested the blood specimens of the complainant, the defendant and the child "for the International OAB, M and N, and C, D, E, and c blood factors by using known blood controls along with the unknowns." . . .

"The data on the International OAB blood group factors are inconclusive because the mating of a type A individual with a type O individual may produce offspring of either type A or type O.

"The data on the M–N factors are inconclusive. . . .

"The data on the Rh blood factor D are inconclusive. . . .

"The data on the Rh blood factor E are inconclusive. . . .

"The data on the [Rh] factor c are inconclusive. . . .

"The data on the Rh factor C however indicate that an exclusion of paternity is established on this basis. Both Hope Steiger and Bruce Gray are negative for the C factor and therefore lack this particular blood

antigen. On the other hand Baby Norma June Steiger is C-positive and therefore possesses this particular blood antigen. Since these blood factors can only be inherited from the parents and since both of these adults lack the C, then some other man than Bruce Gray must be the father of this child.

"In conclusion, an exclusion of paternity is established by the demonstration of the C factor in this child, Norma Steiger, without the presence of this particular blood factor in the blood of either of these two adults, Hope Steiger or Bruce Gray."

Dr. Marsters stated that he and his associates made five separate blood tests and that all proper safeguards were taken to protect the integrity and accuracy of the blood grouping tests. The accuracy of his conclusion of the exclusion of defendant as the father of the child was not rebutted by any counter medical evidence submitted by complainant. . . .

This court further believes that the near unanimity of medical and legal authorities on the question of the reliability of blood grouping tests as an indicator of the truth in questioned paternity cases justifies the taking of judicial notice of the general recognition of the accuracy and value of the tests when properly performed by persons skilled in conducting them. The law does not hesitate to adopt scientific aids to the discovery of the truth which have achieved such recognition. . . .

I hold, further, that because this great weight must be accorded to the blood grouping test results as testified to by Dr. Marsters, complainant has failed to prove the guilt of the defendant by a preponderance of the evidence.

Accordingly, I find the defendant not guilty as charged in the complaint.

Case Questions

1. Why did the defendant not testify in his own behalf?
2. On what does the court base its justification for taking judicial notice?

preponderance of the evidence

The standard of proof required in most civil actions. The party whose evidence, when fairly considered, is more convincing as to its truth has the preponderance of evidence on its side.

guilt beyond a reasonable doubt

The standard of proof that the prosecution must meet in a criminal case.

DISMISSAL MOTIONS

On motion, a judge may end a case because one side has no legal basis for its claims or because no material fact is in dispute and it is time to enter judgment. Because the granting of such motions cuts short further discussion and presentation of facts and denies a person his or her "day in court," the court uses a strict test. Although it is phrased somewhat differently according to the motions, generally it states that the court will test the motion by looking at the case "in the light most favorable to the nonmoving party." This test must be examined by considering the motions. The various dismissal motions are described below and are summarized in Exhibit 7-4.

The Demurrer

The first dismissal motion that can arise in a case is one made by the defendant, attacking the complaint by a "motion to dismiss for failure to state a claim upon which relief can be granted." This is quite a mouthful, so it is abbreviated to "motion to dismiss for failure to state a claim," "motion to dismiss for failure to state a cause of action," or, borrowing from equity, a "**demurrer**." Granting this motion stops the action dead in its tracks. With a demurrer, the defendant argues that the complaint is legally insufficient, that it does not state a cause of action, or that the law has no remedy for the grievance asserted by the plaintiff.

The test used by the court for a demurrer is as follows: If all the allegations of the complaint were true, the complaint would still not allow the plaintiff any relief. In a sense, the demurrer says, "So what?" Some essential ingredient is missing. The *Georgia High School Association* case in Chapter 6 is a case that *should* have been dismissed if

EXHIBIT 7-4 DISMISSAL MOTIONS

TYPE OF MOTION	NAME OF FEDERAL COURT
Demurrer (motion to dismiss)	Asks the court to dismiss a complaint because the complaint is insufficient, the complaint does not state a cause of action, or the law has no remedy for the grievance asserted by the plaintiff
Motion for summary judgment	Asks the court to rule in favor of a party after some discovery has taken place, thus ending the lawsuit in favor of the plaintiff or dismissing a defendant from the lawsuit
Motion for directed verdict	Either a request by the defendant to rule in favor of the defendant at the close of the plaintiff's case-in-chief, or a request by either party at the close of the trial for the judge to rule in favor of the movant
Motion for judgment notwithstanding the verdict (n.o.v.)	Asks the court to enter a judgment contrary to the jury verdict on the basis that, as a matter of law, the verdict is against the manifest weight of the evidence

the trial court judge had taken the position the appellate court did: namely, that the plaintiffs had no property rights that were infringed by the referee's bad call. The law does not allow relief for such a case—no cause of action exists.

The assumption of the truth of a plaintiff's allegations is made only for the purpose of testing the demurrer. By making the demurrer, the defendant does not admit that the allegations are true for any other purpose. If the demurrer is denied (the usual outcome), the defendant may proceed to dispute the facts alleged.

Summary Judgment

A **motion for summary judgment** can be either a trial or a pretrial motion. As a pretrial motion, it is made at some point before trial, when it appears that one side must win. For example, although the complaint may appear to state a cause of action, after all pleadings have been filed and discovery has taken place, the plaintiff's case may reveal some fatal weakness, so the defendant moves for summary judgment. In such a case, the test to be applied is whether, viewing the case in the light most favorable to the plaintiff (the nonmoving party), the plaintiff could not win. Again, if material facts are in dispute, the motion will be denied.

In the Internet age, one might believe that one has been defamed by an online posting but not be able to identify the individual posting the allegedly defamatory message without the help of the Internet service provider. One who posted a message might claim a First Amendment right to express an opinion anonymously. Usually, it is during trial that the plaintiff must present sufficient facts to establish a prima facie case. In *Krinsky*, however, the court examined the likelihood of plaintiff being able to establish a prima facie case at the beginning of the lawsuit. This was the key to the court deciding whether the Internet service provider would have to respond to the subpoena by identifying Doe 6.

demurrer
A motion to dismiss for failure to state a claim upon which relief may be granted; asks the court to dismiss a case because the complaint is legally insufficient (that is, it fails to state a *cause of action*).

motion for summary judgment
A dismissal motion that is a pretrial motion and also a trial motion in a *bench trial*; asks the judge to rule in favor of a party after some discovery or part of the trial has taken place.

Lisa KRINSKY, Plaintiff and Respondent

v.

DOE 6, Defendant and Appellant

Court of Appeal, Sixth District, California

No. H030767

159 Cal. App. 4th 1154, 72 Cal. Rptr. 3d 231

Feb. 6, 2008.

As Internet technology has evolved over the past two decades, computer users have encountered a proliferation of chat rooms and websites that allow them to share their views on myriad topics from consumer products to international diplomacy. Internet bulletin boards, or "message boards," have the advantage of allowing users, or "posters," to express themselves anonymously, by using "screen names" traceable only through the hosts of the sites or their Internet Service Providers (ISPs). One popular forum is the financial message board, which offers posters the opportunity to communicate with others concerning stock trading, corporate behavior, and other finance-related issues.

The conversation on one financial message board devolved into scathing verbal attacks on the corporate officers of a Florida company, prompting a lawsuit by one of those officers, plaintiff Lisa Krinsky. Plaintiff attempted to discover the identity of 10 of the pseudonymous posters by serving a subpoena on the message-board host, Yahoo!, Inc. (Yahoo!). Defendant "Doe 6" moved to quash the subpoena, but the trial court denied the motion. Doe 6 appeals, contending that he had a First Amendment right to speak anonymously on the Internet. Under the circumstances presented, we agree with Doe 6 that his identity should be protected and therefore reverse the order. . . .

Until December 31, 2005 plaintiff was the president, chairman of the board, and chief operating officer of SFBC International, Inc., a publicly traded "global development drug service company" with offices in Florida. In January 2006 plaintiff sued 10 "Doe" defendants in a Florida court. In the action plaintiff alleged that defendants had made "defamatory remarks" about her on Yahoo! message boards and other websites, using screen names to conceal their identities. During the litigation defendant Doe 6 was often referred to as "Senor-Pinche-Wey," the screen name he had used in posting on the Yahoo! Finance message board. . . .

The record contains copies of the alleged defamatory messages posted on the Yahoo! message board devoted to SFBC. Most of the posts derided another SFBC executive, "Jerry 'Lew' Seifer." Seifer was a vice president of legal affairs at SFBC, who apparently resigned in mid-December 2005. . . .

In order to serve the proper defendants, Krinsky served a subpoena on the custodian of records at Yahoo! in Sunnyvale, California. Yahoo! notified Doe 6 that it would comply with the subpoena in 15 days unless a motion to quash or other legal objection was filed. Doe 6 then moved in superior court to quash the subpoena on the grounds that (1) plaintiff had failed to state a claim sufficient to overcome his First Amendment rights for either defamation or interference with a contractual or business relationship, and (2) plaintiff's request for injunctive relief was an invalid prior restraint.

At the April 28, 2006 hearing on the motion, the superior court suggested that Doe 6 was "trying to drive down the price of [plaintiff's] company to manipulate the stock price, sell it short and so forth." The court queried whether it was "protected speech to do that? To deliberately engage in tactics designed to circumvent securities laws to drive the price down to a publicly traded company?" The court also expressed the view that "[a]ccusing a woman of unchastity" and "calling somebody a crook . . . saying that they have a fake medical degree, accusing someone of a criminal act, accusing someone-impinging [*sic*] their integrity to practice in their chosen profession historically have been libel per se." Counsel for Doe 6 maintained, however, that the reference to "crook" was to Seifer, not plaintiff, and that the use of this term was,

in context, mere opinion and therefore protected by the First Amendment. . . .

The parties agree that the viability of the subpoena should be determined by weighing Doe 6's First Amendment right to speak anonymously against plaintiff's interest in discovering his identity in order to pursue her claim. . . . Common to most courts considering the issue is the necessity that the plaintiff make a prima facie showing that a case for defamation exists. Requiring at least that much ensures that the plaintiff is not merely seeking to harass or embarrass the speaker or stifle legitimate criticism. Even the decisions imposing a motion-to-dismiss obligation nonetheless require " 'some showing' " that the tort took place. . . .

"Prima facie evidence is that which will support a ruling in favor of its proponent if no controverting evidence is presented. . . . It may be slight evidence which creates a reasonable inference of fact sought to be established but need not eliminate all contrary inferences." *Evans.* When there is a factual and legal basis for believing libel may have occurred, the writer's message will not be protected by the First Amendment. . . . A private plaintiff in a libel case must prove that the defendant published a false statement about the plaintiff to a third party and that the false statement caused injury to the plaintiff. . . .

When a defamation action arises from debate or criticism that has become heated and caustic, as often occurs when speakers use Internet chat rooms or message boards, a key issue before the court is whether the statements constitute fact or opinion. . . .

In this case, Doe 6's messages, viewed *in context,* cannot be interpreted as asserting or implying objective facts. During November and December 2005 many messages were posted on the Yahoo! Finance "SFCC" message board regarding the management and value of SFBC. Heated discussion focused on plaintiff's credentials and "credibility." Other messages questioned the reputed personal relationship between her and Seifer. . . .

The federal district court in *HIghlands* confronted a similar scenario in granting a motion to quash. Examining the numerous posts on a Yahoo! message board, the magistrate had noted that "[m]any of the messages are crude, indecent, or transparently laughable-and many appear to have nothing whatsoever to do with SGI. Many of the postings include misspellings, grammatical errors, and/or incomplete thoughts and sentences. . . . Messages on this board reflect considerable venting, much tongue-in-cheek, little pretense at sophistication or thoughtfulness, and an ample and obvious sense of irreverence." Thus, the magistrate found, "[v]iewed in context (the only relevant way to view communications), defendant's postings consist of sardonic commentary on a public corporation; through irony and parody, these bulletin board postings express dissatisfaction with the performance of the stock and the way company executives choose to spend company resources." The district court adopted the magistrate's conclusion that plaintiff firm had "failed to demonstrate that a reasonable person perusing the message board at issue would understand the statements as having been made by plaintiff itself, which is plaintiff's theory in support of its defamation and commercial disparagement claims."

We likewise conclude that the language of Doe 6's posts, together with the surrounding circumstances—including the recent public attention to SFBC's practices and the entire "SFCC" message-board discussion over a two-month period—compels the conclusion that the statements of which plaintiff complains are not actionable. Rather, they fall into the category of crude, satirical hyperbole which, while reflecting the immaturity of the speaker, constitute

protected opinion under the First Amendment. It hardly need be said that this conclusion should not be interpreted to condone Doe 6's rude and childish posts; indeed, his intemperate, insulting, and often disgusting remarks understandably offended plaintiff and possibly many other readers. Nevertheless, "the fact that society may find speech offensive is not a sufficient reason for suppressing it. Indeed, if it is the speaker's opinion that gives offense, that consequence is a reason for according it constitutional protection." *Simon & Schuster.* . . .

The order denying Doe 6's motion to quash the subpoena is reversed. The trial court is directed to enter a new order quashing the subpoena to the extent that it commands Yahoo! to disclose the identity of "Senor-Pinche-Wey." Doe 6 is entitled to his costs on appeal.

Case Questions

1. What were Doe 6's two reasons for claiming that the subpoena should be quashed?
2. Why must Krinsky present evidence of a prima facie case this early in the lawsuit?
3. Why does the court distinguish between fact and opinion?
4. How does the court's discussion of *Highlands* help you understand the *Krinsky* decision?

Motion for a Directed Verdict

At trial, after the plaintiff has presented its case-in-chief, the defendant may make a **motion for a directed verdict**. Construing all the evidence in the light most favorable to the plaintiff, the motion will be granted if it appears that the plaintiff has not provided sufficient proof to prevail. If granted, judgment is entered for the defendant and the case is over. Usually there are sufficient facts that a jury *might* find in the plaintiff's favor, so the case will continue. The motion for directed verdict is made routinely, and almost as routinely denied, so that the defendant preserves the right to appeal on the basis of that denial. Even if the plaintiff's case is weak, the judge may be reluctant to take the factfinding away from the jury.

At the close of all the evidence, both sides commonly make motions for a directed verdict. At first glance, it might seem that one would be granted, but because each is measured in terms most favorable to the nonmoving party, if there is a reasonable dispute over the facts, the evidence could be interpreted to support either side. Thus, both motions are denied and that task is left to the jury.

In a nonjury trial, the judge is the factfinder, so the appropriate motions are called *motions for summary judgment*, as the judge may immediately enter judgment. Formerly

motion for a directed verdict

A dismissal motion commonly made by the defendant at the close of the plaintiff's *case-in-chief* and by both sides after presentation of all the evidence; asks the judge to rule in favor of the movant.

judges directed the juries to enter verdicts, which explains the "directed verdict" label of the motion, but this is no longer done. A motion for a directed verdict is also called a *motion for nonsuit* in some jurisdictions.

Motion for Judgment Notwithstanding the Verdict

motion for judgment n.o.v.

A motion made at the end of a trial asking the judge to enter a judgment contrary to the jury's verdict on the ground that the verdict is against the manifest weight of the evidence; also called a *motion for judgment notwithstanding the verdict.* The abbreviation "n.o.v." stands for the Latin *non obstante veredicto,* meaning "notwithstanding the verdict."

After the jury has returned a verdict, either party may make a motion for judgment notwithstanding the verdict, usually referred to as a **motion for judgment n.o.v.**, from the Latin *non obstante veredicto* ("notwithstanding the verdict"). This will be granted if the judge finds as a matter of law that the verdict is against the manifest weight of the evidence. On occasion a jury will return a verdict that appears absurd on the basis of the record, or the jury's factfinding may be legally inconsistent. For example, the jury may find that the plaintiff as well as the defendant was negligent, giving the defendant an absolute defense to the suit (in a state that recognizes contributory negligence), and yet award compensation to the plaintiff. In such a case, the judge would enter a judgment in favor of the defendant on a motion for judgment n.o.v.

Dismissal Motions in Practice

The aforementioned motions terminate the proceedings if granted. Usually they are denied; in most instances a case should not proceed to trial if one side's case is fatally flawed—the case should have been settled short of trial. Nevertheless, the expense of trial is a threat that is used for bargaining, and sometimes both sides are so stubborn in the negotiating process that trial is held regardless of the merits of the case. When the dispute is based on novel or controversial interpretations of the law, the trial may be primarily a prelude to appeal. Negotiations may continue during trial and prior to appeal. In addition, there are posttrial motions designed to set aside the judgment or to ask for a new trial. These and other pretrial procedures will be left to further study. Specific devices of civil procedure vary considerably from one jurisdiction to another, and it is best to learn the peculiarities of the jurisdiction in which one intends to practice.

RES JUDICATA AND COLLATERAL ESTOPPEL

res judicata

Latin for "the thing has been judged"; an affirmative defense that prevents a civil case from being brought a second time.

Although it is possible to obtain a new trial if an appellate court determines that prejudicial error in the first trial justifies relitigating the case, the losing plaintiff does not have the right to a retrial simply by filing the cause of action again. This is the essence of the principle of *res judicata*, Latin for "the thing has been decided." A party may not bring a suit over and over again until a favorable result is achieved. **Res judicata** is an affirmative defense that bars further suit. It is also called *merger and bar,* referring to the principle that the claim of the winning plaintiff is "merged" in the judgment of the court and enforceable by the judgment, but the claim is "barred" from further suit when the plaintiff loses.

Although this seems straightforward, a number of problems complicate the principle. Overlapping state and federal jurisdictions allow a claim in either or both courts. State and federal law may cover similar subjects in different ways. The problem then becomes whether a suit brought in one court is really the same case as that later brought in another. Furthermore, because the law establishes different causes of action that can arise from the same events (e.g., threatening someone with physical harm might be grounds for claims of assault or intentional infliction of mental distress), the question can arise as to whether one suit bars the later suit.

There are important conflicting policies in claim preclusion (*res judicata*). On the one hand, fairness would prevent a defendant from being forced to defend the same case more than once. On the other hand, the plaintiff should have full access to the courts. The court will not invoke *res judicata* if there is a difference in the parties to the claim or if the case involves issues different from those brought in the first case. This discussion seriously oversimplifies *res judicata*, which can become very complex when there are multiple parties and multiple claims.

Collateral estoppel is directly related to *res judicata*; it is a bar to the relitigation of specific issues that have been previously adjudicated, even though the suits may not satisfy the requirements of *res judicata* (if all the issues in a new suit are identical to those in the prior suit, collateral estoppel and *res judicata* may both be said to apply). Occasionally a new suit raises issues presented in a former case as well as additional issues not barred by the prior suit. Nevertheless, those issues raised and decided in the former suit may not again be raised because of collateral estoppel.

Res judicata and collateral estoppel are simple in principle but often difficult in application.

collateral estoppel

Bars the relitigation of issues that have been previously adjudicated.

SUMMARY

Civil procedure has both theoretical and practical importance. Theoretically, examination of our system of civil procedure reveals an adversarial system in which the fairness of the procedural rules takes on special significance. Reliance is placed on procedure to achieve justice. Practically, the legal practitioner must understand the procedure of the jurisdiction, both to enforce the rights of clients and to protect them from the maneuvers of the opposing side.

Lawsuits are initiated by the filing of a complaint and service of process on the defendant. If it is to determine the rights of the parties, the court must have personal jurisdiction over them. In restricted cases, a suit may be filed against a thing (in rem jurisdiction). When there is a choice of courts having jurisdiction over a case, proper venue is determined by the rules and the circumstances of the parties.

Most American jurisdictions follow code pleading, which is a statutory refinement of common law, and equity pleading, which requires that a complaint state a cause of action, to which the defendant files a responsive pleading called an answer. In some cases the plaintiff then files a pleading responding to the answer.

An important feature of pretrial procedure is the discovery process, in which the parties enjoy great latitude in learning about the other side's case through depositions, interrogatories, requests for documents, and so on.

Key features of the jury trial are jury selection and presentation of evidence. Each side has ample opportunity to present evidence and challenge the evidence from the other side. The plaintiff carries the burden of proving the elements of the cause of action.

Each side has at its disposal several motions at the pretrial, trial, and posttrial stages. The most important of these are motions that test the validity of the other side's case, such as a motion for summary judgment. When granted, these motions terminate the litigation at that point.

KEY TERMS

affirmative defense
alienation of affections
answer
attachment
bench trial
breach of promise to
    marry
burden of proof
caption
case-in-chief
cause of action
challenge for cause
charges (to the jury)
collateral estoppel
complaint
counterclaim
criminal conversation
cross-examination
default judgment
demurrer
deposition
direct examination
elements
evidentiary facts
expert witness
forum non conveniens
guilt beyond a reasonable
    doubt

hearsay rule
heart-balm suits
in personam (personal)
    jurisdiction
in rem action
interrogatories
joinder
judicial notice
long-arm statutes
mistrial
motion for a directed
    verdict
motion for judgment
    n.o.v.
motion for summary
    judgment
movant
nonmoving party
opening statements
original service
peremptory challenge
personal service
petition
prayer for relief
preponderance of the
    evidence
pretrial conference
    (hearing)

prima facie case
process
production of
    documents
publication
quasi in rem
recross
redirect
reply
requests for admissions
res
res judicata
seduction
service of process
special appearance
subpoena
substituted service
summation (closing
    argument)
ultimate facts
venue
voir dire
wherefore clause
with prejudice

CHAPTER REVIEW QUESTIONS

1. What is the fundamental premise underlying civil procedure?
2. What two documents are presented to a defendant as part of service of process?
3. Under what circumstances may a court enter a default judgment?
4. Why are in rem actions relatively rare?
5. What is the difference between subject matter jurisdiction and venue?
6. What are the three basic documents in modern code pleading?
7. What is the major criticism of the discovery process?
8. What constitutes a prima facie case?
9. What kind of witness may give opinion testimony?
10. If no material fact is in dispute in a case, what is the next logical step in the case?

CRITICAL THINKING QUESTIONS

1. Some argue that the discovery process incurs delay and expense without improving the result. Is there a better way?
2. Why is fairness usually a procedural question?

CYBER EXERCISE

Opinions of the District Court of Appeals of Florida are accessible through a number of websites, including http://www.flcourts.org/. The Florida District Court of Appeals decided *Funny Cide Ventures, LLC v. Miami Herald Publ'g Co.*, 955 So. 2d 1241 (Fla. Dist. Ct. App., 4th Dist., 2007), on May 16, 2007. The case contained a majority opinion and a concurring opinion. Locate this case through the Florida courts website and answer the following questions:

a. What were the facts?
b. What tort was the basis of the lawsuit, and what does one have to prove to be successful?
c. What was the decision at the trial level?
d. What was the decision on appeal, and what was the court's reasoning?
e. Why did Judge Farmer write a concurring opinion?
f. Why did Judge Farmer include the humorous portion in his opinion?
g. What was Judge Farmer's serious point about special damages and injurious falsehood?

SCENARIO

You represent Fred Goodbody, who is being sued by the Internal Revenue Service (IRS) for unpaid taxes. The IRS challenges his claim of charitable nonprofit status. Fred is a computer consultant for retail businesses. He sets up retail systems with in-store networks that connect point-of-sale computers for collecting cash, checks, and credit card purchases with back-office computers that are designed for tracking inventory, making wholesale purchases, and compiling data for accounting and tax purposes. In short, Fred can go into a store and design a computer system that will take care of all of the store's business needs.

Fred has all payments for his service made by check made out to the Church of Narcissism. Fred received a bachelor's degree in computer science and a master's degree in business administration, both from accredited schools. In addition, Fred has a Doctor of Theology degree from the East Texas Theological Seminary in Dallas, Texas, an unaccredited institution. To obtain his doctorate, Fred sent the seminary a check for $200 and received in return two books: (1) the Holy Bible and (2) *How to Set Up a Tax-Exempt Church*. He was required to submit a letter swearing before God that he had read both books, and in return he received his doctoral diploma. Fred had previously read the Bible while attending Sacred Heart Academy, and he read the other book very carefully. Fred established the Church of Narcissism, registering it with the secretary of state for his state and applying for nonprofit status with the IRS. For two years, Fred has collected his consulting payments in the name of the church and paid taxes only on the salary he pays himself as archbishop of the church. He set up a meditation room in his home, the physical location of the church, where he does yoga and meditation each morning, usually accompanied by his wife, the only other member of the church.

The IRS took no action on his application until recently, when, upon investigation, it claimed that Fred's church was a sham, having no religious purpose.

Fred is about to go to trial, and you are preparing questions for voir dire. Your problem is that you are unsure who would be sympathetic to Fred's device to avoid paying taxes. What questions would you ask? Remember that you have both challenges for cause, which are unlimited, and a limited number of peremptory challenges. Fortunately, the judge is known to be tolerant of voir dire questioning as well as generous in accepting challenges for cause.

List the questions you would ask and then think through the follow-up questions for different answers. Keep in mind that you do not want to offend the jurors if at all possible; in fact, you want them to like you and be predisposed toward your client.

CHAPTER 8

THE LAW OF CRIMINAL PROCEDURE

It is better that ten guilty persons escape than one innocent suffer.

—William Blackstone

THE CONSTITUTIONAL BASIS OF CRIMINAL PROCEDURE

Although criminal procedure follows many of the patterns of civil procedure, there are major differences between them, largely because of the special provisions of the U.S. Constitution (which are usually echoed in state constitutions). The Constitution, and especially the first 10 amendments (the Bill of Rights), expresses a basic code of criminal procedure by enumerating rights of citizens against government intrusion and rights of those accused of crimes. The provisions of the Constitution have been subjected to intense scrutiny by state and federal courts, particularly since the 1950s. Criminal procedure cannot be understood without reference to these rights. Exhibit 8-1 contains excerpts from the Constitution relevant to these rights. The terms italicized in Exhibit 8-1 are annotated or explained in the section following the exhibit.

Annotations

A **writ of habeas corpus** is brought by a petition, the purpose of which is to challenge the lawfulness of a detention by the government. This includes institutions other than prisons, although most habeas corpus petitions are brought by imprisoned criminals. It is often used as a form of federal review after state appeals have failed.

writ of habeas corpus
Brought by petition to challenge the lawfulness of a detention.

EXHIBIT 8-1   EXCERPTS FROM THE CONSTITUTION OF THE UNITED STATES

ARTICLE I

SECTION 9:

2. The privilege of the *Writ of Habeas Corpus* shall not be suspended, unless when in Cases of Rebellion or Invasion the public Safety may require it.
3. No Bill of Attainder or *ex post facto* Law shall be passed.

ARTICLE III

SECTION 2:

3. The trial of all Crimes, except in Cases of Impeachment, shall be by *Jury;* and such Trial shall be held in the State where the said Crimes shall have been committed; but when not committed within any State, the Trial shall be at such Place or Places as the Congress may by Law have directed.

AMENDMENT IV

The right of the people to be secure in their persons, houses, papers, and effects, against *unreasonable searches and seizures;* shall not be violated, and *no warrants shall issue, but upon probable cause, supported by oath or affirmation, and particularly describing the place to be searched, and the persons or things to be seized.*

AMENDMENT V

infamous crime

A major crime for which a heavy penalty may be imposed. Used in the Constitution but now out of date; would probably mean *felony* today.

No person shall be held to answer for a capital, or otherwise **infamous crime**, unless on a presentment or *indictment of a grand jury,* except in cases arising in the land or naval forces, or in the militia, when in actual service in time of war or public danger; nor shall any person be subject for the same offense to be *twice put in jeopardy* of life or limb; nor shall be compelled in any criminal case to be a *witness against himself, nor be deprived of life, liberty, or property, without due process of law;* nor shall private property be taken for public use, without just compensation.

AMENDMENT VI

In all criminal prosecutions, the accused shall enjoy the *right to a speedy and public trial,* by an *impartial jury* of the State and district wherein the crime shall have been committed, which district shall have been previously ascertained by law, and to be informed of the *nature and cause of the accusation,* to be *confronted with the witnesses against him;* to have *compulsory process* for obtaining witnesses in his favor, and to have the *assistance of counsel for his defense.*

AMENDMENT VIII

Excessive bail shall not be required, nor excessive fines imposed, nor *cruel and unusual punishments* inflicted.

AMENDMENT XIV

. . . No State shall make or enforce any law which shall abridge the privileges or immunities of citizens of the United States; nor shall any State deprive any person of life, liberty, or property, without *due process of law;* nor deny to any person within its jurisdiction the *equal protection of the laws. . . .*

 *Failure to Administer the Jury Oath*

Once members of a trial jury are selected, they are administered an oath similar to the following:

> You shall well and truly try the issue formed upon this bill of indictment (or accusation) between the State of [_____] and (name of accused), who is charged with (here state the crime or offense), and a true verdict give according to the evidence. So help you God.

What is the effect of the failure to administer the oath to jurors?

After answering the question, consider whether the following information would alter your answer:

- The defendant was acquitted of one charge and convicted of the other charges.
- The prosecution claims that the case can be retried because the jurors never took the oath.
- The defendant argues that double jeopardy bars retrial of the charge of which he was acquitted.

See Spencer v. State, 640 S.E.2d 267 (Ga. 2007).

An **ex post facto law** is a penal law that operates retroactively. For example, under such a law a person could be charged with a crime for an action that was not a crime at the time it took place, or a person's sentence for a crime could be increased to a greater sentence than was permissible at the time the crime occurred.

Many state constitutions contain provisions similar to those in the United States Constitution. In interpreting a provision of a state constitution, a state court may look to a decision of the United States Supreme Court for guidance, as did the Indiana Supreme Court in *Wallace* in interpreting the ex post facto clause of the Indiana state constitution.

ex post facto law
A penal law that operates retroactively.

Richard P. WALLACE, Appellant (Plaintiff below)

v.

STATE of Indiana, Appellee (Defendant below)

Supreme Court of Indiana

No. 49S02-0803-CR-138

905 N.E.2d 371

April 30, 2009.

The statutes collectively referred to as the Indiana Sex Offender Registration Act ("Act") require defendants convicted of sex and certain other offenses to register with local law enforcement agencies and to disclose detailed personal information, some of which is not otherwise public. In this case we consider a claim that the Act constitutes retroactive punishment forbidden by the Ex Post Facto Clause contained in the Indiana Constitution because it applies to a defendant who committed his offense before the statutes were enacted. We conclude that as applied in this case the Act violates the constitutional provision.

In 1988, Richard Wallace was charged with one count of child molesting as a Class B felony and one count of child molesting as a Class C felony. Under terms of a plea agreement Wallace pleaded guilty to the Class C felony count on February 15, 1989. The trial court imposed a five-year suspended sentence with various conditions of probation. Wallace completed probation in 1992. Two years later the Indiana Legislature passed the Act that, among other things, required probationers and parolees convicted of child molesting on or after June 30, 1994 to register as sex offenders. In 2001 the Act was amended to require all offenders convicted of certain sex offenses to register as sex offenders regardless of conviction date. . . .

After Wallace did not register, he was charged with failing to register as a sex offender [and found guilty]. . . .

The United States Constitution provides that "[n]o State shall . . . pass any . . . ex post facto Law." U.S. Const. art. I, § 10. The Indiana Constitution provides that "[n]o *ex post facto* law . . . shall ever be passed." Ind. Const. art. I, § 24. Among other things "[t]he ex post facto prohibition forbids the Congress and the States to enact any law 'which imposes a punishment for an act which was not punishable at the time it was committed; or imposes additional punishment to that then prescribed.'" *Weaver*. The underlying purpose of the Ex Post Facto Clause is to give effect to the fundamental principle that persons have a right to fair warning of that conduct which will give rise to criminal penalties.

This Court has never addressed whether the analysis of an ex post facto claim under the Indiana Constitution is the same as under the federal Constitution. . . . When interpreting similarly worded provisions in the Indiana Constitution, we often rely on federal authority to inform our analysis, even though the outcome may be different.

When a statute is challenged as an alleged violation of the Indiana Constitution, our standard of review is well settled. Every statute stands before us clothed with the presumption of constitutionality until that presumption is clearly overcome by a contrary showing. The party challenging the constitutionality of the statute bears the burden of proof, and all doubts are resolved against that party.

As noted above, the United States Supreme Court concluded that Alaska's Sex Offender Registration Act, which is very similar to Indiana's Act, did not violate the Ex Post Facto Clause of the United States Constitution. *See Smith*. In reaching its conclusion, the Court applied the "intent-effects" test derived from its prior decisions to determine whether the statute imposed punishment. Under this test a court first determines whether the legislature meant the statute to establish civil proceedings. If the intention of the legislature was to impose punishment, then that ends the inquiry, because punishment results. If, however, the court concludes that the legislature intended a non-punitive regulatory scheme, then the court must further examine whether the statutory scheme is so punitive in effect as to negate that intention[,] thereby transforming what had been intended as a civil regulatory scheme into a criminal penalty.

Although we reach a different conclusion here than the United States Supreme Court reached in *Smith*, we agree that the intent-effects test provides an appropriate analytical framework for analyzing ex post facto claims under the Indiana Constitution. . . .

In assessing a statute's effects, the Supreme Court indicated that . . . seven factors [should be considered]: "[1] Whether the sanction involves an affirmative disability or restraint, [2] whether it has historically been regarded as a punishment, [3] whether it comes into play only on a finding of *scienter*, [4] whether its operation will promote the traditional aims of punishment-retribution and deterrence, [5] whether the behavior to which it applies is already a crime, [6] whether an alternative purpose to which it may rationally be connected is assignable for it, and [7] whether it appears excessive in relation to the alternative purpose assigned." *Mendoza-Martinez*. . . .

Considered as a whole the Act's registration and notification provisions impose substantial disabilities on registrants. When the applicable provisions of the Act are considered together, the first *Mendoza-Martinez* factor clearly favors treating the effects of the Act as punitive when applied to Wallace. . . .

We observe that the Act's requirements also resemble historical common forms of punishment in that its registration and reporting provisions are comparable to conditions of supervised probation or parole. Aside from the historical punishment of shaming, the fact that the Act's reporting provisions are comparable to supervised probation or parole standing alone supports a conclusion that the second *Mendoza-Martinez* factor favors treating the effects of the Act as punitive when applied in this case. . . .

We acknowledge that the Act applies to a few strict liability offenses. However, it overwhelmingly applies to offenses that require a finding of scienter for there to be a conviction. The few exceptions do not imply a non-punitive effect. We conclude that the third *Mendoza-Martinez* factor slightly favors treating the effects of the Act as punitive when applied here. . . .

It is true that to some extent the deterrent effect of the registration and notification provisions of the Act is merely incidental to its regulatory function. . . . Nonetheless it strains credulity to suppose that the Act's deterrent effect is not substantial, or that the Act does not promote "community condemnation of the offender," *Abercrombie*, both of which are included in the traditional aims of punishment. We conclude therefore that the fourth *Mendoza-Martinez* factor slightly favors treating the effects of the Act as punitive when applied to Wallace. . . .

In this jurisdiction the Act applies only to defendants "convicted" of certain specified offenses. We find nothing in the Act that anticipates registration and notification for an offender charged with a sex offense who later by reason of an agreement pleads guilty to another charge for which registration is not required. Nor for example does the Act appear to anticipate that a defendant whose conviction for a sex offense is reversed on appeal (for reasons other than sufficiency of the evidence) is required to register despite having obviously engaged in prohibited conduct. In sum, it is the determination of guilt of a sex offense, not merely the fact of the conduct and potential for recidivism, that triggers the registration requirement. Because it is the criminal conviction that triggers obligations under the Act, we conclude that this factor supports the conclusion that the Act is punitive in effect as to Wallace. . . .

We conclude therefore that the sixth *Mendoza-Martinez* factor clearly favors treating the effects of the Act as regulatory and non-punitive. . . .

In this jurisdiction the Act makes information on all sex offenders available to the general public without restriction and without regard to whether the individual poses any particular future risk. Indeed we think it significant for this excessiveness inquiry that the Act provides no mechanism by which a registered sex offender can petition the court for relief from the obligation of continued registration and disclosure. Offenders cannot shorten their registration or notification period, even on the clearest proof of rehabilitation. Thus, the non-punitive purpose of the Act, although of unquestioned importance, does not serve to render as non-punitive a statute that is so broad and sweeping. We conclude that the seventh *Mendoza-Martinez* factor favors treating the effects of the Act as punitive.

In summary, of the seven factors identified by *Mendoza-Martinez* as relevant to the inquiry of whether a statute has a punitive effect despite legislative intent that the statute be regulatory and non-punitive, only one factor in our view—advancing a non-punitive interest—points clearly in favor of treating the effects of the Act as non-punitive. The remaining factors, particularly the factor of excessiveness, point in the other direction. . . .

Richard Wallace was charged, convicted, and served the sentence for his crime before the statutes collectively referred to as the Indiana Sex Offender Registration Act were enacted. We conclude that as applied to Wallace, the Act violates the prohibition on ex post facto laws contained in the Indiana Constitution because it imposes burdens that have the effect of adding punishment beyond that which could have been imposed when his crime was committed. We therefore reverse the judgment of the trial court.

Case Questions

1. Does it make sense for the court to be guided by but not bound by the way in which the United States

Supreme Court interpreted a similar provision in the United States Constitution?

2. What is the first step in applying the intent-effects test?

3. How is the court's consideration of the seven factors of the intent-effects test helpful?

4. Are you persuaded that the effect of the registration requirement, as applied to Wallace, is punitive?

Case Glossary

scienter

In the context of a criminal case, indicates criminal intent.

jury

With regard to the constitutional right, refers to a petit jury, which is the trier of fact in a criminal case. Also see *grand jury.*

warrant

Written permission given by a judge to arrest a person or conduct a search or make a seizure.

grand jury

A body of citizens who receive complaints and accusations of crime and decide whether an *indictment* should issue.

indictment

A written accusation by a grand jury charging the accused with a criminal act.

The right to a **jury** trial applies to all criminal prosecutions. Disciplinary actions in prisons do not fall into this category.

The right to be free from unreasonable searches and seizures is designed primarily to protect citizens from excessive intrusions by government and police into their homes and persons, but interpretation of search and seizure has extended its application to places of business as well. The reasonableness of a search must necessarily remain a subjective judgment.

". . . [No] **warrants** shall issue, but upon probable cause, supported by oath or affirmation, and particularly describing the place to be searched, and the persons or things to be seized." Warrants are carefully scrutinized by criminal defense attorneys to determine whether they conform to this constitutional requirement. If the warrant or the search exceeds constitutional limits, the evidence seized may be excluded from trial, which is often fatal to the case for the prosecution. For example, drugs illegally seized may not be used as evidence at trial, so the prosecution then has no case.

A **grand jury** indictment requires a hearing before a special body of citizens gathered to review the prosecutor's evidence in support of taking the accused to trial. If the grand jury concludes that there is probable cause to believe the accused committed the crime, it issues an **indictment**, which is a written accusation by the grand jury charging the accused with a criminal act. It is also referred to as a *true bill,* but when the grand jury does not indict, it is called a *no bill.* The grand jury proceeding is controlled by the prosecutor to such an extent that a chief judge of the New York Court of Appeals remarked that a grand jury would indict a ham sandwich if the prosecutor recommended it.

The grand jury differs from a trial jury, a petit jury, in several respects. Grand jury proceedings are not open to the press; a witness before the grand jury does have the right to invoke his Fifth Amendment right not to incriminate himself but does not have the right to be represented by an attorney during the grand jury proceedings. Because of the power of the prosecutor, the grand jury has been used to investigate political activities of dissidents, such as in *Bursey v. United States;* in *Bursey,* the prosecutor used grand jury proceedings to investigate Black Panther Party activities protesting the Vietnam war, including an intention to kill President Nixon and interfere with armed forces in Vietnam.

In 1734, William Cosby, the English governor of New York, sought to have the publisher of a radical newspaper with extremely limited circulation indicted for criminal libel. The grand jury twice refused to indict. Thereafter, the publisher, Peter Zenger, was charged with libel, and one of the most celebrated trials in American history followed. [After a dramatic trial characterized by hostility between an arrogant judge appointed specially by Governor Cosby and a brave and unrelenting defense attorney, Mr. Zenger was found by the jury to be *not guilty,* a historic victory for the people and the cause of freedom of speech and of the press.] It was with this and similar precedents fresh in their memories that our founding fathers incorporated into the Fifth Amendment the requirement that no person shall be held to answer for an infamous crime except upon the presentment or indictment of a grand jury.

Today, courts across this country are faced with an increasing flow of cases arising out of grand jury proceedings concerned with the possible punishment of political dissidents. It would be a cruel twist of history to allow the institution of the grand jury that was designed at least partially to protect political dissent to become an instrument of political suppression.

Bursey v. United States, 466 F.2d 1059, 1089 (9th Cir. 1972).

Double jeopardy prevents a person from being tried twice for the same crime. Jeopardy attaches once the accused has been put on trial before judge or jury; until that time, the case may be postponed without violating this provision. Double jeopardy applies to bringing the same charges in the same jurisdiction even if the courts are different (e.g., a lower criminal court versus a higher criminal court). This does not apply to state and federal jurisdictions. In the famous case of the three civil rights workers who were killed in Mississippi, an acquittal of homicide in the state court was followed by prosecution and conviction in federal court for depriving the victims of their civil rights.

double jeopardy
Prevents a person from being tried twice for the same crime.

 ***Mistrial Declared on September 11, 2001***

A criminal trial began on September 10 and was in progress on September 11, 2001. The judge *sua sponte* (on his own) declared a mistrial on September 11, 2001, because the jurors would be distracted by the acts of terrorism. Does double jeopardy bar retrial of this defendant?

See Walls v. Konteh, 490 F.3d 432 (6th Cir. 2007).

A person cannot be held to be a "witness against himself." This is usually referred to as the **privilege against self-incrimination** and generally is restricted to a testimonial privilege; that is, a person may not be required to testify to matters that would tend to incriminate him or her. Blood tests, fingerprints, and most documents that might incriminate are not considered "testimony" and are not covered by this privilege. This provision of the Fifth Amendment is the basis for the *Miranda* rights, particularly the right to remain silent during a police interrogation. The privilege against self-incrimination in the Fifth Amendment is zealously guarded by the U.S. Supreme Court, as the *Griffin* case demonstrates.

privilege against self-incrimination
Provides that a person accused of a crime cannot be required to testify against himself or herself.

GRIFFIN

v.

CALIFORNIA

U.S. Supreme Court

380 U.S. 609 (1965)

Petitioner was convicted of murder in the first degree after a jury trial in a California court. He did not testify at the trial on the issue of guilt, though he did testify at the separate trial on the issue of penalty. The trial court instructed the jury on the issue of guilt, stating that a defendant has a constitutional right not to testify. But it told the jury:

> As to any evidence or facts against him which the defendant can reasonably be expected to deny or explain because of facts within his knowledge, if he does not testify or if, though he does testify, he fails to deny or explain such evidence, the jury may take that failure into consideration as tending to indicate the truth of such evidence and as indicating that among the inferences that may be reasonably drawn there from those unfavorable to the defendant are the more probable. . . .

Petitioner had been seen with the deceased the evening of her death, the evidence placing him with her in the alley where her body was found. The prosecutor made much of the failure of petitioner to testify:

> . . . He would know how she got down the alley. He would know how the blood got on the bottom of the concrete steps. He would know how long he was with her in that box. He would know how her wig got off. He would know whether he beat her or mistreated her. . . .

> These things he has not seen fit to take the stand and deny or explain.

> And in the whole world, if anybody would know, this defendant would know.

> Essie Mae is dead, she can't tell you her side of the story. The defendant won't.

The death penalty was imposed and the California Supreme Court affirmed. . . .

The question remains whether, statute or not, the comment [on defendant's refusal to testify] rule, approved by California, violates the Fifth Amendment.

We think it does. It is in substance a rule of evidence that allows the State the privilege of tendering to the jury for its consideration the failure of the accused to testify. No formal offer of proof is made as in other situations; but the prosecutor's comment and the court's acquiescence are the equivalent of an offer of evidence and its acceptance. The Court in the *Wilson* case stated: ". . . It is not every one who can safely venture on the witness stand though entirely innocent of the charge against him. . . . [Testifying] will often confuse and embarrass him to such a degree as to increase rather than remove prejudices against him. It is not every one, however honest, who would, therefore, willingly be placed on the witness stand. The statute, in tenderness to the weakness of those who from the causes mentioned might refuse to ask to be a witness, particularly when they may have been in some degree compromised by their association with others, declares that the failure of the defendant in a criminal action to request to be a witness shall not create any presumption against him."

. . . What the jury may infer, given no help from the court is one thing. What it may infer when the court solemnizes the silence of the accused into evidence against him is quite another. That the inference of guilt is not always so natural or irresistible is brought out in the *Modesto* opinion itself: "Defendant contends that the reason a defendant refuses to testify is that his prior convictions will be introduced in evidence to impeach him and not that he is unable to deny the accusations. It is true that the defendant might fear that his prior convictions will prejudice the jury, and therefore another possible inference can be drawn from his refusal to take the stand."

. . . We take that in its literal sense and hold that the Fifth Amendment, in its direct application to the

Federal Government, and in its bearing on the States by reason of the Fourteenth Amendment, forbids either comment by the prosecution on the accused's silence or instructions by the court that such silence is evidence of guilt.

Reversed.

MR. JUSTICE STEWART, with whom MR. JUSTICE WHITE joins, dissenting. . . .

We must determine whether the petitioner has been "compelled . . . to be a witness against himself." Compulsion is the focus of the inquiry. Certainly, if any compulsion be detected in the California procedure, it is of a dramatically different and less palpable nature than that involved in the procedures which historically gave rise to the Fifth Amendment guarantee. When a suspect was brought before the Court of High Commission or the Star Chamber, he was commanded to answer whatever was asked of him, and subjected to a far-reaching and deeply probing inquiry in an effort to ferret out some unknown and frequently unsuspected crime. He declined to answer on pain of incarceration, banishment, or mutilation. And if he spoke falsely, he was subject to further punishment. Faced with this formidable array of

alternatives, his decision to speak was unquestionably coerced.

Those were the lurid realities which lay behind enactment of the Fifth Amendment, a far cry from the subject matter of the case before us. I think that the court in this case stretches the concept of compulsion beyond all reasonable bounds, and that whatever compulsion may exist derives from the defendant's choice not to testify, not from any comment by court or counsel.

Case Questions

1. The case refers to a right not to testify; the Fifth Amendment is commonly described as stating a privilege. What is the difference between a right and a privilege in this context?
2. Why does the majority consider the remarks of the judge and prosecutor sufficiently prejudicial to require a new trial?
3. What reasons does the *Modesto* case give justifying an innocent defendant's refusal to testify? For what other reasons might an innocent person refuse to testify?
4. Why does the dissent dwell on the word *compulsion* in reference to self-incrimination?

The constitutional clause stating that "[no person may . . .] be deprived of life, liberty or property, without due process of law" is an important feature of criminal law because of the inclusion of the words *life* and *liberty,* as the primary means of punishing criminals are execution and incarceration. Any criminal procedure can be scrutinized for fairness on the basis of the due process clause. Although the Fifth Amendment applies to federal action, a similar clause in the Fourteenth Amendment applies to the states, subjecting state action to review by federal courts.

The defendant has a "right to a speedy and public trial." Most state and federal jurisdictions have by statute fixed a time period within which a criminal case must be brought. If the prosecutor exceeds the time limit, the accused may not be tried. The right to a public trial is designed to prevent abuse that might occur in a closed hearing. When appropriate, and with the court's approval, the defendant may waive this right and close the trial to the public.

Usually the delay alleged to violate the defendant's right to a speedy trial is between the arrest and the trial. In *Mendoza*, the delay of eight years was between the indictment and the arrest.

UNITED STATES of America, Plaintiff-Appellee

v.

Paul MENDOZA, Defendant-Appellant

United States Court of Appeals, Ninth Circuit

No. 06-50447

530 F.3d 758

June 20, 2008.

Paul Mendoza appeals his convictions on two counts of subscribing to a false income tax return in violation of 26 U.S.C. § 7201. Mendoza contends that the eight-year delay between his indictment and his arrest violated his Sixth Amendment right to a speedy trial. . . .

During 1989 and 1990, Mendoza embezzled approximately $285,000 from [his employer] by personally collecting some of the clinic's checks and depositing them into his own bank accounts or cashing the checks at a check-cashing company. The money from these transactions was not reported on his 1989 or 1990 tax returns. . . .

Mendoza's wife informed [IRS] Agent Lynn that Mendoza had left her and her children and had been living in the Philippines since June 1995. . . . Mendoza was indicted on April 12, 1996. After the indictment, the government put a warrant out on the law enforcement database so that Mendoza would be detained when he attempted to return to the United States. The warrant was the only attempt the government made to apprehend Mendoza; the government made no attempt to contact Mendoza to inform him that he had been indicted.

Mendoza returned to the United States in June 2004, but was not arrested until October 13, 2004. After his arrest, Mendoza sought and received seven continuances of the scheduled trial date, from December 7, 2004, to March 14, 2006. On January 3, 2006, Mendoza filed a motion to dismiss the indictment because the eight-year delay between his indictment and his arrest violated his Sixth Amendment right to a speedy trial. The district court denied the motion . . . [and] Mendoza was found guilty on two counts of subscribing to a false income-tax return after a jury trial and was sentenced

to a term of imprisonment of thirteen months and restitution in the amount of $79,837.90. . . .

The Sixth Amendment guarantees that criminal defendants "shall enjoy the right to a speedy and public trial. . . ." U.S. Const. amend. VI. To determine whether a defendant's Sixth Amendment speedy trial right has been violated, we balance the following four factors: "[l]ength of delay, the reason for the delay, the defendant's assertion of his right, and prejudice to the defendant." *Barker*. . . .

In this case, the indictment was filed on April 12, 1996, and the trial did not start until April 25, 2006. We find that this ten-year delay creates a presumption of prejudice and triggers an inquiry into the other three factors. . . .

The government has the primary, though not exclusive, responsibility to ensure that the defendant is brought to trial. If . . . the defendant is not attempting to avoid detection and the government makes no serious effort to find him, the government is considered negligent in its pursuit.

In this case, the agent in charge of Mendoza's investigation made no effort to contact Mendoza to inform him that he had been indicted. The government had Mendoza's wife's telephone number and the telephone number of Mendoza's relatives in the Philippines. But rather than attempting to inform Mendoza that he had been indicted through those avenues, the government simply put a warrant out on the law enforcement database so that Mendoza would be detained when he returned to the United States. As a result, Mendoza was not informed he had been indicted until more than eight years after the indictment.

Even though Mendoza left the country prior to his indictment, the government still had an obligation to attempt to find him and bring him to trial. After *Doggett*, the government was required to make some effort to notify Mendoza of the indictment, or otherwise continue to actively attempt to bring him to trial, or else risk that Mendoza would remain abroad while the constitutional speedy-trial clock ticked. However, the government made no serious effort to do so. Further, there is no evidence that Mendoza was keeping his whereabouts unknown. Although he refused to give his own contact information, the government still had his relative's contact information. And when a government agent contacted Mendoza's wife and left a message with his sister, Mendoza returned the call from the Philippines on two different occasions.

Nor does Mendoza's failure to return to the United States as he stated he would support the argument that he was deliberately avoiding contact with the government. Mendoza was unaware of the indictment, so he did not know that he needed to return. And it was not Mendoza's responsibility to contact the government during the investigation. Based on its previous success in contacting Mendoza, the government was negligent when it failed to attempt to inform Mendoza of the indictment by calling either the wife or the relative's telephone number. Therefore, the delay between Mendoza's indictment and arrest was caused by the government's negligence, and this factor weighs in favor of Mendoza. . . .

There is no evidence that Mendoza knew of his indictment, such as evidence that the government had attempted to notify Mendoza by leaving a message with his relatives. Therefore, Mendoza could assert his speedy trial right as to the eight-year period between his indictment and his arrest. . . . However, Mendoza did not assert his right to a speedy trial until after he made numerous requests for continuances and delayed the trial date by over a year. Because Mendoza caused this delay before his assertion of his speedy trial rights, this factor does not weigh in favor of Mendoza nor in favor of the government.

The final factor is prejudice. The Supreme Court has recognized three forms of prejudice that can result from post-indictment delay: (1) oppressive pretrial incarceration, (2) anxiety and concern of the accused, and (3) "the possibility that the [accused's] defense will be impaired by dimming memories and loss of exculpatory evidence." *Doggett.* . . . This final form of prejudice is not only the most important, it is also the most difficult to prove because "time's erosion of exculpatory evidence and testimony 'can rarely be shown.'" In other words, excessive delays can "compromise[ ] the reliability of a trial in ways that neither party can prove or, for that matter, identify."

Due to these concerns, "no showing of prejudice is required when the delay is great and attributable to the government." *Shell.* Instead, we presume prejudice. . . .

If, in this case, the government had pursued Mendoza with reasonable diligence, his speedy trial claim would have failed unless he could show "specific prejudice to his defense." *Doggett.* However, the government did not exercise due diligence. Instead, the government was negligent in pursuing Mendoza, and the eight-year delay between Mendoza's arrest and indictment was attributable to the government. There is, therefore, a strong presumption that Mendoza suffered prejudice, which the Government has not rebutted. . . .

After balancing the *Barker* factors, we conclude that Mendoza's Sixth Amendment speedy-trial right was violated. The eight-year delay between Mendoza's indictment and arrest was a result of the government's negligence, so we presume that Mendoza suffered prejudice. As a result, a dismissal of Mendoza's indictment is warranted.

Case Questions

1. What are the bases of the three types of prejudice resulting from a delay following indictment and prior to trial?
2. How could the government show that a defendant did not suffer prejudice from the third type of delay?

§

The right to an "impartial jury" is fundamental to our criminal justice system, as police and prosecutor assume an accusatorial role. Great pains are often taken to guarantee that the jury is untainted by pretrial publicity or acquaintance with the facts of the case.

Nota bene: The phrase "a jury of one's peers" is commonly thought to be a constitutional right, but it appears nowhere in the U.S. Constitution. The Sixth Amendment only guarantees the right to "a speedy and public trial, by an impartial jury. . . ."

In recent decades, there have been successful challenges to the composition of the jury, especially where minorities appear to have been intentionally and systematically excluded, but these challenges have been based on the equal protection clause of the Fourteenth Amendment rather than the impartial-jury phrase of the Sixth.

The Article III guarantee of a jury trial applies to federal cases. The right to an impartial jury contained in the Sixth Amendment, originally a federal right, applies to the states through the due process clause of the Fourteenth Amendment. Like most of the rights in the Bill of Rights, this federal constitutional right has been "incorporated" by the Fourteenth Amendment to apply to the states. Nonetheless, the right to a jury trial at the state level need not be total. The *Blanton* case, in fact, suggests that there may be quite a large category of criminal cases exempt from the Sixth Amendment right to a jury.

Melvin R. BLANTON and Mark D. Fraley, Petitioners

v.

CITY OF NORTH LAS VEGAS, NEVADA

Supreme Court of the United States

489 U.S. 538 (1989)

Justice MARSHALL delivered the opinion of the Court.

The issue in this case is whether there is a constitutional right to a trial by jury for persons charged under Nevada law with driving under the influence of alcohol (DUI). . . .

DUI is punishable by a minimum term of two days' imprisonment and a maximum term of six months' imprisonment. . . . Alternatively, a trial court may order the defendant "to perform 48 hours of work for the community while dressed in distinctive garb which identifies him as [a DUI offender]." The defendant also must pay a fine ranging from $200 to $1,000. . . . In addition, the defendant automatically loses his driver's license for 90 days, . . . and he must attend, at his own expense, an alcohol abuse education course. . . . Repeat DUI offenders are subject to increased penalties.

Petitioners Melvin R. Blanton and Mark D. Fraley were charged with DUI in separate incidents. Neither petitioner had a prior DUI conviction. The North Las Vegas, Nevada, Municipal Court denied

their respective pretrial demands for a jury trial. On appeal, the Eighth Judicial District Court denied Blanton's request for a jury trial but, a month later, granted Fraley's. Blanton then appealed to the Supreme Court of Nevada, as did respondent city of North Las Vegas with respect to Fraley. After consolidating the two cases along with several others raising the same issue, the Supreme Court concluded, inter alia, that the Federal Constitution does not guarantee a right to a jury trial for a DUI offense because the maximum term of incarceration is only six months and the maximum possible fine is $1,000. . . . We granted certiorari to consider whether petitioners were entitled to a jury trial, . . . and now affirm.

It has long been settled that "there is a category of petty crimes or offenses which is not subject to the Sixth Amendment jury trial provision." . . . In determining whether a particular offense should be categorized as "petty," our early decisions focused on the nature of the offense and on whether it was triable by a jury at common law. . . . In recent years, however, we have sought more "objective indications of the seriousness with which society regards the offense." . . . "[W]e have found the most relevant such criteria in the severity of the maximum authorized penalty."

In using the word "penalty," we do not refer solely to the maximum prison term authorized for a particular offense. A legislature's view of the seriousness of an offense also is reflected in the other penalties that it attaches to the offense. . . . Primary emphasis, however, must be placed on the maximum authorized period of incarceration. . . . Indeed, because incarceration is an "intrinsically different" form of punishment, . . . it is the most powerful indication [of] whether an offense is "serious."

. . . [A] defendant is entitled to a jury trial whenever the offense for which he is charged carries a maximum authorized prison term of greater than six months. . . . The possibility of a sentence exceeding six months, we determined, is "sufficiently severe by itself" to require the opportunity for a jury trial. . . . As for a prison term of six months or less, we recognized that it will seldom be viewed by the defendant as "trivial or 'petty.'" . . . But we found that the disadvantages of such a sentence, "onerous though they may be, may be outweighed by the benefits that result from speedy and inexpensive nonjury adjudications." . . .

. . . A defendant is entitled to a jury trial in such circumstances only if he can demonstrate that any additional statutory penalties, viewed in conjunction with the maximum authorized period of incarceration, are so severe that they clearly reflect a legislative determination that the offense in question is a "serious" one. This standard, albeit somewhat imprecise, should ensure the availability of a jury trial in the rare situation where a legislature packs an offense it deems "serious" with onerous penalties that nonetheless "do not puncture the 6-month incarceration line." . . .

Applying these principles here, it is apparent that petitioners are not entitled to a jury trial. The maximum authorized prison sentence for first-time DUI offenders does not exceed six months. A presumption therefore

exists that the Nevada Legislature views DUI as a "petty" offense for purposes of the Sixth Amendment. Considering the additional statutory penalties as well, we do not believe that the Nevada Legislature has clearly indicated that DUI is a "serious" offense.

Viewed together, the statutory penalties are not so severe that DUI must be deemed a "serious" offense for purposes of the Sixth Amendment. It was not error, therefore, to deny petitioners jury trials. Accordingly, the judgment of the Supreme Court of Nevada is Affirmed.

Case Questions

1. Does it seem that drunken driving is serious enough for national campaigns to stamp it out and levy severe penalties against but not serious enough to guarantee a jury trial? Explain your answer.
2. If you read the Sixth Amendment, would you think that a jury trial would be guaranteed in a criminal proceeding that could result in a six-month incarceration? Explain your answer.
3. Does something in the nature of a DUI charge suggest that a jury is unnecessary? Explain your answer.
4. Consider that many states have reduced the blood alcohol level required for a presumption of drunken driving and are under pressure to reduce it further. Automatic sentences have also been introduced. Is this not conviction by machine? Explain your answer.
5. In many states, some lawyers specialize exclusively in DUI defenses and are apparently very successful (challenging the accuracy of the machine, the way the test was administered, etc.). Is this case an appropriate remedy? Explain your answer.

The defendant must be informed of the *nature and cause of the accusation* in order to prepare a defense. This simply spells out the notice requirement that would otherwise be implied by the due process clause.

The right of the defendant to be *confronted with the witnesses against him* is a protection against anonymous accusers and ensures the right to cross-examine witnesses.

felony

A serious crime, commonly defined by a penalty of a year or more in prison.

Compulsory process refers to the power of the defendant in a criminal case to force witnesses to attend trial under a subpoena issued by the court. If appearance were voluntary, the defendant would be at a severe disadvantage.

In England, at common law, defendants in **felony** cases were forbidden to have an attorney. The Sixth Amendment was intended to do away with this prohibition. Still, the right to effective *assistance of counsel* for the defendant has become a cherished right only in the last few decades. For many years, the right to counsel was considered applicable only to federal cases and then only when the accused could afford to pay or was accused of a capital offense (*Powell v. Alabama*, 287 U.S. 45 [1932])—until the famous exchange between Gideon and the Florida judge:

> *The Court:* Mr. Gideon, I am sorry, but I cannot appoint Counsel to represent you in this case. Under the laws of the State of Florida, the only time the Court can appoint Counsel to represent a Defendant is when that person is charged with a capital offense. I am sorry, but I will have to deny your request to appoint Counsel to defend you in this case.

> *The Defendant:* The U.S. Supreme Court says I am entitled to be represented by Counsel.

Gideon v. Wainwright, 372 U.S. 335 (1963).

Mr. Gideon was not exactly correct when he made this statement, but after he presented his own defense and was convicted, he took the case to the U.S. Supreme Court, which agreed with him. *Argersinger v. Hamlin,* 407 U.S. 25 (1972) extended the right to petty offenses involving possible imprisonment. A defendant who cannot afford an attorney must be furnished one by the government.

The right to be free from the imposition of *excessive bail* is self-explanatory; what is excessive may be judged relative to what is usual bail under similar circumstances. This is a limitation on the judge's discretion.

The right against the imposition of *cruel and unusual punishments* is also a relative concept. This particular principle has been viewed as an evolving standard—what was not considered "cruel and unusual" 50 years ago may be considered uncivilized and barbaric by today's standards.

The *due process* clause demands fair procedure and reasonable laws; it is a standard that the courts can invoke when injustice is apparent.

The *equal protection* clause imposes a test of equality before the law against discriminatory practices. There must be no difference in treatment in the statement of the law itself or in its application. In recent years the differential impact of the laws with regard to minorities has raised equal protection claims; for example, it has been shown statistically that blacks receive a disproportionate number of death sentences.

The defendant's right to due process is ensured by the impartiality of the trial judge and the impartiality of appellate judges, should the defendant appeal. A judge can voluntarily remove (recuse) herself from a case to avoid even the appearance of impropriety; in addition, a party to a case can file a motion to recuse a judge, although such a motion may be made at the risk of angering the judge. Although *Caperton* is not a criminal case, the due process principle discussed is certainly applicable outside the civil context.

Hugh M. CAPERTON, et al., Petitioners

v.

A.T. MASSEY COAL CO., INC., et al.

Supreme Court of the United States

No. 08-22

129 S. Ct. 2252

Decided June 8, 2009.

In this case the Supreme Court of Appeals of West Virginia reversed a trial court judgment, which had entered a jury verdict of $50 million. Five justices heard the case, and the vote to reverse was 3 to 2. The question presented is whether the Due Process Clause of the Fourteenth Amendment was violated when one of the justices in the majority denied a recusal motion. The basis for the motion was that the justice had received campaign contributions in an extraordinary amount from, and through the efforts of, the board chairman and principal officer of the corporation found liable for the damages.

Under our precedents there are objective standards that require recusal when "the probability of actual bias on the part of the judge or decisionmaker is too high to be constitutionally tolerable." *Withrow.* Applying those precedents, we find that, in all the circumstances of this case, due process requires recusal.

In August 2002 a West Virginia jury returned a verdict that found respondents A.T. Massey Coal Co. and its affiliates (hereinafter Massey) liable for fraudulent misrepresentation, concealment, and tortious interference with existing contractual relations. The jury awarded petitioners Hugh Caperton, Harman Development Corp., Harman Mining Corp., and Sovereign Coal Sales (hereinafter Caperton) the sum of $50 million in compensatory and punitive damages. . . .

Don Blankenship is Massey's chairman, chief executive officer, and president. After the verdict but before the appeal, West Virginia held its 2004 judicial elections. Knowing the Supreme Court of Appeals of West Virginia would consider the appeal in the case, Blankenship decided to support an attorney who sought to replace Justice McGraw. Justice McGraw was a candidate for reelection to that court. The attorney who sought to replace him was Brent Benjamin. . . .

To provide some perspective, Blankenship's $3 million in contributions were more than the total amount spent by all other Benjamin supporters and three times the amount spent by Benjamin's own committee. Caperton contends that Blankenship spent $1 million more than the total amount spent by the campaign committees of both candidates combined. . . .

Caperton contends that Blankenship's pivotal role in getting Justice Benjamin elected created a constitutionally intolerable probability of actual bias. Though not a bribe or criminal influence, Justice Benjamin would nevertheless feel a debt of gratitude to Blankenship for his extraordinary efforts to get him elected. . . .

Justice Benjamin was careful to address the recusal motions and explain his reasons why, on his view of the controlling standard, disqualification was not in order. In four separate opinions issued during the course of the appeal, he explained why no actual bias had been established. . . .

Following accepted principles of our legal tradition respecting the proper performance of judicial functions, judges often inquire into their subjective motives and purposes in the ordinary course of deciding a case. This does not mean the inquiry is a simple one. . . .

The judge inquires into reasons that seem to be leading to a particular result. Precedent and *stare decisis* and the text and purpose of the law and the Constitution; logic and scholarship and experience and common sense; and fairness and disinterest and neutrality are among the factors at work. To bring coherence to the process, and to seek respect for the resulting judgment, judges often explain the reasons for their conclusions and rulings. There are instances when the introspection that often attends this process may reveal that what the judge had assumed to be a proper, controlling factor is not the real one at work.

If the judge discovers that some personal bias or improper consideration seems to be the actuating cause of the decision or to be an influence so difficult to dispel that there is a real possibility of undermining neutrality, the judge may think it necessary to consider withdrawing from the case.

The difficulties of inquiring into actual bias, and the fact that the inquiry is often a private one, simply underscore the need for objective rules. Otherwise there may be no adequate protection against a judge who simply misreads or misapprehends the real motives at work in deciding the case. The judge's own inquiry into actual bias, then, is not one that the law can easily superintend or review, though actual bias, if disclosed, no doubt would be grounds for appropriate relief. In lieu of exclusive reliance on that personal inquiry, or on appellate review of the judge's determination respecting actual bias, the Due Process Clause has been implemented by objective standards that do not require proof of actual bias. . . .

We turn to the influence at issue in this case. Not every campaign contribution by a litigant or attorney creates a probability of bias that requires a judge's recusal, but this is an exceptional case. . . . We conclude that there is a serious risk of actual bias—based on objective and reasonable perceptions—when a person with a personal stake in a particular case had a significant and disproportionate influence in placing the judge on the case by raising funds or directing the judge's election campaign when the case was pending or imminent. The inquiry centers on the contribution's relative size in comparison to the total amount of money contributed to the campaign, the total amount spent in the election, and the apparent effect such contribution had on the outcome of the election. . . .

Whether Blankenship's campaign contributions were a necessary and sufficient cause of Benjamin's victory is not the proper inquiry. Much like determining whether a judge is actually biased, proving what ultimately drives the electorate to choose a particular candidate is a difficult endeavor, not likely to lend itself to a certain conclusion. This is particularly true where, as here, there is no procedure for judicial factfinding and the sole trier of fact is the one accused of bias. Due process requires an objective inquiry into whether the contributor's influence on the election under all the circumstances "would offer a possible temptation to the average . . . judge to . . . lead him not to hold the balance nice, clear and true." *Tumey*. In an election decided by fewer than 50,000 votes (382,036 to 334,301), Blankenship's campaign contributions—in comparison to the total amount contributed to the campaign, as well as the total amount spent in the election—had a significant and disproportionate influence on the electoral outcome. And the risk that Blankenship's influence engendered actual bias is sufficiently substantial that it "must be forbidden if the guarantee of due process is to be adequately implemented." *Withrow*.

The temporal relationship between the campaign contributions, the justice's election, and the pendency of the case is also critical. It was reasonably foreseeable, when the campaign contributions were made, that the pending case would be before the newly elected justice. The $50 million adverse jury verdict had been entered before the election, and the Supreme Court of Appeals was the next step once the state trial court dealt with post-trial motions. So it became at once apparent that, absent recusal, Justice Benjamin would review a judgment that cost his biggest donor's company $50 million. Although there is no allegation of a *quid pro quo* agreement, the fact remains that Blankenship's extraordinary contributions were made at a time when he had a vested stake in the outcome. Just as no man is allowed to be a judge in his own cause, similar fears of bias can arise when—without the consent of the other parties—a man chooses the judge in his own cause. And applying this principle to the judicial election process, there was here a serious, objective risk of actual bias that required Justice Benjamin's recusal.

Justice Benjamin did undertake an extensive search for actual bias. But, as we have indicated, that is just one step in the judicial process; objective standards may also require recusal whether or not actual bias exists or can be proved. . . . On these extreme facts the probability of actual bias rises to an unconstitutional level. . . .

Massey and its *amici* predict that various adverse consequences will follow from recognizing a constitutional violation here—ranging from a flood of recusal motions to unnecessary interference with judicial elections. We disagree.

It is true that extreme cases often test the bounds of established legal principles, and sometimes no administrable standard may be available to address the perceived wrong. But it is also true that extreme cases are more likely to cross constitutional limits, requiring this Court's intervention and formulation of objective standards. This is particularly true when due process is violated.

Case Questions

1. Does it make sense for a judge to withdraw from hearing a case or be involuntarily removed from a case even though actual bias has not been shown?
2. Why was Justice Benjamin's explanation of his impartiality insufficient?
3. What circumstances could you imagine in which a criminal defendant could have done something in the past that could be perceived as improperly influencing the judge?

THE EXCLUSIONARY RULE

The exclusionary rule is a special feature of criminal procedure that has developed from a series of U.S. Supreme Court interpretations of the Fourth, Fifth, and Fourteenth Amendments. It applies to excluding evidence illegally obtained by the government and enforces the adversarial principle in criminal proceedings. Because of the disparity between the power and resources of the government and the relative powerlessness of the criminal defendant, a number of protections, such as those enumerated in the Constitution, are afforded the defendant to equalize the respective positions in a criminal proceeding. The exclusionary rule operates to protect the defendant from abusive procedures by a more powerful opponent.

Basically, the exclusionary rule excludes from trial evidence obtained in violation of the defendant's constitutional rights. It first arose in *Weeks v. United States*, 232 U.S. 383 (1914), which held that evidence illegally obtained by federal officers could be excluded from evidence, but *Weeks* failed to apply the principle to the states. *Wolf v. Colorado*, 338 U.S. 25 (1949), held that the search and seizure provisions of the Fourth Amendment were applicable to the states under the due process clause of the Fourteenth Amendment but did not exclude illegally obtained evidence from state prosecutions. *Wolf* was overruled in 1961 by *Mapp v. Ohio*, 367 U.S. 643, which held that the products of a search violating Fourth Amendment rights may not be used in state prosecutions.

Suppose that the police exact a confession from a suspect through torture. Should the confession be presented to the jury and the defendant allowed to disavow the confession because it was involuntary? Should the jury be allowed to weigh the relevance of the confession in light of the circumstances under which it was obtained? Our law answers in the negative. Coerced confessions have no place in the trial. This principle needs little justification; it is a reasonable interpretation of the meaning and intent of the due process clause of the Fourteenth Amendment.

In *Miranda v. Arizona*, 384 U.S. 436 (1966), Chief Justice Warren wrote an opinion that linked the Sixth Amendment right to counsel with the Fifth Amendment privilege against self-incrimination—both applicable to the states under the Fourteenth Amendment due process clause. The four dissenters argued that the Fifth Amendment was historically unconnected to the exclusion of involuntary confessions, but Warren and his four brethren prevailed, and police have been reading *Miranda* rights ever since. (Warren pointed out that these rights had been FBI policy for some time.) The precise requirements were spelled out in Chief Justice Warren's majority opinion:

> Our holding will be spelled out with some specificity in the pages which follow but briefly stated it is this: the prosecution may not use statements, whether exculpatory or inculpatory, stemming from custodial interrogation of the defendant unless it demonstrates the use of procedural safeguards effective to secure the privilege against self-incrimination. By custodial interrogation, we mean questioning initiated by law enforcement officers after a person has been taken into custody or otherwise deprived of his freedom of action in any significant way. As for the procedural safeguards to be employed, unless other fully effective means are devised to inform accused persons of their right of silence and to assure a continuous opportunity to exercise it, the following measures are required. *Prior to any questioning, the person must be warned that he has a right to remain silent, that any statement he does make may be used as evidence against him, and that he has a right to the presence of an attorney, either retained or appointed.* The defendant may waive effectuation of these rights, provided the waiver is made voluntarily, knowingly and intelligently. If, however, he indicates in any manner and at any stage of the process that he wishes to consult with an attorney before speaking there can be no questioning. Likewise, if the individual is alone and indicates in any manner that he does not wish to be interrogated, the police may not question him. The mere fact that he may have answered some questions or volunteered some statements on his own does not deprive him of the right to refrain from answering any further inquiries until he has consulted with an attorney and thereafter consents to be questioned [emphasis added].

In most jurisdictions, a *motion to suppress* (physical evidence or a confession) is a pretrial motion that tests the applicability of the exclusionary rule to the circumstances of the case. If the prosecution's case relies on such evidence, the granting of the motion will be followed by a dismissal of the charges or a motion by the defense for a judgment of acquittal. The motion to suppress is the defense's first line of attack in cases in which confessions or physical evidence are critical elements. A surprising majority of criminal defendants confess in spite of being advised of their right to remain silent and their right to an attorney. When first contacted, the criminal defense attorney's first words of advice are likely to be: "Do not say anything to the police until I get there."

The criminal courts have been inundated for many years by drug crimes. In most of these, the defense's best attack is to suppress the evidence, so search and seizure appeals abound. Search and seizure law has come to draw extremely fine lines between proper and improper searches.

affidavit

A statement in writing sworn to before a person authorized to administer an oath.

To attack evidence seized by police under a search warrant, criminal defense attorneys look to the warrant itself and the **affidavit** underlying it to see if some fatal mistake was made that would make the search itself illegal and the fruits of the search excludable. Police have been protected for a few years by the *good faith* exception, which applies where the warrant proves invalid but the officer reasonably believed it to be valid. *Herring* describes this exception along with a discussion of the validity of search warrants.

Bennie Dean HERRING, Petitioner

v.

UNITED STATES

Supreme Court of the United States

No. 07-513

129 S. Ct. 695

Decided Jan. 14, 2009.

The Fourth Amendment forbids "unreasonable searches and seizures," and this usually requires the police to have probable cause or a warrant before making an arrest. What if an officer reasonably believes there is an outstanding arrest warrant, but that belief turns out to be wrong because of a negligent bookkeeping error by another police employee? The parties here agree that the ensuing arrest is still a violation of the Fourth Amendment, but dispute whether contraband found during a search incident to that arrest must be excluded in a later prosecution.

Our cases establish that such suppression is not an automatic consequence of a Fourth Amendment violation. Instead, the question turns on the culpability of the police and the potential of exclusion to deter wrongful police conduct. Here the error was the result of isolated negligence attenuated from the arrest. We hold that in these circumstances the jury should not be barred from considering all the evidence.

On July 7, 2004, Investigator Mark Anderson learned that Bennie Dean Herring had driven to the Coffee County Sheriff's Department to retrieve something from his impounded truck. Herring was no stranger to law enforcement, and Anderson asked the county's warrant clerk, Sandy Pope, to check for any outstanding warrants for Herring's arrest. When she found none, Anderson asked Pope to check with Sharon Morgan, her counterpart in neighboring Dale County. After checking Dale County's computer database, Morgan replied that there was an active arrest warrant for Herring's failure to appear on a felony charge. Pope relayed the information to Anderson and asked Morgan to fax over a copy of the warrant as confirmation. Anderson and a deputy

followed Herring as he left the impound lot, pulled him over, and arrested him. A search incident to the arrest revealed methamphetamine in Herring's pocket, and a pistol (which as a felon he could not possess) in his vehicle.

There had, however, been a mistake about the warrant. The Dale County sheriff's computer records are supposed to correspond to actual arrest warrants, which the office also maintains. But when Morgan went to the files to retrieve the actual warrant to fax to Pope, Morgan was unable to find it. She called a court clerk and learned that the warrant had been recalled five months earlier. Normally when a warrant is recalled the court clerk's office or a judge's chambers calls Morgan, who enters the information in the sheriff's computer database and disposes of the physical copy. For whatever reason, the information about the recall of the warrant for Herring did not appear in the database. Morgan immediately called Pope to alert her to the mixup, and Pope contacted Anderson over a secure radio. This all unfolded in 10 to 15 minutes, but Herring had already been arrested and found with the gun and drugs, just a few hundred yards from the sheriff's office. . . .

When a probable-cause determination was based on reasonable but mistaken assumptions, the person subjected to a search or seizure has not necessarily been the victim of a constitutional violation. The very phrase "probable cause" confirms that the Fourth Amendment does not demand all possible precision. And whether the error can be traced to a mistake by a state actor or some other source may bear on the analysis. . . .

The fact that a Fourth Amendment violation occurred—*i.e.,* that a search or arrest was unreasonable—does not necessarily mean that the exclusionary rule applies. . . . First, the exclusionary rule is not an individual right and applies only where it " 'result[s] in appreciable deterrence.' " *Leon.* . . . In addition, the benefits of deterrence must outweigh the costs. The principal cost of applying the rule is, of course, letting guilty and possibly dangerous defendants go free—something that "offends basic concepts of the criminal justice system." *Leon.* . . .

These principles are reflected in the holding of *Leon*. When police act under a warrant that is invalid for lack of probable cause, the exclusionary rule does not apply if the police acted "in objectively reasonable reliance" on the subsequently invalidated search warrant. We (perhaps confusingly) called this objectively reasonable reliance "good faith." . . .

To trigger the exclusionary rule, police conduct must be sufficiently deliberate that exclusion can meaningfully deter it, and sufficiently culpable that such deterrence is worth the price paid by the justice system. As laid out in our cases, the exclusionary rule serves to deter deliberate, reckless, or grossly negligent conduct, or in some circumstances recurring or systemic negligence. The error in this case does not rise to that level.

Our decision in *Franks* provides an analogy. In *Franks*, we held that police negligence in obtaining a warrant did not even rise to the level of a Fourth Amendment violation, let alone meet the more stringent test for triggering the exclusionary rule. We held that the Constitution allowed defendants, in some circumstances, "to challenge the truthfulness of factual statements made in an affidavit supporting the warrant," even after the warrant had issued. If those false statements were necessary to the Magistrate Judge's probable-cause determination, the warrant would be "voided." But we did not find all false statements relevant: "There must be allegations of deliberate falsehood or of reckless disregard for the truth," and "[a]llegations of negligence or innocent mistake are insufficient."

Both this case and *Franks* concern false information provided by police. Under *Franks*, negligent police miscommunications in the course of acquiring a warrant do not provide a basis to rescind a warrant and render a search or arrest invalid. Here, the miscommunications occurred in a different context—after the warrant had been issued and recalled—but that fact should not require excluding the evidence obtained. . . .

We have already held that "our good-faith inquiry is confined to the objectively ascertainable question whether a reasonably well trained officer would have known that the search was illegal" in light of "all of the circumstances." *Leon*. These circumstances frequently include a particular officer's knowledge and experience, but that does not make the test any more subjective than the one for probable cause, which looks to an officer's knowledge and experience, but not his subjective intent.

We do not suggest that all recordkeeping errors by the police are immune from the exclusionary rule. In this case, however, the conduct at issue was not so objectively culpable as to require exclusion. In *Leon* we held that "the marginal or nonexistent benefits produced by suppressing evidence obtained in objectively reasonable reliance on a subsequently invalidated search warrant cannot justify the substantial costs of exclusion." The same is true when evidence is obtained in objectively reasonable reliance on a subsequently recalled warrant.

If the police have been shown to be reckless in maintaining a warrant system, or to have knowingly made false entries to lay the groundwork for future false arrests, exclusion would certainly be justified under our cases should such misconduct cause a Fourth Amendment violation. . . . Petitioner's fears that our decision will cause police departments to deliberately keep their officers ignorant are thus unfounded. . . .

Petitioner's claim that police negligence automatically triggers suppression cannot be squared with the principles underlying the exclusionary rule, as they have been explained in our cases. In light of our repeated holdings that the deterrent effect of suppression must be substantial and outweigh any harm to the justice system, we conclude that when police mistakes are the result of negligence such as that described here, rather than systemic error or reckless disregard of constitutional requirements, any marginal deterrence does not "pay its way." *Leon*.

Case Questions

1. Does it make sense to distinguish between a violation of the Fourth Amendment and application of the exclusionary rule?
2. Did the Court strike a good balance between a police officer's difficulty in obtaining a warrant and the defendant's Fourth Amendment right?

PLEA BARGAINING

The criminal justice system cannot be appreciated without an understanding of the custom of plea bargaining. The prosecuting attorney and the defense attorney usually engage in a form of negotiation, which until recent years has been a largely unofficial part of criminal procedure. Nearly all convictions are the result of negotiation. The defendant agrees to plead guilty in return for beneficial treatment by the prosecution. The prosecution may agree to drop some of the charges, reduce the offense—say, from first-degree murder to second-degree murder or from burglary to criminal trespass— thereby lessening the penalty, or recommend a lenient sentence or probation, which recommendation is usually accepted by the judge.

The present system could not work without plea bargaining. If every defendant demanded a jury trial, there would not be enough courts and prosecutors to try all the cases. Less than 5 percent of criminal cases go to trial (the same is true of civil cases). The presumption is that in most cases a trial would result in a conviction, thus encouraging defendants to make the best deal they can. Nevertheless, the custom of plea bargaining has come under severe criticism because negotiation takes place outside of public and judicial scrutiny and suggests a degree of collusion between prosecutors and defense attorneys.

THE STEPS IN PROCESSING A CRIME

The steps in criminal procedure tend to follow a more consistent routine than those of civil procedure because of legal limitations. The burden of proving guilt beyond a reasonable doubt, as opposed to "a preponderance of the evidence," forces police and prosecutor to monitor cases carefully. The exclusionary rule makes evidence or confessions unlawfully obtained inadmissible at trial and thus requires that great care be taken in investigation, arrest, interrogation, and search and seizure of evidence, lest the case fail for improper procedure. The constitutional right to a speedy trial forces police and prosecutor to organize investigation, charges, and trial within a limited timeframe. In addition, the constitutional protections afforded an accused require that cases be carefully prepared to avoid infringement of the accused's rights. (See Exhibit 8-2.)

EXHIBIT 8-2   STEPS IN PROCESSING A CRIME

A large number of crimes go unreported or unsolved. Of those on which action is taken, only a small percentage make it to trial.

The following is an outline of the steps involved in the criminal process, which are followed virtually universally in criminal cases, though the terminology may differ from one jurisdiction to another:

1. Detection of crime.
    a. Report of crime.
    b. Police investigation.

2. Identification of a suspected criminal.
3. Arrest.
   a. Arrest without a warrant before the filing of a complaint.
   b. Arrest with a warrant after the filing of a complaint.
4. Initial appearance before a magistrate.
   a. Inform the accused of the charges and the accused's legal rights.
   b. Set bail or the terms of release from custody.
5. Preliminary hearing.
   a. Determine probable cause that the accused committed a crime.
   b. Release the accused or bind over for grand jury.
6. Indictment.
   a. Grand jury decides whether the accused should be tried, or
   b. Prosecutor indicts by information.
7. Arraignment before the court.
   a. The accused is informed of charges brought.
   b. The accused enters plea.
   i. If plea of guilty or nolo contendere, the accused (defendant) may be sentenced.
   ii. If plea of not guilty, the accused requests or waives jury.
8. Pretrial preparation.
   a. Pretrial motions.
   b. Discovery.
   c. Plea bargaining.
9. Trial.
   a. Acquittal results in release of the defendant.
   b. Conviction leads to sentencing.
10. Optional posttrial motions, appeals, and habeas corpus.

Detection of Crime

The initial intervention of law enforcement officers is prompted by the report of a suspected crime by victims or witnesses or the police themselves, who may witness a crime or discover one during a police investigation into suspected criminal activities. The criminal act may be apparent from the circumstances, as when police encounter bank robbers in the act of robbing a bank, or there may simply be suspicious activities that require investigation or surveillance.

Although it may be clear that a crime has been committed, the identity of the perpetrator may not be immediately apparent. The objective of police inquiry is to establish facts to support the conclusion that a crime has been committed and that a specific person or persons committed that crime. Detection of crime is simply the first step; the police must also furnish the prosecutor with sufficient evidence to form the basis for a probable conviction of the offender.

Statements made in the absence of *Miranda* warnings in the course of a custodial interrogation may be excluded from evidence at trial. What exactly constitutes a *custodial interrogation* has been the subject of numerous cases, including the *Bruder* case.

PENNSYLVANIA
v.
Thomas A. BRUDER, Jr.

U.S. Supreme Court

488 U.S. 9, 109 S. Ct. 205, 102 L. Ed. 2d 172 (1988)

In the early morning of January 19, 1985, Officer Steve Shallis of the Newton Township, Pennsylvania, Police Department observed Bruder driving very erratically along State Highway 252. Among other traffic violations, he ignored a red light. Shallis stopped Bruder's vehicle. Bruder left his vehicle, approached Shallis, and when asked for his registration card, returned to his car to obtain it. Smelling alcohol and observing Bruder's stumbling movements, Shallis administered field sobriety tests, including asking Bruder to recite the alphabet. Shallis also inquired about alcohol. Bruder answered that he had been drinking and was returning home. Bruder failed the sobriety tests, whereupon Shallis arrested him, placed him in the police car and gave him Miranda warnings. Bruder was later convicted of driving under the influence of alcohol. At his trial, his statements and conduct prior to his arrest were admitted into evidence. On appeal, the Pennsylvania Superior Court reversed, on the ground that the above statements Bruder had

uttered during the roadside questioning were elicited through custodial interrogation and should have been suppressed for lack of Miranda warnings. The Pennsylvania Supreme Court denied the State's appeal application.

In *Berkemer v. McCarty,* which involved facts strikingly similar to those in this case, the court concluded that the "noncoercive aspect of ordinary traffic stops prompts us to hold that persons temporarily detained pursuant to such stops are not 'in custody' for the purposes of Miranda." . . .

The facts in this record, which Bruder does not contest, reveal the same noncoercive aspects as the *Berkemer* detention: "a single police officer ask[ing] respondent a modest number of questions and request[ing] him to perform a simple balancing test at a location visible to passing motorists." Accordingly, *Berkemer's* rule, that ordinary traffic stops do not involve custody for purposes of Miranda, governs this case. The judgment of the Pennsylvania Superior Court that evidence was inadmissible for lack of Miranda warnings is reversed.

Case Questions

1. Where does the court draw the line between a custodial and a noncustodial stop?
2. From the language of the case, can we infer that an interrogation did or did not take place?

Arrest and Complaint

Arrest is not an easy term to define in all circumstances and cases, but it generally refers to detaining someone for the purposes of having him or her answer to an allegation of a crime. The *complaint* is the formal allegation that the accused has committed a crime.

arrest
Usually refers to detaining someone to answer for a crime.

Legal process begins with a complaint. The complaint may be filed before or after arrest. When an arrest is made without a warrant during the commission of a crime, the complaint is filed at the defendant's initial appearance before the court or magistrate. When a crime has been completed and the police have information linking a person to the crime, the complaint is filed and an arrest warrant issued, which then serves as the basis for arresting the suspect.

In either case, an initial determination must be made as to whether there is *probable cause* to believe that a crime has been committed and that the defendant committed it. The complaint is accompanied by sworn statements, called *affidavits*, which must present sufficient allegations to persuade the magistrate that a warrant should issue. If an arrest is made without a warrant, the arresting officer must have probable cause to believe that the suspect has committed a crime.

The arrest powers of police are limited by constitutional and statutory requirements. When police exceed their authority in making an arrest, they may subject themselves to civil suit by the arrestee for the tort of false arrest or to a civil rights suit. An arrest made in the good faith belief that it is lawful and under the authority of a warrant and conducted with reasonable force is the ideal standard against which allegedly improper arrests are tested. There is a large body of constitutional cases on arrest, because arrest commonly involves incidental searches and the discovery of evidence later used in prosecution.

Initial Appearance

initial (first) appearance
Opportunity for presence before a magistrate; a person arrested for a crime must be brought before a magistrate promptly after arrest to be informed of the charges and the legal rights of the accused.

State and federal statutes require that an arrestee be brought before a magistrate without undue delay, commonly within 24 hours. This is called **initial** or **first appearance** and is designed to protect individuals from being jailed without charges or bonds in the absence of scrutiny by an impartial magistrate. The accused will be informed of the charges and legal rights, especially the right to an attorney, and that an attorney will be appointed at state expense if the accused does not have funds with which to pay an attorney.

Bail is set at the initial appearance. The purpose of bail is to assure the defendant's appearance at further hearings. The Eighth Amendment prohibits excessive bail, and the defendant may request a hearing to reduce the bail. Under federal law, the court must set the least restrictive conditions to assure appearance. Defendants are frequently released on their own recognizance if, for instance, the defendant has steady employment, has a stable residence, presents little threat to society, and the nature of the crime suggests little likelihood that the defendant will flee the jurisdiction. Extreme circumstances may justify a denial of bail. The court may impose certain conditions for release, such as restrictions on travel.

Preliminary Hearing

preliminary hearing
A criminal defendant's opportunity to challenge the case before the judge in a hearing which determines the sufficiency of the charges without a determination of guilt; ordinarily afforded but not always available.

A **preliminary hearing** is frequently called to examine the basis for the charges against the defendant, although this is frequently waived by the defendant. Because in the American system the prosecutor enjoys unrestricted authority over whether to prosecute, the preliminary hearing provides a defendant the opportunity to challenge the prosecution's case before the court. The preliminary hearing does not determine guilt; rather, it examines the legal basis for the charges against the defendant. The judge determines whether there is sufficient evidence to send the case to the grand jury or whether to release the defendant instead. Not all states require a grand jury indictment, so the preliminary hearing may be the only opportunity to challenge the charges prior to trial.

Grand jury hearings are not truly adversarial; they are secret hearings in which the prosecutor is given wide latitude to present the case for the guilt of the defendant. The grand jury does not decide guilt but instead determines whether probable cause exists that the defendant committed the crime. If the grand jury finds no probable cause, the defendant is discharged; otherwise, the defendant is indicted and the case goes to trial.

In *Corra*, the indictment differed from the evidence produced at trial and from the jury instruction.

Indictment and Information

Although the Constitution requires a grand jury for **infamous crimes** and many states require a grand jury indictment for **felonies**, many cases are brought on the basis of an **information**, which is a written accusation by a public prosecutor. The practice differs from jurisdiction to jurisdiction, but the defendant must be formally charged by an indictment or information.

infamous crime

A major crime, for which a heavy penalty may be awarded. Used in the Constitution but now out of date and would probably mean felony today.

felony

A serious crime, commonly defined by a penalty of a year or more in prison.

information

A written accusation made by a public prosecutor.

STATE of West Virginia, Appellee

v.

Jeff CORRA, Defendant Below, Appellant

Supreme Court of Appeals of West Virginia

No. 33911

678 S.E.2d 306

Decided Feb. 27, 2009.

In this appeal from the Circuit Court of Wood County, defendant Jeff Corra was indicted and convicted of knowingly furnishing "alcoholic liquors" to persons under the age of 21 years in violation of W.Va. Code, 60-3-22a(b) [1986]. At trial, the State introduced evidence that the defendant furnished Coors Light beer to persons under the age of 21 years, and asserted that the furnishing of Coors Light was sufficient to convict the defendant of furnishing "alcoholic liquors" as alleged in the indictment. In addition, the circuit court instructed the jury that the defendant could be found guilty if he furnished "beer" to persons under the age of 21 years.

On appeal, the defendant argues that Coors Light is defined by statute as a "nonintoxicating beer" and that the indictment charging a crime under W.Va. Code,

60-3-22a(b) [1986] requires that "alcoholic liquor" be furnished before he could be convicted of violating this statute. Essentially, the defendant asserts that the indictment charged him with the crime of "furnishing alcoholic liquors," but the State convicted him of committing the different crime of "furnishing nonintoxicating beer." . . .

Facts and Background

At the time of the alleged crime, the defendant, Jeff Corra, was a 50-year-old resident of Wood County and a divorced father of a 20-year-old daughter, Ashley. On the night of August 5, 2006, Ashley invited a number of her friends to her father's home. All of her guests were under the age of 21 years. . . .

Several of Ashley's friends admitted buying and bringing beer (Budweiser) and alcoholic liquor (Jagermeister) to the appellant's house, and consuming it on the premises. The State does not contend that the defendant furnished Budweiser or Jagermeister to the persons at the party. However, some of Ashley's friends drank Coors Light beer which the defendant had previously purchased and placed in his refrigerator. Although the defendant did not give Coors Light to anyone at the party, there was testimony that the defendant knew, but did nothing to stop his daughter's friends from taking his Coors Light from the refrigerator and drinking it.

In the early morning hours of August 6, 2006, four individuals under the age of 21 left the defendant's residence together in a vehicle. The vehicle—driven by 20-year-old Courtney McDonough—left the roadway and collided with a tree. Two occupants were killed and a third was seriously injured. . . .

Discussion . . .

We begin by noting that, from our review of the record, it is apparent that neither the prosecutor nor defense counsel read the statutes relating to the crime of furnishing "alcoholic liquors" before the jury reached its verdict. The prosecutor mistakenly informed a busy trial judge that beer was the same as alcoholic liquor for the purpose of proving the indictment. Likewise, it is not disputed that when the circuit court asked at the charge conference whether he should instruct the jury on the definition of alcoholic liquor, defense counsel stated that an instruction was not necessary because beer was an alcoholic liquor.

The central theme of the trial was whether the defendant committed acts which could be considered as "furnishing beer." However, the main issue should have been whether the defendant could be convicted under an indictment charging the "furnishing of alcoholic liquor" to persons under the age of 21 years when the State could only prove the "furnishing of beer." . . .

[The court reviewed the statute under which Corra was convicted and the statutes defining "alcoholic liquor" and "nonintoxicating beer."]

"Nonintoxicating beer" shall mean all cereal malt beverages or products of the brewing industry commonly referred to as beer, lager beer, ale and all other mixtures and preparations produced by the brewing industry, including malt coolers and containing at least one half of one percent alcohol by volume, but not more than four and two-tenths percent of alcohol by weight, or six percent by volume, whichever is greater, all of which are hereby declared to be nonintoxicating and *the word "liquor" as used in chapter sixty of this code shall not be construed to include or embrace nonintoxicating*

beer nor any of the beverages, products, mixtures or preparations included within this definition.

This statute, too, makes it clear that the Legislature intended for "nonintoxicating beer" and "liquor" to be treated differently in Chapter 60 of the *W.Va.Code,* and makes it clear that alcoholic liquors have more alcohol content than nonintoxicating beers. . . .

There is no doubt that the defendant was convicted of a different crime than that for which he was indicted. He was indicted for "furnishing alcoholic liquor" but convicted of "furnishing non-intoxicating beer." The *West Virginia Constitution* provides that a defendant can only be convicted of the offense for which he or she has been fully and plainly charged. . . .

The law in West Virginia requires that any substantial amendment to an indictment, direct or indirect, must be resubmitted to the grand jury. . . . When the evidence at trial differs from the allegations in the indictment, then a variance has occurred. It is only when the defendant is prejudiced by the variance that a reversal is required. . . . However, not every variation between an indictment and proof at trial creates reversible error. . . .

On the other hand, when either the evidence or the jury instructions, or both, vary materially and prejudicially from the charge contained in the indictment, there is a constructive amendment of the indictment and any conviction under the indictment cannot stand and must be reversed. . . .

The difference between a harmless variance and a reversible constructive amendment (fatal variance) was said best by Justice McHugh in . . . *State v. Johnson* . . . :

If the proof adduced at trial differs from the allegations in an indictment, it must be determined whether the difference is a variance or an actual or a constructive amendment to the indictment. If the defendant is not misled in any sense, is not subjected to any added burden of proof, and is not otherwise prejudiced, then the difference between the proof adduced at trial and the indictment is a variance which does not usurp the traditional safeguards of the grand jury. However, if the defendant is misled, is subjected to an added burden of proof, or is otherwise prejudiced, the difference between the proof at trial and the indictment is an actual or a constructive amendment of the indictment which is reversible error.

"Whether the difference between the indictment and proof adduced at trial is merely a variance or whether the difference is an actual or a constructive amendment of the indictment will have to be determined on a case-by-case basis." *State v. Johnson.*

There is no doubt that a substantial variation amounting to a constructive amendment of the indictment occurred in this case. The proof and the jury instructions both added new charges which are not minor discrepancies from the body of the indictment. . . .

We therefore hold that when a defendant is charged with a crime in an indictment, but the State convicts the defendant of a charge not included in the indictment, then *per se* error has occurred, and the conviction cannot stand and must be reversed. We wish to make clear, however, that under this holding a defendant may still be convicted of a crime that is a lesser-included offense of the primary offense—the key is that the primary offense must be fully and plainly charged in the indictment, such that a defendant may be on notice to mount a defense to both the primary offenses and any lesser-included offense.

In the case at bar, the variation between the indictment and the evidence, along with the jury instruction, "destroyed the defendant's substantial right to be tried only on charges presented in an indictment returned by a grand jury. Deprivation of such a basic right is far too serious to be treated as nothing more than a variance and then dismissed as harmless error. The very purpose of the requirement that a man be indicted by grand jury is to limit his jeopardy to offenses charged by a group of his fellow citizens acting independently of either prosecuting attorney or judge." *Stirone.*

Therefore, we conclude that the defendant's conviction must be reversed. Because there was insufficient evidence to convict the defendant of the charges for which he was indicted, a retrial is prohibited.

Case Questions

1. What errors were committed by the prosecution?
2. Why was furnishing a light beer to a minor not a lesser included offense of furnishing an alcoholic liquor to a minor?

Arraignment

After indictment or upon an **information**, the defendant is brought before the court to answer the charge. At **arraignment**, the defendant makes a plea from one of three pleas available (see Exhibit 8-3). In minor crimes (misdemeanors), the arraignment may be part of the preliminary hearing—the defendant is informed of the charges and asked to make a plea. Felonies requiring a grand jury and indictment separate the preliminary hearing and the arraignment, which follows the indictment.

information
A written accusation made by a public prosecutor.

arraignment
Brings the defendant before the court to make a plea.

EXHIBIT 8-3 PLEAS AT ARRAIGNMENT

1. *Not guilty.* A plea of not guilty results in a trial. The defendant may waive a jury, but the Constitution guarantees the right to a jury trial in criminal cases.
2. *Guilty.* The defendant admits commission of the crime and submits to the sentence of the court. Guilty pleas are usually the result of a plea negotiation (bargain) between the prosecution and the defense attorney, with the acquiescence of the defendant.

nolo contendere (Latin)

Plea known by its Latin name, meaning "I do not want to contest"; accepts responsibility without an admission of guilt.

3. **Nolo contendere** (not available in some jurisdictions; often not available in felony cases). Literally meaning "I do not wish to contest," nolo contendere is equivalent to a guilty plea except that it does not admit guilt. It is treated the same as a guilty plea for the purposes of sentencing, but it cannot be used in later civil or criminal cases as an admission of guilt.

The court has discretion to accept a guilty or nolo contendere plea. The court may require a defendant to plead guilty or not guilty rather than nolo contendere and may also in its discretion refuse to accept a guilty plea. If the defendant refuses to make a plea, the court will assume this refusal to be a plea of not guilty and set the case for trial.

not guilty by reason of insanity

A plea in a criminal case that admits commission of the acts charged but denies intent on the basis of the defendant's insanity.

A special plea of **not guilty by reason of insanity** is available in many jurisdictions; this subject is more fully covered in Chapter 9. This plea admits commission of the acts with which the defendant is charged but negates the critical element of criminal intent on the basis of the defendant's insanity.

Pretrial

In many respects the pretrial phase is reminiscent of civil procedure. Pretrial motions are available, such as the motion to suppress evidence. Discovery procedures are similar except for protections against self-incrimination. Plea bargaining bears some resemblance to the strategies for negotiating settlements in civil cases.

Trial

In most respects the criminal trial is conducted in the same way as a civil trial. The prosecutor has the burden of proving the case. Each side presents its witnesses and cross-examines witnesses for the other side. There are opening statements, closing arguments, and so on. The major difference in the nature of the proceedings comes from the much higher standard that the prosecution must meet: that of proving guilt beyond a reasonable doubt. Another major difference is that the defendant may not be compelled to testify. In one respect this right is illusory. It is human nature to expect the defendant to take the witness stand and declare innocence. If a criminal defendant declines to testify, the judge will instruct the jurors that they should not draw any conclusions from this because the defendant is exercising a constitutional right. Human nature, however, slants jurors toward a negative inference when the defendant refuses to take the opportunity to urge his or her innocence.

 *Jurors Questioning Witnesses*

The usual practice is for the attorneys to question witnesses during trial, though on occasion the judge asks a question of the witness. Would it be appropriate for the judge to allow the jurors to question a witness?

After answering the question, consider whether the following questions:
- If it is appropriate to allow jurors to question a witness, are there any safeguards that should be in place?
- Would it be appropriate for the jurors to question a criminal defendant?

See *Ex parte* Malone, 12 So. 3d 60 (Ala. 2008).

Sentencing

Sentencing procedures differ widely among the states. Historically, judges had wide discretion in sentencing because the range of imprisonment was broad (e.g., "one to ten years"). Now, though, some states have adopted guidelines that establish customary sentences for crimes. The judge must justify imposing a sentence more severe than the guidelines or risk reversal on appeal. Some crimes in some states now call for mandatory minimum imprisonment, limiting the judge's discretion. Federal prosecutions follow **sentencing guidelines** as well.

There are a number of alternatives to incarceration. In recent times, judges have become reluctant to send convicted criminals to jail. This is partly because our jails are full and partly because numerous studies have shown that incarceration tends to breed career criminals rather than prepare them for a return to society. It is now rare for a person to be sent to prison on first conviction of nonviolent lesser crimes.

Among alternatives to incarceration, the oldest is probation. **Probation** is ordered for a fixed period of time, during which the probationer is subject to stringent conditions, the violation of which may result in incarceration. The probationer is monitored by a probation officer, who ideally not only checks for violations of probation but also serves as a personal counselor to aid the probationer in obtaining employment and making appropriate choices in conduct and career.

A convicted criminal may be sentenced to perform community service. The accused may also avoid conviction by having the judge withhold adjudication under specified conditions. Some jurisdictions allow **pretrial diversion** that postpones and usually obviates the need for trial if the accused meets certain conditions, typically the performance of community service. The criminal justice system recognizes that incarceration can be detrimental not only to the criminal but also to society. In addition, the effect of conviction may be a serious impediment to a person's career, so young first offenders are often treated leniently.

Prison alternatives are frequently the result of plea bargaining and offer the judge considerable discretion in the treatment of offenders. This feature of the criminal justice system distinguishes it from civil procedure. In criminal cases, the court is not concerned simply with the determination of guilt and the award of penalties but also with the regulation of conduct and the protection of society.

Appeal

Criminal appeals are similar in most respects to those in civil procedure. Appellate courts, however, jealously guard against infringements of basic constitutional rights,

sentencing guidelines
State-adopted guidelines that establish specific sentences for specific crimes. Some states have also adopted minimum sentences for certain crimes.

probation
An alternative to incarceration that sets a period of time during which the probationer must adhere to conditions set by the court and be supervised by a probation officer. Violation of the conditions may result in incarceration.

pretrial diversion
Postpones and usually obviates the need for trial if the accused meets certain conditions, typically the performance of community service.

pro bono (publico) (Latin)

"For the (public) good." Traditionally, members of the bar were under a moral obligation to render free services to the public, typically to provide services to people who could not afford to pay. States now make this a requirement of membership in the bar, typically with specific minimum contributions of time.

such as involuntary confessions and illegal searches and seizures, in an effort to ensure fairness to the accused. The right to counsel is the subject of many appeals. Indigent defendants are appointed counsel from the public defender's office or private counsel. Public defenders typically have heavy caseloads and may not always be able to devote as much attention to each case as it deserves. Private attorneys often serve on a **pro bono** basis and are under pressure to devote their time to paying clients. This may or may not result in neglect of criminal cases, but those who are convicted often use this argument to claim ineffective assistance of counsel, in an effort to obtain a new trial.

Although prejudicial error is the basis for reversal of rulings on the law, jury instructions, and so on, as in civil cases, the test of error in factfinding is necessarily different in a criminal trial because the test is guilt beyond a reasonable doubt. On appeal, a verdict of guilty is tested against a standard that asks whether "no trier of fact could have found proof beyond a reasonable doubt." Like "clearly erroneous" and "substantial evidence," this test shows great deference to factfinding at trial and makes it difficult to challenge on this basis.

 *Habeas Corpus Relief for the Prosecution Striking All African-Americans during Jury Selection*

Should a court grant a criminal defendant habeas corpus relief when the prosecution used its peremptory challenge to exclude all African-Americans from the jury?

After answering the question, consider whether the following information would alter your answer:

- This was a death penalty case.
- The alleged crime occurred more than 30 years ago.
- There was evidence of racial prejudice in the community in which the defendant was tried.

See Reed v. Quarterman, 555 F.3d 364 (5th Cir. 2009).

Habeas Corpus

The writ of habeas corpus provides prisoners with a remedy not available in civil cases. Because it challenges the lawfulness of detention, habeas corpus is often used in addition to appeal as a means to obtain review of a case.

Usually an application for a writ of habeas corpus is filed by one in prison after being convicted. In *Bond*, however, the criminal defendant was awaiting a second trial after the judge at the first trial declared a mistrial. The court granted Bond's application for a writ of habeas corpus and held a hearing to determine whether a second trial would constitute double jeopardy. Bond seems to have had difficulty in finding an attorney who could provide him with effective assistance of counsel. During the first trial, the attorney failed to appear in court, and the attorney representing him here on the appeal was overzealous, which conduct may result in the attorney being disciplined.

In a footnote the court stated: "Counsel's argument goes beyond the limits of zealous advocacy. He has misrepresented the facts, distorted the record, and falsely accused the trial court of highly unprofessional and unethical conduct. In our opinion, counsel's statements exceed the very broad scope of permissible argument set forth in rule 301 of the Texas Disciplinary Rules of Professional Conduct."

Marvin P. BOND, Appellant

v.

The STATE of Texas, Appellee

Court of Appeals of Texas, Houston (1st Dist.)

No. 01-03-00599-CR

176 S.W.3d 397

Sept. 16, 2004.

Appellant, Marvin Bond, appeals the trial court's denial of relief on his pretrial application for a writ of habeas corpus seeking relief from double jeopardy. We affirm.

Background

Appellant was indicted for the felony offense of driving while intoxicated. [On July 30, 2002, the fifth day of Bond's jury trial, Bond's attorney failed to show up in court. The judge issued a writ of attachment and a show cause order for Fisch, which two deputies took to Fisch's home. The deputies were unable to locate Fisch.] When court resumed on July 31, Fisch did not appear, but he was represented by Mr. Mitcham, who said he understood that Fisch was still ill. . . .

Appellant told the trial court that he had talked to Fisch for about three minutes the previous evening. They did not talk about the case, but Fisch asked whether the court had said anything in front of the jury and whether the court was upset. Appellant said that Fisch complained that "they" were harassing his family. The court explained to appellant that it could not remove Fisch as counsel because appellant had retained Fisch, but that the court could appoint an attorney to explain appellant's options to him under the circumstances. Appellant said he would like to do that, and the court appointed an attorney, Ms. Miller,

for appellant for the sole purpose of advising appellant as he decided how he wanted to proceed.

After a recess, the court stated several options that were available to appellant, including the option of sending the jury home and asking them to return the next day, when it could be determined whether Fisch would appear. Because appellant had had only one three-minute conversation with Fisch since the time that Fisch had claimed to be ill, and that conversation, according to appellant, did not include anything about the case or any advice about how to proceed, the court said, "It appears to this Court that he has abandoned you as a client." When asked what he wanted to do, appellant said, "Well, I can't proceed with him. I don't want to proceed with him. I don't think I can get a fair trial. The jury probably knows by now. If they don't, they have some kind of idea. So I have nothing else to do." . . .

> THE COURT: All right. . . . I just want to make doubly sure. You are requesting me to declare a mistrial. Ms. Miller has explained to you what a mistrial is. . . . Do you understand what that means?
>
> [APPELLANT]: Yes, Ma'am.
>
> THE COURT: Then I'll allow you to fire Mr. Fisch. Is that what you want?
>
> [APPELLANT]: Yes, ma'am.
>
> . . . .
>
> THE COURT: I don't want to put words in your mouth. I want you to tell me what you want.
>
> [APPELLANT]: I cannot continue with him. I can't use him as a lawyer.
>
> THE COURT: What do you want me to do with this jury?

[APPELLANT]: I don't believe they can be fair toward me or anybody in my situation as it stands right now.

THE COURT: Are you requesting to declare a mistrial?

[APPELLANT]: Yes, ma'am.

The court then found that the mistrial was not due to any act of the prosecution, but was based solely on the conduct of Fisch, who had abandoned appellant as a client. The court observed that the jury was angry and concluded that there was no way to know how that might affect the trial. Because appellant had been laid off from his job and had spent his savings to hire Fisch, the court appointed Ms. Miller to represent appellant in the DWI case.

Approximately one month later, appellant filed a pretrial application for writ of habeas corpus seeking relief from double jeopardy. Appellant contended that the mistrial was caused by the intentional and/or reckless conduct of the court by coercion, duress, and intimidation. Appellant argued that a second prosecution of the cause would constitute double jeopardy under the Fifth and Fourteenth Amendments of the United States Constitution.

The court issued the writ of habeas corpus and held a hearing on the matter. At the hearing, Fisch testified that, on the sixth day of appellant's trial, Fisch woke up feeling nauseated, throwing up, and having cold sweats. He said that he went to the emergency room of a hospital and also went to a doctor. He stated that he was unable to attend the trial that day or the next and that he learned that a mistrial had been declared while he was ill. He also testified that he was still the attorney of record on the case.

The trial court asked appellant whom he had wanted to be his attorney in the trial, and appellant testified that, when Fisch did not show up in the courtroom, he was very confused. Appellant said that he did not recall whether he had had any say over whether a mistrial had been declared. When asked whether he had wanted the impaneled jury to continue on his case, he said he could not answer that and had been "really confused." He then agreed, in response to questions by the court, that he would have been happy to continue with Fisch and had wanted the same jury to continue to the conclusion of the case. Under

cross-examination, appellant clarified that he thought that, if the events leading up to the mistrial had not happened, he could have got a fair trial. The court denied the requested relief. . . .

The Fifth Amendment of the United States Constitution prohibits the State from putting a person in jeopardy twice for the same offense. In a jury trial, jeopardy attaches when the jury is impaneled and sworn. An exception to this rule exists if the defendant consents to a retrial or if a retrial is mandated by manifest necessity. Manifest necessity is not an issue in this case because appellant requested a mistrial. Therefore, we must determine whether, in spite of his request, appellant did not give his effective consent to the mistrial.

Appellant's contention that he was not represented at the time he requested a mistrial is not supported by the record. The record reflects that the trial court appointed counsel to advise appellant regarding the effect of a mistrial and the options available to appellant. The trial court asked appellant on the record whether counsel had explained that a mistrial meant that the jurors would be excused and the case would start over as if there had been no trial. Appellant responded, "Yes, ma'am." Thus, the record establishes that appellant was represented by counsel at the time he requested the mistrial.

Appellant contends that the trial court "provoked and prodded" appellant into requesting a mistrial and that the trial court created "a coercive and threatening environment." Appellate counsel has again misrepresented the record. The trial court scrupulously honored appellant's right to counsel and to be informed of what was occurring. Trial counsel's conduct showed an egregious disregard for the welfare of his client. Furthermore, appellate counsel's characterization of the trial court, including "despotic" and "erratic and irrational," is offensive to this Court. We conclude that the trial court did not abuse its discretion in denying appellant's requested relief.

Case Questions

1. Why should a defendant's right to double jeopardy be based on the conduct of the prosecutor rather than on the conduct of defendant's attorney?
2. What are the two exceptions to double jeopardy?
3. Are you persuaded that Bond freely consented to a mistrial?

SUMMARY

Criminal procedure is similar to civil procedure in the steps it follows from pretrial to trial, in the presentation of evidence, and in the adversarial nature of the proceedings. There are important differences, however, many of which are based on constitutional rights of the accused. The Bill of Rights forms a skeletal code of criminal procedure that has been elaborated through appellate decisions. Among the more important rights guaranteed an accused are the privilege against self-incrimination, the right to an attorney even for those who cannot afford one, the right to a speedy and public trial, the right to be free of cruel and unusual punishment, and the right against imposition of excessive bail.

Criminal procedure involves initial steps to assure that the accusation of crime is well grounded in the requirements of probable cause for arrest and for warrants (arrest or search warrants), of initial appearance before a magistrate after arrest, of preliminary hearing, and of grand jury indictment and arraignment.

The major differences between criminal and civil trials are the right of the accused in a criminal trial not to be compelled to testify, the exclusion of improperly obtained evidence, and the burden of proof on the prosecution to prove guilt beyond a reasonable doubt.

KEY TERMS

affidavit	infamous crime	pretrial diversion
arraignment	information	privilege against self-
arrest	initial (first) appearance	incrimination
double jeopardy	jury	*pro bono (publico)*
ex post facto law	nolo contendere	probation
felony	not guilty by reason of	sentencing guidelines
grand jury	insanity	warrant
indictment	preliminary hearing	writ of habeas corpus

CHAPTER REVIEW QUESTIONS

1. What is an ex post facto law? Can you think of an example?
2. With what is the Fourth Amendment concerned?
3. What is the specific language of the Constitution that describes what is commonly referred to as the "privilege against self-incrimination"?
4. What is meant by the phrase "compulsory process" used in the Constitution?
5. What right was established in the case *Gideon v. Wainwright* (1963)?
6. What two rights did *Miranda v. Arizona* link, and how did it affect the exclusionary rule?
7. What is nolo contendere, and at what stage of the procedure may it be found?
8. What are the two types of formal charges in criminal cases, and which one is associated with a grand jury?
9. Why do prisoners often bring petitions for a writ of habeas corpus?
10. State the test for determining an error in factfinding in a criminal case at the appellate level.

CRITICAL THINKING QUESTIONS

1. Is the requirement of a unanimous verdict of guilt beyond a reasonable doubt an unreasonably difficult standard to meet?

2. Do those accused of crime enjoy too many procedural advantages?

CYBER EXERCISES

1. Opinions of the United States Supreme Court are accessible at a number of websites, in particular http://www.supremecourtus.gov/. The United States Supreme Court decided *Herring v. United States*, 129 S. Ct. 695 (2009) on January 14, 2009. The case contained two dissenting opinions in addition to the majority opinion excerpted in this chapter. Locate the case at the Supreme Court website and answer the following questions:

   a. In her dissent, what is Justice Ginsburg's argument in support of the defendant concerning the Fourth Amendment?

   b. How would Justice Ginsberg have applied the exclusionary rule?

   c. Why did Justice Breyer join in Justice Ginsberg's dissenting opinion and author a separate dissenting opinion?

   d. In his dissenting opinion, how would Justice Breyer have applied the exclusionary rule, and what case was the basis for his argument?

2. Opinions of the United States Supreme Court are accessible at a number of websites, in particular http://www.supremecourtus.gov. The United States Supreme Court decided *Caperton v. A.T. Massey Coal Co., Inc.*, 129 S. Ct. 2252 (2009), on June 8, 2009. The case contained the majority opinion, excerpted in this chapter, and two separate dissenting opinions. Locate the case at the Supreme Court website and answer the following questions:

   a. In his dissenting opinion, what does Justice Roberts think will be the outcome of the application of the majority opinion to future cases?

   b. How does Justice Scalia's dissenting opinion differ from that of Justice Roberts?

   c. Do you agree more with the majority opinion or with either of the dissenting opinions and why?

SCENARIO

Note: The following scenario is loosely based on Florida law and Florida fact; it is fictional but not unrealistic.

The state of Florida is the southernmost of the continental United States and, as such, is one of the favorite entry points for illegal drugs coming from the Caribbean and South America. Miami and its environs play a major part in the drug traffic. Dealers and distributors commonly drive Interstate I-95 through Florida to Miami, bringing money to Miami and drugs back north. I-95 passes through Ambrosia County, which has discovered a lucrative device to fund the county and especially the sheriff's department. The deputy sheriffs of Ambrosia County have "profiles" of likely drug dealers, described by race, type of car, driving habits, and so on, which allows the deputies to stop cars most likely to be driven by drug dealers. The deputies can either stop the cars for actual traffic or safety violations or manufacture them, for example, failure to signal when changing lanes. Once stopped, the deputies are adept at judging the likelihood that the detained persons are drug dealers, letting the apparently innocent go with a warning while wheedling a consent to search out of most of the apparently guilty.

Ambrosia County deputies concentrate on southbound vehicles because, as Willie Sutton put it, in reference to the banks he robbed, "That's where the money is." Florida law provides that law enforcement officers may confiscate money they have a reasonable suspicion is being used or is about to be used for illegal purposes. The Florida Supreme Court has held that anyone carrying more than $5,000 on his person without a clearly defined legitimate purpose (for example, bank courier) raises such a reasonable suspicion. On this basis, the deputies have successfully confiscated about $3 million per year for the past three years. Although the purpose of the law is the forfeiture of money destined for an illegal purpose, the sheriff's department often keeps the money even when criminal charges are dropped. The forfeiture is classified as civil in nature, but many attorneys have argued that the label is a sham because the money is forfeited in connection with alleged criminal activity. Owners of the seized money must sue to get it back if the sheriff's department does not voluntarily return it. Of course, if the owners are convicted of crimes such as drug possession or other drug crimes, they will not succeed in getting their money returned.

John and Nanci Martinez are driving down I-95 to Miami, where they will stay with relatives while they look for work and housing, intending to move from New York City to Miami. Because John does not trust banks, he keeps his money in cash. They sold most of their possessions in New York, and they have $12,000 in cash, $6,000 in John's wallet and $6,000 in Nanci's purse. While driving through Ambrosia County, they are stopped by Deputy Birddog for driving in the left lane when not passing. Deputy Birddog asks if he can search the car and the persons of John and Nanci. They agree, believing they have done nothing wrong and not knowing about cash forfeitures. Birddog discovers the money, confiscates it, and finds the remains of a marijuana cigarette underneath John's (the driver's) seat. Birddog arrests John and Nanci. Later, when the state attorney's office is presented with the case, it declines to prosecute because of a policy to dismiss cases involving less than 0.1 ounces of marijuana. When John and Nanci ask for the return of their money, the sheriff's department refuses, claiming that the money was forfeited in connection with drug activity and was about to be used to purchase drugs to be sold out of state. They cite the fact that John was convicted five years previously in New York of purchasing an ounce of marijuana. (He was given three years probation, which he served without incident.) The sheriff's department offers to return half of the money that was in Nanci's possession if John and Nanci will sign a release promising not to sue for the rest of the money.

You are the attorney for John and Nanci. Although the letter of the law seems to support Ambrosia County, a new circuit court judge has been elected and is handling this case. This judge has been known to criticize the forfeiture law and will entertain wide-ranging arguments on behalf of your clients. Build an argument drawing from whatever principles you can find in criminal procedure and the Bill of Rights to obtain the return of their money.

CHAPTER 9

CRIMINAL LAW

INTRODUCTION

With a basic knowledge of criminal procedure, we can now turn to the substantive law of crimes. Because substantive criminal law varies from state to state, a concise catalog of American crimes is not possible. Instead, this chapter concentrates on underlying issues related to criminal concepts of fault and culpability involved in the criminal act and in criminal intent, especially the latter.

CRIMINAL LAW IN PRACTICE

public defender's office

A government agency that provides criminal defense services to indigents.

Many criminal defense attorneys work as sole practitioners or in small firms where a large staff is not cost efficient. The government employs lawyers and paralegals in prosecutors' offices and in **public defenders' offices**. In addition, many government agencies have positions in which legal training and skills are useful. No understanding of American law is complete, however, without studying the basics of criminal law.

DEFINITION

crime

An act that violates the criminal law. (If this seems redundant, compare *Orans*: "Any violation of the government's penal laws. An illegal act.")

There is no adequate substantive definition of **crime**. The condemnation of heinous acts against persons, such as murder, is a common feature of human societies; but property crimes, crimes against the state, and regulatory crimes—and the penalties for

244

their violation—reflect arbitrary decisions of rulemakers that vary considerably from nation to nation and even from one American state to another, depending on perceived needs to regulate behavior. The criminal law as presently constituted is a compilation of specific prohibited acts. In a sense, a *crime* may be defined simply as an act that violates the criminal law. In the American legal system, a line has been drawn between acts that are regulated by criminal law process and those for which redress is sought through the civil law process, depending on whether punishment or compensation is sought. In many instances, a specific act may give rise to both civil and criminal legal actions.

Thus, **criminal law** may be defined as the list of crimes promulgated by the state. This list is essentially arbitrary in the sense that the state may penalize conduct that was formerly not criminal and may decriminalize conduct that was formerly criminal. Slavery was once legal in the United States; now it is not. Using cocaine was once legal; now it is not. It was once criminal to libel the president; now it is not.

Criminal law may be practically defined by concentrating on procedural distinctions. *Crime* is defined as a "wrong against society." This really indicates that the means to redress that wrong are monopolized by the state. Our system has evolved to put the redress of criminal conduct wholly in the hands of public officials, so we have created agencies of police, prosecutors, and judges to accomplish the task. A criminal case can be distinguished from a civil case by the fact that it is brought by the public prosecutor, enforcing a criminal statute.

As *Christopherson* shows, a crime is a crime because the legislature (or in some cases the court) says it is a crime.

criminal law

The list of crimes promulgated by the state, including the mental states required for particular crimes, for example, specific intent and premeditation.

The PEOPLE of the State of Illinois, Appellee

v.

Jenna M. CHRISTOPHERSON, Appellant

Supreme Court of Illinois

No. 105928

899 N.E.2d 257

Nov. 20, 2008.

At issue is whether minors may be charged with delivery of alcoholic liquor to a minor (235 ILCS 5/6-16 (a)(iii) (West 2006)). We hold that they may.

Background

The State charged defendant, Jenna M. Christopherson, with unlawful delivery of alcoholic liquor to a minor. The information alleged that defendant provided a 30-pack of Icehouse beer and two cases of Bud Light beer to Jamie L. Smith, a person under the age of 21. Smith died in a one-car accident after drinking some of the beer allegedly provided by defendant.

Defendant moved to dismiss the information, arguing that the statutory subpart under which she was charged was not intended to apply to minors. . . .

Analysis

Because this issue concerns the construction of a statute, it is a question of law, and our standard of review is *de novo*. The principles guiding our review are familiar. The primary objective in construing a statute is to give effect to the legislature's intent, presuming the legislature did not intend to create absurd, inconvenient or unjust results. Accordingly, courts should consider the statute in its entirety, keeping in mind the subject it addresses and the legislature's apparent objective in enacting it. The best indication of legislative intent is the statutory language, given its plain and ordinary meaning. When the statutory language is clear and unambiguous, it must be given effect without resort to other tools of interpretation.

[5] We hold that the statutory language is clear and unambiguous and that we may not resort to statutory construction [aids]. Section 6-16(a)(iii) forbids any "person" from giving, selling, or delivering alcoholic liquor to a person under the age of 21. . . . We believe that the legislature's intent in this section was to prohibit any person of any age from providing alcoholic liquor to a minor. When considering the entirety of section 6-16, it is clear that the legislature's intent in this section is keeping alcoholic liquor out of the hands of minors and intoxicated persons. In addition to the general prohibition against providing alcohol to minors in subsection (a)(iii), section 6-16 also contains provisions forbidding those who hold liquor licenses from providing alcohol to minors and forbidding common carriers from delivering alcoholic liquor to persons under 21. This section also prohibits the renting of hotel rooms with knowledge that the room will be used for consumption of alcohol by minors. Section 6-16 contains further prohibitions against the furnishing of fraudulent identification to minors and the use of fraudulent identifications by minors to obtain alcohol. Additionally, section 6-16 prohibits parents or guardians from using their homes to allow violations of the Act. Finally, section 6-16 prohibits any person from having alcoholic liquor on his person on school district property on days when children are present. Section 6-16 represents a comprehensive attempt by the legislature to keep alcohol out of the hands of minors. Construing section 6-16(a)(iii) to apply to all persons effectuates this intent. The tragic facts of this case indicate that the potential harm when alcohol reaches the hands of minors is no different when the alcohol is provided by another minor rather than by an adult. Because we construe the statute in this manner, we find irrelevant the cases defendant cites for the proposition that courts may sometimes depart from clear statutory language if necessary to effectuate the legislature's intent. No such departure is required here.

Moreover, we do not find that the context of section 6-16 as a whole creates an ambiguity in subsection (a)(iii). Defendant argues that because subsection (a)(i), which is directed at licensees (such as taverns, restaurants, and liquor stores), and subsection (a)(ii), which is directed at common carriers who transport alcoholic beverages, apply to those who are legally entitled to possess alcohol, then "person" in subsection (a)(iii) should be construed as referring to persons who are lawfully entitled to possess alcohol. We disagree. If anything, a consideration of the entire statute makes it even more clear that the legislature intended section 6-16(a)(iii) to apply to minors. First, defendant's suggestion that section 6-16 is directed only at those persons who are entitled to possess alcoholic liquor themselves is simply not true. One portion of section 6-16 is specifically directed at minors. Section 6-16(a) makes it a Class A misdemeanor for persons "under the age of 21 years" to use false or fraudulent identification to obtain or to attempt to obtain alcoholic beverages. Thus, it is clear that section 6-16 regulates the conduct of both minors and adults. Further, the legislature uses age limitations throughout section 6-16 whenever it means to limit the meaning of the term "person." Section 6-16 is replete with such phrases as "at least 21 years of age," "under the age of 21 years," "under 21 years of age," "over the age of 21 years," and "less than 21 years of age." The fact that no such limitation appears after the term "no person" in section 6-16(a)(iii) is further evidence that the legislature did not intend to exclude minors from its reach. Thus, far from creating an ambiguity, considering section 6-16(a)(iii) in the context of the entire statute confirms the lack of ambiguity. . . .

Conclusion

Section 6-16(a)(iii) unambiguously prohibits the delivery of alcohol to minors by all persons. Therefore, the appellate court correctly reversed the judgment of the circuit court, which improperly dismissed the charge against defendant on the basis that she is under 21, and remanded the cause for further proceedings.

Case Questions

1. Do you think that Christopherson would have been charged with a crime had the person to whom Christopherson furnished the beer not died?
2. Why would Christopherson think that the statute did not apply to her?

CRIME AND MORALITY

There is a cliché that says, "You can't legislate morality." This is patently false, as that is exactly what law, especially criminal law, does. However, if the statement is really intended to say that immorality cannot be eliminated simply by passing criminal laws, then the statement is correct.

To say that a crime is a wrong against society is to assert that the subject action is immoral; otherwise, it might merely be a wrong against a person and of little consequence to the public at large. There are certain offenses, like murder, that are virtually universally condemned in our society, and others, such as using marijuana, over which there is widespread disagreement. As social mores change, so too will the law. In part, the criminal law is a reflection of societal values, but it is also an effort by lawmakers to control and regulate conduct they consider politically undesirable. In the latter sense, the criminal law may impose morality rather than merely reflect it.

Mala in Se and *Mala Prohibita*

Some crimes, such as murder, are considered inherently wrong—*mala in se*. Others, which are not wrong in themselves but are nonetheless penalized (usually as a regulatory measure, such as failure to file an income tax return), are called *mala prohibita*. The recent proliferation of the latter offenses is derived from the growth of a highly bureaucratized and regulated political organization in the form of the state.

Consider the difference in nature between driving while intoxicated and driving with an expired automobile registration. The former represents a danger to the public and is *mala in se*, whereas the latter is primarily designed for revenue collection and recordkeeping and is *mala prohibita*.

In simpler times, a person could rely, with good reason, on the shared values of society to avoid breaking the moral injunctions of the law. Today, the bewildering complexity of a regulated society requires its members to consult the requirements of the law at every turn. The moral basis of the penal law has become obscure.

The confusion is exacerbated by rules penalizing offenses that are not criminal, a development of recent decades. Parking violations may no longer be misdemeanors (smaller crimes), as they were in the past. That ne'er-do-well who lets his auto registration expire will most certainly pay an extra fee when he renews, but why is he penalized? He was not caught, not charged, not convicted; he incurred no extra administrative expense. No doubt the late fee is called a *civil penalty,* something of a contradiction in terms. It is not labeled criminal, but it looks like a wrong and certainly not a private wrong, which would be a tort and covered by compensation law (see Chapter 10).

In short, a crime is not a crime if the legislature says it is not a crime.

mala in se (Latin)
"Wrong in and of itself"; crimes that are morally wrong.

mala prohibita (Latin)
"Prohibited wrongs"; crimes that are not inherently evil (usually regulatory crimes).

NOTE ON THE *MODEL PENAL CODE*

The American Law Institute, which publishes the *Restatement of Torts* and the *Restatement of Contracts,* is also responsible for the *Model Penal Code,* an additional attempt to encourage uniformity in state law. Some areas of criminal law present a bewildering assortment of treatments among the states, and the *Model Penal Code* is often a leader in these areas rather than merely a restatement of the law. Many state laws are a hodgepodge of custom, past practice, and reformulation of the common law of crimes. The *Model Penal Code* attempts a more consistent and coherent statement of criminal law, but it has no official standing and is not authoritative when state law departs or varies from it. Nevertheless, it is perhaps the most modern statement of American criminal law available and so is occasionally referred to here. It is an important research resource for those examining the law and is often quoted in judicial opinions.

FAULT

punishment (retribution)
The primary goal of criminal law: punishing a person for criminal conduct. The other theories regarding the treatment of criminals are *deterrence* of crime; *incapacitation*, which consists of removing the criminal from society through incarceration; and *rehabilitation*, in which the criminal is helped toward a productive role in society.

Fault is as much a part of public wrongs (crimes) as it is of private wrongs (torts). In criminal law, however, the element of intent to do wrong is far more important than in tort law or contract law, where the focus of the law is on the injured party. Criminal law is primarily concerned with **punishment**, or **retribution**, of the criminal and the **deterrence** of crime; Anglo-American law aims at punishing those who deserve it. Traditionally, two components have been required to hold a person responsible for a crime: criminal act and criminal intent.

CRIMINAL ACT AND CRIMINAL INTENT

To find a person guilty of a crime, there first must be a criminal act or ***actus reus***: conduct that the law prohibits or absence of conduct that the law requires. With most crimes there must also be criminal intent or ***mens rea*** (literally, "criminal mind"). Before discussing these requisites for a crime any further, consider the cases briefly outlined in Exhibit 9-1. Do you think that the individuals charged with crimes should be convicted? It would be interesting for you to consider whether your assessment of the cases changes after you read the rest of this chapter. These cases might also lead to an enlightening class discussion.

deterrence
Theory in criminal law holding that the purpose of the sanctions imposed by the law is to avoid or keep criminal conduct from occurring (*deter*), rather than simply punish those who commit crimes.

Criminal Act

Under early English law, most crimes were treated in the courts as common law crimes. Today, most crimes are statutory, though many of these are simply statutory refinements of the old common law crimes (e.g., murder, rape, burglary, embezzlement, etc.). In an earlier, settled, agricultural society, values relating to wrongs against persons and property were widely shared and understood, so that the courts could turn to customary values and religious principles to define criminal misconduct. Today, in our diverse and complex society, it is not always clear exactly what should be prohibited and what should not. The underlying policy of the criminal law is that a person should not be punished for conduct not expressly prohibited by the law. This requires the articulation of criminal law by the legislatures rather than the courts. All states have criminal statutes, and most do not allow conviction for common law crimes. Judges are not supposed to impose their perceptions of wrongful conduct; instead, they must find that the accused's conduct falls clearly within a criminal statute in order to hold a person guilty of a crime. Ultimately, a court must determine the meaning of the statute as it applies to a particular incident, but, as already noted, criminal statutes are strictly construed.

actus reus
Criminal act; conduct that the law prohibits or absence of conduct that the law requires.

mens rea
Literally, "criminal mind"; criminal intent.

EXHIBIT 9-1 CRIMINAL CHARGES

1. A prostitute, knowing that she has AIDS, continues to ply her trade and is charged with attempted murder.

2. Four seamen adrift in a lifeboat for 20 days decide that one of them must be sacrificed and eaten in order to save the rest. A young cabin boy in weakened condition is killed and eaten. The others are charged with murder.

3. A parent who belongs to a religious sect that believes that physical illness must be cured by prayer and faith refuses medical aid for a child suffering from leukemia. When the child dies, the parent is charged with manslaughter.

4. A young woman is kidnapped by a revolutionary gang, put in a closet for several weeks, and occasionally raped by her kidnappers. For several months she is subjected to political indoctrination and finally agrees to participate in a bank robbery with her abductors to get funds to further their revolutionary cause. When finally found, she is charged with bank robbery.

5. A man meets a young woman in a bar; when asked by the bartender for identification proving her age, she shows a driver's license and is served a beer. She states to the man that she is 20, and he believes it. Later they go to his apartment and have sexual relations. He is later charged with the crime of statutory rape, "sexual relations with a person under the age of 18."

6. A woman believes her husband to be dead and remarries. When her first husband reappears, she is charged with bigamy.

7. A man picks up the wrong suitcase at an airport, believing it to be his, but later discovers his mistake and returns the suitcase. He is charged with theft.

8. A physician assists a terminally ill person to commit suicide by preparing and providing the means to end her life in a painless and comfortable way. The physician is charged with murder.

9. A game warden makes an image of a deer and puts it in the woods. When hunters shoot at the deer, the game warden arrests them for hunting deer out of season.

10. A man shoots a person intending to kill. It later turns out that the victim was already dead, although the shooting would have killed him if he had still been alive. The shooter is charged with homicide.

Actus reus requires that the criminal act be **voluntary**. At first blush, this would seem to be a feature of the mental state of the accused, part of the criminal intent (*mens rea*). *Voluntariness*, however, refers to whether the act was a product of free will and does not address issues of motivation specific to *mens rea*. Examples of involuntary acts are those occurring during sleep, unconsciousness, or hypnosis and those caused by reflexes or convulsions.

Thoughts alone are not criminal; an act must occur. In general, speech is protected by the First Amendment, but speech is conduct and sometimes constitutes a crime, as with inciting to riot or promoting a conspiracy.

voluntary

When used in reference to criminal law, means an act of free will, though this is different from its use in contract law, where coercion may negate voluntariness. In criminal law, acts are not voluntary when they occur during sleep, unconsciousness, or hypnosis or by reflex or convulsions.

The failure to act, an omission, may also constitute *actus reus* in cases in which the law imposes a duty to act; for instance, when a parent fails to provide nourishment to a child or a person with knowledge of a felony fails to report such knowledge (misprision of a felony). Failure to meet a *moral* obligation to act is not a crime if there is no *legal* duty to act. Historically, American law has not recognized a duty to rescue; a person may stand by and watch another drown, even if saving the drowning person offers no risk to the potential rescuer. A duty arises only if the rescuer was in some way responsible for the peril or enjoys a status requiring rescue, such as a lifeguard.

Because criminal act is typically shown by physical evidence, it presents far fewer problems than criminal intent, in which a mental state must usually be inferred from the circumstances of the events of the crime.

Criminal Intent

An act may be voluntarily accomplished without entailing *mens rea.* The man who mistakenly took the wrong suitcase at the airport acted voluntarily but without criminal intent. The nature of the intent required for guilt varies significantly from one crime to another, and some strict liability crimes require no proof of criminal intent. (See Exhibit 9-2 and the following discussion.)

General Intent

general intent

For criminal law, requires merely that the actor intended a harmful act, not necessarily the specific result of the action. Also see *specific intent.*

The broadest form of intent is called **general intent**, to be distinguished from specific intent, discussed in the next subsection. General intent is the traditional form of *mens rea* derived from the common law. It requires that the actor have intended a harmful act but not that the specific result be intended. This may extend to reckless and negligent acts in which the actor acted with a "conscious disregard of a substantial and unjustifiable risk of harm" (recklessness) or, though lacking conscious disregard, nevertheless acted when a "reasonable person would have recognized a substantial and unjustifiable

EXHIBIT 9-2   CRIMINAL INTENT OR A SUBSTITUTE

MENS REA OR A SUBSTITUTE	DESCRIPTION
General intent	The actor intended a harmful act but not the specific result
Specific intent	The actor intended the precise result of a harmful act
Strict liability	Eliminates the prosecution's burden of proving *mens rea* or shifts to the defendant the burden of proving innocent motive

risk" (negligence). A person throwing a firecracker into a crowd of people would be guilty of any resulting harm covered by a crime requiring only general intent.

Criminal intent is more convincingly shown if malice can be proven. General intent is a somewhat cloudy area because of the variety of harmful acts and the mysteries of the human mind and human motivation. With a few exceptions requiring powerful deterrents, the law and judicial decisions reflect a desire not to punish involuntary, innocent, and accidental acts. The elements that make up a specific crime indicate the intention required.

Specific Intent

As a rule of thumb, statutes that use the words "knowingly," "willfully," or "maliciously" require **specific intent**. These statutes are most easily satisfied when the defendant intended the precise results of the wrongful act (e.g., shooting someone in the head at close range). Defendants will naturally assert a lack of intent or knowledge, but courts and juries are disinclined to accept such assertions. It may be enough that a knowledge of a high risk was present, as measured by what a reasonable person would know. The problem is that this is a subjective measure, that is, what the defendant knew or intended. Because only the defendant knows for certain what his or her knowledge and intent were, the defendant theoretically is the most reliable witness as to that intent. However, in practice, the defendant's statements are highly unreliable because self-interest often distorts the truth. What was intended may be inferred from the defendant's conduct, and the defendant's self-serving statements may be treated with skepticism. The *Jewell* case demonstrates the court's reluctance to accept a defendant's self-serving assertions.

Mens rea is a confusing area of criminal law because it attempts to define subjective knowledge, volition, and intent. To paraphrase one justice's comments about the definition of contracts, perhaps the definition of *mens rea* consists of the totality of the cases that define it. As a practical matter, this means that applying criminal intent to a given case requires fitting that case into a framework established by similar cases of the past. It then becomes clear that the method of the common law prevails even in an area that ostensibly has been preempted by statute.

Long ago, *mens rea* may have appeared to be a relatively simple concept, but as we come to know more about the complexity of the human psyche, the legal concept has become more and more difficult to state with certainty. In questionable cases, a great deal of research into precedents may be appropriate.

All the research in the world, however, means little to the jury. Through its deliberations, the jury mysteriously arrives at conclusions about the defendant's intent. The jury is likely to pay more attention to common sense and experience than the technicalities of the jury instructions. In the *Jewell* case, some jurors must have asked, "Why did he have a secret compartment in his trunk? Surely he must have known, or at least guessed, there was marijuana in the secret compartment." Preparation of a jury case must pay at least as much attention to the mentality of the jury as to the law.

specific intent
In criminal law, requires that the actor have intended the precise result of a harmful act. Also see *general intent*.

UNITED STATES of America,
Plaintiff-Appellee

v.

Charles Demore JEWELL, Defendant-Appellant

U.S. Court of Appeals, 9th Circuit

532 F.2d 697 (9th Cir. 1976)

[This is an appeal from a conviction for violating the Comprehensive Drug Abuse Prevention and Control Act of 1970. Jewell was found to have knowingly transported marijuana in the trunk of his car from Mexico to the United States. The marijuana was concealed in a secret compartment behind the back seat of his car. Jewell insisted that he did not know the marijuana was in the secret compartment. Whether he knew or did not know was a fact question for the jury. If he knew, he was guilty of the crime; but the trial judge was concerned that even a lack of knowledge could have been the result of "deliberate ignorance" and gave the following instruction to the jury:

> The Government can complete their burden of proof by proving, beyond a reasonable doubt, that if the defendant was not actually aware that there was marijuana in the vehicle he was driving when he entered the United States his ignorance in that regard was solely and entirely a result of his having made a conscious purpose to disregard the nature of that which was in the vehicle, with a conscious purpose to avoid learning the truth.

Jewell appealed on the grounds that this instruction was not an accurate statement of the law with regard to criminal intent and that the jury should have been instructed that to find guilt, they must find that he knew he was in possession of marijuana. The court of appeals upheld the trial court's jury instruction with the following reasoning:]

The substantive justification for the rule is that deliberate ignorance and positive knowledge are equally culpable. The textual justification is that in common understanding one "knows" facts of which he is less than absolutely certain. To act "knowingly," therefore, is not necessarily to act only with positive knowledge, but also to act with an awareness of the high probability of the existence of the fact in question. When such awareness is present, "positive" knowledge is not required.

* * *

[D]efining "knowingly" makes actual knowledge unnecessary. "[T]hose who traffic in heroin will inevitably become aware that the product they deal with is smuggled, *unless they practice a studied ignorance to which they are not entitled.*"

. . . Holding that this term [*knowingly*] introduces a requirement of positive knowledge would make deliberate ignorance a defense. It cannot be doubted that those who traffic in drugs would make the most of it. This is evident from the number of appellate decisions reflecting conscious avoidance of positive knowledge of the presence of contraband—in the car driven by the defendant or in which he is a passenger, in the suitcase or package he carries, in the parcel concealed in his clothing.

* * *

The conviction is affirmed.

Kennedy, J., dissenting: [T]he "conscious purpose" jury instruction is defective in three respects. First, it fails to mention the requirement that Jewell have been aware of a high probability that a controlled substance was in the car. It is not culpable to form "a conscious purpose to avoid learning the truth" unless one is aware of facts indicating a high probability of that truth. . . .

The second defect in the instruction as given is that it did not alert the jury that Jewell could not be convicted if he "actually believed" there was no controlled substance in the car. . . .

Third, the jury instruction clearly states that Jewell could have been convicted even if found ignorant or "not actually aware" that the car contained a controlled substance. This is unacceptable because true ignorance, no matter how unreasonable, cannot provide a basis for criminal liability when the statute requires knowledge.

Case Questions

1. Why did the majority not adopt the dissent's approach?

2. In a portion of the dissenting opinion omitted in this case, the dissenting judge declared his approval of *Model Penal Code* § 2.02(7), which reads:

Requirement of Knowledge Satisfied by Knowledge of High Probability. When knowledge of the existence of a particular fact is an element of an offense, such knowledge is established if a person is aware of a high probability of its existence, unless he actually believes that it does not exist.

Does this imply the dissent's conclusion that "true ignorance, no matter how unreasonable, cannot provide a basis for criminal liability when the statute requires knowledge"?

3. Perhaps when Jewell spoke with his attorney, the attorney said, "The statute requires that you *knowingly* transported controlled substances. You didn't know that what was in the secret compartment was *actually* marijuana, *did* you?" And suppose Jewell responded, "I didn't actually *see* marijuana put in the car; I didn't actually *know* there was marijuana in there." Can attorney and client then in good conscience go to court and base their defense on lack of knowledge? Is it unethical for the attorney to lead the client in this way? Argue both sides.

4. Is not subjective knowledge always arguable? If Jewell actually knew there was marijuana placed in the secret compartment but he left his car for an hour, would he *know* the marijuana was still there if he did not check to see? Does this deliberate ignorance principle furnish a reasonable alternative to the philosophical problem of knowledge?

5. Does the rule in *Jewell* accord with the principle of strict construction of criminal statutes? Explain.

6. Do you think the jury would have found differently if it had been instructed as the dissent suggested?

CRIMINAL INTENT AND SPECIFIC CRIMES

The nature and degree of criminal intent required varies from crime to crime. In some instances, *intent* refers simply to the knowledge the accused must have. For example, crimes involving theft commonly require that the defendant intended to deprive someone permanently of property, knowing that the property belonged to another. Such a requirement would save the man in our airport suitcase mistake example because there was neither an intent to permanently deprive nor a knowledge of true ownership at the time of the taking.

Crimes against property, such as burglary, embezzlement, and larceny, are usually economically motivated, so intent can readily be inferred. Unless these involve violence or large amounts of money, they receive only modest attention in the press, which tends to focus on bizarre and violent crime. As a result, the popular conception of crime is distorted.

Other crimes require special ingredients for criminal intent that make them quite distinct. Murder, rape, conspiracy, and attempt are examples.

Murder

Murder is the unlawful killing by one human being of another with malice aforethought. It is distinguished from manslaughter (also called murder in the second degree) by the requirement of "malice aforethought," often referred to as *premeditation* or *malice prepense*, depending on one's preference for Old English, new Latin, or French. The requirement of premeditation removes from this most heinous of crimes homicides that are accidental but blameworthy (i.e., caused by culpable negligence) and those occurring in a moment of passion or anger. At the very least, murder requires some reflection about what one is doing or sufficient time between the beginning of

murder

The wrongful killing of another human being with malice aforethought (premeditation).

the act and its completion to provide an opportunity to desist from following through. Obviously, a planned killing satisfies premeditation. In other cases, proof of premeditation typically takes the form of showing that the accused thought about what he or she was doing and then did it.

Murder cases present a very distorted picture of the criminal law. One reason is the requirement of evil intent; another is the availability of the death penalty upon conviction of murder in most states. Because of our fear of sending an innocent person to be executed—a mistake that can never be corrected—the propriety of conduct by the police and prosecution and the conduct of the trial are scrutinized to a degree unusual in other cases. Because of media attention to these cases, the public forms a strange picture of the criminal law and criminal procedure.

Rape

rape

At common law, forcible sexual intercourse by a man on a woman against her will. Modern *statutory rape* makes consent irrelevant because of the status or mental state of the victim. Modern law recognizes a variety of sexual assaults.

Forcible **rape** is the most serious of sex crimes. At present, there is little uniformity either in terminology or definition among the states with regard to sex crimes. On the one hand, we have seen a strong movement toward decriminalizing consensual sexual relations, but different states have shown different approaches depending on whether the partners are married, heterosexual, or homosexual. On the other hand, there has been a movement to refine the definitions of sex crimes to protect specific categories of victims—the young, the elderly, the mentally and physically handicapped. Because this is presently a dynamic area of legislation, we encounter a lack of uniformity among the states.

With regard to the mental state required for forcible rape, the problem is compounded by its nonconsensual element. Not only the defendant's mental state is at issue but also the victim's. It is a defense to forcible, as opposed to statutory, rape that the alleged victim consented to the sexual act. Because sexual relations usually occur in private without witnesses, ascertaining the mental states of perpetrator and victim presents difficult problems of proof.

An essential element of rape is the use of force. What constitutes force is problematic, and the relationship between force and consent raises additional questions. If a man holds a knife to a woman's throat and asks her if she wants to have sexual relations, is her affirmative answer consent? Consent under duress is not consent at all.

Rape is a serious crime that occurs with significant frequency in our society and is likely to leave victims with permanent emotional damage, yet it is difficult to prove and usually goes unreported. The commands of the criminal law have failed to control primal urges toward violence and sex.

Recently, focus has changed toward victim-oriented services and enlightened treatment of victims in court. Because of the consent defense, victims have in the past been questioned regarding their prior sexual contacts and sexual conduct in general. Much of this has been curtailed by law because of its questionable relevance; the factual issue is always whether the victim actually consented in this particular instance. A great many jurisdictions have also turned to victim advocacy and fought antifemale stereotypes on the part of traditionally male-dominated law enforcement. Officers have been sensitized to the plight of the victim and her responses to the trauma of rape. Rape counselors are often called in to assist in the aftermath of rape.

Conspiracy

Conspiracy presents problems with both *mens rea* and *actus reus* in that it addresses the planning of crime rather than its actual commission. The elements of conspiracy are an agreement to commit a crime and an overt act in furtherance of the crime. An affirmative defense is renunciation of criminal purpose, which typically is an overt act that prevents the crime from occurring.

Under these rules, one may effectively be charged with conspiracy for participating in the planning of a bank robbery even if one did not plan to participate in the actual bank robbery, conduct that society may appropriately condemn as criminal. However, the crime of conspiracy may cast a wide net to include many persons marginally associated with others engaged in criminal conduct.

An interesting wrinkle on conspiracy has been the ever-expanding use of the Racketeer Influenced and Corrupt Organizations Act (RICO), which was originally designed to be used against organized crime and corrupt labor unions. In recent years, RICO has been applied generously in white-collar crime where "racketeering" has been given a broad interpretation. In particular, a variety of financial and stock manipulations have been attacked under RICO.

The *Recio* case illustrates a feature of conspiracy law that is not inherently logical; namely, that a conspiracy can exist even when the police have made commission of the crime impossible. Persons may conspire to commit a crime that has no chance of success. *Recio* also illustrates an important feature of U.S. Supreme Court decision making. The Court primarily hears, or one might say grants review (by writ of certiorari) for, cases that have resulted in the circuit courts of appeals formulating different rules. In *Recio*, the Ninth Circuit did not follow the conspiracy law of the other circuits. The Supreme Court needed to resolve this inconsistency in the law and among the circuit courts.

conspiracy
A crime involving two or more persons who agree to commit a crime or agree to plan a crime.

United States

v.

Francisco Jimenez RECIO and Adrian Lopez-Meza

537 U.S. 270 (2003)

ON WRIT OF CERTIORARI TO THE UNITED STATES COURT OF APPEALS FOR THE NINTH CIRCUIT

We here consider the validity of a Ninth Circuit rule that a conspiracy ends automatically when the object of the conspiracy becomes impossible to achieve—when, for example, the Government frustrates a drug conspiracy's objective by seizing the drugs that its members have agreed to distribute. In our view, conspiracy law does not contain any such "automatic termination" rule. . . .

In *United States v. Cruz,* . . . the Ninth Circuit . . . wrote that a conspiracy terminates when " 'there is affirmative evidence of abandonment, withdrawal, disavowal *or defeat of the object of the conspiracy.*' " (Emphasis added.) It considered the conviction of an individual who, the Government had charged, joined a conspiracy (to distribute drugs) after the Government had seized the drugs in question. . . . The Circuit held that the conspiracy had terminated with that "defeat," *i.e.,* when the Government seized the drugs. Hence the individual, who had joined the conspiracy after that point, could not be convicted as a conspiracy member.

In this case the lower courts applied the *Cruz* rule to similar facts: On November 18, 1997, police stopped a truck in Nevada. They found, and seized, a large stash of illegal drugs. With the help of the truck's two drivers, they set up a sting. The Government took the truck to the drivers' destination, a mall in Idaho. The drivers paged a contact and described the truck's location. The contact said that he would call someone to get the truck. And three hours later, the two defendants, Francisco Jimenez Recio and Adrian Lopez-Meza, appeared in a car. Jimenez Recio drove away in the truck; Lopez-Meza drove the car away in a similar direction. Police stopped both vehicles and arrested both men.

The Court has repeatedly said that the essence of a conspiracy is "an agreement to commit an unlawful act." *Iannelli v. United States.* . . . That agreement is "a distinct evil," which "may exist and be punished whether or not the substantive crime ensues." *Salinas v. United States.* . . . The conspiracy poses a "threat to the public" over and above the threat of the commission of the relevant substantive crime—both because the "[c]ombination in crime makes more likely the commission of [other] crimes" and because it "decreases the probability that the individuals involved will depart from their path of criminality." *Callanan v. United States.* . . . Where police have frustrated a conspiracy's specific objective but conspirators (unaware of that fact) have neither abandoned the conspiracy nor withdrawn, these special conspiracy-related dangers remain. . . . So too remains the essence of the conspiracy— the agreement to commit the crime. That being so, the Government's defeat of the conspiracy's objective will not necessarily and automatically terminate the conspiracy. . . .

[T]he view we endorse today is the view of almost all courts and commentators but for the Ninth Circuit. . . . The *Cruz* majority argued that the more traditional termination rule threatened "endless" potential liability. To illustrate the point, the majority posited a sting in which police instructed an arrested conspirator to go through the "telephone directory . . . [and] call all of his acquaintances" to come and help him, with the Government obtaining convictions of those who did so. . . . The problem with this example, however, is that, even though it is not necessarily an example of entrapment itself, it draws its persuasive force from the fact that it bears certain resemblances to entrapment. The law independently forbids convictions that rest upon entrapment. . . . And the example fails to explain why a different branch of the law, conspiracy law, should be modified to forbid entrapment-like behavior that falls outside the bounds of current entrapment law. . . . In tracing the origins of the statement of conspiracy law upon which the *Cruz* panel relied, we have found a 1982 Ninth Circuit case, *United States v. Bloch* . . . in which the court, referring to an earlier case, *United States v. Krasn* . . . , changed the language of the traditional conspiracy termination rule. *Krasn* said that a conspiracy is " 'presumed to continue unless there is affirmative evidence that *the defendant* abandoned, withdrew from, or disavowed the conspiracy *or defeated its purpose.*' " . . . (emphasis added). The *Bloch* panel changed the grammatical structure. It said that "a conspiracy is presumed to continue until *there is* . . . defeat of the purposes of the conspiracy" . . . (emphasis added). Later Ninth Circuit cases apparently read the change to mean that a conspiracy terminates, not only when the *defendant* defeats its objective, but also when *someone else* defeats that objective, perhaps the police. In *Castro,* the panel followed *Bloch.* . . . In *Cruz,* the panel quoted *Castro.* . . . This history may help to explain the origin of the *Cruz* rule. But, since the Circuit's earlier cases nowhere give any reason for the critical change of language, they cannot help to justify it.

We conclude that the Ninth Circuit's conspiracy-termination law holding set forth in *Cruz* is erroneous in the manner discussed. We reverse the present judgment insofar as it relies upon that holding.

Case Questions

1. Does it seem fair that a person could be convicted of a crime that is impossible to complete?
2. The sort of conspiracy dealt with here is really a "sting" situation, which comes very close to entrapment. Is the line between entrapment and a legitimate sting operation involving conspiracy clear?

Attempt

The **attempt to commit a crime** is also a crime. In its simplest form, an *attempt* is a crime that failed. The deterrent aspect of the criminal law should apply with equal force to attempts as to successful crimes (for instance, it would seem useful to deter bank robbers whether or not they are successful). The punitive aspect of the criminal law, however, has traditionally been more lenient with attempted crimes, which are usually of lesser grade or carry a lesser sentence. *Model Penal Code* § 5.05(1) treats attempts as equal to the crime attempted, and a few states have adopted this policy.

Significant traps lie in wait for charges of attempt to commit a crime, depending in large part on the reason the crime was not consummated. One of the most perplexing comes from *impossibility* theories. Impossibility is an issue in *Guffey* and *Dlugash*. Although the issue of impossibility has resulted in varied responses in various jurisdictions, most courts have struggled with distinguishing *legal* and *factual* impossibility:

1. If the intended act is not criminal, there can be no criminal liability for an attempt to commit the act. This is sometimes described as a "legal impossibility."
2. If the intended substantive crime is impossible of accomplishment because of some physical impossibility unknown to the accused, the elements of a criminal attempt are present. This is sometimes described as "impossibility in fact."

United States v. Thomas, 13 C.M.A. 278 ([U.S. Court of Military Appeals] 1962).

Simple in the abstract, this is most difficult to apply, as will be seen in the following cases.

attempt to commit a crime
An act that goes beyond mere preparation to commit a crime but that is not completed.

State

v.

GUFFEY et al.

Springfield Court of Appeals, Missouri

262 S.W.2d 152 (1953)

[Missouri Conservation agents set up a stuffed deer hide in a field about fifty yards from the roadside, then lay in wait for "some citizen who might come that way, see the tempting bait and with visions of odoriferous venison cooking in pot or pan, decide not to wait until" the beginning of deer season. The defendants drove by with a spotlight and noticed the deer; the car stopped and there was a shotgun blast. The defendants were thereupon arrested, and despite their testimony that they were out frog-hunting and shot at the "deer" thinking it was a wolf, they were convicted

of the misdemeanor of pursuit and taking of wildlife against rules and regulations.]

Appellants were convicted of violating Section 252.040, V.A.M.S. and regulations of the Missouri Conservation Commission and have appealed. The section of the statute is as follows:

'No wild life shall be pursued, taken, killed, possessed or disposed of except in the manner, to the extent and at the time or times permitted by such rules and regulations; and any pursuit, taking, killing, possession or disposition thereof, except as permitted by such rules and regulations, are hereby prohibited. Any person violating this section shall be guilty of a misdemeanor.'

* * *

Bearing these definitions [of *pursue* and *pursuit*] in mind, it seems to us that the State has wholly failed to make its case when it stands upon the proposition that defendants 'pursued' a deer. In the first place there was no deer. The hide of a doe long since deceased, filled with boards, excelsior and rods with eyes made of a reflective scotch tape, was not a deer within the meaning of the statute and Section 33 of the 'Wildlife Code of Missouri'. The dummy, such as it was, was a stationary affair, it could not run, could not jump, it could not flee from the rifle slug of a hunter. It was not wild and it had no life.

* * *

Undoubtedly the words 'pursued' as used in the statute and 'pursue' as used in Section 33 of the Code means to follow with the intention of overtaking, or to chase.

* * *

The State's evidence shows that one of the defendants did shoot the dummy but did they pursue, chase or follow a *deer* by shooting this stuffed defunct doe hide? It was not a deer. If the dummy had been actually taken (it could not be pursued), defendants would not have committed any offense. It is no offense to attempt to do that which is not illegal. See Burdick's Law of Crime, Vol. 1, Sec. 143, et seq. (1946). Neither is it a crime to attempt to do that which it is legally impossible to do. For instance, it is no crime to attempt to murder a corpse because it cannot be murdered. [Citation omitted.] 'Neither can one be convicted of an attempt to commit a crime unless he could have been convicted if his attempt had been successful; thus, where the act, if accomplished, would not constitute the crime intended, as a matter of law,

then there is no indictable attempt.' 22 C.J.S., Criminal Law, § 74, page 138.

If all which an accused person intends to do would, if done, constitute no crime, it cannot be a crime to attempt to do with the same purpose a part of the thing intended. If the State's evidence showed an attempt to take the dummy, it fell far short of proving an attempt to take a deer. We hold that the State wholly failed to make a case. Appellants contend that there was an unlawful search and seizure, also that they were entrapped by the agents of the Missouri Conservation Commission. From the view we take of this case, it is unnecessary to pass upon these questions.

The judgment and sentence of the trial court should be reversed and the appellants discharged. It is so ordered.

Case Questions

1. *Guffey* was overruled by state statute. See Mo. Ann. Stat. § 564.011.2 (Vernon 1979) ("no defense to a prosecution . . . that the offense attempted was, under the actual attendant circumstances, factually or legally impossible of commission, if such offense could have been committed had the attendant circumstances been as the actor believed them to be"). Why?
2. Did the state's case fail because of an absence of *actus reus* or *mens rea*? Does the answer to this question help to explain how someone may be convicted of an attempt in a situation where a conviction of the crime would not be available?

The PEOPLE of the State of New York

v.

Melvin DLUGASH

Court of Appeals of New York

41 N.Y.2d 725, 363 N.E.2d 1155, 395 N.Y.S.2d 419 (1977)

[Dlugash, Bush, and Geller had been drinking until three o'clock in the morning. Several times Geller,

in whose apartment the incident occurred, had demanded that Bush pay $100 toward the rent since Bush had moved in with Geller. Bush threatened to shoot Geller if he would not shut up, and on the final demand Bush fired three shots at Geller, one of which went through Geller's lung and into his heart. A few minutes later, Dlugash fired several shots into Geller's head. When the investigating detective asked Dlugash why he did this, he said at first he did not really know, but when asked the third time, Dlugash said, "well, gee, I guess it must have been because I was afraid of Joe Bush." At trial, medical experts testified that the chest wounds would have killed Geller without prompt medical attention, but it was not clear whether Geller was still alive when Dlugash fired into his head. Dlugash did not testify at trial, but after the jury found him guilty of murder, he moved to set the verdict aside on the grounds that he was certain Geller was dead before Dlugash shot him, and his shots were made because Bush held a gun on him and said he would kill Dlugash if Dlugash did not shoot the body. On appeal, it was held that the state failed to prove beyond a reasonable doubt that Geller had been alive at the time Dlugash shot him; and also held him not guilty of attempted murder. The highest court came to a somewhat different conclusion:]

The criminal law is of ancient origin, but criminal liability for attempt to commit a crime is comparatively recent. At the root of the concept of attempt liability are the very aims and purposes of penal law. The ultimate issue is whether an individual's intentions and actions, though failing to achieve a manifest and malevolent criminal purpose, constitute a danger to organized society of sufficient magnitude to warrant the imposition of criminal sanctions. . . . [One] concern centers on whether an individual should be liable for an attempt to commit a crime when, unknown to him, it was impossible to successfully complete the crime attempted. . . . The 1967 revision of the Penal Law approached the impossibility defense to the inchoate crime of attempt in a novel fashion. The statute provides that, if a person engages in conduct which would otherwise constitute an attempt to commit a crime, "it is no defense to a prosecution for such attempt that the crime charged to have been attempted was, under the attendant circumstances, factually or legally impossible of commission, if such crime could have been committed had the attendant circumstances been as such person believed them to be." (Penal Law, s 110.10.) This appeal presents to us, for the first time, a case involving the application of the modern statute. We hold that, under the proof presented by the People at trial, defendant Melvin Dlugash may be held for attempted murder, though the target of the attempt may have already been slain, by the hand of another, when Dlugash made his felonious attempt.

[There follows a long discussion of the facts followed by the conclusion that the appellate division was correct in overturning the conviction for murder. The court then discusses the history of impossibility theory, concluding that legal impossibility was a defense, citing *Guffey* ("it is not crime to attempt to do that which is legal"), but holding that factual impossibility was not a defense ("Thus, a man could be held for attempted grand larceny when he picked an empty pocket").]

In the belief that neither of the two branches of the traditional impossibility arguments detracts from the offender's moral culpability . . . the Legislature substantially carried the code's treatment of impossibility into the 1967 revision of the Penal Law. . . . Thus, a person is guilty of an attempt when, with intent to commit a crime, he engages in conduct which tends to effect the commission of such crime. . . . It is no defense that, under the attendant circumstances, the crime was factually or legally impossible of commission, "if such crime could have been committed had the attendant circumstances been as such person believed them to be." . . . Thus, if defendant believed the victim to be alive at the time of the shooting, it is no defense to the charge of attempted murder that the victim may have been dead.

The jury convicted the defendant of murder. Necessarily, they found that defendant intended to kill a live human being. Subsumed within this finding is the conclusion that defendant acted in the belief that Geller was alive. Thus, there is no need for additional fact findings by a jury. Although it was not established beyond a reasonable doubt that Geller was, in fact, alive, such is no defense to attempted murder since a murder would have been committed "had the attendant circumstances been as (defendant) believed them to be." (Penal Law, s 110.10.) The jury necessarily found that defendant believed Geller to be alive when defendant shot at him.

The Appellate Division erred in not modifying the judgment to reflect a conviction for the lesser included offense of attempted murder. An attempt to commit a murder is a lesser included offense of murder (see CPL 1.20, subd. 37) and the Appellate Division has the authority, where the trial evidence is not legally sufficient to establish the offense of which the defendant was convicted, to modify the judgment to one of conviction for a lesser included offense. . . .

Case Questions

1. From *Dlugash*: "A further example is Francis Wharton's classic hypothetical involving Lady Eldon and her French lace. Lady Eldon, traveling in Europe, purchased a quantity of French lace at a high price, intending to smuggle it into England without payment of the duty. When discovered in a customs search, the lace turned out to be of English origin, of little value and not subject to duty. The traditional view is that Lady Eldon is not liable for an attempt to smuggle." Would Lady Eldon be convicted under New York law?

2. Consider the following fact situations:
   a. A person shoots a corpse in the head, knowing that the corpse is dead.
   b. A person shoots a corpse in the head, believing the corpse to be alive.
   c. A person intending to kill shoots at a figure in a bed, but there is no one there.
   d. A person shoots at someone, intending to kill, but misses.

   Which of these actions is the law of attempts designed to punish? Which would be attempts under the reasoning of *Dlugash*?

---

strict criminal liability

Attaches to a few crimes that may be proven without proving intent; see *strict liability*.

felony-murder rule

Allows a conviction of murder when someone is killed during the commission of a felony; premeditation need not be proven.

STRICT LIABILITY

Underlying the *mens rea* requirement is the traditional legal principle in criminal law of a *presumption of innocence*. *Mens rea* imposes a burden on the prosecution to show that the defendant acted out of evil intent. In recent years, however, legislatures have sometimes imposed strict criminal liability, thereby either eliminating the burden of proving *mens rea* or shifting to the defendant the burden of proving innocent motive.

Some precedent for **strict criminal liability** can be found in the common law **felony-murder rule**, under which a person can be found guilty of murder without proof of premeditation if a person is killed during the perpetration of a felony. Some justification for the rule can be found in an attempt to deter the use of unreasonable force in the commission of a felony, but on rare occasions the rule has been applied with peculiar results, as when one of the felons is killed by police and the other co-felons are held accountable for felony-murder. The felony-murder rule has been subject to much criticism, as noted in *Heemstra*, and is severely qualified in some jurisdictions.

STATE of Iowa, Appellee

v.

Rodney Neil HEEMSTRA, Appellant

Supreme Court of Iowa

No. 04-0058

721 N.W.2d 549

Aug. 25, 2006.

Rodney Heemstra was convicted by a jury of first-degree murder under Iowa Code sections 707.1 and 707.2. . . .

Rodney Heemstra and Tom Lyon were farmers in Warren County, Iowa. Since 1998 Lyon had rented a portion of land belonging to a Rodgers family. In July 2002 Heemstra purchased the land with a closing date set for March 10, 2003. As the renter in possession, Lyon was legally entitled to remain on the Rodgers farm until March 1, 2003. After Heemstra purchased the land, relations between Lyon and Heemstra became strained over who would have possession of it pending transfer of title. Lyon had hoped to purchase the farm, and he was upset that Heemstra bought it. . . .

On January 13, 2003, Heemstra and Lyon, both driving pickups, were traveling in the same direction on a county road near Lyon's home. According to Heemstra, he was driving behind Lyon, who stopped his truck and angled it to block the road. Both men left their trucks. Heemstra testified that Lyon was hostile, contorted with rage, saying he was going to make "goddamn sure that I did not end up with that farm." Heemstra, feeling threatened, retrieved a rifle from his truck "to neutralize [the] situation," according to him. Heemstra testified that, as he was getting the gun, Lyon shouted obscenities at him, saying "[I didn't] have the balls to pull the trigger, and he lunged at me, and I shot him." Lyon's body was later recovered in a cistern located on land farmed by Heemstra about a quarter of a mile from Lyon's abandoned truck. Lyon had sustained a single gunshot to the head, as well as other injuries resulting from being dragged behind Heemstra's truck to the cistern. The medical examiner could not determine whether these injuries occurred before or after Lyon died.

The following day, officers went to Heemstra's home. . . . When questioned, Heemstra initially denied knowledge of any harm to Lyon and said he had not seen him for several days. Heemstra consented to the officers searching his truck, where they found what they thought were blood and hair. Heemstra then admitted he had been present at Lyon's death and finally confessed to shooting him. When he was asked by the officers whether Lyon had anything in his hands, Heemstra said, "no, I shot a defenseless man." . . .

At trial, Heemstra claimed self-defense. He introduced evidence that Lyon had talked about harming or killing Heemstra and that Lyon could be a violent person. Evidence was also presented that suggested Lyon may have had mental health problems. . . .

The district court instructed on both alternatives for first-degree murder: willful, deliberate, and premeditated murder under section 707.2(1) and felony murder under section 707.2(2). . . .

The State argues that the pointing of the gun or displaying it in a dangerous manner constituted willful injury. There is no dispute that Heemstra pointed the gun at Lyon and did so intentionally; he admits that. He argues, however, that the act of "point[ing] a firearm . . . or display[ing] a dangerous weapon in a threatening manner" does not fit the statutory definition of willful injury and cannot provide the basis for felony murder. . . .

On appeal Heemstra claims that, if the jury found he had committed willful injury, it would be permitted

to find first-degree murder under the felony-murder instruction without finding the elements of deliberation, premeditation, and specific intent to kill. He further argues that, while forcible felonies may infer such elements under the felony-murder rule, that was not the case here because the act specified in the court's felony-murder instruction was not a forcible felony. . . .

The State counters that Heemstra failed to preserve error on his argument that pointing a gun at a person cannot be considered willful injury under the felony-murder instruction. Heemstra's trial counsel objected to the instruction by stating:

> By submitting willful injury as the predicate felony, it plainly permits the jury to find the defendant guilty of murder in the first degree without proof of deliberation, premeditation and specific intent to kill, and additionally, by permitting the jury to infer malice from the commission of the offense of willful injury permits the jury to find the defendant guilty of first-degree murder without proof of malice.

We believe this objection was sufficient to alert the court to the problem inherent in the felony-murder instruction, i.e., if the jury found Heemstra pointed the gun at Lyon intending to cause serious injury and that serious injury resulted, it could find felony murder, despite the fact that the gun pointing was not a forcible felony for purposes of felony murder and without proof of willfulness, deliberation, and premeditation. . . .

First-degree murder under Iowa Code section 707.2 (1) requires proof that the murder was committed "willfully, deliberately, and with premeditation." In contrast, first-degree murder based on the felony-murder rule under section 707.2(2) does not require proof of any of these elements; they are presumed to exist if the State proves participation in the underlying forcible felony. . . .

The rationale of the felony-murder rule is that certain crimes are so inherently dangerous that proof of participating in these crimes may obviate the need for showing all of the elements normally required for first-degree murder. This reduced quantum of proof in establishing first-degree murder has caused the felony-murder doctrine to be called "[o]ne of the most controversial doctrines in the field of criminal law. . . ." Erwin S. Barbre, [ALR] Annotation. The California Supreme Court [in Washington] has observed that:

The felony-murder rule has been criticized on the grounds that in almost all cases in which it is applied it is unnecessary and that it erodes the relation between criminal liability and moral culpability. Although it is the law in this state, it should not be extended beyond any rational function that it is designed to serve.

Even if the acts of the defendant were considered to be willful injury, as the State argues, the question remains whether willful injury may be considered a predicate for felony murder under the facts of this case. A long line of Iowa cases have answered that question in the affirmative, but we believe we must revisit the issue and reach a contrary conclusion. . . .

Although the State argues that merger principles should not apply to these facts, nothing in any of the statutes relied upon to support that argument suggests that the legislature had any intent to abolish the principle of merger under the circumstances of this case. Furthermore, we should not defer to the legislature for a signal for us to adopt a legal principle that is the responsibility of the court and within the power of the court to apply, based on legal precedent, common sense, and fairness.

We now hold that, if the act causing willful injury is the same act that causes the victim's death, the former is merged into the murder and therefore cannot serve as the predicate felony for felony-murder purposes. . . . We realize that this view is inconsistent with our prior cases, including *Beeman* and its progeny. We therefore overrule those cases, insofar as they hold that the act constituting willful injury and also causing the victim's death may serve as a predicate felony for felony-murder purposes. . . .

When a general verdict does not reveal the basis for a guilty verdict, reversal is required. . . .

Because we have no indication as to which basis of guilt the jury accepted, we must reverse and remand for a new trial.

Case Questions

1. What is the rationale for the felony-murder rule?
2. Why is the felony-murder rule disfavored?
3. Why might it be unfair to convict Heemstra of murder by using the felony-murder rule?

Another example of traditional strict liability is covered in the crime of statutory rape, in which sexual relations with a person under a certain age eliminate the defense of consent and in many states deny the defendant the defense of a good faith belief that the victim was above the prescribed age. Again, a reasonable objective of protecting young and innocent or naive girls from predatory older males is used to justify strict liability. It should be noted that older *females* have been charged and convicted of such crimes even though the stereotypical sexual predator is male.

The growth of strict liability, however, has occurred primarily in regulatory statutes. Strict liability has been justified when a class of persons, such as the young, seem to warrant special protection or when the danger to the public is particularly hazardous, as with alcohol, firearms, drugs, and poisons.

Although common law crimes have been done away with, criminal intent continues the common law tradition, except when the legislature passes a new regulatory law, *malum prohibitum* (the singular form of *mala prohibita*). Typically, such regulatory law is silent about intent, and the courts have shown an inclination to interpret such legislative acts as strict liability crimes when they cannot be classified as civil penalties.

THE INSANITY DEFENSE

No discussion of *mens rea* would be complete without mention of the insanity defense. A criminal defendant may plead "not guilty by reason of insanity." This plea acknowledges commission of the criminal act but negates criminal intent because of the defendant's insanity. The policy basis for the defense is to hold accountable for crimes only those persons who freely chose to commit crimes. An additional reason for the defense is the inappropriateness of putting insane persons in with the general prison population. The insanity defense is very much like the defense of an involuntary act or the absence of criminal intent. The difference lies in acknowledging insanity, which typically results in commitment to a mental institution if insanity is proven.

The principal problem with insanity is defining it. Understanding the subjective states of the human mind is difficult even for psychologists and psychiatrists with extensive training and experience. Although some persons may be found to be insane by almost any measure, the line between sanity and insanity cannot be drawn with accuracy—yet the law requires that the line be drawn.

The English rule originating in the nineteenth-century *M'Naghten* case (10 Cl. & F. 200, 8 Eng. Rep. 718 [1843]) is still followed, with some modifications, in many American jurisdictions. Daniel M'Naghten suffered delusions that the prime minister was out to get him; M'Naghten shot and killed the prime minister's secretary, mistakenly believing the secretary to be the prime minister. Public outrage over M'Naghten's acquittal ultimately led to a consideration of the insanity defense by the House of Lords (England's "Supreme Court"). Consensus resulted in what is often called the "right-wrong test," namely, whether the accused suffered from a defect of mind such that he did not understand the nature of his act or did not know that it was wrong. This is a difficult test to meet because it requires a very serious mental imbalance.

In recent decades, the fields of psychology and psychiatry have shown that we are much less in control of our minds and actions than was formerly believed, so other insanity tests have been adopted that lower the threshold of insanity for legal purposes. The issue of legal accountability for acts committed by someone with diminished mental capacity is very murky at present.

Insanity defenses frequently involve several highly paid expert witnesses. As in *Clark*, prosecution witnesses testify that the defendant was sane at the time of the act, while defense witnesses argue precisely the opposite; the jury must attempt to arrive at the "truth" of the defendant's mental state as described by experts who reconstruct that mental state after the fact.

A satisfactory resolution of these and other problems related to the insanity defense does not appear to be forthcoming.

Eric Michael CLARK, Petitioner

v.

ARIZONA

Supreme Court of the United States

No. 05-5966

548 U.S. 735

Argued April 19, 2006.

Decided June 29, 2006.

The case presents two questions: whether due process prohibits Arizona's use of an insanity test stated solely in terms of the capacity to tell whether an act charged as a crime was right or wrong; and whether Arizona violates due process in restricting consideration of defense evidence of mental illness and incapacity to its bearing on a claim of insanity, thus eliminating its significance directly on the issue of the mental element of the crime charged (known in legal shorthand as the *mens rea*, or guilty mind). We hold that there is no violation of due process in either instance.

In the early hours of June 21, 2000, Officer Jeffrey Moritz of the Flagstaff Police responded in uniform to complaints that a pickup truck with loud music blaring was circling a residential block. When he located the truck, the officer turned on the emergency lights and siren of his marked patrol car, which prompted petitioner Eric Clark, the truck's driver (then 17), to pull over. Officer Moritz got out of the patrol car and told Clark to stay where he was. Less than a minute later, Clark shot the officer, who died soon after but not before calling the police dispatcher for help. Clark ran away on foot but was arrested later that day with gunpowder residue on his hands; the gun that killed the officer was found nearby, stuffed into a knit cap. . . .

Clark waived his right to a jury, and the case was heard by the court.

At trial, Clark did not contest the shooting and death, but relied on his undisputed paranoid schizophrenia at the time of the incident in denying that he had the specific intent to shoot a law enforcement officer or knowledge that he was doing so, as required by the statute. Accordingly, the prosecutor offered circumstantial evidence that Clark knew Officer Moritz was a law enforcement officer. The evidence showed that the officer was in uniform at the time, that he caught up with Clark in a marked police car with emergency lights and siren going, and that Clark acknowledged the symbols of police authority and stopped. The testimony for the prosecution indicated that Clark had intentionally lured an officer to the scene to kill him, having told some people a few weeks before the incident that he wanted to shoot police officers. . . .

In presenting the defense case, Clark claimed mental illness, which he sought to introduce for two purposes. First, he raised the affirmative defense of insanity, putting the burden on himself to prove by clear and convincing evidence that "at the time of the commission of the criminal act [he] was afflicted with a mental disease or defect of such severity that [he] did not know the criminal act was wrong," § 13-502(A). Second, he aimed to rebut the prosecution's evidence of the requisite *mens rea*, that he had acted intentionally or knowingly to kill a law enforcement officer.

The trial court ruled that Clark could not rely on evidence bearing on insanity to dispute the *mens rea*.

The court cited *State v. Mott* which "refused to allow psychiatric testimony to negate specific intent," and held that "Arizona does not allow evidence of a defendant's mental disorder short of insanity . . . to negate the *mens rea* element of a crime." . . .

Clark first says that Arizona's definition of insanity, being only a fragment of the Victorian standard from which it derives, violates due process. The landmark English rule in *M'Naghten's Case*, states that

> "the jurors ought to be told . . . that to establish a defence on the ground of insanity, it must be clearly proved that, at the time of the committing of the act, the party accused was laboring under such a defect of reason, from disease of the mind, as not to know the nature and quality of the act he was doing; or, if he did know it, that he did not know he was doing what was wrong."

The first part asks about cognitive capacity: whether a mental defect leaves a defendant unable to understand what he is doing. The second part presents an ostensibly alternative basis for recognizing a defense of insanity understood as a lack of moral capacity: whether a mental disease or defect leaves a defendant unable to understand that his action is wrong.

[The court reviewed the insanity standards adopted by various states.] . . . With this varied background, it is clear that no particular formulation has evolved into a baseline for due process, and that the insanity rule, like the conceptualization of criminal offenses, is substantially open to state choice. . . . Clark can point to no evidence bearing on insanity that was excluded. His psychiatric expert and a number of lay witnesses testified to his delusions, and this evidence tended to support a description of Clark as lacking the capacity to understand that the police officer was a human being. There is no doubt that the trial judge considered the evidence as going to an issue of cognitive capacity, for in finding insanity not proven he said that Clark's mental illness "did not . . . distort his perception of reality so severely that he did not know his actions were wrong,"

We are satisfied that neither in theory nor in practice did Arizona's 1993 abridgment of the insanity formulation deprive Clark of due process. . . .

Clark's second claim of a due process violation challenges the rule adopted by the Supreme Court of Arizona in *Mott*. . . . The state court held that testimony of a professional psychologist or psychiatrist about a defendant's mental incapacity owing to mental disease or defect was admissible, and could be considered, only for its bearing on an insanity defense; such evidence could not be considered on the element of *mens rea*, that is, what the State must show about a defendant's mental state (such as intent or understanding) when he performed the act charged against him.

Understanding Clark's claim requires attention to the categories of evidence with a potential bearing on *mens rea*. First, there is "observation evidence" in the everyday sense, testimony from those who observed what Clark did and heard what he said; this category would also include testimony that an expert witness might give about Clark's tendency to think in a certain way and his behavioral characteristics. This evidence may support a professional diagnosis of mental disease and in any event is the kind of evidence that can be relevant to show what in fact was on Clark's mind when he fired the gun. Observation evidence in the record covers Clark's behavior at home and with friends, his expressions of belief around the time of the killing that "aliens" were inhabiting the bodies of local people (including government agents), his driving around the neighborhood before the police arrived, and so on. . . .

Second, there is "mental-disease evidence" in the form of opinion testimony that Clark suffered from a mental disease with features described by the witness. As was true here, this evidence characteristically but not always comes from professional psychologists or psychiatrists who testify as expert witnesses and base their opinions in part on examination of a defendant, usually conducted after the events in question. The thrust of this evidence was that, based on factual reports, professional observations, and tests, Clark was psychotic at the time in question, with a condition that fell within the category of schizophrenia.

Third, there is evidence we will refer to as "capacity evidence" about a defendant's capacity for cognition and moral judgment (and ultimately also his capacity to form *mens rea*). This, too, is opinion evidence. Here, as it usually does, this testimony came from the same experts and concentrated on those specific details of the mental condition that make the difference between sanity and insanity under the Arizona definition. In their respective testimony on these details the experts disagreed: the defense expert gave his opinion that the symptoms or effects of the disease in Clark's case included inability to appreciate the nature of his action and to tell that it was wrong, whereas the State's psychiatrist was of the view that Clark was a schizophrenic who was still sufficiently able to appreciate the reality of shooting the officer and to know that it was wrong to do that. . . .

Clark's argument that the *Mott* rule violates the Fourteenth Amendment guarantee of due process turns on the application of the presumption of innocence in criminal cases, the presumption of sanity, and the principle that a criminal defendant is entitled to present relevant and favorable evidence on an element of the offense charged against him.

The first presumption is that a defendant is innocent unless and until the government proves beyond a reasonable doubt each element of the offense charged, including the mental element or *mens rea*. . . . The presumption of sanity is equally universal in some variety or other, being (at least) a presumption that a defendant has the capacity to form the *mens rea* necessary for a verdict of guilt and the consequent criminal responsibility. This presumption dispenses with a requirement on the government's part to include as an element of every criminal charge an allegation that the defendant had such a capacity. . . .

[E]vidence tending to show that a defendant suffers from mental disease and lacks capacity to form *mens rea* is relevant to rebut evidence that he did in fact form the required *mens rea* at the time in question; this is the reason that Clark claims a right to require the factfinder in this case to consider testimony about his mental illness and his incapacity directly, when weighing the persuasiveness of other evidence tending to show *mens rea*, which the prosecution has the burden to prove. . . .

No one, certainly not Clark here, denies that a State may place a burden of persuasion on a defendant claiming insanity. . . . But if a State is to have this authority in practice as well as in theory, it must be able to deny a defendant the opportunity to displace the presumption of sanity more easily when addressing a different issue in the course of the criminal trial. . . . [I]f a jury were free to decide how much evidence of mental disease and incapacity was enough to counter evidence of *mens rea* to the point of creating a reasonable doubt, that would in functional terms be analogous to allowing jurors to decide upon some degree of diminished capacity to obey the law, a degree set by them, that would prevail as a stand-alone defense. . . .

Are there, then, characteristics of mental-disease and capacity evidence giving rise to risks that may reasonably be hedged by channeling the consideration of such evidence to the insanity issue on which, in States like Arizona, a defendant has the burden of persuasion? We think there are: in the controversial character of some categories of mental disease, in the potential of mental-disease evidence to mislead, and in the danger of according greater certainty to capacity evidence than experts claim for it.

To begin with, the diagnosis may mask vigorous debate within the profession about the very contours of the mental disease itself. . . .

Next, there is the potential of mental-disease evidence to mislead jurors (when they are the factfinders) through the power of this kind of evidence to suggest that a defendant suffering from a recognized mental disease lacks cognitive, moral, volitional, or other capacity, when that may not be a sound conclusion at all. . . . The limits of the utility of a professional disease diagnosis are evident in the dispute between the two testifying experts in this case; they agree that Clark was schizophrenic, but they come to opposite conclusions on whether the mental disease in his particular case left him bereft of cognitive or moral capacity. . . .

There are, finally, particular risks inherent in the opinions of the experts who supplement the mental-disease classifications with opinions on incapacity: on whether the mental disease rendered a particular defendant incapable of the cognition necessary for moral judgment or *mens rea* or otherwise incapable of understanding the wrongfulness of the conduct charged. Unlike observational evidence bearing on *mens rea*, capacity evidence consists of judgment, and judgment fraught with multiple perils: a defendant's state of mind at the crucial moment can be elusive no matter how conscientious the enquiry, and the law's categories that set the terms of the capacity judgment are not the categories of psychology that govern the expert's professional thinking. Although such capacity judgments may be given in the utmost good faith, their potentially tenuous character is indicated by the candor of the defense expert in this very case. . . .

In sum, these empirical and conceptual problems add up to a real risk that an expert's judgment in giving capacity evidence will come with an apparent authority that psychologists and psychiatrists do not claim to have. We think that this risk, like the difficulty in assessing the significance of mental-disease evidence, supports the State's decision to channel such expert testimony to consideration on the insanity defense, on which the party seeking the benefit of this evidence has the burden of persuasion.

Case Questions

1. What is the difference between the *M'Naghten* definition of insanity and Arizona's definition of insanity?
2. Why does the Court say that it is appropriate for the defendant to bear the burden of proof on the defendant's insanity claim rather than have the factfinder consider evidence of insanity while considering whether the defendant had the requisite *mens rea* to commit the crime?

SUMMARY

Although the practice of criminal law tends to focus on problems of proof and other procedural issues, the substantive law of crimes is largely the concern of legislative enactments. There is considerable variability in the definitions of specific crimes from state to state. A general definition of crime is difficult to state, but crime may be identified procedurally by recourse to statutes that define crimes and delegate authority to police and prosecutors for the resolution of misconduct so labeled.

The criminal law penalizes conduct that offends the moral sentiments of the people. However, in our diverse society, moral commands are not always a matter of consensus. In addition, lawmakers provide criminal and civil penalties to encourage people to conform to an increasingly regulated state.

Traditionally, a crime requires both a criminal act and criminal intent on the part of the actor. The criminal act is defined by the elements of specific crimes, and it is up to the courts to determine whether a particular act falls within the prohibitions of the law.

Criminal intent, or *mens rea,* requires that the defendant in a criminal case be shown to have had a specific state of mind at the time of commission of the criminal act. Because subjective states of mind are difficult to ascertain, the intent of the defendant is frequently at issue in trials. Specific crimes often require or infer a specific state of mind. Questions of motivation, willfulness, premeditation, accident, knowledge, and intent are fact questions for the jury that may be quite confusing and difficult to resolve. The insanity defense is particularly problematic because of the inconsistency of legal and psychiatric definitions of insanity.

KEY TERMS

actus reus	felony-murder rule	public defender's office
attempt to commit a crime	general intent	punishment (retribution)
conspiracy	*mala in se*	rape
crime	*mala prohibita*	specific intent
criminal law	*mens rea*	strict criminal liability
deterrence	murder	voluntary

CHAPTER REVIEW QUESTIONS

1. How can you tell a criminal case from a civil case?
2. What is the difference between a crime that is *mala in se* and one that is *mala prohibita*?
3. What are the translations of *actus reus* and *mens rea*?
4. Distinguish between general and specific intent (to commit a crime).
5. What unique requirement for intent is made in the case of murder?
6. Renunciation of criminal purpose would be a defense to a charge of what crime?
7. When might the felony-murder rule apply?
8. Describe the *M'Naghten* test for insanity.
9. What is the difference between the penalties for a crime and an attempt to commit that crime under the *Model Penal Code*?
10. What is the defense to a charge of rape?

CRITICAL THINKING QUESTIONS

1. Does it matter that psychologists and psychiatrists generally feel that the legal test for insanity (e.g., the *M'Naghten* rule) bears no resemblance to any scientific definition of *insanity*?
2. Are current drug laws misguided?

CYBER EXERCISES

1. Opinions of the United States Supreme Court are accessible at a number of websites, in particular http://www.supremecourtus.gov. The United States Supreme Court decided *Clark v. Arizona*, 548 U.S. 735 (2006), on June 29, 2006. The case contained the majority opinion, excerpted in this chapter, an opinion concurring in part and dissenting in part, and a dissenting opinion. Locate the case at the Supreme Court website and answer the following questions:

    a. What was Justice Breyer's reasoning for dissenting in part?

    b. From which portions of the majority opinion did Justice Breyer dissent?

    c. How does Justice Kennedy's dissenting opinion differ from the majority opinion?

    d. With the information presented to you and the facts of the case laid out, how would you have ruled if you had been sitting on the Supreme Court of the United States?

2. Opinions of the Supreme Court of Iowa can be accessed at a number of websites, including http://www.iowacourts.gov/. The Iowa Supreme Court decided *State v. Heemstra*, 721 N.W.2d 549 (Iowa 2006), on August 25, 2006. The case contained the majority opinion, excerpted in this chapter, and two separate dissenting opinions. Locate the case at the Supreme Court of Iowa website and answer the following questions:

    a. In his dissenting opinion, how does Justice Carter contrast the definition of felony-murder and what the defendant did?

    b. How does Justice Carter use *State v. Beeman* to support his dissent?

    c. In his dissenting opinion, why does Justice Cady state that the court should not overrule precedent?

SCENARIO

Scenario 1

A woman and a man meet in a bar; the woman is scantily clad, with a hemline that reveals that she is wearing no underwear. She agrees to have sexual intercourse with the man for money, and they leave in his van. She later accuses him of rape. She has prior convictions for prostitution and, on a prior occasion, charged rape against another man under roughly similar circumstances. The present defendant is wanted in another state on a rape charge. He promised the woman money for sex but refused to pay her up front, and she claims she refused to have sex with him.

Assume that in the trial for rape, the prior convictions are admitted into evidence as relevant to the issue of consent (but not necessarily proving consent).

1. Frame the argument for the prosecution, telling the story as she would have represented it.

2. Frame the argument for the defense, telling the story as he would have represented it.

Briefly give the discussion a jury of six men and six women would have had to come up with a unanimous verdict of guilty or not guilty. In other words, how do you think a jury would evaluate the parties' stories? Remember that the standard of proof is guilt beyond a reasonable doubt.

Scenario 2

A man and a woman meet in a singles bar. The woman is dressed provocatively and plays the temptress. After many drinks, they end up in her apartment. She puts on a nun's habit and declares that she is a virgin and married to God. Then she takes her clothes off and has intercourse with the man; all the while, she is saying, "No. No. No. I'm a virgin" (which she is not). The man is of below-average intelligence. He acknowledges overcoming some slight efforts of physical resistance on her part.

The woman is diagnosed as psychotic by a prosecution psychiatrist, although a defense psychiatrist testifies from his interviews with the woman that she has emotional problems without delusionary tendencies and does not have multiple personalities. On the witness stand, she is emotional but otherwise appears normal.

1. Frame the argument for the prosecution.
2. Frame the argument for the defense.

Briefly give the discussion a jury of six men and six women would have had to come up with a unanimous verdict of guilty or not guilty. In other words, how do you think a jury would evaluate the parties' stories? Remember that the standard of proof is guilt beyond a reasonable doubt.

CHAPTER 10

TORTS, PERSONAL INJURY, AND COMPENSATION

INTRODUCTION

torts

A major area of substantive law including causes of action to redress injuries that arise out of noncontractual events. Tort includes three major divisions: *intentional torts, negligence,* and *strict liability.*

The traditional term for the field of personal injury and compensation law is **torts**. Generally, torts have specific legal labels, each considered a different cause of action, such as trespass, **slander**, negligence, and product liability. They often seem to have little in common except the law's recognition that private interests can be subject to injury, the remedy for which is typically compensation if responsibility for the injury can be attributed to another party. The difference in terminology reflects a difference in attitude. The term *torts* suggests a set of fixed, labeled causes of action; the phrase *compensation for injuries* reflects a more flexible category that can accommodate new interests as tort law evolves. For example, electronic eavesdropping has come to be recognized as an impermissible intrusion on privacy subsumed under the cause of action invasion of privacy. Despite the more descriptive and realistic "compensation for injuries," *torts* continues to be favored for saving seven syllables or twenty keystrokes.

DEFINITION

In the word *tort* we have a rare example of legal custom providing a doctrinaire but reliable definition: "A tort is a private wrong not arising out of contract." Unfortunately, the definition states what a tort is *not*, without stating exactly what it *is*. It is not a public wrong; that is, it is not a crime, and it is not based on a contract. Exhibit 10-1 contains information from the following two sections.

Tort versus Crime

Legal scholars have argued whether in ancient times crime and tort were separable. In modern times, the distinction between the two is clear because the rise of the modern state resulted in the state's assumption of authority over misconduct it deemed criminal. Public wrongs are often characterized as "wrongs against society." It is doubtful that the victim of a rape or robbery meditates on the social impact of the crime. Nevertheless, in our legal system the public has a legitimate interest in preventing such crimes.

Distinguishing tort from crime is clearest from a procedural standpoint. If the public prosecutor seeks a remedy (usually punishment) for misconduct, the wrong is public—it is a crime. If the victim sues in his or her own right for compensation, the wrong is private and the cause of action lies in tort. If conduct constituting a public wrong causes injury to person or property, there is nearly always a private action in tort available to the injured party in addition to prosecution available to the state. The public and private actions are independent of each other and are procedurally distinct. In some cases the causes of action may have similar names; for example, battery is a criminal offense as well as a civil cause of action in tort. The crime of rape, in contrast, fits best into the civil cause of action called *battery* (some states have renamed the crime "sexual battery").

Not all torts involve criminal conduct. Because crimes ordinarily require intentional conduct, unintentional infliction of injuries, such as through negligence (e.g., causing an auto accident, medical malpractice) and liability for unsafe products (product liability), is usually not considered criminal even though the wrongdoer, a **tortfeasor**, may be subject to severe financial liability in tort.

slander
An injury to reputation ordinarily caused by the communication of lies to third parties. It is the spoken form of defamation, *libel* being written defamation.

tortfeasor
A person who engages in tortious conduct.

EXHIBIT 10-1 TORT, CRIME, AND CONTRACT

BASIS OF A LAWSUIT	ATTRIBUTES
Tort	The victim sues in his or her own right for compensation for an injury to person or property
Crime	The public prosecutor seeks a remedy (usually punishment) for a public wrong, that is, a wrong against society
Contract	A party to an agreement sues another party who breached the agreement

Civil cases can be distinguished from criminal cases by the titles of the cases. *Montagu v. Capulet* and *Hatfield v. McCoy* are civil cases, whereas *Commonwealth v. Ripper, People v. Samson,* and *State v. Miranda* (when the defendant appeals to the U.S. Supreme Court, it becomes *Miranda v. Arizona* or *Ripper v. Massachusetts*) are criminal cases. This distinction is not infallible, however, as states may be parties to civil suits as well.

Tort versus Contract

Private wrongs fall into two categories: tort and contract. Because torts are "private wrongs not arising out of contract," noncontract actions based on wrongful conduct are necessarily torts. The reason for defining tort by what it is *not* can be attributed to the fact that the field of torts consists of a number of causes of action that have little in common, whereas contract actions are predicated on the existence of a valid contract.

The legal significance of this distinction rests on the source of the duty imposed on the defendant. In contract cases, the duties are created by the agreement between the parties and do not exist without it. If a young man offers to mow a neighbor's lawn for $10 and the neighbor agrees, the neighbor is obligated by this contract under the law to pay the $10 if the man mows the lawn. In contrast, if the young man simply mows the lawn in the neighbor's absence without any agreement and then demands payment, the neighbor has no obligation to pay; there was no contract. In fact, going on the neighbor's land without consent could technically constitute the tort of trespass.

Rights and duties in tort actions, by contrast, are based on obligations imposed by law. For example, our law recognizes both an individual's right to a good reputation and a corresponding duty on others not to spread lies that injure the individual's reputation. If such an injury occurs, the injured party may sue in tort under a cause of action for **defamation**. Liability is based on the breach of duties established by law (statutes and cases) rather than on an agreement between the parties found in the terms of a contract.

defamation

An injury to reputation; includes *slander* and *libel.*

In a cause of action for breach of contract, the court looks to the contract to determine whether it is valid and enforceable under contract law and then (if the contract is found to be valid) to the terms of the contract to determine precisely what obligations were created. If one party failed to fulfill promises made in the contract, liability may be imposed for a resulting injury to the other party. In principle this is simple, but life is complex, so a large body of law has developed to fit this principle to a variety of circumstances (discussed fully in Chapter 11). It should be kept in mind that although the law sets the rules for the enforcement of contracts, the specific duties on which suits are based are to be found in the private agreement of the parties, the contract itself. In a sense, the duty imposed by the law of contracts simply embodies a policy that the law favors the fulfillment of promises made between private parties.

In a cause of action for tort, duties to be enforced must be found in the law. A basic policy of protecting person, property, reputation, or the like is not sufficient. The court needs guidance to determine whether liability should be imposed under the unique circumstances presented by a given case. This is the reason that the common law has been extremely important in the development of tort law. Whenever possible, the court will look to similar cases from past decisions to determine how the duties have been defined. If duties have been established by statute, these may serve as the basis for judicial enforcement in tort. In fact, legislatures often create or redefine tort actions. For example, Congress provided in 42 U.S.C. § 1983 (Civil Rights Act of 1871) for private actions to be brought against state officials who wrongfully deprive individuals of their civil rights.

Often tort actions arise between persons who have relations such that the cause of action may appear to be a contract action. For example, medical malpractice cases arise in a contract relationship: a physician agrees to furnish services in return for payment, a rather typical exchange of promises between parties to a contract. If the physician negligently treats a patient, thereby causing injury, the patient may sue for malpractice in tort based on the duties imposed by law on the physician rather than the duties expressed by the terms of the contract. Although this seems to be a wrong arising out of contract, in fact, the court looks to the law rather than the contract to determine the duties between the parties. There is also a tort called **wrongful interference with contractual relations**, which occurs when a person *not* a party to a contract improperly disrupts the contractual relationship of others, as when a theater owner persuades a singer to break a contract at another theater. Obviously the tort is predicated on a contract, but in this case the contract is not one between the plaintiff and the defendant.

> **wrongful interference with contractual relations**
> When a person not a party to a contract improperly disrupts the contractual relationship of others.

Elements of Tort

As suits for personal injury developed over the centuries, the courts distinguished types of wrongful conduct. It seemed clear that the intentional infliction of physical injury, for example, was quite different in nature from an injury to reputation, so each required its own definition. Even the *threat* of physical injury—**assault**—was distinguished from the *infliction* of injury—**battery**. The definitions of specific causes of action in tort were framed in terms of *elements* (crimes are also defined by elements). To succeed in a tort action, the plaintiff must allege sufficient facts in a complaint to satisfy each element of a particular cause of action. If the plaintiff fails to do this, the complaint may be dismissed for failure to state a cause of action (the defendant would make a motion to dismiss "for failure to state a claim upon which relief can be granted"). Of course, the plaintiff must prove these allegations at trial to win the case.

> **assault**
> Putting someone in apprehension of a *battery*. The actor must have the ability to carry out the threatened battery.

Battery provides a time-tested example of the elements of a tort. It has been defined traditionally as an "unconsented, unprivileged, offensive contact." The definition contains the elements of battery as well as the defenses to battery. Exhibit 10-2 lists the three elements of and the two defenses to battery.

> **battery**
> An unconsented, unprivileged, offensive contact.

Battery is rooted in injury caused by fists or weapons but has been extended generally to offensive bodily contacts, such as sexual touching. It must be intentional and not simply accidental or careless, though this latter might constitute a cause of action for negligence. There must be a contact and not merely a threat of contact (assault). The contact must be offensive. Although a particular form of contact may ordinarily constitute a battery, consent may prevent recovery, as with prizefighters and football players. The contact may be privileged, as when a parent strikes a child as a reasonable disciplinary measure or a policeman subdues a criminal by using reasonable force.

EXHIBIT 10-2 BATTERY

ELEMENTS:
1. Intent
2. Bodily contact (extended to clothing, etc.)
3. Offensive in nature

DEFENSES:
1. Consent to the contact
2. Privilege

Tort Law: An Evolving Field

Preparation of a tort suit begins with the search for an appropriate cause of action and an examination of whether a client's case fits comfortably within the elements of one or more torts. Tort law has experienced and continues to experience an evolution in both its definition as a whole and the definition of specific causes of action. Not only does our notion of appropriate conduct change, but opportunities for injury change as well.

For example, the tort labeled "intentional infliction of mental distress" is a product of the twentieth century and has undergone considerable growth and refinement. Courts of the past were reluctant to compensate for emotional suffering unless accompanied by some physical injury, but modern courts have come to recognize emotional injuries as compensable when caused intentionally by malice or outrageous conduct. Harassing telephone calls, unscrupulous bill collectors, impersonal public and private bureaucracies, and perhaps even the lowering of standards of courtesy on many fronts have all contributed to a recognition that the potential for serious harm to one's emotional well-being is a fact of modern life. The courts have come to impose a legal duty on conduct that custom has always disapproved but not legally condemned. The recognition of **intentional infliction of mental distress** is not designed to compensate for every insult or affront or to encourage the overly sensitive to sue. Nevertheless, some individuals engage in conduct aimed at causing suffering in ways that the courts feel compelled to condemn. (Example: A man was held liable when he jokingly told a woman that her husband had been in a serious accident and persuaded her to rush down to the hospital.)

The judicial creation of a new tort starts with a dispute before a judge, who will be inclined to recognize right and duty when faced with a compelling set of facts. Tort law has evolved to be highly individualized, based on a recognition of an individual's right to be free from unjustified intrusions on person, personality, personal dignity, and private property. Establishment of a new right of action occurs when an appropriate case demands the redress of a harm that is socially acknowledged and fits within the basic policy of general tort law. In short, the court is unwilling to refuse an injured party a

intentional infliction of mental distress
Almost self-explanatory; usually requires unreasonable or outrageous conduct and serious mental distress.

remedy even if the case does not fit precisely into the elements of some traditional cause of action. Whether such a single decision will give rise to a cause of action depends on whether other courts agree and allow the precedent to stand or whether they criticize it, thus cutting short its life.

As our society changes or as our perception of harm changes, the law comes to recognize new forms of compensable injuries. For example, the law in the twentieth century developed theories of liability for unreasonable intrusions on personal dignity in the form of four varieties of invasion of privacy. In the 1990s, attention was directed to a particularly troublesome phenomenon called *stalking*. Some high-profile celebrities were the victims of stalking, and it was soon noted that ordinary citizens were also victims of stalking. The court in *Troncalli v. Jones* was asked to recognize stalking as a new tort. This conduct appears to fall within the tort of invasion of privacy in such a way that this and other courts will address the issues of whether an invasion of privacy is sufficient to warrant compensate and protect the victims of stalking and whether stalking is such a serious problem as to deserve to become a tort of its own.

Troncalli is complicated by the fact that the Georgia legislature has seen fit to create the new crime of *stalking*. Thus far, we have treated torts as the evolutionary products of judicial decisions. Legislatures, however, may create civil liability through the enactment of statutes. They may also create liability by implication through the passage of criminal statutes. The Supreme Court of Georgia was asked in *Troncalli* to imply a *tort* of stalking by virtue of the *crime* of stalking. Courts are often asked to determine whether such crimes give rise to civil liability. In some cases, a court may find a legislative intent to create liability, whereas other cases may result in the opposite conclusion. The court can always fall back on the argument that the legislature had the power to create civil liability had it so desired. In reading this case, note that the conduct denominated "stalking" was used to establish other causes of action, so that the plaintiff had strong grounds for a remedy even if the stalking argument lost.

Troncalli

v.

Jones

Court of Appeals of Georgia

237 Ga. App. 10, 514 S.E.2d 478 (1999)

Regina Jones sued Tom Troncalli. Her complaint set forth one count of stalking; a claim for **intentional infliction of emotional distress**; a claim for **negligent infliction of emotional distress**; a claim for invasion of privacy; and a claim for assault and battery. In addition to the claim for compensatory damages, the complaint sought punitive damages.

The case was tried to a jury; at the conclusion of the evidence, the trial court directed a verdict on the claim for negligent infliction of emotional distress. The jury then returned a general verdict in Jones' favor for $45,000 in compensatory damages; the jury also found that the evidence warranted punitive damages and that Troncalli had acted with specific intent to cause harm. The punitive damages portion of the trial was then held, and the jury awarded $245,891 in punitive damages. The trial court entered judgment, Troncalli appeals, and based on our conclusion in Division 1 that stalking is not a tort, we reverse the judgment.

[The evidence in the case is then discussed. The incidents began when Jones and Troncalli were at a party at a mutual friend's home. Troncalli inappropriately "brushed up" against Jones' breasts on two separate occasions during the night. This act appeared to be intentional and resulted in Jones leaving the party. Troncalli followed her closely despite her reckless driving. Jones eventually spotted police and asked for assistance. Troncalli gave Jones a threatening gesture from his car but was then asked to leave by the police. Jones did not file a report until a week later, a week during which Troncalli harassed her in public and came by her home. Jones "developed shingles, experienced nausea and vomiting, became frightened and depressed, and sought psychological counseling."]

Troncalli testified at trial and claimed that Jones' account of the above incidents was erroneous.

1. In his first enumeration of error, Troncalli claims that the trial court erred in denying his motion for directed verdict on Jones' claim of stalking. Troncalli argues that the court's holding that a tort of stalking was created when the legislature created a criminal statute on stalking was erroneous. Jones argues that the court did not err in denying the motion for directed verdict and that the court's charge on stalking simply set forth a duty, which Troncalli breached. Jones claims that because there was a general verdict from the fact that stalking was included as an offense was, at most, harmless error.

The enactment of OCGA § 16-5-90, which defines the crime of stalking, did not automatically create a tort of stalking. It is well settled that "[t]he violation of a penal statute does not automatically give rise to a civil cause of action on the part of one who is injured thereby." . . .

Here, although OCGA § 16-5-90 establishes the public policy of the state, nothing in its provisions creates a private cause of action in tort in favor of the victim. Because there is no cause of action for stalking, the court should have granted Troncalli's motion for directed verdict on this basis.

Jones' argument that there was no harmful error because the jury returned a general verdict lacks merit. In fact, the opposite of this is true: "[S]ince the jury found a general verdict for the plaintiff against [the] defendant, the verdict cannot stand for the reason that this court cannot determine whether the verdict was entered upon a proper basis. [Cits.]" . . .

Similarly, Jones' arguments that the jury was appropriately charged on stalking because the charge outlined Troncalli's duty and because all of the evidence regarding stalking would have been otherwise admissible under other theories are without merit. Stalking was one of Jones' main theories of recovery in the case; it formed a separate count of the complaint. Jones' opening statement listed stalking as the first theory of recovery. In its closing charge, the court gave the jury a lengthy charge regarding stalking, tracking the statutory definition which is set forth in OCGA § 16-5-90. Contrary to Jones' argument, the court did not instruct the jury that stalking simply defined a duty and Jones' argument that stalking was peripheral to her recovery is without merit.

3. Troncalli contends that the trial court erred in denying his motion for directed verdict on Jones' claim of intentional infliction of emotional distress. He argues that his actions did not rise to the level of egregiousness necessary to maintain a claim of this nature. We do not agree.

Judgment reversed.

Case Questions

1. Even though the legislature did not create civil liability for stalking, could the court have created a new tort of stalking? Explain.
2. Might the plaintiff have fared better if she had argued for a separate tort of stalking, independent of the legislative enactment and legislative intent, perhaps citing the crime of stalking as evidence of a serious social problem that the state legislature was attempting to ameliorate? Do you think the plaintiff made this argument as well but the court did not address it? Explain.
3. Do you think there should be a special tort of stalking? Explain.

Case Glossary

intentional infliction of emotional distress; negligent infliction of emotional distress

Causes of action based on severe emotional distress. Although most states recognize the intentional tort, generally requiring outrageous conduct, few recognize the cause of action based on negligence.

EXTRANEOUS FACTORS INFLUENCING TORT LAW

The law develops in a social, economic, and political context. As Oliver Wendell Holmes declared in 1881, "The life of the law has not been logic; it has been experience." Law-making is not simply a process of refining abstract rules, nor is the process of deciding disputes controlled by the simple expedient of applying abstract rules to concrete events. Tort law has a strong component of logic and common sense. The rights represented by tort law generally reflect what most Americans consider their rights should be (e.g., a person can use force against another person in self-defense). In a sense, tort law more than any other area of law reflects our social values with regard to interpersonal conduct. Nevertheless, there are some special factors that play a large part in tort suits and influence actual outcomes but have little to do with the values expressed in substantive principles.

The Doctrine of *Respondeat Superior* (Vicarious Liability)

The English legal historian Plucknett attributes the birth of this doctrine to Lord Holt, who, in deciding a case in 1691, stated, "Whoever employs another is answerable for him, and undertakes for his care to all that make use of him." Until that time, the doctrine of **respondeat superior**, which places liability on the employer for injuries caused by an employee within the scope of employment, had only been applied to certain public officials when their underlings could not pay damages. Nothing inherent in tort law requires this principle, which is a peculiarity of Anglo-American common law. It contradicts a fundamental principle of tort law, namely, that fault should be the basis for liability. Nonetheless, an employer may be liable without acting wrongfully.

respondeat superior

A principle of agency whereby a principal is held responsible for the negligent acts of an agent acting within the scope of the agency (e.g., an employer is liable for the negligence of an employee); also called vicarious liability.

The influence of *respondeat superior* on modern tort litigation is great. Personal injury cases are costly to litigate, and it is futile to sue a defendant who has limited resources. If, however, a person is injured by a worker who is on the job for a large corporation, the suit becomes economically feasible. The resources of employees are generally far more limited than those of their employers. As a practical matter, juries tend to be less concerned about the pocketbooks of large businesses than they are about those of workers.

As a result, the availability of compensation may depend more on who may be liable than on the legal merits of the case. When we read in the newspapers of unusually high awards, we can be relatively certain that some "deep pocket" was available to be sued. *Respondeat superior* creates many deep pockets.

In *Adames*, the family of a young boy who died tragically attempted to hold the Cook County, Illinois, Sheriff's Office liable. The court had to consider whether the gun owner was acting within the scope of his employment when storing the gun. If not, then the sheriff's office could not be liable under the doctrine of *respondeat superior*.

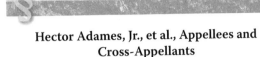

Hector Adames, Jr., et al., Appellees and Cross-Appellants

v.

Michael F. Sheahan, in His Official Capacity as Cook County Sheriff, Appellant and Cross-Appellee

Hector Adames, Jr., et al., Appellees and Cross-Appellants

v.

Beretta U.S.A. Corporation, Appellants and Cross-Appellees

Supreme Court of Illinois

Nos. 105789, 105851

909 N.E.2d 742

March 19, 2009.

On May 5, 2001, William (Billy) Swan accidentally shot and killed his friend Joshua (Josh) Adames while playing with his father's service weapon. At the time, Billy's father, David Swan, was employed by the Cook County sheriff's department as a correctional officer. . . . At issue in this case are plaintiffs' claims against defendant Michael F. Sheahan (Sheahan), in his official capacity as Cook County sheriff. . . .

[The following version of the facts is from Billy Swan's deposition.] On the morning of May 5, 2001, Billy Swan, who then was 13 years old, was home alone. . . . Billy called his friend Josh Adames and invited him over to play. . . . Billy knew that both going into his parents' bedroom and inviting friends over when no one else was home were against house rules. [Billy found three guns, including a Beretta 92FS handgun, in a box on the top shelf of the closet. Billy claimed that the box was unlocked, while his father claimed that the box was locked.] . . . Billy knew that the Beretta was loaded when the magazine was in the gun, but thought it was unloaded when the magazine was taken out. He thought that the bullet came out of the top of the magazine when the handgun was fired, and did not know that a bullet remained in the chamber. . . .

Billy showed Josh the guns and the boys began playing around. While Billy was holding the Beretta, Josh tried to reach for it to take it out of Billy's hand. Billy pushed the button on the Beretta, took the magazine out and put it in his pocket. At this point, Josh was by the front door. Billy pretended that he was firing the gun, then pulled the trigger, discharging the gun. The gunshot was loud, causing Billy's ears to ring. Billy was afraid he would be in trouble if the neighbors heard the noise, so he ran upstairs and put the guns away.

When Billy came back downstairs, he saw Josh sitting against the door holding his stomach. Josh told Billy that he had been shot. Billy first thought that Josh was kidding, but when he moved Josh's hand, he saw a hole. Billy called 911 and told the dispatcher that he had found a gun and accidentally shot his friend while playing. Billy testified that he knew he was handling a real firearm and real ammunition when he shot Josh. . . .

Sheahan's executive director and weapons training officers testified concerning Sheahan's orders and training instructions. Those orders and training instructions required all weapons to be locked up when stored at home. Weapons must be stored so they are inaccessible to children, and officers are taught to expect their children to look everywhere in their homes. . . .

Gerald O'Sullivan, retired executive director of the Cook County sheriff office's training program, testified that Cook County Sheriff's Office correctional officers do not need a weapon to perform their duties. O'Sullivan said that only court deputies and sheriff's police officers need a weapon. The only authorized purpose for a correctional officer's duty firearm would be for external operations outside the jails. . . .

With regard to Sheahan, plaintiffs' third amended complaint contained a wrongful-death claim and a survival claim. Plaintiffs alleged that Sheahan assumed and exercised control over David Swan as Sheahan's employee and servant with regard to the safe and secure handling and storage of David's duty firearm and ammunition. Plaintiffs alleged, ***inter alia***, that David Swan negligently stored his firearm, as well as his ammunition, in a manner that allowed his 13-year-old son to gain access to it. . . .

Plaintiffs alleged that, as a result of one or more of David's negligent acts, Billy accessed David's firearm and bullets, and used the firearm to shoot and kill Josh. In addition, the wrongful death of Josh was proximately caused by David's negligence in the course of his employment as a deputy Cook County sheriff, while motivated to serve Sheahan's interests and the terms of David's employment. Plaintiffs asserted that Sheahan was **vicariously** liable for David's negligent acts and/or omissions in the scope of his employment as an officer of the Cook County sheriff's office, both at common law and pursuant to statute.

Sheahan moved for summary judgment on the ground that the shooting did not occur within the course and scope of David's employment as a Department of Corrections officer. . . .

Turning to the substance of the appellate court's ruling, we find that the appellate court erred in finding that David was acting within the scope of his employment and that Sheahan is liable for David's tortious acts. Contrary to the appellate court's conclusion, this case is factually distinguishable from *Gaffney*.

In contrast to *Gaffney*, David testified that he was not required to own a gun and did not need to carry a gun to work once he was promoted to lieutenant in 1997 or 1998. David testified that he did not get rid of his guns, even though he did not carry a weapon in performing his duties, because he wanted the guns for protection and in case he was transferred to a different position where he would need a weapon. In fact, the last time David had seen or touched the Beretta prior to the May 5, 2001, shooting was in the summer of 2000, when David did his yearly qualification with the sheriff's department at the firing range. David also testified that when he was off duty, he was not required to respond to a crime by attempting to stop the crime himself. Rather, his duty was to call 911 and report the crime to the proper authorities. . . .

Based on the preceding testimony, we find as a matter of law that none of the three general criteria for determining whether an employee's acts are within the scope of employment have been met in this case. With regard to the first criteri[on], David's negligent storage of his guns was not the kind of conduct David was employed to perform, nor was it incidental to his employment. . . .

For the same reasons, David's negligent storage of the gun was not within the authorized time and space limits of his employment. Unlike the police officer in

Gaffney, David was not on call 24 hours a day, was not required to respond to emergencies at all times, and was not required to respond to a crime by attempting to stop the crime himself. In contrast to *Gaffney*, David's employment was not unlimited with respect to actions incidental to his response to an emergency. Consequently, even under the most liberal interpretation of the time and space requirement, it is clear that David's negligent storage of the gun in this case was not within the scope of his employment.

Similarly, there is no evidence that David was motivated, at least in part, by a desire to serve his employer when he negligently stored his gun. . . . As discussed, David did not keep the Beretta unlocked in order to respond to an emergency. David kept the Beretta, and thus stored the Beretta, for his own protection and in case he needed it in the future.

Although summary judgment is generally inappropriate when scope of employment is at issue, if no reasonable person could conclude from the evidence that an employee is acting within the course of employment, a court should hold as a matter of law that the employee was not so acting. Here, no reasonable person could conclude from the evidence that David was acting within the scope of his employment when he negligently stored his weapon. Consequently, Sheahan was entitled to summary judgment in his favor on the issue of *respondeat superior.* The appellate court erred in finding that David was acting within the scope of employment and that Sheahan was thereby liable for David's allegedly tortious acts.

Case Questions

1. What are the three general criteria used to determine if someone is acting within the scope of employment?
2. What is the reason for using *respondeat superior* to hold the employer liable?

Case Glossary

inter alia
    (Latin) Among other things.
vicariously
    Indirectly responsible.

Insurance

insurance

The pooling of risk among many insureds, typically enabled by a corporation that sells insurance contracts.

The rise of the modern **insurance** industry has abetted tort litigation. The basic principle of insurance is pooling risk. A homeowner who buys fire insurance contributes a small amount to a large pool for protection against the possible but unlikely prospect of a fire. Although the risk of fire is small, the result if it occurs is likely to be financial catastrophe for the uninsured. The insurance company is the pooling agency, collecting payments and maintaining funds from which the unlucky are reimbursed for their losses. The homeowner usually has a homeowner's policy that includes protection against suits from those who may be injured in some way while on the homeowner's property. Loss may be a simple economic loss that can be fairly easily established (such as that from a fire), but the situation is quite different when the child next door wanders over and drowns in the swimming pool. The value of that child's life is not easy to determine, and the attempt to do so will likely produce protracted negotiations between the insurance company and the bereaved parents (through their attorneys). Insurance companies differ greatly in their willingness to make reasonable settlement offers, so the threat of lawsuit is often necessary. When a settlement cannot be reached, the dispute may be resolved by trial.

The presence of insurance encourages lawsuits for the very reason *respondeat superior* does: the insurance company has great financial resources. The economic costs of this system are great. Attorneys reap large rewards, insurance companies make handsome profits, and injured parties suffer through long delays to receive their (presumably) just compensation.

Given the realities of the economic system and tort law, however, alternative choices are often too risky. For example, physicians commonly pay enormous premiums for malpractice insurance. One might think that a competent, diligent physician need not carry insurance, as the likelihood of suit is minimal. But dedicated, ethical physicians are more concerned with treatment than with liability. Under the law they are held to a high standard of professional care. A simple error of judgment may result in death or serious permanent injury. The potential injuries are so severe that a physician practices without insurance at the peril of financial ruin. The alternative is to practice medicine with the primary purpose of avoiding liability, something neither the medical profession nor the public finds desirable.

Contingency Fees

contingency fees

Arrangement between an attorney and a client in which the attorney will receive compensation in the form of a percentage of money recovered in a lawsuit; used predominantly in personal injury cases.

The prominence of personal injury lawsuits in the practice of law is encouraged by the custom of **contingency fees**. These fees are set by a contract between the lawyer and the client under which the lawyer receives compensation measured by the settlement negotiated with the defendant or the award determined by the court. Rather than charging an hourly fee or a fee fixed in advance, the attorney agrees to represent the client for a percentage of the award. Typically, the minimum fee is one-third for a settlement, and 40 percent if the case goes to trial.

Ethically, contingency fees have always been suspect. They not only encourage suits if the potential award is great, but they also give the attorney an interest in the lawsuit, which presents a temptation for the attorney to act on the basis of personal gain rather than in the interests of the client or the law. The contingency fee arrangement is a peculiarly American institution and is not allowed in most countries. The justification for the arrangement most often given is that most injured parties could not afford to pursue a lawsuit if they were forced to pay attorneys as the case proceeds. They would be forced by economic circumstances to settle for much less than their injuries are worth. The individual of limited resources who sues an insurance company or a large corporation that has sufficient funds to pay attorneys to delay awards indefinitely is necessarily at a great disadvantage. The contingency-fee arrangement somewhat equalizes the disparity between the parties. One must question, however, whether this is a natural or artificial product of the tort law.

Contingency fees encourage some sorts of lawsuits and discourage others. If an injury is severe and permanent, especially if it is disabling or disfiguring, compensation may be very great and thus justify the costs of litigation. If the defendant has no financial resources, a lawsuit is unlikely.

FAULT

The concept of fault is central to the development of legal theories of tort. Ultimately, the resolution of a tort suit involves the question of a transfer of wealth from the defendant to the plaintiff. If someone suffers an injury or a loss, should there be a source of compensation? The law looks to the cause of the injury. If caused by an "act of God," as when someone is struck by lightning, the law cannot allocate compensation because there is no party at fault.

In contrast, if the cause of the injury can be attributed to human forces, allocation of liability may be appropriate. At that point a question of fairness arises. Would it be fair for this person or this organization to surrender some of its resources to the injured party? An affirmative answer to this question is easiest when the injury can be shown to have been caused directly by wrongful conduct of another party to an injured party who is utterly blameless. Unfortunately, causation and blameworthiness are frequently obscure or difficult to prove. What should be the result, for example, when a commercial airline crashes, killing all aboard, but the cause of the crash cannot be determined? Should a widow of one of the passengers be compensated for her loss by the airline? Our sympathies are naturally with the widow, but should the airline compensate her even though she cannot prove fault on the part of the airline? The famous case of *Cox v. Northwest Airlines, Inc.*, 379 F.2d 893 (7th Cir. 1967), resolved this issue through the often-criticized principle of *res ipsa loquitur* ("the thing speaks for itself"). *Res ipsa* is used to infer negligence, specifically a failure of due care, when it would appear that the injury would not have occurred if due care had been exercised. An airplane does not crash without some fault attributable to those in control of it (is this really true?). In this case the principle could be applied without pangs of conscience. The deceased was clearly blameless. The airline was in control of the airplane. In other words, it seems fair that the airline should pay, essentially making the airline the insurer of its passengers, but the fact that fault was established in the absence of proof is troubling to those demanding logic and consistency in the law. Put another way, would it not be better simply to charge airlines (and other common carriers) with the duty to ensure the safety of their passengers rather than apply the questionable principle of *res ipsa loquitur*? Practically speaking, the doctrine of *res ipsa loquitur* is merely a device to get the issue of negligence to the jury.

A different problem of fault was encountered in another famous case, *Summers v. Tice*, 33 Cal. 2d 80, 199 P.2d 1 (1948). Summers was one member of a hunting party who was injured when two of his companions fired simultaneously at a quail, hitting Summers in the eye. It was not possible to determine which hunter's shot was responsible for Summers's injury. Logically one was at fault, while the other was not, but the California Supreme Court held both liable because both were negligent in firing in Summers's direction, even though only one could have been the actual *cause* of the injury. "To hold otherwise would be to exonerate both from liability, although each was negligent, and the injury resulted from someone's negligence" (199 P.2d at 3). The court refused to make Summers suffer the burden of his injuries simply because he could not prove which companion fired the shot that hit his eye.

A similar problem is encountered in the DES (diethylstilbestrol) cases in which an antimiscarriage drug has been alleged to be the cause of cancer in the later life of children born to women who took the drug while pregnant. Assuming the truth of the allegations and assuming that the several drug companies who marketed the drug were legally responsible for the later injuries, who should pay when the medical records, prescriptions, and the mother's memory do not establish which company sold the drug that caused the cancer? One solution proposed to this problem is **enterprise liability** (also known as *market share liability*). Because several companies produced the drug, liability could be pooled among the companies according to their shares of the market for the drug (i.e., if one company sold 15 percent of the drug, it would pay 15 percent of the damages). Although enterprise liability is still controversial, it reflects the capacity of tort law to find novel remedies for unusual situations.

Enterprise liability also represents the modern trend in tort law away from the technicalities of finding fault and toward emphasis on a search for compensating the innocent victim. The courts and legislatures have been increasingly sensitive to the plight of the consumer, the workforce, the motorist, the homemaker, and the man on the street. Unfortunately, the principles that have arisen do not correct the inequities of the legal system itself. Compensable injuries go uncompensated when the economics of litigation pose an impediment. If there is no "deep pocket" or the injuries are less than the costs of litigation, personal injury attorneys will decline to pursue a case.

The legal profession has the ethical responsibility to provide services to the public in general, not just in cases in which legal fees are readily obtained. The American Bar Association has shown concern for this very problem, but it is up to attorneys to shoulder the responsibility or assist in finding a solution. One promising alternative in this regard is in the growing body of well-trained paralegals. Many of the services provided by attorneys could be provided by paralegals at a much lower cost—not only do paralegals provide their services at a lower fee, but they can operate within restricted areas with lower overhead. Full utilization of paralegals by lawyers can significantly reduce costs to clients. Economic necessity together with ethical obligation should result in a employment growth area for paralegals. This would serve the public and enhance the

enterprise liability

Method of apportioning damages when an injury can be attributed to a number of companies in an industry; allocates damages according to the market share of each.

image of the legal profession. For paralegals this would be a welcome development; helping the nonwealthy may be more personally rewarding than protecting the rich and corporate America.

Should a business enterprise be liable for the intentional torts of a third party on its premises? That is the question in the *Goggin* case. It represents both the search for fault and the plaintiff's search for an affluent defendant.

One of the defenses to negligence is **assumption of risk**, under which the plaintiff voluntarily encounters a known risk (e.g., someone employed to detonate explosives). In *Goggin,* the court not only finds the defendant free of negligence for the harm caused by a third party but also suggests that the plaintiff knew what he was getting into. At the same time, the court acknowledges that the owners of premises open to the public have duties with regard to the safety of patrons. The case raises interesting issues with regard to the assignment of fault.

assumption of risk

May prevent liability for negligence when the plaintiff voluntarily encounters a known risk.

Harold J. Goggin

v.

New State Ballroom

Supreme Judicial Court of Massachusetts, Suffolk

355 Mass. 718, 247 N.E.2d 350 (1969)

On March 17, 1960, the plaintiff, accompanied by a lady companion, entered the New State Ballroom in Boston at approximately 8:45 P.M. in anticipation of an evening with Terpsichore. Having paid the admission of $2 each and checked clothing, they commenced dancing when the music began. At this time there were approximately 900 people in the hall. The dance floor was waxed and polished and was about 125 feet long with a width of 90 feet. By 9:30 P.M. the crowd had grown to 1,200, and by 10 P.M. it had increased to the point where there were 1,800 to 1,900 people on the dance floor. These dancers were "noisy and boisterous, kicking their feet, bumping into people and doing some real kicking." This kicking occurred in connection with the execution of such dances as the "cha cha and jitterbug," and was accompanied by "bumping." The plaintiff, however, "only danced the waltz and refrained from the cha cha or the jitterbug." . . . While the plaintiff's partner claimed she saw no attendants, there was testimony from the defendant's manager that two police officers, plus a sergeant, were on duty "along with two employees of the Ballroom who were on the dance floor." This detail was evidently insufficient to aid

the plaintiff, for at 10 P.M. "he was dancing the waltz with his partner in a corner as there was one fellow he was trying to keep away from. When it is crowded like that you really can get bumped." He and his partner remained in the corner "but this fellow kept coming and all of a sudden, bang! 'We were pushed right over!'" The plaintiff went down, his head hit the floor, and his partner fell on top of him and ripped her dress in the descent. The plaintiff had been no stranger to the physical activity which took place at the ballroom for he was a regular attendant there on every Saturday evening between March 17, 1959, and March 17, 1960. He also repaired to the ballroom during that period on any holiday nights that fell on a weekday.

On this evidence the defendant moved for a directed verdict on a count in an action of tort brought by the plaintiff wherein he alleged that he was on the defendant's premises by invitation, that he had paid an admission, and that he was injured by reason of the defendant's negligence in its failure to conduct its establishment in an orderly manner and in compliance with statutes, ordinances and rules relating to it. The motion was denied, there was a verdict for the plaintiff, and the defendant is here on an exception to that denial.

The law in these circumstances has been often stated. The defendant, which opened its ballroom to the public in furtherance of its business, owed the duty to the plaintiff [**business invitee**], who paid to enter, of reasonable care that no injury occur to the plaintiff through the actions of a third person whether such acts were accidental, negligent or intentional. . . . The defendant, however, was not an insurer of the plaintiff's safety. . . . Its liability in this instance must arise from its knowledge, or the fact that it should have known of or anticipated, in the exercise of reasonable care, the disorderly or rowdy actions of third persons which might lead to injury to the plaintiff. . . . Furthermore, where in a ballroom such as this conditions existing at the time of the accident are open and obvious to any person of ordinary intelligence, the defendant is under no duty to warn the plaintiff even where a substantial crowd has gathered. . . .

The plaintiff in this case chose on an evening not noted for restraints on exuberance in the city of Boston to go with his lady to a public dance hall where he knew the patrons were lovers of the cha cha and the jitterbug. He knew these dances involved muscular contortions and a degree of abandon not associated with a minuet. A certain amount of innocent bumping in a large crowd would be unavoidable. That the bump which floored the plaintiff may have been deliberate was, in our view, not such a happening that the defendant was bound to anticipate it. It was unusual

and not reasonably to be apprehended and affords no basis for treating the defendant as negligent. . . . The vagaries of fashions in the dance and their consequences are better left subject to the judgment of those who engage in them or frequent establishments where they may be found, absent circumstances which may in the light of the principles herein discussed provide a basis for liability. . . .

Exceptions sustained. Judgment for the defendant.

Case Questions

1. To what duty does the court hold the ballroom with regard to the plaintiff invitee?
2. What language in the case suggests assumption of risk?

Case Glossary

business invitee

The most common form of an invitee. Businesses, especially retail stores, are often open to the public. By implication, businesses invite members of the public to enter their premises, and they owe a duty of care to those who enter their stores.

FAULT AND THREE AREAS OF TORT LAW

Tort law covers a variety of areas of injury to person and property, but three areas constitute the bulk of tort litigation:

1. Intentional torts
2. Negligence
3. Strict liability (represented primarily by the booming area of product liability)

The most ancient category is intentional torts; negligence flowered in the nineteenth and twentieth centuries; and product liability has come to fruition only in recent decades. It is not possible here to discuss any of these in sufficient detail to suggest a mastery of them, which must be left for later study. They are discussed primarily with regard to the different ways in which they relate to concepts of fault in its historical legal evolution (see Exhibit 10-3).

Intentional Torts

A number of causes of action are lumped together as **intentional torts**. Many of them are quite ancient, such as battery, assault, trespass, false imprisonment, and the like.

intentional torts
Torts that require proof of intentional wrongful conduct.

EXHIBIT 10-3   THREE CATEGORIES OF TORT WITH STANDARD OF FAULT REQUIRED

TORT CATEGORY	SPECIFIC TORTS	STANDARD OF FAULT
Intentional torts	Battery, trespass, defamation, invasion of privacy, intentional infliction of emotional distress, nuisance, wrongful interference with contractual relations, etc.	Intentional
Negligence	Negligence (including malpractice)	Breach of standard of care (reasonable person standard)
No-fault torts	Absolute liability, strict liability (including extrahazardous activities), and product liability	No proof of fault required

Some are recent in origin, such as invasion of privacy and intentional infliction of mental distress. Their common bond is the essential element of intent. Intent to do some harm (sometimes the intent to do specific harm) must be alleged and be proven if the plaintiff is to prevail. Neither malicious motive nor criminal intent is required for an intentional tort, though **malicious prosecution** specifically requires a showing of malice. Absence of malice may in some cases be a defense against libel (hence the movie *Absence of Malice*).

The requirement of intent demands a proof of fault against the defendant and requires a willful act on the part of the defendant. The law of intentional torts assumes that human beings act from free will and can conform their conduct to societal rules. When they fail to do so and that failure results in harm to others, they will be held responsible for their acts to the injured party. If a harmful act was intended, punitive damages are often awarded in addition to compensation. Punitive damages are not ordinarily awarded for nonintentional torts.

The plaintiff must prove intentional conduct, but the defendant has the opportunity to rebut intent. Intent is commonly inferred from the events that gave rise to the injury. In the colorful case of *Katko v. Briney*, 183 N.W.2d 657 (Iowa 1971), an Iowa farmer protected his wife's often-vandalized, unoccupied farmhouse by wiring a shotgun to a bedroom door to go off when someone opened the door. Katko, a trespasser looking for old bottles, had the misfortune of opening the door and suffered permanent injury to his leg. Briney's attempt to negate intent by stating on the witness stand that he "did not intend to injure anyone" was not believed by the jury, which found that he had acted maliciously and awarded Katko $20,000 in compensatory and $10,000 in punitive damages.

Conversely, when a five-year-old child pulled a lawn chair out from under a woman who was about to sit in it, the Supreme Court of Washington held that it was insufficient that the child's act was intentional and remanded the case to the trial judge to determine whether the child realized with a "substantial certainty" that the harmful contact would result (*Garrett v. Dailey*, 46 Wash. 2d 197, 279 P.2d 1091 [1955]). Liability was thus predicated on the knowledge and understanding of a five-year-old. (On remand, the trial court found that the child did in fact have such knowledge.)

malicious prosecution

When someone initiates or causes a groundless suit to be brought out of malice. To succeed in this claim, it is essential that the original suit be terminated in favor of the person later suing for malicious prosecution.

In addition to intent, a plaintiff must allege and prove all the other elements of the specific cause of action, as discussed earlier.

 *Alleged Invasion of Privacy by the Husband*

The husband installed a video camera and surreptitiously taped his wife's activities while she was in their bedroom alone. Can the wife hold the husband liable for invasion of privacy?

After answering the question, consider whether the following information would alter your answer:

- The husband had filed a petition for dissolution of marriage.
- The wife included the invasion of privacy claim in her answer to the petition.
- It was unclear whether the husband and wife were separated at the time of the videotaping.
- The videotaped material did not contain any offensive material.

See *In re* Marriage of Tigges, 758 N.W.2d 824 (Iowa 2008).

Negligence

The Industrial Revolution of the nineteenth century and the automobile of the twentieth both caused a marked increase in serious personal injuries. These injuries were caused by machines and the human beings that control them. Injury was usually accidental rather than intentional, so the traditional notions of intentional fault required elaboration.

A complete listing of the names of the causes of action in tort would be dominated by intentional torts, but the cases actually brought for personal injuries would be dominated by the single cause of action called *negligence.* Most people are injured accidentally and not intentionally. In negligence law, liability arises through a different notion of fault than intent. In a sense, negligence is simply culpable carelessness. Poor judgment, momentary inattention, and lack of foresight often result in injury. Negligence law sought and found a measure by which the failure to exercise due care could be categorized as fault and thereby incur liability.

The standard of care is embodied in the *reasonable man* test. Tradition uses the generic male for the standard, but today the test is more properly put as "what a reasonably prudent *person* would have done under the circumstances." Whether someone should be found at fault and held liable is measured by a standard of care based on reasonableness rather than subjective mental state or intent.

Negligence has four elements, as listed in Exhibit 10-4.

The breach of the duty establishes fault. Because negligence applies to the myriad injuries incurred daily through oversight and carelessness, it is not possible

EXHIBIT 10-4   ELEMENTS OF NEGLIGENCE

1. Duty (standard of care)
2. Breach of the duty (conduct falling below the standard of care)
3. Causation (the breach must be the cause of the injury)
4. Injury

to cover in the elements the precise circumstances that give rise to liability; they are simply too numerous. The reasonable person standard acknowledges that what may be prudent conduct in one situation may not be prudent in another. The test must be applied on a case-by-case basis, with the standard of care determined by the jury. The "reasonable man" (now usually called the "reasonable person") is a hypothetical person of ordinary understanding but prudent in conduct; individuals are not expected to exercise extraordinary care, nor are they excused by the fact that most people are often careless. It would undoubtedly be negligent not to fence in a swimming pool in a neighborhood full of small children but perhaps not imprudent not to do so on a country estate with no neighboring children; it is up to the jury to decide what is reasonable and prudent.

 *Golf Course Injury*

Sometimes a golfer inadvertently hits a golf shot that strikes another golfer. Does one golfer owe another golfer a duty of care such that the first golfer could be liable for unintentionally striking the second golfer with a golf shot?

After answering the question, consider whether the following information would alter your answer:

- The plaintiff golfer and the defendant golfer were in a golf threesome.
- The defendant golfer hit a "duck hook," which was a shot that veered sharply to the left at a great speed.
- The plaintiff golfer had proceeded along the side of the course in a golf cart to determine whether the preceding group of golfers were out of the way and assumed that the defendant golfer would not tee off before the plaintiff golfer returned to the tee.
- The plaintiff golfer was not watching the defendant golfer and did not realize that the defendant golfer was teeing off.

See Zeidman v. Fisher, 980 A.2d 637 (Pa. Super. Ct. 2009).

The standard of care for negligence may vary from the reasonable person standard. Thus, if a statutory standard fits the case, it usually serves as the standard of care. For example, if a motorist runs a stop sign and causes an accident, the breach of the standard of care is satisfied by a statute that requires a full stop at stop signs, so the jury need not question whether a reasonably prudent person stops at stop signs.

For professionals, the standard of care is measured by professional standards in the community in which the professional practices or by a national standard for specialists. It would hardly do for a jury to decide what a reasonably prudent person would do when performing brain surgery. At present, paralegals are not professionals in this legal sense, so negligence on their part ordinarily would result in a suit against the supervising attorney. Should a paralegal who has been certified as a legal assistant by NALA be subject to suit if the paralegal represents himself or herself as a "Certified Paralegal"? At present, many states are questioning whether paralegals should be licensed, which would presumably make them professionals and subject to suit for their negligent mistakes.

Contributory Negligence/Comparative Negligence

With the rise of negligence suits in the nineteenth century, the requirement of fault (breach of the standard of care) also gave rise to a defense based on fault. It did not seem just to allow recovery if the plaintiff shared some responsibility for causing the injury. A plaintiff's fault was called *contributory negligence* and constituted a complete defense to a suit for negligence. (It is an affirmative defense that has been replaced by *comparative negligence* in most states.) The courts soon realized that the result of using this doctrine was not always just or fair. In some cases a minor fault of the plaintiff would preclude recovery. Railroad workers, for example, often worked under dangerous conditions in which a moment's inadvertence could result in serious injury or death. It was not sufficient for the widow and children to prove that the employer had been responsible for the dangerous conditions; if the employee had not been careful, there could be no recovery.

workers' compensation

A statutory scheme whereby fixed awards are made for employment-related injuries. This commonly takes the form of state-regulated employers' insurance arrangements.

Legislatures responded to dangers in the workplace by establishing **workers' compensation**, and many courts and legislatures responded with comparative negligence for nonworkplace accidents. Under comparative negligence schemes, many of which are statutory, fault is *apportioned*; that is, if the plaintiff is negligent as well as the defendant, the plaintiff's award is reduced by the plaintiff's percentage of fault. Thus, if the jury, under the judge's instructions, determines that 80 percent of the fault rests with the defendant and 20 percent is the fault of the plaintiff, the plaintiff is entitled only to 80 percent of the amount of the injuries. If the jury values the plaintiff's injuries at $50,000, the plaintiff would receive $40,000. The percentages are arbitrary approximations, but the jury must estimate them if it allocates fault to both parties. Many states will not allow the plaintiff to recover if the jury assigns 50 percent or more of the fault to the plaintiff. Automobile accidents often involve injuries to both drivers, each of whom claims the other was at fault. The final award can differ greatly depending on whether the jurisdiction uses contributory negligence or comparative negligence ("pure" or modified).

In *Bjorndal*, the court does away with a jury instruction that had modified the standard of care to allow the plaintiff to recover even if the plaintiff was partly at fault. As the court noted, this jury instruction was no longer necessary with the abolition of contributory negligence.

Brenda Bjorndal, Petitioner on Review

v.

Jay Weitman, Respondent on Review

Supreme Court of Oregon, En Banc

(CC 031320; CA A131325; SC S054837)

184 P.3d 1115

Decided May 8, 2008.

In this personal injury action arising out of an automobile accident, we consider-and, having done so, reject-the use of the so-called "emergency instruction" in such cases. The trial court gave that jury instruction at defendant's request and over plaintiff's objection, and the jury returned a verdict in defendant's favor. Plaintiff appealed, arguing that the evidence did not establish an "emergency" that would support giving the instruction. . . . We allowed review and now hold that the emergency instruction, as used in ordinary vehicle negligence cases, is an inaccurate and confusing supplement to the instructions on the law of negligence and, therefore, should not be given. For that reason, we reverse the rulings of the Court of Appeals and the trial court and remand the case to the trial court for further proceedings.

Plaintiff was driving east on Highway 22 in Linn County and looking for her father, whose car had broken down along the highway. Defendant had been following plaintiff for approximately 20 minutes, and there was no evidence that defendant was following too closely during that time. Plaintiff then spotted her father ahead on the right side of the road. Defendant testified that he had watched plaintiff's father, who was waving his hands and gesturing, for two seconds and then, assuming "that there was some sort of emergency situation, a hazard, or something that we needed to be aware of and looked-I did glance to my left and I scanned the horizon [for about a second] to try and identify what this possible hazard or emergency was." Defendant testified that, when he returned his eyes to the road ahead of him, he noticed that plaintiff, who was driving a van, had rapidly decelerated or was in the process of decelerating. He estimated that plaintiff slowed from a speed of 50 miles per hour to 10 miles per hour within one second.

Defendant testified that he then applied his brakes and, seeing that there was no oncoming traffic, decided to steer to his left to pass plaintiff on her left. Plaintiff, however, had planned to turn left because she had been told that there was a snowpark on the left side of the highway where she could stop. As she slowed to make the left turn, she signaled and steered to the left. Defendant testified that he did not see plaintiff's left turn signal until after the van started to move to the left and at that point he was unable to avoid colliding with plaintiff's van.

Plaintiff brought this negligence action against defendant, seeking damages for her injuries and medical expenses arising out of the collision. The case was tried to a jury. Defendant requested, and the trial court gave, the "emergency instruction" as set forth in Oregon Uniform Civil Jury Instruction 20.08:

> "People who are suddenly placed in a position of peril through no negligence of their own, and who are compelled to act without opportunity for reflection, are not negligent if they make a choice as a reasonably careful person placed in such a position might make, even though they do not make the wisest choice." . . .

The reasons for the development of the emergency instruction can be understood by examining several cases where this court approved similar instructions. [Here the court reviewed several cases.] The cases just discussed suggest that the emergency instruction originated as a means to allow the jury to avoid the harsh result of finding that a defendant was negligent *per se* for violating a statute or ordinance, as in *Marshall*, or that a plaintiff was contributorily negligent and therefore barred from recovering damages against a negligent defendant, as in *Durnford*. In recent decades, courts in some states have abolished the emergency instruction because the tort doctrines that it was intended to ameliorate have themselves been changed. . . .

A person is negligent if the person fails to exercise reasonable care, a standard that "is measured by what a reasonable person of ordinary prudence would, or would not, do in the same or similar circumstances." *Woolston*. The emergency instruction, however, tells the jurors that, notwithstanding the instruction that a person must exercise reasonable care, if there was an emergency, they nevertheless may conclude that the person whose actions are at issue was "*not* negligent" (emphasis added), even if the person made a choice that is not the "wisest choice," as long as it was a choice a "reasonably careful person" in those circumstances "might" make. Jurors would understandably view that instruction as permitting them to find a defendant "not negligent," even when the defendant makes an "unwise" choice. To be sure, the reasonable care standard does not *always* require a defendant to make the "wisest choice." But neither does it mean that a defendant was "not negligent" simply because the defendant's "unwise choice" was made in the context of an emergency.

Given the wide range of factual settings in vehicle negligence cases, there certainly are circumstances in which a reasonable jury could conclude that any choice other than the "wisest choice" was *not* a reasonably prudent choice and therefore was negligent. The emergency instruction is erroneous because it introduces into the liability determination additional concepts that are not part of the ordinary negligence standard— whether the person had a "choice," whether the person made a "choice" that a reasonable person "might" make, and whether the person made the "wisest" choice or not. The addition of those new, otherwise-undefined concepts to the standard of reasonable care in light of all the circumstances injects a likely source of juror confusion as to the legal standard to be applied. . . .

Parties may of course introduce evidence, and may argue about, the "emergency" nature of the circumstances in which the parties acted and whether or not various "choices" of conduct, wise or not, were available. The *existence* of "emergency" circumstances in vehicle accident cases—sudden actions by other drivers, unexpected weather events, roadway hazards—is

indisputably appropriate for a jury to consider in determining whether a person has used reasonable care in attempting to avoid harming others. . . . But this court has never articulated the *legal* standard of negligence as turning on those considerations. Rather, the negligence standard focuses on whether a person acted with reasonable care to avoid harm to others, in light of all the circumstances, including any "emergency." Thus, the general negligence standard embodied in Uniform Civil Jury Instruction 20.02 encompasses any legitimate concerns about "emergency" circumstances, without introducing misleading concepts of the extent to which a "choice" available to the person was "unwise," "wise," "wiser," or "wisest." Moreover, the negligence instruction already refers to facts that may create an emergency situation when it speaks of the "dangers apparent or reasonably foreseeable when the events occurred" and the "circumstances" that are to be considered in determining whether a person used reasonable care. . . .

To summarize: the emergency instruction, at least as used in vehicle accident cases, misstates the law of negligence by introducing an inquiry respecting whether a person has made the "wisest choice," rather than focusing on whether the person used reasonable care, given all the circumstances. Because the instruction misstates the law, it should not be given. The trial court here erred in giving the emergency instruction.

Case Questions

1. How does the emergency instruction modify the defendant's duty?
2. What were the two older tort doctrines that led to development of the emergency instruction?

Strict Liability/Product Liability

The age of technology has confounded the concept of fault in tort. The American consumer acquires a bewildering assortment of machines, appliances, and pharmaceutical drugs as well as other products that pose unseen dangers. Manufacturers may exercise reasonable precautions to make their products safe and certainly do not intend to injure their customers, so it is difficult to assign fault under theories of negligence or intentional tort. The purchase of products creates a contractual relationship, but ordinary contract remedies do not contemplate compensation for personal injury.

Early in the twentieth century, judges were troubled by innocent victims of defective products who could not prove fault on the part of the producer. As America became a mighty industrial power, courts became less concerned about protecting business from ruinous lawsuits and more concerned about the hapless victims of their products. It did not seem just that a company could reap large profits from sales of its products without compensating those injured by them. A number of cases strained at the concept of fault to protect innocent parties, and in 1963 Justice Traynor of the California Supreme Court wrote the opinion, in *Greenman v. Yuba Power Products, Inc.,* 59 Cal. 2d 57, 377 P.2d 897, that announced the birth of product liability. Greenman had purchased a combination power tool for his home workshop that one day inexplicably ejected a piece of wood, striking him in the forehead. Justice Traynor reasoned that traditional requirements of proof of fault were no longer tenable and set the standard for the plaintiff in the case as follows:

> To establish the manufacturer's liability it was sufficient that plaintiff proved that he was injured while using the Shopsmith in a way it was intended to be used as a result of a defect in design and manufacture of which plaintiff was not aware that made the Shopsmith unsafe for its intended use . . .

Perhaps no case in the common law has had a more immediate and far-reaching effect on American law. The *Restatement of Torts* responded two years later with § 402A, which elaborated on the *Greenman* decision. Section 402A was adopted in some form by state after state in rapid succession. In a few short years, numerous cases served to refine the principles of product liability. Never has such a vast body of law so quickly fixed a cause of action so firmly in the law.

This was a revolution in tort law waiting to happen. Traynor could appeal to precedent in **implied warranty** theory, which held sellers responsible for the fitness for use of the products they sell. The consumer reasonably relied on the seller to deliver a product fit for use. Implied warranties were in addition to the express warranties given by the seller. The advent of the automobile made implied warranties important because the purchaser was rarely in a position to determine whether the product was properly designed or assembled.

The adoption of the cause of action for product liability was justified on policy grounds, which were stated succinctly by Judge Jacobson in a concurring opinion in *Lechuga, Inc. v. Montgomery,* 12 Ariz. App. 32, 467 P.2d 256:

> It is apparent from a reading of the Restatement, and the leading cases on this subject, that the doctrine of **strict liability** has evolved to place liability on the party primarily responsible for the injury occurring, that is, the manufacturer of the defective product. This, as Justice Traynor stated in his concurring opinion in *Escola v. Coca Cola Bottling Co. of Fresno,* 24 Cal. 2d 453, 150 P.2d 436 (1944), is based on reasons of public policy: "If public policy demands that a manufacturer of goods be responsible for their quality regardless of negligence there is no reason not to fix that responsibility openly." 150 P.2d, at 441.

These public policy considerations have been variously enumerated as follows:

1. The manufacturer can anticipate some hazards and guard against their recurrence, which the consumer cannot do. . . .

implied warranty

A promise imposed by law (e.g., an implied warranty of fitness for use or consumption), as distinguished from an express warranty stated in a contract.

strict liability

A principle, largely applied to *product liability,* which creates liability without proof of fault (e.g., liability for a "dangerously defective product"); virtually interchangeable with *absolute liability.*

2. The cost of injury may be overwhelming to the person injured while the risk of injury can be insured by the manufacturer and be distributed among the public as a cost of doing business. . . .

3. It is in the public interest to discourage the marketing of defective products. . . .

4. It is in the public interest to place responsibility for [the product] reaching the market. . . .

5. That this responsibility should also be placed upon the retailer and wholesaler of the defective product in order that they may act as the conduit through which liability may flow to reach the manufacturer, where ultimate responsibility lies. . . .

6. That because of the complexity of present day manufacturing processes and their secretiveness, the ability to prove negligent conduct by the injured plaintiff is almost impossible. . . .

7. That the consumer does not have the ability to investigate for himself the soundness of the product. . . .

8. That this consumer's vigilance has been lulled by advertising, marketing devices and trademarks. . . .

Inherent in these policy considerations is not the nature of the transaction by which the consumer obtained possession of the defective product but rather the character of the defect itself, that is, one occurring in the manufacturing process and the unavailability of an adequate remedy on behalf of the injured plaintiff.

The theory in products liability is that the commercial manufacturer of a product sold to the public should be strictly liable for the product failure. The situation becomes slightly more complicated where a commercial manufacturer supplies a component that another commercial manufacturer incorporates in a product sold to consumers. In *Sylvan*, the product failed because the component was faulty. The second manufacturer dealt with the consumers, replaced or repaired the product at a substantial cost, and then sued the first manufacturer for costs incurred due to the defective component.

Sylvan R. Shemitz Designs, Inc.

v.

Newark Corporation, et al.

Supreme Court of Connecticut

No. 17998

967 A.2d 1188

Decided April 21, 2009.

Under . . . the Connecticut Product Liability Act (act)[,] commercial losses, in contrast to damage to property, are not recoverable in a product liability action as between commercial parties. In this case, Elliptipar, Inc. (Elliptipar), a division of the plaintiff company, Sylvan R. Shemitz Designs, Inc. (plaintiff), sold to its customers a product containing a defective part that had been manufactured by the defendant General Electric Company (General Electric) and the defendant Regal-Beloit Corporation (Regal). Thereafter, the plaintiff incurred costs for replacing the part and otherwise repairing damage to its product that had been caused by the defective part. The issue presented by this appeal is whether, under the act, those costs constitute damage to property and, therefore, are recoverable by the plaintiff against the defendants, or whether the costs represent unrecoverable commercial losses. We conclude, contrary to the determination of the trial court, that the costs constitute damage to property that the plaintiff may recover. . . .

The plaintiff is a manufacturer of commercial and residential lighting fixtures. For many years, one of its divisions, Elliptipar, purchased capacitor boots (boots), an insulation product that is used in lighting fixtures, from Newark Corporation, a distributor of such products. The boots were manufactured by General Electric until 2004, when Regal acquired the manufacturing operation of General Electric. Since that time, Regal has manufactured the boots. Elliptipar used those boots in the manufacture of the lighting fixtures that it sold to its customers.

In approximately July, 2004, Elliptipar began receiving reports from its customers that lighting fixtures containing the boots were failing, often within two weeks of the time that the fixtures had been placed in operation. Elliptipar conducted an investigation and determined that the failure of the lighting fixtures was caused by a defect in the boots that resulted in arcing and ignition. In response to the problem, Elliptipar repaired and, when necessary, replaced the lighting fixtures that had been damaged by the boots. Elliptipar also replaced the boots in those fixtures that had been sold but not yet damaged. . . .

We . . . note, preliminarily, that the defendants do not dispute that the damages that the plaintiff seeks to recover in connection with its product liability claim represent the costs that the plaintiff actually incurred in remedying the damage to the lighting fixtures that had been caused by the defective boots. In other words, the defendants do not contend that the damages that the plaintiff seeks are for consequential economic loss such as lost profits, loss of commercial opportunities or damage to business reputation. The defendants' sole contention is that the term "damage to property" in § 52-572m(d) pertains only to property that is owned by the party seeking to recover under the act. . . .

Our disagreement with the statutory interpretation urged by the defendants and adopted by the trial court stems from the fact, first, that the language of the act imposes no express requirement that a claimant own the property that has been damaged in order to bring an action seeking compensation for damage to that property. Under General Statutes § 52-572n(a),

a product liability action may be brought only for "harm caused by a product." Although "harm" is defined in General Statutes § 52-572m(d) as "damage to property, including the product itself, and personal injuries including wrongful death," as between commercial parties, "harm" does not include "commercial loss" caused by a product. General Statutes § 52-572n(c). The act, however, contains no definition of the term "commercial loss." Thus, under the construction advocated by the defendants, we would be required to read into the term a prohibition against recovery for economic losses suffered by a claimant resulting from damage to property that the claimant no longer owns. . . .

In addition, as the plaintiff notes, the act expressly contemplates and provides for the allocation of liability along a product's chain of distribution. . . . We doubt that the legislature intended for the term "commercial loss" in § 52-572m(d) to encompass costs incurred by a commercial party in remedying property damage caused by a defective product because such an interpretation of the act contravenes these fundamental precepts of statutory construction.

We recognize that there is a split of authority in the Superior Court as to whether the act permits claims for contribution and indemnification as between commercial parties for costs incurred in repairing damage to property otherwise covered by the act. . . . [W]e find persuasive and adopt the view of the trial court cases that have determined that the term "commercial loss" does not encompass costs incurred by a commercial party in repairing or replacing a defective product, or in repairing property damage caused by a defective product.

Furthermore, although there is little legislative history surrounding the 1984 amendment to the act that added the language prohibiting the recovery of commercial loss[,] what little there is strongly suggests that the term "commercial loss" does not encompass the type of damages that the plaintiff seeks in the present case. . . .

Finally, our construction of the term "commercial loss" "is consistent with the public policy rationales supporting the imposition of strict products liability"; *Potter*; which include, among others, "that the seller, by marketing his product for use and consumption, has undertaken and assumed a special responsibility toward any member of the consuming public who may be injured by it . . . [and] that the public has the right to and does expect, in the case of products which it needs and for which it is forced to rely [on] the seller, that reputable sellers will stand behind their goods. . . ." Consistent with these policies, the plaintiff in the present case stood behind the light fixtures that it sold to its customers and voluntarily repaired or replaced the fixtures that had been damaged by the boots, thus relieving the customers of the trouble and expense of commencing and prosecuting an action to recover damages. We agree with the plaintiff that the trial court's determination that the damages in the pres-

ent case represent a nonrecoverable commercial loss contravenes not only the express provisions of the act that permit and promote the allocation of liability along a product's chain of distribution to the ultimate responsible party but, also, the act's purpose of engendering responsible business practices.

Case Questions

1. What is consequential economic loss?
2. On what basis did the defendant argue that it should not be held liable?

absolute liability

Liability without fault or negligence; often used interchangeably with *strict liability*, though many would contend that there is a difference.

In addition to implied warranty as a ground for product liability, the principle of **absolute liability** for extrahazardous activities furnished precedent. Under this principle, parties engaged in especially dangerous activities, such as the use of explosives, were held liable regardless of fault. The policy grounds were similar. It appeared to the courts unjust that innocent parties could be injured through the direct cause of another's activities and be left without a remedy simply because those engaged in the activities had exercised due care.

Behind liability for dangerously defective products and extrahazardous activities lies a foreseeability issue. Clearly, engaging in activities that present a significant risk to the public makes injury foreseeable in a general sense, even if neither the victim nor the manner of occurrence is precisely foreseeable. Likewise, when a manufacturer makes products that are potentially dangerous, the risk of injury has a degree of foreseeability. The law now holds that those who incur risks should bear the cost of the injuries that result. Foreseeability lurks everywhere in tort law. Because of the nature of lawsuits, the foreseeability issue always arises from hindsight—what may seem foreseeable in looking back on the course of events may not have been even remotely foreseen at the beginning. The foreseeability issue is both argued and ignored, but further study is beyond the scope of our present discussion.

DAMAGES

A person who loses an arm, a leg, or an eye or is left paraplegic suffers a loss of lifestyle as well. The courts have long considered a reduction in earning potential to be recoverable, but recently attorneys have argued, sometimes successfully, that injured parties should collect for "hedonic" losses, meaning essentially a decrease in enjoyment of life. Imagine an artist made blind by another's wrongful conduct. The artist may lose not only a career and earnings but also much of the meaning and enjoyment of life. The next few years will tell how far courts are willing to go in recognizing such losses as compensable.

Compensatory Damages

Compensatory damages are generally easy to understand when they consist of provable concrete economic losses, such as medical expenses, property damage, loss of work, and so on. Compensation is also allowed for pain and suffering, which are real injuries even though difficult to value. In recent years, courts of many states have allowed compensation for **hedonic losses**, roughly speaking, losses of the pleasure of living. How is this measured, and how can someone qualify as an expert in determining that value?

Punitive (or Exemplary) Damages for Intentional Tort

If compensatory damages aim at returning the plaintiff to the condition enjoyed before the wrongful injury by way of monetary compensation, punitive damages are reserved to punish the outrageous conduct of the defendant. They have nothing to do with compensation and are a windfall to the plaintiff (after paying 30 or 40 percent of the award to the plaintiff's attorney, the windfall is likely to be erased). Punitive damages are relative to the wealth of the defendant. While $10,000 was an onerous amount for Briney, the Iowa farmer discussed earlier in this chapter, Ford Motor Co. was assessed many millions when two women burned to death in a Ford Pinto as a result of a defect known to the company. Asking for punitive damages may allow the plaintiff to present evidence of defendant's worth, which can influence the jury.

Because punitive damages go beyond compensation in order to punish outrageous conduct and deter similar conduct, the amount of punitive damages may greatly exceed the award of compensatory damages. The richer the defendant, the greater the award needed to punish.

The following case, *Biomet v. Finnegan*, is the second of two cases involving Biomet. In the first case, Biomet was found liable at trial for more than $7 million in compensatory damages and $20 million in punitive damages. A major portion of the award was for Biomet's alleged infringement of a patent. The attorney made the decision to appeal the patent infringement decision but not to appeal the punitive damages award. The decision not to appeal the punitive damages award was based on the combination of *BMW v. Gore* (a then-recent United States Supreme Court decision on punitive damages) and Biomet's conduct, which the jury found to be "particularly reprehensible." On appeal, the attorney was successful in having the patent infringement decision reversed. After the case was remanded, the trial court lowered the compensatory damages liability to $520 but did nothing with the $20 million punitive damages award because punitive damages had not been at issue on appeal.

Biomet was understandably upset with still being liable for millions of dollars in punitive damages, so it sued the attorney for malpractice in *Biomet v. Finnegan*. The question before the court in the legal malpractice case was whether an attorney may be held liable by a former client when the attorney made a tactical decision that made sense at the time but was very wrong in light of a later (and severe) reduction in the client's liability for compensatory damages.

compensatory damages
Awarded to an injured party to make her whole: in tort, damages to compensate for all injuries, and, in contract, to put the nonbreaching party in the position he would have been in if the contract had been performed. Also referred to as actual damages.

hedonic losses (damages)
Money awarded in some lawsuits for loss of the ability to enjoy life's pleasures; a recent and controversial basis for awarding damages.

Biomet Inc., Appellant

v.

Finnegan Henderson LLP, Appellee

District of Columbia Court of Appeals

No. 07-CV-813

967 A.2d 662

Decided March 19, 2009.

Biomet Inc. ("Biomet") appeals from the grant of summary judgment in favor of Finnegan Henderson LLP ("Finnegan") by the trial court. Below, the trial court found that, as a matter of law, Finnegan could not be held liable for legal malpractice in this case and granted summary judgment. . . .

This case involves a legal malpractice claim brought by Biomet, a manufacturer of orthopedic devices, against Finnegan, a law firm, alleging that Finnegan failed to preserve a constitutional challenge to excessive punitive damages resulting in waiver of the issue. Briefly, the relevant facts include the following. In 1991, Dr. Raymond Tronzo brought a suit against Biomet in the United States District Court for the Southern District of Florida alleging that Biomet infringed and misused his patent and other confidential information. In 1996, following a jury verdict, the district court awarded $7,134,000 in compensatory damages and $20 million in punitive damages against Biomet for patent infringement, fraud, and violation of a confidential relationship. The district court also enjoined Biomet from manufacturing the device that used the infringed patent. Finnegan was hired by Biomet to assist with the post-trial motions in the district court and to handle Biomet's appeal to the Federal Circuit, if necessary.

After the district court rejected Biomet's post-trial motions for relief, Finnegan handled Biomet's appeal to the Federal Circuit challenging the district court's ruling that the plaintiff had presented sufficient evidence to support a jury verdict of patent infringement. Finnegan did not appeal the punitive damage award as unconstitutional at that time because the ratio of punitive to compensatory damages after the initial trial was only 3:1, and the jury had found Biomet's conduct to be particularly reprehensible[,] making such an argument

extremely difficult. On appeal, Finnegan successfully obtained reversal of the patent infringement finding and the injunction. The Federal Circuit then remanded the case for recalculation of damages in light of its ruling.

On remand from the Federal Circuit, the district court determined that Biomet was liable for only $520 in compensatory damages. Following the significant reduction in the compensatory damages, Finnegan moved for a reduction of the $20 million punitive damage award in light of the Supreme Court's ruling in *BMW v. Gore*, which held that excessive punitive damages can violate constitutional due process. The district court agreed that the new 38,000:1 ratio of punitive to compensatory damages was unconstitutionally excessive and reduced the punitive damages to $52,000. On appeal . . . , the Federal Circuit held that because punitive damages were not challenged in the initial appeal, Biomet had waived its right to seek relief from the punitive damage award while the case was on remand. Therefore, the Federal Circuit reinstated the $20 million punitive damage award. . . .

Under District of Columbia law, to prevail on a claim of legal malpractice, a plaintiff must establish the applicable standard of care, a breach of that standard, and a causal relationship between the violation and the harm complained of. . . . The issue before us is whether Finnegan could be found to have breached its duty of care to Biomet by failing to include a constitutional challenge to punitive damages in its initial appeal to the Federal Circuit. . . .

It has long been recognized that an attorney is not liable for mistakes made in the honest exercise of professional judgment. . . . Today, that same basic proposition is often recognized as professional judgment immunity or judgmental immunity. . . . Essentially, the judgmental immunity doctrine provides that an informed professional judgment made with reasonable care and skill cannot be the basis of a legal malpractice claim. . . .

In order to find that the trial court properly granted summary judgment for Finnegan based on judgmental immunity, we must be satisfied that (1) the alleged error is one of professional judgment, and (2) the attorney exercised reasonable care in making his or her judgment. Neither party disputes the fact that

Finnegan's decision about how to structure the initial appeal was an exercise of professional judgment. . . .

Because Finnegan's decision not to challenge the punitive damage award as unconstitutional in the initial appeal was an exercise of professional judgment, we now must determine whether that professional judgment was reasonable at the time it was made, not whether a different strategy may have resulted in a more favorable judgment. . . .

The Supreme Court's decision in *BMW*, the first case where the Court found punitive damages to be unconstitutionally excessive, was issued a year before Finnegan filed the initial appeal on behalf of Biomet. As the Court's latest word on the issue of unconstitutionally excessive punitive damages, the *BMW* opinion provided litigants the best guidance on the criteria used to evaluate the excessiveness of punitive damage awards, and the three primary considerations for evaluating the excessiveness of punitive damages advanced in *BMW* were reprehensibility, ratio, and criminal and civil sanctions for comparable misconduct. . . . In sum, a fair reading of *BMW* suggests that while a high ratio of punitive to compensatory damages could be unconstitutionally excessive, a low ratio would not be, and that, a ratio of 10:1 punitive to compensatory damages is not excessive. . . .

We are satisfied Finnegan's decision not to initially appeal punitive damages was a reasoned exercise of informed judgment that cannot under any circumstances be found to be negligent. We agree with the trial court that, prior to the Federal Circuit's ruling, whether the constitutionality of the punitive damage award could be raised for the first time following a reduction in compensatory damages occasioned by a favorable appeal was a debatable point of unsettled law. Based on relevant Supreme Court precedent, it was reasonable for Finnegan to believe that, because of the original, low 3:1 ratio of punitive to compensatory damages awarded by the judge after the trial and the jury's finding of Biomet's reprehensible conduct, Biomet did not have a viable constitutional challenge

to the punitive damage award at the time of the initial appeal. Further, it was reasonable for Finnegan to conclude that, because the compensatory damages could be reduced following a favorable appeal, a challenge to excessive punitive damages in Biomet's case was contingent upon a reduction in the compensatory damages and creation of a higher damages ratio, and that such a contingent claim was "not ripe for adjudication" in the initial appeal. *Texas*. Granted, the Federal Circuit disagreed with Finnegan's arguments about contingency and ripeness. But, prior to the Federal Circuit's ruling, reasonable attorneys, including, as the trial court noted, a district court judge and a number of past presidents of the Federal Circuit Bar Association, agreed with Finnegan that the constitutionality of the punitive damage award was properly raised for the first time on remand despite the Federal Circuit's mandate.

Because there was a substantial question, as to whether a constitutional challenge to punitive damages had to be raised during an initial appeal when the punitive damage award at that time was not unconstitutionally excessive when compared with the compensatory damage award, and because there was no clear precedent one way or the other prior to the Federal Circuit's opinion in the underlying case, and thus, reasonable attorneys could disagree, we are satisfied that, as a matter of law, there was no legal malpractice in this case.

Therefore, for the foregoing reasons, we affirm the trial court's grant of summary judgment in favor of Appellee.

Case Questions

1. What is professional judgment immunity?
2. What are the two issues the court considered in determining whether professional judgment immunity was a valid defense?
3. What do you think led to the development of professional judgment immunity?
4. Should professional judgment immunity have been applied in this case?

SUMMARY

Tort has traditionally been defined as "a private wrong not arising out of contract." This definition distinguishes between public wrongs, which are classified as crimes, and private wrongs, which are wrongful conduct causing injury to a private party. The public prosecutor is responsible for bringing actions in criminal cases; private parties bring actions on their own behalf to redress private wrongs. The definition also distinguishes between torts and contract causes of action. In contract, the legal obligations are created by mutual agreement of the parties; the law of contracts simply establishes the requisites for enforcement. In tort law, obligations are imposed by law. Tort law establishes protected private interests relating to person, property, reputation, and so on that are not premised on a contractual relationship, though one may exist (e.g., doctor–patient in medical malpractice).

There are numerous causes of action in tort, each having elements, each of which must be present for the court to accept a lawsuit based on a specific cause of action. However, tort law is a continually evolving field. New causes of action arise with some regularity, and courts exercise flexibility in allowing cases that do not fit into textbook definitions if conduct is clearly wrongful and injury is apparent.

Many factors influence the course of tort law independent of the interest sought to be protected. New law cannot be made by the courts unless disputes are brought, yet the economics of litigation usually influence which suits may be economically rewarding for a plaintiff.

Among the factors facilitating suit is the doctrine of *respondeat superior*, which holds an employer liable for the wrongful acts of an employee, thus making suits feasible when the wrongdoer/employee has limited funds and the employer has substantial resources. Similarly, the widespread use of insurance presents the opportunity to collect full compensation for injuries sustained, which might not be possible if the defendant were uninsured and without assets.

In personal injury cases, customary practice includes the use of contingency-fee arrangements whereby attorneys receive as their compensation a percentage of the settlement or award at the termination of the case. A great many cases could not be brought if the injured party were required to provide compensation to a lawyer as the case progressed.

Although these factors address practical questions, they affect the development of tort law, as certain sorts of cases are frequently pursued while others remain impractical.

Traditionally, the basis for requiring a defendant to compensate an injured plaintiff was fault fixed on the defendant for a wrongful act. The degree of fault required for a particular tort distinguishes between major categories of tort. The common element of intentional torts is an intentional act, whereas in negligence the standard is not what the defendant intended but the failure to act in a reasonable and prudent manner, the so-called reasonable man or reasonable person standard.

The relatively new field of product liability establishes liability without the necessity of proving fault. Manufacturers, in particular, are held liable for distributing dangerously defective products despite a lack of intent to harm or lack of care in production. Although product liability has developed primarily over the past three decades, its roots can be found in much older theories of implied warranty and absolute liability for extrahazardous activities.

An important aspect of tort law is damages, or monetary compensation. Any determination of the amount of compensation depends on what can be included, but the object is to put the injured party in the position occupied before the wrongdoing occurred, that is, compensation for the difference in the plaintiff's life that the injury imposed. In some cases, punitive damages may be available to punish the wrongdoer. These go beyond actual compensation and require malicious or outrageous conduct on the part of the defendant.

KEY TERMS

absolute liability	hedonic losses (damages)	slander
assault	implied warranty	strict liability
assumption of risk	insurance	tortfeasor
battery	intentional infliction of	torts
compensatory damages	mental distress	workers' compensation
contingency fees	intentional torts	wrongful interference with
defamation	malicious prosecution	contractual relations
enterprise liability	*respondeat superior*	

CHAPTER REVIEW QUESTIONS

1. How are duties created in tort, as opposed to contract?
2. Why is it not practical to catalog the causes of action in tort?
3. When a person is injured by the negligence of an employee, it is sometimes possible to sue the employer under what principle?
4. Why does the custom of contingency fees encourage lawsuits?
5. What are the three major categories of tort?
6. What are the elements of negligence?
7. What is the difference between criminal battery and civil battery?
8. What is the difference between contributory and comparative negligence?
9. What are *hedonic losses*?
10. Punitive damages are most commonly available for which category of tort?

CRITICAL THINKING QUESTIONS

1. Because punitive damages are by definition not compensatory, should they not be awarded to the state rather than to the injured party?
2. Does tort law (or practice) need reform?

CYBER EXERCISE

Opinions of the United States District Courts are accessible at a number of websites, including the Google Scholar website, http://scholar.google.com/. The United States District Court for the Southern District of New York decided *Smith ex rel. Smith v. Islamic Emirate of Afghanistan*, 262 F. Supp. 2d 217 (S.D.N.Y. 2003) in May of 2003, (docket number 01 CIV. 10132[HB]). Locate the case and answer the following questions concerning the case:

a. Who brought this lawsuit and who were the defendants?
b. What is required to recover treble damages under the Antiterrorism Act of 1991?
c. What level of proof is needed to obtain a default judgment against a foreign state under the Foreign Sovereign Immunities Act?

  d. Did the plaintiffs meet the requisite level of proof?

  e. What are solatium damages?

  f. What amounts of damages did the judge award the plaintiffs?

SCENARIO

Northeastern Printing Corporation of Worcester, Massachusetts, was remodeling its old plant and hired Berkshire-Worcester Electric to rewire part of the plant for a computer laboratory. Berkshire assigned two of its electricians, Fitzgerald and Saltonstall, to complete the work. In the course of rewiring, the electricians drilled holes in the existing countertops, walls, and ceiling. Unbeknownst to them, the countertops contained asbestos fibers. Although the laboratory manager knew of this, he did not warn the workmen of it until they were almost finished and had not used protective gear. It is undisputed that the workers inhaled some dust containing asbestos fibers, although the extent of exposure could not be established. It is also undisputed that the inhalation of asbestos fibers can lead to potentially lethal lung cancer. Expert witnesses testified that the likelihood of Fitzgerald and Saltonstall getting cancer from the asbestos was about 1 in 100 and would probably not occur, if at all, for another 20 years (both were 35 years old).

Some 18 months later, Fitzgerald and Saltonstall were examined by Dr. Nathaniel Hawthorne, to whom they had been referred by their attorney. Although Dr. Hawthorne concluded that neither had any asbestos-related disease, they sued Northeastern Printing for mental anguish damages caused by its having negligently exposed them to asbestos fibers.

Dr. Hawthorne testified that the two workmen had been injured by their exposure to asbestos and inhalation of asbestos fibers at the Northeastern Printing lab. He estimated that the chances of their developing a disease as a "high possibility" but not a probability.

Dr. Sigmund Jung, a noted psychiatrist, testified that the men were suffering serious mental distress due to fear of acquiring serious disease from the inhalation of asbestos fibers.

The trial court granted summary judgment in favor of Northeastern Printing on the ground that Fitzgerald and Saltonstall had not suffered any injury for which they could recover mental anguish damages. (Northeastern Printing argued that the plaintiffs' claims for fear of the mere possibility of developing some disease in the future amounted to nothing more than negligent infliction of emotional distress, for which they could not recover. The plaintiffs responded that their inhalation of asbestos fibers was a real, physical injury that could eventually lead to disease and that they were entitled to be compensated for their anxiety over that eventuality.)

The case is now on appeal to the court of appeals.

1. Make the argument appealing the summary judgment for plaintiff-appellants, Fitzgerald and Saltonstall.

2. Counter those arguments on behalf of Northeastern Printing.

3. How would you find if you were the court of appeals judge? Which argument is most compelling?

CHAPTER 11
CONTRACTS AND COMMERCIAL LAW

CHAPTER OUTLINE

INTRODUCTION

There are two fundamental—and conflicting—conceptions of contractual obligations. The earlier, pre–nineteenth-century conception embodied equitable principles, emphasizing fairness along with concepts of property, and relying especially on transfer of title. The nineteenth century gave rise to the modern law of contracts, in which the obligations of contracts were cast in the light of the agreement itself, the bargain relationship, and the intent (will) of the parties.

    The title theory of exchange works well for the simultaneous exchange of things of fixed value, as when one pays for groceries at the supermarket. The will theory is

executory contract

A contract that has not yet been fully performed; one that has been fully performed is an *executed* contract.

more effective for **executory contracts**, that is, contracts relying on promises of future performance. For example, if a food processor contracts with farmers to buy crops for delivery at a fixed price in the future, principles of transfer of property rights at the making of the contract prove very awkward, whereas an examination of the bargain and the intent of the parties usually provides a basis for the enforcement of promises. The will theory is far more suitable for merchants and manufacturers in a commercial society and was gradually adopted by nineteenth-century courts, which viewed the encouragement of commerce and manufacturing as an important instrument of national growth.

Mechanical adherence to the will theory, however, encourages ruthless competition, so many of the adjustments to contract law in the twentieth century were designed to ensure fairness in the market and protection against unfair exploitation. Equitable concepts of fairness are used by the courts to prevent the excesses of the unscrupulous. In addition, legislatures have been active in passing laws, such as recent consumer-oriented legislation, to protect a vulnerable public. For example, many consumer contracts now include a three-day grace period during which a purchaser can disavow a contract, as a protection against high-pressure salespersons.

CONTRACT LAW IN PRACTICE

Most contract obligations are discharged by performance of the parties according to the terms of the agreement. When full performance is not feasible, the parties usually compromise their differences without recourse to law or litigation. Except for the specialist in commercial litigation, lawyer and paralegal alike are most often concerned with making rather than breaking contracts. Most of their work consists of aiding in contract negotiation and drafting contracts. Precision and clarity of language are the skills most needed for drafting and should be taught as part of a legal writing course (but often are not).

It may appear that we devote an inordinate amount of space in this chapter to contract formation and the conflicting principles that surround it. Although the approach here may seem unduly theoretical in a text for practitioners, the object is to avoid the morass of confusion presented by comprehensive contract texts and the omissions and simplifications of texts on business law.

DEFINITION

Like so many legal concepts, *contract* is not easily defined. There is a difference between tort and contract in that for contracts obligations are determined from the mutual agreements of the parties as opposed to obligations imposed by the law of torts. Even this distinction becomes seriously blurred when a court imposes terms or conditions on parties that they never bargained for and never agreed to. Tort and contract often overlap.

The important feature of contract law is not the contract itself but rather the contractual relations it creates, and it is the regulation of relationships that is the subject of this chapter. If a court declares a contract void because one of the parties was coerced into agreement, it is saying something not about the nature of contracts but about the nature of contractual relationships. With this caveat in mind, let us look at some definitions of *contract*.

A contract is a promise or set of promises for the breach of which the law gives a remedy, or the performance of which the law in some way recognizes as a duty.

Restatement (Second) of Contracts § 1 (1981).

"Contract" means the total legal obligation which results from the parties' agreement as affected by this Act and any other applicable rules of law.

Uniform Commercial Code (UCC) § 1–201(11).

The *Restatement* takes the traditional view of contract as an exchange of promises (e.g., "I promise to pay you $10,000 if you promise to give me title to your automobile") that the law recognizes as enforceable. The UCC avoids promissory language and describes a contract as an enforceable agreement. At any rate, it is clear that individuals may make promises or agreements, some of which are legally enforceable and are called *contracts.*

The *Restatement* definition of contract reflects the will theory mentioned previously, which is henceforth referred to as the *classical* approach to contracts, reflecting developments in contracts arena in the nineteenth and early twentieth centuries. It comprises what most legal practitioners need to know about contracts (along with the UCC) in order to draft contracts. Classical contract theory treats the essentials of contract formation in terms of the discrete elements necessary to make a valid contract namely offer, acceptance, and consideration. It attempts to treat contract law as logical, precise, and self-contained.

Unfortunately, when the promises made at the formation stage are not fulfilled, issues of fairness and morality arise that are not so neatly resolved. A body of law that conflicts with classical theory has evolved to deal with contractual relations. This approach might be called the *moral* or *reliance theory* and is embodied in the somewhat obscure language of § 90 of the first *Restatement:*

A promise which the promisor should reasonably expect to induce action or forbearance of a definite and substantial character on the part of the promisee and which does induce such action or forbearance is binding if injustice can be avoided only by enforcement of the promise.

In many cases, this principle allows the court to weigh the fairness of enforcement or nonenforcement of contract claims. Although theories of reliance and moral obligation may be of little significance in drafting contracts, they are important once a contract dispute arises. Failure to appreciate that there are two competing theories of contract inevitably leads to confusion. The classical model will be addressed along with the issue of contract formation, and the reliance model will be introduced in connection with breach of contract and contract remedies.

CONTRACT FORMATION: THE CLASSICAL MODEL

The requirements of contract formation established in the nineteenth century cast the bargain relationship in idealized form. Parties to contracts were seen as individuals negotiating from equal positions of power, freely arriving at a "meeting of the minds," in which the agreement that constituted the contract was complete and its subject matter and terms were understood by both parties. When such was the case, if one of the parties failed to fulfill contractual promises, it would be necessary only for the court to apply the appropriate remedy for the injured party. Under this scheme, the court inquired into whether the elements of offer, acceptance, and consideration were present; it then interpreted the terms of the contract.

Offer

offer

A proposal; the first of the three requirements of traditional contract formation: *offer, acceptance,* and *consideration.*

Contract negotiations typically begin with an **offer**; the party making the offer is the *offeror.* The contract is not complete until an offer has been accepted by an *offeree.* The elements of an offer are set forth in Exhibit 11-1. The failure of any of the requisites of an offer may nullify contract formation.

What appears to be an offer may fail because it lacks intent on the part of the offeror. Offers are often distinguished from invitations to negotiate or even solicitations for offers. "No reasonable offer refused," "Would you go as high as $1,000?," or "I might sell it for as little as $500" are illusory offers in this category. The circumstances of the offer may also indicate that intent is lacking, as when the offer is made in jest, anger, or intoxication ("I'd sell that money-sucking car for two cents!"). The offeror's post hoc claim that a serious offer was not intended is not sufficient to avoid the contract; the test is whether a reasonable person would conclude from the circumstances that a serious offer had been made.

The offer may be made in terms so indefinite as to render the contract unenforceable; in such a situation, it is usually found that no meeting of the minds was present. Indefiniteness of price, for example, is usually fatal ("Just pay me a fair price." [The UCC takes exception to the indefinite-price rule in the sale of goods when certain conditions are met; *see* UCC § 2–305.])

A valid and intended communication must be made to the offeree. The classic example in this category is the offer of a reward. Someone not aware of an offer of a reward who returns a lost dog is not legally entitled to the reward.

acceptance

In contract law, the final act in concluding negotiations, when an offeree accepts all the terms of the offer.

Acceptance

An offer does not bind the offeror until it is accepted by the offeree. Prior to **acceptance**, the offeror may revoke the offer, so acceptance subsequent to revocation does not bind the offeror. The elements of acceptance are set forth in Exhibit 11-2.

EXHIBIT 11-1 ELEMENTS OF AN OFFER

An offer requires:

1. Intent to make an offer on the part of the offeror
2. Definite terms
3. Communication to the offeree

EXHIBIT 11-2   Elements of Acceptance

Acceptance requires:

1. Communication to the offeror
2. Acceptance of the terms of the offer

Because a valid acceptance creates a contract, it is essential that the acceptance be communicated to the offeror. Acceptance has traditionally been classified in two forms:

1. Acceptance by a return promise ("I will pay the $4,000 you are asking for your car")

2. Acceptance by performance required by the offer (acceptance of the offer of a reward for lost property is made by returning the property, not by promising to return the property)

When an offer calls for a return promise, it is called a **bilateral contract**. When the offer calls for acceptance in terms of performance, it is called a **unilateral contract**. Because most contracts are bilateral, it is important for the offeror who insists on performance (rather than a promise to perform) to make this condition quite clear. To "I will pay you $500 to clear my lot by Thursday, October 20" should be added "If you cannot finish by the end of Thursday, do not undertake the job because I will not pay."

The offeror is *master of the offer* and may set specific terms or manner of acceptance. When the offer is silent as to the manner of acceptance, the law has developed a complex set of rules governing the communication of acceptance, to which the UCC has made exceptions with regard to sales of goods.

A valid acceptance requires that the offeree agree to the specific terms of the offer. This is the so-called *mirror-image rule,* which has been changed drastically for sales of goods covered by the UCC. If the offeree attempts to change the terms of the offer, the attempted acceptance will be treated as a counteroffer rather than an acceptance, and the offeror and offeree change places. If the offeror offers to sell "my first edition of *Moby Dick* for $500," offeree's response of "I'll pay $400" is a counteroffer rather than an acceptance, and the purchaser has become the offeror and the owner the offeree ("I accept your offer of $400" would constitute acceptance and create a contract). Similarly, "I will pay $500 if you furnish a certificate of authenticity" is a counteroffer because it has added a term not present in the original offer.

The meeting-of-the-minds/mirror-image formula is technically simple, but transactions in the real world often defy its application. For example, in something as simple as the first-edition sale, when the offeree appears with the personal check for $500, the offeror may insist on cash or a cashier's check. When they agreed on $500, did this mean "cash"? Can the offeror insist on cash? Does the offer to clear land "by" Thursday mean "before" Thursday (midnight Wednesday) or "on" Thursday (before Friday)? An apparent meeting of the minds rarely includes every last detail of performance,

bilateral contract

A contract accepted by a return promise. It is an exchange of promises, supported by consideration. Compare to *unilateral contract.*

unilateral contract

A contract in which acceptance is accomplished by performance; for example, offer of a reward is accepted by performing the reward request. Compare to *bilateral contract.*

and the courts do not require perfection in offer and acceptance; but those who draft contracts must be particularly careful in the precision of their language and use their imaginations to include essential terms and conditions of the contract.

The goal of the attorney may conflict with that of the contracting parties. The attorney aims at protecting a client and providing a contract, the terms of which are sufficiently clear that litigation can be avoided; or, if litigation is necessary, so that the court could apply the contract terms as originally intended. The contracting parties, in contrast, are interested in a mutually satisfactory result. Businesspersons are often more concerned about flexibility, cooperation, and continuing good relations than they are about technical problems of contract law. A good legal team should not assume that contracting parties are adversaries; contract relations are ordinarily created because both sides have found a mutual benefit in working together.

If a contract is formed by a "meeting of the minds," what happens when one of the parties later claims that the intentions were different? If anyone could avoid a contract simply by asserting a secret intent at the time of making of the contract, no contract could be reliable. The courts have developed an "objective" standard for assessing the intent of the parties similar to the reasonable person standard of torts: What would a reasonable person have inferred from the circumstances and conduct of the parties? Such a standard was applied in *Lucy v. Zehmer.*

W.O. LUCY and J.C. Lucy
v.
A. H. ZEHMER and Ida S. Zehmer
Supreme Court of Appeals of Virginia
196 Va. 493, 84 S.E.2d 516 (1954)

This suit was instituted by W.O. Lucy and J.C. Lucy, complainants, against A.H. Zehmer and Ida S. Zehmer, his wife, defendants, to have specific performance of a contract by which it was alleged the Zehmers had sold to W.O. Lucy a tract of land owned by A.H. Zehmer in Dinwiddie county containing 471.6 acres, more or less, known as the Ferguson farm for $50,000. J.C. Lucy, the other complainant, is a brother of W.O. Lucy, to whom W. O. Lucy transferred a half interest in his alleged purchase.

The instrument sought to be enforced was written by A.H. Zehmer on December 20, 1952, in these words: "We hereby agree to sell to W.O. Lucy the Ferguson Farm complete for $50,000, title satisfactory to buyer," and signed by the defendants, A.H. Zehmer and Ida S. Zehmer.

The answer of A.H. Zehmer admitted that at the time mentioned W.O. Lucy offered him $50,000 cash for the farm, but that he, Zehmer, considered that the offer was made in jest; that so thinking, and both he and Lucy having had several drinks, [he] wrote out "the memorandum quoted above and induced his wife to sign it; that he did not deliver the memorandum to Lucy, but that Lucy picked it up, read it, put it in his pocket, attempted to offer Zehmer $5 to bind the bargain, which Zehmer refused to accept, and realizing for the first time that Lucy was serious, Zehmer assured him that he had no intention of selling the farm and that the whole matter was a joke. Lucy left the premises insisting that he had purchased the farm.

* * *

The defendants insist that the evidence was ample to support their contention that the writing sought to be enforced was prepared as a bluff or dare to force Lucy to admit that he did not have $50,000; that the whole matter was a joke; that the writing was not delivered to Lucy and no binding contract was ever made between the parties.

It is an unusual, if not bizarre, defense. When made to the writing admittedly prepared by one of the defendants and signed by both[,] clear evidence is required to sustain it.

In his testimony Zehmer claimed that he "was high as a Georgia pine," and that the transaction "was just a bunch of two doggoned drunks bluffing to see who could talk the biggest and say the most." That claim is inconsistent with his attempt to testify in great detail to what was said and what was done. It is contradicted by other evidence as to the condition of both parties, and rendered of no weight by the testimony of his wife that when Lucy left the restaurant she suggested that Zehmer drive him home. The record is convincing that Zehmer was not intoxicated to the extent of being unable to comprehend the nature and consequences of the instrument he executed, and hence that instrument is not to be invalidated on that ground. It was in fact conceded by defendants' counsel in oral argument that under the evidence Zehmer was not too drunk to make a valid contract.

The evidence is convincing also that Zehmer wrote two agreements, the first one beginning "I hereby agree to sell." Zehmer first said he could not remember about that, then that "I don't think I wrote but one out." Mrs. Zehmer said that what he wrote was "I hereby agree," but that the "I" was changed to "We" after that night. The agreement that was written and signed is in the record and indicates no such change. Neither are the mistakes in spelling that Zehmer sought to point out readily apparent.

The appearance of the contract, the fact that it was under discussion for forty minutes or more before it was signed; Lucy's objection to the first draft because it was written in the singular, and he wanted Mrs. Zehmer to sign it also; the rewriting to meet that objection and the signing by Mrs. Zehmer; the discussion of what was to be included in the sale, the provision for the examination of the title, the completeness of the instrument that was executed, the taking possession of it by Lucy with no request or suggestion by either of the defendants that he give it back, are facts which furnish persuasive evidence that the execution of the contract was a serious business transaction rather than a casual, jesting matter as defendants now contend.

* * *

If it be assumed, contrary to what we think the evidence shows, that Zehmer was jesting about selling his farm to Lucy and that the transaction was intended by him to be a joke, nevertheless the evidence shows that Lucy did not understand it but considered it to be a serious business transaction and the contract to be binding on the Zehmers as well as on himself. The very next day he arranged with his brother to put up half the money and take a half interest in the land. The day after that he employed an attorney to examine the title. The next night, Tuesday, he was back at Zehmer's place and there Zehmer told him for the first time, Lucy said, that he wasn't going to sell and he told Zehmer. "You know you sold that place fair and square." After receiving the report from his attorney that the title was good he wrote to Zehmer that he was ready to close the deal.

Not only did Lucy actually believe, but the evidence shows he was warranted in believing, that the contract represented a serious business transaction and a good faith sale and purchase of the farm.

In the field of contract, as generally elsewhere, "We must look to the outward expression of a person as manifesting his intention rather than to his secret and unexpressed intention. 'The law imputes to a person an intention corresponding to the reasonable meaning of his words and acts.'"

* * *

"The law, therefore, judges of an agreement between two persons exclusively from those expressions of their intentions which are communicated between them." . . . [T]he law imputes to a person an intention corresponding to the reasonable meaning of his words and acts. . . . [I]t is immaterial what may be the real but unexpressed state of his mind.

So a person cannot set up that he was merely jesting when his conduct and words would warrant a reasonable person in believing that he intended a real agreement.

Whether the writing signed by the defendant and now sought to be enforced by the complainants was the result of a serious offer by Lucy and a serious acceptance by the defendants, or was a serious offer by Lucy and an acceptance in secret jest by the defendants, in either event it constituted a binding contract of sale between the parties.

* * *

The complainants are entitled to have specific performance of the contract sued on. . . .

Reversed and remanded.

Case Questions

1. Zehmer had bought the farm eleven years before for $11,000 and had refused an offer seven years prior by Lucy for $20,000. If the contract had been for $10,000, would the court have enforced it? Why or why not?

2. What if Lucy had known the contract was a joke but proceeded as if it had not been? How might the facts have been different?

3. Could Zehmer have succeeded if he had argued that he was drunk at the time, claiming intoxication as a defense?

Consideration

consideration

A requirement in classical contract formation that consists of an exchange of something of value, although this may in some cases be largely symbolic.

Consideration is a somewhat anomalous requirement for contract formation. It is the symbolic proof that the contract was the result of bargaining. In its broadest conception, consideration is represented by the exchange of something of value. Many form contracts include a pro forma recital of consideration, typically one dollar or ten dollars, to satisfy the consideration requirement. Although this is artificial and often illusory (often no money actually changes hands), many courts developed or adopted the doctrine that the sufficiency of consideration is not to be questioned.

The bargain aspect of consideration is exemplified by § 71 of the *Restatement:* "To constitute consideration, a performance or a return promise must be bargained for." The "something of value" may simply be a return promise. The original purpose of consideration appears to have been the refusal to enforce promises of gifts when the promisee does nothing in return. If Grandmother says to Grandson, "When you reach 25, I'll give you $10,000," and Grandson replies, "I'll be glad to receive it," the appearance is that of acceptance; but when Grandmother's junk bonds become worth 20 cents on the dollar, the court is loath to enforce the agreement, arguing that Grandson neither conferred a benefit on Grandmother nor suffered a "detriment" by forbearing to do something he was entitled to do, so there was no consideration on his part for the contract. In contrast, when Uncle promised Nephew $5,000 on his twenty-fifth birthday if until that time Nephew would refrain from drinking and smoking, the court may find consideration in that Nephew suffered a legal detriment by forbearing doing something he had a legal right to do. Courts have on occasion found consideration based on "love and affection" to support the promise of a gift when a relative has provided aid and support. It would seem that the courts have attempted to avoid unfairness by invoking the existence of consideration or its absence and have stretched logic to justify their conclusions. Any other explanation suggests a logic and consistency to the concept of consideration that is not corroborated by the cases.

Love and affection have on occasion been construed to be consideration to support enforcement of a contract between persons in close relationships, even though material consideration is lacking. The *Rose* court, however, was unwilling to find consideration on this basis.

Consideration is an artificial legal concept rarely of concern to those engaged in the bargaining relationship. Gilmore traces the rise of the concept to Holmes's *The Common Law,* where it appears mysteriously and without authority. The effect of the

Leah ROSE, Plaintiff-Appellant

v.

Samuel ELIAS, Defendant-Respondent

Supreme Court, Appellate Division, First Department

177 A.D.2d 415, 576 N.Y.S.2d 257 (1991)

Order . . . entered May 14, 1990, which granted defendant's motion to dismiss the complaint for failure to state a cause of action, unanimously affirmed, without costs.

Defendant, a married man, promised in writing to purchase an apartment for the plaintiff, his female companion, in return for the "love and affection" that she provided to him during the prior three years. We agree with the [lower] court that the love and affection provided by plaintiff were insufficient consideration for defendant's promise to purchase an apartment for her.

Nor is a cause of action stated by virtue of plaintiff's claim that she forbore job opportunities at defendant's oral request, since defendant's written promise to provide an apartment for plaintiff was unambiguous and complete, and it is apparent that the parties did not view plaintiff's forbearance from accepting job opportunities as consideration for the promise. " 'Nothing is consideration . . . that is not regarded as such by both parties.' "

The defendant asserted that his relationship with the plaintiff was primarily a sexual relationship, and plaintiff did not deny that sexual relations were a part of the relationship. Plaintiff admitted that the proposed purchase of an apartment was intended to facilitate a "comfortable" life together with the defendant. "Agreements tending to dissolve a marriage or to facilitate adultery are closely scrutinized to determine whether the main objective of the agreement is aimed to produce that result." The [lower] court concluded that the words "love and affection" in the circumstances presented suggest adultery, and thus illegal consideration. Since there was found to be no severable legal component of the consideration for defendant's promise, the court correctly ruled in the alternative that the contract was void as against public policy.

We have considered plaintiff's arguments based on theories of estoppel and unjust enrichment, and find them to be without merit.

Case Questions

1. Is there more than a promise to make a gift here?
2. How critical to this decision is the fact that the defendant was married?

consideration requirement is to negate many contracts that would be enforceable without it. It is a device that can be used by a court to declare that contract formation was flawed and therefore unenforceable. It is probably of little practical importance to the attorney except as a strategy on behalf of a client who is trying to avoid enforcement of a contract. Nevertheless, when custom dictates a recital of consideration, it is wise to follow established practice.

Consideration is important in option contracts. Because offers may be revoked prior to acceptance, one way to keep an offer open is to pay for it. A person may purchase an option on land—for example, by paying $1,000 for an option to purchase land for $50,000 before January 1. In this way, the offer to sell the land may not be revoked until the expiration of the option (January 1). Because consideration has been paid, a contract has been formed. Of course, if January 1 passes without action, the contract ends, as do the duties of the parties.

LIMITATIONS ON CONTRACT FORMATION

fraud

In contract law, a contract induced by intentionally false misrepresentations; such a contract is voidable.

misrepresentation

A false representation; may be innocent or intentional. A contract based on an innocent misrepresentation is still *voidable* by the person to whom the false representation was made.

rescind

To annul or cancel a contract, putting the parties back in the position they were in before, as if no contract had been made.

Even when offer, acceptance, and consideration are present, the law will not recognize a contract if the bargaining process was flawed by misconduct (fraud, misrepresentation, duress, or undue influence), defect in agreement (mistake), the incapacity of one of the parties (minority or mental incompetence), or illegal purpose. In addition, the law requires that certain contracts be in writing to be enforceable (Statute of Frauds). Each of these is treated in summary fashion here (see Exhibit 11-3).

Contract Induced by Misconduct of One of the Parties

Although parties have great latitude in the promises they exchange in a bargaining relationship, the absence of a bargain may be found if one of the parties was deceived as to the bargain or deprived of free will in bargaining.

Fraud and **misrepresentation** are generally distinguished on the basis of intentional false representations (fraud) and innocent false representations (misrepresentation). If a used car dealer sells a 1979 model as a 1980 model while knowing it to be a 1979 model, it would be fraud; if the dealer believed it to be a 1980 model, it would be misrepresentation. In either case, the innocent party should have the option to accept the contract or to **rescind** it, returning the car and receiving the return of payments made. Such contracts are **voidable**, meaning the innocent party may avoid the contract by returning to the conditions prior to the agreement. This is distinguished from contracts that are *void* (see discussion of illegality later in this section).

EXHIBIT 11-3   VOID, VOIDABLE, AND UNENFORCEABLE CONTRACTS*

TYPE	EXAMPLES	EFFECT
Void	Contract for an illegal purpose; in some states a person legally insane at time of making contract; some forms of mistake may make a contract void	Unenforceable by either party; *void ab initio* (never was a contract).
Voidable	Lack of capacity, duress, misrepresentation, undue influence, mutual mistake	Valid until one of the parties avoids the contract by raising a defense. In case of misconduct (e.g., misrepresentation), only the aggrieved party may avoid. Some contracts, such as contracts with minors, may be ratified when the impediment is removed.
Unenforceable	A contract that conflicts with public policy or a legal requirement (e.g., an oral contract required by the Statute of Frauds to be in writing) may not be enforced	The court will not enforce the contract.

*These terms are used inconsistently; the distinction between *void* and *unenforceable* is particularly blurry. The concept of mistake is complex and beyond the scope of this text.

A contract is also voidable if it can be shown that one of the parties could not exercise free will in the bargaining process (duress). **Duress** occurs when one party is threatened with harm to induce agreement. The threatened harm is ordinarily physical or emotional harm directed against the party, the party's family, or the party's property. Usually economic pressure is not sufficient to constitute duress, nor is the threat to bring a civil action ("If you don't sell, I'll foreclose").

Undue influence occurs when relentless pressure so weakens a party's will that the bargain is not freely obtained. Undue influence also occurs when the parties have a confidential relationship, such as close family relations, attorney-client, physician-patient, or the like.

Mistake

Mutual, or bilateral, **mistake of fact** makes the contract voidable by either party. For example, in one famous case, the violinist Efrem Zimbalist purchased two violins believed by both purchaser and seller to have been made by Guarnerius and Stradivarius. Zimbalist was able to avoid the contract when the violins proved to be nearly worthless. Note, though, that this example somewhat oversimplifies the complex and confusing area of mistake.

Lack of Capacity to Form a Contract

Lack of capacity may be due to lack of legal competence based on status (minor), lack of mental capacity to form contracts, or temporary incapacitation (intoxication).

In most states, the age of majority is 18. Until reaching the age of majority, persons are not legally competent, which includes an incapacity to bind themselves contractually. Exceptions are sometimes made for **emancipated minors**. Contracts with minors may be avoided by the minor but can be **ratified** when the minor reaches the age of majority. Contracts for "necessaries," such as food and clothing, are usually enforceable against minors.

The invalidity of contracts involving lack of mental capacity is based on the notion that lack of capacity prevents an individual from understanding the bargain. A person may display peculiarities that indicate mental illness yet understand fully the subject matter and obligations entered into by contract, in which case the contract may not be avoided. A person determined to be mentally incompetent by legal authority is not legally competent, and contracts with such persons are in some states void from their inception.

Inability to understand the nature and purpose of contractual obligations may also be established by the intoxication of one of the parties at the time the contract was formed. Intoxication includes all drugs that affect one's mental state and ability to understand the consequences of the bargain. The intoxicated person may later affirm or disaffirm the contract. There is significant variation among jurisdictions as to proof and legal effect of intoxication.

There is a story about Sophocles, the great dramatist of ancient Athens, who had amassed significant wealth from prizes for his plays. When he reached the ripe old age of 80, his children, then in their fifties, grew tired of waiting for their inheritance

voidable
Describes a contract that the innocent party (the other party having contracted wrongfully in certain recognized ways) may avoid by returning the parties to their conditions prior to the agreement.

duress
Threats of harm made to induce agreement by one party to a contract.

undue influence
Relentless pressure, especially from one in a confidential relationship, to induce a party to agree to a contract.

mistake of fact
In contract formation, one or both parties believe some essential fact about the transaction to be other than it really is; makes the contract *voidable*.

emancipated minor
A person under the age of majority who is totally self-supporting or married; varies by state.

ratify
To approve, as when one suffering a disability approves a contract after the disability has terminated; for example, a minor reaches age of majority and agrees to a contract made when he or she was still a minor.

and brought Sophocles before the court of Athenian citizens to have him declared senile so that they could manage his wealth. As his only defense, Sophocles read to those assembled a play he had just written. The jury found him to be of sound mind, and his children had to wait another 10 years to collect their inheritance. Sophocles would undoubtedly have enjoyed the result in the *Hanks* case.

Hanks

v.

McNEIL COAL CORPORATION et al.

Colorado Supreme Court

114 Colo. 578, 168 P.2d 256 (1946)

Lee A. Hanks, who was a prosperous farmer and businessman in Nebraska, came to Colorado with his family in 1918, at first settling on a farm in Weld county, which included the coal lands involved in this proceeding; then, in 1920 moving to Boulder where he purchased a home, engaged in the retail coal business, and thereafter resided. . . . Shortly after 1922 Lee Hanks discovered that he was afflicted with diabetes, and members of his family noticed a progressive change in his physical and mental condition thereafter. He became irritable and easily upset, very critical of his son's work, and increasingly interested in the emotional type of religion. He began to speculate in oil and other doubtful ventures with money needed for payment of debts and taxes. About 1934 he sent his son what he denominated a secret formula for the manufacture of medicine to cure fistula in horses, which was compounded principally of ground china, brick dust, burnt shoe leather and amber-colored glass. If the infection was in the horse's right shoulder, the mixture was to be poured in the animal's left ear, and if on the left shoulder then in the right ear. In 1937 Mr. Hanks started to advertise this medicine through the press under the name of Crown King Remedy. Thereafter he increasingly devoted his efforts and money to the compounding and attempted sale of this concoction, his business judgment became poor and he finally deteriorated

mentally to the point that on May 25, 1940, he was adjudicated insane and his son was appointed conservator of his estate.

[In 1937, before being adjudicated insane, Hanks sold property to the coal company, which he had learned was hauling coal over his lands. His son, the conservator of his estate, brought this suit to avoid the contract.]

. . . The legal test of Hanks' insanity is whether "he was incapable of understanding and appreciating the extent and effect of business transactions in which he engaged."

. . . One may have insane delusions regarding some matters and be insane on some subjects, yet capable of transacting business concerning matters wherein such subjects are not concerned, and such insanity does not make one incompetent to contract unless the subject matter of the contract is so connected with an insane delusion as to render the afflicted party incapable of understanding the nature and effect of the agreement or of acting rationally in the transaction.

. . . Patently Hanks was suffering from insane delusion in 1937 with reference to the efficacy of the horse medicine, but there is no evidence of delusions or hallucinations in connection with this transaction or with his transaction of much of his other business at that time; there is no basis for holding voidable his sale here involved on the ground of his insanity.

Case Questions

1. What difference would it have made if Hanks had been adjudicated insane prior to the sale?
2. Of what significance was the horse medicine?

Illegality

Agreements to do an unlawful act, including tortious as well as criminal acts, or for an unlawful purpose are deemed void by the courts and will not be enforced. A number of problems, such as what exactly is unlawful and how to handle a contract that is in part unlawful and in part lawful, have had different results in different jurisdictions.

Statute of Frauds

An oral contract binds the parties as much as a written one, though a written contract provides more certain evidence of the terms of a contract than personal recollection of what was orally agreed. In 1677, the **Statute of Frauds** was enacted, making certain contracts unenforceable unless written. In 1677 the law of contracts was poorly developed, as were the laws of evidence and proof; the statute was an attempt to prevent fraudulent abuse of legal process. The Statute of Frauds remained largely intact during the creation of American law, often with only minor modifications. Although the statute identified five categories in which a written contract was required, two remain of major importance in the practice of law: (1) contracts for the conveyance of interests in land; (2) contracts not to be performed within one year. The UCC has created its own version of the Statute of Frauds, requiring that certain contracts be in writing, the most notable of which covers the sale of goods for more than $500 and the sale of other forms of personal property valued at more than $5,000.

Statute of Frauds
An ancient doctrine requiring that certain contracts be in writing and signed.

Today the Statute of Frauds can actually invite fraud, as, for instance, when a person attempts to avoid an obligation by invoking the statute while at the same time benefiting from another's performance. The courts have displayed considerable creativity in getting around the statute when the interests of justice are not served by strict adherence to it.

COMPENSATORY DAMAGES FOR BREACH OF CONTRACT

Because contract law is modeled largely on business relations and contractual relations are created by the parties to the contract, the remedy for breach of contract is quite different from tort remedies. Injuries that are not foreseeable or not within the contemplation of the parties are not a usual element of compensatory damages. Physical or emotional injuries are not recoverable except where tort principles have invaded contract territory (e.g., malpractice and product liability).

The overriding policy in compensatory damages for breach of contract is to put the "nonbreaching party in the position he would have been in had the contract been performed." This may include lost profits if they are roughly ascertainable and within the contemplation of the parties. It may mean paying the cost of completion, as with unfinished construction contracts, or the cost of replacement, or the difference between contract price and market price. Damages are often phrased as "giving the nonbreaching party the benefit of his bargain." Several different measures of damages have developed for different categories of contracts, and the Uniform Commercial Code provides its own special rules. The diversity of rules is designed to ensure that the nonbreaching party does not suffer a loss or enjoy a windfall. Although breach represents the fault aspect of contract law, the breaching party is to be protected rather than penalized (punitive damages are rare in contract cases).

This brief summary of damages ignores numerous complicating factors, such as **anticipatory breach**, **substantial performance**, and cases in which both parties breach, which are normally covered in some detail in contract and business law texts.

PROBLEMS WITH THE CLASSICAL MODEL

Classical contract theory, which developed during the period before and after the turn of the twentieth century, constructed a logical set of rules based on offer, acceptance, and consideration for the formation of contract and compensatory damages for the resolution of contract disputes. This scheme is satisfactory for a great many contracts, but the diversity of contract relationships creates a variety of situations that defy mechanical solutions. Exhibit 11-4 contains a number of short fact patterns that do not fit within classical contract theory. Spend a few minutes deciding how you would deal with these situations if you were the judge. Then keep the fact patterns and your solutions in mind as you read the balance of the chapter. Did your classmates develop any other principles to deal with these situations? Were your solutions similar to what a court would do?

Fault

Historically, judges were naturally reluctant to leave an innocent injured party without a remedy. This presented no problem if the contract was clearly enforceable and one party had breached. If a damages remedy fully compensated the injured party, an easy and just result was available. The breaching party was at fault under contract law, and liability was fixed. In many cases, though, such as those previously listed, contract principles were unavailing. Judges employed a number of devices to avoid unjust results, some of them old, notably equitable remedies and principles; some of them new; and some of them fictitious.

When fault under common law contract theory was unworkable, the courts frequently resorted to the developing law of torts. Negligence theory provided a ready remedy for professional malpractice, especially medical malpractice, where compensatory contract damages were inappropriate because the injury was not loss of profits but disability, death, or pain and suffering. The duty of due care was imposed by law rather than by contract, so these cases jumped the fence from contract to tort at an early date without much resistance from the courts. The foreseeability of serious injury from medical malpractice, viewed from either a contract or a tort law perspective, strengthens the imposition of liability. A high standard of professional care also places the burden on the physician in the doctor-patient relationship, a standard easily implied to the contract.

The shift of product liability from contract to tort was more tortuous (forgive the pun). Although Justice Traynor finally justified the imposition of tort liability for defective

anticipatory breach

Occurs when one party to a contract expresses an intention not to perform; the other party may then treat the contract as *breached* and pursue an appropriate remedy rather than wait for nonperformance (actual breach).

substantial performance

Occurs when one party has attempted to complete performance in good faith but that performance varied in minor ways from the specific terms of the contract. Under the equitable principle of substantial performance, the court may enforce the contract and declare it performed, though possibly reducing the payment for performance because of the minor breach.

EXHIBIT 11-4 FACT PATTERNS NOT ADEQUATELY DEALT WITH UNDER THE CLASSICAL CONTRACT MODEL

1. *A person promises to make a gift.* A brother offers his sister the free use of his second home on a permanent basis. She sells her own house and moves her belongings and family. Brother later gets a good offer on the house and reneges on his promise. Under classical consideration principles, the sister has no enforceable contract rights.
2. *Charitable pledges.* A church solicits pledges from its parishioners to build a new annex, then enters into a building contract. Was there consideration to support enforcement of the pledges?
3. *Confidential professional relationships.* Doctor and patient enter a contract for treatment, but the treatment is negligently performed. Compensatory damages for breach of contract do not compensate for the injuries sustained.
4. *Indefinite oral contracts.* Buyer and seller agree to transfer title to an automobile, but time and place of performance are not mentioned.
5. *Unilateral contracts requiring performance as acceptance when promisee has begun to perform and promisor revokes the offer.* Property owner offers $2,500 to roofer when roof is completed to "owner's satisfaction." Roofer moves trucks and men out to do the work, only to find that owner has hired someone else.
6. *Contracts in which the parties leave the details to be worked out later.*
7. *Performance without a contract.* Contractor blacktops the wrong driveway while owner stands by and watches silently, later disclaiming any liability in the absence of a contract.
8. *Contracts for which compensatory damages create an unfair result.* Seller of house lot refuses to deliver deed as required by contract because a second buyer has offered a higher price. First buyer's costs attributable to the breach of contract are minimal.
9. *Inducements to contract cause a party to incur costs relying on the inducement, but the contract is never completed.* Offer of hardware franchise induces potential franchisee to sell business at loss and work as manager/trainee to learn business. Franchisor later refuses to enter contract.
10. *Strict adherence to the Statute of Frauds will have grossly unfair results.* Seller and buyer agree orally to transfer land for a fixed price. Buyer clears the land and puts in a foundation for a house, and seller decides not to sell. Under the Statute of Frauds, the contract is unenforceable.
11. *Manufacturer claims no responsibility for person injured by a product because purchaser bought the product from a dealer and had no contractual relation with manufacturer.*

products on policy grounds (see Chapter 10), his landmark decision in *Greenman v. Yuba Power Products* rested on a line of cases developed from Judge Cardozo's opinion in *MacPherson v. Buick Motor Co.,* 217 N.Y. 382, 111 N.E. 105 (1916), dispensing with the **privity of contract** requirement and holding the manufacturer as well as the dealer liable. Product liability ultimately rested on the principle of implied warranty, under which the law imposes duties beyond the express terms of the contract. Although product liability is said to be strict liability without the need to prove fault, the plaintiff must show that the product was "dangerously defective when it left the manufacturer" and that the user was using the product in the manner for which it was designed. In many cases, the plaintiff's burden of proof is not significantly less than showing a manufacturer's negligence.

privity of contract

The relationship between two parties to a contract. Originally, this was a bar to a suit brought by a consumer against a manufacturer when the consumer bought through a dealer and not directly from the manufacturer. Modern product liability law does away with this impediment.

contracts of adhesion

Contracts in which all the bargaining power (and the contract terms) favor one side; often seen when the seller uses a preprinted form contract to unfair advantage.

rescission

Aims at destroying the contract and its obligations, thereby putting the parties back in the positions they occupied prior to making the agreement.

reformation

Aims at correcting a contract to reflect the actual intention of the parties.

In other cases, fault in the sense of a legal wrong (e.g., breach of contract, tortious conduct) may be absent, but concepts of commercial morality, such as "good faith," present convenient analogies.

Deceptive Practices

Unscrupulous businesses are very inventive in seducing the innocent consumer into agreements with obscure provisions, penalties, and duties. Most consumers are confronted frequently with contracts that have confusing fine print, often in quite simple transactions where costs appear to be standard and reasonable. Though we may not be especially sympathetic to the consumer who signs without reading, neither are we sympathetic to the business that crafts contracts that are indecipherable or misleading, even if they do not contain intentional misrepresentations. Form contracts that do not allow change or negotiation are called **contracts of adhesion**, are viewed skeptically by the courts, and are interpreted against the party who creates the form and all its terms. Some practices aimed at deceiving the public have become so common that many state legislatures have passed laws to protect consumers against unfair business practices that might otherwise stand up in court.

EQUITABLE REMEDIES

When compensatory damages are inadequate, equitable remedies may be available. Some exist as alternative remedies if certain defects in contract formation can be shown (rescission and reformation). Others ask for something other than money (specific performance and injunctive relief).

Rescission and Reformation

Rescission aims at destroying the contract and its obligations and putting the parties back in the positions they occupied prior to the agreement. Grounds for rescission are defects in formation already mentioned: illegality, undue influence, insanity, and so on. **Reformation** aims at correcting the contract to reflect the actual intent of the parties, usually where mutual mistake exists.

As we have seen from the discussion of equity in Chapter 6, a court that is exercising its equitable jurisdiction enjoys considerable discretion to do justice to the parties. Equity is particularly interesting in contract actions because the relationships between contracting parties and their circumstances present every conceivable possibility. Unusual cases call for equitable remedies such as rescission. What should happen when an innocent purchaser buys a haunted house, the unfortunate character of which is known to everyone except the out-of-town purchaser? Just such a situation presented itself in *Stambovsky v. Ackley*. The ancient principle of *caveat emptor*, "let the buyer beware," urges the purchaser to check out his purchase at his peril, but who asks the realtor whether a house on the market is haunted? One might expect the court to be reluctant to acknowledge the "phantasmal" character of property or give any relief, yet *Stambovsky* resulted in a three-to-two split among the judges on this question (the dissent is omitted). The case presents interesting questions of equity, contract, and property law.

Jeffrey M. STAMBOVSKY

v.

Helen V. ACKLEY

Supreme Court of New York, Appellate Division, First Department

169 A.D.2d 254; 572 N.Y.S.2d 672 (N.Y. App. Div. 1991)

Plaintiff, to his horror, discovered that the house he had recently contracted to purchase was widely reputed to be possessed by poltergeists, reportedly seen by defendant seller and members of her family on numerous occasions over the last nine years. Plaintiff promptly commenced this action seeking rescission of the contract of sale. Supreme Court reluctantly dismissed the complaint, holding that plaintiff has no remedy at law in this jurisdiction.

The unusual facts of this case, as disclosed by the record, clearly warrant a grant of equitable relief to the buyer who, as a resident of New York City, cannot be expected to have any familiarity with the folklore of the Village of Nyack. Not being a "local," plaintiff could not readily learn that the home he had contracted to purchase is haunted. Whether the source of the spectral apparitions seen by defendant seller are parapsychic or psychogenic, having reported their presence in both a national publication (*Readers' Digest*) and the local press (in 1977 and 1982, respectively), defendant is **estopped** to deny their existence and, as a matter of law, the house is haunted. More to the point, however, no divination is required to conclude that it is defendant's promotional efforts in publicizing her close encounters with these spirits which fostered the home's reputation in the community. . . . The impact of the reputation thus created goes to the very essence of the bargain between the parties, greatly impairing both the value of the property and its potential for resale. . . .

While I agree with Supreme Court that the real estate broker, as agent for the seller, is under no duty to disclose to a potential buyer the phantasmal reputation of the premises and that, in his pursuit of a legal remedy for fraudulent misrepresentation against the seller, plaintiff hasn't a ghost of a chance, I am nevertheless moved by the spirit of equity to allow the buyer to seek rescission of the contract of sale and recovery of his down payment. . . .

. . . New York adheres to the doctrine of caveat emptor and imposes no duty upon the vendor to disclose any information concerning the premises [with exceptions, especially affirmative misrepresentation].

Caveat emptor is not so all-encompassing a doctrine of common law as to render every act of nondisclosure immune from redress, whether legal or equitable. . . . Where fairness and common sense dictate that an exception should be created, the evolution of the law should not be stifled by rigid application of a legal maxim.

The doctrine of caveat emptor requires that a buyer act prudently to assess the fitness and value of his purchase. . . . It should be apparent, however, that the most meticulous inspection and the search would not reveal the presence of poltergeists at the premises or unearth the property's ghoulish reputation in the community. Therefore, there is no sound policy reason to deny plaintiff relief for failing to discover a state of affairs which the most prudent purchaser would not be expected to even contemplate. . . .

Where a condition which has been created by the seller materially impairs the value of the contract and is peculiarly within the knowledge of the seller or unlikely to be discovered by a prudent purchaser exercising due care with respect to the subject transaction, nondisclosure constitutes a basis for rescission as a matter of equity.

In the case at bar, defendant seller deliberately fostered the public belief that her home was possessed. Having undertaken to inform the public-at-large, to whom she has no legal relationship, about the supernatural occurrences on her property, she may be said to owe no less a duty to her contract vendee. . . . Where, as here, the seller not only takes unfair advantage of the buyer's ignorance but has created and perpetuated a condition about which he is unlikely to even inquire, enforcement of the contract (in whole or in part) is offensive to the court's sense of equity. Application of the remedy of rescission, within the bounds of the narrow exception to the doctrine of caveat emptor set forth herein, is entirely appropriate to relieve the unwitting purchaser from the consequences of a most unnatural bargain.

Accordingly, the judgment . . . should be modified, on the law and the facts, and in the exercise of discretion, and the first cause of action seeking rescission of the contract reinstated, without costs.

Case Questions

1. We will encounter estoppel principles shortly under the discussion of reliance theory, but it is critical in this case. Does estoppel relieve the court from the embarrassing position of ruling that a house may be haunted?

2. Should caveat emptor require a purchaser to inquire into the supernatural character of a house about to be purchased?

Case Glossary

estopped
Prevented, stopped. In equity, a person may be "estopped" from making assertions contrary to prior assertions on which another has relied to his or her detriment.

Specific Performance

Specific performance asks the court to order the breaching party to perform rather than compensate, that is, to deliver the goods or the deed to real property. This remedy is available when goods are unique, such as a Stradivarius violin (land is always considered unique, hence the availability of specific performance for enforcing real property sales contracts). This remedy, however, is premised on a valid contract and does not cure formation and consideration problems. (See *Lucy v. Zehmer,* p. 000).

In *White*, the seller and the buyer were mistaken in the belief that a driveway leading to an adjoining property did not encroach on the property offered for sale. This mutual mistake of fact could have led either to the contract being rescinded or to the contract being reformed to reflect a driveway easement. Instead, the buyer asked the Chancery Court judge, referred to in the opinion as the "chancellor," to order specific performance. Remember from Chapter 6 that historically chancery courts had jurisdiction over a request for an equitable remedy.

W. E. WHITE

v.

Glenn COOKE, Dennis Massey and Steve Weeks

Supreme Court of Mississippi

No. 2007-CA-01511-SCT

4 So. 3d 330

Jan. 15, 2009.

William Earl White attended a public auction at which he successfully bid for and contracted to purchase four tracts of land from Glenn Cooke, Dennis Massey, and Steve Weeks (hereinafter collectively referred to as "Cooke"). Prior to closing, a survey revealed that the driveway on a separate property owned by Cooke actually extended onto one of the tracts that White had contracted to purchase. After efforts to reach a compromise with White proved unproductive, Cooke sold this separate property to Roberta Jamison-Ross and granted her an easement across White's tract. As a result, White filed suit for specific performance of the real-estate contract without the burden of an easement.

The chancellor dismissed White's complaint. We affirm the chancellor's denial of specific performance, but reverse and render the award of attorney fees to Cooke.

For specific performance to be granted, a contract must be reasonably complete and reasonably definite on material terms. . . . If the contract does not pass this test of specificity, it should be rendered unenforceable, and specific performance should be denied.

A contract may be set aside, however, where both parties at the time of the agreement were operating under a mutual mistake of fact. . . . In any event, the mistake must relate to a past or present material fact to relieve a party(s) from liability.

The chancellor found that "there was a contract to sell land by deed closing within thirty days; however, there was an error in the description." He determined that the "as is" clause within the contract afforded Cooke an "escape clause." He found the forty feet of frontage and the easement to be "vital important facts" to the contract, but stated that Cooke could not convey something that they did not own. He construed the later surveys, which White rejected, as "being in the nature of [ ] counter-offers." He then dismissed the action, concluding that "there could be no closing within thirty days and there cannot be specific performance of the sale of the property. . . ."

Our review of the chancellor's opinion leads us to conclude that he denied specific performance because the parties failed to have a "meeting of the minds" on a material term of the contract. Thus, he found that no enforceable contract existed due to a mutual mistake and dismissed the entire action, including Cooke's counterclaim.

We find that the chancellor did not abuse his discretion in denying specific performance and dismissing the case. At the time of the contract, both parties were laboring under a mistaken belief that the driveway on tract ten did not intrude onto tract nine. The existence of the driveway constituted a material term in that it interfered with White's ability to access the property with his farm equipment and afforded the sole means of ingress and egress to the house on tract ten. Thus, the driveway was an essential term of the contract based on its importance or substantial effect upon each tract. Because the parties were mistaken about a material fact, we find that the chancellor did not abuse his discretion in rescinding the contract. . . .

Whether the Chancellor Erred in Awarding Attorney Fees to Cooke

The chancellor awarded attorney fees to Cooke on the basis that White failed to act in good faith after the mistake was discovered. The chancellor found that "by rejecting the additional plats and by filing this action for specific performance, which was denied, White caused damage to Cooke, et al[.] in the nature of attorney fees."

We find that White did not act in bad faith and that the chancellor abused his discretion in awarding Cooke attorney fees. In rejecting the additional surveys and filing for specific performance, White merely sought to enforce what he believed he had contracted for—the property without the easement. Had a valid contract been found, White likely would have been entitled to specific performance subject to the easement, with the right to recover damages for breach of contract.

Case Questions

1. What were the facts leading the chancellor to conclude that there was no enforceable contract?
2. What problem did the driveway create for White?
3. Why would the owner of tract ten need to use tract nine?

Injunctive Relief

Injunctive relief is sometimes available to order someone not to do something that is prohibited by a contract (e.g., to prevent someone from building a carport in a development where deed restrictions require garages and prohibit carports). Such relief also is premised on valid contractual obligations.

LIBERAL CONSTRUCTION OF CONSIDERATION

One means of avoiding the arbitrariness of the classical model of contract formation was to construe consideration in the broadest possible terms in order to create a contract. This method was a favorite of Judge Cardozo of the New York Court of Appeals. Cardozo enforced a father's promise to pay an annuity to his daughter following her marriage by finding consideration in her forbearance from breaking off the engagement. *DeCicco v. Schweizer*, 221 N.Y. 431, 117 N.E. 807 (1917). In another case, he found consideration for a pledge to a college endowment campaign in an implied duty of the college to memorialize the donor. *Allegheny College v. National Chatauqua Bank*, 246 N.Y. 369, 159 N.E. 173 (1927). In both of these cases, classical theory should have found a promise to make a gift without consideration on the part of the promisee.

When consideration was designed to deny contracts even when offer and acceptance were present, the liberal construction of consideration undercut its importance. When a powerful moral, as opposed to legal, obligation was present or when a promisee changed position in reliance on a promise, judges at first strained to find consideration.

MORAL OBLIGATION AND RELIANCE THEORY

Consider the following examples taken from those listed earlier:

1. Contractor makes a contract with Thomas to blacktop Thomas's driveway at 116 Spring Street for $2,000. Contractor mistakenly blacktops Henry's driveway at 114 Spring Street (the two houses are in an urban subdivision where the houses bear a striking similarity to each other). Variations on the facts might be: Henry is away on vacation while the blacktopping occurs and has no knowledge of it until he returns; Henry watches through his window but remains silent, all the while knowing that Thomas was planning to blacktop and that Contractor is mistaken.

2. George, the owner of a small business, opens negotiations with a national hardware chain for a franchise. Franchisor insists that George get experience as a manager/trainee in one of the branches and assures George that training plus $25,000 will result in a franchise, although no guarantees are made. George sells his business, moves to another city, and works as a trainee. Franchisor increases the cost of the franchise to $35,000. George sells his house to raise the money, but Franchisor decides not to grant the franchise.

quasi-contract

Concept arising from the theory that a "contract" is created on the basis of moral obligation, called *unjust enrichment,* in which one party receives a benefit to the detriment of another, that begs for *restitution,* not an actual contract.

Moral Obligation: Quasi-Contract

In example 1, there was no contract, but Henry has received a benefit at Contractor's expense. There was no contract, no offer, no acceptance, and no consideration on Henry's part, but it would seem unfair for Henry to retain the benefit, particularly if he failed in his moral obligation to inform Contractor of the mistake. In such a situation the court may impose contractual obligations in the name of **quasi-contract**, which is not an actual contract but a "non-contractual obligation that is to be treated procedurally as if it were a contract." *Continental Forest Products, Inc. v. Chandler Supply Co.,* 95 Idaho 739, 518 P.2d 1201 (1974).

Quasi-contract is also called *contract implied in law*—distinguished from a **contract implied in fact**—and is based on the concepts of **unjust enrichment** and **restitution**. Unjust enrichment is an equitable principle asserting that one receiving a benefit at another's loss owes restitution to the other. Because fairness is the goal of equity, the imposition of contractual obligations depends on the specific circumstances of each case and cannot easily be reduced to mechanical rules. Typically, quasi-contract requires that the recipient of the benefit have the opportunity to decline the benefit and yet fail to do so. In the driveway example, the court might imply such failure if Henry sat idly by and watched the work proceed. It is doubtful that the court would impose the same obligation if Henry had no knowledge of the work (for example, if he was on vacation).

Reliance: Promissory Estoppel

Example 2 presents a different problem, that of **promissory estoppel**. Although a contract was never complete, George's course of action was determined by assurances made in the course of contract negotiations. George incurred significant costs in reasonably relying on those assurances. The national chain received no benefit at George's expense, so unjust enrichment/quasi-contract is not appropriate, but George has certainly suffered because of the chain's conduct. To impose liability on the chain, the court may resort to another equitable principle called **equitable estoppel**, under which liability is incurred if one by language or conduct leads another to do something he or she would not otherwise have done. This is the basis for the mysterious language of the first *Restatement* § 90:

> A promise which the promisor should reasonably expect to induce action or forbearance of a definite and substantial character on the part of the promisee and which does induce such action or forbearance is binding if injustice can be avoided only by enforcement of the promise.

This section applies to George's plight; it is a concise statement of *reliance theory.* Promises were made on which George relied to his detriment. Although a contract never quite passed the negotiation stage, it would be unjust for George to be left without some compensation.

Hoffman is a classic case of promissory estoppel. The plaintiff was induced into a course of conduct by the defendant with the promise of a forthcoming contract that never arrived. Good faith and reliance on one side were met with vacillation and chicanery on the other. Nevertheless, promissory estoppel is not the same as breach of contract, and the case was ultimately set for new trial on the issue of the amount the plaintiff should receive. Omitted from the case excerpt is the following quotation from Corbin, one of the leading contributors to the *Restatement of Contracts,* the supreme master of reliance theory, showing just how elusive promissory estoppel can be:

> Enforcement of a promise does not necessarily mean Specific Performance. It does not necessarily mean Damages for breach. Moreover the amount

contract implied in fact
A contract that can be inferred by the conduct of the parties in the absence of a verbal or express contract.

unjust enrichment
An equitable principle asserting that one receiving a benefit at another's loss owes *restitution* to the other.

restitution
In contract law, usually the amount that returns the plaintiff back to his or her precontract financial position.

promissory estoppel
An equitable principle that enforces a promise in the absence of a completed contract. When a person makes a promise to another to induce that other to act to his detriment and that other does so act in reliance on the promise, the court may prevent (estop) the first person from denying or negating the promise.

equitable estoppel
Being stopped by one's own prior acts or statements from claiming a right against another person who has legitimately relied on those acts or statements.

law merchant

The generally accepted customs of merchants; often used to refer to early commercial law developed by the merchants themselves, which later formed the basis for much of commercial common law.

allowed as Damages may be determined by the plaintiff's expenditures or change of position in reliance as well as by the value to him of the promised performance. Restitution is also an "enforcing" remedy, although it is often said to be based upon some kind of a rescission. In determining what justice requires, the court must remember all of its powers, derived from equity, **law merchant**, and other sources, as well as the common law. Its decree should be molded accordingly.

Joseph HOFFMAN

v.

RED OWL STORES, INC., a foreign corp., et al., Appellants

Supreme Court of Wisconsin

26 Wis. 2d 683, 133 N.W.2d 267 (1965)

[An agent for Red Owl Stores engaged in continuing negotiations with Hoffman, who operated a bakery but wanted to run a Red Owl supermarket. Negotiations took more than two years, during which Hoffman sold his bakery at the agent's request and bought and worked in a small grocery store. During this period, the price of the franchise was raised from $18,000 to $24,000 to $26,000. When Red Owl insisted that $13,000 put up by Hoffman's father-in-law be considered a gift, Hoffman balked.]

The record here discloses a number of promises and assurances given to Hoffman by Lukowitz in behalf of Red Owl upon which plaintiffs relied and acted upon to their detriment.

Foremost were the promises that for the sum of $18,000 Red Owl would establish Hoffman in a store. After Hoffman had sold his grocery store and paid the $1,000 on the Chilton lot, the $18,000 figure was changed to $24,100. Then in November, 1961, Hoffman was assured that if the $24,100 figure were increased by $2000 the deal would go through. Hoffman was induced to sell his grocery store fixtures and inventory in June, 1961, on the promise that he would be in his new store by fall. In November,

plaintiffs sold their bakery building on the urging of defendants and on the assurance that this was the last step necessary to have the deal with Red Owl go through.

We determine that there was ample evidence to sustain the answers of the jury to the questions of the verdict with respect to the promissory representations made by Red Owl, Hoffman's reliance thereon in the exercise of ordinary care, and his fulfillment of the conditions required of him by the terms of the negotiation had with Red Owl.

There remains for consideration the question of law raised by defendants that agreement was never reached on essential factors necessary to establish a contract between Hoffman and Red Owl. Among these were the size, cost, design, and layout of the store building; and the terms of the lease with respect to rent, maintenance, renewal, and purchase options. This poses the question of whether the promise necessary to sustain a cause of action for promissory estoppel must embrace all essential details of a proposed transaction between promisor and promisee so as to be the equivalent of an offer that would result in a binding contract between the parties if the promisee were to accept the same.

Originally the doctrine of promissory estoppel was involved as a substitute for consideration rendering a gratuitous promise enforceable as a contract. In other words, the acts of reliance by the promisee to his detriment provided a substitute for consideration. If promissory estoppel were to be limited to only those situations where the promise giving rise to the cause of action must be so definite with respect to all details that a contract would result were the promise supported by consideration, then the defendants' instant promises to Hoffman would not meet this test. However, [the *Restatement of Contracts*] does not impose the requirement that the promise giving rise to the cause of action must be so comprehensive in scope as to meet the requirements of an offer that would ripen into a contract if accepted by the promisee. Rather[,] the conditions imposed are:

1. Was the promise one which the promisor should reasonably expect to induce action or forbearance of a definite and substantial character on the part of the promisee?
2. Did the promise induce such action or forbearance?
3. Can injustice be avoided only by enforcement of the promise?

We deem it would be a mistake to regard an action grounded on promissory estoppel as the equivalent of a breach of contract action. . . .

While the first two of the above listed three requirements of promissory estoppel present issues of fact which ordinarily will be resolved by a jury, the third requirement, that the remedy can only be invoked where necessary to avoid injustice, is one that involves a policy decision by the court. Such a policy decision necessarily embraces an element of discretion.

We conclude that injustice would result here if plaintiffs were not granted some relief because of the failure of defendants to keep their promises which induced plaintiffs to act to their detriment.

* * *

Plaintiffs contend that in a breach of contract action damages may include loss of profits. However, this is not a breach of contract action.

The only relevancy of evidence relating to profits would be with respect to proving the element of goodwill in establishing the fair market value of the grocery inventory and fixtures sold. Therefore, evidence of profits would be admissible to afford a foundation for expert opinion as to fair market value.

Where damages are awarded in promissory estoppel instead of specifically enforcing the promisor's promise, they should be only such as in the opinion of the court are necessary to prevent injustice. Mechanical or rule of thumb approaches to the damage problem should be avoided.

* * *

"The wrong is not primarily in depriving the plaintiff of the promised reward but in causing the plaintiff to change position to his detriment. It would follow that the damages should not exceed the loss caused by the change of position, which would never be more in amount, but might be less, than the promised reward."

* * *

At the time Hoffman bought the equipment and inventory of the small grocery store at Wautoma he did so in order to gain experience in the grocery store business. At that time discussion had already been had with Red Owl representatives that Wautoma might be too small for a Red Owl operation and that a larger city might be more desirable. Thus Hoffman made this purchase more or less as a temporary experiment. Justice does not require that the damages awarded him, because of selling these assets at the behest of defendants, should exceed any actual loss sustained measured by the difference between the sales price and the fair market value.

Since the evidence does not sustain the large award of damages arising from the sale of the Wautoma grocery business, the trial court properly ordered a new trial on this issue.

Case Questions

1. What is the difference in the measure of damages between breach of contract and promissory estoppel?
2. The court cites and rejects the argument that promissory estoppel creates a substitute for consideration. Williston was the foremost proponent of the classical model (offer, acceptance, and consideration) in contract law. *Restatement* § 90 was written by Corbin, the foremost critic of the classical model. How does the court choose one over the other?

FAILURE OF THE CLASSICAL MODEL

Out of the chaos of contract law in the nineteenth century, an effort was made by scholars, particularly Langdell and Holmes in the United States, to reduce contract law to logical principles in the common law. The effort was doomed from the start because of the nearly infinite variety of promissory situations and bargaining relations. Judges were disinclined to apply mechanical formulas when the results were clearly unjust. The concepts of fairness and good faith in principles of equity provided alternative remedies in some cases, and in other cases alternatives were found in the foundations for quasi-contract and promissory estoppel. The result has been an uneasy coexistence of two contradictory conceptions of contract.

Evidence of the demise of the classical model can be found in the Uniform Commercial Code, which departs from that model at every turn. The UCC emphasizes assisting contract formation rather than restricting it. Consideration is transformed, the mirror-image rule is banished, indefinite terms may be implied or determined by the custom of the marketplace, and so on.

For the practitioner, the classical model of offer, acceptance, and consideration must be kept in mind while constructing contracts, but the full range of principles must be appreciated when an agreement fails.

THE FIELD OF COMMERCIAL LAW

Contract law is the starting point for the study of commercial law, as most commercial relationships are contractual in nature. Just as the intricacies of contract law are beyond the scope of this book, so too are the various specialized areas of commercial law, each of which deserves a course by itself in law school curricula. Although they are very important to the paralegal, only a brief introduction to the subject matter of the major subfields of commercial law is presented here to acquaint the paralegal with topics covered more fully elsewhere.

The Uniform Commercial Code

The Uniform Commercial Code was designed to establish a set of rules governing commercial transactions, modernizing the concepts of contract and commercial law to suit the marketplace. The UCC encouraged uniformity in state law regarding commercial transactions, and in this it has been largely successful, having been adopted with only minor variations in all states except Louisiana, which has adopted only four of its articles. Separate sections (articles) of the UCC cover the following subjects:

Sales

Commercial paper

Bank deposits and collections

Letters of credit

Bulk transfers

Warehouse receipts, bills of lading, and other documents of title

Investment securities

Secured transactions; sales of accounts, contract rights, and chattel paper

Except for the specialist, the key sections of the UCC concern sales, commercial paper, and secured transactions. Of these, Article 2 (Sales) is extremely important because it clarifies and modifies existing principles of contract law, some of which have been noted earlier. The one transactional area *not* covered in detail by the UCC is real property transactions, in which long-standing principles differ widely among the states, defying attempts at unification. The UCC as incorporated in state law should be consulted on any question that comes within its ambit.

Commercial Paper

Commercial paper, or **negotiable instruments**, consists of substitutes for cash used to facilitate commercial transactions. **Checks, drafts, promissory notes**, and **certificates of deposit** are all considered commercial paper. Commercial paper is thus a signed writing representing an unconditional promise to pay money. It is regulated by Article 3 of the UCC.

Secured Transactions

A **secured transaction** takes place when the payment of a debt is protected by **collateral**. The most common secured transactions are (1) real property **mortgages**, in which the purchaser or owner of land borrows money, pledging interests in real property to satisfy the debt in case of default, and (2) purchase money installment contracts for personal property (such as an automobile), in which the seller retains rights of repossession in case of default. Article 9 of the UCC covers secured transactions of personal property except for interests arising by operation of law, such as **mechanic's liens**. Secured interests in real property fall outside the UCC, so the law of each state must be consulted for applicable rules.

Obligations to pay money that are unsecured are covered by the state law of debtor and creditor. Discharge of debt through bankruptcy falls within federal jurisdiction under the U.S. Constitution.

Business Organizations

Business organizations consist of variations on three forms: **corporations**, **partnerships**, and **sole proprietorships**. Attorneys are regularly called upon to advise clients on the choice of business organization that will best suit their needs. Personal liability, tax consequences, and financing are major considerations that affect the choice, but size of the organization, its structure, and its long-range goals are also important factors. Paralegals frequently draft the documents that create and control business organizations. Once formed, businesses not only must conform to their own rules but also are subject to numerous requirements of state and federal law with which the commercial lawyer and the paralegal must be familiar.

negotiable instruments
"Commercial paper"; consists of cash substitutes, such as *checks, drafts, promissory notes,* and *certificates of deposit.*

check
Written order to a bank to pay money to a named person.

draft
An order to pay money; a *drawer* orders a *drawee* to pay money to a *payee.* A *check* is a draft on a bank payable on demand.

promissory note
Promise by the maker of the note to pay money to a payee; usually involved in loans and debts.

certificates of deposit
Promises by banks to repay money deposited with the bank, ordinarily with interest.

**secured
transaction**

Takes place when the payment of a debt is protected by *collateral*. The most common secured transactions are (1) real property *mortgages*, in which the purchaser or owner of land borrows money, pledging interests in real property to satisfy the debt in case of default, and (2) purchase money installment contracts for personal property, in which the seller retains rights of repossession in case of default. Article 9 of the UCC covers secured transactions of personal property except for interests arising by operation of law, such as *mechanic's liens*. Secured interests in real property fall outside the UCC.

collateral

Property pledged to pay a debt; a security interest.

mortgage

A written instrument creating an interest in land as collateral for the payment of a debt.

mechanic's lien

Arises when someone is not paid for work done on or improvements made to property; the debt or obligation to pay money becomes a burden on the property. Ordinarily created by law under state statutes.

SUMMARY

The law of contracts is concerned with private agreements that the law recognizes as enforceable. Unlike torts, the obligations to be enforced are established by the agreement rather than the law. Under the classical model of contract formation, the requisites for making an enforceable contract consisted of offer, acceptance, and consideration. In its simplest form, consideration is an exchange of promises to perform agreed-upon obligations. The contract is not complete until offeror and offeree agree upon identical terms; an attempted acceptance of an offer that alters a term of the contract is considered a counteroffer rather than acceptance.

Even when offer, acceptance, and consideration are present, contract formation can be corrupted by misconduct of one of the parties, mistake, lack of contractual capacity, or illegality. Certain kinds of contracts are required to be in writing by the Statute of Frauds and the Uniform Commercial Code, the latter making significant changes in the model of offer, acceptance, and consideration.

When a contract is not fulfilled, compensatory damages are available to put the nonbreaching party in the position he or she would have been in had the contract been performed. Punitive damages and recovery for emotional damages are not ordinarily available in contract, but the lines between contract and tort have become increasingly blurred, as demonstrated by medical malpractice and product liability.

Strict adherence to the classical model provides little flexibility in the nearly infinite variety of contractual situations, so the courts have devised a number of ways around what appear to be unjust results. The classical model based on the common law must compete with traditional concepts of fairness emanating from equity. A number of equitable remedies are available that depart from monetary compensation. In addition, equitable principles have given rise to enforcement of moral obligations in the form of quasi-contract, whereby the law imposes a contract to avoid unjust enrichment, and promissory estoppel, whereby a party suffers a detriment in relying on inducements made by another when a contract is not enforceable under common law principles. Although common law contract principles and theories of moral obligation and reliance in equity exist side by side, they are intrinsically contradictory, resulting in inconsistency in contract law.

The field of commercial law covers a large number of subfields, such as commercial paper, secured transactions, and business organization. Much of the law in this area is statutory, including the Uniform Commercial Code, which has been adopted by most states and which provides uniformity in interstate commercial transactions.

KEY TERMS

acceptance	collateral	duress
anticipatory breach	consideration	emancipated minor
bilateral contract	contract implied in fact	equitable estoppel
business organizations	contracts of adhesion	executory contract
certificate of deposit	corporation	fraud
check	draft	law merchant

mechanic's lien

misrepresentation

mistake of fact

mortgage

negotiable instruments

offer

partnership

privity of contract

promissory estoppel

promissory note

quasi-contract

ratify

reformation

rescind

rescission

restitution

secured transaction

sole proprietorship

Statute of Frauds

substantial performance

undue influence

unilateral contract

unjust enrichment

voidable

business organizations

Consist of variations on three forms: *corporations*, *partnerships*, and *sole proprietorships*. Attorneys are regularly called upon to advise clients on the choice of business organization that will best suit their needs. Personal liability, tax consequences, and financing are major considerations, but the size of the organization, its structure, and its long-range goals are also important. Once formed, businesses not only must conform to their own rules but also are subject to numerous requirements of state and federal law.

corporation

A fictional person chartered by a government; a business organization that protects owners and managers from personal liability.

partnership

Unincorporated business association lacking the limited liability of a corporation, so that debts that cannot be satisfied by partnership property may go after the personal assets of the partners.

sole proprietorship

An unincorporated business owned by one person.

CHAPTER REVIEW QUESTIONS

1. Why are lawyers often more concerned with writing rather than litigating contracts?
2. What is an executory contract?
3. What are the three requirements of contract formation under the so-called classical model?
4. How do we label a contract that is accepted by performance rather than by a return promise of performance?
5. The meeting-of-the-minds model of contract formation characterizes which model of contract?
6. What does the Statute of Frauds require?
7. What is the exception to minors' lack of contractual capacity?
8. What is the measure of damages for breach of contract?
9. The concept of "unjust enrichment" is the basis for which contract remedy?
10. What is the justification for creating obligations of contract under promissory estoppel when the elements of contract formation (offer, acceptance, and consideration) have not been satisfied?

CRITICAL THINKING QUESTIONS

1. Why is professional malpractice based on tort law rather than contract law?
2. To what extent should consumer protection override traditional obligations of contract?

CYBER EXERCISE

Opinions of the Supreme Court of Mississippi can be found at a number of websites, including http://www.mssc.state.ms.us/. The Mississippi Supreme Court decided *White v. Cooke*, 4 So. 3d 330 (Miss. 2009), on January 15, 2009. The case contained the majority opinion, excerpted in this chapter, and a dissenting opinion. Locate the case at http://www.mssc.state.ms.us/ and answer the following questions:

a. In his dissenting opinion, why does Justice Dickinson side with the plaintiff?
b. How does Justice Dickinson apply race/notice in his opinion?

SCENARIO

In general, parties to a contract are free to set whatever terms and conditions they please if they are legally competent and the contract does not have an illegal purpose. The following contract is unusual and untested in the courts, to the best of this author's knowledge. The first author came across the contract on which this example is modeled on the World Wide Web and soon discovered several other similar contracts. There is a private world of "bondage enthusiasts," for want of a better term, who take such contracts quite seriously.

Master and Slave Contract

I hereby offer myself in slavery to my Master in consideration of his love and affection. I make these promises voluntarily out of a desire to serve my Master whom I love and adore. This contract shall begin _____ and end _____.

Terms and Conditions

The slave agrees to obey her Master in every way. Her body is available for her Master at all times and she agrees that he may determine whether others may use her body and for what purpose. The slave accepts that her Master may hurt her to gain pleasure for himself. The slave may on appropriate circumstances utter the *safeword,* a word agreed upon entering this contract, that temporarily suspends the obligations of this contract.

The slave will address the Master as "Master" or "Sir" and will always show him deference and respect. On days when the Master works, the slave will greet him at his return wearing wrist restraints, a neck collar with a leash, or such garments as the Master shall desire. She must ask the Master for permission to leave the room, to eat, and to use the toilet. Failure in any of these will result in a punishment of the Master's choosing.

None of the foregoing terms and conditions shall interfere with the slave's career. She is expected to work hard and dress and act as expected in her career.

I consign my body and soul to my Master according to the terms set herein.

(*signature*) _____ Slave _____ date

I accept my slave's promise of obedient service and take responsibility for her care and discipline to see that she serves my will.

(*signature*) _____ Master _____ date

As an attorney, you are visited by the "slave" who signed this contract. She acknowledges that she was strongly attracted to sexual bondage and sadomasochism, but her "master," a man of independent wealth, beat her so severely over several months that she has lost the use of her left hand and has several permanent scars on her body. She wants to sue in tort for her injuries. What part does this contract play in such a suit? On what grounds can the contract be attacked? How can the "master" use the contract as a defense to suit for battery?

CHAPTER 12
THE LAW OF PROPERTY

CHAPTER OUTLINE

INTRODUCTION

The previous chapters have probably given the impression that disputes and litigation form the core of the law, but this is a false impression of the practice of law. Particularly in the area of property, litigation is rare because good "lawyering" work prevents the need for litigation. A properly drafted and executed will should avoid all but unreasonable challenges. A carefully executed real estate transaction transfers title without loose ends and settles all important future questions about ownership.

Property law is extremely important for paralegals because it involves a great deal of work that does not require an attorney except as legal advisor and supervisor. Within the area of property law are a number of important subfields, such as real estate transactions, landlord and tenant law, estates and trusts, estate planning, planning and zoning, environmental law, and commercial leases. Other areas present specialized property law aspects, such as community property, equitable distribution, and marital estates in family law and leases and real property transactions in contract law. Taxation is an important consideration in legal advising on all aspects of property law. There are specific causes of action in tort to protect property interests: trespass, **nuisance**, and ejectment, among many others. In recent years government regulation of property via planning, zoning, and environmental laws has placed severe restrictions on land use and created a need for legal specialization in these areas. Bankruptcy, **foreclosure**, mortgages, and mechanic's liens concern rights of third parties in property.

nuisance
Basically, a continuing trespass, as when one discharges polluting effluents that seep into a neighbor's pond (this constitutes a *private* nuisance).

foreclosure
The process whereby real property is sold to satisfy a mortgage under default.

In short, all of private law that is not concerned with wrongful misconduct (and much that is) revolves around property law. Perhaps in no other field of law is a more comprehensive knowledge of law required for legal advice, even on what may appear to be a relatively simple problem or transaction, than in the area of real property law.

PROPERTY IS AN ABSTRACTION

Natural property does not exist. From a legal point of view, a mountain is not property, nor a lake, nor a book. Until we assign legal rights in a thing, it is not property. When a person building a new home says, "I am going out to the property," we understand that there is a building site, a piece of land, in its natural or altered state, but we also understand that the statement asserts rights of ownership over something that has been defined on a map with boundaries, the title to which has been transferred from one hand to another and recorded in the records of the county in which it is situated. But the most important, albeit often unconscious, assertion in this use of the word *property* is that the owner has rights that the law will defend. The definition, determination, and allocation of these rights are the subject matter of property law.

The abstract nature of property may be illustrated by a few examples contained in Exhibit 12-1.

EXHIBIT 12-1   EXAMPLES OF THE ABSTRACT NATURE OF PROPERTY

condominium

A form of ownership in real property where owners typically share ownership in common areas, such as the land, sidewalks, swimming pool, and so on, but have individual rights in a building, as if each owner owned an apartment or townhouse.

franchise

A collaborative relationship in which the franchisee pays a franchisor for the use of the franchisor's trade name and products; may also include a business model or system.

1. A retailer builds up a profitable business over many years and then decides to sell it and retire. Not only may the retailer sell the premises and the inventory of the store, but a major part of the sales price may be for "goodwill," which is valuable property.
2. A professional basketball player is paid a very large sum of money just to have his name associated with a line of sneakers. He has property rights in his name.
3. A person buys a fifth-story **condominium** on the beach before it is built. Until constructed, ownership is of a piece of air.
4. Someone pays for a **franchise** to operate a fast-food restaurant.
5. Amazon.com invents a software program to keep online buyer information to enable one-click purchases from repeat buyers. Amazon patents the process and successfully stops Barnes & Noble from using a virtually identical program for its online shoppers.
6. A state university professor receives **tenure**, which grants a right to permanent employment at the university.
7. Someone registers the Internet domain name http://www.beautiful.com with Network Solutions and is later offered (and accepts) $1 million for the domain name.
8. A physician challenges antiabortion statutes on the ground that they unconstitutionally restrict the right to practice medicine.

All these examples express valuable property rights of which the law takes cognizance. Note that the government not only restricts property rights (example 8) but also creates them (examples 5 and 6). In fact, the government through its laws can create or destroy property rights, subject only to due process of law and just compensation for property taken for a public purpose.

The law may recognize something as property for one purpose but not for another. In New York, for example, a professional license may be "marital property," the value of which can be divided in a divorce, but it is not property for the purposes of sale or gift. In *Community Redevelopment Agency v. Abrams*, 15 Cal. 3d 813, 543 P.2d 905, 126 Cal. Rptr. 423 (1975), the California Supreme Court held that goodwill in a pharmacy that was taken in order to redevelop an urban center was not property, even though it would be property for the purposes of a private sale of the pharmacy. In relation to this last example, Professor Berger asked the unanswerable question, "Did the pharmacist lose because he had no property or did he have no property because he lost?" Goodwill is an abstract concept, but goodwill as property raises it to an even higher level of abstraction. Property itself is an abstraction of the rights that the law recognizes.

A condominium owner's interest in the property is subject to restrictions typically found in the *condominium declaration*, the document establishing the condominium; and the *condominium bylaws*, the document that further defines the condominium owner's rights and duties. The condominium declaration contains more basic provisions than do the bylaws; it is typically recorded in the public records and thus puts the public on notice of its provisions. The condominium declaration anticipates that bylaws will further define condominium ownership and that any bylaws must be in conformance with the condominium declaration. Bylaws usually contain condominium rules, are not recorded in the public records, and are amended more frequently than the condominium declaration.

In *Apple Valley*, the court references the tension between an individual owner and restrictions imposed by the condominium documents. Perhaps there was even more tension for the individual who originally developed the condominium but later became the owner of one condominium unit. Here the former developer transitioned from a position of power, as developer, to the position of an individual owner, subject to the condominium restrictions just like any other owner.

tenure

In higher education, job security granted to faculty members, usually after a period of several years and based on an extensive approval process. Tenured faculty cannot be fired without cause.

APPLE VALLEY GARDENS ASSOCIATION, INC., Plaintiff-Respondent

v.

Gloria MacHUTTA and Steven MacHutta, Defendants-Appellants-Petitioners

Supreme Court of Wisconsin

No. 2007AP191

763 N.W.2d 126

Decided March 27, 2009.

This is a review of a published decision of the court of appeals affirming the entry of summary judgment in favor of Apple Valley Gardens Association, Inc. (the "Association") by the Circuit Court for Waukesha County, Paul F. Reilly, Judge. Three issues are presented. First, may a condominium complex prohibit the rental of condominium units through an amendment to the bylaws, or must such a restriction be placed in the condominium's declaration? Second, does the condominium declaration at issue here create a right to rent that precludes the enforcement of a bylaws amendment prohibiting condominium rentals? And third, does a prohibition on the rental of condominium units render title to those units unmarketable in violation of Wis. Stat. § 703.10(6) (2007-08)?

Spouses Gloria and Steven MacHutta (collectively, "the MacHuttas") each currently own one condominium unit in the Apple Valley Gardens condominium complex. Steven MacHutta developed the complex in the late 1970s. The declaration of condominium, recorded in July 1979 to establish the condominium (the "declaration"), contained no restriction regarding rental of the units. However, on December 18, 2002, the Association amended the condominium bylaws (the "bylaws amendment") to prohibit rental of the condominium units. In 2004, Gloria MacHutta leased her condominium unit to a new tenant over the Association's objection, claiming that the rental prohibition was ineffective because it had not been added to the condominium declaration. The Association then filed an action in the circuit court seeking an order for declaratory judgment that the bylaws amendment was enforceable. The circuit court ultimately entered summary judgment in favor of the Association, which the court of appeals affirmed.

We hold that the condominium bylaws amendment prohibiting the rental of condominium units is permissible under Wis. Stat. § 703.10(3). We further conclude that the condominium declaration in this case does not conflict with the bylaws amendment prohibiting unit rental. Having been duly adopted by the Association, the bylaws amendment is therefore enforceable under Wis. Stat. § 703.10(1). Additionally, in accord with Wis. Stat. § 703.10(6), the bylaws amendment constitutes a mere restriction on the use of the condominium units, and does not in any way affect the quality of the units' title or marketability. Under the undisputed facts of this case, the Association is entitled to summary judgment as a matter of law. Accordingly, we affirm the decision of the court of appeals. . . .

In 2002, the Association membership duly amended Article VI, ¶ 6.1(j) of the condominium bylaws to prohibit rental of the condominium's units as follows:

j. *Owner occupied.*

i. Effective January 1, 2003, all units are required to be owner occupied. No residential unit owner shall rent, lease or otherwise so demise any residential unit or any part therein. Owners shall not permit the use of said unit by any party other than owner or owner's immediate family member.

ii. An owners' [*sic*] observance of and performance under a rental agreement, lease, or other instrument granting occupancy in a residential unit in effect as of December 18, 2002 shall not be a violation of this subparagraph (j). . . . When the existing tenants . . . vacate their respective units, said units shall become owner occupied under this subparagraph (j), irrespective of the effective date of the rental agreement, lease, or other instrument granting occupancy in a residential unit.

The Association also duly amended the bylaws to include a provision in Article IX, ¶ 9.1 requiring written consent from the board of directors for the renewal or extension of any lease or rental agreement.

In 2004, Gloria MacHutta's then-tenant vacated the rental unit. Wishing to lease the unit to a new tenant, Gloria MacHutta submitted a lease application to the Association's board of directors for its consent. The board refused, however, invoking the 2002 bylaws amendment. Undeterred, Gloria MacHutta proceeded to lease her unit to the new tenant. . . .

It is true that condominium declarations do and must include information regarding the usage of the units. Wis. Stat. § 703.09(1)(g) requires that a declaration contain a "[s]tatement of the purposes for which the building and each of the units are intended and restricted as to use." The use restrictions in mind here are general in nature. Nothing in this provision or in any other section of the Wisconsin Condominium Ownership Act (Wis. Stat. ch. 703) requires that *all* restrictions on use must be identified in the declaration. Similarly, no statute suggests that a prohibition on the rental of condominium units must be placed in the declaration to be effective. Declarations are not required to be exhaustive as to permissible uses of condominium units.

This is where bylaws come in. Bylaws govern the administration of condominiums. Wisconsin Stat. § 703.10(1) explains:

(1) BYLAWS TO GOVERN ADMINISTRATION. The administration of every condominium shall be governed by bylaws. Every unit owner shall comply strictly with the bylaws and with the rules adopted under the bylaws, as the bylaws or rules are

amended from time to time, and with the covenants, conditions and restrictions set forth in the declaration or in the deed to the unit. Failure to comply with any of the bylaws, rules, covenants, conditions or restrictions is grounds for action to recover sums due, for damages or injunctive relief or both maintainable by the association or, in a proper case, by an aggrieved unit owner.

This section requires strict compliance with restrictions that are added to a condominium's bylaws after the declaration is recorded.

Wisconsin Stat. § 703.10(3) expressly authorizes the placement of additional use restrictions in condominium bylaws:

PERMISSIBLE ADDITIONAL PROVISIONS. The bylaws also may contain any other provision regarding the management and operation of the condominium, including *any restriction on or requirement respecting the use and maintenance of the units* and the common elements. (Emphasis added.)

This provision does not contain limitations on the types of restrictions that can be implemented through bylaw amendments. Therefore, as long as use restrictions do not conflict with the declaration (an issue taken up in Section IV.B. below) or with state or federal law, they are valid and enforceable.

We recognize that this empowers condominium associations to take actions that limit the rights of individual owners. There is an inherent tension between the competing interests of supermajority owners and individual owners. A unit owner might be frustrated, financially or otherwise, by the loss of her ability to rent out her unit. But the statutes are clear that associations have this power. Condominium ownership is a statutory creation that obligates individual owners to relinquish rights they might otherwise enjoy in other types of real property ownership. When purchasing a condominium unit, individual owners agree to be bound by the declaration and bylaws as they may be amended from time to time.

The MacHuttas' argument, then, that a restriction on the rental of condominium units must be placed in the declaration, simply does not square with the applicable statutes. The fact that lenders and purchasers rely on recorded declarations is irrelevant. If lenders and purchasers wish to know whether and under what conditions a condominium unit may be rented out, they may easily inquire of both the declaration and the bylaws. Even so, the association, if not prohibited by the declaration, could choose to withdraw an owner's ability to rent out his or her unit at a later date. This is one of the sacrifices of condominium ownership under the current statutory scheme.

Case Questions

1. Why would there be a prohibition on condominium rental?
2. What can the condominium do if one of the unit owners violates a provision of the condominium declaration or the bylaws?

REAL PROPERTY'S "BUNDLE OF RIGHTS" MODEL

In an effort to simplify the abstraction of property, legal scholars refer to a *bundle of rights* that a person may enjoy. This model is used to explain the complex laws of real property ownership. Real property consists of land and its improvements (buildings, fences, wells, etc.—those valuable changes that humans inflict on their land). Other things that may be owned, such as money, goods, stocks and bonds, and the like, are called *personal property* and come with a much smaller bundle of rights.

The most important property rights are rights of possession, use, and transfer. Each of these includes other rights. The *right of possession* allows one not only

tenancy by the entirety
A form of co-ownership with a *right of survivorship* that can be held only by husband and wife.

dower and curtesy

Formerly, interests in property held by a wife (dower) and a husband (curtesy), the primary purpose of which was to guarantee real property interests for a surviving spouse. The husband was favored, and these interests have been equalized or combined in recent times so as not to discriminate.

restrictive covenants

Mandates concerning what may or may not be done with, to, or on real property; take many forms, including minimum square footage for a house, lawn and yard maintenance, ability to rent the property, and signage. Racially restrictive covenants and other discriminatory practices have long been held unconstitutional.

easement

A right of use in another's property, for example, when someone has a right-of-way to cross another's land.

lease

An agreement by an owner of property (the *lessor*), with a renter (a *tenant* or *lessee*) whereby the lessee pays for the right of possession and use but does not acquire title.

to be present on the land but also to exclude others. The causes of action for trespass, ejectment, and nuisance are based on this right. *Use rights* include the right to improve the land, to exploit it for agriculture, mining, timber cutting, and so on. The *right of transfer or conveyance* includes the right to sell, lease, or give away real property. Real property is also transferred at death by will or intestate succession; these are important rights of ownership.

The nature and duration of these rights are restricted by a number of features of property law and property rights. Consider a married couple that "owns" a home. If they acquired the home after they were married, it is likely that they have a form of co-ownership called a **tenancy by the entirety**, whereby the surviving spouse would own the entire property in the event of the other's death. Even if title to the home is held in only one name, the other may have a marital interest based on **dower** or **curtesy** or on community property rights in some states. If there is a mortgage on the home, someone else has a right to sell the property in foreclosure if the couple defaults on the payments, and their capacity to sell the property may be severely restricted by the terms of their mortgage.

What they can do with their land may be subject to many limitations—**restrictive covenants**—placed in their deed if the home was part of a housing development. The use of their land is limited by local, state, and federal law. For example, they may not be allowed to cut down a tree or have a garage sale without a permit. If their house is on a city street, the city has an **easement** along the street that gives the city a number of rights and the owners little but duties. The electric company has an easement for lines across the property, as does the city water department. There could be other private easements allowing other persons a right-of-way across their land. They might not own the mineral rights below the surface of their land. The city, county, state, or federal governments could take away their property to build a highway or for other public use, only providing them with just compensation. Despite these restrictions, they are taxed on the value of the entire property, which could be sold for nonpayment of the taxes.

The duration of property rights may also be limited. If possession is held by a **lease**, the right of possession is subject to limitations of time as well as any other conditions the lessor includes in the lease agreement. A title may be limited in duration, such as for life (life estate) or until the fulfillment of a condition. When title has a limited duration, someone other than the present possessor has a future interest in the property, so that the present possessor has duties and limitations on use for the benefit of the future interest.

The bundle of rights may be viewed as the totality of rights and restrictions on rights held by a person with regard to real property. In view of the complexities of property rights, the term *ownership* has limited usefulness in the field of real property. The law deals with rights, and the extent of a person's ownership depends on how much of the bundle a person has.

In *Saddlehorn*, the subdivision association claims that it has a recreation easement over lots owned by the Dyers. If the recreation easement exists, the easement would restrict the Dyers' use of the lots.

SADDLEHORN RANCH LANDOWNER'S,
INC.; William Cheney; Nathan Gaston; Robert
Krechter; Michael & Tracy McFadin; Thomas
Phillips; Lawrence M. Thompson, Plaintiffs-
Counterdefendants-Respondents-Cross
Appellants

v.

Christy B. DYER; Dan Dyer; and Christy B. Dyer
as trustee of the Christy B. Dyer Children's Trust
Fund, Defendants-Counterclaimants-Appellants-
Cross Respondents

Supreme Court of Idaho, Twin Falls, November
2008 Term

No. 34605

203 P.3d 677

Jan. 21, 2009.

This case arises out of a dispute over ownership of
two parcels of land in the Saddlehorn Ranch subdivision. Christy and Dan Dyer, husband and wife, (the
Dyers) and Christy Dyer as trustee of the Christy
B. Dyer Children's trust fund (the Trust) appeal the
district court's decision granting in part, and denying in part, the parties' cross-motions for summary
judgment. Saddlehorn Ranch Landowner's, Inc. (the
Association) cross-appeals to this Court.

Factual and Procedural Background

In 1982 the Dyers entered into a contract of sale
for their property to Dale and Janet Sykes (the Sykes).
The agreement required the Sykes, who intended
to develop the property into a residential subdivision, to make periodic payments to the Dyers and,
in exchange, the Dyers would release certain parcels
to the Sykes to be sold. The Sykes subdivided and
recorded the original **plat** in 1982 under the name of
Le Emeraude. The R-Lots are referenced in the 1982
plat and appear exactly the same in the 1996 plat.
The disputed parcels are labeled as "R" lots on the plat

recorded in 1982 by the Sykes and re-recorded in 1996
by Christy Dyer. The plat legend defines "R" lots as
"Reserved." Lot 1-R is labeled as "Gravel Pit and Future
Recreation Lot" and lot 4-R is labeled as "Recreation
Center." As the Sykes made payments on the property,
the Dyers released portions of the property to the
Sykes and the Sykes subsequently sold those parcels.
The Sykes recorded the "Amended master declaration
of restrictive covenants and conditions for Le Emer-
aude subdivision" (the Covenants) in March of 1984.

In 1987 the Sykes defaulted on the contract and
the Dyers initiated foreclosure proceedings. The
Dyers acquired 73 of the original 123 lots in the
subdivision by **sheriff's deed** in 1990. In 1994, after
the foreclosure proceedings were complete, Christy
Dyer incorporated the Association and subsequently
re-filed the plat in 1996. The name of the subdivision
was changed to Saddlehorn Ranch in 1994 following
incorporation.

The following are the relevant portions of the
Covenants which reference any common areas
or recreation areas in the subdivision. The 1984
covenants were referenced and reiterated when
Christy Dyer incorporated the subdivision in 1994.

Paragraph 12 states "COMMON AREA, if any, shall
mean any area that may be designated on any current
plat as common area."

Section 2.08 reads "Zoning Regulations. No lands
within the subdivision shall ever be occupied or used
by or for any building or purpose or in any manner
which is contrary to the zoning regulations applicable
thereto validily [sic] in force from time to time. Buildings shall be restricted to single family dwelling units
and associated structures only."

Article IV "COMMON AREA" reads "The following
conditions shall apply to the common area, if any:
Section 4.01 Common area. The common area, if any,
and any improvements or facilities located thereon shall
be owned by the Master Association and shall be subject
to the rules and regulations of the Master Association."

Section 5.04 "Duties of the Master Association"
recites "C. Operation of Le Emeraude Common Area.
To operate and maintain, or provide for the operation

and maintenance of the common area and to keep all Improvements of whatever kind and for whatever purpose from time to time located thereon in good order and repair, including but not limited to all recreation facilities, utilities, waterworks and sewage facilities located therein."

In 1994 and 1999 Christy Dyer, as president of the Association[,] signed and recorded amendments to the master declaration. None of the amendments reference any of the provisions listed above. . . .

The following [issue is] presented to this Court on appeal: . . .

Whether the district court erred by failing to consider the "surrounding circumstances" in finding that the Dyers dedicated the R-lots to the Association. . . .

The district court did not err by failing to consider the "surrounding circumstances" when it found that the Dyers dedicated the R-lots to the Association.

The district court held that the Dyers retained title to the R-lots, but that the Association holds an easement for recreational purposes. The district court further held that the Association "is responsible to maintain that easement and any developments thereon, as contemplated by the Declaration of Covenants, Conditions and Restrictions."

The elements of public and private common law dedication are the same, requiring "(1) an offer by the owner clearly and unequivocally indicating an intent to dedicate the land and (2) an acceptance of the offer." *Ponderosa*. This doctrine protects the interest of purchasers who rely on the value of these public areas.

The offer for dedication must be clear and unequivocal, thereby indicating the owner's intent to dedicate the land. The burden of proof is on the party alleging that the land owner's act or omission manifested an intent to dedicate the land for public use. . . .

The Dyers emphasize the language in the Covenants which consistently states "if any" after the word "common area" as an indication that there was not an intent to dedicate the R-lots to the Association. The plat labels the lots as "reserved" on the map legend, and they are more specifically labeled as "gravel pit and future recreation lot" and "recreation center." No homeowner's association existed when the Covenants were filed, and

it was Christy Dyer who incorporated and created the Association in 1994 thereby making the contemplated homeowner's association a reality. Similarly, Christy Dyer also made any contemplated common areas a reality when she re-filed the plat in 1996. There is no single act in this stream of events which would constitute a common law dedication. However, through several purposeful acts, Christy Dyer took the Covenants, plat and subdivision that the Sykes only contemplated and made them all a reality. Her actions show a clear intent to develop the subdivision as originally contemplated, which includes a dedication of the R-lots to the Association for recreational purposes. She continued to sell lots with reference to the plat, with knowledge that those purchasers would rely on her acts as positive assertions that the common areas were dedicated to the Association. This Court finds that the R-lots were dedicated to the Association and that the Association has a valid easement on the R-lots for recreational purposes.

This Court further finds that the district court did not fail to analyze the "surrounding circumstances". . . . It is clear that the district court analyzed every aspect of the plat recording process and all the events preceding the actual 1996 re-recording of the subdivision plat and the continual sale of parcels with reference to the re-recorded 1996 plat.

Case Questions

1. What could the owner of a lot subject to a recreation easement do with the property?
2. What are the two elements necessary to dedicate land?
3. What protection does the court provide to landowners who purchased lots in reliance on the recorded plat?

Case Glossary

plat
A map showing the division of an area of real property into lots, streets, parks, etc., and indicating easements.

sheriff's deed
The deed given to the buyer of real property at an auction ordered by a court to satisfy the debt of the property owner.

§

THE DEED

A will must satisfy rigid formalities to be valid. **Deeds** are the documents that express the intention to transfer real property interests from one owner, the **grantor**, to another, the **grantee**. A **warranty deed** is desirable because it includes certain promises of the grantor, especially the promise to defend the title. The requirements of a deed are listed in Exhibit 12-2.

deed

A document that describes a piece of real property and its transfer of title to a new owner.

 *Delivery of a Deed*

A homeowner signed a deed transferring his home to a friend, rented a safe deposit box in his and the friend's name, and placed the deed in the safe deposit box. Under the homeowner's will, the home would not have gone to the friend. If the deed remained in the safe deposit box when the homeowner died, would the friend own the home, or would the home pass to the individuals named in the will?

After answering the question, consider whether the following information would alter your answer:

- The friend was a married woman that the homeowner would have married had she been single.
- His stepchildren would own the home had the home not previously passed to the lady friend under the deed.

See Moseley v. Zieg, 146 N.W.2d 72 (Neb. 1966).

EXHIBIT 12-2   REQUIREMENTS OF A DEED

Generally, a deed has the following requirements:

- The deed must be in writing.
- The grantor must be competent.
- The grantee must be identified.
- There must be an adequate description of the property.
- Consideration—a mere recital of consideration is usually sufficient.
- The grantor must sign.
- Witnesses are commonly required.
- The deed must be delivered to the grantee.

ESTATES IN LAND

grantor

A party that transfers an interest in real property to another, the *grantee*.

grantee

A party to which an interest in real property is transferred by the *grantor*.

warranty deed

A *deed* that includes promises or warranties, especially the promise to defend the title.

In a highly commercial society such as ours, real estate is often perceived as a commodity to be bought and sold for investment or speculation. As the real estate market boomed in 2004 and 2005, a new term, *flipping*, became popular, referring to purchase and almost immediate resale of residential property. A speculative surge initiates all sorts of "creative" financing and property transfers. Nevertheless, real estate is not a commodity like pencils, where monetary payment and delivery of the goods pass title from one hand to the next without either side considering problems of title. Even the simplest real estate sale involves lawyers, title companies, tax stamps, recording at the courthouse, realtors, closing agents, mortgage companies, and so forth. The need for all of these has a lot to do with the ancient law of estates.

The law of tort and contract is a model of common sense compared to property law. Law based on private wrong must adapt to changing values and daily life, whether personal or commercial. Property law, in contrast, reflects the accumulation of technical principles establishing ownership rights. Land law is conservative; many basic principles have changed little over the centuries.

The conservatism of land law is partly due to concern on the part of those who have property that their rights remain secure and partly because, over the centuries, those with wealth in property have either made the law or had extraordinary influence over those who make the law. Thus, tinkering with the rules of property rights has been disfavored. Another reason for the conservatism lies in the very law that has given us the bundle-of-rights principles. Title to land, as we have seen, is a complex matter. Intrusions into ownership rights may take place at any time—a second mortgage, a tax lien, a lease, or marriage or divorce can occur during the course of possession and will affect how various rights are distributed and limited. When someone sells real estate, the buyer will want to know the status of all rights pertaining to the property in question. The current status of a piece of real property depends upon its history. A search of the history—**chain of title**—of the property may even reveal that the seller's claims of ownership are much in doubt, that someone else claims to be the owner, or that there are restrictions that make the property unsuitable for the purchaser's intended use.

chain of title

The history of the transfer of title to real property; comprised of a series of grantor-to-grantee transfers leading to a showing of who is the present holder of title.

Often a plaintiff obtains a judgment against a defendant requiring the defendant to pay the plaintiff money even though the defendant has no money to pay the plaintiff. The plaintiff can take the official document setting forth the judgment and have it recorded in the public records for the county where the defendant lives or where the plaintiff anticipates that the defendant will purchase property. Should the defendant purchase real property, the judgment would attach to any real property the defendant owns in a county where the judgment is recorded.

A crucial element, in addition to recording of the judgment, is proper indexing of the recorded judgment, by the custodian of the public records, to reflect the defendant's name. *Hinnant* concerns a situation in which the defendant's name on the recorded judgment was missing one letter.

Charles H. HINNANT and Dorothy W. Hinnant,
Plaintiffs

v.

Richard B. PHILIPS and Sheila A. Philips,
Defendants

and

Pedro Martinez Espinosa; Cecilia M. Rodriguez;
John T. Matthews, Trustee

and

Mortgage Electronic Registration Systems, Inc.,
Defendant/Intervenors

Court of Appeals of North Carolina

No. COA06-1308

645 S.E.2d 867

June 19, 2007

Defendant-intervenors, Pedro Espinosa and Cecilia Rodriguez; John Matthews, Trustee; and Mortgage Electronic Registration Systems, Inc. (MERS), appeal from an order granting the motion of plaintiffs Charles and Dorothy Hinnant for execution on a judgment obtained against Richard and Sheila Phillips (defendants). We affirm.

The factual and procedural history of this case began in 1982 when plaintiffs loaned money to defendants, secured by a promissory note executed by the parties. Defendants failed to make the required payments, and plaintiffs filed a complaint to collect the balance of the loan. Their complaint was captioned *Hinnant v. Phillips*, 87 CVD 1689. Plaintiffs obtained a default judgment on 18 March 1988, which was docketed and indexed with "Richard Barry Phillips and Sheila Ann Phillips" named as defendants.

In July 1988, after the docketing of the judgment in 87 CVD 1689, defendants bought a parcel of land in Johnston County (the subject property). Approximately ten years later, in 1998, plaintiffs filed a complaint to renew their judgment against

defendants. The complaint, 98 CVD 272, was again captioned with the parties' names, but the last name "Phillips" was spelled "Philips" with one "L." In February 1998 plaintiffs obtained judgment in their favor; this judgment and the copy docketed by the Clerk of Court also spelled "Phillips" as "Philips."

In 2005 plaintiffs filed a motion in the cause seeking to collect on the judgment through sale of the subject property. However, by 2005 the property had changed hands several times. Defendants had defaulted on their mortgage, and the lender foreclosed on the property; thereafter, it was conveyed to a financial corporation. The subject property was then conveyed to Espinosa, who executed a promissory note in favor of MERS and its trustee, John Matthews.

In May 2006 the trial court allowed appellants to intervene in the case, to protect their rights in the subject property. At the hearing conducted 8 May 2006, appellants argued that the judgment against plaintiffs was not an effective lien as against a *bona fide* purchaser. Appellants asserted that the claimed lien was invalid because it did not appear in the chain of title in a search for "Phillips" with two L's. Plaintiffs presented expert testimony that the standard of care for a title search includes checking for common spelling variants of a name, and that the approved practice is to enter part of a name (in this case, P-H-I-L) in order to catch minor errors or spelling variations. . . .

N.C. Gen.Stat. § 1-233 (2005) sets out requirements for docketing a judgment, and provides in relevant part that:

> Every judgment . . . affecting title to real property, or requiring . . . the payment of money, shall be indexed and recorded by the clerk of said superior court on the judgment docket of the court. The docket entry must contain the file number for the case in which the judgment was entered, [and] the names of the parties[.] . . . The clerk shall keep a cross-index of the whole, with the dates and file numbers thereof[.] . . .

Under N.C. Gen.Stat. § 1-234 (2005), a judgment docketed in accordance with G.S. § 1-233 creates a lien that is effective against third parties:

> Upon the entry of a judgment . . . affecting the title of real property, or directing . . . the payment of money, the clerk of superior court shall index and record the judgment on the judgment docket [.] . . . The judgment lien is effective as against third parties from and after the indexing of the judgment as provided in G.S. § 1-233. The judgment is a lien on the real property in the county where the same is docketed[.] . . .

G.S. § 1-234.

Docketing a judgment provides notice of the existence of the lien on the property, and a judgment that is not docketed is ineffective as to third parties. . . .

The issue presented is whether the judgment docketed under the name "Philips" instead of "Phillips" nonetheless provided sufficient notice, actual or constructive, to create a valid lien on the subject property. We conclude that on the facts of this case, the judgment was a lien on the property. . . .

Plaintiffs argue that a judgment docketed and indexed in substantial compliance with the pertinent statutes will establish a lien on the judgment debtor's property, while defendants contend that the statutory requirements must be strictly followed in all respects. . . .

The relationship between the standard of care for title examination and the question of the efficacy of the judgment to create a lien is as follows: If a title examiner exercising the standard of care would have found the judgment at issue, then it sufficiently complies with G.S. § 1-233 to create a lien on the property. In the instant case, plaintiffs established by uncontradicted expert testimony that in this case the standard of care for a reasonably prudent title examiner would be to search under part of the last name, such as "P-H-I-L," which would have revealed the judgment at issue. Additionally, even a search under "Phillips" would indicate defendants' involvement in several other proceedings, including a foreclosure; this should have spurred further inquiry. We conclude that plaintiffs substantially complied with G.S. § 1-233, and agree with the trial court's findings and conclusions.

Appellants, however, assert that the statutory requirements for indexing a judgment require "strict compliance" and that any spelling error automatically renders the judgment unenforceable against a third party purchaser. Under the pertinent case law, . . . we have reached a different conclusion. Moreover, the cases cited by appellants are neither binding precedent nor persuasive authority, as none are factually similar. In *Holman*, cited by appellants, the court's decision was based on the fact that the judgment in question had not been docketed in a timely manner and *not* on any defect or spelling error in the docketing. Thus, the Court's discussion of docketing practices dating back to "the reign of Henry VIII" is mere dicta. In *Trust Co. v. Currie*, also cited by appellants, the judgment in question was indexed under a totally different last name: "Quick," rather than "Currie."

Case Questions

1. What was the chain of title of the real property once owned by the Phillips?
2. Is it fair to hold subsequent owners liable for the judgment amount?
3. Should the court require substantial compliance or strict compliance with the indexing statute?

To many, our land law is simply a cumbersome relic of the past, but it is self-perpetuating; its technical complexity makes it difficult to change. What may appear to be a minor change may turn out to require adjustments throughout the entire system, and anything that potentially casts doubt on ownership is unfavorably viewed by property owners, lawyers, and those who make the law. Modernization of land law would be a monumental task and an agonizing ordeal that few seem ready to undertake.

The result of this conservatism is land law based on an ancient system that bears little relation to present realities. At the core of land law are the common law estates that were developed in the first centuries following the Norman Conquest in 1066. These came into being during England's feudal period, when a person's status in society depended almost entirely on rights in land. Society and government were built on a military model with the king at its apex. Technically, all land was held by the king, but it was divided among his subjects, who thereby owed the king certain fees and military service. Thus, a certain baron might control a certain area of land and the peasants working the land and be required to furnish his overlord with fees and a specified number of knights and soldiers in time of conflict. The overlord, in turn, was similarly responsible to his overlord and so forth up to the king. At the base of the pyramid were the peasants who worked the land, providing a portion of their crops and personal service to the landlord, who was their protector. Although no one owned the land in the modern sense of the word, the status attached to the land passed from father to eldest son—by **primogeniture**—as long as the son was acceptable to the lord and swore fealty to the lord. A baron's (or count's) land was inherited by his son (land could not be passed by will until the Statute of Wills in 1540), who then became the baron.

Although the system of primogeniture and certain other features of aristocratic land ownership were not adopted in the United States, the system of common law estates continues to this day. The estates were divided between freehold and nonfreehold estates (see Exhibit 12-3); freeholders were free men, and nonfreeholders were called "villeins." Except for the last term, which has come to mean something quite different, the terms have been preserved intact. It is more common to call a nonfreehold a leasehold estate with a lease, a lessor, and a lessee.

Fee Simple Absolute

The inheritable freehold estates were called *fees*; the most important one, then and today, was the **fee simple absolute**. This estate represents the maximum bundle of rights with

primogeniture
A system under the common law whereby title to land passed to the eldest son (*primo-*, first-; *geni-*, born).

fee simple absolute
An estate in land having the maximum rights, that is, without future interests.

EXHIBIT 12-3 ESTATES IN LAND

TYPE OF ESTATE	NAME OF ESTATE	DESCRIPTION
Freehold	Fee simple absolute	The estate having the maximum rights, such that the owner can sell or give it away, the owner can pass it by will, and it will pass to the owner's heirs if there is no will
Freehold	Life estate	An estate that lasts during the life tenant's lifetime, such that the life tenant can sell or give away the estate (with such sale or gift effective only during the life tenant's lifetime) but the estate cannot pass by will or pass to the life tenant's heirs if there is no will
Nonfreehold	Lease	The right to possession and occupancy of the leased premises

inheritable

The character of an estate in land that may pass to heirs upon death (with no will). Personal property is usually inheritable. *Inheritable* has the same meaning as *heritable*.

devisable

The character of an estate in land that is capable of being passed by will upon death. Personal property is usually devisable.

life estate

An estate, especially in land, that lasts until someone dies (the *life tenant*).

life tenant

A person who has an interest in an estate (especially in land) that lasts until that person (or another specified person) dies.

remainder

A future interest in land that follows a *life estate*.

the fewest strings attached. Among its important features are that it is *alienable* (it can be sold or given away), **inheritable**, and **devisable** (it can be passed by will). A fee simple absolute is unconditional and has potentially infinite duration. Standard real estate sales contracts call for a fee simple absolute, and that is what purchasers want and expect, whether or not they are familiar with its name. Such an estate still represents what it did several hundred years ago: the complete bundle of rights to possession, use, and transferability.

Life Estate

Contrast fee simple absolute with **life estate**, which is a freehold estate that is not inheritable. A life estate is created to last for a person's lifetime. It cannot be inherited or passed by will because it ends immediately upon the death of the owner, the **life tenant**. Otherwise, it has the attributes of a fee simple absolute: It can be sold, leased, or given away. Of course, the life tenant cannot transfer more than he has—the purchaser gets an estate that lasts only as long as the original life tenant is alive. A life estate always creates a future interest; someone must have title after the life tenant dies, which imposes a duty on the life tenant to preserve the estate or be liable for "waste." For example, a father conveys real property "to my son Michael for life, and then to my grandson George." If no other limiting language is included, when Michael dies, George will hold the property in fee simple absolute (while Michael is alive, George's future interest is called a **remainder**).

It might be expected that a spouse who remarries later in life and who had grown children from the first marriage might provide in the will a life estate for the second spouse and the remainder to the grown children. The *Hershman-Tcherepnin* court reached a different conclusion.

Sue-Ellen HERSHMAN-TCHEREPNIN

v.

Nicholas TCHEREPNIN & others [Stefan Tcherepnin, Sergei Tcherepnin, and Sarina Tcherepnin-Morris]

Supreme Judicial Court of Massachusetts, Middlesex

891 N.E.2d 194

Decided July 31, 2008.

This case is before this court on an application for further appellate review of a judgment by the Probate and Family Court declaring that Ivan Tcherepnin (testator), through his will, devised his home as follows: a life estate to his wife, Sue-Ellen Hershman-Tcherepnin (wife), and a one-fifth future interest in remainder to her and each of his four children by an earlier marriage. . . .

Although it is clear that the testator granted the wife and each of his four children a one-fifth ownership interest in the house, it is not clear whether those interests are present estates or future (remainder) estates, in light of the additional grant to the wife of the "right to remain there for as long as she desires." That language creates an ambiguity because it is susceptible to two meanings: a life estate or a mere right of occupancy (a right or privilege not to be removed from the house). Put another way, the phrase leaves some doubt about the property bequeathed, i.e., the quantum of the estate given to the wife. . . .

Typically, "a conveyance 'to B during his life' or 'to B until his death' or other similar words of limitation will create a life estate in B." H.J. Alperin. Here, the testator used neither "life" nor "death," nor did he use comparable wording. Where a will does not employ the language typically used to create a life estate, the will may nonetheless create a life estate if other factors are present, such as where the will grants the premises to the person in question or requires that person to maintain the property and pay taxes and insurance on it.

In this case, however, the testator did not give or grant the premises—i.e., the entire house—to the wife for so long as she desired to live there; he gave her only one-fifth of the house and the right to remain there for as long as she desired. . . .

Another reason that we conclude that the will did not create a life estate and five remainder interests is the absence of remainder language. Ordinarily, a future estate is created by language such as: " 'to B for life, remainder to C and his heirs'—B has a present life estate, and C has a remainder in fee simple." Alperin. . . . Here, no such comparable language was used.

Moreover, to read the will to grant the wife a life estate would be to give her a disproportionate share of the house—a one-fifth interest *plus* a life estate. The will and the circumstances under which it was created belie that reading and instead show that the testator intended to divide the house equally. The specific bequests in clauses six and ten through thirteen give the wife and each child a one-fifth interest in the house and its furnishings (with the wife getting first choice of the furnishings). And the seventeenth clause provides: "Any specific bequest or residuary bequest made in this will to two or more beneficiaries shall be shared equally among them, unless unequal shares are specifically indicated." The testator did not specify unequal shares in ownership of the house—he did not give the wife a life estate *plus* a one-fifth ownership interest; he gave her and each child only a one-fifth ownership interest.

The wife began living in the home only in 1995—relatively late compared to the children, who had grown up in the house in the 1980's. And even after the sons moved away, they continued to maintain their bedrooms in the house; "everyone," including the testator, considered the house the " 'family' home." Moreover, at the time the will was created, Stefan was living in the house, and Sergei was visiting nearly every weekend. When the testator died, he had been married to the wife for a few months. Those circumstances support the view that the testator intended to give the wife not a disproportionate share of the house, but to give her and each child equal shares of the property.

By giving the wife and the children equal, present shares in the house, the testator created a tenancy in common. . . . But the testator also gave the wife something above and beyond what he gave the other cotenants: the "right to remain" in the house "for as long as she desires." The testator was not an attorney, and so we consider the literal meaning of the words he used. . . . Accordingly, even though a tenancy in common, by its very nature, protects each cotenant from exclusion or ouster, it is reasonable to conclude (in the absence of evidence indicating that the testator understood the legal rights created by a tenancy in common) that the testator used the "right to remain" language to ensure that the children understood that, despite her relatively short time in the house and in the family, and despite the fact that the children were given four-fifths of the house, the wife was entitled to stay in the house after the testator's death. In other words, the "right to remain" language gave the wife not an estate in the property but a right or privilege not to be excluded from the home.

That the law of tenancies in common protects each cotenant from ouster is not to say, however, that the "right to remain" language is mere surplusage. We must give effect to that language, if possible. We conclude that the "right to remain" language, while unnecessary to ensure the wife's protection from ouster, is meaningful as a means to accomplish the testator's intent to provide the wife with a home insofar as it protects her from losing her possessory interest through a partition (a point conceded by the children).

While a tenancy in common carries with it protection from ouster, it also carries with it an absolute right to partition. . . . Pursuant to the absolute right to partition, each cotenant is potentially vulnerable to being divested of his possessory interest in the property if another cotenant seeks partition and a physical division of the property is inconvenient or nonadvantageous.

Thus, consistent with the testator's intent that the wife be protected against removal from the house by the children, we conclude—consistent with the children's concession—that he intended that she be protected against partition. In other words, we conclude that, in these circumstances, the testator's use of the "right to remain" language is tantamount to a restraint on the children's ability to partition the property for as long as the wife chooses to remain there (i.e., no longer than her lifetime). . . . That is not to say, however, that the testator did not give the children the right to enter or live in the house. By creating a tenancy in common, he gave them such rights; but through the "right to remain" language he also prevented them from removing the wife from the house by partition.

Although we conclude that the testator granted the wife protection from partition, in the particular circumstances of this case we conclude that the wife relinquished that protection by seeking partition. First, although she contended in her petition for partition that she held a life estate in the property and that she and each child held a one-fifth remainder interest, on that view she would not have held a concurrent possessory interest with the children and thus would not have been entitled to a partition at all. . . .

In any event, that the wife could have pursued a partition as an owner of a one-fifth interest in the property as a tenant in common with the children does not guarantee that the wife would have been able to obtain sole possession of the house by purchasing the children's shares, or that she would even have been able to remain in the house. In fact, unless the house can be partitioned in kind, which seems doubtful, it will have to be sold. That the wife anticipated the sale of the house is buttressed by the fact that she not only petitioned for partition, but she also moved for the appointment of a commissioner and an order directing that the property be sold. In sum, while not relinquishing her one-fifth ownership interest in the house, the wife, by seeking to partition the property, has demonstrated her willingness to give up her "right to remain" there "for so long as she desires." . . .

The testator's will devised to the wife and each of the four children one-fifth ownership of the house as tenants in common. Through the "right to remain" language, the will also granted the wife protection against partition. In the particular circumstances of this case, however, the wife terminated that protection by seeking a partition.

Case Questions

1. What facts would support a life estate to the wife and the remainder to the children?
2. What facts would support the interpretation that the wife and children were tenants in common?
3. Does the court's interpretation of the language make sense?

§

Nonfreehold Estates

Nonfreehold estates are also called **leasehold estates** and are most commonly represented by formal leases, commercial or residential, which spell out rights, duties, commencement, and termination as well as rental terms. Because these are contractual in nature and do not pass title, problems are resolved under contract law and state landlord and tenant law. Oral and informal arrangements present special problems that are usually handled in small claims court, as most rentals involving substantial amounts of money are evidenced by written contracts that are the products of professional legal advice.

Co-Ownership

Title may be held by more than one owner. Mention has been made of tenancy by the entirety, which is a species of co-ownership that can be held only by husband and wife. It includes a **right of survivorship**, as does **joint tenancy**, which can be held by two or more people as equal owners with equal rights of use and possession. Under the right of survivorship, if one co-owner dies, the share of the deceased is owned equally by the survivors. Sale or gift prior to death defeats the right of survivorship, but an attempted gift by will fails because death terminates all property interests in a joint tenancy or tenancy by the entirety. A remaining form of co-ownership is **tenancy in common**, which does not have a right of survivorship and which permits unequal shares among the co-owners.

An important example of co-ownership today is the condominium, in which owners of individual housing units are also tenants in common with regard to common areas—stairs, walkways, parking lots, and so on—and are equally obligated for their maintenance. Time-share arrangements are a relatively new phenomenon commonly associated with a condominium-like land use. Under time-share, owners are tenants in common but restricted in their use to certain time periods during the year. States in which condominiums and time-share are common have adopted comprehensive statutes governing them.

When a married couple purchases a home in both their names, the co-ownership is usually a tenancy by the entireties. Because only married couples can enjoy this type of co-ownership, it is destroyed by divorce, and if the property continues to be owned by both it will become a tenancy in common by "operation of law," unless otherwise agreed (the marital settlement agreement could provide for a joint tenancy with right of survivorship).

Principles of co-ownership are summarized in Exhibit 12-4.

As explained in *Smith v. Korstad*, when a spouse dies the surviving spouse becomes the sole owner of the property by operation of law. The question considered in *Smith* is whether a creditor of the decedent can obtain a **writ of execution** on the home now owned by the surviving spouse.

right of survivorship
An incident to certain forms of co-ownership whereby a co-owner, if there are but two co-owners, will own the entire interest upon the death of the other co-owner.

joint tenancy
A form of co-ownership that includes a *right of survivorship*.

tenancy in common
A form of co-ownership that does not have a *right of survivorship* and that permits unequal shares.

writ of execution
A demand that property be sold to satisfy a debt of the property owner.

EXHIBIT 12-4   CO-OWNERSHIP

TYPE OF CO-OWNERSHIP	OWNERS	ATTRIBUTES
Tenancy by the entirety	Spouses	Owners have equal interests, with rights of use and possession, and the tenancy includes a right of survivorship
Joint tenancy	Joint tenants	Owners have equal interests, with rights of use and possession, and the tenancy includes a right of survivorship
Tenancy in common	Tenants in common	Owners' interests may be unequal and, upon an owner's death, the owner's interest passes by will or, if there is no will, to the owner's heirs

Mike SMITH d/b/a Wasilla Concrete, Petitioner

v.

Raymond KOFSTAD, individually and d/b/a Busch Concrete, and Marguerite Kofstad, Respondents

Supreme Court of Alaska

No. S-12679

206 P.3d 441

April 24, 2009.

Mike Smith, d/b/a Wasilla Concrete, sued Raymond Kofstad, d/b/a Busch Concrete, over nonpayment for construction materials and supplies. Smith obtained a **default judgment** against Raymond for $41,589.41 in September 1995. The judgment was **recorded** the next month in the Palmer Recording District, where Raymond and Marguerite owned a home as tenants by the entirety. Raymond died in January 2001.

Smith first sought a writ of execution in August 2005, almost ten years after entry of judgment and more than four years after Raymond died. Smith filed a motion in the district court requesting leave to execute on the Kofstad home. . . . The motion was accompanied by an affidavit explaining that Smith had not previously obtained a writ of execution because he "did not believe that the judgment debtor had assets with net value capable of satisfying a portion of the judgment." He further stated: "I also became aware that the defendant was deceased during the Fall of 2000 [sic]. I checked property records and discovered that a number of IRS liens had been recorded, which would have made execution upon the judgment debtor's real property fruitless. I believe the IRS liens have since expired." Smith served the motion, affidavit, and a summons on Marguerite. She opposed the motion, and the district court denied leave to execute without explanation. . . .

A judgment creditor generally can obtain a writ of execution as a matter of course within five years of the judgment. There is no definitive time limitation on the commencement of executions of judgment, but if the judgment creditor does not seek a writ of execution within five years, "no execution may issue except by order of the court in which judgment is entered." The court shall grant leave to execute only if it determines "there are just and sufficient reasons for the failure to obtain the writ of execution within five years after the entry of judgment." We have held that a judgment debtor's previous lack of assets that could satisfy the judgment, rendering execution futile, is a just and sufficient reason to permit leave to execute under AS 09.35.020.

The parties disagree whether, as a matter of law, a judgment creditor must diligently try to verify the lack of assets during the five year period to merit permission to later execute on the judgment. But because execution is now futile—when Raymond died and Marguerite took full ownership of their home by operation of survivorship, Smith's ability to execute on Raymond's share of the property was extinguished—we need not reach the question raised by the parties.

When an individual judgment debtor dies, his or her property generally is transferred through probate proceedings to heirs or devisees, subject to creditor claims against the decedent. If a judgment creditor has an existing lien on specific property owned by the judgment debtor, the lien survives the judgment debtor's death and can be foreclosed as if the judgment debtor were still living. Alternatively the judgment creditor can file a claim in the probate proceedings to have the debt satisfied from the decedent's estate.

But when property is owned by husband and wife as tenants by the entirety and one spouse dies, the decedent's share in the property does not pass through probate. Instead, the decedent's share is extinguished at death and the surviving spouse takes full ownership of the property by operation of law from the original conveyance: "The common law theory . . . is that the decedent's interest vanishes at death, and therefore no probate is necessary because no interest passes to the survivor at death." When the decedent's share in unsevered survivorship property extinguishes, so therefore must the putative interest of any creditor in that property. Courts in other jurisdictions have uniformly assumed, if not expressly stated, that with respect to unsevered survivorship property, the death of a judgment debtor and the consequent destruction of the judgment debtor's share in the property also destroys any interest of a judgment creditor in that share. This is an issue of first impression for this court.

We hold, in accordance with the uniform practice in other jurisdictions and with the logic of tenancy by the entirety, that: (1) recording a judgment against a judgment debtor, thus creating a judgment lien against property owned by the judgment debtor, does not sever a tenancy by the entirety between the judgment debtor and spouse, and (2) a judgment creditor's interest, if any, in a judgment debtor's interest in an unsevered tenancy by the entirety is extinguished when the judgment debtor predeceases the spouse. We observe that a judgment creditor may take action to sever a tenancy by the entirety. [AS 09.38.100 provides]:

> If an individual and another own property in this state as tenants in common or tenants by the entirety, a creditor of the individual . . . may obtain a levy on and sale of the interest of the individual in the property. A creditor who has obtained a levy, or a purchaser who has purchased the individual's interest at the sale, may have the property partitioned or the individual's interest severed.

Severance terminates a tenancy by the entirety, nullifying survivorship and thus protecting a judgment creditor's interest in the judgment debtor's share of the property. We express no opinion on when in the execution process a tenancy by the entirety is actually severed. Smith never attempted to levy on the Kofstads' home prior to Raymond's death, and the Kofstads' tenancy by the entirety therefore remained unsevered; Raymond's death consequently extinguished his interest in the home.

Because Smith is unable to execute on the Kofstad home, his application under AS 09.35.020 for leave to execute on the home is futile.

Case Questions

1. Why must the judgment creditor ask a court for a writ of execution if the judgment is more than five years old?
2. Why is the judgment creditor treated differently when the decedent's property was held by tenancy by the entirety rather than by tenancy in common?

Case Glossary

default judgment
A judgment obtained by the plaintiff when the defendant fails to answer the complaint within the allotted time.

record
The act of putting the public on notice of a document affecting property ownership by placing the document in the public records.

§

Implications

Clearly, the holder of a life estate is missing some of the rights enjoyed by the owner in fee simple absolute. There are other, less frequently used freehold estates that are not described here, but keep in mind that in a sale of land, the purchaser ordinarily expects a fee simple absolute, and it is the responsibility of the person examining the land's past to determine whether the asserted owner does in fact have a clear title with the full bundle of rights.

The purchaser must be informed of any encumbrances. Attorneys are called upon to search titles, that is, to examine the records to establish the present owner and the extent of ownership. If any of the previously mentioned numerous intrusions on ownership appear in the records, the purchaser should know of these and their legal ramifications, for instance, the significance of a utility easement that allows the electric company to cross the land to serve other properties. Inconsistencies and questions should be resolved: Has an old mortgage been satisfied even though satisfaction of mortgage has not been recorded? What was the effect of the divorce of a prior owner? An attorney may be retained not only to help conduct the transaction but also to provide a title opinion describing the current status of the title. Title insurance companies, which maintain extensive records on land within the territory they cover, offer additional protection to the prudent buyer.

Title searches, title opinions, and title insurance are made necessary by the system of estates that has been inherited over the centuries. Land sales call for a methodical approach that typically follows an orderly checklist to prepare for a smooth closing at which the purchase price is exchanged for delivery of a deed to the property. Much of the work in real property transactions can and should, for reasons of cost, be done by paralegals. In fact, a person who specializes in such transactions, or even one who specializes in residential or commercial sales or leases, is preferable to a general practitioner. Experience develops an awareness of the myriad problems that may arise.

LIABILITY OF LANDOWNERS

invitee

At common law, usually a person who enters upon real property to pursue business with the landowner, by invitation express or implied (e.g., customer of a retail store who enters the store).

licensee

At common law, a person who enters upon real property, not by invitation (express or implied), for his or her own purpose (e.g., a pharmaceutical vendor visiting a physician's office).

trespasser

A person who enters land wrongfully without consent, invitation, or privilege (e.g., a "squatter").

Landowners have duties toward others present on their land. The common law distinguished three major categories of people who entered another's land: **invitee**, **licensee**, and **trespasser**. In this order, the landowner (or occupier of land) owed a diminishing duty. To the *trespasser* was owed almost no duty at all, except perhaps a duty not to set hidden traps; a trespasser is on the land wrongfully, without consent or invitation, express or implied. The *invitee* is usually someone who enters premises on business involving the landowner, by invitation express or implied; this is most usually a business visitor. The invitee is owed a duty of protection against dangers that are known, or reasonably should have been known, to the landowner. The *licensee* is a person privileged to enter the land by permission or consent, express or implied, but whose purpose is the licensee's, not any interest of the landowner. The licensee is owed a lesser standard of care than the invitee. The difference today between a licensee and an invitee is blurred or nonexistent. The courts are more likely to look at reasonable duty of care in either case. Trespassers are a different story, however.

YOU be the JUDGE   *Liability of Landowner*

A parent hosts a party for her underage child and the child's friends at the parent's home. Some of the party attendees are drinking alcohol, and one attendee injures another attendee. Can the parent be held liable for the attendee's injuries?

After answering the question, consider whether the following information would alter your answer:

- At least 70 underage individuals attended the party.
- Two kegs of beer were available.
- After the injury occurred, the parent offered no assistance, retreating into the house and locking the door.

See Martin v. Marciano, 871 A.2d 911 (R.I. 2005).

TITLE

The word **title** has been used frequently thus far; its definition cannot be postponed. It is an important concept but one that is often misunderstood. The definition of title is curiously absent from or cursorily treated in law texts covering real property—possibly because the concept of title is abstract to the point of mystery.

In its beginnings, title was embodied in the concept of *seisin,* which originally meant possession but gradually came to signify possession under the right to claim a freehold estate. Seisin originally referred to what seems today to have been a rather mystical relationship between an owner and his land; seisin was passed from one man to another by a ritual called *livery of seisin,* symbolized by handing over a twig or a clump of dirt from the land. When seisin passed, so did the right of possession.

The concept of title is similar. Its definition takes three forms, as listed in Exhibit 12-5.

Title is not a document, such as a deed, though the term is often loosely used in such a reference. A deed is simply one of many bits of evidence of title. In a sense, title is held by the one who holds the greatest number of the bundle of rights that constitute a freehold estate; a lessee does not have title despite having the right of possession.

The three definitions of title treat different aspects of title. As evidence of title, there are numerous documents that, combined in a somewhat mystical union, tell us who has title. Documents alone may not be sufficient. One in wrongful possession for a sufficient period of time may acquire title by **adverse possession**. Treating title as a means of claiming possession refers to the need, on occasion, for one holding title to prove title against other claimants for title or possession. Finally, the right of ownership represented by the concept of title is its most common meaning, especially when ownership is not in question. "Right of ownership" must remain abstract because the law is normally concerned with acknowledging and enforcing specific rights.

If the concept of title still seems obscure, that is because it is relative and abstract. It is used in preference to *ownership* because it signifies application of all the rules that identify ownership. Perhaps it is best explained by the barb, "I don't own the house, the bank owns it." This is an obvious reference to the lender on a mortgage, who usually puts up a far greater portion of the purchase price than the actual purchaser. In most states, however, the bank merely holds a lien on the property and no part of the title. Nevertheless, the title to the land in question is encumbered by the mortgage, and no prudent purchaser would buy the land without resolving the mortgage question. (A mortgage may not prevent a sale of land, but because the mortgage is secured by the land, a failure to pay the mortgage could result in foreclosure no matter who has title.)

title
Formal ownership of property; has many nuances of meaning.

adverse possession
A means of acquiring title by occupying and using land for a certain length of time even though the occupier does not have title. The period at common law was 20 years, but this period has been shortened in most states by statute.

EXHIBIT 12-5 TITLE

1. The right to ownership and possession of land
2. The means whereby an owner of land has just possession
3. The evidence of ownership of land

Personal Property

Title to personal property does not usually raise the complex problems associated with chain of title to real property. Because tangible personal property is commonly exchanged by sale or gift, mere possession is significant evidence of exchange of title. Most problems arise with bailments and lost, stolen, or abandoned property, which is usually covered by well-established legal rules. The Uniform Commercial Code gives specific guidance on sale of goods and intangible personal property in the form of negotiable instruments.

What happens to an engagement ring when the marriage does not take place? Devising fair principles is not as easy as it may seem. The problem is complicated by the intersection of contract law, tort law, family law, and property law, as more fully explained in Exhibit 12-6.

The basic principles that developed concerning return of an engagement ring were as follows: (1) If the donee breaks off the engagement without fault on the part of the donor, the donor is entitled to its return. (2) If the donor breaks off the engagement, the donee keeps the ring. (3) An engagement broken by mutual consent obliges the return of the ring.

In the state of New York, these common law rules applied until 1935, when the legislature abolished actions for breach of promise to marry, which was interpreted by the courts to bar an action for recovery of engagement rings. In 1965, the legislature enacted a law to allow recovery of engagement rings when "justice so requires." This moral tone is echoed in the *Cohen* case, in which the fiancé was killed in an auto accident shortly before the wedding and the personal representative of his estate attempted to recover the ring.

A somewhat similar case was decided in Massachusetts a few years before, but with different results. In *DeCicco v. Barker*, 339 Mass. 457, 159 N.E.2d 534 (1959), a married man gave several rings to a woman, at least one of which, a six-carat diamond ring,

EXHIBIT 12-6   LAW RELATED TO OWNERSHIP OF AN ENGAGEMENT RING WHEN THE MARRIAGE DOES NOT TAKE PLACE

1. *Contract law.* Is an engagement a contract? If the contract is breached, is restitution in the form of return of the engagement ring an appropriate remedy?
2. *Tort law.* There was at one time an action at common law called "breach of promise to marry," with a consequent suit for damages. Many states have abolished this cause of action. Could the engagement ring be an element of damages? Does abolishing the cause of action put the ring beyond reach?
3. *Family law.* Should the marriage (and engagement) contract be treated like any other contract, or should the state's interest in the sanctity of the family treat this contract specially, including the right to the engagement ring? If the state's public policy is not to force incompatible couples to marry, how should the court decide on the ring?
4. *Property law.* Is the engagement ring a gift? Consideration for a contract? A pledge? Has title passed?

was apparently an engagement ring. His wife was in the hospital at the time, and the engagement was conditioned on her death, which occurred two months later. Subsequent to the wife's death, the woman broke the engagement but kept the engagement ring.

When he sued to get the engagement ring back, she relied on the Massachusetts legislature's abolition of the cause of action for breach of promise to marry; the court gave him the six-carat ring, stating,

> . . . It is a proceeding not to recover damages, either directly or indirectly for breach of the contract to marry but to obtain on established equitable principles restitution of property held on a condition which the defendant was unwilling to fulfil [sic]. It seeks to prevent unjust enrichment.

Carol Cohen's ring was worth only $1,000. In *Lowe v. Quinn*, the ring was valued at $60,000, which explains why she wanted to keep it and he went to the highest state court to get it back. Although she broke off the engagement, he was in a special dilemma—he was still married.

COHEN

v.

BAYSIDE FEDERAL SAVINGS AND LOAN ASSOCIATION

Supreme Court of New York

62 Misc. 2d 738, 309 N.Y.S.2d 980 (1970)

Some courts have propounded a pledge theory. Other courts state that principles of unjust enrichment govern and the most popular rationale is that the ring is given as a gift on condition subsequent. It is not always clear, however, whether it is the actual marriage of the parties or the donee's not performing any act that would prevent the marriage that is the actual condition of the "transaction."

Thus a confusing body of law has grown up around the engagement ring and, after careful consideration of these principles, this court has decided that Carol should keep the ring because that result is equitable and because "justice so requires". . . .

I cannot believe that the age-old ritual of giving an engagement ring to bind the mutual premarital vows can be or is intended to be treated as an exchange of consideration as practiced in the everyday market place. Can it be seriously urged that the giving of this ring by the decedent "groom" to his loved one and bride-to-be can be treated as the ordinary commercial or business transaction requiring the ultimate in consideration and payment? I think not. To treat this special and usually once in a lifetime occasion, one as requiring quid pro quo, is a mistake and unrealistic.

EDWIN S. LOWE, Appellant

v.

JAYNE D. QUINN, Respondent

Court of Appeals of New York

27 N.Y.2d 397, 267 N.E.2d 251 (1971)

An engagement ring "is in the nature of a pledge for the contract of marriage" and, under the common law, it was settled—at least in a case where no impediment existed to a marriage—that, if the recipient broke the "engagement," she was required, upon demand, to return the ring on the theory that it constituted a conditional gift. However, a different result is compelled where, as here, one of the parties is married. An agreement to marry under such circumstances is void as against public policy, and it is not saved or rendered valid by the fact that the married individual contemplated divorce and that the agreement was conditioned on procurement of the divorce. Based on such reasoning, the few courts which have had occasion to consider the question have held that a plaintiff may not recover the engagement ring or any other property he may have given the woman. . . .

[The court goes on to argue that the legislative reenactment of the right to recover an engagement ring did not apply to a situation in which either of the parties is married at the time of the gift of the ring.]

Case Questions

1. Is *Cohen* decided on the basis of contract, tort, family, or property law, as suggested in the comments prior to the cases?
2. Is *Lowe* decided on the basis of contract, tort, family, or property law, as suggested in the comments prior to the cases?

ESTATE PLANNING

An important area of law practice is estate planning, which deals with the orderly distribution of assets at death. If no provision is made in advance, the property of a deceased person, called the *estate* or *decedent's estate,* passes by intestate succession as ordered by state law. Most persons would distribute their property somewhat differently than will the state and should so provide in advance by will and/or trust. The estate planner not only assists in preparing the documents of distribution but also advises clients on tax and other legal consequences of different distributions. Though advice is legal and financial, it can be very personal as well.

Wills

The primary purpose of a will is distribution of the financial assets of the deceased according to directions provided prior to death in the will itself. Many persons wish to control the use of their property long after death or want to specify in great detail how everything they own will pass to intended beneficiaries. All this can be accomplished through a will. However, unnecessary complexity not only makes administration of the estate cumbersome but also tends to anger and frustrate beneficiaries and encourage suits to contest the validity of the will. When specific problems, such as a spendthrift child or spouse, warrant limitations on the distribution or use of property, a trust is often the more appropriate solution.

Will drafting is often left to paralegals, who can use the language and form of past models to express the intent of the testator, as long as the document is reviewed by the responsible attorney before the testator and witnesses sign it. Today, drafting wills can be greatly facilitated by computers programmed with standard clauses and paragraphs that reflect the requirements of state law. In some instances, an attorney or paralegal may simply follow a checklist of questions, the answers to which are entered into a computer, which then prints a will. If the computer program is comprehensive, the possibility of human error is minimized.

Each state requires specific formalities for the signing and attesting of wills that must be strictly adhered to in order to create a valid will. The legal advisor's goal should be to give force to the intent of the testator in a form that will discourage and overcome legal challenge. The process of settling an estate through the court is called *probate,* and the court responsible is commonly called *probate* or *surrogacy* court.

Working with clients who wish to have wills drafted calls for delicacy, tact, common sense, and a basic understanding of human nature. Contemplation of death is unpleasant at best, and letting go of the acquisitions of a lifetime is not easy.

A special note is warranted here. Making a will for a client usually results in the attorney and staff acquiring a detailed knowledge of the client's finances and personal relationships. All of this information is strictly confidential, and all members of the legal staff must scrupulously avoid revealing any knowledge thus acquired.

Trusts

A *trust* is a device dating back to the fourteenth century, when it was used to avoid certain features of the ownership of common law freehold estates. It was enforced in the courts of equity and is still governed by equity today. A trust involves a transfer of title of real or personal property to a trustee who is charged with a duty to hold the property for the benefit of another, a *beneficiary* (*cestui que* trust). The trust instrument provides instructions for the trustee to follow in distributing property to the beneficiary.

By setting up a **living (inter vivos) trust**, a person can put property into the trust that will go to named parties immediately or when the donor dies. In this way the trust can be used as a will substitute and has the advantage of making possible detailed instructions as to the distribution of property at the same time that it avoids probate of the property. When a trust is used as a will substitute, the donor can make himself or herself trustee and beneficiary for his or her lifetime and thereby both control and benefit from the property. Trusts can also be used to transfer property without regard to death, as with a trust fund to send one's children to college; the donor may relinquish any control (*irrevocable trust*).

The advantage of a trust over a will is that it names a trustee to carry out the wishes of the donor. Without such an arrangement, future decisions would be based on interpretations of the intent of the testator, which might prove inappropriate as times and situations change. The donor may provide for flexibility that would not be possible in an outright distribution. Also, the trustee has a fiduciary duty toward the beneficiary that can make the trustee more accountable than someone who misuses distributed property. For someone with minor children or others who cannot properly take care of their affairs, a trust can be established that provides temporarily for financial needs while preserving assets for later distribution. In short, the trust can be tailored to very special problems that would be very awkward to handle in a will.

A good deal of the work involving trusts can be efficiently done by paralegals.

living (inter vivos) trust
An ordinary trust, as opposed to a trust established by a will at death (*inter vivos*—"between living persons").

GOVERNMENT REGULATION OF REAL PROPERTY

Ownership of real property today is subject to many intrusions by government. Most of these take the form of restrictions on use. In addition, governments may take property under the power of eminent domain, and the federal government has authority over navigable waters. Former rights to airspace above an owner's property have been restricted primarily because of the advent of the airplane.

Eminent Domain

The Fifth Amendment to the U.S. Constitution, the repository of basic rights in criminal law, ends with the clause, "nor shall private property be taken for a public use, without just compensation." This, along with similar language in state constitutions, is the basis for the power our governments exercise called **eminent domain**. This power is used to take property for highways, parks, urban redevelopment, and protection of the environment. "Public use" has been broadly defined to cover laws allowing private railroads to acquire property for their routes, electric utilities to obtain rights-of-way, and so forth.

Compensation for the taking of property is often subject to dispute, but state and federal governments have procedures designed to determine fair market value and to give the opportunity to challenge assessments. The major issue in litigation has been interpretation of the word *taking*. When government takes title to an entire piece of property, the solution may be simple: pay fair market value. If, however, the state builds a new highway, reducing traffic on an old highway and thereby making a filling station unprofitable, there is no "taking"—it is considered *damnum absque injuria,* a harm without a legal injury, and not compensable. Thus, some effects of government action constitute taking, and some do not. The issue arose early in the last century with planning and zoning.

The United States Supreme Court was much criticized for its decision in *Kelo* because the Court found that a governmental entity's power of eminent domain included the power to take private land to promote economic development.

eminent domain

The power of the government to take private property for a public use, for which just compensation is required by the Constitution.

Susette KELO, et al., Petitioners

v.

CITY OF NEW LONDON, CONNECTICUT, et al.

Supreme Court of the United States

No. 04-108

545 U.S. 469

Decided June 23, 2005.

In 2000, the city of New London approved a development plan that, in the words of the Supreme Court of Connecticut, was "projected to create in excess of 1,000 jobs, to increase tax and other revenues, and to revitalize an economically distressed city, including its downtown and waterfront areas." In assembling the land needed for this project, the city's development agent has purchased property from willing sellers and proposes to use the power of eminent domain to acquire the remainder of the property from unwilling owners in exchange for just compensation. The question presented is whether the city's proposed disposition of this property qualifies as a "public use" within the meaning of the Takings Clause of the Fifth Amendment to the Constitution. . . .

Petitioner Susette Kelo has lived in the Fort Trumbull area since 1997. She has made extensive improvements to her house, which she prizes for its water view. Petitioner Wilhelmina Dery was born in her Fort Trumbull house in 1918 and has lived there her entire life. Her husband Charles (also a petitioner) has lived in the house since they married some 60 years ago. In all, the nine petitioners own 15 properties in

Fort Trumbull—4 in parcel 3 of the development plan and 11 in parcel 4A. Ten of the parcels are occupied by the owner or a family member; the other five are held as investment properties. There is no allegation that any of these properties is blighted or otherwise in poor condition; rather, they were condemned only because they happen to be located in the development area.

In December 2000, petitioners brought this action in the New London Superior Court. They claimed, among other things, that the taking of their properties would violate the "public use" restriction in the Fifth Amendment. . . . Two polar propositions are perfectly clear. On the one hand, it has long been accepted that the sovereign may not take the property of *A* for the sole purpose of transferring it to another private party *B*, even though *A* is paid just compensation. On the other hand, it is equally clear that a State may transfer property from one private party to another if future "use by the public" is the purpose of the taking; the condemnation of land for a railroad with common-carrier duties is a familiar example. Neither of these propositions, however, determines the disposition of this case.

As for the first proposition, the City would no doubt be forbidden from taking petitioners' land for the purpose of conferring a private benefit on a particular private party. . . . Nor would the City be allowed to take property under the mere pretext of a public purpose, when its actual purpose was to bestow a private benefit. The takings before us, however, would be executed pursuant to a "carefully considered" development plan. The trial judge and all the members of the Supreme Court of Connecticut agreed that there was no evidence of an illegitimate purpose in this case. Therefore, as was true of the statute challenged in *Midkiff*, the City's development plan was not adopted "to benefit a particular class of identifiable individuals."

On the other hand, this is not a case in which the City is planning to open the condemned land—at least not in its entirety—to use by the general public. Nor will the private lessees of the land in any sense be required to operate like common carriers, making their services available to all comers. But although such a projected use would be sufficient to satisfy the public use requirement, this "Court long ago rejected any literal requirement that condemned property be put into use for the general public." *Midkiff*. Indeed, while many state courts in the mid-19th century endorsed "use by the public" as the proper definition of public use, that

narrow view steadily eroded over time. Not only was the "use by the public" test difficult to administer (*e.g.*, what proportion of the public need have access to the property? at what price?), but it proved to be impractical given the diverse and always evolving needs of society. Accordingly, when this Court began applying the Fifth Amendment to the States at the close of the 19th century, it embraced the broader and more natural interpretation of public use as "public purpose." Thus, in a case upholding a mining company's use of an aerial bucket line to transport ore over property it did not own, Justice Holmes' opinion for the Court stressed "the inadequacy of use by the general public as a universal test." *Strickley*. We have repeatedly and consistently rejected that narrow test ever since.

The disposition of this case therefore turns on the question [of] whether the City's development plan serves a "public purpose." Without exception, our cases have defined that concept broadly, reflecting our longstanding policy of deference to legislative judgments in this field. [The Court reviews several cases it previously decided.] . . .

Those who govern the City were not confronted with the need to remove blight in the Fort Trumbull area, but their determination that the area was sufficiently distressed to justify a program of economic rejuvenation is entitled to our deference. The City has carefully formulated an economic development plan that it believes will provide appreciable benefits to the community, including—but by no means limited to—new jobs and increased tax revenue. As with other exercises in urban planning and development, the City is endeavoring to coordinate a variety of commercial, residential, and recreational uses of land, with the hope that they will form a whole greater than the sum of its parts. To effectuate this plan, the City has invoked a state statute that specifically authorizes the use of eminent domain to promote economic development. Given the comprehensive character of the plan, the thorough deliberation that preceded its adoption, and the limited scope of our review, it is appropriate for us, as it was in *Berman*, to resolve the challenges of the individual owners, not on a piecemeal basis, but rather in light of the entire plan. Because that plan unquestionably serves a public purpose, the takings challenged here satisfy the public use requirement of the Fifth Amendment.

To avoid this result, petitioners urge us to adopt a new bright-line rule that economic development does not qualify as a public use. Putting aside the unpersuasive suggestion that the City's plan will provide only purely economic benefits, neither precedent nor logic supports petitioners' proposal. Promoting economic development is a traditional and long-accepted function of government. There is, moreover, no principled way of distinguishing economic development from the other public purposes that we have recognized. In our cases upholding takings that facilitated agriculture and mining, for example, we emphasized the importance of those industries to the welfare of the States in question. . . .

It is further argued that without a bright-line rule nothing would stop a city from transferring citizen *A*'s property to citizen *B* for the sole reason that citizen *B* will put the property to a more productive use and thus pay more taxes. Such a one-to-one transfer of property, executed outside the confines of an integrated development plan, is not presented in this case. While such an unusual exercise of government power would certainly raise a suspicion that a private purpose was afoot, the hypothetical cases posited by petitioners can be confronted if and when they arise. They do not warrant the crafting of an artificial restriction on the concept of public use.

Alternatively, petitioners maintain that for takings of this kind we should require a "reasonable certainty" that the expected public benefits will actually accrue. Such a rule, however, would represent an even greater departure from our precedent. . . . The disadvantages of a heightened form of review are especially pronounced in this type of case. Orderly implementation of a comprehensive redevelopment plan obviously requires that the legal rights of all interested parties be established before new construction can be commenced. A constitutional rule that required postponement of the judicial approval of every condemnation until the likelihood of success of the plan had been assured would unquestionably impose a significant impediment to the successful consummation of many such plans.

Just as we decline to second-guess the City's considered judgments about the efficacy of its development plan, we also decline to second-guess the City's determinations as to what lands it needs to acquire in order to effectuate the project. . . .

In affirming the City's authority to take petitioners' properties, we do not minimize the hardship that condemnations may entail, notwithstanding the payment of just compensation. We emphasize that nothing in our opinion precludes any State from placing further restrictions on its exercise of the takings power. Indeed, many States already impose "public use" requirements that are stricter than the federal baseline. Some of these requirements have been established as a matter of state constitutional law, while others are expressed in state eminent domain statutes that carefully limit the grounds upon which takings may be exercised. As the submissions of the parties and their *amici* make clear, the necessity and wisdom of using eminent domain to promote economic development are certainly matters of legitimate public debate. This Court's authority, however, extends only to determining whether the City's proposed condemnations are for a "public use" within the meaning of the Fifth Amendment to the Federal Constitution. Because over a century of our case law interpreting that provision dictates an affirmative answer to that question, we may not grant petitioners the relief that they seek.

Case Questions

1. What did the city's economic development plan entail?
2. What is the distinction between public use and public purpose, and which of the two does the Court apply?
3. Is it permissible for the states to place more restrictions on eminent domain than those permissible under the United States Constitution?

Planning and Zoning

The most direct intrusions into a private property owner's rights have come from governmental attempts to regulate land use. For both residential and commercial owners, planning and zoning have resulted in severe restrictions on property owners' rights.

The classic example of planning that is still to be found everywhere is the comprehensive zoning ordinance. Starting in the 1920s, cities and counties throughout the country adopted the practice of mapping land use zones, which restrict areas to categories of use such as residential, professional, commercial, and industrial. Generally these zones reflect contemporary uses but restrict future development. The object of zones is to diminish the effects of urban blight, save agricultural and green areas, and prevent the intrusion of incompatible uses in adjacent areas. Because zoning clearly represents the government depriving property owners of use rights they would otherwise enjoy, it was challenged as a taking under eminent domain for which no compensation was provided.

The U.S. Supreme Court, in *Euclid v. Ambler*, 272 U.S. 365, 47 S. Ct. 114, 71 L. Ed. 303 (1926), upheld comprehensive zoning in the village of Euclid, Ohio, under the state's power to regulate health, safety, and welfare. In contrast, it found a taking in *Nectow v. City of Cambridge*, 277 U.S. 183, 48 S. Ct. 447, 72 L. Ed. 842 (1928), where zoning effectively deprived the owner of any economically feasible use of his property (property zoned residential, though adjacent properties were occupied by industrial enterprises). The judgment relied on the Fourteenth Amendment's prohibition of deprivation of property without due process of law. Subsequent constitutional history has affirmed the resulting balancing test between the rights of communities to control land use and the rights of individual property owners to make reasonable use of their land.

Today planning has taken on additional tasks. Zoning maps are only a temporary solution to the problems that intensive growth has created in many areas. Comprehensive, long-range planning prevails in populous states, along with environmental concerns. Residential and commercial development are frequently carried out on a grand scale, and federal and state laws have been enacted to require exhaustive studies of the impact of such development on the environment and the capacity of local resources to support new building. Government has taken a serious role in controlling and directing growth. Major projects, airports, shopping malls, large residential developments, and the like are subject to intense scrutiny to assure compliance with the law, and it is unlikely that such legal requirements will decrease in the future.

Lawyers find much work in this area in advising, negotiating, and facilitating cooperation between developers and local governmental bodies. Paralegals can be invaluable in the process.

A developer must have a working knowledge of any applicable building code. When in doubt, it seems reasonable to request an interpretation of the building code from a building official. *Chamberlain* illustrates an instance in which the developer was not protected by obtaining an interpretation from the city's building official.

CHAMBERLAIN, L.L.C., Appellant	Supreme Court of Iowa
v.	No. 06-1487
CITY OF AMES, Iowa and Ames Board of Appeals, Appellees	757 N.W.2d 644
	Nov. 21, 2008.

An Ames developer planned to build an apartment complex with loft space that could be used for sleeping or storage. Uncertain whether the lofts were permissible under the Ames Municipal Code, the developer requested an interpretation of the code from the city's building official, who concluded [that] the lofts were permissible. When the building was completed, the city denied the developer's application for a certificate of occupancy because it found the lofts violated the ceiling height requirements for habitable space. The developer appealed to the city's board of appeals[,] which upheld the denial of certification. The developer then filed actions in the district court on this issue as well as asserting recovery on the basis of promissory estoppel, equitable estoppel, and vested rights. . . .

Today we decide whether the building official's initial interpretation of the building code vis-à-vis the lofts is entitled to preclusive effect. . . . An agency determination may be entitled to preclusive effect if the parties had a full and fair opportunity to litigate the issue and if the determination was considered final.

The building official's interpretation of the code was not entitled to preclusive effect because the interpretation was not a final decision. Chamberlain argues the city was required to file a writ of certiorari if it disagreed with the building official's interpretation. Because the time for filing a writ of certiorari has long since passed, Chamberlain claims the city acted illegally when it refused to issue a certificate of occupancy. We disagree.

The fact that the city failed to file a writ of certiorari challenging the building official's interpretation does not make the building official's decision "final." Both the International Building Code, adopted by the City of Ames, and the Ames Municipal Code contain provisions confirming the conditional nature of the building official's interpretation. . . . Thus, although the building official is empowered to provide interpretations of the code, he is restricted from being able to make interpretations that directly contradict or ignore the plain provisions of the code.

The Ames Municipal Code also indicates that the building official's interpretations cannot be considered final adjudications by which the building official and the city will forever be bound unless the city files a timely writ-of-certiorari action. Regardless of prior interpretations, the building official can

deny a building permit application if the plans do not conform "to the requirements of the Code and other pertinent laws and ordinances." Ames, Iowa, Mun. Code § 5.106(4). Moreover, even after an interpretation has been made and/or a building permit has been issued, the Ames Municipal Code provides:

> The issuance of a permit or approval of plans and specifications shall not be construed to be a permit for or approval of any violation of any of the provisions of this Code. No permit appearing to give authority to violate or cancel the provisions of this Code shall be valid. . . . The issuance of a permit based upon plans and specifications shall not prevent the Building Official from thereafter requiring the correction of errors in said plans and specifications or from preventing building operations being carried on thereunder when in violation of this Code or of any other ordinance of the City.

Id. § 5.106(5). Finally, even after the certificate of occupancy has been granted, various officials are empowered, regardless of prior interpretations, to initiate abatement action against a building if it is "manifestly unsafe" or violates any code, ordinance, or regulation. Ames, Iowa, Mun.Code § 5.131(1), (2); Int'l Bldg. Code § 110.4.

These provisions demonstrate [that] an interpretation of the code by the building official is not an adjudication of rights unalterable by the city. The city is empowered to deny an occupancy permit based on safety concerns or when the building does not comply with the provisions of the code. Ames, Iowa, Mun. Code § 5.106(5); Int'l Bldg. Code § 105.4. In our case, the fire chief/acting building official determined [that] the lofts were both unsafe and in violation of the building code. Int'l Bldg.Code § 1208.2. The lofts had only forty-five inches of headroom, and the building code requires seven and one-half feet for habitable spaces. *Id.* Even though the building official interpreted the loft areas to be extensions of other code compliant rooms, thus excluded from ceiling height restrictions, such an interpretation directly contradicts the plain provisions of the code. The loft areas were the size of a standard bedroom (148 square feet), and considering a space of that size to be an extension of another room seems illogical and plainly contrary to the code requirements. *See* Int'l Bldg.Code § 1208.3.

If a prior interpretation is later altered, the building owner has the right to a hearing in front of the board of appeals and afterwards judicial review. Int'l Bldg. Code § 112. Chamberlain exhausted these remedies when it appealed the city's interpretation that the lofts violated the ceiling height restrictions of the code and lost. The building official's initial interpretation of the code was not a final decision, and therefore, we hold it is not entitled to preclusive effect.

A building official's interpretation of the building code may be binding in certain instances under the doctrine of vested rights. Generally, a city is not estopped from revoking a validly issued building permit. However, when the permit holder makes expenditures in reliance on the permit, he may acquire vested rights in that permit, and the city may be estopped from revoking the permit. But, if the permit was not validly issued or if the building does not comply with applicable requirements, a permit can be revoked notwithstanding the permit holder's reliance.

As the building official has statutory authority to provide interpretations that are consistent with the code, an interpretation by the building official is akin to a building permit for the purposes of a vested rights analysis. Thus, so long as the interpretation does not contradict the plain provisions of the building code, an individual may acquire vested rights in that interpretation if he or she made expenditures in reliance on the interpretation. When the building official's interpretation resolves some kind of ambiguity or interprets an indefinite provision of the building code, a party can enforce that interpretation under the theory of vested rights.

In this case, however, the lofts, measuring 148 square feet (the size of a standard room) with forty-five inches of headroom, did not comply with the building code, which requires a ceiling height of seven and one-half feet for all habitable spaces. Int'l Bldg.Code § 1208.2. Although the building code does permit the building official to approve alternate designs, these designs must comply with the intent of the code and meet applicable safety requirements. *Id.* § 104.11. Thus, even though Chamberlain made substantial expenditures in reliance on the building inspector's interpretation and the building permit, Chamberlain did not acquire vested rights to an occupancy certificate since the lofts violated the plain provisions of the code.

Because the building official's interpretation of the code with respect to the lofts was not a final decision, Chamberlain is not entitled to utilize the doctrine of issue preclusion. Further, as the lofts do not comply with the building code, Chamberlain did not acquire vested rights in the building official's interpretation. Therefore, we affirm the decision of the court of appeals and the judgment of the district court.

Case Questions

1. According to the city, what was the problem with the lofts?
2. How could the developer have protected itself in this situation?
3. Why is the city given so much leeway, allowing it to revoke a building permit and to file an abatement action after the certificate of occupancy has been issued?
4. What is the doctrine of issue preclusion?

SUMMARY

Property is an abstract concept, not a natural or physical object or feature. It is best explained in terms of legal rights, such as rights to possess, exclude, and transfer. Rights can also be limited in time, such as a lease or a life estate, and in the nature of use and transferability. Rights may be restricted by a deed, by zoning ordinances, and by rights of others, such as utility easements and rights-of-way.

Property is divided into real and personal property. Real property, which consists of land and its improvements, is based on common law estates, which have endured for many centuries because of the basic conservatism of real property law. Under this system a person owns rights in land (the bundle-of-rights concept) rather than owning the land itself. When a person owns the maximum bundle of rights, the estate is called a fee simple absolute and corresponds to what we casually refer to as ownership. Lesser estates may be held, of which the most common is the life estate, which allows the life tenant to exercise rights over the property while alive. Upon death, the rights automatically transfer to a person who until that time held only a future interest.

Leasehold (or nonfreehold) estates involve the temporary transfer of the right of possession and are regulated by landlord and tenant laws of each state.

Title is an important concept in property law. It is not a document like a deed but an abstraction based on the history of the ownership of property that describes the extent of rights and limitations on rights; it can be determined by examining the records of transactions dealing with a particular piece of land. Title to personal property is generally much simpler, especially when physical property is directly exchanged for cash or a cash equivalent—title passes instantaneously.

An important aspect of the practice of property law is estate planning, that is, preparing for the distribution of a person's estate (the totality of one's property, real and personal). The most common devices used in estate planning are wills and trusts. A will provides for the distribution of property at death. A trust may distribute property at death or during one's lifetime; it establishes a trustee who distributes property to a beneficiary according to instructions in the trust instrument.

Today property is extensively regulated by government. Particularly affecting real property are restrictions on land use covered by local government planning and zoning, but state and federal governments have become more and more active in limiting land use, especially in the area of environmental law.

KEY TERMS

adverse possession	grantor	nuisance
chain of title	inheritable	primogeniture
condominium	invitee	remainder
deed	joint tenancy	restrictive covenants
devisable	lease	right of survivorship
dower and curtesy	licensee	tenancy by the entirety
easement	life estate	tenancy in common
eminent domain	life tenant	tenure
fee simple absolute	living trust (inter vivos trust)	title
foreclosure		trespasser
franchise	nonfreehold estate (leasehold estate)	warranty deed
grantee		writ of execution

CHAPTER REVIEW QUESTIONS

1. Are stocks and bonds personal property or real property?
2. Why have we preserved the ancient law of estates?
3. Why is it necessary to examine the chain of title prior to a purchase of real estate?

4. Why are real property transactions so much more complicated than personal property transactions?

5. What are nonfreehold estates called?

6. What are the elements of negligence?

7. What is the name for the acquisition of title by virtue of long-term possession (rather than by transfer)?

8. What is a bailment?

9. What is the advantage of a trust over a will in passing property to beneficiaries?

10. What is equal ownership with right of survivorship?

CRITICAL THINKING QUESTIONS

1. Why is real property law so conservative?

2. There are some who believe that all law is based on property rights. Why would they hold such beliefs?

CYBER EXERCISES

1. Opinions of the Supreme Court of Wisconsin can be found at a number of websites, including http://www.wisbar.org/. The Wisconsin Supreme Court decided *Apple Valley Gardens Ass'n, Inc. v. MacHutta*, 763 N.W.2d 126 (Wis. 2009), on March 27, 2009. The case contained the majority opinion, excerpted in this chapter, and a dissenting opinion. Locate the case at the Wisconsin Bar website and answer the following questions:

    a. What is the basis for Judge Prosser's conclusion in his dissent that condominium owners have the right to rent their condominium units?

    b. How do the facts in *La Fevbre* differ from the *Apple Valley Gardens* facts?

2. Opinions of the Florida Supreme Court are accessible at a number of websites, including the website for the Florida Supreme Court, http://www .floridasupremecourt.org/. Opinions of the U.S. Supreme Court are accessible at a number of websites, including the United States Supreme Court website, http://www.supremecourt.gov. The Florida Supreme Court decided *Walton County v. Stop Beach Renourishment, Inc.*, 998 So. 2d 1102 (Fla. 2008), on September 29, 2008; as of the writing of this book, the U.S. Supreme Court was expected to decide the case during its 2009 term. Locate the Florida Supreme Court case at the Florida Supreme Court website, locate the U.S. Supreme Court case at the U.S. Supreme Court website, and answer the following questions concerning the cases:

    a. What was the holding of the Florida Supreme Court, and what was the court's reasoning?

    b. What was the holding of the United States Supreme Court, and what was the court's reasoning?

    c. How might the decision of the United States Supreme Court be applied to other states?

3. Opinions of the United States Supreme Court are accessible at a number of websites, in particular http://www.supremecourt.gov/. The United States Supreme Court decided *Kelo v. City of New London, Conn.*, 545 U.S. 469 (2005), on June 23, 2005. The case contained the majority opinion, excerpted in this chapter, a concurring opinion, and two dissenting opinions. Locate the case at the Supreme Court website and answer the following questions:

   a. In his concurring opinion, Justice Kennedy cites *Hawaii Housing Authority v. Midkiff* and *Berman v. Parker*. How do these cases relate to eminent domain issues?

   b. In her dissenting opinion, Justice O'Connor quotes from a two-centuries-old case. Does it make sense to continue to follow the principles of that case, and why or why not?

   c. Justice Thomas dissents, stating that what the Pfizer Corporation is promising is vague and possibly purposeless. Do you think what Pfizer is proposing is for "public use" or for something different?

   d. Would you agree more with the majority opinion or with either of the dissenting opinions, and why?

4. Opinions of the Court of Appeals of North Carolina can be found at a number of websites, including http://www.aoc.state.nc.us/www/public/html/opinions.htm. The North Carolina Court of Appeals decided *Hinnant v. Philips*, 645 S.E.2d 867 (N.C. Ct. App. 2007), on June 19, 2007. The case contained the majority opinion, excerpted in this chapter, and a concurring opinion. Locate the case at the North Carolina Courts website and answer the following questions:

   a. In his concurring opinion, what did Judge Steelman state was the only evidence shown at trial concerning the appropriate standard of care?

   b. Why does Judge Steelman concur in the result but not join in the majority opinion?

SCENARIO

Eileen Slipslope was staying at the Holiday Six Hotel in Williwonky, Maryland, when she was injured walking from the parking lot to the hotel. Mrs. Slipslope slipped on some ice and fell forward onto the sloping pavement.

The court is considering Holiday Six's motion for summary judgment and Slipslope's response, which present contrasting legal bases for Slipslope's claim. The Holiday Six argues that it has no liability to Slipslope under the Maryland "ridges and hills" doctrine regarding liability for snow and ice accumulation. In her response, Slipslope argues that she does not rely on the "ridges and hills" doctrine but, instead, alleges a design defect in the parking lot.

The "ridges and hills" doctrine is a long-standing and well-entrenched legal principle that protects an owner or occupier of land from liability for generally slippery conditions resulting from ice and snow where the owner has not permitted the ice and snow to unreasonably accumulate in ridges or elevations. To show liability under such circumstances, the plaintiff must demonstrate (1) that snow and ice had accumulated on the sidewalk in ridges or elevations of such size and character as to unreasonably obstruct travel and constitute a danger to pedestrians traveling thereon; (2) that the property owner had notice, either actual or constructive, of the existence of such condition; and (3) that it was the dangerous accumulation of snow and ice that caused the injury.

Application of this doctrine has been extended to cases in which a business invitee falls on snow or ice covering a parking lot. The parties stipulate that Slipslope was a business invitee of the Holiday Six and that the parking lot in question belonged to the Holiday Six.

Assume the following facts: The evidence shows that snow stopped falling only about 10 hours before the accident and that temperatures had not risen to the point where the snow might have melted away. Thus, there is no disputed issue of material fact over whether "generally slippery conditions" existed in the Holiday Six's parking lot on that March 8 evening. Similarly, there is no dispute that the ice that allegedly caused Mrs. Slipslope's fall had not accumulated in a "hill" or "ridge" but instead was evidently barely perceptible.

Thus, if it applies, the "ridges and hills" doctrine prevents Slipslope from holding the Holiday Six liable for the existence of the patch of ice on the parking lot.

Slipslope argues that she does not rely on the "ridges and hills" doctrine. Instead, she contends that there was a design defect in the parking lot, which "at a minimum, was a concurrent cause of the accident coupled with the inclement weather." In particular, she alleges that the portion of the parking lot on which she fell is "too steep a slope for any pedestrian to traverse, and creates a danger in all inclement weather."

Slipslope offered the testimony of an expert witness who testified that the area in question "could have easily been more gradually graded as was done at the other parking lanes." He also performed an analysis of the forces operating on a 150-pound adult attempting to walk down a snow- or ice-covered surface sloped as the one at issue and concluded that there would always exist a downhill force causing the pedestrian to lose balance.

Assignment

Sitting as the judge in this case, write an opinion discussing the issues on each side and explain why you think one side should win rather than the other. In your discussion, consider the following persuasive authority.

The *Restatement (Second) of Torts* § 343 reads:

A possessor of land is subject to liability for physical harm caused to his invitees by a condition on the land if, but only if, he

(a) knows or by the exercise of reasonable care would discover the condition and should realize that it involves an unreasonable risk of harm to such invitees, and

(b) should expect that they will not discover or realize the danger or will fail to protect themselves against it, and

(c) fails to exercise reasonable care to protect them against the danger.

CHAPTER 13

FAMILY LAW

CHAPTER OUTLINE

INTRODUCTION

Writing a textbook anticipates that the book will be printed a few months after final editing, ordered for classes the next semester or the semester following, and then used for three to five years. Unfortunately, life and law are sufficiently dynamic that changes in some areas will render today's comments out of date. We are aware that the area of family law is at a crossroad. Not having quite recovered from the problems of a high divorce rate, both parents working, latchkey children, deadbeat parents failing to pay child support, the sexual revolution, and the women's movement of the past half century, family law now faces the daunting questions that same-sex marriage presents.

The study of family law is fascinating because it reflects the nature of the basic unit of our society. In America, perhaps more than elsewhere, the family unit is constantly transforming, and this shows no sign of abating.

HISTORICAL ROOTS OF FAMILY LAW

Probably no area of law has changed more in American history than family law. Family and family life have changed radically, and the law has changed along with them. Regulation of the family by legislatures and courts has followed a tortuous course. The degree to which the state should intrude into family relationships has always been controversial. For example, public policy supports the protection of children from abuse and neglect, but traditional values also protect parental authority against interference by the government.

Regulation of the family involves limiting choices by law in an area of human life where choices are jealously guarded. Should individuals be free to marry, **divorce**, and bear children at their whim? In our society, some would place severe restrictions on each of these; others would insist that each is purely a matter of individual choice and not a concern of government.

divorce
The severance of the bonds of matrimony; also referred to as *dissolution of marriage.*

Whereas other areas of law, such as the law of property, may be seen as a logical evolution from ancient English roots, family law is largely an American creation, consciously departing from English legal traditions. For example, Connecticut allowed absolute divorce long before England did. Divorce is really an American legal institution.

The archetypal family consists of a father, a mother, and their children. Although there are contemporary pressures to define *family* in much broader terms, the legal foundations of family law are premised on legitimizing a sexual relation between husband and wife that encourages childbearing and child rearing. American courts have, throughout their history, regarded themselves as the protectors of the family, often invoking rules on purely moral grounds.

The moral basis of family law was formalized when the Church assumed responsibility for regulating domestic relations in the late Middle Ages. At that time, **marriage** became a sacrament, subjecting the marital relationship to regulation by the Church. Our family law originated in the **canon law**, the law of the ecclesiastical courts. Because America did not employ ecclesiastical courts or canon law, the area of domestic relations was subsumed under the courts of equity, except in colonies like Connecticut and Massachusetts that refused to adopt courts of equity. At the founding of the American republic, the division between courts of equity and common law courts was still very strong. There was no common law tradition of family law except for property rights, and the common law was most appropriately charged with handling formal legal matters such as the remedies for injury to person or property, for crimes, and for breach of contract.

marriage
The legal joining together of husband and wife, having among its important effects the legitimation of their offspring; also, the Christian sacrament that joins husband and wife.

canon law
Church, or ecclesiastical, law traditionally associated with the Roman Catholic Church, which in English law was continued by the Church of England. Separation of church and state in the United States created gaps in the law, most notably in the area of domestic relations (family law).

Despite the American rejection of ecclesiastical law, the marriage contract retains some elements of its former sacred character. In former times, the betrothal was the critical event in marriage, as marriage partners were chosen by the parents of the bride and groom as part of a family alliance that benefited the respective families as well as the couple. In recent times, the wedding has become the significant event, as people have become free to choose their own partners. Both church and state have retreated from their former authority, leaving individuals free to form and dissolve the marital union.

child custody

The rights and duties of those legally entrusted with the care and control of a child, usually the parents.

child support

An obligation of parents; the payments due from one parent to another for the care of children following divorce.

alimony

Payments for personal maintenance from one ex-spouse to the other following divorce.

community property

A regime in which the earnings of husband and wife during marriage are owned equally by both. Nine states, borrowing from French (Louisiana) or Spanish (Texas west to California) law, have incorporated the concept of community property into marital law.

equitable distribution

Designed to equalize the marital shares of husband and wife for purposes of divorce; many states that are not *community property* states follow principles of equitable distribution.

LAW AND MARRIAGE

The legal requirements for marriage are minimal. The bride and groom must meet minimum age requirements, they must ordinarily be of different sexes (at least for the moment), they must have legal capacity to contract marriage, they must not be married to someone else, and they must not be closely related by blood. In short, it is easy to get married. Lawyers are rarely consulted.

Divorce, in contrast, is far more complicated. The principal subjects of family law are in one way or another concerned with divorce and its aftermath: **child custody**, **child support**, spousal support (**alimony**), **community property**, and **equitable distribution**.

Marriage as Contract

The marriage itself is traditionally viewed as a contractual arrangement because the parties voluntarily assume the relationship of husband and wife, but the most important duties are those imposed by law rather than the agreement of the parties. For example, husband and wife are obligated to provide mutual support for each other and support and nurture for their children. Individuals may avoid these duties by agreement only under special circumstances allowed by the law.

Although marriage has long been characterized as a contract, it has not been an ordinary contract in the eyes of the law, that is, one that could be freely made, altered, and broken. The sacred aspect of the family and procreation argued for a sacred contract. In recent decades, however, the states, which in America have assumed responsibility for domestic regulation, moved toward making the marriage contract much more like other contracts, in which the contracting parties controlled the relationship. Many of the features of family law can be explained by the tension between the special regard with which we view marriage and the family and the objective contractual rights and duties that the law imposes on family relationships.

It is also to be observed that, although marriage is often termed by text writers and in court decisions as a civil contract—generally to indicate that it must be founded upon the agreement of the parties and does not require any religious ceremony for its solemnization—it is something more than a mere contract. The consent of the parties is of course essential to its existence, but when the contract to marry is executed by the marriage, a relation between the parties is created which they cannot change. Other contracts may be modified, restricted, or enlarged, or entirely released upon consent of the parties. Not so with marriage. The relation once formed, the law steps in and holds the parties to various obligations and liabilities. It is an institution in the maintenance and purity of which the public is deeply interested, for it is the foundation of the family and of society, without which there would be neither civilization nor progress. *Maynard v. Hill*, 125 U.S. 190, 210 (1888).

Marriage as a Partnership

From an economic standpoint, the marriage contract establishes an ongoing, cooperative unit like a business partnership. In some instances, the reciprocal nature of the business is clear, as when the wife works as a secretary to support her husband while he gets through law school, with the understanding that once the husband's practice is prospering, the wife will quit working and bear and raise the couple's children. Success of the partnership depends upon each spouse meeting the terms of the contract. Other marriage partners may be business partners in an objective sense; that is, they may jointly manage their own commercial enterprise. Often the division of profits does not take place in the way unmarried partners would ordinarily conduct a business, but in every other respect the differences may be insignificant. Perhaps the majority of marriages do not have the usual characteristics of a business venture, but nearly all marriages involve important cost and savings sharing for mutual benefit, similar to a business enterprise.

Divorce may be treated like the dissolution of a business partnership. To the extent that property assets have been acquired by the joint efforts of the spouses, this model may, when used with caution, effect a fair distribution of the marital property.

Same-Sex Marriage

To those outside the field of family law, same-sex marriage seems like a simple question of whether the right to marry should be extended to same-sex couples, thereby allowing them to enjoy marital bliss (as it was once called) and, more importantly, to avail such relationships of the *benefits* that married status confers under the law. These benefits are not inconsiderable; they include all-important health benefits, pension benefits, and social security, to mention but a few.

The ramifications of same-sex marriage are far-reaching. For example, the opponents of same-sex marriage argue that the purpose of marriage is procreation, whereas the proponents point out that heterosexual couples who intend never to have children are not denied marriage licenses, nor are infertile couples denied licenses. Same-sex couples frequently desire to have children, and the technology exists to help them do so. Still, we encounter problems such as the following: A California Court of Appeals held that a woman who donated her eggs so that her same-sex partner could become pregnant via in vitro fertilization is not the mother of the resulting twins; the woman who carried the twins, who had no genetic relationship to the children, was the only legal parent. Apparently that court gave priority to bearing children over the genetic relationship, disregarding other factors that may have been involved in the case. Some might point out that the surrogacy problem first arose with opposite-sex couples (the *Baby M* case), but it is clear that surrogacy, in vitro fertilization, or adoption is essential to same-sex couples wishing to establish a legal parental relationship. Some states outlaw surrogacy contracts. If male same-sex couples could legally marry, such prohibitions would be challenged on equal protection grounds. One hopes that unusual cases like this will be rare, but we can expect that in some instances the constitutional issues will ultimately arrive at the U.S. Supreme Court after a significant lapse of time. Perhaps the issue that looms largest will be whether one state must honor a same-sex marriage obtained in another state, under the full faith and credit clause of the Constitution.

Unfortunately, a consensus is lacking on whether to confer marital eligibility to same-sex couples. Although American society has moved from strongly held values antagonistic to homosexuals toward a more tolerant attitude toward sexual preference, a strong majority, judging by votes in the states on prohibiting same-sex marriage, opposes extending that tolerance to marriage. In many instances, that antagonism is part of emotionally charged religious doctrine. Nor should we ignore powerful emotional reactions to sexual practices that many find offensive. Because the sides are socially, emotionally, and legally polarized, the resolution of the same-sex marriage issue may be even more dramatic than anyone presently anticipates, though one hopes that will not be the case. With an aging U.S. Supreme Court, new appointments may be threatened by the marriage issue. Certainly politicians will fight over family values. Congress and the state legislatures are currently grappling with the Defense of Marriage Act (DOMA), and more law may be forthcoming. Trial courts will reflect the polarization, with one judge finding a constitutional right to marry and another upholding the state laws against same-sex marriage (e.g., 2005, in Oregon and Nebraska). The situation is compounded by the wide variations in marriage and divorce law among the various states, encouraged by the *domestic relations exception* that federal courts have long observed by a hands-off policy toward state laws and actions with regard to spousal and parental determinations. The Constitution seems not to have contemplated federal intrusion on the family.

Strauss v. Horton deals with the interplay of law, constitution, different branches of government, and different levels of government, along with the sovereignty of the people, in amending the state constitution. When these interrelationships come into conflict, courts inevitably become involved to determine where authority lies and how it must be exercised under the law.

Divisive issues such as the legality of same-sex marriage, abortion, and the death penalty present moral issues that society cannot reconcile, so they end up in court. A careful reading of *Strauss* shows how the court concentrates on legal process so as to resolve the problem in an orderly fashion. In so doing, the court deals with the relation of local versus state authority, legislative versus administrative authority, and the authority to make the laws, interpret them, and carry them out. In addition, we have an example of the authority and power of the people to amend the state constitution within the context of majority rule versus rights claimed by a minority.

As you read *Strauss*, resist the temptation to agree or disagree with the reasoning because you like or dislike the result. Save any biases until you have read the case objectively. Note that this was not a unanimous decision. You can consider the other opinions (two concurring opinions and one opinion concurring in part and dissenting in part) if you answer the question concerning *Strauss* at the end of this chapter.

Karen L. STRAUSS et al., Petitioners

v.

Mark B. HORTON, as State Registrar of Vital Statistics, etc., et al., Respondents;

Dennis Hollingsworth et al., Interveners.

Robin Tyler et al., Petitioners

v.

The State of California et al., Respondents;

Dennis Hollingsworth et al., Interveners.

City and County of San Francisco et al., Petitioners

v.

Mark B. Horton, as State Registrar of Vital Statistics, etc., et al., Respondents;

Dennis Hollingsworth et al., Interveners.

Supreme Court of California

Nos. S168047, S168066, S168078

207 P.3d 48

May 26, 2009.

For the third time in recent years, this court is called upon to address a question under California law relating to marriage and same-sex couples.

In *Lockyer*, we were faced with the question [of] whether public officials of the City and County of San Francisco acted lawfully by issuing marriage licenses to same-sex couples in the absence of a judicial determination that the California statutes limiting marriage to a union between a man and a woman were unconstitutional. We concluded in *Lockyer* that the public officials had acted unlawfully in issuing licenses in the absence of such a judicial determination, but emphasized in our opinion that the substantive question of the constitutional validity of the marriage statutes was not before our court in that proceeding.

In *In re Marriage Cases*, we confronted the substantive constitutional question that had not been addressed in *Lockyer*—namely, the constitutional validity, under the then-controlling provisions of the California Constitution, of the California marriage statutes limiting marriage to a union between a man and a woman. A majority of this court concluded in the *Marriage Cases* that same-sex couples, as well as opposite-sex couples, enjoy the protection of the constitutional right to marry embodied in the privacy and due process provisions of the California Constitution, and that by granting access to the designation of "marriage" to opposite-sex couples and denying such access to same-sex couples, the existing California marriage statutes impinged upon the privacy and due process rights of same-sex couples and violated those couples' right to the equal protection of the laws guaranteed by the California Constitution.

Proposition 8, an initiative measure approved by a majority of voters at the November 4, 2008 election, added a new section—section 7.5—to article I of the California Constitution, providing: "Only marriage between a man and a woman is valid or recognized in California." The measure took effect on November 5, 2008. In the present case, we address the question [of] whether Proposition 8, under the governing provisions of the California Constitution, constitutes a permissible change to the California Constitution, and—if it does—we are faced with the further question of the effect, if any, of Proposition 8 upon the estimated 18,000 marriages of same-sex couples that were performed before that initiative measure was adopted.

In a sense, this trilogy of cases illustrates the variety of limitations that our constitutional system imposes upon each branch of government—the executive, the legislative, and the judicial.

In addressing the issues now presented in the third chapter of this narrative, it is important at the outset to emphasize a number of significant points. First, . . . our task in the present proceeding is not to determine whether the provision at issue is wise or sound *as a matter of policy* or whether we, as individuals, believe it *should* be a part of the California Constitution. Regardless of our views as individuals on this question of policy, we recognize as judges and as a court our responsibility to confine our consideration to a determination of the constitutional validity and legal effect of the measure in question. It bears emphasis in this regard that our role is limited to interpreting and applying the principles and rules embodied in the California Constitution, setting aside our own personal beliefs and values.

Second, it also is necessary to understand that the legal issues before us in this case are entirely distinct from those that were presented in either *Lockyer* or the *Marriage Cases*. Unlike the issues that were before us in those cases, the issues facing us here do not concern a public official's authority (or lack of authority) to refuse to comply with his or her ministerial duty to enforce a statute on the basis of the official's personal view that the statute is unconstitutional, or the validity (or invalidity) of a *statutory* provision limiting marriage to a union between a man and a woman *under state constitutional provisions that do not expressly permit or prescribe such a limitation.* Instead, the principal issue before us concerns the scope of *the right of the people, under the provisions of the California Constitution, to change or alter the state Constitution itself* through the initiative process so as to incorporate such a limitation as an explicit section of the state Constitution. . . .

[A]s numerous decisions of this court have explained, although the initiative process may be used to propose and adopt *amendments* to the California Constitution, under its governing provisions that process may not be used to *revise* the state Constitution. Petitioners' principal argument rests on the claim that Proposition 8 should be viewed as *a constitutional revision* rather than as *a constitutional amendment,* and that this change in the state Constitution therefore could not lawfully be adopted through the initiative process. . . .

In analyzing the constitutional challenges presently before us, we first explain that the provision added to the California Constitution by Proposition 8 . . .

properly must be understood as having a considerably narrower scope and more limited effect than suggested by petitioners in the cases before us. Contrary to petitioners' assertion, Proposition 8 does not *entirely repeal* or *abrogate* the aspect of a same-sex couple's state constitutional right of privacy and due process that was analyzed in the majority opinion in the *Marriage Cases*—that is, the constitutional right of same-sex couples to "choose one's life partner and enter with that person into a committed, officially recognized, and protected family relationship that enjoys all of the constitutionally based incidents of marriage." Nor does Proposition 8 *fundamentally alter* the meaning and substance of state constitutional equal protection principles as articulated in that opinion. Instead, the measure carves out a narrow and limited exception to these state constitutional rights, reserving the official *designation* of the term "marriage" for the union of opposite-sex couples as a matter of state constitutional law, but leaving undisturbed all of the other extremely significant substantive aspects of a same-sex couple's state constitutional right to establish an officially recognized and protected family relationship and the guarantee of equal protection of the laws. . . .

Taking into consideration the actual limited effect of Proposition 8 upon the preexisting state constitutional right of privacy and due process and upon the guarantee of equal protection of the laws, and after comparing this initiative measure to the many other constitutional changes that have been reviewed and evaluated in numerous prior decisions of this court, we conclude [that] Proposition 8 constitutes a constitutional amendment rather than a constitutional revision. As a quantitative matter, petitioners concede that Proposition 8—which adds but a single, simple section to the Constitution—does not constitute a revision. As a qualitative matter, the act of limiting access to the designation of marriage to opposite-sex couples does not have a substantial or, indeed, even a minimal effect on *the governmental plan or framework of California* that existed prior to the amendment. Contrary to petitioners' claim in this regard, the measure does not transform or undermine the judicial function; this court will continue to exercise its traditional responsibility to faithfully enforce *all* of the provisions of the California Constitution, which now include the new section added through the

voters' approval of Proposition 8. Furthermore, the judiciary's authority in applying the state Constitution always has been limited by the content of the provisions set forth in our Constitution, and that limitation remains unchanged. . . .

The Attorney General, in his briefing before this court, has advanced an alternative theory—not raised by petitioners in their initial petitions—under which he claims that even if Proposition 8 constitutes a constitutional amendment rather than a constitutional revision, that initiative measure nonetheless should be found invalid under the California Constitution on the ground that the "inalienable rights" embodied in article I, section 1 of that Constitution are not subject to "abrogation" by constitutional amendment without a compelling state interest. The Attorney General's contention is flawed, however, in part because, like petitioners' claims, it rests inaccurately upon an overstatement of the effect of Proposition 8 on both the fundamental constitutional right of privacy guaranteed by article I, section 1, and on the due process and equal protection guarantees of article I, section 7. . . . Proposition 8 does not abrogate any of these state constitutional rights, but instead carves out a narrow exception applicable only to access to the *designation* of the term "marriage," but not to any other of "the core set of basic *substantive* legal rights and attributes traditionally associated with marriage . . ." (*Marriage Cases*), such as the right to establish an officially recognized and protected family relationship with the person of one's choice and to raise children within that family. . . .

Accordingly, we conclude that each of the state constitutional challenges to Proposition 8 advanced by petitioners and the Attorney General lacks merit. Having been approved by a majority of the voters at the November 4, 2008 election, the initiative measure lawfully amends the California Constitution to include the new provision as article I, section 7.5.

In a sense, petitioners' and the Attorney General's complaint is that it is just too easy to amend the California Constitution through the initiative process.[1] But it is not a proper function of this court to curtail that process; we are constitutionally bound to uphold it. . . .

[1] In contrast to the process by which the California Constitution may be amended, in both Connecticut

and Iowa—two states in which supreme courts recently have held that a statute limiting marriage to opposite-sex couples violates the provisions of their respective state constitution (see *Kerrigan v. Commissioner of Public Health* (2008); *Varnum v. Brien* (2009))—the state constitution may not be amended through the initiative process, and in each state an amendment proposed by a majority of the legislators in each house must be approved in two successive legislative sessions before it can be submitted to the voters for ratification at the next general election. . . .

In Massachusetts—the other state in which a statute limiting marriage to opposite-sex couples has been found unconstitutional under the state constitution (see *Goodridge v. Department of Public Health* (2003))—the state constitution may in some circumstances be amended through the initiative process, but in that state, after an initiative petition has been signed by the requisite number of electors, the proposed constitutional amendment must be approved by one-fourth of the state legislators in two successive legislative sessions before it can be placed on the ballot.

In Vermont, where the state legislature recently amended [2009] that state's marriage statute (over a gubernatorial veto) to permit same-sex couples to marry, the state constitution may not be amended through the initiative process, and an amendment proposed by the legislature must be approved in two successive legislative sessions before it can be submitted to the voters for ratification.

In Maine, where the state legislature also recently amended [2009] that state's marriage statute to permit same-sex couples to marry, the state constitution similarly may not be amended through the initiative process. In that state, an amendment to the state constitution may be proposed by a two-thirds vote of both houses of the legislature, and becomes effective if approved by a majority of voters at the next biennial statewide election.

Finally, we consider whether Proposition 8 affects the validity of the marriages of same-sex couples that were performed prior to the adoption of Proposition 8. Applying well-established legal principles pertinent to the question [of] whether a constitutional provision should be interpreted to apply prospectively or retroactively, we conclude that the new section cannot properly be interpreted to apply retroactively. Accordingly, the marriages of same-sex couples performed prior to the effective date of Proposition 8 remain valid and must continue to be recognized in this state.

Case Questions

1. According to the court, what is the principal issue before it?
2. Why is the distinction between a constitutional amendment and a constitutional revision significant?
3. Are you persuaded by the court's reasoning?
4. Why does the court include footnote 1, providing information concerning what other states have done?

Children

Family law, often called **domestic relations**, might more properly be titled the *law of intimate relations,* especially in this period in our society when couples exercise considerable freedom in the partners they choose and the lifestyles those partnerships express. Even though we have moved away from the traditional marriage-and-children model of adult relationships, the idealized model of the family continues to be a heterosexual union having as its major motivation the creation and nurture of children. Children add a dimension to family law that distinguishes it from other areas of law: Family law commonly deals with the welfare of human beings who have not reached the age of legal

domestic relations

The field of law governing the rights and duties of family relations, particularly divorce; usually synonymous with *family law.*

competence (majority), who are vulnerable to abuse or exploitation, and who must be protected by society through its legal institutions when the family, the primary social institution, fails. Problems in other areas of law are often neatly handled by the transfer of wealth from one pocket to another; family law involves issues that are not readily measured in dollars and cents.

Family Law and the Adversarial Process

American legal procedure has developed around an adversarial process in which disputing parties arm themselves with legal representatives and ultimately try their cases before an impartial judge if the lawyers and the parties cannot reach an agreement. The sides are viewed as hostile, and the lawyers are duty-bound to fight for the interests of their clients. This model quite naturally tends to focus and intensify the dispute, one of the reasons the states have attempted to soften the process by adopting no-fault divorce statutes. Divorcing couples with minor children pose a serious problem for the legal system. We assume that parents will care for the interests of their children, but divorcing parents often aggravate the damage that divorce causes to children by drawing them into a continuing dispute.

ANNULMENT

annulment

Ends the relation of husband and wife by invalidating the marriage contract, as if they were never married.

An examination of **annulment** is valuable because it reveals the requirements for a valid marriage. An action for annulment challenges the validity of the original marriage contract. Annulment is uncommon today largely because the adoption of no-fault divorce statutes has made divorce easier than annulment. Nevertheless, for religious or other reasons, some individuals may prefer to seek annulment.

The most important aspect of the difference between annulment and divorce relates to the grounds for ending the marriage. Annulment is based on a defect in existence when the marriage was contracted. Divorce is based on grounds arising during the marriage itself. For instance, it is often possible to obtain an annulment if one of the parties to the marriage was impotent or sterile at the time of the marriage (usually assuming this fact was unknown to the other party); impotence or sterility developing after the marriage contract would not ordinarily be grounds for annulment—the complaining party would be forced to resort to divorce to get out of the marriage.

Divorce terminates the marriage from the time of the final decree, but annulment operates retroactively to invalidate the marriage from its beginning. This is so because the cause of action for annulment asserts some impediment to the formation of the marriage contract itself—if the contract was invalid, no marriage resulted. One of the important consequences of annulment is the general unavailability of alimony, which most American courts award only upon dissolution of a valid marriage, although alimony has become almost as rare as annulment.

Void or Voidable?

Under traditional contract theory, some contracts are deemed void and some are merely voidable. A *void contract* is one that was never valid; a *voidable contract* is valid until a court declares it invalid. Through the passage of time and removal of the impediment to validity, a voidable contract may become enforceable. Marriage contracts are similarly subject to the void–voidable distinction. Because of the special nature of the marriage contract, though, the grounds for invalidity are somewhat different from other contracts.

Marriages generally considered void include:

1. **Bigamous** marriage, when one of the parties is already married
2. **Incestuous** marriage, within a prohibited relationship for marriage (e.g., brother–sister)
3. **Mental incompetence**, when one of the parties lacks mental capacity to contract marriage
4. **Nonage**, when at least one of the parties is below the minimum age to marry

Marriages may be merely voidable on the ground of *formalities*, that is, failure to meet the formal requirements for a licensed marriage, or for *fraud*. Fraud, which accounts for the largest number of attacks on marriages through annulment proceedings, includes three categories:

1. *Fraud with regard to the essentials of marriage.* Many courts have adopted the rule that fraud as to the essentials of marriage must be of an extreme nature. This is often referred to as the *Massachusetts rule*, derived from *Reynolds v. Reynolds*, 85 Mass. (3 Allen) 605 (1862), in which an annulment was granted to a husband whose wife had represented herself as chaste even though she was already pregnant by another man. An annulment was granted to the husband.
2. *Fraud with regard to inability or unwillingness to have children.* Perhaps the oldest ground for annulment known to our law has to do with sex and procreation. When one spouse misrepresents his or her ability to have children, the law traditionally permits annulment.
3. *Fraud on the court or legal process.* Certain cases of collusion between parties involve fraud on the legal system rather than fraud on the other party. This occurs with sham marriages, wherein some purpose other than marriage, cohabitation, and procreation is intended, such as marrying to qualify for a visa or legitimize a child. When there was no intent to consummate the marriage and the marriage was not in fact consummated, annulment may be available.

Consequences of Annulment

Historically, annulment treated the marriage as if it had never occurred, but the harshness of this rule has been softened in recent times. In particular, annulment should not bastardize the offspring of an annulled marriage. The Uniform Marriage and Divorce Act (UMDA), in § 207(c), states, "Children born of a prohibited marriage are legitimate." (The UMDA was drafted by the National Conference of Commissioners on Uniform State Laws to propose legislation for the states that would cover the principal subject of marriage and divorce. Several states have adopted the Act, and many judicial opinions cite it as supporting authority.)

Alimony is another matter. Under the common law, it was the duty of the husband to provide for the wife, and this extended to legal separations (i.e., divorce from bed and board) as well as absolute divorce. This duty, however, depended upon a valid marital contract and was therefore inconsistent with annulment. A number of states have passed legislation allowing alimony following annulment under restricted circumstances, as when the receiving spouse is an innocent party.

bigamous
Describes the marriage of a person who is already married to another person. Bigamy is a crime, and a bigamous marriage is void.

incestuous
Marriage within a prohibited degree of relationship (e.g., brother–sister).

mental incompetence
In relation to marriage, condition that exists when one of the parties lacks mental capacity to contract marriage.

nonage
The condition of being a minor, not having reached the age of majority.

elective share

The phrase representing what was formerly *dower* and *curtesy* in the common law; the share of a surviving spouse in the deceased spouse's property that the surviving spouse may choose (elect) to take instead of the property that a will would distribute.

antenuptial (premarital) agreement

A contract agreed to by persons before their marriage; primarily concerned with the distribution of personal and marital assets in the event of divorce or death.

postnuptial agreement

An agreement between spouses, usually concerned with distributing family property in the event of death or divorce.

separation agreement (property settlement agreement)

A contract between husband and wife, after they have already married, to distribute property in case of death or divorce. Such an agreement is usually executed in preparation for divorce, but it is occasionally used between couples who merely wish to live separately.

ANTENUPTIAL (PREMARITAL) AGREEMENTS

Dower and curtesy under the common law, and their modern representatives such as **elective share**, provide that a surviving spouse is entitled to a large share of the decedent's estate despite testamentary provisions (the laws of intestacy apply when no valid will exists). Community property and equitable distribution schemes both favor a 50–50 split in case of divorce. In most states, the only way to decrease this share upon death or divorce is through an agreement signed before the marriage: an **antenuptial** or **premarital agreement**. Until the twentieth century, such agreements were judicially disapproved as violating public policy, which disfavored any agreement tending to promote divorce. By the end of the twentieth century, this trend had reversed, and now most states enforce antenuptial contracts, especially when financial disclosure precedes the contract and coercive conduct is absent.

Antenuptial agreements are private contracts setting the terms of the marital contract in advance. Both their popularity and their use have increased in recent years. In the practice of law, the important features of antenuptial agreements concern the distribution of property at death or divorce. Jurisdictions that approve antenuptial agreements have tended to treat them in most respects like other contracts. Their validity may be challenged on traditional contract grounds, such as voluntariness, fraud, and conscionability. Some jurisdictions, however, have been reluctant to treat antenuptial agreements like other contracts, expressing traditional public policy concerns for the stability of the family and protection of its members.

Certain situations are ready-made for antenuptial agreements, as when someone remarries and wants to ensure that a major portion of his or her assets will be preserved for children of a prior marriage. Spouses, most commonly women, who sacrifice to put their spouses through a long and expensive education may want to protect themselves in case of divorce so that they recoup their investments.

POSTMARITAL CONTRACTS

Postmarital contracts may be labeled **postnuptial agreements**, **separation agreements**, or **property settlement agreements**. Postnuptial agreements executed while the marriage is still harmonious are subject to the same public policy challenge as antenuptial agreements, and they lack the consideration essential to a valid contract. Separation agreements and property settlements executed in contemplation of an impending divorce are generally exempt from these attacks. The modern trend in most states increasingly favors recognition of the validity of postmarital agreements.

A major issue regarding agreements submitted to the courts in divorce proceedings concerns whether the agreement is merged into the final decree, so that it loses its separate existence as a contract. On the answer to this question rests the availability of a suit or petition for modification to change or extend the terms of the agreement at a later date. The means of enforcement also depend on whether the agreement is said to be merged into the decree. If merged, contempt of court is available to enforce compliance, on the ground that noncompliance defies the order of the court. Without merger, traditional contract actions may be necessary to remedy noncompliance. If the agreement is merged so that its terms are ordered by the court, those orders may be modified like other orders (custody and support) emanating from the court. If the agreement is not merged, the contract may be modified only by mutual agreement of the parties.

The common exception to this concerns children, whose interests most courts will not allow to be bargained away.

DIVORCE: PROPERTY SETTLEMENTS

The principal legal issues at divorce are the division of property and rights and duties with regard to children. These issues should be explicitly resolved in the property settlement or marital settlement agreement. Although the judge in a divorce case is ultimately responsible for recognizing the agreement or setting its provisions, most judges will avoid making difficult choices if at all possible. Because the judge in a divorce case is vested with great discretion, lawyers are extremely reluctant to take chances on the vagaries of judicial choice and advise their clients against such a course. This means that the lawyers will hammer out a property settlement, often through extended negotiations with obstinate spouses. The negotiations are limited by principles enunciated by state legislatures and the courts.

The distribution of assets at divorce is treated differently in different states, but the underlying goal is fairness to both parties. In the past, a major theme of distribution was the effort to protect dependent spouses. More recently, this has been restated in terms of valuing homemaking in the distribution of marital assets. Now that wives have taken their place in the workforce, the valuation of respective contributions has an added feature in divorce calculations. The questions that arise in this context concern classification and valuation. Fairness requires that the courts be open to a variety of economic claims that were rare a few decades ago. For example, is a spouse entitled to share in the value of a professional license acquired by the other spouse during the marriage? Are future pension benefits classified as property, marital property, or something else? What if one of the spouses dissipates marital assets (say, through gambling or extravagance)? Does this entitle the other spouse to a larger share of what is left? The answer to these questions is yes, in *some* states. Regardless of the nature of the property that is subject to distribution, its valuation is a major problem when market value is less than obvious.

In community property states (Arizona, California, Idaho, Louisiana, New Mexico, Nevada, Texas, Washington, and Wisconsin), property acquired during the marriage is owned equally, so disputes in divorce concern whether property is community or *separate property*. The latter consists of property owned prior to the marriage or acquired during the marriage by gift, will, or inheritance. Separate property can be transmuted into community property by transfer or gift or by commingling funds so as to render them untraceable as separate property.

Community property embodies a partnership model that has been borrowed in so-called common law states with the label *equitable distribution*. This scheme is designed to treat the partners fairly, especially in considering domestic contributions equal to financial contributions. Although equitable distribution generally takes a broad, inclusive view of marital property, it distinguishes between marital and separate property in a fashion similar to community property. It would be a mistake, however, to conclude that divorces in any of the states involved will result in either a 50–50 split in property or a division regarded as fair by both sides.

Under basic community property theory, property acquired during marriage is owned equally by husband and wife because they are a community. What exactly may be included varies somewhat from state to state. In the *Lynch* case, the court argues that the rules may be drastically opposed in different states.

LYNCH

v.

LYNCH

Court of Appeals of Arizona

164 Ariz. 127, 791 P.2d 653 (1990)

A man who won the lottery before the pending dissolution of his marriage seeks to reverse the trial court's grant of half his winnings to his wife. We hold that the winnings were community property and affirm. . . .

Michael Lynch (husband) and Bonnie Lynch (wife) were married in 1968. Their only child was born in 1971. The couple separated in 1985, and within a year husband began living with a woman named Donna Williams. Wife filed for dissolution shortly after.

Wife's petition was uncontested, and at a default hearing on February 10, 1987, wife testified that the marriage was irretrievably broken. A decree of dissolution is ordinarily entered at the conclusion of a default hearing. However, on February 10, the trial court took the matter under advisement and, on February 19, vacated the hearing because husband had received untimely notice. . . .

On February 21, husband and Donna Williams won a $2.2 million jackpot in the Arizona State Lottery. Each owned half a share of the winning ticket. Wife then filed an amended petition in the unconcluded dissolution seeking half of husband's share. This time husband answered, the case went on to trial, and in the ultimate decree of dissolution the trial court awarded wife half of husband's lottery share.

Husband has appealed the trial court's ruling on three grounds. . . . By each argument, he attempts to establish that the parties acquired no community property after February 10, 1987, when the invalid default hearing was held. First, he argues that a marital community lasts only as long as the parties' will to union and that these parties' will to union had ended by the time of wife's testimony on February 10 that the marriage was irretrievably broken. Second, he argues that, by this testimony, wife waived her community interest in his future acquisitions. Last, he contends that, because wife's lawyers gave untimely notice of the

February 10 hearing, wife is estopped from denying that the marital community ended on that date.

Community Duration

When an Arizona spouse acquires an asset before marital dissolution, Arizona law treats the asset as community property unless it falls within one of several statutory exceptions. . . . A marriage endures in Arizona—and thus the acquisition of community property continues—"until the final dissolution is ordered by the court."

In some jurisdictions, acquisition of community property ceases when spouses begin to live separate and apart. In Arizona, however, demarcation by decree "avoids the factual issue of when the couple began living apart, and provides appropriate treatment for the on-again off-again manner in which some couples try to resolve their differences and patch up their marriages."

An Arizona couple that wishes to end the acquisition of community property before (or without) dissolution has a statutory means to do so. [State statute] provides for entry of a decree of legal separation that terminates "community property rights and liabilities. . . . as to all property, income and liabilities received or incurred after [its] entry." In the absence of a decree of legal separation, however, acquisition of community property continues in Arizona until the decree of dissolution is filed.

[The court then rejected husband's argument based on the will-to-union doctrine, a Spanish rule which holds that property acquired after the union of the wills has ceased would not be community property. On the facts, the court found some basis to doubt that the will to union had really ceased.]

Waiver

Husband makes the related argument that wife waived any interest in his further acquisitions on February 10 when she testified that the marriage was irretrievably broken, expecting a decree of dissolution to issue on that date. We disagree. Waiver is the intentional relinquishment of a known right. Wife surely waived her interest in husband's acquisitions beyond the dissolution of their marriage, but her waiver went no further. She did not relinquish what might accrue to the marital community if the marriage lasted beyond its anticipated end. . . .

ended equitably, though not formally, before the winning ticket was acquired. We have given our reasons for rejecting his arguments. The judgment of the trial court is affirmed.

Conclusion

This case displays the hand of chance. Fortune favored husband with a jackpot, but, because his marriage had not ended, fortune dealt his wife a share. Though the lottery was a windfall, spouses marry for better or for worse and share no less in windfalls than in labor's wages. Husband claims that his marriage

Case Questions

1. Why wasn't a default entered on February 10, 1987? What would its effect have been if it had been entered? Do you think Bonnie Lynch could have challenged a default if entered?
2. Bonnie Lynch's attorney made a mistake in the hearing notice procedure. Was she mad at him? Explain.

ALIMONY

The traditional term for **spousal support** was *alimony*. In many jurisdictions it is called *maintenance,* and all three terms may be used interchangeably in many states. For some, alimony has a negative connotation because it is associated with an earlier time when a husband had a lifelong duty to support his dependent wife, whether married or divorced. Because of equal rights guaranteed by the Constitution, alimony today requires that a husband may receive alimony if a wife can. In recent times, courts and legislatures have come to disfavor both permanent alimony and alimony in general. Most awards of alimony today come in the form of periodic payments lasting a few months or years, classified as **rehabilitative alimony** and designed to return a homemaker to the job market (i.e., to help a dependent spouse get through the postdivorce period of adjustment to self-sufficiency). **Lump-sum alimony** is occasionally awarded, often to provide compensation for contributions by one spouse, such as one spouse who worked to put the other through a professional education.

Alimony is part of a more comprehensive plan dividing the resources and obligations of the spouses. The distribution of assets and child support are the other two important economic ingredients of this plan.

Alimony is characterized by a high degree of discretion on the part of the judiciary, although most states have provided more or less detailed guidelines for judges to weigh when awarding alimony. Alimony is principally based on the need of the recipient and the other spouse's ability to pay. Need is a relative concept, depending to a large degree on the standard of living enjoyed during the marriage. Alimony is usually terminated by the death of either party or by remarriage of the recipient. Depending on the jurisdiction, this may be waived in the property settlement agreement.

A postdivorce procedure in the form of a petition for **modification** is available to increase or decrease alimony or to extend or shorten the period during which payments are made. The key element in a successful suit for modification is proof of *changed circumstances* justifying modification. For the recipient of alimony to obtain an upward modification, it must be shown that the payor has the ability to pay the increased amount.

spousal support

Payments made to an ex-spouse following divorce that are designed as support rather than a division of the marital property. Traditionally this was called *alimony,* and in many jurisdictions the term *maintenance* is used.

rehabilitative alimony

Ordinarily a form of periodic payment, temporary in duration, designed to provide for an ex-spouse until he or she can become self-supporting.

lump-sum alimony

Alimony that is established as one lump-sum amount, usually in the form of one payment but occasionally in installments.

modification

When applied to divorce, a court-approved change in the amount or terms of alimony, child support, or child custody.

The *Brown* case traces the history of alimony in Florida over more than a century. Although the dates may differ from state to state, the path from a preference for permanent periodic monthly payments for a divorced wife to the general disfavor in which alimony is held today is echoed in state after state. In most instances, changes in the law of alimony directly reflect the changing status of women in our society.

BROWN

v.

BROWN

First District Court of Appeal of Florida
300 So. 2d 719 (Fla. Dist. Ct. App. 1974)

For at least forty years prior to the recent enactments repealing divorce and instituting dissolution of marriage (commonly referred to as no fault), the courts awarded a divorced wife periodic alimony almost as a matter of constitutional right. In *Phelan v. Phelan*, 12 Fla. 449 (1868) the Supreme Court [said:] "Permanent alimony is not a sum of money or a specific proportion of the husband's estate given absolutely to the wife. It is a continuous allotment of sums payable at regular periods for her support from year to year."

This definition of permanent alimony was reaffirmed in . . . 1948 [in a case holding that a wife was entitled to periodic alimony based upon her needs and her husband's ability to pay. The court refused to apply retroactively a newly enacted statute permitting the award of lump-sum alimony.]

The next development in the law of alimony was the appearance of the doctrine of special equity. As early as 1919, the Supreme Court . . . , after noticing that the wife, mother of six children, had contributed generously in funds and by her personal exertion and industry through a long period of time to the acquisition and development of [the] home and other property and the establishment of [a] fortune, held that the wife possessed a special equity in the property which she aided in acquiring and possessing.

In 1932, the Supreme Court utilized the doctrine of special equity to relieve a wife from the harshness of the statutory prohibition of awarding alimony to an adulteress.

* * *

[The court was again confronted with the question of lump-sum alimony in 1968. The original final judgment for payment of periodic alimony by the husband to the wife was amended to provide lump-sum alimony payable in monthly installments.]

In 1955, Justice Roberts, speaking for our Supreme Court, announced:

Times have now changed. The broad, practically unlimited opportunities for women in the business world of today are a matter of common knowledge. Thus, in an era where the opportunities for self-support by the wife are so abundant, the fact that the marriage has been brought to an end because of the fault of the husband does not necessarily entitle the wife to be forever supported by a former husband who has little, if any, more economic advantages than she has.

This pronouncement marks the entry in the jurisprudence of this state of the concept of rehabilitative alimony. Rehabilitative means the restoration of property that has been lost. The concept of rehabilitative alimony appeared in the statutory scheme of this state in 1971 when the legislature made a major change. . . . The salient provisions are:

[T]he court may grant alimony to either party, which alimony may be rehabilitative or permanent in nature. In any award of alimony, the court may order periodic payment or payments in lump sum or both. . . .

In determining a proper award of alimony, the court may consider any factor necessary to do equity and justice between the parties.

In 1966, [another Florida district court] clearly stated the rule that prevailed as to awarding alimony prior to the dissolution of marriage act in 1971 as: "The accepted principles are that a divorced wife is entitled to alimony which will permit her to live in a manner commensurate with that provided by her husband during coverture, if he has the ability to pay."

Post 1971 Alimony

[In 1972], the trial court found (as is probably true in more than 90 percent of marriage failures) that although neither party was without fault, "the preponderance of the equities lies with appellant husband and he is entitled to a divorce from appellee wife on the ground of habitual intemperance and indulgence in alcoholic beverages." [The court reversed an award of $100 per month permanent alimony with the following statement:]

> They now occupy a position of equal partners in the family relationship resulting from marriage, and more often than not contribute a full measure to the economic well-being of the family unit. Whether the marriage continues to exist or is severed through the device of judicial decree, the woman continues to be as fully equipped as the man to earn a living and provide for her essential needs. The fortuitous circumstance created by recitation of the marriage vows neither diminishes her capacity for self-support nor does it give her a vested right in her husband's earnings for the remainder of her life. . . .

> The new concept of the marriage relation implicit in the so-called no fault divorce law enacted by the legislature in 1971 places both parties to the marriage on a basis of complete equality as partners sharing equal rights and obligations in the marriage relationship and sharing equal burdens in the event of dissolution.

. . . Either spouse may contribute either by working in the market place or by working as a homemaker. The fact that in one marital venture a spouse is gainfully employed in the market place and pays a housekeeper to rear the children and keep house is not distinguishable from the spouse who devotes his or her full time to the profession of homemaker. The primary factual circumstance is each spouse's contribution to the marital partnership. In the case sub judice, the wife has been short changed. The wife has not been adequately compensated for the contribution that she made as a full time mother and homemaker to the equal partnership marriage. We hold that the trial court abused its discretion in awarding the wife a pittance of the material assets accumulated in the husband's name during 21 years.

McCORD, Judge (specially concurring):

[Rehabilitative alimony is defined as] financially supporting an ill spouse until his or her health is restored, or financially supporting a spouse until he or she can be trained for employment, or, in some circumstances, until the spouse has a reasonable time to recover from the trauma of the dissolution.

Case Questions

1. Why does Judge McCord's definition of rehabilitative alimony fit the commonly accepted meaning of the phrase better than the definition given in the main opinion?
2. How does the evolution of alimony reflect the changing status of American women?

CHILD SUPPORT

After divorce, one parent usually becomes the primary caregiver of the children. When one parent is responsible for the physical custody of the children more than the other, the primary caregiver is entitled to contribution for providing more than his or her share of support. Today both parents are obligated to support their children, and that obligation is measured in terms of their respective ability to pay and the needs of the children. Legal issues with regard to child support range from the basic questions of how much support should be paid and how to collect arrearages to questions of who should pay and what should be covered. Legislation in this area has focused on establishing precise guidelines for payment and the means to enforce them.

Parental Duty to Support

As the duty of support was first legally recognized, it applied only to the father. In the twentieth century, the duty of support was extended to mothers as *secondarily* liable for support. This concept was destined to fail as focus on the equal protection clause of the Fourteenth Amendment was applied with greater force to legal distinctions based on gender. Eventually, the law required equal duty of support from mother and father.

Unmarried fathers are also obligated to support their offspring. Adoptive parents are legally bound to support their adoptive children—adoption severs the legal bond between a child and its natural parents and treats the child as having the same legal relationship to its adoptive parents as a natural child would have. There is even a trend toward recognizing stepparents' legal obligations to support their stepchildren.

Need and Ability to Pay

Like alimony, child support is based on (children's) *need* for support and (parents') *ability to pay*. Even when the mother is the primary custodian of the children, her resources may be considered in the amount ordered to be paid by the father, as she is obligated to support her children, too. Similarly, when the father has custody of the children, the mother may be ordered to pay child support to the father. Unlike alimony, the resources of the beneficiary have only a limited impact on the award. A child's resources (e.g., a trust set up by grandparents) do not ordinarily reduce the parental obligation to furnish necessaries.

Need is a relative concept. The courts do not limit parental contributions to necessaries after divorce. In this instance, the child of divorce may be entitled to more (and usually receives less) than the child of an intact family, who has only a right to necessaries. The rationale is that a child should not be required to drastically reduce an accustomed lifestyle simply because one of the parents has moved to other quarters.

Setting and Enforcing Child Support

During the 1980s and 1990s, both states and the federal government made a major effort at reducing welfare costs by collecting child support arrearages. A federal law made crossing state lines to avoid paying child support a federal crime. The motivation for government action was not a simple and direct response to the woeful record of support payments, even though statistics in that regard demanded attention and action. Rather, the governments aimed to reduce the governments' share in welfare payments to single-parent families. In many instances, public assistance provided support when parents (fathers in particular) failed to meet their legal support obligations. New laws provide means for collecting arrears that can then be credited to welfare amounts that have been paid.

These efforts were begun primarily through the Office of Child Support Enforcement of the U.S. Department of Health and Human Services, beginning in 1974, and are presently collecting several billion dollars yearly. The federal government furnishes funds for state enforcement programs at the same time that it imposes requirements on the states that receive the funds. Amendments to the law (the Federal Enforcement Initiative of 1974) in 1984 and 1988 have added more requirements and made more drastic the means of enforcement. Applicants for Aid to Families with Dependent Children (AFDC applicants) assign their uncollected support rights to the state and must assist efforts to collect. Both the states and the federal government maintain records to assist in locating parents who are in arrears.

Under the requirements imposed on the state, new laws must require employee withholding of child support from paychecks of those in arrears. Arrears in excess of $1,000 must be deducted from state and federal income tax refunds. Under the 1988 amendments, orders for support or orders modifying support cause support payments to be automatically deducted from paychecks whether the payor is in arrears or not. The 1988 amendments also provided new standards for paternity and federal funds for paternity testing in an obvious effort to make unwed fathers financially responsible for their offspring.

Child Support Guidelines

One of the most far-reaching requirements of the 1984 amendments provided, "Each state, as a condition for having its State plan approved under this part, must establish guidelines for child support award amounts within the state. The guidelines may be established by law or by judicial or administrative action." Although need and ability to pay are the foundation for determining the amount of child support the noncustodial parent must pay, a powerful movement toward establishing statutory (sometimes judicial) guidelines has resulted in numerous schemes, from criteria to formulas to lengthy tables, by which to calculate child support.

Interstate Enforcement: URESA

The Uniform Reciprocal Enforcement of Support Act (URESA)—and its latest revised version (RURESA)—was produced by the National Conference of Commissioners on Uniform State Laws. URESA was formulated because of the national problem with interstate enforcement of child support orders. URESA provides a means of enforcement when defaulted payments have not been reduced to judgment, as well as providing for when the defaulting obligor has been ordered in contempt of court. It is a means by which the recipient of child support payments may bring an action in his or her own state that will be tried in the state of the debtor. This solves the problem of lack of personal jurisdiction over the debtor by the state of the creditor and saves the creditor the expense of traveling to the debtor's state.

A complaint is filed in the appropriate court in the creditor's state. The complaint is forwarded to the court having jurisdiction over the debtor-defendant, and the case is tried there, with a local official representing the creditor.

Once the case is decided, the state ordering compliance receives the payments and forwards them to the court of the creditor. Failure to pay subjects the debtor to the usual sanctions (contempt, garnishment, etc.) available in the state with personal jurisdiction over the defendant.

Unwed fathers may also be subject to URESA. If paternity has already been adjudicated, they may be treated the same as divorced fathers. URESA also provides for the responding state to adjudicate paternity.

CHILD CUSTODY

Battles over custody of children may be the most intense of all legal encounters. The introduction of no-fault divorce did not seriously change the volatile nature of custody cases, which pose special problems. Those most deeply affected—namely, minor children—are not parties to the lawsuit. In custody battles, children often become pawns in a political struggle between men and women. Complicating this situation is the fact that the court departs from its usual role of resolving a dispute over *past* events and must predict the best course of action for the *future* welfare of the children.

Historical Overview

The English common law carried on the Western European tradition of Roman law, which gave the father absolute control over his children. Because the father-husband enjoyed and exercised legal rights in behalf of the family, his duty of support was balanced by custodial rights. In America, where divorce was early recognized, issues of custody and support became problems for ordinary people. As the revolutionary family was cast in the companionate mold, with the wife responsible for home and children, the father's right to custody was disputed and lost, particularly for children of tender years.

It was not until the twentieth century that this custodial double standard was challenged. The movement for equality of women caused two ideological changes in the legal view of custody. First, if the sexes are equal and should have equal rights, as embodied in the equal protection clause of the Fourteenth Amendment, the tender years doctrine could no longer stand. Second, as the country grew more prosperous and new opportunities for employment of women became available, judicial opinions began to argue that women were no longer unable to join men in the workplace. The custodian of the children then became a matter of choice, giving rise to the ultimate standard, the best interests of the child.

The most recent turn in this story has been a shift from parental rights toward parental responsibilities. The best-interests-of-the-child standard emphasizes rights of the child rather than those of the parents. This change of focus has encouraged extensive study of children of divorce, single-parent families, and adopted and foster children, all of which we now have in large supply. Psychological and sociological studies have influenced both statute and court decisions. Child custody is but one part of a larger picture in which many of our youth appear to be at risk.

joint custody
The continued sharing of rights and duties with regard to children following divorce.

sole custody
The award of *child custody* exclusively to one parent upon divorce; the other parent usually enjoys visitation rights.

Many states have attempted to reduce the injury that divorce does to children by adopting **joint custody** as the preferred form of parental responsibility. Formerly, **sole custody** was granted to one parent, who made all decisions for the children, while the other parent was granted visitation rights. Under the joint custody scheme, both parents share in the decision making about the vital concerns of the children, and both have frequent contact with the children. There is a fundamental weakness in the premise of joint custody: We are asking two individuals who were unable to cooperate effectively while married to cooperate after the destructive ordeal of divorce. Fortunately, most parents continue to love their children long after they have lost their love for each other and may be able to cooperate for the sake of the children. That, at least, is the hope that joint custody offers.

Best Interests of the Child

Case after case insists that the polestar of custody decisions is the best interests of the child. This is a significant departure from the older common law, paternal-rights approach, but the common law rule really acted as a presumption in favor of the father and existed in an era when divorce was rare (largely available only to rich and powerful men who could well afford to support children in their care). Today, despite the best-interests standard, custody decisions are made in the context of presumptions, preferences, and legislative and judicial guidelines. For example, the tender years doctrine, popular during the latter part of the nineteenth century and most of the twentieth, expressed a presumption or preference, depending on the state, that young children should be in the custody of their mother. Even in jurisdictions that have clearly abolished the tender years doctrine by judicial decision, the mother of small children represents an unspoken claim that judges are likely to heed. After all, the suckling infant will not be forcibly weaned in the name of parental equality. Other policies underlying custody decisions include the wishes of the child; avoidance of splitting siblings; minimizing dislocation of children from school, community, and extended family; and protecting parents' rights against third parties.

Formerly, the adultery of the mother could cause her to lose custody; a strict moral code was in force, including a double standard censuring extramarital conduct on the part of the wife and mother. Not only was a woman at fault with regard to the divorce itself, but the moral code presumed that her conduct would have a bad impact on the children. This sometimes overcame the preference in favor of awarding custody to the mother. More recently, however, sexual misconduct has generally been abandoned as grounds to deny custody, unless the father can demonstrate that the mother's sexual behavior has a detrimental impact on the children. The issue continues to be cloudy, however, because judges have very different perceptions of improper sexual conduct and different beliefs about the impact of parental sexuality on children.

Modification

Custody awards may be modifiable, like alimony and child support, but modification is more difficult to obtain than alimony and child support because of judges' reluctance to switch custody and remove a child from a stable environment. Many states have adopted provisions prohibiting modification of custody for two years following a custody order, absent a showing of danger to the child posed by its environment. The most common form of modification attack addresses the sexual misconduct of a custodial mother—the "moral leper" approach used to gain custody at divorce. When the single mother begins to date, the ex-husband may use this to seek custody (and sometimes as a device to negotiate reductions in support payments). Formerly, courts concluded without proof that extramarital sexual encounters by the mother automatically created an immoral environment for children. Sensitivity in the courts to the impropriety of a sexual double standard, along with a focus on the welfare of the child rather than the rights of the parents, has reversed this custom. Today, a mother's sexuality does not justify modification of custody without a clear showing that the mother's conduct has an injurious effect on the children.

The Natural Father

When children are born to unmarried parents, a special set of problems arises. On the one hand, there is no body of law from which to fashion rights of the unofficial family. On the other hand, the recognition of Fourteenth Amendment equal protection rights has generated a continuing inquiry into discrimination against the relationships within a nonmarital family. As a general rule, nonmarital relationships should not invoke different treatment. The unwed father should have the same rights as the man married to a child's mother. Although it may pose a moral issue for some, the nonmarital family does not pose a legal quandary when it is an intact family or when an intact family splits up. In many cases, however, the illegitimate child is the product of a relatively brief relationship, sometimes terminating before the child's birth. This may constitute abandonment of a relationship that was never established except biologically.

Uniform Child Custody Jurisdiction Act

The outcome of custody disputes can be radically different in different states. In the past, a parent could grab the kids, run to another state, and thwart the other parent's custodial rights not only by hiding but also by making recovery of the children dependent on a cumbersome process in which state jurisdiction became a legal issue of considerable complexity. The Uniform Child Custody Jurisdiction Act (UCCJA) was proposed to ameliorate this situation, discourage child snatching, and provide a uniform basis for jurisdiction that could be applied reciprocally by the states.

The UCCJA resolves three problems that arose in the past. First, jurisdiction was commonly premised on the physical whereabouts of the child, which encouraged child snatching and interstate flight as well as forum shopping. Second, parents often attempted to undo custody orders by seeking modification in another state. Although full faith and credit applied to the original order, this did not prevent another state from assuming jurisdiction for the sake of modification. Third, the UCCJA promotes swift enforcement of the custody orders of other states.

ADOPTION

adoption

In family law, the legal establishment of parent–child bonds between persons who did not formerly have them; commonly, this also entails the severance of those bonds with a former parent.

Adoption creates bonds of parent and child between persons who did not previously have this relationship. Ordinarily this involves the severance of legal bonds between a child and its natural parent or parents and the substitution of a new parent or parents, with all the legal consequences of the parent–child relationship.

Adoption was not recognized in England until 1926. The American law of adoption traces its roots to Massachusetts statutes in 1851. Until recently, adoption was primarily concerned with finding children for childless couples; providing parents for children was an incidental benefit. As the focus of public policy turned away from parental rights toward the interests of children, some reorientation in adoption has taken place. An early issue in the law of adoption was the degree to which judicial intervention was appropriate. Today governmental administrative agencies concern themselves with the adoption process, and legislatures have enacted increasing numbers of laws to regulate the adoption process.

Government has entered the adoption process in favor of children with special needs, creating subsidies for parents to adopt children when their resources would otherwise be insufficient. The National Conference of Commissioners on Uniform State Laws published the Uniform Adoption Act in 1953 and revised it in 1969; the federal Department of Health, Education, and Welfare proposed a model act for the states called "An Act for the Adoption of Children."

The Parties

Other than the status of adulthood, the states place few statutory requirements on the prospective adopting parent. Administrative or judicial approval, however, is another matter. The law has been reluctant to grant anyone a *right* to adopt, but clear preferences may be found in the law and in the decisions approving and disapproving particular adoptions. An examination of some of the most common situations clarifies the adoption picture:

1. *Blood relatives.* By custom, orphans became the wards of their close relatives. For divorced parents with minimal resources or for working single mothers, parental duties may be overwhelming, and children are often placed in the care of grandparents or aunts and uncles. Although these may be purely temporary placements, with legal custody remaining with the parent or parents, the desire to adopt may arise for many reasons. With orphans, de facto adoption may be followed by legal adoption. The court or agency looks for the same factors applicable to custody disputes—wholesome environment, continuity of care (same home, school, neighborhood, etc.), keeping siblings together.

2. *Foster parents.* Children who have been placed in the care of strangers may remain with them via adoption even though the foster care administered through the state was traditionally conditioned on the **foster parents** not attempting adoption.

    foster parents
    Caretakers of children who are not their parents, stepparents, nor adoptive parents, whom the law has recognized as parental caretakers, commonly when children are taken away from their parents for cause.

3. *Stepparents.* One of the most common relationships involved in adoption is stepparent–stepchild. A typical scenario: A stepfather is actively involved in raising his wife's children by a former marriage, with the natural father mostly or completely absent and perhaps totally neglecting support obligations. The greatest stumbling block to such an adoption is denial of consent by the natural parent. Although this may be overcome by a court finding that abandonment or neglect has severed the bonds between parent and child, the law so strongly favors continuance of the biological bond as a legal bond that lack of consent in many instances is fatal to the adoption process. Adoption severs the natural parents' rights with regard to the child, something that courts are extremely reluctant to do.

4. *Childless strangers.* Couples unable to bear children are most likely to go to adoption agencies or lawyers to seek children to adopt. Adoption agencies are usually extensively regulated and subject to statutory restriction. Potential adoptive parents are in theory carefully scrutinized both for the environment they can provide and their capacity to be good parents. The process may be lengthy and cumbersome, so many couples employ attorneys to facilitate the process.

illegitimate

Refers to a child born to an unwed mother. In most states, the acknowledgment of paternity by a natural father may legitimate the child despite its being born out of wedlock.

5. *Unwed (nonmarital) fathers.* Until recent years, fathers of **illegitimate** offspring had no rights or legal relationship with their children. With the advent of financial responsibility through paternity suits, the fathers could expect to have rights as well. Visitation rights were forthcoming, and custody was possible when the mother died or her custody was detrimental to the child. Still, because the father had not married the mother and usually had not otherwise acknowledged paternity, his rights inevitably threatened the maternal bond. Courts and legislatures have created a balancing act between recognition of the special place of the mother without depriving the father of rights.

6. *Same-sex couples.* By statute (upheld by the Florida Supreme Court), Florida does not allow adoption by homosexuals.

Surrogacy

surrogacy contract

A contract by which the natural father takes custody of a child and the mother relinquishes custody in favor of adoption by the father's wife.

Because of the *Baby M* case in 1988, much public attention was directed at so-called **surrogacy contracts**. In surrogacy contracts, the natural father takes custody of the child, while the mother relinquishes custody in favor of adoption by the natural father's wife. Conception is ordinarily achieved by artificial insemination with the contracting father's sperm or by implanting a fertilized ovum in the surrogate mother. In the former case, the childbearer is the genetic mother but not in the latter case. Although in theory surrogacy contracts are simple, their subject matter is unique. From one point of view, they seem to be agreements to sell babies and thus clearly illegal. In contrast, because the natural fathers are assuming custody, they cannot be said to be buying something to which they have no right. These contracts have also been considered offensive because they imply that women's bodies may be rented for a period of time, suggesting exploitation of the poor by the rich. Additionally, surrogacy involves the psychobiology of rending an infant from its natural mother, whose feelings and state of mind have undoubtedly changed considerably since the time of contracting. For all these (and perhaps other) reasons, the *Baby M* case, in which a surrogate mother changed her mind after the birth of the child, prompted a diversity of intense emotional and intellectual responses, and state legislatures hurriedly passed legislation to regulate surrogacy contracts.

Same-sex marriage may require a rethinking of statutes that prohibit surrogacy contracts, on equal protection grounds.

FEDERAL INVOLVEMENT IN FAMILY LAW

Not long ago, the federal government left family law to the states. The Supreme Court stood by the family law exception to deny certiorari to marriage, divorce, and custody decisions of the state courts and Congress left legislating to the states. Attitudes of elected politicians changed, however, when "family values" became an issue for both political parties. Sexual intimacy is now one of the Court's favorite issues, which suggests that same-sex marriage, adoption, and benefits will be heard in the high court and thus serve to further undermine the family law exception. Meanwhile, Congress has discovered the need to regulate the family. Foremost among the new laws is the Defense of Marriage Act:

28 U.S.C. § 1738C. Certain acts, records, and proceedings and the effect thereof

No State, territory, or possession of the United States, or Indian tribe, shall be required to give effect to any public act, record, or judicial proceeding of any other State, territory, possession, or tribe respecting a relationship between persons of the same sex that is treated as a marriage under the laws of such other State, territory, possession, or tribe, or a right or claim arising from such relationship.

A majority of states have enacted laws under the auspices of DOMA to deny recognition to same-sex marriages performed in other states. The purpose of DOMA is to give the states authority to override the full faith and credit clause of the Constitution. This is an unusual way to "amend" the Constitution, an act that will shortly be challenged. Interestingly, states have always had public policy to attack orders and decrees from other states (i.e., a state could refuse to honor an official act of a sister state where that act violated the public policy of the state asked to give it full faith and credit). This has been rarely used because very few acts that are proper in one state are highly offensive in another. Same-sex marriage, however, might qualify. We will see many cases in many places, possibly resolving the major issues about the time the fifth edition of this text is printed.

SUMMARY

Family law has undergone continuous revision since the founding of American law, changing to keep up with American society. The principal subject of family law is divorce, although annulment remains an alternative. Divorce inevitably raises the issues of distribution of marital property, spousal and child support, and child custody. Although these are the most litigated issues of family law, in most instances their resolution occurs outside of court during lawyers' negotiations. This is due in part to the uncertainty created by the vast discretion judges exercise when forced to decide domestic relations issues.

Adoption and premarital, or antenuptial, agreements pose additional areas of legal concern in family law.

KEY TERMS

adoption	domestic relations	nonage
alimony	elective share	postnuptial agreement
annulment	equitable distribution	property settlement
antenuptial (premarital)	foster parents	agreement
agreement	illegitimate	rehabilitative alimony
bigamous	incestuous	separation agreement
canon law	joint custody	sole custody
child custody	lump-sum alimony	spousal support
child support	marriage	surrogacy contract
community property	mental incompetence	
divorce	modification	

CHAPTER REVIEW QUESTIONS

1. What is the difference between annulment and divorce?
2. What is the usual purpose of an antenuptial agreement?
3. Why has alimony come to be disfavored?
4. What are the different forms of child custody?
5. What is the overriding consideration in awarding custody?
6. What is *surrogacy*?
7. What are the two parameters for modification of child support?
8. What does URESA stand for?
9. What was the catalyst for the states legislating child support guidelines?
10. Why has no-fault divorce become the law in the states?

CRITICAL THINKING QUESTIONS

1. Could you define *family* in a way that would be legally useful?
2. Do you imagine that family law will be changing in the future?

CYBER EXERCISES

1. Opinions of the Supreme Court of California are accessible at a number of websites, including http://www.courtinfo.ca.gov/. The California Supreme Court decided *Strauss v. Horton*, 207 P.3d 48 (Cal. 2009), on May 26, 2009. The case contained three concurring opinions and one dissenting opinion. Locate the case at the California Supreme Court website and answer the following questions:
   a. What does Judge Kennard's concurring opinion conclude?
   b. Judge Werdegar filed a concurring opinion containing one major disagreement with the majority's analysis of the court's prior decision. What does he believe the majority did wrong in this particular case?
   c. Why did Judge Moreno file a dissenting opinion in addition to his concurring opinion? Do you feel that he is right?
2. The Opinions of the Supreme Court of Connecticut are accessible at a number of websites, including http://www.jud.ct.gov/. The Connecticut Supreme Court decided *Kerrigan v. Commissioner of Public Health*, 957 A.2d 407 (Conn. 2008), on October 28, 2008. The case contained three dissenting opinions. Locate the case through the Connecticut Supreme Court website and answer the following questions:
   a. What was the ruling of the majority concerning the legality of same-sex marriages in Connecticut?
   b. What was the basis of the decision?
   c. What is the basis for each of the three dissenting opinions?
   d. Which of the opinions is more persuasive?
3. Same-sex marriage is a hot topic, with states dealing with the topic by provisions in the state constitutions, by statute, and by case law. Much information on same-sex

marriage is available at http://www.freedomtomarry.org/. Using that website, answer the following questions:

    a. Which states have dealt with same-sex marriage by provisions in the state constitutions, and to what effect?

    b. Which states have statutes sanctioning same-sex marriage?

    c. Which states have dealt with same-sex marriage by case law, and to what effect?

    d. Would a state that has not spoken on the legality of same-sex marriage recognize the validity of a same-sex marriage sanctioned by another state?

    e. What if a same-sex couple marry in a state allowing same-sex marriage, move to a state prohibiting same-sex marriage, and then decide to divorce?

    f. What is the law in your state concerning same-sex marriage?

SCENARIO

Henry A. Fuller (Henry) was born to Audrey Fuller (Audrey) in 1951. Paternity was never established. Audrey decided to give up her son for adoption. In 1957, the Columbia County Juvenile Court entered a parental termination order stating that Audrey was "permanently deprived of any and all maternal rights and interests in and to the said Baby Boy Fuller." The order also placed Henry into the permanent custody of the Catholic Charities of the Diocese, authorizing that organization to consent to his adoption. Henry was never adopted. The parent–child relationship between Henry and Audrey was never reestablished.

    Henry died intestate in 1996. He was not married and had no children. Two biological relatives survived Henry—his biological mother and his half-brother, William Gilbert, who was born to Audrey after she terminated her parental rights to Henry.

    In 1998, the personal administrator of Henry's estate, Renfrew, filed a petition for determination of heirship. She asked the court to find that Audrey and Gilbert were not entitled to inherit from Henry because by court order all maternal rights had been terminated. She argued that Henry's estate should escheat to the state because he died intestate without any legal heirs.

    Audrey and Gilbert filed a response and objection to the petition. The superior court commissioner agreed with Renfrew and ruled that the estate should escheat to the state because Henry was without legal heirs. The commissioner found that the 1957 order terminating Audrey's maternal rights to Henry also extinguished her right to inherit intestate and that Gilbert could not inherit from Henry because there was no longer a common ancestor between them.

    Audrey died soon after the commissioner ruled. Gilbert was appointed personal representative of her estate. After her death, Gilbert continued to assert a claim to Henry's estate, filing a motion in superior court to revise the ruling of the commissioner. The superior court upheld the commissioner's order.

    The statute in effect at the time of the court-ordered surrender of Henry provided that when a parent surrendered a child to a charitable organization, "the rights of its natural parents or of the guardian of its person (if any) shall cease and such corporation shall become entitled to the custody of such a child."

The statute regarding intestate succession reads as follows:

(1) Shares of others than surviving spouse. The shares of the net estate not distributable to the surviving spouse, or the entire net estate if there is no surviving spouse, shall descend and be distributed as follows:

  (a) To the issue of the intestate. . . .

  (b) If the intestate not be survived by issue, then to the parent or parents who survive the intestate.

  (c) If the intestate not be survived by issue or by either parent, then to those issue of the parent or parents who survive the intestate[.]

If no person qualified to inherit under the intestate law, the property belongs to the state.

  Query: There are two ways that Gilbert might acquire Henry's estate. Make an argument that will favor Gilbert using two alternative ways that could happen. Argue the intent of the legislature. Argue policy—why the law would favor an interpretation that would give Gilbert the estate rather than the state. Argue justice—why the facts of the case are special and the equities are in Gilbert's favor. How can you define "apparent" in such a way that Gilbert can prevail?

CHAPTER 14
ADMINISTRATIVE LAW AND PROCEDURE

INTRODUCTION

Administrative law refers to the law that governs administrative action by government. It regulates the relationship between the citizen and the government. Although it is poorly understood by laypersons and many practitioners, it has a greater impact on the daily lives of Americans than any other area of law. Most people have few, if any, brushes with criminal law, few are often involved in personal injury law, and contract and property law are matters of occasional concern for the nonbusinessperson. But the rules and regulations of government agencies are encountered throughout a lifetime. The water we drink, the air we breathe, the places we work, the schools we attend, the Social Security system, and a host of other facets of our lives are subject to regulation by agencies governed by administrative law.

administrative law

The body of law that controls the way in which administrative agencies operate if covered by state and federal Administrative Procedure Acts; also deals with regulations issued by administrative agencies.

THE FIELD OF ADMINISTRATIVE LAW

Administrative law was born in the twentieth century. In theory, it can be traced back through the centuries, but the field as it is defined today emanates principally from the U.S. Constitution as it has come to be interpreted in recent decades. The federal Administrative Procedure Act, first enacted in 1946, may have been the most important event in administrative law, although its provisions drew heavily on prior case law. Because

bureaucracy
That part of the government composed of agencies staffed by civil servants; forms the major part of the administrative branch.

administrative law is relatively young, it is still dynamic and changing. Our **bureaucracy** has expanded and blossomed, particularly in the years since Roosevelt's New Deal. The greatest expansion has come in social services agencies, such as Social Security, the Veterans Administration, Medicare, and the social welfare agencies. The new agencies and the expanding scope of government activities have presented numerous problems that have encouraged the growth of administrative law and the litigation that often shapes it. Charting new ground for law has left a confusing array of cases and rules that makes administrative law a great challenge.

Substantive Law

The academic study of administrative law is generally confined to procedural law because of the impossibility of learning the substantive law. Each agency has its own set of substantive rules and regulations, sometimes a product of the legislature and sometimes the legislative product of the agency itself. The regulations of the Social Security Administration bear little resemblance to those of the Securities and Exchange Commission or the Environmental Protection Agency. The regulations of all the agencies are collected in the *Code of Federal Regulations,* which is a huge compendium that no one has ever mastered. It would be a major undertaking simply to gain a relatively complete understanding of the rules and regulations of the Social Security Administration.

Procedural Law

Administrative procedural law encompasses most of what is usually meant when the term *administrative law* is used. There are certain principles governing administrative action regardless of the agency concerned. Administrative agencies pose a special problem for the law because most agencies engage in all three governmental functions. Although they belong to the executive branch of government, most agencies engage in rulemaking, which is the administrative agency equivalent of legislation, and most large agencies (and many small agencies) have an adjudicatory function as well.

Administrative procedure is particularly concerned with the legislative (rulemaking) and adjudicatory functions of agencies. Because these involve state or federal action, they are constrained by the due process clauses of the Fifth and Fourteenth Amendments requiring fundamental fairness in substance and procedure. What makes administrative procedural law different from the procedural principles that apply in suits between private parties derives from the nature of the parties involved.

Every administrative law case potentially involves weighing the important interests of the individual against the interests of society as represented by government. A prime example is sovereign immunity from suit. In the nineteenth century, the courts and some state legislatures concluded that it made no sense for a private citizen to sue the government. At that time, of course, government was small, offered few services, and intruded very little into private affairs. A democratic government was perceived as benevolent, as representing the people, so it was illogical for the people to sue themselves. By the 1960s and 1970s, it had become apparent that a democratic government could indeed be intrusive and abusive and that sovereign immunity was often viewed as a license for government to run roughshod over private interests.

ADMINISTRATIVE LAW IN PRACTICE

The study of administrative law is a worthwhile endeavor for the paralegal student, for a number of reasons. Only by studying administrative law can a person gain a deep understanding of the basic process by which the rights of the citizen are upheld or defended against the intrusions of government. It is also a rewarding education in constitutional law. Nonetheless, the study of administrative law can also be very practical. Litigation against the government increases as the scope of government activities increases, and there seems to be no end to this increase. Administrative law cases frequently involve lengthy litigation with copious amounts of research that should be done by paralegals for reasons of cost efficiency. In addition, many agencies, such as the Social Security Administration and other social service agencies, permit claimants to be represented by anyone of their choosing. The California Bar Association issued an opinion in 1989 allowing paralegals employed by law firms to represent the firm's clients in administrative hearings. This affords paralegals an opportunity to do trial work. Many legal aid offices employ paralegals to represent indigents at administrative hearings. Administrative law thus presents a promising area for employment of paralegals. Although many (perhaps most) paralegals will never handle administrative law work, others will become administrative law specialists.

INDEPENDENT REGULATORY AGENCIES

Administrative law questions ultimately concern the power of government to regulate and the right of private parties to challenge regulation. Most of the major principles of the law of administrative procedure grew out of challenges to government regulation of business, against government agencies established for the purpose of regulating business.

The discussion of administrative law in this chapter uses federal administrative procedure as its model. Most states have adopted comprehensive administrative procedure statues, modeled on the federal act with modifications. Nevertheless, administrative law at the federal level has tended to lead the way—the federal Administrative Procedure Act (APA) pre-dates state acts by two to four decades. Congress and the federal courts naturally became involved at an earlier stage because of the creation of **independent regulatory agencies** with national authority and great power.

Independent regulatory agencies were originally created to control the devastating effects of cutthroat competition in certain industries. The first great agency to be created was the Interstate Commerce Commission, created in 1887. Since that time Congress has periodically created new agencies; there now exist a dozen major independent regulatory agencies and more than fifty smaller ones. Regulating an industry is essentially anticompetitive and counter to a pure market model of free enterprise. Americans, especially politicians, often speak of free enterprise as if it has always characterized—and continues to characterize—the American economy. Even a cursory review of world history shows that free enterprise unregulated by government probably never existed, though the United States may have come closest to the model at one time or another. In a legal sense, we have been more committed to a *fair* market than a *free* market. It is the nature of government to allocate and distribute power and wealth, which makes it inevitable that business will be taxed and regulated.

independent regulatory agencies
Those agencies of the government that exercise relative autonomy because their heads cannot be removed at the whim of the chief executive, for example, the president; distinguished from departments, which are under the direct control of secretaries, who serve at the pleasure of the president.

The Interstate Commerce Commission (ICC) is a good illustration of the rationale of regulation. The ICC was formed to serve the railroad industry and the public. Vicious competition combined with monopolistic practices often undermined individual companies on the one hand and allowed excessive rates on the other. The industry was unstable at a time when the railroads were a major vehicle for economic growth of the country. Railroads are different from some other businesses in that they must operate on fixed routes—the investment in land and track must result in a level of use that will repay the investment. If one hundred railroads build tracks from Chicago to St. Louis, none of them will make money until most have abandoned the route. The ICC was charged with regulating routes and rates in such a way that the railroads could make a reasonable profit while charging rates that business and the public could afford, so that everyone would benefit. As part of the movement toward deregulation, the ICC was terminated in 1995. Regulatory schemes are not perfect—sometimes they benefit the country, and sometimes they are a burden—but the fact remains that some business activities are so central to the national economy that the government is unlikely to relinquish control.

Some activities must be controlled because they are by nature monopolistic. Public utilities are the prime example. The furnishing of water, sewer, gas, and electricity is an activity that can be accomplished efficiently by only one company serving a community, locality, or region. In fact, these activities are often performed by government. Where they are not, public service commissions monitor their activities and particularly their rates. Because these activities provide absolutely essential services to the community, government does not allow the utilities a free rein.

Independent agencies may be distinguished on the federal level by the following rule of thumb: an independent agency is one whose head cannot be removed by the president without cause. By contrast, cabinet chiefs (the secretaries of state, labor, defense, etc.) occupy their positions at the pleasure of the president. Although the president must obtain Congress's approval for appointment, he can remove a cabinet secretary at any time. The president may remove the chiefs or commissioners of the independent regulatory agencies only upon showing just cause for their removal.

Since the Roosevelt New Deal era, Congress has moved away from creating new industry-regulating agencies toward the establishment of social service agencies, such as the Social Security Administration; the Occupational Safety and Health Review Commission, created under the Occupational Safety and Health Act; and the Consumer Product Safety Commission.

The importance of independent regulatory agencies for administrative law is twofold. First, the creation of these agencies brought into question the authority of Congress to delegate its legislative powers granted by the Constitution. Second, authority was delegated to administrative agencies with a degree of independence from the executive branch of government of which they were a part. Because the agencies often regulated national industries and administrative activities, the regulations they promulgated, the enforcement procedures they sued, and their activities were frequently challenged by business interests that could afford to pursue their remedies all the way to the U.S. Supreme Court. As the initial legal issues were basic constitutional questions, many of the fundamental principles of administrative procedure were formulated in the context of the regulation of business.

Thus, many of the landmark cases in administrative law seem remote from daily life. For example, *United States v. Morgan*, 313 U.S. 409 (1941), involved the fixing of rates for buying and selling livestock at the Kansas City Stock Yards, but it went to the U.S. Supreme Court four times and ultimately set standards for the extent to which litigants could inquire into the decisionmaking of high-level policymakers. *Abbott Laboratories v. Gardner*, 387 U.S. 136 (1967), concerned Food and Drug Administration regulation of drug labeling but set forth the fundamental interpretation of judicial review under the APA, namely, that agency action is presumptively reviewable by the courts.

Research and argument in administrative procedural law differ from other areas of law because the cases deal with myriad agencies. In most private law cases, especially substantive questions of law, the researcher looks for cases with a similar fact pattern (argument in a slip-and-fall case will usually revolve around prior slip-and-fall decisions). In contrast, administrative procedure arguments are constructed from a line of precedent-setting cases that bear no fact resemblance other than the procedural issue raised.

DELEGATION OF LEGISLATIVE AUTHORITY

In the nineteenth century, the courts frequently repeated the doctrine that Congress could not delegate its legislative authority, on the ground that the Constitution restricted this authority to Congress. In actual fact, Congress from the very beginning delegated its authority to administrative agencies, but the courts did not strike down such delegation until 1935, when a broad delegation of authority under the National Industrial Recovery Act was held by the U.S. Supreme Court to be unconstitutional in two cases. Since then, the nondelegation doctrine has been all but dead, though it was partially resurrected in *Immigration and Naturalization Service v. Chadha*, 462 U.S. 919 (1983). The principle is still occasionally raised in administrative law cases with state agencies.

JUDICIAL REVIEW OF AGENCY ACTION

Critical topics in the field of administrative law are judicial review and the scope of judicial review. These issues address basic questions concerning whether a dispute over agency action is a matter for the courts, who may bring such an action, and exactly what the courts should consider. These problems are constitutional issues. Because the U.S. Constitution establishes the doctrine of separation of powers, it was thought in the nineteenth century that the courts had no authority to question actions by the executive branch of government. An opposing constitutional premise, however, is that the executive branch may not violate the Constitution, and because the federal courts are responsible for interpreting the Constitution, logically the courts should be the forum for preventing the executive branch from exceeding its constitutional authority.

The demise of the doctrine of nonreviewability was signaled by *American School of Magnetic Healing v. McAnnulty*, 187 U.S. 94 (1902), in which the postmaster general prohibited the school from using the mail. It was clear that the postmaster general did not have such authority, and the court was faced with either dismissing the case for nonreviewability, thereby allowing the postmaster general unbridled authority, or reviewing the case and limiting the postmaster general to his legal authority. There really was no choice; our democratic legal principles could not allow a public official to act unlawfully. The postmaster general lost, and judicial review assumed respectability. Thereafter, the doctrine of judicial review was formulated in a series of cases that culminated in the enactment of Chapter 7 of the APA, which states in relevant part the following:

§ 701. Application; definitions

(a)   This chapter applies, according to the provisions thereof, except to the extent that—
    (1)   statutes preclude judicial review; or
    (2)   agency action is committed to agency discretion by law.

§ 704. Actions reviewable

Agency action made reviewable by statute and final agency action for which there is no other adequate remedy in a court are subject to judicial review.

What exactly these two sections mean in combination has been the subject of much commentary and will undoubtedly continue to require clarification. What is clear, in theory if not always in fact, is that § 701(a)(1) means that Congress may specifically exempt some agency action from court review by statute, but when review is specifically authorized by statute, review is available. If Congress states that action cannot be reviewed, it cannot be reviewed; if Congress states that action can be reviewed, it can be reviewed. This is simple enough—except that Congress is usually silent with regard to review. In that situation, § 704 would seem to indicate that review is available, except where "agency action is committed to agency discretion by law," a proviso that is less than crystal clear. *Abbott Laboratories v. Gardner*, 387 U.S. 136 (1967), resolved the issue by ignoring the lack of clarity in the language of the APA and stating that the APA expresses a "presumption of reviewability." The courts and Congress seem content with that principle and have left the debate over the nuances of the APA to legal scholars.

Review of Discretionary Acts of Officials

The actions of public officials often fall within areas of discretion recognized by the law. The very term *discretion* implies unreviewability, and the statement in § 701(a)(2) that "agency action is committed to agency discretion by law" suggests that discretionary action may not be reviewed. Nevertheless, "committed . . . by law" invites various interpretations. Certainly Congress may use statutory language specifically using the term *discretion* or *discretionary* to leave no doubt of its delegation of authority. If a court concludes that such a delegation is proper, it is unlikely to challenge an exercise of discretion. In many instances, the statutory language suggests a delegation of discretion that a court might conclude was not fully committed by law. In addition, the precise scope of discretion may be unclear, and an official might act within the scope of her duties without acting within the area of committed discretion. At the highest levels of government, official decisions are commonly policy decisions, not only discretionary but also protected by principles of separation of powers. At lower levels of action, decision making enjoys less respect, and when decisions affect rights, assuming a quasi-judicial flavor, the separation-of-powers protection is less persuasive.

When the exercise of discretion is challenged, the standard of review is different from the standards of review applied in lower courts of law; instead, it follows equity. Recall from our discussion of equity in Chapter 6 that courts of equity have always enjoyed considerable discretion. Discretionary acts of public officials are judged by the same standard: abuse of discretion. Logically, when the people, the government, and the law give someone official discretion, that discretion must not be abused. Here is another way of putting this: Courts, in our system of separate powers, are reluctant to question the acts of other branches of government, or the acts of officials of those other branches; no one has absolute power, and every official must act within reasonable bounds. We must have some basis to hold officials accountable for clearly unreasonable actions.

The litigation surrounding the presidential election of 2000 offers an illustration of the application of abuse of discretion at the state level. Katherine Harris, the Florida secretary of state, was invested by the Florida legislature with the authority to certify the electors for the State of Florida along with the responsibility to supervise voting standards and procedures. Although she had great discretion, that discretion was limited. Judge Lewis of the Circuit Court for Leon County recognized this discretion but commanded her to exercise discretion within the limits appropriate to her task. In *McDermott v. Harris* [*McDermott* I], Judge Lewis describes in precise terms the nature of official discretion and its limitation in the election controversy.

[McDermott I]

McDERMOTT

v.

HARRIS

Florida Circuit Court, Leon County

No. 00-2700 (Fla. 2d Cir. Ct. Nov. 14, 2000)

The heart of the issue raised by the Motion [for declaratory judgment] is this: Section 102.166, Florida Statutes, contemplates that upon request a county canvassing board may authorize a manual recount of votes cast in an election. Both Volusia and Palm Beach Counties have so authorized, and are in the process of conducting, a manual recount. The Boards are concerned that the manual recounts may not be completed by 5:00 P.M. today, November 14, 2000, which is the deadline imposed upon them by Section 102.112, Florida Statutes,

to certify and report the election returns to the Secretary of State. This Section provides that if the returns are not received by the deadline, such returns *may* be ignored by the Secretary in her certification of results statewide.

The Plaintiffs insist that the Secretary of State *must* consider the certified results from Volusia and Palm Beach Counties, even if they are filed late, if they are still engaged in the manual recount of the votes. The Secretary of State insists that, absent an Act of God such as a hurricane, any returns not received by the statutory deadline *will* not be counted in the statewide tabulations and certification of the election results. For the reasons set forth below, I find that the County Canvassing Boards must certify and file what election returns they have by the statutory deadline of 5:00 P.M. of November 14, 2000, with due notification to the Secretary of State of any pending manual recount, and may thereafter file supplemental or corrective returns. The Secretary of State may ignore such late filed returns, but may not do so arbitrarily, rather, only by the proper exercise of discretion after consideration of all appropriate facts and circumstances. . . .

It is unlikely that the Legislature would give the right to protest returns, but make it meaningless because it could not be acted upon in time. . . .

To determine ahead of time that such returns *will* be ignored, however, unless caused by some Act of God, is not the exercise of discretion. It is the abdication of that discretion. . . .

I can lawfully direct the Secretary to properly exercise her discretion in making a decision on the returns, but I cannot enjoin the Secretary to make a particular decision, nor can I rewrite the Statute that, by its plain meaning, mandates the filing of returns by the Canvassing Boards by 5:00 P.M. on November 14, 2000. . . .

Accordingly, it is ORDERED AND ADJUDGED that the Secretary of State is directed to withhold determination as to whether or not to ignore late filed returns, if any, from Plaintiff Canvassing Boards, until due consideration of all relevant facts and circumstances consistent with the sound exercise of discretion. In all other respects, the Motion for Temporary Injunction is denied.

§

In response to Judge Lewis's warnings, Secretary Harris instructed the county canvassing boards to furnish reasons for submitting amended vote counts based on manual counts. Furnished with their reasons, Harris rejected the changes in vote on the ground that none of the reasons were justified by the statutes, which she interpreted to include acts of God, machine malfunction, and fraud, none of which had been given as reasons.

Secretary Harris's conclusions were challenged as the case returned to Judge Lewis, who gave a brief order [*McDermott* II]. (Subsequent legal history of the 2000 presidential election is difficult to decipher from a nonpartisan perspective.)

[McDermott II]

McDERMOTT

v.

HARRIS

Florida Circuit Court, Leon County

No. 00-2700 (Fla. 2d Cir. Ct. Nov. 17, 2000)

Order denying emergency motion to compel compliance with and for enforcement of injunction

The limited issue before me on this Motion is whether the Secretary of State has violated my Order of November 14, 2000. The Plaintiffs assert that she has acted arbitrarily in deciding to ignore amended returns from counties conducting manual recounts. I disagree.

As noted in my previous Order, Florida law grants to the Secretary, as the Chief Elections Officer, broad discretionary authority to accept or reject late filed returns. The purpose and intent of my Order was to insure that she in fact properly exercised her discretion, rather than automatically reject returns that came in after the statutory deadline.

On the limited evidence presented, it appears that the Secretary has exercised her reasoned judgment to determine what relevant factors and criteria should be considered, applied them to the facts and circumstances pertinent to the individual counties involved, and made her decision. My Order requires nothing more.

Accordingly, it is ORDERED AND ADJUDGED that the Motion is hereby denied. . . .

Case Questions

1. Are these two cases consistent?
2. Was the judge motivated by political considerations? Explain your answer.

§

Scope of Review

The reluctance of the early courts to review administrative action was due in part to a desire to avoid retrying the facts. When an agency had made a determination of rights, especially if a hearing had been provided, the courts saw no need to conduct another hearing. When facts were found by the agency, the courts did not want to engage in a new round of factfinding. In addition, the agency was presumably better at finding facts because it employed experts in the field for which it was established. It was reasoned, for example, that the ICC was better able to understand the intricacies of the railroad business than were ordinary judges and juries, so the courts were reluctant to interfere with policymaking by the agencies entrusted with that function.

The resolution of this problem came about through the gradual transformation of judicial review into an appellate procedure, with the agencies serving in the place of trial courts (conducting the hearings, finding fact, and applying rules) and the court of appeals reviewing agency determinations much like an appellate court reviews an appeal from a trial court. Today, nearly all judicial review in both state and federal courts takes place at the appellate level.

In this way, the courts have limited the scope of judicial review to the legal questions with which appellate judges are competent and comfortable. Issues of jurisdiction, the interpretation of statutes, and due process raise questions that the courts treat on a daily basis. When factfinding is questioned, the courts borrow the substantial evidence test used for appellate review of jury factfinding. By limiting the scope of review, the courts remove themselves from making policy decisions and assume responsibility for monitoring the fairness of procedure.

A celebrated example of this was *Environmental Defense Fund, Inc. v. Ruckelshaus,* 439 F.2d 584 (D.C. Cir. 1971), in which the secretary of agriculture was sued by an environmental group in an effort to ban the pesticide DDT. Judge Bazelon separated the questions of fact from the questions of law. He declined to examine the conclusion of the secretary that DDT did not present an "imminent hazard," which would warrant summary suspension—this was a fact question left to the determination of the agency. However, the issue raised by the Environmental Defense Fund concerning whether the standard of proof used by the secretary conflicted with legislative intent in the applicable statute was a legal question appropriate for judicial determination. In this way, the court avoided making policy as to whether DDT should be banned and restricted the scope of review to whether the agency acted properly within the statute.

In *Unistar*, we see the Connecticut court of last resort deferring to the administrative agency by limiting its review to the question of whether the agency's factfinding was supported by substantial evidence. This should remind you of the role of the appellate court introduced in Chapter 5.

UNISTAR PROPERTIES, LLC	Supreme Court of Connecticut
v.	No. 18321
CONSERVATION AND INLAND WETLANDS COMMISSION of the TOWN OF PUTNAM et al.	977 A.2d 127
	Decided Aug. 18, 2009.

The plaintiff, Unistar Properties, LLC, appeals from the judgment of the trial court dismissing its appeal from the denial of its application for a wetlands permit by the named defendant, the conservation and inland wetlands commission (commission) of the town of Putnam (town), in connection with a proposed subdivision on its property. The principal issue in this certified appeal is whether the commission properly denied the plaintiff's application for a wetlands permit as incomplete because it was missing certain information, including a sufficiently detailed wildlife inventory and an analysis of alternatives to the proposed activity. . . .

The plaintiff is the co-owner of a sixty-two acre parcel (property) located on Five Mile River Road in the town. The property contains five distinct wetland areas, including two "vernal pools" located in the center of the property that contain various wildlife and plant species. On May 3, 2006, the plaintiff filed an application for a wetlands permit with the commission in connection with a proposed thirty-four lot subdivision to be developed on the property. The subdivision was to be built outside the regulated area but included a roadway and cul-de-sac that would encircle the two vernal pools in the center of the property. Accompanying the application was a report dated May 1, 2006, written by Ian T. Cole, a soil scientist, that described the wetlands on the property and concluded: "The wetlands on-site primarily serve as areas of groundwater recharge and discharge, in addition to providing wildlife habitat. In my professional opinion, protection of the wetlands should focus on water quality. To preserve the wildlife habitat attributes of the wetlands there will be no disturbance of any inland wetlands or watercourses, or within the [fifty] foot upland review area." The report also noted that an artificial wetland would be constructed on the property and that the majority of any stormwater discharge from the property would be treated and diverted away from the natural wetlands and into the constructed wetland to avoid infiltrating the natural wetlands.

The commission forwarded the application to the Eastern Connecticut Conservation District, Inc. (conservation district) for its assessment. The conservation district identified two major concerns with the proposed subdivision. First, it identified the vernal pool wetlands in the center of the property as "high-quality"

and recommended that the plaintiff increase the buffer area around those pools to 200 feet to protect the "function" of the pools. Second, the report concluded that, because surface runoff would be redirected away from the wetlands by the proposed roadway and other structures, the water supply to the wetlands would be "seriously compromised."

The commission conducted a public hearing on the plaintiff's application over the course of four evenings held over several months. The plaintiff provided expert evidence to support its conclusion that its proposed subdivision would not affect the wetlands on the property. Several neighboring property owners, two of whom had filed a timely notice of intervention (intervenors), provided expert evidence that contradicted the plaintiff's conclusion. The intervenors' expert opined that the plaintiff's plan likely would affect the wetlands within the property adversely, but concluded that additional information was required to determine the extent of that impact. Finally, an expert retained by the commission concluded that the application was missing certain information required for compliance with the regulations, including an inventory of plant and wildlife species on the property and an evaluation of the impact of the proposed subdivision on those species. The plaintiff thereafter submitted a modified plan and additional evidence in an attempt to address some of these issues, but the intervenors' expert maintained that an adverse impact still was likely despite the modifications and that the application continued to lack sufficient detail to determine the extent of that impact. . . .

It is well established that in challenging the decision of an administrative agency, such as an inland wetlands commission, the plaintiff carries the burden of proof to show that the challenged action is not supported by the record. . . . This so-called substantial evidence rule is similar to the sufficiency of the evidence standard applied in judicial review of jury verdicts, and evidence is sufficient to sustain an agency finding if it affords a substantial basis of fact from which the fact in issue can be reasonably inferred. . . .

[The court details the evidence presented at the four sessions of the public hearing.]

In light of this record, the trial court properly concluded that the commission's decision was supported by substantial evidence. At the outset, it is clear that the plaintiff's contention that no evidence was presented that there would be a change in the physical characteristics of the wetlands is not supported by the record. Throughout the course of the public hearing, evidence clearly demonstrated that the wetlands would be impacted in a variety of ways, and the commission needed to resolve whether that impact would be adverse. Significantly, the plaintiff's own expert testified that the natural waterflow to the vernal pools would be interrupted by the proposed roadway and that the wetlands would be replenished by stormwater from the development that had been filtered to public health standards. Experts retained both by the intervenors and by the commission noted that, due to the fact that the vernal pools were highly productive, they were "hydrologically vulnerable" to changes in their water supply. . . .

As is well settled, the board's decision must be affirmed if there is any ground to support it. In the present case, at least two of the reasons cited by the commission for concluding that that the application was incomplete are supported by substantial evidence, namely, that the application lacked: (1) a specific wildlife inventory and an analysis of the impact of the proposed subdivision on that wildlife; and (2) an analysis of alternatives to the proposed development to address issues that had been raised. With respect to the first reason, as we previously have noted, the town's regulations specify that applications must contain *"a sufficiently detailed description of the proposed activity to permit the [c]ommission to evaluate its impact on the regulated area"* and note that applicants may be required to produce an inventory of plant and animal species on the property and the effects of the proposed activity on those species. (Emphasis added.) Putnam Wetlands and Water Courses Regs., § 6.1. In the present case, although on the last day of the public hearing, the plaintiff provided a list of vegetation and wildlife that was either known to be present or likely to be present, there was testimony that this inventory lacked the requisite specificity for the commission to determine whether the wetlands would be impacted. . . . Finally, the application contains no analysis of the effects of the proposed subdivision on any of the species other than the conclusory statement of the plaintiff's expert, unsupported by analysis, that there would be no adverse effect. It is well established that credibility and factual determinations are solely within the province of the commission and the commission "is not required to believe any witness, even an expert, nor is it required to use in any particular fashion any of the materials presented to it so long as the conduct of the hearing is fundamentally fair." *Huck.*

With respect to whether the application lacked an analysis of alternatives to the proposed subdivision, it is undisputed that the plaintiff consistently failed to provide an analysis of alternatives, maintaining that, because there would be no adverse effect on the wetlands, no alternatives analysis was necessary. It is well established, however, that a commission is authorized to request information concerning alternatives to the proposed activity and, significantly, such information permits the commission "to determine the likelihood that the proposed activity may or may not impact or affect the resource, and whether an alternative exists to lessen such impact." *Queach.* Moreover, as we previously have noted, the evidence clearly established that the plaintiff's plan would result in a physical change to the wetlands.

It is clear that the commission was acting pursuant to its regulations when it requested a wildlife inventory and an alternatives analysis, and those regulations do not condition receipt of such information on a finding of an adverse impact to the wetlands. The plaintiff has made no challenge to those regulations. Therefore, in light of the evidence contained in the record, we conclude that the trial court properly determined that substantial evidence supported the commission's determination that the application was incomplete.

Case Questions

1. Why did the court state that the commission split the public hearing into four sessions, which occurred over several months, and detail what transpired during the sessions?
2. What information did Unistar fail to provide?
3. Why did the court opine that the commission was acting pursuant to regulations and Unistar had not challenged the regulations?

RULEMAKING

The major innovation made by the APA was § 553, "Rule Making." With acceptance of Congress's authority to delegate its legislative powers, a standard was needed to ensure that those powers were exercised with procedural fairness. **Rulemaking** is simply the name applied to the agency's legislative function. In some cases, Congress specifically charges an agency with rulemaking authority; sometimes Congress is silent, but rulemaking authority is implied from the agency's statutory mission, and occasionally Congress denies an agency rulemaking authority (the Federal Trade Commission, for example, is an investigatory rather than a regulatory agency).

rulemaking

Generic meaning of making rules; specific meaning referring to the legislative function of administrative agencies, as distinguished from their usual administrative functions.

When an agency engages in rulemaking, it must follow the procedure of the APA, or the rule is invalid and unenforceable. The steps required by the APA are simple:

§ 553. Rule Making

(b) General notice of proposed rule making shall be published in the Federal Register, unless persons subject thereto are named and either personally served or otherwise have actual notice thereof in accordance with law. The notice shall include—
   (1) A statement of the time, place, and nature of public rule making proceedings;
   (2) reference to the legal authority under which the rule is proposed; and
   (3) either the terms or substance of the proposed rule or a description of the subjects and issues involved.

* * *

(c) After notice required by this section, the agency shall give interested persons an opportunity to participate in the rule making through submission of written data, views, or arguments with or without opportunity for oral presentation. After consideration of the relevant matter presented, the agency shall incorporate in the rules adopted a concise general statement of their basis and purpose. . . .

(d) The required publication or service of a substantive rule shall be made not less than 30 days before its effective date [with exceptions].

Although § 553 presents some burden to the agencies, the steps are not cumbersome. Basically it requires public notice of proposed rules and an opportunity for public input. Legally there is nothing to prevent an agency from making rules despite major opposition as long as it follows the procedure. The innovation of § 553 is its requirement that the process be public and provide for public participation. The weaknesses and unpopularity of a proposed rule may thus be brought into the open. An agency cannot long defy the public interest without a response from Congress and the president, who ultimately control the power that the agency exercises.

Section 553 has some significant exceptions. Internal housekeeping rules, those concerning personnel and internal management, are not covered by it. So-called interpretative rules need not go through the § 553 procedure. In a loose sense, *interpretative rules* are those that carry out the meaning of a statute, interpreting it rather than adding to it. The distinction between interpretative and legislative or substantive rules is far from clear—a technical question that several cases have confused rather than clarified. The question seems purely academic until an agency attempts to make an interpretative rule without going through § 553 procedure, only to run up against a complaining party asserting that the rule is substantive and therefore invalid for lack of proper procedure. If the court agrees with the complaining party and concludes that the rule is substantive (legislative), the failure to follow § 553 procedure makes the rule invalid.

When Congress specifically authorizes an agency to make rules under § 553, those rules are said to have the "binding force of law," meaning that the courts will accord them the same respect as if the rules had been passed by Congress. Interpretative rules do not enjoy this stature, though as a practical matter they ordinarily are enforced by the courts.

THE RIGHT TO BE HEARD

Section 553 leaves to the agency the discretion to allow oral presentation and argument and the scope of any such presentations, but some rules call for more than the mere opportunity for written submission of argument. Some questions are better left to an adjudicatory process by the agency.

An issue that often arises in suits against governmental bodies is whether the plaintiffs have *standing;* that is, do they have the right to sue, or, as it is described in *Norris,* do they have a "legally cognizable interest"?

As discussed in earlier chapters, legislation and adjudication are different processes appropriate to different situations. In the administrative field, two cases arising in Colorado have been used repeatedly as examples of this distinction. In *Bi-Metallic Investment Co. v. State Board of Equalization,* 239 U.S. 441 (1915), the state had increased the valuation of all real estate in Denver by 40 percent. The court denied a suit for an injunction by the company, holding that no hearing was necessary. The court distinguished the earlier case of *Londoner v. Denver,* 210 U.S. 373 (1908), in which it had required a hearing ("by argument however brief, and, if need be, by proof, however informal") on the assessment of the plaintiff's land for the cost of paving a street. The distinction was made on the difference between policy that treated the entire community equally (*Bi-Metallic*) and a decision in which a few persons were affected individually (*Londoner*). In other words, the decision to set valuations in general is a legislative question, whereas assessing costs individually and differentially is an adjudicative question, as the individual may have special reasons why the assessment is unfair. Highly particularized disputes of this sort call for a hearing.

Donald L. NORRIS, et al., Petitioners/Plaintiffs

v.

Town of WHEATLAND, et al., Respondents/Defendant

Supreme Court, Monroe County, N.Y.

613 N.Y.S.2d 817 (1994)

After eighteen months of divisive debate about the future of their police department, the Town of Wheatland voters elected two board members and a supervisor who stood for its abolition. Upon taking office in January 1994, the Town Board, by a three to two vote, immediately approved the Wheatland Police Department for only three months. On March 3, 1994 the Town Board proposed, and on March 30, 1994 passed, Local Law No. 1 abolishing the Wheatland Police Department as of June 1, 1994.

This action was brought . . . seeking to set aside and annul the decision of the Wheatland Town Board pursuant to Local Law No. 1. The Petitioners, which include the Wheatland Police Chief and 41 residents of the town, allege the Town Board acted improperly by: 1) not procedurally complying with the appropriate provisions of the State Environment Quality Review Act (SEQRA) and by failing to consider the "socioeconomic effect" of the Local Law; 2) acting arbitrarily and capriciously; 3) failing to comply with the requirements of the Municipal Home Rule Law; 4) not referring the Local Law to a referendum; and 5) one of the Board Members voting in favor of the Local Law No. 1 not being a resident of the Town of Wheatland at the time of the vote.

In rejoinder, the respondents deny the allegations of the petition and questioned whether the petitioners have standing to bring the action.

Standing

. . . "It is established law that to be entitled to seek judicial review of an administrative determination, the petitioning party must have a legally cognizable interest that is or will be affected by the determination. A showing of special damage or actual injury is not necessary to establish a party's standing."

Unlike a zoning matter, the abolition of a town police department is all-pervasive. To require a showing of special damage or actual injury to one resident vis-à-vis another is unlikely and counteracts the intent of SEQRA, which is "to assure that those charged with decision-making responsibility are aware of their obligations to protect the environment for the use and enjoyment of this and all future generations." Furthermore, to deny standing in this matter would be to insulate governmental action from scrutiny. In a matter affecting a town-wide service, either all residents have standing, or none do. In this matter, any resident of the Town of Wheatland has standing.

* * *

[In a lengthy discussion of whether the Board had properly complied with the procedural requirements related to abolishing the police force, the court concluded that it had.]

Seqra Compliance—Substantive

It must now be reviewed whether the Town Board, as lead agency, by issuing a Negative Decision, "...determine(d) either that there will be no environmental effect or that the identified environmental effects will not be significant," and did the Town Board "...take a hard look at all relevant impacts... in making this decision and document its reasons in writing."

Those supporting the retention of the Police Department provided the Town Board with reports, letters and testimony which raised questions as to the environmental, economic and social effects on the community. In addition, there existed a thorough and comprehensive task force report supporting the retention.

In response, the Town Board undertook the following steps: 1. The Town solicited comments from all the Town Supervisors in Monroe County who relied on the Monroe County Sheriff's Department for their police services. The request for information specifically related questions concerning response time, community involvement, professionalism and effectiveness. 2. The Town contacted the Monroe County Sheriff's Office and requested information concerning its ability to provide police services to the Town of Wheatland. Sheriff Andrew Meloni, in part, stated: "I am confident that the Monroe County Office of Sheriff has all the necessary resources to provide professional, effective and efficient services to the Town of Wheatland." 3. The Supervisor conducted a review of crime statistics, the capacity of Monroe County Sheriff's Office, the degree of activities of various districts of the Monroe County Sheriff's Office and the ability of the Monroe County Sheriff's Office to handle the Town of Wheatland. The Town of Wheatland invited the public to comment on issues including environmental significance of the proposed action and heard all parties wishing to address the issue and received and filed all documents concerning this subject. The Town Board also held a public informational meeting on March 1, 1994 at which the public addressed questions to Undersheriff O'Flynn.

The Court's role in reviewing SEQRA determinations is to, first, review the agency procedures to determine whether they were lawful. As set forth above, the only procedural defect, an inadvertent reference to a hearing, has been satisfactorily resolved. Second, courts may review the record to determine whether the agency identified the relevant areas of environmental concern, took a "hard look" at them, and made a "reasoned elaboration" of the basis for its determination. When doing so the Courts are to remember that an agency's substantive obligations under SEQRA must be viewed in light of a rule of reason. Although agencies have considerable latitude in evaluating environmental effects and choosing among alternatives, "[n]othing in the law requires an agency to reach a particular result on an issue, or permits the courts to second-guess the agency's choice, which can be annulled only if arbitrary, capricious or unsupported by substantial evidence."

[T]he court finds that the Wheatland Town Board identified the relevant areas of environmental concern, took a hard look at them and made a "reasoned elaboration" for the basis of its determination.

* * *

Arbitrary and Capricious

Considering its extensive experience with and regard for local police, this Court does not necessarily agree with the Board's abolition of the Police Department. However, it cannot be said that the Board's actions, as set forth in the legislative findings, are unsupportable or were arbitrary or capricious. Ultimately, in the representative democracy of Wheatland, New York, the wisdom of the abolition of the police department by the Town Board can be reviewed by the voters on November 7, 1995.

Case Questions

1. Can a town through its elected representatives abolish the police force? Explain.
2. On what basis do the plaintiffs have standing?
3. Why is the statute (SEQRA) at issue here?

What Kind of a Hearing?

The right to a hearing in administrative law does not necessarily mean an on-the-record, trial-type, or evidentiary hearing. Such events present a significant burden to an agency, which may devote significant resources and time when the full complement of rights and procedures must be respected. The extent of a person's rights in a hearing run the gamut from extremely informal meetings to hearings that are virtually indistinguishable from trials. The extremes are represented by *Goss v. Lopez,* 419 U.S. 565 (1975), and *Goldberg v. Kelly,* 397 U.S. 254 (1970). *Goss* involved ten-day suspensions of high school students. The U.S. Supreme Court held that they were entitled to a hearing but that the students' rights were limited to (1) notice of the charges against them, (2) explanation of the evidence against them, and (3) the opportunity to present their side of the facts. By contrast, *Goldberg* concerned the right of a welfare recipient to a hearing prior to termination of benefits. The court held that she was entitled to a hearing before termination, including the following rights in connection with the hearing:

1. Notice with reasons for the termination
2. Confrontation of witnesses against her
3. Oral argument

4. Cross-examination of adverse witnesses

5. Disclosure of evidence for the other side

6. Representation by an attorney

7. Determination on the record

8. Statement of reasons relied on for decision

9. Impartial decisionmaker

Practically speaking, this is a catalog of the rights ordinarily enjoyed in a civil trial.

Administrative Hearings

Most agencies establish procedural steps within the agency for processing grievances and complaints. Judicial review is premised on "final agency action," which requires some authoritative determination of rights; the APA allows agencies to require that a claimant exhaust some or all of these steps prior to seeking judicial review. Prior to enactment of the APA, claimants were required to exhaust all administrative remedies before judicial review, and many states still require this.

Agencies are hierarchical bureaucracies and typically provide aggrieved parties the opportunity to pursue review of determinations from lower levels all the way to the top of the bureaucratic pyramid. Someone once counted thirty-three steps in the Social Security system that would have to be completed to fully exhaust the administrative remedies available. It is unrealistic to think that the reviewing court would reverse a consistent determination through all these steps except on the ground that the procedure itself was constitutionally defective.

Hearings at the highest level are held by hearing officers called *administrative law judges*, who are employed by the government to hold recorded hearings, make findings of fact, and recommend action to the highest level of the agency. In most instances, the agency will follow the recommendations of the administrative law judge.

LIABILITY OF GOVERNMENT AND ITS OFFICERS

Recent decades have seen a major change in liability for agency action. When sovereign immunity was in its heyday, the only remedy for a person injured by official action was a suit against the public employee who caused the injury. Even then, the courts developed a doctrine of official immunity for injuries caused by "discretionary" acts within the scope of the employee's duties. Policymakers and planners were thus immunized for most of their acts.

The death knell of sovereign immunity for tort suits came with enactment of the Federal Tort Claims Act (FTCA) in 1947. The FTCA continued the judicial doctrine of discretionary immunity and exempted a number of intentional torts but held the federal government "liable, respecting the provisions of this title relating to tort claims, in the same manner and to the same extent as a private individual under like circumstances." This formally enacted a judicial doctrine that had developed to disallow governmental immunity when the activities were the same as those performed by private enterprise, the so-called governmental-proprietary function test. The states gradually followed suit, though they did so with a variety of statutes, many of which retained varying degrees of immunity.

With the availability of suits against the government, the courts became more protective of government officers. Not only was the discretionary immunity expanded, but also a form of *qualified immunity* was invented that immunized from suit officers acting in good faith and under a reasonable belief that their actions were proper. This was a logical result of the dilemma in which public officers, especially police, found themselves when acting pursuant to statutory authority, only to have a court hold the statute unconstitutional. For example, a police officer makes an arrest under a state statute, but the statute is found by the court to be unconstitutional, so the arrest was illegal, and the officer is subject to suit for false arrest and false imprisonment. If the standards of the doctrine are met, the officer enjoys qualified (as distinguished from absolute) immunity.

42 U.S.C. § 1983

To protect former slaves from abuse at the hands of white authorities following the Civil War, Congress passed the Civil Rights Act of 1871, from which 42 U.S.C. § 1983 reads,

> Every person who, under color of any statute, ordinance, regulation, custom, or usage, of any State or Territory, subjects, or causes to be subjected, any citizen of the United States or other person within the jurisdiction thereof to the deprivation of any rights, privileges, or immunities secured by the Constitution and laws, shall be liable to the party injured in an action at law, suit in equity, or other proper proceeding for redress.

The broad provisions of this act were rarely used until 1961, when a suit brought against Chicago police officers and the City of Chicago was successful (*Monroe v. Pape*, 365 U.S. 167). *Monroe* held that the city was not a "person" under the act and could not be sued, but in 1978 the U.S. Supreme Court overruled *Monroe* and allowed a suit against the City of New York (*Monell v. Department of Social Services*, 436 U.S. 658). Since *Monell*, § 1983 suits have proliferated and are a constant concern of local governments, especially for the conduct of their police; a §1983 suit was even brought against the governor of Ohio over the National Guard shootings of Kent State University students during antiwar demonstrations in 1970. (The U.S. Supreme Court held that the governor had qualified immunity.) The broad scope of the language of § 1983 and its expanding application have made it a frequent basis for litigation.

Although the scope of 42 U.S.C. § 1983 has been greatly expanded with regard to suing state and local governments, suits against government officials have confronted increasing recognition of absolute and qualified immunities. The courts have been steadfast in upholding absolute immunity of judges acting in their judicial capacity. *Stump v. Sparkman* expresses the most extreme application of judicial immunity. The mother of a "somewhat retarded" daughter petitioned Judge Stump of an Indiana Circuit Court for an order permitting the daughter to be sterilized. Judge Stump met with the mother in chambers and wrote and signed the order. The sterilization procedure was performed, the daughter being told that her appendix was being removed. When the daughter married two years later, she soon discovered what had happened. She sued Judge Stump under § 1983. The U.S. District Court held that the judge enjoyed immunity from suit, but the Court of Appeals reversed, and the case reached the U.S. Supreme Court on certiorari.

STUMP

v.

SPARKMAN

U.S. Supreme Court

435 U.S. 349 (1978)

The governing principle of law is well established and is not questioned by the parties. As early as 1872, the Court recognized that it was "a general principle of the highest importance to the proper administration of justice that a judicial officer, in exercising the authority vested in him, [should] be free to act upon his own convictions, without apprehension of personal consequences to himself." For that reason the Court held that "judges of courts of superior or general jurisdiction are not liable to civil actions for their judicial acts, even when such acts are in excess of their jurisdiction, and are alleged to have been done maliciously or corruptly." Later we held that this doctrine of judicial immunity was applicable in suits under § 1 of the Civil Rights Act of 1871, 42 U.S.C.A. § 1983, for the legislative record gave no indication that Congress intended to abolish this long-established principle.

* * *

Perhaps realizing the broad scope of Judge Stump's jurisdiction, the Court of Appeals stated that, even if the action taken by him was not foreclosed under the Indiana statutory scheme, it would still be "an illegitimate exercise of his common law power because of his failure to comply with elementary principles of procedural due process." This misconceives the doctrine of judicial immunity. A judge is absolutely immune from liability for his judicial acts even if his exercise of authority is flawed by the commission of grave procedural errors. . . .

Disagreement with the action taken by the judge, however, does not justify depriving that judge of his immunity. Despite the unfairness to litigants that sometimes results, the doctrine of judicial immunity is thought to be in the best interests of "the proper administration of justice . . . for it allows] a judicial officer, in exercising the authority vested in him [to] be free to act upon his own convictions, without apprehension of personal consequences to himself." The fact that the issue before the judge is a controversial one is all the more reason that he should be able to act without fear of suit. . . .

Mr. Justice STEWART, with whom Mr. Justice MARSHALL and Mr. Justice POWELL join, dissenting.

It is established federal law that judges of general jurisdiction are absolutely immune from monetary liability "for judicial acts, even when such acts are in excess of their jurisdiction, and are alleged to have been done maliciously or corruptly." It is also established that this immunity is in no way diminished in a proceeding under 42 U.S.C.A. § 1983. But the scope of judicial immunity is limited to liability for "judicial acts," and I think that what Judge Stump did on July 9, 1971, was beyond the pale of anything that could sensibly be called a judicial act.

* * *

When the Court says that what Judge Stump did was an act "normally performed by a judge," it is not clear to me whether the Court means that a judge "normally" is asked to approve a mother's decision to have her child given surgical treatment generally, or that a judge "normally" is asked to approve a mother's wish to have her daughter sterilized. But whichever way the Court's statement is to be taken, it is factually inaccurate. In Indiana, as elsewhere in our country, a parent is authorized to arrange for and consent to medical and surgical treatment of his minor child. And when a parent decides to call a physician to care for his sick child or arranges to have a surgeon remove his child's tonsils, he does not, "normally" or otherwise, need to seek the approval of a judge. On the other hand, Indiana did in 1971 have statutory procedures for the sterilization of certain people who were *institutionalized.* But these statutes provided for *administrative proceedings* before a board established by the superintendent of each public hospital. Only if, after notice and an evidentiary hearing, an order of sterilization was entered in these proceedings could there be review in a circuit court.

* * *

Mr. Justice POWELL, dissenting.

While I join the opinion of Mr. Justice STEWART, I wish to emphasize what I take to be the central feature of this case—petitioner's preclusion of any possibility for the vindication of respondent's rights elsewhere in the judicial system.

* * *

But where a judicial officer acts in a manner that precludes all resort to appellate or other judicial remedies that otherwise would be available, the underlying assumption of the *Bradley* doctrine is inoperative. . . . The complete absence of normal judicial process

foreclosed resort to any of the "numerous remedies" that "the law has provided for private parties."

Case Questions

1. Was Judge Stump's order a judicial act? Explain.
2. Judicial immunity was again tested in the U.S. Supreme Court in 1988 in *Forrester v. White,* 108 S. Ct. 538, in which a female probation officer was fired by Judge White, who was responsible for hiring and firing probation officers. Ms. Forrester sued under § 1983 on the ground that she had been discriminated against because of her sex. Writing the opinion of the Court, Justice O'Connor applied the "judicial function" test that asserts absolute immunity for a judge's actions while exercising a judicial function. Justice O'Connor concluded that Judge White's authority over personnel was an administrative function separate from his judicial function, rendering him amenable to suit for improper actions in his administrative function, and the suit was allowed to proceed. Can you reconcile *Forrester* with *Stump*?

§

SUMMARY

Administrative law covers the rules relating to legal action taken against the administrative agencies of the government. Although each agency has its own substantive rules and regulations, procedural law has evolved and is still evolving, first from the Constitution and more recently from the enactment of federal and state administrative procedure legislation.

The past hundred years have witnessed reversals in the major areas of administrative law. In the nineteenth century, sovereign immunity was doctrine throughout the United States—officers could be sued but not the government. It was presumed that Congress could not delegate its legislative authority to other government agencies. There was a presumption of nonreviewability of administrative action by the courts. All of these doctrines met their demise in the twentieth century. Rather than challenging legislative delegation, the courts have concentrated on the question of whether the agencies adhere to legislative intent. Rather than refusing to review, the courts have limited the scope of review along lines similar to appellate review. With the erosion of sovereign immunity, the courts have expanded the liability of government and narrowed the liability of public officers.

The enactment of the APA in 1946 put administrative law on a firm footing. The major innovation of the APA was its provisions for rulemaking, requiring public notice and the opportunity for public input prior to the promulgation of agency rules.

Administrative law was forced to change as government changed from performing relatively few services into an immense bureaucracy regulating every aspect of our daily lives. Administrative law changed to hold government more accountable to the public.

KEY TERMS

administrative law   independent regulatory   rulemaking
bureaucracy   agencies

CHAPTER REVIEW QUESTIONS

1. What determines whether an agency of government is an independent regulatory agency?
2. Why do courses on administrative law concentrate almost exclusively on administrative procedure?
3. What is the legal source of authority for federal rulemaking?
4. Where may the substantive rules of federal administrative agencies be found?
5. Why are public utilities subject to regulatory agencies?
6. What special role can the paralegal play in administrative law that is not available in private law cases?
7. Where does the "presumption of reviewability" come from?
8. What is meant by "judicial review" in administrative law?
9. When is oral argument available in § 553 rulemaking?
10. Can a person sue a city under 42 U.S.C. § 1983?

CRITICAL THINKING QUESTIONS

1. Why do we need administrative law?
2. Should the decisions of government agencies be reviewable in court?

CYBER EXERCISES

1. Washburn Law School maintains a well-known website, Washlaw Web, accessible at http://www.washlaw.edu/. Use this website to access information concerning federal agencies and federal regulations.
2. The portion of the FindLaw website located at http://news.findlaw.com/ contains current legal news articles. Determine whether any of the listed articles relates to administrative law. Read any of the articles relating to administrative law.
3. The U.S. government official Web portal is located at http://www.firstgov.gov/. Use this website to access an alphabetical listing of federal agencies. Select and read about two agencies.

SCENARIO

Morgan Pierpont, a small-time investor in common stocks who had about a million dollars in the market at the height of his powers, has lost two-thirds of his wealth in a recent crash of the stock market. The catalyst for the crash seems to have been the decision of the Federal Reserve Board (the Fed) to raise the interest rate at which the

Fed lends funds to member banks a full point, which it made at a surprise meeting of the Fed called by Alan Redspan, its chairman and dominant leader and policymaker. The Fed interest rate, especially when raised or cut, for a long time has been considered the single most important means by which the stock market can be sent up or down, especially when the change is unanticipated by investors and especially when the change is a half point or more. Although the effect of interest rate changes on the economy as a whole tends to take six months or a year, the effect on the stock market can be instantaneous. Redspan and the Fed have consistently expressed their overriding concern for inflation, which they fight aggressively with rate hikes, although they tend to gradually lower interest rates when inflationary pressures are minimal and the specter of recession looms on the horizon. The reason for the sudden raise in the Fed rate, as expressed publicly by Redspan, was the announcement three days before of an unexpected rise of 5 percent of the consumer price index (CPI), an indicator of inflation, which reached a level much higher than anticipated and well beyond the level Redspan finds acceptable. A month later, when all the data were in, the CPI was adjusted downward for March to 3.5 percent, but by then the damage had been done. The market had gone into a steady downward spiral and consumer confidence was at a ten-year low.

Pierpont and other investors are both impoverished and furious. Pierpont brings a lawsuit against the president of the United States demanding that the president fire the chairman of the Federal Reserve Board. Pierpont bases his standing on the economic losses he sustained because of government action and as a taxpayer. The Federal District Court dismisses for lack of standing. Pierpont appeals to the Circuit Court of Appeals, which acknowledges that economic losses due to government action have traditionally established standing. Because the lower court made no findings of fact with regard to the nexus between the action of the government and actual damages to the plaintiff/appellant, the Circuit Court of Appeals proceeds beyond the standing question to dismiss the case on other grounds.

Discuss the many policy grounds that might support the dismissal of Pierpont's lawsuit. Section 701 of the Administrative Procedure Act regarding judicial review of agency action may be a useful starting point, but many commonsense arguments apply here as well. Common sense, however, makes a good legal argument only when accompanied by an understanding of the law and the legal system, as well as a basic understanding of constitutional principles, which extends to administrative law. Pierpont really has nothing going for him, but your job is to frame his weaknesses in lawyerly arguments.

APPENDIX A

HOW TO READ A CASE

INTRODUCTION

Reported judicial decisions have a style and format all their own. This discussion is designed to acquaint readers with the form and the nature of judicial decisions. Although judges have considerable freedom in how they write opinions, some uniformity of pattern comes from the similarity of purpose for decisions, especially decisions of appellate courts, which frequently serve as authority for later cases.

Similarity is also a product of custom. The influence of West, which publishes the regional reporter series and the federal reporters, as well as the Westlaw® database, has been great. Some of this material repeats discussions in the first chapters of the book, but this appendix is designed to be read at almost any point during the book—the sooner, the better, as judicial decisions are interspersed throughout the text.

WHICH COURT?

Knowing which court issued the opinion is extremely important. As a general rule, the higher the court, the more compelling its authority. The binding force of precedent depends on the relationship between the court that issues it and the court that applies it. A decision of the Iowa Supreme Court has no precedential power over courts in Tennessee because each state has its own laws and legal system. Iowa courts may not dictate to Tennessee what Tennessee law is or should be. However, decisions of the Supreme Court of Tennessee, the highest court of that state, are binding precedent on other state courts in Tennessee; lower courts must follow the law as stated by a higher court in their jurisdiction.

Federal and State Courts

The United States has two parallel legal structures. Each state has its own set of laws and courts. In addition, the federal government has a separate legal authority through courts located in every state. Federal courts are not superior to state courts but parallel to them, having authority over different types of cases. For example, the U.S. Constitution restricts authority over patents and copyrights to the federal government. Thus, a patent case will be heard in federal court but not in a state court. In contrast, there are both federal and state civil rights laws, so a particular case might be filed in one or the other. When federal and state courts have concurrent jurisdiction of this sort, exercise of authority is governed by custom or law, but when state and federal law overlap and conflict, state law must yield to federal law.

Trial and Appellate Courts

State and federal courts are divided into trial and appellate courts. Most cases originate in trial courts, where evidence is presented, witnesses are questioned, and a judgment determining the rights of the parties is entered. If one of the parties to the case is dissatisfied with the result, the case may be appealed; an appellate court is petitioned to review the proceedings of the lower, or trial, court to determine if errors were made that would justify changing the outcome of the case.

The federal system provides a model followed in general terms by a majority of state systems. The U.S. District Court is the primary federal trial court. The next higher federal court is the United States Court of Appeals. It is called an intermediate appellate court because it is subordinate to the highest court, the U.S. Supreme Court.

Most states name their highest court Supreme Court; New York, a notable exception, calls its highest court the Court of Appeals and uses the designation Supreme Court for lower courts. Some states do not have intermediate appellate courts. There is also considerable variety in state trial courts and the names applied to them.

The careful researcher always takes note of the court issuing a decision because the higher the court, the greater the force of its decision. The decision of a court is binding on lower courts within its jurisdiction, meaning that the rules it lays down must be followed by lower courts faced with the same issue.

FOR WHOM ARE JUDICIAL OPINIONS WRITTEN?

In evaluating any written material, the reader should assess the audience the writer is addressing and the writer's goals. Judges write decisions for two reasons. The first is to inform the parties to the dispute who won and who lost, giving the rules and reasoning the judge applied to the facts. The second is to inform the legal profession, attorneys and judges, of the rules applied to a given set of facts and the reasons for the decision.

Attorneys and Judges Read Judicial Opinions

Very few laypersons ever enter a law library to find and read cases. The people found in the county law library are usually lawyers, paralegals, and judges. With the advent of the Internet and the ready availability of a wealth of legal materials, including cases and statutes, undoubtedly more laypersons are conducting legal research. However, few persons untrained in legal research can navigate their way through the maze of materials, much less interpret them with any confidence.

Cases are rarely intended to be entertaining, and judges are not motivated to make their cases "reader friendly." Their tasks are quite specific. Because any case may serve as precedent, or at least form a basis for subsequent legal arguments, judges are especially concerned with conveying a precise meaning by carefully framing the rules and providing the reasoning behind them. The higher the court, the greater this concern will be. Imagine writing an opinion—which may well affect important rights of citizens in the future—for a highly skilled, highly intelligent readership that critically analyzes every word and phrase.

Judicial writing is different from most other kinds of writing in that its goal is neither simply to pass on information nor to persuade the reader of the author's point of view. The judge is stating the law and making a final judgment but must do so with caution so that the statements are not misinterpreted or misused. An appreciation of the judge's dilemma is essential to critical evaluation of cases.

The Effect of Setting Precedent

The cost of litigation is great, and appeal of a decision incurs significant additional cost. It makes sense to appeal if the losing party reasonably concludes that the lower court was incorrect in its application of the law. It would be quite foolish to spend large sums of money to go to the higher court if the chances of winning were slim and the stakes were small. This means that the cases we read from appellate courts, and especially from the highest courts, generally involve questions with strong arguments on both sides. The judges of these courts are faced with difficult decisions and must respect the reasonable arguments of both sides in deciding which side will prevail.

Clarity versus Confusion

Judicial writing is often difficult and obscure, but such criticism of judicial writing often fails to recognize not only that the issues are difficult to present with clarity but also that often the importance of narrowing the application of the decision encourages tortuous reasoning. For example, when faced with a landmark case of reverse discrimination (a white applicant for medical school was denied admission, while less qualified minority students were admitted), the U.S. Supreme Court was expected to lay down a rule concerning the constitutionality of such admissions programs. Those expectations were disappointed. The justices wrote divergent opinions that made it very difficult to discover exactly what the rule was. At the time the issue was quite controversial, and the decision potentially could have affected efforts by the administration and Congress to help the position of disadvantaged minorities. Any precedent of the Court would have far-reaching consequences. Although the plaintiff won and subsequently entered medical school, there was some confusion as to why he won. The effect of the decision was to stifle future efforts to pursue reverse discrimination cases. Each justice of the Court viewed the problem in a different light, and the result was a resolution of the dispute without a clear picture of the rule to be applied in such cases.

Thus, the reader of cases should be aware that the complex reasoning of a judge's writing is not always due to the complexity of the issues but may also be caused by the judge's desire to narrow the effect of the precedent.

Most appellate decisions are the product of three or more judges. A unanimous or majority opinion is not the reasoning of a single person. The author of an opinion must take into consideration the views of the judges who join in the opinion. In some cases, especially with the nine justices of the U.S. Supreme Court, achieving a majority involves negotiation—one justice may vote with the majority only if a key point in his or her reasoning is included or only if the rule is narrowed to cover a limited number of situations. The author of the opinion may thus be stating someone else's reasoning or opinion or may be stating the argument to appease a justice who is reluctant to join in the opinion. The politics of decision making may make it quite difficult to write a cohesive opinion that makes everyone happy.

Doing Justice to the Parties

It is a mistake to assume that judges are dispassionate, totally rational, and objective interpreters of the law. The notion that judges reason directly from the facts to the law in a rather mechanical fashion neglects the obvious fact that judges are human beings doing their best to dispense justice. We must suspect that in any given case, the judge or judges form an opinion as to which side should win and then select rules and arguments to support that side. (If justice clearly favors one side, it is usually not difficult to frame a convincing legal argument for that side to win.)

Sometimes a strict application of the law causes a very undesirable result. The Kentucky Court of Appeals was faced with such circumstances in *Strunk v. Strunk*, 445 S.W.2d 145, in which a man was dying of a kidney problem and his brother was the only appropriate donor for a lifesaving kidney transplant. The problem was that the brother with the healthy kidneys was severely mentally retarded and therefore legally incompetent to consent to the operation. The issue facing the court was whether the mother of the two brothers could consent to the operation, acting as the guardian of the retarded brother. Kentucky precedents (cited by the dissenting judges but ignored by the majority) seemed to show clearly that a guardian's authority did not extend to making such a decision. Faced with a heartrending life-or-death decision, four of seven judges deciding the case ignored prior precedents. Three of the judges disagreed, and one wrote a vigorous dissenting opinion. The reasoning of the majority opinion was weak, but it is difficult to fault the judges under the circumstances.

THE FORMAT FOR A REPORTED DECISION

The cases found in the reporters generally follow a uniform format with which researchers must become familiar. The first part of the case has no official authority. Authoritative statements begin with the actual text of the opinion.

All of the comments and the example that follows represent the print version of the cases, following a format developed by West Publishing Company many years ago and cross-indexed to its many publications. Naturally, the appearance is different from the electronic versions found on Westlaw®, but the elements will be familiar to anyone conversant with the print version. The **headnotes** with accompanying "key numbers" are a West invention and therefore copyrighted and not found on other electronic versions unless West has given its permission. The decision itself is a public document

headnotes
Statements of the major points of law discussed in a case; found in the law reports published by West, formerly West Publishing Company.

syllabus

A summary of a case often included with a report decision and preceding the official text of the opinion.

and falls within the public domain exception to copyright. This sometimes presents a problem because the **syllabus** section of the case may have been written by a court official or by the private reporter, for example, West. Whether it falls under copyright protection must be determined by examination. Although this may not be significant to the reader, copyright issues are important to the author of this book and others who publish from the cases.

Other electronic versions may have a different style, but the case itself should be identical. The great advantage of electronic versions is the inclusion of links to cited materials and related authorities; in other words, speed and convenience of research far surpass that afforded by print materials. Although many law firms are converting to electronic law libraries, virtually every lawyer working today started with the books and many prefer to read from the printed page, whether it is a book or the "hard copy" of a digital version. The effect of the electronic law library on the format and style of legal writing has yet to be determined. For the time being, it is best to become familiar with the format of the printed version.

Format Preceding the Opinion

West publishes the reporter series for which it has established a uniform format. The first page of *United States v. National Lead Co.*, 438 F.2d 935 (8th Cir. 1971), illustrates all the elements (Exhibit A-1).

The Citation

The heading of the page indicates the citation: "UNITED STATES v. NATIONAL LEAD COMPANY" and "Cite as 438 F.2d 935 (1971)." This is the name of the case and where it can be found, namely, on page 935 in Volume 438 of the *Federal Reporter, Second Series*. Note that this differs from the official citation, *United States v. National Lead Co.*, 438 F.2d 935 (8th Cir. 1971), that would be used in legal texts and opinions. The official citation indicates that the case was decided by the U.S. Court of Appeals for the Eighth Circuit.

EXHIBIT A-1

UNITED STATES v. NATIONAL LEAD COMPANY

Cite as 438 F.2d 935 (1971)

UNITED STATES of America, Plaintiff-Appellant,

v.

NATIONAL LEAD COMPANY, a Corporation, and Chemical Workers' Basic Union Local 1744, AFL-CIO, Defendants-Appellees.

No. 20427.

United States Court of Appeals, Eighth Circuit.

Feb. 26, 1971.

Action by government against company and union for alleged violations of Civil Rights Act of 1964. The United States District Court for the Eastern District of Missouri, Roy W. Harper, Senior District Judge, 315 F.Supp. 912, denied government's motion for preliminary injunction, and government appealed. The Court of Appeals, Bright, Circuit Judge, held that although, under facts, some vestiges of employer's past discrimination seemed preserved in employer's transfer and promotion procedures, in view of fact that actual impact of this discrimination upon black employees possessing seniority dating back prior to end of discrimination was unclear, and in view of fact that an appropriate solution was not readily apparent from partial development of facts, denial of relief by way of a preliminary injunction was not error.

Affirmed and remanded.

1. Civil Rights 3

Employment policies which appear racially neutral but build upon bias that existed prior to enactment of 1964 Civil Rights Act to produce present discrimination are actionable. Civil Rights Act of 1964, § 701 et seq., 42 U.S.C.A. § 2000e et seq.

2. Civil Rights 3

Policy of 1964 Civil Rights Act is not fulfilled by a showing that black employees may enjoy substantially equal pay with others in similar capacities; the test is whether all employees possess an equal opportunity to fully enjoy all employment rights. Civil Rights Act of 1964, §§ 703(h), 706(g), 42 U.S.C.A. §§ 2000e–2(h), 2000e–5(g).

3. Injunction 137(4)

Although, under facts, some of vestiges of employer's past discrimination seemed preserved in employer's transfer and promotion procedures, in view of fact that actual impact of this discrimination upon black employees possessing seniority dating back prior to end of discrimination was unclear, and in view of fact that an appropriate solution was not readily apparent from partial development of facts, denial of relief by way of a preliminary injunction was not error. Civil Rights Act of 1964, §§ 701 et seq., 707(a) 42 U.S.C.A. §§ 2000e et seq., 2000e–6(a).

4. Injunction 147

In view of evidence disclosing that in recent years blacks had filled three of six vacancies for guard positions and that employer planned no immediate expansion of present guard force or filling of any existing vacancies, no need for preliminary injunction was shown with respect to guard force. Civil Rights Act of 1964, §§ 701 et seq., 707(a), 42 U.S.C.A. §§ 2000e et seq., 2000e–6(a).

Jerris Leonard, Asst. Atty. Gen., Daniel Bartlett, Jr., U. S. Atty., David L. Rose, Stuart P. Herman, Attys., Dept of Justice, Washington, D.C., for plaintiff-appellant.

Edward Weakley, Howard Elliott, Boyle, Priest, Elliot & Weakley, St. Louis, Mo., for National Lead Co.

Harry Moline, Jr., Thomas, Busse, Cullen, Clooney, Weil & King, St. Louis, Mo., for Chemical Workers' Basic Union, Local 1744, AFL-CIO.

Before GIBSON and BRIGHT, Circuit Judges, and McMANUS, Chief District Judge.

BRIGHT, Circuit Judge.

The United States by its Attorney General brings this action seeking . . .

The Caption

Exhibit A-2 shows the caption of the case, which names the parties. Note that the citation names only one party for each side, whereas the caption includes a codefendant, a union local of the AFL-CIO. The caption also indicates the status of the parties with regard to the suit as "Plaintiff-Appellant" and "Defendants-Appellees." We can surmise from this that the United States brought the original suit as plaintiff and then also the appeal, apparently having lost the original suit.

Commonly, the caption simply states "appellant" and "appellee," and the reader must discover from the text who brought the suit originally. It is important to note who is appellant and who is appellee because many opinions refer to the parties by those terms. In *National Lead,* Judge Bright refers to "the government" and "National Lead," which makes reading much less confusing.

Below the parties we find "No. 20427," the docket number, which is a number assigned to the case upon initial filing with the clerk of the court and by which it is identified prior to assigning it a volume and page number in the reporter series. This number is important when attempting to research the case prior to its official

EXHIBIT A-2

UNITED STATES OF AMERICA, Plaintiff-Appellant,	Basic Union Local 1744, AFL-CIO, Defendants-Appellees.
v.	No. 20427.
NATIONAL LEAD COMPANY, a Corporation, and Chemical Workers'	United States Court of Appeals, Eighth Circuit. Feb. 26, 1971.

EXHIBIT A-3

Action by government against company and union for alleged violations of Civil Rights Act of 1964. The United States District Court for the Eastern District of Missouri, Roy W. Harper, Senior District Judge, 315 F. Supp. 912, denied government's motion for preliminary injunction, and government appealed. The Court of Appeals, Bright, Circuit Judge, held that although, under facts, some vestiges of employer's past discrimination seemed preserved in employer's transfer and promotion procedures, in view of fact that actual impact of this discrimination upon black employees possessing seniority dating back prior to end of discrimination was unclear, and in view of fact that an appropriate solution was not readily apparent from partial development of facts, denial of relief by way of a preliminary injunction was not error.

Affirmed and remanded.

publication. Below the docket number is the name of the court issuing the decision and the date of the decision.

The Syllabus

Following the caption is a brief summary of the case called the *syllabus* (Exhibit A-3). Although this is sometimes written by the court or a reporter appointed by the court, it is a narrow condensation of the court's ruling and cannot be relied upon as the precise holding of the court. The syllabus can be useful in obtaining a quick idea of what the case concerns—a summary of the issue and the holding of the court. Frequently, legal researchers follow leads to cases that upon reading prove to be unrelated to the issue being researched. Reading the syllabus may make reading the entire opinion unnecessary. However, if the syllabus suggests that the case may be important, a careful reading of the entire text of the opinion is usually necessary.

Headnotes

Exhibit A-4 illustrates the *headnotes*, which are statements of the major points of law discussed in the case. With limited editing, the headnotes tend to be nearly verbatim statements lifted from the opinion. The headnotes are listed in numerical order, starting

EXHIBIT A-4

3. Injunction 137(4)

Although, under facts, some of vestiges of employer's past discrimination seemed preserved in employer's transfer and promotion procedures, in view of fact that actual impact of this discrimination upon black employees possessing seniority dating back prior to end of discrimination was unclear, and in view of fact that an appropriate solution was not readily apparent from partial development of facts, denial of relief by way of a preliminary injunction was not error. Civil Rights Act of 1964, §§ 701 et seq., 707(a) 42 U.S.C.A. §§ 2000e et seq., 2000e–6(a).

4. Injunction 147

In view of evidence disclosing that in recent years blacks had filled three of six vacancies for guard positions and that employer planned no immediate expansion of present guard force or filling of any existing vacancies, no need for preliminary injunction was shown with respect to guard force. Civil Rights Act of 1964, §§ 701 et seq., 707(a), 42 U.S.C.A. §§ 2000e et seq., 2000e–6(a).

EXHIBIT A-5

Jerris Leonard, Asst. Atty. Gen., Daniel Bartlett, Jr., U. S. Atty., David L. Rose, Stuart P. Herman, Attys., Dept of Justice, Washington, D.C., for plaintiff-appellant.

Edward Weakley, Howard Elliott, Boyle, Priest, Elliot & Weakley, St. Louis, Mo., for National Lead Co.

Harry Moline, Jr., Thomas, Busse, Cullen, Clooney, Weil & King, St. Louis, Mo., for Chemical Workers' Basic Union, Local 1744, AFL-CIO.

Before GIBSON and BRIGHT, circuit judges, and MCMANUS, chief district judge.

at the beginning of the opinion, so that the reader may look quickly for the context of a point expressed by a headnote. For example, the part of the text that deals with a particular point made in the headnote will have the number of the headnote in brackets (e.g., [4]) at the beginning of the paragraph or section in which it is discussed. This is very helpful when researching lengthy cases in which only one issue is of concern to the researcher.

To the right of the headnote number is a generic heading, such as "Civil Rights," and a *key number*. Because this reporter is published by West Law, Inc., it uses an indexing title and number that can be used throughout the many West indexes, reporters, and encyclopedias.

Although syllabi and headnotes are useful, they are not authoritative.

Attorneys for the Parties

Exhibit A-5 shows the *attorneys for the parties* as well as the judges sitting on the case. These are listed just above the beginning of the opinion, shown in Exhibit A-6.

EXHIBIT A-6

BRIGHT, Circuit Judge.
The United States by its Attorney General brings this action seeking . . .

FORMAT OF THE OPINION

Following the names of the attorneys and a list of the judges sitting on the case, the formal opinion (i.e., the official discussion of the case) begins with the name of the judge writing the opinion, for example, "Bright, Circuit Judge," in *National Lead*. The author of the opinion has considerable freedom in presentation. Some opinions are written mechanically; a few are almost poetic. The peculiarities of any particular case may dictate a special logical order of their own. Nevertheless, the majority of opinions follow a standard format. When this format is followed, reading and understanding are simplified, but no judge is required to make an opinion easy reading. The following format is the one most frequently used.

Procedure

Most opinions begin with some reference to the outcome of the trial in the lower court and the basis for appeal. In a criminal case, for example, the opinion may state that the defendant was found guilty of aggravated assault and is appealing the judge's ruling to admit certain evidence over the defendant's objections that the evidence was prejudicial to the defendant's case. Often the remarks about procedure are brief and confusing, especially if the reader is not familiar with procedural rules. If the procedure is important to the opinion, a more elaborate discussion is usually found in the body of the opinion. Many things in the opinion become clear only upon further reading, and many opinions must be read at least twice for a full understanding. An opinion is like a jigsaw puzzle—the reader must put the parts together to see the full picture.

The Facts

Most of the text of an opinion in appellate decisions is concerned with a discussion of the law, but because a case revolves around a dispute concerning events that occurred between the parties, no opinion is complete without some discussion of the events that led to the trial. Trials generally explore these events in great detail and judge or jury settle the facts, so appellate opinions usually narrow the fact statement to the most relevant facts. In an interesting case, the reader is often left wanting to know more about what happened, but the judge is not writing a story. The important element in the opinion is the application of law.

The Issue

Following a summary of relevant facts, many writers describe the questions of law that must be decided. Rarely, this is made quite clear: "The only issue presented to the court is . . ." Unfortunately, few writers pinpoint the issue in this fashion, so the reader must search the text for the issue. At this point it is appropriate to introduce a favorite term used by attorneys: *caveat.* This means "warning" or, literally, "Let him beware."

Caveat: The issue is the most important element in an opinion. If the issue is not understood, the significance of the rule laid down by the court can easily be misunderstood. This point cannot be emphasized too strongly. Law students study cases for three years with one primary goal: "Identify the issues." Anyone can fill out forms, but a competently trained person can go right to the heart of a case and recognize its strengths and weaknesses.

The Discussion

The main body of the text of an opinion, often 90 percent of it, discusses the meaning of the issue(s) and offers a line of reasoning that leads to a disposition of the case and explains why a certain rule or rules must apply to the dispute. This part of the opinion is the most difficult to follow. The writer has a goal, but the goal is often not clear to the reader until the end. For this reason, it is usually helpful to look at the final paragraph in the case to see whether the appellate court affirmed (agreed with the lower court) or reversed (disagreed with the lower court). Many judges seem to like to hold the reader in suspense, but the reader need not play this game. By finding out the outcome of the decision, the reader can see how the writer of an opinion is building the conclusion. By recognizing the issue and knowing the rule applied, the reader can see the structure of the argument. The discussion section is the writer's justification of the holding.

The Holding

The **holding** states the **rule of the case**, that is, the rule the court applies to conclude whether the lower court was correct. The rule is *the law,* meaning that it determines the rights of the parties unless reversed by a higher court. It binds lower courts faced with a similar dispute in future cases. It is best to think of the holding as an answer to the issue.

Let us give a real-life example. A woman is suing for wrongful death. Her husband was killed in an auto accident, and she is attempting to collect damages based on the income her husband would have received had he lived, in which income she would have shared. Since the death, however, she has married an affluent man, and her lifestyle has not diminished. The issue is whether the jury can be informed of her remarriage. The court holds that the fact of her remarriage may not be kept from the jury. The court also holds that evidence of her new husband's earnings may *not* be presented to the jury. In this instance, the holding goes a bit beyond the issue and clarifies it. (This particular issue has been answered quite differently in different states.) The reasoning for the holding is as follows: There is no justification for deliberately

holding

The core of a judge's decision in a case; that part of the written opinion that applies the law to the facts of the case. It expresses the *rule of the case,* as distinguished from *dicta.*

rule of the case

That part of a written judicial opinion that decides the case; it is what the case stands for as far as applying a rule to the facts of the case.

deceiving the jury about the woman's marital status. However, her current husband's earnings are irrelevant to the damage she suffered in losing her former husband. Fairness on this issue is difficult.

EVALUATING CASES

Once the purpose, style, and structure of appellate decisions have been grasped, mastering the content is a matter of concentration and experience. Researching cases generally has one or more of the following three goals:

1. Finding statements of the law
2. Assessing the law in relation to the client's case
3. Building an argument

Finding the Law

Research of cases is done for a number of reasons. The principles that apply to a dispute may be unknown, unfamiliar, or forgotten. With experience, legal professionals come to develop a knack for guessing how a dispute will be decided and can even predict what rules will be applied. Once the issues of a case are recognized, a reasonable prediction of a fair outcome can be made. This is, however, merely tentative; the researchers must check their knowledge and memory against definitive statements of the law. In some instances, a statute clearly defines the rights and duties that pertain to the case at hand; in others, the elaboration of the law in the cases leaves little room for doubt. Frequently, however, the issue in a client's case is complex or unique, and no case can be found that is directly "on point." Ideally, research will result in finding a case that contains a fact situation so similar to that of the client that an assumption can be made that the same rule will apply. A case with a factual background identical to that of the client is said to be *on point*, as illustrated in the following example.

Suppose Laura Lee, while waiting for a bus, was hit and injured by an automobile. The driver had lost control because of a defective steering mechanism. Laura was seriously injured, and the driver has minimal insurance (and may not have been at fault). The issue is whether the manufacturer of the automobile is liable. The owner could sue the automobile manufacturer, but can a bystander sue as well? A search reveals several cases involving bystanders who were injured by vehicles with defective brakes and were able to sue the manufacturer for product liability. Although the facts are not identical, these cases are on point because the issue is not what kind of defect caused the accident but whether a bystander can sue.

Distinguishing Cases

In some instances, the facts of a dispute are used to *distinguish* it from similar cases. For example, in researching Laura Lee's case, a case is encountered in which a bystander was injured by an automobile with a defective steering mechanism. In that case, the bystander did not collect damages from the manufacturer. The case was distinguishable because the driver was intoxicated. The driver's negligence was not merely passive, such as procrastinating in obtaining repairs, but was actively caused by his intoxication. The intoxication was the true cause of the injury, so it would have been unfair to place liability on the manufacturer. (The manufacturer would probably be sued anyway simply because it has the resources to compensate for the injury.)

Only experience and knowledge of the law will develop the keen sense it takes to separate cases that are on point from those that are distinguishable. It is often the advocate's job to persuade on the basis of threading a way through a host of seemingly conflicting cases.

SUMMARY

Judicial opinions are unique as a literary form in that their statements of law as defined by the court become precedent for future legal arguments and decisions. Judges must not only do justice to the parties but also remain aware that their decisions determine rights of other parties in the future. Complex issues often result in opinions that are difficult to follow. Controversial issues may cause judges to be evasive in their conclusions.

A standard publishing format is followed in reported judicial decisions. In addition, custom has dictated a format for the text of the opinion itself. Judges are under no requirement to follow this format, and it is up to the reader to ferret out the issues and follow the reasoning.

APPENDIX B

THE CONSTITUTION OF THE UNITED STATES OF AMERICA

PREAMBLE

We the People of the United States, in Order to form a more perfect Union, establish Justice, insure domestic Tranquility, provide for the common defence, promote the general Welfare, and secure the Blessings of Liberty to ourselves and our Posterity, do ordain and establish this Constitution for the United States of America.

ARTICLE I

Section 1   All legislative Powers herein granted shall be vested in a Congress of the United States, which shall consist of a Senate and House of Representatives.

Section 2   (1) The House of Representatives shall be composed of Members chosen every second Year by the People of the several States, and the Electors in each State shall have the Qualifications requisite for Electors of the most numerous Branch of the State Legislature.

(2) No Person shall be a Representative who shall not have attained to the age of twenty-five Years, and been seven Years a Citizen of the United States, and who shall not, when elected, be an Inhabitant of that State in which he shall be chosen.

(3) Representatives and direct Taxes shall be apportioned among the several States which may be included within this Union, according to their respective Numbers, which shall be determined by adding to the whole Number of free Persons, including those bound to Service for a Term of Years, and excluding Indians not taxed, three fifths of all other Persons. The actual Enumeration shall be made within three Years after the first Meeting of the Congress of the United States, and within every subsequent Term of ten Years, in such Manner as they shall by Law direct. The Number of Representatives shall not exceed one for every thirty Thousand, but each State shall have at Least one Representative; and until such enumeration shall be made, the State of New Hampshire shall be entitled to chuse three, Massachusetts eight, Rhode Island and Providence Plantations one, Connecticut five, New York six, New Jersey four, Pennsylvania eight, Delaware one, Maryland six, Virginia ten, North Carolina five, South Carolina five, and Georgia three.

(4) When vacancies happen in the Representation from any State, the Executive Authority thereof shall issue Writs of Election to fill such Vacancies.

(5) The House of Representatives shall chuse their Speaker and other Officers; and shall have the sole Power of Impeachment.

Section 3   (1) The Senate of the United States shall be composed of two Senators from each State, chosen by the Legislature thereof, for six Years; and each Senator shall have one Vote.

(2) Immediately after they shall be assembled in Consequence of the first Election, they shall be divided as equally as may be into three Classes. The Seats of the Senators of the first Class shall be vacated at the Expiration of the second Year, of the second Class at the Expiration of the fourth Year, and of the third Class at the Expiration of the sixth Year, so that one third may be chosen every second Year; and if Vacancies happen by Resignation, or otherwise, during the Recess of the Legislature of any State, the Executive thereof may make temporary Appointments until the next Meeting of the Legislature, which shall then fill such Vacancies.

(3) No Person shall be a Senator who shall not have attained to the Age of thirty Years, and been nine Years a Citizen of the United States, and who shall not, when elected, be an Inhabitant of that State for which he shall be chosen.

(4) The Vice President of the United States shall be President of the Senate, but shall have no Vote, unless they be equally divided.

(5) The Senate shall chuse their other Officers, and also a President pro tempore, in the Absence of the Vice President, or when he shall exercise the Office of the President of the United States.

(6) The Senate shall have the sole Power to try all Impeachments. When sitting for that Purpose, they shall be on Oath or Affirmation. When the President of the United States is tried, the Chief Justice shall preside: And no Person shall be convicted without the Concurrence of two thirds of the Members present.

(7) Judgment in Cases of Impeachment shall not extend further than to removal from Office, and disqualification to hold and enjoy any Office of honor, Trust or Profit under the United States: but the Party convicted shall nevertheless be liable and subject to Indictment, Trial, Judgment and Punishment, according to Law.

Section 4   (1) The Times, Places and Manner of holding Elections for Senators and Representatives, shall be prescribed in each State by the Legislature thereof; but the Congress may at any time by Law make or alter such Regulations, except as to the Places of chusing Senators.

(2) The Congress shall assemble at least once in every Year, and such Meeting shall be on the first Monday in December, unless they shall by Law appoint a different Day.

Section 5   (1) Each House shall be the Judge of the Elections, Returns and Qualifications of its own Members, and a Majority of each shall constitute a Quorum to do Business; but a smaller Number may adjourn from day to day, and may be authorized to compel the Attendance of absent Members, in such Manner, and under such Penalties as each House may provide.

(2) Each House may determine the Rules of its Proceedings, punish its Members for disorderly Behaviour, and, with the Concurrence of two thirds, expel a Member.

(3) Each House shall keep a Journal of its Proceedings, and from time to time publish the same, excepting such Parts as may in their Judgment require Secrecy; and the Yeas and Nays of the Members of either House on any question shall, at the Desire of one fifth of those Present, be entered on the Journal.

(4) Neither House, during the Session of Congress, shall, without the Consent of the other, adjourn for more than three days, nor to any other Place than that in which the two Houses shall be sitting.

Section 6   (1) The Senators and Representatives shall receive a Compensation for their Services, to be ascertained by Law, and paid out of the Treasury of the United States. They shall in all Cases, except Treason, Felony and Breach of the Peace, be privileged from Arrest during their Attendance at the Session of their respective Houses, and in going to and returning from the same; and for any Speech or Debate in either House, they shall not be questioned in any other Place.

(2) No Senator or Representative shall, during the Time for which he was elected, be appointed to any civil Office under the Authority of the United States, which shall have been created, or the Emoluments whereof shall have been encreased during such time; and no Person holding any Office under the United States, shall be a Member of either House during his Continuance in Office.

Section 7   (1) All Bills for raising Revenue shall originate in the House of Representatives; but the Senate may propose or concur with Amendments as on other Bills.

(2) Every Bill which shall have passed the House of Representatives and the Senate, shall, before it become a Law, be presented to the President of the United States; If he approve he shall sign it, but if not he shall return it, with his Objections to that House in which it shall have originated, who shall enter the Objections at large on their Journal, and proceed to reconsider it. If after such Reconsideration two thirds of that House shall agree to pass the Bill, it shall be sent, together with the Objections, to the other House, by which it shall likewise be reconsidered, and if approved by two thirds of that House, it shall become a law. But in all such Cases the Votes of both Houses shall be determined by Yeas and Nays, and the Names of the Persons voting for and against the Bill shall be entered on the Journal of each House respectively. If any Bill shall not be returned by the President within ten Days (Sunday excepted) after it shall have been presented to him, the Same shall be a Law, in like Manner as if he had signed it, unless the Congress by their Adjournment prevent its Return, in which Case it shall not be a Law.

(3) Every Order, Resolution, or Vote to which the Concurrence of the Senate and House of Representatives may be necessary (except on a question of Adjournment) shall be presented to the President of the United States; and before the Same shall take Effect, shall be approved by him, or being disapproved by him, shall be repassed by two thirds of the Senate and House of Representatives, according to the Rules and Limitations prescribed in the Case of a Bill.

Section 8   (1) The Congress shall have Power To lay and collect Taxes, Duties, Imposts and Excises, to pay the Debts and provide for the common Defence and general Welfare of the United States; but all Duties, Imposts and Excises shall be uniform throughout the United States;

(2) To borrow Money on the credit of the United States;

(3) To regulate Commerce with foreign Nations, and among the several States, and with the Indian Tribes;

(4) To establish an uniform Rule of Naturalization, and uniform Laws on the subject of Bankruptcies throughout the United States;

(5) To coin Money, regulate the Value thereof, and of foreign Coin, and to fix the Standard of Weights and Measures;

(6) To provide for the Punishment of counterfeiting the Securities and current Coin of the United States;

(7) To establish Post Offices and post Roads;

(8) To promote the Progress of Science and useful Arts, by securing for limited Times to Authors and Inventors the exclusive Right to their respective Writings and Discoveries;

(9) To constitute Tribunals inferior to the Supreme Court;

(10) To define and punish Piracies and Felonies committed on the high Seas, and Offenses against the Law of Nations;

(11) To declare War, grant Letters of Marque and Reprisal, and make Rules concerning Captures on Land and Water;

(12) To raise and support Armies, but no Appropriation of Money to that Use shall be for a longer Term than two Years;

(13) To provide and maintain a Navy;

(14) To make Rules for the Government and Regulation of the land and naval Forces;

(15) To provide for calling forth the Militia to execute the Laws of the Union, suppress Insurrections and repel Invasions;

(16) To provide for organizing, arming, and disciplining, the Militia, and for governing such Part of them as may be employed in the Service of the United States, reserving to the States respectively, the Appointment of the Officers, and the Authority of training the Militia according to the discipline prescribed by Congress;

(17) To exercise exclusive Legislation in all Cases whatsoever, over such District (not exceeding ten Miles square) as may, by Cession of particular States, and the Acceptance of Congress, become the Seat of the Government of the United States, and to exercise like Authority over all Places purchased by the Consent of the Legislature of the State in which the Same shall be, for the Erection of Forts, Magazines, Arsenals, dock-Yards, and other needful Buildings;—And

(18) To make all Laws which shall be necessary and proper for carrying into Execution the foregoing Powers, and all other Powers vested by this Constitution in the Government of the United States, or in any Department or Officer thereof.

Section 9   (1) The Migration or Importation of such Persons as any of the States now existing shall think proper to admit, shall not be prohibited by the Congress prior to the Year one thousand eight hundred and eight, but a Tax or Duty may be imposed on such Importation, not exceeding ten dollars for each Person.

(2) The Privilege of the Writ of Habeas Corpus shall not be suspended unless when in Cases of Rebellion or Invasion the public Safety may require it.

(3) No Bill of Attainder or ex post facto Law shall be passed.

(4) No Capitation, or other direct, Tax shall be laid, unless in Proportion to the Census or Enumeration herein before directed to be taken.

(5) No Tax or Duty shall be laid on Articles exported from any State.

(6) No Preference shall be given by any Regulation of Commerce or Revenue to the Ports of one State over those of another; nor shall Vessels bound to, or from, one State, be obliged to enter, clear or pay Duties in another.

(7) No Money shall be drawn from the Treasury, but in Consequence of Appropriations made by Law; and a regular Statement and Account of the Receipts and Expenditures of all public Money shall be published from time to time.

(8) No Title of Nobility shall be granted by the United States: And no Person holding any Office of Profit or Trust under them, shall, without the Consent of the Congress, accept of any present, Emolument, Office, or Title, of any kind whatever, from any King, Prince or foreign State.

Section 10   (1) No State shall enter into any Treaty, Alliance, or Confederation; grant Letters of Marque and Reprisal; coin Money; emit Bills of Credit; make any Thing but gold and silver Coin a Tender in Payment of Debts; pass any Bill of Attainder, ex post facto Law, or Law impairing the Obligation of Contracts, or grant any Title of Nobility.

(2) No State shall, without the Consent of Congress, lay any Imposts or Duties on Imports or Exports, except what may be absolutely necessary for executing its inspection Laws: and the net Produce of all Duties and Imposts, laid by any State on Imports or Exports, shall be for the Use of the Treasury of the United States; and all such Laws shall be subject to the Revision and Controul of the Congress.

(3) No State shall, without the Consent of Congress, lay any Duty of Tonnage, keep Troops, or Ships of War in time of Peace, enter into any Agreement or Compact with another State, or with a foreign Power, or engage in War, unless actually invaded, or in such imminent Danger as will not admit of Delay.

ARTICLE II

Section 1   (1) The executive Power shall be vested in a President of the United States of America. He shall hold his Office during the Term of four Years, and, together with the Vice President, chosen for the same Term, be elected, as follows:

(2) Each State shall appoint, in such Manner as the Legislature thereof may direct, a Number of Electors, equal to the whole Number of Senators and Representatives to which the State may be entitled in the Congress: but no Senator or Representative, or Person holding an Office of Trust or Profit under the United States, shall be appointed an Elector.

The Electors shall meet in their respective States, and vote by Ballot for two Persons, of whom one at least shall not be an Inhabitant of the same State with themselves. And they shall make a List of all the Persons voted for, and of the Number of Votes for each; which List they shall sign and certify, and transmit sealed to the Seat of the Government of the United States, directed to the President of the Senate. The President of the Senate shall, in the presence of the Senate and House of Representatives, open all the Certificates, and the Votes shall then be counted. The Person having the greatest Number of Votes shall be the President, if such Number be a Majority of the whole Number of Electors appointed; and if there be more than one who have such Majority, and have an equal Number of Votes, then the House of Representatives shall immediately chuse by Ballot one of them for President; and if no Person have a Majority, then from the five highest on the List the said House shall in like Manner chuse the

President. But in chusing the President, the Votes shall be taken by States, the Representation from each State having one Vote; a quorum for this Purpose shall consist of a Member or Members from two thirds of the States, and a Majority of all the States shall be necessary to a Choice. In every Case, after the Choice of the President, the Person having the greatest Number of Votes of the Electors shall be the Vice President. But if there should remain two or more who have equal Votes, the Senate shall chuse from them by Ballot the Vice President.

(3) The Congress may determine the Time of choosing the Electors, and the Day on which they shall give their Votes; which Day shall be the same throughout the United States.

(4) No Person except a natural born Citizen, or a Citizen of the United States, at the time of the Adoption of this Constitution, shall be eligible to the Office of President; neither shall any Person be eligible to that Office who shall not have attained to the Age of thirty five Years, and been fourteen Years a Resident within the United States.

(5) In Case of the Removal of the President from Office, or of his Death, Resignation, or Inability to discharge the Powers and Duties of the said Office, the Same shall devolve on the Vice President, and the Congress may by Law provide for the Case of Removal, Death, Resignation or Inability, both of the President and Vice President, declaring what Officer shall then act as President, and such Officer shall act accordingly, until the Disability be removed, or a President shall be elected.

(6) The President shall, at stated Times, receive for his Services, a Compensation, which shall neither be increased nor diminished during the Period for which he shall have been elected, and he shall not receive within that Period any other Emolument from the United States, or any of them.

(7) Before he enter on the Execution of his Office, he shall take the following Oath or Affirmation:—"I do solemnly swear (or affirm) that I will faithfully execute the Office of President of the United States, and will to the best of my Ability, preserve, protect and defend the Constitution of the United States."

Section 2 (1) The President shall be Commander in Chief of the Army and Navy of the United States, and of the Militia of the several States, when called into the actual Service of the United States; he may require the Opinion, in writing, of the principal Officer in each of the executive Departments, upon any Subject relating to the Duties of their respective Offices, and he shall have Power to grant Reprieves and Pardons for Offenses against the United States, except in Cases of Impeachment.

(2) He shall have Power, by and with the Advice and Consent of the Senate, to make Treaties, provided two thirds of the Senators present concur; and he shall nominate, and by and with the Advice and Consent of the Senate, shall appoint Ambassadors, other public Ministers and Consuls, Judges of the supreme Court, and all other Officers of the United States, whose Appointments are not herein otherwise provided for, and which shall be established by Law: but the Congress may by Law vest the Appointment of such inferior

Officers, as they think proper, in the President alone, in the Courts of Law, or in the Heads of Departments.

(3) The President shall have Power to fill up all Vacancies that may happen during the Recess of the Senate, by granting Commissions which shall expire at the End of their next Session.

Section 3 He shall from time to time give to the Congress Information of the State of the Union, and recommend to their Consideration such Measures as he shall judge necessary and expedient; he may, on extraordinary Occasions, convene both Houses, or either of them, and in Case of Disagreement between them, with Respect to the Time of Adjournment, he may adjourn them to such Time as he shall think proper; he shall receive Ambassadors and other public Ministers; he shall take Care that the Laws be faithfully executed, and shall Commission all the Officers of the United States.

Section 4 The President, Vice President and all Civil Officers of the United States, shall be removed from Office on Impeachment for, and Conviction of, Treason, Bribery, or other high Crimes and Misdemeanors.

ARTICLE III

Section 1 The judicial Power of the United States, shall be vested in one supreme Court, and in such inferior Courts as the Congress may from time to time ordain and establish. The Judges, both of the supreme and inferior Courts, shall hold their Offices during good Behaviour, and shall, at stated Times, receive for their Services, a Compensation, which shall not be diminished during their Continuance in Office.

Section 2 (1) The judicial Power shall extend to all Cases, in Law and Equity, arising under this Constitution, the Laws of the United States, and Treaties made, or which shall be made, under their Authority;—to all Cases affecting Ambassadors, other public Ministers and Consuls;—to all Cases of admiralty and maritime Jurisdiction;—to Controversies to which the United States shall be a party;—to Controversies between two or more States;—between a State and Citizens of another State;—between Citizens of different States;—between Citizens of the same State claiming Lands under Grants of different States, and between a State, or the Citizens thereof, and foreign States, Citizens or Subjects.

(2) In all Cases affecting Ambassadors, other public Ministers and Consuls, and those in which a State shall be Party, the supreme Court shall have original Jurisdiction. In all the other Cases before mentioned, the supreme Court shall have appellate Jurisdiction, both as to Law and Fact, with such Exceptions, and under such Regulations as the Congress shall make.

(3) The Trial of all Crimes, except in Cases of Impeachment, shall be by Jury; and such Trial shall be held in the State where the said Crimes shall have been committed; but when not committed within any State, the Trial shall be at such Place or Places as the Congress may by Law have directed.

Section 3 (1) Treason against the United States, shall consist only in levying War against them, or in adhering to their Enemies, giving them Aid and Comfort. No Person shall be convicted of Treason unless on the Testimony of two Witnesses to the same overt Act, or on Confession in open Court.

(2) The Congress shall have Power to declare the Punishment of Treason, but no Attainder of Treason shall work Corruption of Blood, or Forfeiture except during the Life of the Person attainted.

ARTICLE IV

Section 1 Full Faith and Credit shall be given in each State to the public Acts, Records, and judicial Proceedings of every other State. And the Congress may by general Laws prescribe the Manner in which such Acts, Records and Proceedings shall be proved, and the Effect thereof.

Section 2 (1) The Citizens of each State shall be entitled to all privileges and Immunities of Citizens in the several States.

(2) A Person charged in any State with Treason, Felony, or other Crime, who shall flee from Justice, and be found in another State, shall on Demand of the executive Authority of the State from which he fled, be delivered up, to be removed to the State having Jurisdiction of the Crime.

(3) No Person held to Service of Labour in one State, under the Laws thereof, escaping into another, shall, in Consequence of any Law or Regulation therein, be discharged from such Service or Labour, but shall be delivered up on Claim of the Party to whom such Service or Labour may be due.

Section 3 (1) New States may be admitted by the Congress into this Union; but no new State shall be formed or erected within the Jurisdiction of any other State; nor any State be formed by the Junction of two or more States, or Parts of States, without the Consent of the Legislatures of the States concerned as well as of the Congress.

(2) The Congress shall have power to dispose of and make all needful Rules and Regulations respecting the Territory or other Property belonging to the United States; and nothing in this Constitution shall be so construed as to Prejudice any Claims of the United States, or of any particular State.

Section 4 The United States shall guarantee to every State in this Union a Republican Form of Government, and shall protect each of them against Invasion; and on Application of the Legislature, or of the Executive (when the Legislature cannot be convened) against domestic Violence.

ARTICLE V

The Congress, whenever two thirds of both Houses shall deem it necessary, shall propose Amendments to this Constitution, or, on the Application of the Legislatures of two thirds of the several States, shall call a Convention for proposing Amendments, which, in either Case, shall be valid to all Intents and Purposes, as Part of this Constitution, when ratified by the Legislatures of three fourths of the several States, or by Conventions in three fourths thereof, as the one or the other Mode of Ratification may be proposed by the Congress; Provided that no Amendment which may be made prior to the Year One thousand eight hundred and eight shall in any Manner affect the first and fourth Clauses in the Ninth Section of the first Article; and that no State, without its Consent, shall be deprived of its equal Suffrage in the Senate.

ARTICLE VI

(1) All Debts contracted and Engagements entered into, before the Adoption of this Constitution, shall be as valid against the United States under this Constitution, as under the Confederation.

(2) This Constitution, and the Laws of the United States which shall be made in Pursuance thereof; and all Treaties made, or which shall be made, under the Authority of the United States, shall be the supreme Law of the Land; and the Judges in every State shall be bound thereby, any Thing in the Constitution or Laws of any State to the Contrary notwithstanding.

(3) The Senators and Representatives before mentioned, and the Members of the several State Legislatures, and all executive and judicial Officers, both of the United States and of the several States, shall be bound by Oath or Affirmation, to support this Constitution; but no religious Test shall ever be required as a Qualification to any Office or public Trust under the United States.

ARTICLE VII

The Ratification of the Conventions of nine States, shall be sufficient for the Establishment of this Constitution between the States so ratifying the Same.

ARTICLES IN ADDITION TO, AND AMENDMENT OF, HE CONSTITUTION OF THE UNITED STATES OF AMERICA, PROPOSED BY CONGRESS, AND RATIFIED BY THE SEVERAL STATES, PURSUANT TO THE FIFTH ARTICLE OF THE ORIGINAL CONSTITUTION

AMENDMENT I (1791)

Congress shall make no law respecting an establishment of religion, or prohibiting the free exercise thereof; or abridging the freedom of speech, or of the press; or the right of the people peaceably to assemble, and to petition the Government for a redress of grievances.

AMENDMENT II (1791)

A well regulated Militia, being necessary to the security of a free state, the right of the people to keep and bear Arms, shall not be infringed.

AMENDMENT III (1791)

No Soldier shall, in time of peace be quartered in any house, without the consent of the Owner, nor in time of war, but in a manner to be prescribed by law.

AMENDMENT IV (1791)

The right of the people to be secure in their persons, houses, papers, and effects, against unreasonable searches and seizures, shall not be violated, and no Warrants shall issue, but upon probable cause, supported by Oath or affirmation, and particularly describing the place to be searched, and the persons or things to be seized.

AMENDMENT V (1791)

No person shall be held to answer for a capital, or otherwise infamous crime, unless on a presentment or indictment of a Grand Jury, except in cases arising in the land or naval forces, or in the Militia, when in actual service in time of War or public danger; nor shall any person be subject for the same offence to be twice put in jeopardy of life or limb; nor shall be compelled in any criminal case to be a witness against himself, nor be deprived of life, liberty, or property, without due process of law; nor shall private property be taken for public use, without just compensation.

AMENDMENT VI (1791)

In all criminal prosecutions, the accused shall enjoy the right to a speedy and public trial, by an impartial jury of the State and district wherein the crime shall have been committed, which district shall have been previously ascertained by law, and to be informed of the nature and cause of the accusation; to be confronted with the witnesses against him; to have compulsory process for obtaining witnesses in his favor, and to have the Assistance of Counsel for his defence.

AMENDMENT VII (1791)

In Suits at common law, where the value in controversy shall exceed twenty dollars, the right of trial by jury shall be preserved, and no fact tried by a jury, shall be otherwise re-examined in any Court of the United States, than according to the rules of the common law.

AMENDMENT VIII (1791)

Excessive bail shall not be required, nor excessive fines imposed, nor cruel and unusual punishments inflicted.

AMENDMENT IX (1791)

The enumeration in the Constitution, of certain rights, shall not be construed to deny or disparage others retained by the people.

AMENDMENT X (1791)

The powers not delegated to the United States by the Constitution, nor prohibited by it to the States, are reserved to the States respectively, or to the people.

AMENDMENT XI (1798)

The Judicial power of the United States shall not be construed to extend to any suit in law or equity, commenced or prosecuted against one of the United States by Citizens of another State, or by Citizens or Subjects of any Foreign State.

AMENDMENT XII (1804)

The Electors shall meet in their respective states and vote by ballot for President and Vice-President, one of whom, at least, shall not be an inhabitant of the same state with themselves; they shall name in their ballots the person voted for as President, and in distinct ballots the person voted for as Vice-President, and they shall make distinct lists of all persons voted for as President, and of all persons voted for as Vice-President, and of the number of votes for each, which lists they shall sign and certify, and transmit sealed to the seat of the government of the United States, directed to the President of the Senate;—The President of the Senate shall, in the presence of the Senate and House of Representatives, open all the certificates and the votes shall then be counted;—The person having the greatest number of votes for President, shall be the President, if such number be a majority of the whole number of Electors appointed; and if no person have such majority, then from the persons having the highest numbers not exceeding three on the list of those voted for as President, the House of Representatives shall choose immediately, by ballot, the President. But in choosing the President, the votes shall be taken by states, the representation from each state having one vote; a quorum for this purpose shall consist of a member or members from two-thirds of the states, and a majority of all the states shall be necessary to a choice. And if the House of Representatives shall not choose a President whenever the right of choice shall devolve upon them, before the fourth day of March next following, then the Vice-President shall act as President, as in the case of the death or other constitutional disability of the President—The person having the greatest number of votes as Vice-President, shall be the Vice-President, if such number be a majority of the whole number of

Electors appointed, and if no person have a majority, then from the two highest numbers on the list, the Senate shall choose the Vice-President; A quorum for the purpose shall consist of two-thirds of the whole number of Senators, and a majority of the whole number shall be necessary to a choice. But no person constitutionally ineligible to the office of President shall be eligible to that of Vice-President of the United States.

AMENDMENT XIII (1865)

Section 1   Neither slavery nor involuntary servitude, except as a punishment for crime whereof the party shall have been duly convicted, shall exist within the United States, or any place subject to their jurisdiction.

Section 2   Congress shall have power to enforce this article by appropriate legislation.

AMENDMENT XIV (1868)

Section 1   All persons born or naturalized in the United States and subject to the jurisdiction thereof, are citizens of the United States and of the State wherein they reside. No State shall make or enforce any law which shall abridge the privileges or immunities of citizens of the United States; nor shall any State deprive any person of life, liberty, or property, without due process of law; nor deny to any person within its jurisdiction the equal protection of the laws.

Section 2   Representatives shall be apportioned among the several States according to their respective numbers, counting the whole number of persons in each State, excluding Indians not taxed. But when the right to vote at any election for the choice of electors for President and Vice-President of the United States, Representatives in Congress, the Executive and Judicial officers of a State, or the members of the Legislature thereof, is denied to any of the male inhabitants of such State, being twenty-one years of age, and citizens of the United States, or in any way abridged, except for participation in rebellion, or other crime, the basis of representation therein shall be reduced in the proportion which the number of such male citizens shall bear to the whole number of male citizens twenty-one years of age in such State.

Section 3   No person shall be a Senator or Representative in Congress, or elector of President and Vice President, or hold any office, civil or military, under the United States, or under any State, who, having previously taken an oath, as a member of Congress, or as an officer of the United States, or as a member of any State legislature, or as an executive or judicial officer of any State, to support the Constitution of the United States, shall have engaged in insurrection or rebellion against the same, or given aid or comfort to the enemies thereof. But Congress may by a vote of two-thirds of each House, remove such disability.

Section 4   The validity of the public debt of the United States, authorized by law, including debts incurred for payment of pensions and bounties for services in suppressing insurrection or rebellion, shall not be questioned. But neither the United States nor any State shall assume or pay any debt or obligation incurred in aid of insurrection or rebellion against the United States, or any claim for the loss or emancipation of any slave; but all such debts, obligations and claims shall be held illegal and void.

Section 5   The Congress shall have power to enforce, by appropriate legislation, the provisions of this article.

AMENDMENT XV (1870)

Section 1   The right of citizens of the United States to vote shall not be denied or abridged by the United States or by any State on account of race, color, or previous condition of servitude.

Section 2   The Congress shall have power to enforce this article by appropriate legislation.

AMENDMENT XVI (1913)

The Congress shall have power to lay and collect taxes on incomes, from whatever source derived, without apportionment among the several States, and without regard to any census or enumeration.

AMENDMENT XVII (1913)

The Senate of the United States shall be composed of two Senators from each State, elected by the people thereof, for six years; and each Senator shall have one vote. The electors in each State shall have the qualifications requisite for electors of the most numerous branch of the State legislatures.

When vacancies happen in the representation of any State in the Senate, the executive authority of such State shall issue writs of election to fill such vacancies: *Provided*, That the legislature of any State may empower the executive thereof to make temporary appointments until the people fill the vacancies by election as the legislature may direct.

This amendment shall not be so construed as to affect the election or term of any Senator chosen before it becomes valid as part of the Constitution.

AMENDMENT XVIII (1919)

Section 1   After one year from the ratification of this article the manufacture, sale, or transportation of intoxicating liquors within, the importation thereof into, or the exportation thereof from the United States and all territory subject to the jurisdiction thereof for beverage purposes is hereby prohibited.

Section 2   The Congress and the several States shall have concurrent power to enforce this article by appropriate legislation.

Section 3   This article shall be inoperative unless it shall have been ratified as an amendment to the Constitution by the legislatures of the several States, as provided in the Constitution, within seven years from the date of the submission hereof to the States by the Congress.

AMENDMENT XIX (1920)

The right of citizens of the United States to vote shall not be denied or abridged by the United States or by any State on account of sex.

Congress shall have power to enforce this article by appropriate legislation.

AMENDMENT XX (1933)

Section 1   The terms of the President and Vice President shall end at noon on the 20th day of January, and the terms of Senators and Representatives at noon on the 3d day of January, of the years in which such terms would have ended if this article had not been ratified; and the terms of their successors shall then begin.

Section 2   The Congress shall assemble at least once in every year, and such meeting shall begin at noon on the 3d day of January, unless they shall by law appoint a different day.

Section 3   If, at the time fixed for the beginning of the term of the President, the President elect shall have died, the Vice President elect shall become President. If a President shall not have been chosen before the time fixed for the beginning of his term, or if the President elect shall have failed to qualify, then the Vice President elect shall act as President until a President shall have qualified; and the Congress may by law provide for the case wherein neither a President elect nor a Vice President elect shall have qualified, declaring who shall then act as President, or the manner in which one who is to act shall be selected, and such person shall act accordingly until a President or Vice President shall have qualified.

Section 4   The Congress may by law provide for the case of the death of any of the persons from whom the House of Representatives may choose a President whenever the right of choice shall have devolved upon them, and for the case of the death of any of the persons from whom the Senate may choose a Vice President whenever the right of choice shall have devolved upon them.

Section 5   Sections 1 and 2 shall take effect on the 15th day of October following the ratification of this article.

Section 6   This article shall be inoperative unless it shall have been ratified as an amendment to the Constitution by the legislatures of three-fourths of the several States within seven years from the date of its submission.

AMENDMENT XXI (1933)

Section 1   The eighteenth article of amendment to the Constitution of the United States is hereby repealed.

Section 2   The transportation or importation into any State, Territory or possession of the United States for delivery or use therein of intoxicating liquors, in violation of the laws thereof, is hereby prohibited.

Section 3   This article shall be inoperative unless it shall have been ratified as an amendment to the Constitution by conventions in the several States, as provided in the Constitution, within seven years from the date of the submission hereof to the States by the Congress.

AMENDMENT XXII (1951)

Section 1   No person shall be elected to the office of the President more than twice, and no person who has held the office of President, or acted as President, for more than two years of a term to which some other person was elected President shall be elected to the office of the President more than once. But this Article shall not apply to any person holding the office of President when this Article was proposed by the Congress, and shall not prevent any person who may be holding the office of President, or acting as President, during the term within which this Article becomes operative from holding the office of President or acting as President during the remainder of such term.

Section 2   This Article shall be inoperative unless it shall have been ratified as an amendment to the Constitution by the legislatures of three-fourths of the several States within seven years from the date of its submission to the States by the Congress.

AMENDMENT XXIII (1961)

Section 1   The District constituting the seat of Government of the United States shall appoint in such manner as the Congress may direct:

A number of electors of President and Vice President equal to the whole number of Senators and Representatives in Congress to which the District would be entitled if it were a State, but in no event more than the least populous State; they shall be in addition to those appointed by the States, but they shall be considered, for the purposes of the election of President and Vice President, to be electors appointed by a State; and they shall meet in the District and perform such duties as provided by the twelfth article of amendment.

Section 2   The Congress shall have power to enforce this article by appropriate legislation.

AMENDMENT XXIV (1964)

Section 1   The right of citizens of the United States to vote in any primary or other election for President or Vice President, for electors for President or Vice President, or for Senator or Representative in Congress, shall not be denied or abridged by the United States or any State by reason of failure to pay any poll tax or other tax.

Section 2   The Congress shall have power to enforce this article by appropriate legislation.

AMENDMENT XXV (1967)

Section 1   In case of the removal of the President from office or of his death or resignation, the Vice President shall become President.

Section 2   Whenever there is a vacancy in the office of the Vice President, the President shall nominate a Vice President who shall take office upon confirmation by a majority vote of both Houses of Congress.

Section 3   Whenever the President transmits to the President pro tempore of the Senate and the Speaker of the House of Representatives his written declaration that he is unable to discharge the powers and duties of his office, and until he transmits to them a written declaration to the contrary, such powers and duties shall be discharged by the Vice President as Acting President.

Section 4   Whenever the Vice President and a majority of either the principal officers of the executive departments or of such other body as Congress may by law provide, transmit to the President pro tempore of the Senate and the Speaker of the House of Representatives their written declaration that the President is unable to discharge the powers and duties of his office, the Vice President shall immediately assume the powers and duties of the office as Acting President.

Thereafter, when the President transmits to the President pro tempore of the Senate and the Speaker of the House of Representatives his written declaration that no inability exists, he shall resume the powers and duties of his office unless the Vice President and a majority of either the principal officers of the executive department or of such other body as Congress may by law provide, transmit within four days to the President pro tempore of the Senate and the Speaker of the House of Representatives their written declaration that the President is unable to discharge the powers and duties of his office. Thereupon Congress shall decide the issue, assembling within forty-eight hours for that purpose if not in session. If the Congress, within twenty-one days after receipt of the latter written declaration, or, if Congress is not in session, within twenty-one days after Congress is required to assemble, determines by two-thirds vote of both Houses that the President is unable to discharge the powers and duties of his office, the Vice President shall continue to discharge the same as Acting President; otherwise, the President shall resume the powers and duties of his office.

AMENDMENT XXVI (1971)

Section 1   The right of citizens of the United States, who are eighteen years of age or older, to vote shall not be denied or abridged by the United States or by any State on account of age.

Section 2   The Congress shall have power to enforce this article by appropriate legislation.

AMENDMENT XXVII (1992)

No law varying the compensation for the services of the senators and representatives shall take effect, until an election of representatives shall have intervened.

GLOSSARY

A

absolute liability Liability without fault or negligence; often used interchangeably with *strict liability,* though many would contend that there is a difference.

acceptance In contract law, the final act in concluding negotiations, when an offeree accepts all the terms of the offer.

actus reus Criminal act; conduct that the law prohibits or absence of conduct that the law requires.

adjudication The formal act of deciding disputes by a court or tribunal.

administrative law The body of law that controls the way in which administrative agencies operate if covered by state and federal Administrative Procedure Acts; also deals with regulations issued by administrative agencies.

administrator A person appointed by a court to manage the distribution of the estate of a deceased person.

admiralty Branch of law pertaining to maritime commerce and navigation.

adoption In family law, the legal establishment of parent-child bonds between persons who did not formerly have them; commonly, this also entails the severance of those bonds with a former parent.

adversarial system The U.S. legal system in which litigants, typically represented by attorneys, argue their respective sides in a dispute before an impartial judge and jury; often contrasted with an inquisitorial system in which an accused is questioned by officials without rights of defense in a relentless search for the truth.

adverse possession A means of acquiring title by occupying and using land for a certain length of time even though the occupier does not have title. The period at common law was twenty years, but this period has been shortened in most states by statute.

affidavit A statement in writing sworn to before a person who is authorized to administer an oath.

affirmative defense A claim made by the defendant that, if it prevails, will negate the plaintiff's case.

aggravated Circumstance that increases the severity of a crime.

alienation of affections Taking away the love, companionship, or help of another person's husband or wife; still recognized in a few states.

alimony Payments for personal maintenance from one ex-spouse to the other following divorce.

annulment Ends the relation of husband and wife by invalidating the marriage contract, as if they were never married.

answer A pleading that responds to the complaint, admitting and denying specific allegations and presenting defenses.

antenuptial (premarital) agreement A contract agreed to by persons before their marriage; primarily concerned with the distribution of personal and marital assets in the event of divorce or death.

anticipatory breach Occurs when one party to a contract expresses an intention not to perform; the other party may then treat the contract as *breached* and pursue an appropriate remedy rather than wait for nonperformance (actual breach).

appellant The party bringing an appeal against the other party, the *appellee.*

appellate brief A formal statement submitted to the appellate court. When a case is appealed, the appellant submits a written statement to the appellate court raising legal issues to be decided. The appellee then has a period within which to file an appellee's brief, challenging the appellant's arguments on the issues.

appellate courts As distinguished from *trial courts,* courts that function primarily to correct errors of the lower, trial courts and do not ordinarily serve as factfinders. The two common forms of appellate courts are intermediate appellate courts, usually called courts of appeal(s), and the highest courts, usually called supreme courts.

appellee The party against whom an appeal is brought.

arraignment Brings the defendant before the court to make a plea.

arrest Usually refers to detaining someone to answer for a crime.

assault Putting someone in apprehension of a *battery*. The actor must have the ability to carry out the threatened battery.

associate The title usually given to a full-time member of a law firm who has not yet been elevated to partner.

assumption of risk May prevent liability for negligence when the plaintiff voluntarily encounters a known risk.

attachment Formal seizure of property to bring it under the control of the court; usually done by getting a court order to have a law enforcement officer take control of the property.

attempt to commit a crime An act that goes beyond mere preparation to commit a crime but that is not completed.

attorney-client privilege Legal protection whereby confidential statements made by a client to an attorney may not be disclosed to others by the attorney without the client's permission.

B

bailiff An officer of the court charged with keeping order in the courtroom, having custody over prisoners and the jury.

bailment When the owner of personal property delivers possession without intent to pass title, such as when one leaves an automobile with an auto mechanic.

bankruptcy Generally, the situation in which a person, business, or government cannot or will not pay its debts, so its property is entrusted to a "trustee in bankruptcy" who distributes the property to creditors.

bar 1. The term used to refer collectively to licensed members of the legal profession. 2. To defeat or estop.

bar examination A written test required of applicants for a license to practice law.

barrister An English lawyer who specializes in trial work.

battery An unconsented, unprivileged, offensive contact.

bench Drawn from the term referring to the seat occupied by judges in court; refers to all judges collectively.

bench trial A case decided by a judge, without a jury; a nonjury trial.

bicameral Refers to a legislature with two bodies, such as a House of Representatives and a Senate; only Nebraska has a single, or *unicameral*, legislature.

bigamous Describes the marriage of a person who is already married to another person. Bigamy is a crime, and a bigamous marriage is void.

bilateral contract A contract accepted by a return promise. It is an exchange of promises, supported by consideration. Compare to *unilateral contract*.

black-letter law Lawyers' slang for the basic, well-established rules of law.

breach of contract When a party fails to render the performance required by a contract.

breach of promise to marry A cause of action based on breaking off an engagement to marry.

burden of proof The duty of proving a fact that is in dispute. In a trial, the plaintiff has the burden of proving, through the presentation of evidence, the allegations on which the case is brought. If the plaintiff fails to present sufficient evidence to prevail even if that evidence were believed, the burden of proof has not been met and the case should be dismissed in the defendant's favor.

bureaucracy That part of the government composed of agencies staffed by civil servants; forms the major part of the administrative branch.

business invitee The most common form of an invitee. Businesses, especially retail stores, are often open to the public. By implication, businesses invite members of the public to enter their premises, and they owe a duty of care to those who enter their stores.

business organizations Consist of variations on three forms: *corporations*, *partnerships*, and *sole proprietorships*. Attorneys are regularly called upon to advise clients on the choice of business organization that will best suit their needs. Personal liability, tax consequences, and financing are major considerations, but the size of the organization, its structure, and its long-range goals are also important. Once formed, businesses not only must conform to their own rules but also are subject to numerous requirements of state and federal law.

C

canon law Church, or ecclesiastical, law traditionally associated with the Roman Catholic Church, which in English law was continued by the Church of England. Separation of church and state in the United States created gaps in the law, most notably in the area of domestic relations (family law).

canons of construction Rules of statutory interpretation.

caption The heading of a court paper, which usually includes the names of the parties, the court, and the case number.

case and controversy Terms used in Article III, § 2, of the U.S. Constitution regarding the judicial power; the terms have been interpreted to mean that the courts have authority over real disputes between real parties, as opposed to hypothetical disputes or nonadversarial parties. The courts do not answer questions about the law but decide actual disputes.

case-in-chief The main evidence offered by one side in a lawsuit; does not include evidence offered to oppose the other side's case.

case method A means of studying law that consists of reading judicial opinions (cases) and analyzing them under the law professor's questioning; since its introduction by Dean Langdell at Harvard Law School, this method has been the standard approach to law school instruction in the United States.

case of first impression A case presenting a fact situation that has never been decided before by that court.

cause of action Subject of a statement required to bring a lawsuit, identifying the theory or law under which the plaintiff is suing. The court must recognize the action (suit) as one of the many kinds that the court can decide. In a sense, a cause of action is a label for a type of lawsuit. For example, slander, breach of contract, invasion of privacy, and trespass are causes of action.

cease and desist order A court directive prohibiting someone from continuing to take a specific action.

certificates of deposit Promises by banks to repay money deposited with the bank, ordinarily with interest.

certify a question A procedure by which a lower court asks a higher court to answer a specific question posed by the lower court.

certiorari To be informed of; to be made certain in regard to.

chain of title The history of the transfer of title to real property; comprised of a series of grantor-to-grantee transfers leading to a showing of who is the present holder of title.

challenge for cause In qualifying jurors during *voir dire*, either party may challenge the seating of a juror for bias or other disqualification. Challenges for cause are unlimited.

chambers The private office of a judge where matters not required to be heard in open court can be discussed and appropriate orders issued.

chancellor (master in equity) A judge of a court of chancery or court of equity.

chancery Equity, equitable jurisdiction, a court of equity; a court that administers justice and decides controversies in accordance with the rules, principles, and precedents of equity and that follows the forms and procedure of chancery; as distinguished from a court having the jurisdiction, rules, principles, and practice of the common law.

charges [to the jury] Jury instructions, given to the jurors before their deliberations.

check Written order to a bank to pay money to a named person.

child custody The rights and duties of those legally entrusted with the care and control of a child, usually the parents.

child suvpport An obligation of parents; the payments due from one parent to another for the care of children following divorce.

clean hands doctrine An *equitable maxim* according to which a court of equity will refuse to provide a remedy to a petitioner who has acted in bad faith (with "unclean hands").

clearly erroneous The test or standard used at the appellate level to determine if *judicial* factfinding at trial constitutes prejudicial error. Highly deferential toward the trial court.

clinical programs Programs found in most law schools and sanctioned by the courts and the bar in which students provide legal services to the public under the supervision of law professors; some schools require enrollment, but in most law schools "clinic" is a voluntary course for credit.

codification May refer to the simple process of turning a custom or common law rule into legislation but usually refers to the making of a *code*, that is, a set of written rules.

cohabitation Living together in a marital-like relationship; sometimes simply refers to a sexual relationship.

collateral Property pledged to pay a debt; a security interest.

collateral estoppel Bars the relitigation of issues that have been previously adjudicated.

common law Judge-made law.

common law tradition In the first century after the Norman Conquest, the Normans established a legal regime for the entire kingdom of England, with laws common to all inhabitants of the realm. Under that system, three common law courts were established (King's bench, common pleas, exchequer). The decisions of these courts and especially the decisions of the appeals of these courts became binding precedents on lower courts under a doctrine called *stare decisis*.

community property A regime in which the earnings of husband and wife during marriage are owned equally by both. Eight states, borrowing from French (Louisiana) or Spanish (Texas west to California) law, have incorporated the concept of community property into marital law.

comparative negligence A principle whereby damages are apportioned between plaintiff and defendant according to their relative fault in a negligence case where both are found to have been at fault.

compensatory damages Awarded to an injured party to make her whole; in tort, damages to compensate for all injuries and, in contract, to put the nonbreaching party in the position he would have been in if the contract had been performed. Also referred to as actual damages.

complaint The initial pleading in a civil action, in which the plaintiff alleges a cause of action and asks that the wrong done to the plaintiff be remedied by the court.

condominium A form of ownership in real property where owners typically share ownership in common areas, such as the land, sidewalks, swimming pool, and so on, but have individual rights in a building, as if each owner owned an apartment or townhouse.

conflict of laws Also called *choice of law*; concerns the problem that arises when there is a question about which state's law should apply in a particular case.

consideration A requirement in classical contract formation that consists of an exchange of something of value, although this may in some cases be largely symbolic.

conspiracy A crime involving two or more persons who agree to commit a crime or agree to plan a crime.

construe The verb from which the noun *construction* is derived; very close in meaning to *interpret*.

contempt An action taken in violation of a prior court directive.

contingency fees Arrangement between an attorney and a client under which the attorney receives compensation in the form of a percentage of the money recovered in a lawsuit; used predominantly in personal injury cases.

contract An agreement that creates a legal relationship and obligations between two or more parties.

contract implied in fact A contract that can be inferred by the conduct of the parties in the absence of a verbal or express contract.

contracts of adhesion Contracts in which all the bargaining power (and the contract terms) favor one side; often seen when the seller uses a preprinted form contract to unfair advantage.

contributory negligence A principle by which recovery will be denied to a plaintiff for defendant's negligence if plaintiff is also found to have been at fault. It is an affirmative defense that has been replaced by *comparative negligence* in most states.

controversion In a dispute, one party's statement of the facts.

copyright A right in literary property, giving an author exclusive rights over her or his works for a limited period of time.

corporation A fictional person chartered by a government; a business organization that protects owners and managers from personal liability.

counterclaim A cause of action brought by a defendant against the plaintiff in a single case; for example, in an auto collision, both drivers often sue each other, with one filing a complaint and the other counterclaims.

court reporter A person who makes verbatim recordings of court proceedings and other sworn statements, such as depositions, which can be reduced to printed transcripts.

crime An act that violates the criminal law. (If this seems redundant, compare *Orans*: "Any violation of the government's penal laws. An illegal act.")

criminal conversation Causing a married man or woman to commit adultery. Despite its name, this is a tort, not a crime, and it has generally been abolished in most states as a cause of action.

criminal law The list of crimes promulgated by the state, including the mental states required for particular crimes, for example, specific intent and premeditation.

cross-examination The questioning of an opposing witness during a trial or hearing.

D

declaratory judgment A binding judgment that specifies the rights of the parties but orders no relief. It is the appropriate remedy for the determination of an actionable dispute when the plaintiff's legal rights are in doubt.

deed A document that describes a piece of real property and its transfer of title to a new owner.

defamation An injury to reputation; includes *slander* and *libel*.

default judgment May be entered against a party that fails to file a required document in a lawsuit, particularly for failing to file an answer. A judgment entered by the court for the plaintiff when the plaintiff filed a complaint that the defendant failed to answer; a judgment obtained by the plaintiff when the defendant fails to answer the complaint within the allotted time.

demurrer A motion to dismiss for failure to state a claim upon which relief may be granted; asks the court to dismiss a case because the complaint is legally insufficient (i.e., it fails to state a *cause of action*).

deportation Removal of someone not a United States citizen from the United States and transfer to the country of origin.

deposition Oral examination of a witness transcribed by a court reporter. Ordinarily, attorneys for both sides are present, one having requested the deposition. A deposition is part of the pretrial procedure called *discovery* and is usually conducted without any participation by the judge.

deterrence Theory in criminal law holding that the purpose of the sanctions imposed by the law is to avoid or keep criminal conduct from occurring (*deter*) rather than simply punish those who commit crimes.

devisable The character of an estate in land that is capable of being passed by will upon death. Personal property is usually devisable.

dictum (dicta, obiter dictum) *Dictum* is a Latin word meaning "said" or "stated." *Obiter* means "by the way" or "incidentally." *Obiter dictum,* then, means something stated incidentally and not necessary to the discussion, usually shortened to *dictum* or its plural *dicta.* In law, it refers to a part of a judicial decision that goes beyond the scope of the issues and is considered mere opinion and not binding precedent.

direct examination The first questioning of a witness in a trial by the side that called the witness.

directed verdict The judge may order a verdict against the plaintiffs when they have failed to meet their burden of proof. Formerly the judge ordered the jury to enter a verdict against the plaintiff. Today the judge grants a motion for a directed verdict and enters a judgment.

disbarment The most severe professional disciplinary sanction, canceling an attorney's license to practice law.

discovery A pretrial procedure in which parties to a lawsuit ask for and receive information such as testimony, records, or other evidence from each other.

diversity of citizenship The subject matter jurisdiction of federal courts to hear cases between citizens of different states.

divorce The severance of the bonds of matrimony; also referred to as *dissolution of marriage.*

docket The court calendar of proceedings.

domestic relations The field of law governing the rights and duties of family relations, particularly divorce; usually synonymous with *family law.*

double jeopardy Prevents a person from being tried twice for the same crime.

dower Property interests acquired in a husband's estate upon marriage. At old common law, a wife was entitled to one-third of her husband's real property upon his death. Today, husband and wife have the same rights as surviving spouses, but these vary from state to state.

dower and curtesy Formerly, interests in property held by a wife (dower) and a husband (curtesy), the primary purpose of which was to guarantee real property interests for a surviving spouse. The husband was favored, and these interests have been equalized or combined in recent times so as not to discriminate.

draft An order to pay money; a *drawer* orders a *drawee* to pay money to a *payee*. A *check* is a draft on a bank payable on demand.

due process clause The Fifth Amendment and the Fourteenth Amendment to the U.S. Constitution, which guarantee that law administered through courts of justice is equally applied to all under established rules that do not violate fundamental principles of fairness. The process that is due before government may deprive a person of life, liberty, or property.

duress Threats of harm made to induce agreement by one party to a contract.

E

easement A right of use in another's property; for example, when someone has a right-of-way to cross another's land.

effective date [of a statute] The date on which the statute can first be applied.

ejectment A common law cause of action designed to return rightful possession of real property; commonly called *eviction* in modern landlord/tenant law.

elective share The phrase representing what was formerly *dower* and *curtesy* in the common law; the share of a surviving spouse in the deceased spouse's property that the surviving spouse may choose (elect) to take instead of the property that a will would distribute.

elements The specific parts of a *cause of action* that must be alleged and proved to make out that cause of action.

emancipated minor A person under the age of majority who is totally self-supporting or married; varies by state.

eminent domain The power of the government to take private property for a public use, for which just compensation is required by the Constitution.

enterprise liability Method of apportioning damages when an injury can be attributed to a number of companies in an industry; allocates damages according to the market share of each.

equal protection of the laws A constitutional guaranty specifying that every state must give equal treatment to every person who is similarly situated or to persons who are members of the same class; this protection is a requirement of the Fourteenth Amendment, originally enacted to protect former slaves.

equitable distribution Legal scheme of property ownership designed to equalize the marital shares of husband and wife for purposes of divorce; many states that are not *community property* states follow principles of equitable distribution.

equitable estoppel Being stopped by one's own prior acts or statements from claiming a right against another person who has legitimately relied on those acts or statements.

equitable maxim A general rule or principle guiding decision-making in courts of equity, often serving the function that *precedent* would serve in a common law court.

equitable remedy A special remedy, such as an injunction or specific performance, not available at common law.

equity A system for ensuring justice in circumstances where the remedies customarily available under conventional law are not adequate to ensure a fair result. Also see *chancery*.

estate Has several legal meanings; when used in reference to a decedent, it means the property rights to be distributed following death.

estopped Prevented, stopped. In equity, a person may be "estopped" from making assertions contrary to prior assertions on which another has relied to his or her detriment.

ethics Concerns right or proper conduct; often refers to the fairness and honesty of a person's character. In philosophy, it covers the area of inquiry into right conduct.

evidence The information presented at trial; the rules of evidence are part of the procedural law.

evidentiary facts The specific facts presented at trial, as distinguished from the more general *ultimate facts*.

ex post facto clause A provision of the U.S. Constitution, Article I, § 10, prohibiting a state from passing a statute with retrospective application.

ex post facto law A penal law that operates retroactively.

executory contract A contract that has not yet been fully performed; one that has been fully performed is an *executed* contract.

expert witness A witness who is qualified (by education, licensing, experience, etc.) to offer opinion testimony, which would be objectionable in a "lay" witness.

F

federal question Issues in cases arising under the Constitution, laws, and treaties of the United States, over which federal courts have subject matter jurisdiction.

fee simple absolute An estate in land having the maximum rights, that is, without future interests.

felony A serious crime, commonly defined by a penalty of a year or more in prison.

felony-murder rule Allows a conviction of murder when someone is killed during the commission of a felony; premeditation need not be proven.

foreclosure The process whereby real property is sold to satisfy a mortgage under default.

forum non conveniens Doctrine stating that if two or more courts both have proper *venue* for a case, a judge of one such court may rule that the lawsuit must be brought in the other court for either the convenience of or fairness to the parties.

foster parents Caretakers of children who are not their parents, stepparents, or adoptive parents whom the law has recognized as parental caretakers, commonly when children are taken away from their parents for cause.

franchise A collaborative relationship in which the franchisee pays a franchisor for the use of the franchisor's trade name and products; may also include a business model or system.

fraud In contract law, a contract induced by intentionally false misrepresentations; such a contract is voidable.

full faith and credit The Constitution requires that each state respect the legal pronouncements of sister states: "Full faith and credit shall be given in each State to the public acts, records, and judicial proceedings of every other State" (Article IV).

G

garnishment An action by which one who is owed a debt may collect payments through a third party, often an employer.

general intent For criminal law, requires merely that the actor intended a harmful act, not necessarily the specific result of the action. Also see *specific intent*.

general retainer The first payment made in hiring an attorney. A general retainer occurs when a client furnishes a sum of money to an attorney to ensure that the attorney will represent the client in whatever legal matters may arise.

general subject matter jurisdiction A court's authority to hear and decide a broad range of cases.

grand jury A body of citizens who receive complaints and accusations of crime and decide whether an *indictment* should issue.

grantee A party to which an interest in real property is transferred by the *grantor*.

grantor A party that transfers an interest in real property to another, the *grantee*.

gratuitous bailment A bailment for which no compensation is made.

gross negligence Negligence reflecting a reckless disregard for the rights of others; in contrast to *ordinary negligence*, which is commonly characterized by simple carelessness or inattention.

guilt beyond a reasonable doubt The standard of proof that the prosecution must meet in a criminal case.

H

headnotes Statements of the major points of law discussed in a case; found in the law reports published by West, formerly West Publishing Company.

hearing The presentation of evidence and argument before a tribunal. Under *procedural due process,* the hearing (usually the trial) must be fair and evenhanded. Most of the elements of a fair hearing have been established by custom and precedent.

hearsay rule Excludes from testimony out-of-court statements made by a person not present in court; a complex rule with many exceptions.

heart-balm suits Now largely discredited lawsuits for emotional injuries, such as *seduction, breach of promise to marry, criminal conversation,* and *alienation of affections.*

hedonic losses (damages) Money awarded in some lawsuits for loss of the ability to enjoy life's pleasures; a recent and controversial basis for awarding damages.

holding The core of a judge's decision in a case; that part of the written opinion that applies the law to the facts of the case. It expresses the *rule of the case,* as distinguished from *dicta.*

house counsel Full-time attorneys employed by many corporations and other businesses as part of the administrative staff; distinguished from "outside counsel."

I

illegitimate Refers to a child born to an unwed mother. In most states, the acknowledgment of paternity by a natural father may legitimate the child despite its being born out of wedlock.

implied warranty A promise imposed by law (e.g., an implied warranty of fitness for use or consumption), as distinguished from an express warranty stated in a contract.

in absentia Without physically presence; here, without the client or attorney being present.

in personam (personal) jurisdiction The power a court has over the person of a defendant to subject that person to decisions and rulings made in a case.

in rem action A lawsuit brought to enforce rights in a thing against the whole world, as opposed to one brought to enforce rights against another person; see *in personam jurisdiction*.

In the matter of Indicates that this case does not involve two parties; that is, this is not plaintiff versus defendant. "In the matter of" is converted to "In re" in references, so that this case would be referred to as *In re Estep.*

incestuous Marriage within a prohibited degree of relationship (e.g., brother–sister).

independent regulatory agencies Those agencies of the government that exercise relative autonomy because their heads cannot be removed at the whim of the chief executive, for example, the president; distinguished from departments, which are under the direct control of secretaries, who serve at the pleasure of the president.

indictment A written accusation by a grand jury charging the accused with a criminal act. Also called a "true bill." When the grand jury does not indict, it is called a "no bill."

ineffective assistance of counsel Advice and assistance of an attorney that falls below the standard expected by the legal community.

infamous crime A major crime for which a heavy penalty may be imposed. Used in the Constitution but now out of date; would probably mean *felony* today.

information A written accusation made by a public prosecutor.

inheritable The character of an estate in land that may pass to heirs upon death (with no will). Personal property is usually inheritable. *Inheritable* has the same meaning as *heritable*.

initial (first) appearance Opportunity for presence before a magistrate; a person arrested for a crime must be brought before a magistrate promptly after arrest to be informed of the charges and the legal rights of the accused.

Inns of Court Place in London where English lawyers were trained; for centuries, students learned the law there by association with legal scholars, lawyers, and judges.

insurance The pooling of risk among many insureds, typically enabled by a corporation that sells insurance contracts.

integrated bar A state bar association in which membership is required in order to practice law.

intentional infliction of emotional distress; negligent infliction of emotional distress Causes of action based on severe emotional distress. Although most states recognize the intentional tort, generally requiring outrageous conduct, few recognize the cause of action based on negligence.

intentional infliction of mental distress Almost self-explanatory; usually requires unreasonable or outrageous conduct and serious mental distress.

intentional torts *Torts* that require proof of intentional wrongful conduct.

inter alia (Latin) Among other things.

interlocutory appeal An appeal of a matter crucial to the lower court decision prior to the lower court reaching a final decision of the case.

interrogatories Pretrial written questions sent from one party to the other party in a lawsuit; one of several *discovery* devices.

intestate A person who dies without a will. Also used as an adjective to refer to the state of dying without a will.

invitee At common law, usually a person who enters upon real property to pursue business with the landowner, by invitation express or implied (e.g., customer of a retail store who enters the store).

J

J.D. The basic law degree; stands for "juris doctor" and is equivalent to the more traditional LL.B.

joinder The bringing in of a new person who joins together with the plaintiff as a plaintiff or the defendant as a defendant.

joint custody The continued sharing of rights and duties with regard to children following divorce.

joint tenancy A form of co-ownership that includes a *right of survivorship*.

judgment The official decision of a court about the rights and claims of each side in a lawsuit; usually a final decision after trial based on findings of fact and making conclusions of law.

judicial notice The judge recognizing a certain fact as true without a party furnishing evidence; ordinarily judicial notice is taken on the basis of common knowledge of a fact.

judicial restraint An accepted, customary policy of courts to restrict themselves to consideration of the questions presented to them and to restrain from legislating or interfering unduly with the executive or legislative branches. The principle also refers to the customary restraint federal courts exercise to leave questions of state law to state courts.

judicial review Review by an appellate court of a determination by a lower court; also, the power of the federal courts to declare acts contrary to the Constitution null and void.

jurisdiction The authority, capacity, power, or right of a court to render a binding decision in a case.

jurisprudence Commonly defined as the science or philosophy of law; it is generally concerned with the nature of law and legal systems.

jury With regard to the constitutional right, refers to a petit jury, which is the trier of fact in a criminal case. Also see *grand jury*.

jury instructions Detailed directions (instructions) given by the judge to the jury about its functions in the lawsuit.

Justice The title given to the judges of the Supreme Court of the United States and to the judges of the appellate courts of many of the states.

L

laches An equitable principle roughly equivalent to a statute of limitations at common law; it prevents a party from bringing a petition (suit) when there has been unreasonable delay in doing so.

law clerk A law school student who works summers or part time for private attorneys; also, top law students who obtain clerkships with judges after graduating from law school.

law merchant The generally accepted customs of merchants; often used to refer to early commercial law developed by the merchants themselves, which later formed the basis for much of commercial common law.

law review Publication issued by most accredited law schools, on a quarterly basis, with scholarly articles and comments on legal issues.

Law School Admissions Test (LSAT) A written, largely multiple-choice, test required for admission at most law schools.

lease An agreement by an owner of property (the *lessor*), with a renter (a *tenant* or *lessee*), whereby the lessee pays for the right of possession and use but does not acquire title.

legal ethics Synonymous with "professional responsibility"; the legal profession promulgates specific rules to cover important areas of professional misconduct and disciplines transgressors.

legal remedy A remedy under the common law, as distinguished from an *equitable remedy*.

legal technician Person who provides legal services for compensation without attorney supervision.

legislation The act of giving, making, or enacting laws; preparation and enactment of laws; lawmaking, ordinarily the prerogative of legislatures or legislative bodies.

legislative history Recorded events that provide a basis for determining the legislative intent underlying a statute enacted by a legislature; the sources for legislative history include legislative committee hearings and debates on the floor of the legislature.

legislative intent That which the legislature wanted or intended to achieve when it enacted a statute; the determination of which is the goal of the court when the language of a statute is in question, ambiguous, or called into doubt.

lex loci delicti (Latin) "The law of the place of the wrong." In a *conflict-of-laws* question in a tort action, this ancient rule held that the court would apply the law of that place (state) where the last act necessary to complete the tort occurred or the last act necessary to make the actor liable occurred.

licensee At common law, a person who enters upon real property, not by invitation (express or implied), for his or her own purpose (e.g., a pharmaceutical vendor visiting a physician's office).

life estate An estate, especially in land, that lasts until someone dies (the *life tenant*).

life tenant A person who has an interest in an estate (especially in land) that lasts until that person (or another specified person) dies.

limited subject matter jurisdiction A court's restricted authority to decide only certain kinds of cases; for example, a probate court hears only cases concerning decedents' estates.

litigation A dispute brought to court; derived from the Latin *lis*, which means lawsuit.

living trust (inter vivos) trust An ordinary trust, as opposed to a trust established by a will at death (*inter vivos*—"between living persons").

LL.B. The basic law degree, a "bachelor of laws," replaced in most law schools today by J.D. (juris doctor).

long-arm statutes Statutes that provide a state with jurisdiction over persons or entities ordinarily beyond its territory and usual jurisdiction.

lump-sum alimony *Alimony* that is established as one lump-sum amount, usually in the form of one payment but occasionally in installments.

M

mala in se (Latin) "Wrong in and of itself"; crimes that are morally wrong.

mala prohibita (Latin) "Prohibited wrongs"; crimes that are not inherently evil (usually regulatory crimes).

malicious prosecution When someone initiates or causes a groundless suit to be brought out of malice. To succeed in this claim, it is essential that the original suit be terminated in favor of the person later suing for malicious prosecution.

malpractice Professional negligence; those who are licensed professionals are held to a higher standard of care for their services than is required in ordinary negligence.

marital settlement agreement A contract between spouses concerning division and ownership of property acquired during the marriage and entered into in contemplation of separation or divorce.

marriage The legal joining together of husband and wife, having among its important effects the legitimation of their offspring; also, the Christian sacrament that joins husband and wife.

mechanic's lien Arises when someone is not paid for work done on or improvements made to property; the debt or obligation to pay money becomes a burden on the property. Ordinarily created by law under state statutes.

mediation A form of conflict resolution often used in conjunction with litigation or as an alternative to it. Mediation deals with adversarial parties, as in divorce mediation, but is not an adversarial process. The mediator's task is to facilitate agreement and resolution, bringing the parties together without taking sides.

medical malpractice A form of professional misconduct restricted to negligence in the medical field; an important field of legal specialization.

memorandum decision (per curiam opinion) A court's decision that gives the ruling (what it decides and orders done) but no opinion (reasons for the decision). A *memorandum opinion* is the same as a *per curiam opinion*, which is an opinion without a named author, usually a brief and unanimous decision.

mens rea Literally, "criminal mind"; criminal intent.

mental incompetence In relation to marriage, condition that exists when one of the parties lacks mental capacity to contract marriage.

misrepresentation A false representation; may be innocent or intentional. A contract based on an innocent misrepresentation is still *voidable* by the person to whom the false representation was made.

mistake of fact In contract formation, occurs one or both parties believe some essential fact about the transaction to be other than it really is; makes the contract *voidable*.

mistrial A trial that the judge ends and declares will have no legal effect because of a major defect in procedure or because of the death of a juror, a deadlocked jury, or other major problem.

modification When applied to divorce, a court-approved change in the amount or terms of alimony, child support, or child custody.

mortgage A written instrument creating an interest in land as collateral for the payment of a debt.

motion Generally, a formal request by a party for a ruling by the court in favor of that party. There are many types of motions; dismissal motions are discussed in Chapter 7.

motion for a directed verdict A dismissal motion commonly made by the defendant at the close of the plaintiff's *case-in-chief* and by both sides after presentation of all the evidence; asks the judge to rule in favor of the movant.

motion for judgment n.o.v. A motion made at the end of a trial asking the judge to enter a judgment contrary to the jury's verdict on the ground that the verdict is against the manifest weight of the evidence; also called a *motion for judgment notwithstanding the verdict*. The abbreviation "n.o.v." stands for the Latin *non obstante veredicto*, meaning "notwithstanding the verdict."

motion for summary judgment A dismissal motion that is a pretrial motion and also a trial motion in a *bench trial*; asks the judge to rule in favor of a party after some discovery or part of the trial has taken place.

movant The party making a motion.

Multistate Bar Examination A standardized national test of general legal subjects, such as property, contracts, and constitutional law.

murder The wrongful killing of another human being with malice aforethought (premeditation).

N

negligence A cause of action based on a failure to meet a reasonable standard of conduct, which failure results in an injury.

negotiable instruments "Commercial paper"; consists of cash substitutes, such as *checks, drafts, promissory notes,* and *certificates of deposit.*

no-fault divorce Contemporary method divorce that does away with the need to prove fault (i.e., state grounds) against the other spouse.

nolo contendere (Latin) Plea known by its Latin name, meaning "I do not want to contest"; accepts responsibility without an admission of guilt.

nonage The condition of being a minor, not having reached the age of majority.

nonfreehold estate (leasehold estate) An interest in real property that does not include holding of title. This is primarily the right of possession and occupancy, as in a lease agreement.

nonmoving party The party against whom a motion is made.

not guilty by reason of insanity A plea in a criminal case that admits commission of the acts charged but denies intent on the basis of the defendant's insanity.

notice In law, represents the requirement of timely notification of the opposing party. Under *procedural due process,* the fairness of legal procedure requires that a party have sufficient notice to prepare a response to legal action.

nuisance Basically, a continuing trespass, as when one discharges polluting effluents that seep into a neighbor's pond (this constitutes a *private* nuisance).

O

offer A proposal; the first of the three requirements of traditional contract formation: *offer, acceptance,* and *consideration.*

opening statements The introductory statements made at the start of a trial by the lawyers for each side. The lawyers typically present a version of the facts that best supports their side of the case, explain how these facts will be proved, and state how they think the law applies to the case.

ordinance Legislation at the local level, typically created or passed by city councils or county commissions.

original service The first presentation of legal documents to the defendant, after which service is usually made to the defendant's attorney.

output contract A contract that binds the buyer to buy and the seller to sell the entire product produced by the seller.

P

paralegal (legal assistant) Generally, an employee in a law office who performs legal tasks under attorney supervision but who is not licensed to practice law. Some states allow paralegals to provide limited legal services without supervision. "Paralegal" as a title and a job is usually interchangeable with "legal assistant."

partnership Unincorporated business association lacking the limited liability of a corporation, so that debts that cannot be satisfied by partnership property may go after the personal assets of the partners.

patent An exclusive right, granted by the government, to use one's invention.

peremptory challenge Exclusion of a juror that does not require justification. Each side is allowed a limited number of peremptory challenges, as dictated by statute.

perjury Knowingly making a false statement under oath in a judicial proceeding; the false statement must concern a material issue or fact in the proceeding.

personal service The presentation of the summons and complaint upon the defendant personally.

persuasive authority Authority that carries great weight even though not qualifying as precedent, for example, decisions of other state courts.

petition A formal, written request, addressed to a person or body in a position of authority, that alleges a cause of action; sometimes also known as a *complaint* or *pleading.*

physical evidence Physical objects introduced as evidence, such as a gun, a lock, drugs, and so on.

plain meaning rule A rule of statutory construction stating that if the language of a statute is unambiguous, the terms of the statute should be construed according to their ordinary meaning.

plat A map showing the division of an area of real property into lots, streets, parks, and so on and indicating easements.

plea bargaining One accused of a crime can "bargain" through her attorney with the prosecutor; the bargain usually involves an agreement by the accused to plead guilty in return for favorable treatment, such as a lenient sentence, reduction to a lesser charge, or probation in lieu of incarceration.

pleadings Written formal documents framing the issues of a lawsuit, consisting primarily of what is alleged on the one side (e.g., the plaintiff's complaint) or denied on the other (e.g., the defendant's answer).

postnuptial agreement An agreement between spouses, usually concerned with distributing family property in the event of death or divorce.

prayer for relief Also known as *demand for relief;* the portion of a complaint or claim for relief that specifies the type of relief to which the plaintiffs feel they are entitled and that they are requesting. See *wherefore clause.*

precedent Prior decisions of the same court or a higher court that a judge must follow in deciding a subsequent case presenting similar facts and the same legal problem. Precedent consists of the rule applied in a case and encompasses the reasoning that requires it. In a given decision, the precedent may be distinguished from *dictum,* which includes extraneous or conjectural statements that are not necessary to the decision and are not binding on future decisions.

preemption The principle or doctrine that federal statutes that overlap or are in conflict with state statutes will take precedence and prevail (be preferred), even to the point of invalidating state statutes entirely.

prejudicial error (reversible error) Mistakes made at trial that are sufficiently serious to prejudice the result.

preliminary hearing A criminal defendant's opportunity to challenge the case before the judge in a hearing that determines the sufficiency of the charges without a determination of guilt; ordinarily afforded but not always available.

preponderance of the evidence The standard of proof required in most civil actions. The party whose evidence, when fairly considered, is more convincing as to its truth has the preponderance of evidence on its side.

pretrial conference (hearing) A meeting of attorneys in a case with the judge to discuss the issues in the case and plan for the trial.

pretrial diversion Postpones and usually obviates the need for trial if the accused meets certain conditions, typically the performance of community service.

prima facie case A case that will win unless the other side comes forward with evidence to disprove it.

primogeniture A system under the common law whereby title to land passed to the eldest son (*primo-,* first-; *geni-,* born).

prior restraint An action by the government to impose limits on the exercise of free speech, especially publication, prior to its exercise, as distinguished from punishing a person after publication.

privilege against self-incrimination Provides that a person accused of a crime cannot be required to testify against himself or herself.

privity of contract The relationship between two parties to a contract. Originally, this was a bar to a suit brought by a consumer against a manufacturer when the consumer bought through a dealer rather than directly from the manufacturer. Modern product liability law does away with this impediment.

pro bono (publico) (Latin) "For the (public) good." Traditionally, members of the bar were under a moral obligation to render free services to the public, typically to provide services to people who could not afford to pay. States now make this a requirement of membership in the bar, typically with specific minimum contributions of time.

pro se (Latin) "For oneself," "in one's own behalf." American law recognizes not only the right to be represented by an attorney but also the right to represent oneself in court.

probation An alternative to incarceration that sets a period of time during which the probationer must adhere to conditions set by the court and be supervised by a probation officer. Violation of the conditions may result in incarceration.

procedural due process Due process that is concerned with the fairness of *notice* and *hearing* provided by government in the adjudication of rights and duties.

procedural law The part of the law that deals with procedures and the proper or authorized method of doing things.

process In criminal law, the document commanding a party to do or not to do something; see *service of process.*

product liability A branch of tort law that assigns liability to a manufacturer when injury occurs due to a "dangerously defective product." It dispenses with traditional requirements of proving fault, as in intentional torts and negligence.

production of documents Requests used in *discovery* to obtain from the other side of a case documents that are pertinent to issues in the case.

promissory estoppel An equitable principle that enforces a promise in the absence of a completed contract. When a person makes a promise to another to induce that other to act to his detriment, and that other does so act in reliance on the promise, the court may prevent (estop) the first person from denying or negating the promise.

promissory note Promise by the maker of the note to pay money to a payee; usually involved in loans and debts.

prosecutor The attorney charged with prosecuting criminal cases on behalf of a state or the United States; a public employee commonly titled state attorney, district attorney, or United States attorney.

prospective Occurring in the future; with respect to a statute, enforcement or application of the statute as to circumstances occurring on or after the statute's *effective date.*

public defender's office A government agency that provides criminal defense services to indigents.

publication In reference to *service of process,* a means of service by publishing notice in the legal section of a newspaper periodically as prescribed by statute. In reference to tort law, making a statement publicly, orally, or in writing, that is, to a third person.

punishment (retribution) The primary goal of criminal law: punishing a person for criminal conduct. The other theories regarding the treatment of criminals are *deterrence* of crime; *incapacitation,* which consists of removing the criminal from society through incarceration; and *rehabilitation,* in which the criminal is helped toward a productive role in society.

punitive damages Sometimes awarded beyond mere compensation (see *compensatory damages*) to punish a defendant for outrageous conduct in tort.

Q

quasi-contract Concept arising from the theory that a "contract" is created on the basis of moral obligation, called *unjust enrichment,* in which one party receives a benefit to the detriment of another that begs for *restitution*; not an actual contract.

quasi in rem Describes an action that is really directed against a person but is formally directed only against property.

question (issue) of fact A question for the jury in a jury trial or for the judge in a bench trial. Fact questions are evidentiary questions concerning who, when, where, and what.

question of law A question for the judge, that is, a question as to the appropriate law to be applied or the correct interpretation of the law.

R

rape At common law, forcible sexual intercourse by a man on a woman against her will. Modern *statutory rape* makes consent irrelevant because of the status or mental state of the victim. Modern law recognizes a variety of sexual assaults.

ratify To approve, as when one suffering a disability approves a contract after the disability has terminated; for example, a minor reaches age of majority and agrees to a contract made when he or she was still a minor.

real estate closing Culmination or completion of a real estate transaction(s), at which numerous documents are signed and exchanged, payment is made, and property deeds are transferred.

record (noun) All the evidence presented at trial, whether or not recorded.

record (verb) The act of putting the public on notice of a document affecting property ownership by placing the document in the public records.

recross The questioning of a witness by the party that did not call the witness following *redirect.*

redirect The questioning of a witness by the party that called the witness following *cross-examination.*

reformation Aims at correcting a contract to reflect the actual intention of the parties.

rehabilitative alimony Ordinarily a form of periodic payment, temporary in duration, designed to provide for an ex-spouse until he or she can become self-supporting.

remainder A future interest in land that follows a *life estate.*

remand Sending a case back to a lower court; done by a higher court.

replevin A common law cause of action to recover personal property wrongfully possessed by another person.

reply A pleading made by a plaintiff when a defendant makes a counterclaim or affirmative defenses that require a response.

requests for admissions Discovery device through which one side in a lawsuit gives a list of facts to the other side and asks that the facts be admitted or denied; those admitted need not be proved at trial.

res Thing. (In Latin, nouns have different forms for subjective and objective positions in the sentence. Thus, *res* is the same noun as the *rem* in "in rem," except that the latter takes a different ending because it follows the preposition. Note that "in personam" also adds an "m" to "persona" because it follows the preposition.)

res judicata Latin for "the thing has been judged"; an affirmative defense that prevents a civil case from being brought a second time.

rescind To annul or cancel a contract, putting the parties back in the position they were in before, as if no contract had been made.

rescission Aims at destroying the contract and its obligations, thereby putting the parties back in the positions they occupied prior to making the agreement.

respondeat superior A principle of agency whereby a principal is held responsible for the negligent acts of an agent acting within the scope of the agency (e.g., an employer is liable for the negligence of an employee); also called vicarious liability.

Restatements of the Law Compilations of general interpretations of major fields of common law, sponsored and published by the American Law Institute (founded in 1923).

restitution In contract law, usually the amount that returns the plaintiff back to his or her precontract financial position.

restrictive covenants Mandates concerning what may or may not be done with, to, or on real property; take many forms, including minimum square footage for a house, lawn and yard maintenance, ability to rent the property, and signage. Racially restrictive covenants and other discriminatory practices have long been held unconstitutional.

retroactive (retrospective) Applying to past circumstances or occurrences; with respect to a statute, enforcement or application of the statute as to events and actions that occurred before the statute became law.

right of survivorship An incident to certain forms of co-ownership whereby a co-owner, if there are but two co-owners, will own the entire interest upon the death of the other co-owner.

rule of the case That part of a written judicial opinion that decides the case; it is what the case stands for as far as applying a rule to the facts of the case.

rule to show cause A court directive that someone appear in court to explain why the court should not take the contemplated action (in this case, why Estep should not be held in contempt).

rulemaking Generic meaning of making rules; specific meaning referring to the legislative function of administrative agencies, as distinguished from their usual administrative functions.

rules of construction A tradition of customs for statutory interpretation.

S

scienter In the context of a criminal case, indicates criminal intent.

secondary authority Authoritative statements of law other than statutes and cases, such as law review articles, treatises, and the Restatements.

secured transaction Takes place when the payment of a debt is protected by *collateral*. The most common secured transactions are (1) real property *mortgages*, in which the purchaser or owner of land borrows money, pledging interests in real property to satisfy the debt in case of default, and (2) purchase money installment contracts for personal property, in which the seller retains rights of repossession in case of default. Article 9 of the UCC covers secured transactions of personal property except for interests arising by operation of law, such as *mechanic's liens*. Secured interests in real property fall outside the UCC.

seduction Inducing (usually by deception or promise to marry) a person (usually a chaste, unmarried woman) to have sex.

sentencing guidelines State-adopted guidelines that establish specific sentences for specific crimes. Some states have also adopted minimum sentences for certain crimes.

separation agreement (property settlement agreement) A contract between husband and wife, after they have already married, to distribute property in case of death or divorce. Such an agreement is usually executed in preparation for divorce, but it is occasionally used between couples who merely wish to live separately.

separation of powers Effect of the constitutional prohibition on any branch of government carrying out a government function of another branch. The federal government is divided into three branches, with the legislative branch responsible for passing legislation, the judicial branch responsible for interpreting law and deciding cases, and the executive branch responsible for carrying out law. The powers of each branch are separate and unique to that branch.

service of process Delivery of a summons, writ, complaint, or other process to the opposite party or other person entitled to receive it, in such manner as the law prescribes.

sheriff's deed The deed given to the buyer of real property at an auction ordered by a court to satisfy the debt of the property owner.

show cause A court may issue a rule to show cause when it wants a hearing on the question of why it should not take certain action. A party shows cause by providing a compelling reason to prevent the action.

significant relationship test The modern rule followed in a *conflict-of-laws* setting; it is used in both tort and contract contexts and makes the court apply the law of the state that had the most "significant relationship" to the cause of action.

slander An injury to reputation ordinarily caused by the communication of lies to third parties. It is the spoken form of defamation, *libel* being written defamation.

sole custody The award of *child custody* exclusively to one parent upon divorce; the other parent usually enjoys visitation rights.

sole proprietorship An unincorporated business owned by one person.

solicitation In legal ethics, using improper means to drum up business. For example, the practice of "ambulance chasing," such as approaching hospital patients to solicit business, is unethical.

solicitor A lawyer in England who handles all legal matters except trial work.

special appearance An appearance in court by a defendant, for the purpose of challenging personal jurisdiction, that does not confer personal jurisdiction, as an appearance would otherwise do.

specific intent In criminal law, requires that the actor have intended the precise result of a harmful act. Also see *general intent*.

specific performance An equitable remedy that asks the court to order a party to a contract to perform the terms of the contract.

spousal support Payments made to an ex-spouse following divorce that are designed as support rather than a division of the marital property. Traditionally this was called *alimony*, and in many jurisdictions the term *maintenance* is used.

standing A person's right to bring a lawsuit because he or she is directly affected by the issues presented, having a stake in the outcome of the suit.

stare decisis The doctrine that judicial decisions stand as precedents for cases arising in the future. It is a fundamental policy of our law that, except in unusual circumstances, a court's determination on a point of law will be followed by courts of the same or lower rank in later cases presenting the same legal issue. It means to "stand by a decision." The conventional translation (probably not very helpful) is "Let the decision stand."

Statute of Frauds An ancient doctrine requiring that certain contracts be in writing and signed.

statute A law enacted by the legislative branch of government declaring, commanding, or prohibiting something.

statute of limitations A federal or state law that specifies time limits within which suits must be filed for civil and criminal actions; they vary from state to state and from action to action.

strict construction Narrow interpretation by a very literal reading; criminal statutes in particular are *strictly construed*.

strict criminal liability Attaches to a few crimes that may be proven without proving intent; see *strict liability*.

strict liability A principle, largely applied to *product liability*, which creates liability without proof of fault (e.g., liability for a "dangerously defective product"); virtually interchangeable with *absolute liability*.

subject matter jurisdiction The jurisdiction of a court to hear and determine the type of case before it. For example, in Florida, election contests are heard in the circuit court but not in county court. The reference to Leon County in "the Circuit Court for Leon County" refers only to the location of the court—it is a circuit court, not a county court.

subpoena A court's order to a person that he or she appear in court to testify in a case.

substantial evidence The test or standard used at the appellate level to determine if *jury* factfinding at trial constitutes prejudicial error. Often used interchangeably with *clearly erroneous*.

substantial performance Occurs when one party has attempted to complete performance in good faith but that performance varied in minor ways from the specific terms of the contract. Under the equitable principle of substantial performance, the court may enforce the contract and declare it performed, though possibly reducing the payment for performance because of the minor breach.

substantive due process A theory of due process that emphasizes judging the content of a law by a subjective standard of fundamental fairness; the government may not act arbitrarily or capriciously in making, interpreting, or enforcing the law.

substantive law The part of law that creates, defines, and regulates rights; compare to *procedural law*, which deals with the method of enforcing rights.

substituted service Service of process to someone other than the defendant, such as a relative living at the defendant's abode; requirements are usually defined by statute.

substitution of judgment The standard of review of conclusions of law made by a lower court.

summation (closing argument) Each lawyer's presentation of a review of the evidence at the close of trial.

supersedeas An order staying the execution of judgment by a trial court; suspension of the trial court's power, as when an appeal halts the court's power to execute judgment.

supremacy clause Article VI of the U.S. Constitution, which provides: "This Constitution and the laws of the United States which shall be made in pursuance thereof; and all treaties made, or which shall be made, under the authority of the United States, shall be supreme law of the land, and the Judges in every State shall be bound thereby, any thing in the Constitution or laws of any State to the contrary notwithstanding."

surrogacy contract A contract by which the natural father takes custody of a child and the mother relinquishes custody in favor of adoption by the father's wife.

syllabus A summary of a case often included with a report decision and preceding the official text of the opinion.

T

tenancy by the entirety A form of co-ownership with a *right of survivorship* that can be held only by husband and wife.

tenancy in common A form of co-ownership that does not have a *right of survivorship* and that permits unequal shares.

tenure In higher education, job security granted to faculty members, usually after a period of several years and based on an extensive approval process. Tenured faculty cannot be fired without cause.

title Formal ownership of property; has many nuances of meaning.

toll Suspension of the running of a time period.

tolled Held in abeyance; kept from running.

tolling statute A statute that stops the clock on the running of a statute of limitation while a given circumstance exists.

tortfeasor A person who engages in tortious conduct.

torts A major area of substantive law including causes of action to redress injuries that arise out of noncontractual events. Tort includes three major divisions: *intentional torts, negligence,* and *strict liability*.

trademark A distinctive mark, in symbols or words, used to distinguish products of manufacturers or merchants.

transcript A written verbatim version of an oral statement. In law, transcripts are used most frequently in reference to depositions and trials.

treatises In the legal context, scholarly books about the law, usually covering one of the basic fields of law, such as torts or contracts, or a significant subfield of the law, such as workers compensation.

trespass Originally covered a wide variety of wrongs, one species of which, trespass *quare clausum fregit*, constituted "trespass to land," which is a wrongful intrusion on the land of another.

trespasser A person who enters land wrongfully without consent, invitation, or privilege (e.g., a "squatter").

trial A judicial examination, in accordance with the law, of a criminal or civil action. It is an "on-the-record hearing," which means the determination is to be made on the basis of what is presented in court. It is a trial of fact with judgment entered on the law.

trier of fact Also called *factfinder;* the entity that determines fact in a trial. In a jury trial, the jury is entrusted with factfinding; in a bench trial, the judge necessarily must find the facts as well as make conclusions of law.

trust A device whereby title to property is transferred to one person, the trustee, for the benefit of another, the beneficiary.

trust account In the practice of law, a special bank account in which fees paid by clients are kept until an attorney may properly claim the funds for fees or expenses.

U

ultimate facts The general statements of fact that support a cause of action, for example, the allegations of fact in the complaint. Compare to *evidentiary facts.*

undue influence Relentless pressure, especially from one in a confidential relationship, to induce a party to agree to a contract.

Uniform Commercial Code (UCC) Commonly referred to simply as the UCC, a set of comprehensive statutes governing most commercial transactions; has been adopted in every state except Louisiana.

unilateral contract A contract in which acceptance is accomplished by performance; for example, offer of a reward is accepted by performing the reward request. Compare to *bilateral contract.*

unjust enrichment An equitable principle asserting that one receiving a benefit at another's loss owes *restitution* to the other.

V

venue Place; specifically, the place where jurisdiction is exercised. Many courts may have jurisdiction over a case, but it is filed in only one place (venue).

verdict The factfinding by a jury. For example, in a civil case, the jury might find the defendant liable in a dollar amount; in a criminal case, the verdict is usually *guilty* or *not guilty* of each criminal charge.

vicariously Indirectly responsible.

void for vagueness A constitutional principle of substantive due process used to invalidate legislation that fails to give a person of ordinary intelligence fair notice that his or her contemplated conduct is forbidden by the legislation.

voidable Describes a contract that the innocent party (the other party having contracted wrongfully in certain recognized ways) may avoid by returning the parties to their conditions prior to the agreement.

voir dire The examination of potential jurors to qualify them for the trial.

voluntary When used in reference to criminal law, means an act of free will, though this is different from its use in contract law, where coercion may negate voluntariness. In criminal law, acts are not voluntary when they occur during sleep, unconsciousness, or hypnosis or by reflex or convulsions.

W

warrant Written permission given by a judge to arrest a person or conduct a search or make a seizure.

warranty deed A *deed* that includes promises or warranties, especially the promise to defend the title.

wherefore clause The *prayer for relief;* the final clause in a complaint that asks the court for some sort of remedy: "Wherefore, the plaintiff prays that. . . ." *Wherefore* means "for this reason."

will A document through which a person directs how his or her property will be distributed after the person's death.

with prejudice A dismissal with prejudice precludes the plaintiff from filing an amended complaint in the lawsuit.

workers' compensation A statutory scheme whereby fixed awards are made for employment-related injuries. This commonly takes the form of state-regulated employers' insurance arrangements.

writ A written order directing that a specific act be performed.

writ of certiorari A writ issued by a higher court to a lower court requiring the certification of the record in a particular case so that the higher court can review the record and correct any actions taken in the case that were not in accordance with the law. The method used by the United States Supreme Court to invoke its discretionary jurisdiction over a case.

writ of execution A demand that property be sold to satisfy a debt of the property owner.

writ of habeas corpus Brought by petition to challenge the lawfulness of a detention.

writ of mandamus An order requiring a public officer to perform a duty.

writ of prohibition An order by a higher court directing a lower court not to do something.

wrongful interference with contractual relations When a person not a party to a contract improperly disrupts the contractual relationship of others.

Z

zoning variance Exception to or specific modification of a zoning code or ordinance. It is customary in the United States for local governments to create *zones* within city and county boundaries with restrictions primarily on the form of use, for example, agricultural, residential, commercial, and so on.

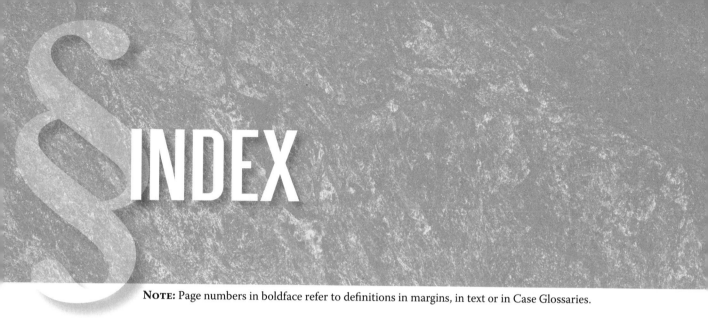

INDEX